W9-AZM-675

ANTIQUE TRADER BOOKS

# POTTERY
# AND
# PORCELAIN
# CERAMICS
## PRICE GUIDE

### 2ND EDITION

Edited by Kyle Husfloen

Contributing Editor Susan N. Cox

ATB

Antique Trader Books
P.O. Box 1050
Dubuque, IA 52004

ISBN: 0-930625-73-0
Library of Congress Catalog Card Number: 97-72626

Assistant Editor: *Elizabeth Stephan*
Editorial Assistant: *Ruth Willis*
Editorial Assistant: *Pat Scott*
Designer: *Darryl Keck*
Production Assistant: *Aaron Wilbers*
Cover Design: *Jaro Sebek*

*Printed in the United States of America*

To order additional copies of this
book or a catalog please contact:

**Antique Trader Books**
P.O. Box 1050
Dubuque, Iowa 52004
1-800-334-7165

# Introduction

For over twenty-five years The Antique Trader has been producing general price guides covering all types of antiques and collectibles. Since the founding of our new Antique Trader Books & Price Guides division in 1994, we have greatly expanded our offerings in the category of price guides as well as other specialized references for the collecting field.

Our first product for our expanded price guide coverage was *Antique Trader Books Pottery & Porcelain—Ceramics Price Guide,* released in early 1994. This well-illustrated reference covered all major categories of pottery and porcelain, foreign and domestic, and was well received by the collecting community. Now we are bringing you a completely new Second Edition. Similar in size and format to our first edition, we have gathered all-new and updated data for the numerous categories included and have increased the number and size of our photographs to add to their usefulness and eye-appeal. As in the first volume, this edition covers ceramics produced as far back as the eighteenth century in Europe, but also includes expanded sections on popular twentieth century American chinawares and pottery. Whatever segment of the vast ceramics market you find most appealing, we'll have information included here.

As with our earlier book, we pride ourselves on providing the most accurate and detailed descriptions possible for each item included. These authoritative listings are highlighted by an abundance of fine black and white photographs since these are so important to a better understanding and appreciation of particular pieces and categories.

Ceramics, like most collecting specialties, has a vocabulary all its own. To give you a better understanding of terms used throughout this guide we begin with a general introduction to the collecting of ceramics followed by several pages of sketches showing a wide variety of pieces and forms you will find listed. The sketches include brief notes on the forms and body parts which will make it easier to study and use our guide. As an additional reference source we are including, at the conclusion of our price listings, a Glossary of Selected Ceramics Terms followed by several special Appendices covering individual collecting groups, museums of interest and references to pottery and porcelain marks. Since English ceramics of the nineteenth and early twentieth century make up quite a large portion of collectible ceramic wares found in this country, we also include an appendix explaining the unique system of English Registry Marks.

My staff and I have put many hours of effort into producing an attractive and useful guide and it took many hands and hearts to produce the volume you now hold. A special note of thanks goes to our Contributing Editor Susan N. Cox for preparing a variety of categories covering some of today's most popular and collectible twentieth century American ceramics. Her special expertise has helped us present a well rounded and comprehensive guide.

I sincerely hope that all who add *Antique Trader Books Pottery & Porcelain—Ceramics Price Guide* to their library will find it handy, easy to use and authoritative. Use it as a guide in your collecting pursuits and it should serve you well. If you have special comments or questions, we'll be happy to answer your inquiries. Enjoy this guide and may it bring you new knowledge and appreciation of your ceramic treasures and those waiting your discovery.

Kyle Husfloen, Editor

# Photography Credits

Photographers who have contributed to this volume include: Edward Babka, East Dubuque, Illinois; Stanley L. Baker, Minneapolis, Minnesota; Dorothy Beckwith, Platteville, Wisconsin; Rodney L. Bourdeau, Danbury, Connecticut; Susan N. Cox, El Cajon, California; J.D. Dalessandro, Cincinnati, Ohio; Loretta DeLozier, Bedford, Iowa; Jim Martin, Monmouth, Illinois; Louise Paradis, Sparta, Wisconsin; Joyce Roerig, Waltersboro, South Carolina; and Tom Wallace, Chicago, Illinois.

For other photographs, artwork, data or permission to photograph in their shops, we sincerely express appreciation to the following auctioneers, galleries, museums, individuals and shops:

Bell Tower Antique Mall, Covington, Kentucky; Brown Auctions, Mullinville, Kansas; Butterfield & Butterfield, San Francisco, California; The Cedars - Antiques, Aurelia, Iowa; Norm and Diana Charles, Hagerstown, Indiana; Christie's, New York, New York; Christie's, South Kensington, England; Cincinnati Art Galleries, Cincinnati, Ohio; Collector's Sales & Services, Middletown, Rhode Island; D & L Antiques, North Berwick, Maine; DuMouchelles, Detroit, Michigan; Dunning's Auction Service, Elgin, Illinois; T. Ermert, Cincinnati, Ohio; The Galena Shoppe, Galena, Illinois; Garth's Auctions, Delaware, Ohio; Morton M. Goldberg Auction Galleries, New Orleans, Louisiana; Robert Gordon, San Antonio, Texas; Grunewald Antiques, Hillsborough, North Carolina; Vicki Harman, San Marcos, California; Gene Harris Antique Auction Center, Marshalltown, Iowa; Leslie Hindman Auctioneers, Chicago, Illinois; Jackson's Auctions, Cedar Falls, Iowa; Doris Johnson, Rockford, Illinois; Agnes Koehn Antiques, Cedar Rapids, Iowa; Bev Kubesheski, Dubuque, Iowa; Joy Luke Gallery, Bloomington, Illinois; J. Martin, Mt. Orab, Ohio; Dave Rago, Lambertville, New Jersey; Jane Rosenow, Galva, Illinois; Skinner, Inc., Bolton Massachusetts; Sotheby's, New York, New York; Michael Strawser, Wolcottville, Indiana; Temples Antiques, Minneapolis, Minnesota; Town Crier Auction Service, Burlington, Wisconsin; Treadway Gallery, Cincinnati, Ohio, Lee Vines, Hewlett, New York; Bruce & Vicki Waasdorp, Clarence, New York; Wolf's Fine Arts & Auctioneers, Cleveland, Ohio; Woody Auctions, Douglass, Kansas; and Yesterday's Treasures, Galena, Illinois.

**ON THE COVER:** Top left to lower right - An early Adams' Rose pattern 9" d. plate, $100-125; Van Briggle Pottery conch shell in matte blue, $75-125; 7" d. hand-painted porcelain plate, $25; Red Wing Pottery 'Random Harvest' cup and saucer, $10-15; Noritake porcelain covered sugar bowl, ca. 1920s, $35-45; hand-painted Nippon low open-handled dish, $45-65; Lily-of-the-Valley ironstone sugar bowl with Tea Leaf decoration, $225-275; late 19th century Japanese Satsuma pottery hand-decorated small vase, $100-125.

Cover design by Jaro Sebek. Photographs courtesy of The Galena Shoppe, Galena Illinois and a private collection. Photography by Elite Images, Eric Misko.

# Collecting Guidelines

Whenever I'm asked about what to collect, I always stress that you should collect what you like and want to live with. Collecting is a very personal matter and only you can determine what will give you the most satisfaction. With the wide diversity of ceramics available, everyone should be able to find a topic they will enjoy studying and collecting.

One thing that every collector should keep in mind is that to get the most from their hobby they must study it in depth, read everything they can get their hands on, and purchase the best references available for their library. New research material continues to become available for collectors and learning is an ongoing process.

It is also very helpful to join a collectors' club where others who share your enthusiasm will support and guide your learning. Fellow collectors often become your best friends and sources for special treasures to add to your collection. Dealers who specialize in a ceramics category are always eager to help educate and support collectors and many times they become a mentor for a novice who is just starting out on the road to the 'advanced collector' level.

With the very ancient and complex history of ceramic wares, it's easy to understand why becoming educated about your special interest is of paramount importance. There have been collectors of pottery and porcelain for centuries, and for nearly as long collectors have had to be wary of reproductions or 'reissues.' In Chinese ceramics, for instance, it has always been considered perfectly acceptable to copy as closely as possible the style and finish of earlier ceramics and even mark them with period markings on the base. The only problem arises when a modern collector wants to determine whether their piece, 'guaranteed' antique, was produced over two hundred years ago or barely a century ago.

With European and, to some extent, American wares, copying of earlier styles has also been going on for many decades. As far back as the mid-nineteenth century, 'copies' and 'adaptions' of desirable early wares were finding their way onto the collector market. By the late nineteenth century, in particular, revivals of eighteenth century porcelains and even some early nineteenth century earthenwares were available, often sold as decorative items and sometimes clearly marked. After a hundred years, however, these early copies can pose a real quagmire for the unwary.

Again, education is the key. As you're building your store of knowledge and experience, buy with care from reliable sources.

Another area that calls for special caution on the part of collectors, especially the tyro, is that of damaged and repaired pieces. A wise collector will always buy the best example they can find and it is a good policy to save up to buy one extra fine piece rather than a handful of lesser examples. You never want to pass up a good buy. But, in the long run, a smaller collection of choice pieces will probably bring you more satisfaction (and financial reward) than a large collection of moderate quality.

Purchasing a damaged or clearly repaired piece is a judgment only the collector can make. In general I wouldn't recommend it unless the piece is so unique that another example is not likely to come your way in the near future. For certain classes of expensive and rare ceramics, especially early pottery that has seen heavy use, a certain amount of damage may be inevitable and more acceptable. The sale price, however, should reflect this fact.

Restoration of pottery and porcelain wares has been a fact of life for many decades. Even in the early nineteenth century before good glues were available, 'make-do' repairs were sometimes done to pieces using small metal staples and today some collectors seek out these quaint examples of early recycling. Since the early twentieth century glue and repainting have been common methods used to mask damages to pottery and porcelain and these repairs can usually be detected today with a strong light and the naked eye.

The problem in recent decades has been the ability of restorers to completely mask any sign of previous damages using more sophisticated repair methods. There is nothing wrong with a quality restoration of a rare piece as long as the eventual purchaser is completely aware such work has been done.

It can take more than the naked eye and a strong light to detect some invisible repairs today and that's where the popular 'black light,' using ultraviolet rays, can be of help. Many spots of repair will fluoresce under the 'black light.' I understand, however, that newer glues and paints are becoming available which won't show up under the black light. The key then, especially for the beginner, is know your ceramic or your seller and be sure you have a money-back guarantee when making a major purchase.

I certainly don't want to sound too downbeat and discourage anyone from pursuing what can be a wonderfully fun and fulfilling hobby, but starting from a position of strength, with confidence and education, will certainly pay-off in the long run for every collector.

Ceramics, in addition to their beauty and charm, also offer the collecting advantage of durability and low-maintenance. It's surprising how much pottery and porcelain from two centuries ago is still available to collect. There were literally train-cars full of it produced and sold by the late nineteenth century, and such wares are abundantly available and often reasonably priced. Beautiful dinnerwares and colorful vases abound in the marketplace and offer exciting collecting possibilities. They look wonderful used on today's dining tables or gracing display shelves.

A periodic dusting and once-a-year washing in mild sudsy, warm water is about all the care they will require. Of course, it's not recommended you put older pottery and porcelains in your dishwasher where rattling and extremely hot water could cause damage. Anyway, it's more satisfying to hold a piece in your hand in warm soapy water in a rubber dishpan (for added protection) and caress it carefully with a dishrag. The tactile enjoyment of a ceramic piece brings a new dimension to collecting and this sort of T.L.C. can be nearly as satisfying as just admiring a piece in a china cabinet or on a shelf.

Whatever sort of pottery or porcelain appeals to you most, whether it be eighteenth century Meissen or mid-twentieth century California-made pottery, you can take pride in the fact that you are carrying on a collecting tradition that goes back centuries when the crowned heads of Europe first began vying for the finest and rarest ceramics with which to accent their regal abodes.

Kyle Husfloen

# Typical Ceramic Shapes

The following line drawings illustrate typical shapes found in pottery and porcelain pitchers and vases. These forms are ferred to often in our price listings.

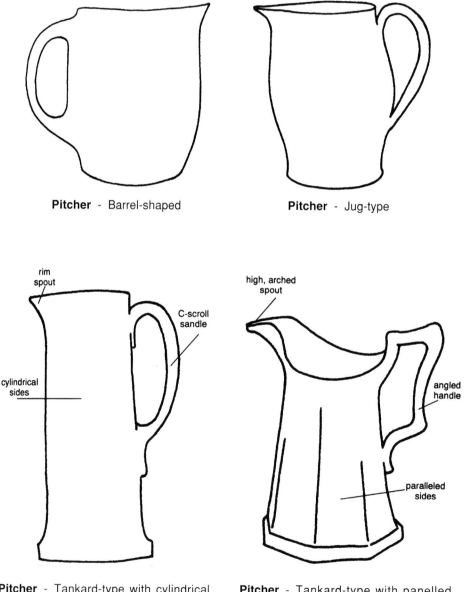

**Pitcher** - Barrel-shaped

**Pitcher** - Jug-type

rim spout

C-scroll sandle

cylindrical sides

high, arched spout

angled handle

paralleled sides

**Pitcher** - Tankard-type with cylindrical sides, C-scroll handle, and rim spout.

**Pitcher** - Tankard-type with panelled (octagonal) sides, angled handle and high, arched spout.

# Vases

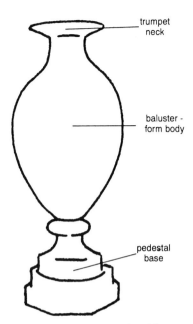

trumpet
neck

baluster -
form body

pedestal
base

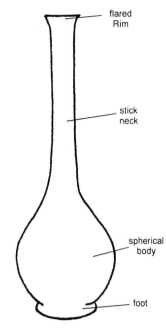

flared
Rim

stick
neck

spherical
body

foot

**Vase** - Baluster-form body with trumpet neck on a pedestal base.

**Vase** - Bottle-form — Spherical footed body tapering to a tall stick neck with flared rim.

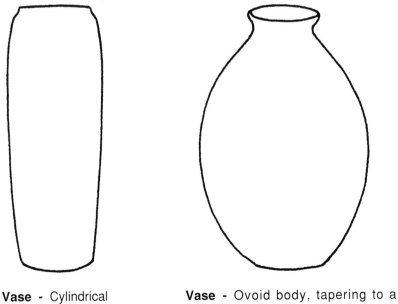

**Vase -** Cylindrical

**Vase -** Ovoid body, tapering to a short, flared neck.

# Vases (Continued)

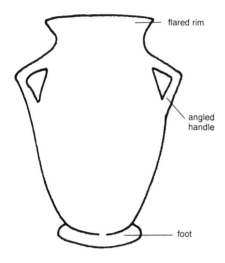

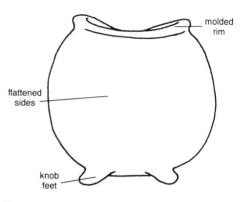

**Vase** - Pillow-shaped with molded rim; on knob feet.

**Vase** - Ovoid, footed body with flared rim & angled handles.

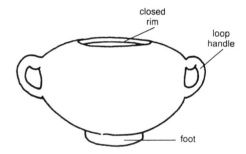

**Vase or bowl vase** - Spherical, footed body with closed rim and loop handles.

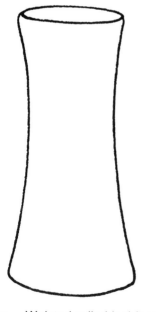

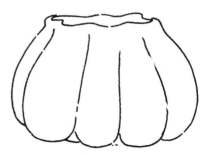

**Vase** - Waisted cylindrical form.

**Vase** - Squatty bulbous body with lobed sides.

# ABINGDON

*From about 1934 until 1950, Abingdon Pottery Company, Abingdon, Illinois, manufactured decorative pottery, mainly cookie jars, flowerpots and vases. Decorated with various glazes, these items are becoming popular with collectors who are especially attracted to Abingdon's novelty cookie jars.*

*Abingdon Marks*

**Book ends,** figural horse head, white, w/labels, pr. .................... **$70.00**

**Bowl,** 12" d., shell-shaped, No. 533, yellow ................................. **20.00**

**Console set:** large bowl & pr. candleholders; No. 532 & No. 575, blue, 3 pcs. ........................ **35.00**

**Cookie jar,** "Jack-in-the-Box" ......................................... **550.00**

**Cookie jar,** "Money Bag" ............. **80.00**

*Abingdon "Mother Goose" Cookie Jar*

**Cookie jar,** "Mother Goose" (ILLUS.) .................................... **495.00**

**Cookie jar,** "Pumpkin" (Jack o' Lantern) ................... **350.00 to 450.00**

**Figure,** woman, gold hair & trim, holding basket w/flower decal, 10" h. ........................................ **200.00**

**Sugar bowl,** cov., cherry finial ...... **35.00**

**Vase,** 7" h., Abbey, No. 575, pink .. **20.00**

**Vase,** 10" h., Classic, No. 117, green .......................................... **40.00**

**Vase,** 11" h., Swirl, No. 514, chartreuse or blue, each ............. **40.00**

**Vase,** 11" h., Swirl, decorated w/rose decals, gold flowers & stipple, tan & orange ground ....... **95.00**

**Wall pocket,** figural lily, white ....... **75.00**

# AREQUIPA

*Fine Arequipa Jardiniere*

*Dr. Philip King Brown established The Arequipa Sanitorium in Fairfax, California in the early years of the 20th century. In 1911 he set up a pottery at the facility as therapy for his female tuberculosis patients since he had been impressed with the success of the similar Marblehead pottery in Massachusetts.*

*The first art director was the noted ceramics designer Frederick H. Rhead who had earlier been art director at the Roseville Pottery.*

*In 1913 the pottery was separated from the medical facility and incorporated as The Arequipa Potteries. Later that year Rhead and his wife, Agnes, one of the pottery instructors, left Arequipa and Albert L. Solon took over as the pottery director. The corporation was dissolved in 1915 and the pottery closed in 1918 although the sanitorium remained in operation until 1957.*

*Arequipa Marks*

**Jardinere & pedestal,** a squatty bulbous jardiniere resting atop a tall slender pedestal base flared at the top & foot, squeezebag decoration of stylized circular blossoms in deep rose w/yellow centers on twisting vines & leaves against a dark ground, stylized geometric rim band, signed w/a raised "R" at base, probably designed by Frederick Rhead, jardiniere 13½" d., 8" h., overall 24½" h., 2 pcs. (ILLUS. previous page) .......... **$825.00**

**Vase,** 3¼" h., 5" d., squatty bulbous body w/a wide short flat neck, decorated around the wide shoulder w/a band of stylized leaves in squeezebag under a matte cobalt blue glaze, designed by Frederick Rhead, Rhead-period blue mark ....... **3,960.00**

**Vase,** 4" h., 4½" d., bulbous ovoid body w/a rounded shoulder to the short cylindrical neck, decorated w/hand-tooled jonquils over deeply incised stems under a smooth matte greyish blue glaze, die-stamp mark & "HD 2" ...................... **3,630.00**

**Vase,** 5¼" h., 3½" d., ovoid body w/a rounded shoulder to the short cylindrical neck, decorated around the shoulder w/an incised band of stylized flowers & Greek key pattern under a matte dark brown glaze, die-stamped mark ................. **1,870.00**

**Vase,** 6½" h., 3¾" d., slender ovoid body w/a low rolled rim, relief-carved w/morning glories on tall leafy stems under a satin raspberry pink & grey glaze, incised "Arequipa - NN - 11" .... **825.00**

**Vase,** 8¾" h., 6" d., wide ovoid body tapering sharply at the shoulder to the wide flat mouth, decorated in squeezebag around the upper half w/panels of scrolling stylized florals in green on a brick red ground against a green dripping over a periwinkle blue glaze, probably by Frederick Rhead ............. **3,410.00**

# AUSTRIAN

*Numerous potteries in Austria produced good-quality ceramic wares over many years. Some factories were established by American entrepreneurs, particularly in the Carlsbad area, and other factories made china under special brand names for American importers. Marks on various pieces are indicated in many listings. Also see ROYAL VIENNA.*

*Austrian Marks*

*Ornate Austrian Dessert Set*

**Cheese & cracker server,**
decorated w/small roses,
9½" d. (M.Z. Austria)................ **$45.00**

**Chocolate pot,** cov., portrait
decoration of Philippe d'Orleans,
Regent of Louis the XV, cobalt
blue ground, ca. 1891-1918,
9" h. (Victoria Carlsbad)............ **475.00**

**Dessert set:** 5" h., 8½" d. open
compote & six 8½" d. matching
plates; Alhambra patt., each w/a
slightly scalloped rim & a wide
border band composed of gold &
green fan devices alternating
w/dark green & white & dark
maroon & gold arrowheads, a
white center w/a central starburst
in maroon, dark green & gold, the
set (ILLUS. top) ......................... **330.00**

**Ewer,** decorated w/h.p. cherub,
5" d., 7½" h. (Victoria
Carlsbad) .................................. **175.00**

**Figures,** a male & female
standing wearing 18th c.
costume, late 19th c., 12¼" h.,
pr. ............................................ **431.00**

**Fish set,** 20" l. platter & eight 8¼"
plates; each decorated w/a
different game fish (LS&S,
Carlsbad Austria) ..................... **335.00**

*Rose-decorated Austrian Pitcher*

**Pitcher,** 4¼" h., 4¼" d., wide
ovoid body w/a wide gently
flared mouth & small spout,
angled loop handle, h.p. w/dark
red & bright yellow roses &
green leaves on a pastel
background, marked "Vienna
Austria" (ILLUS.) ........................ **45.00**

**Pitcher,** 8" h., ovoid form w/a
bacchante mask molded under
the spout, decorated w/a scene
of a girl w/a dove & roses, artist-
signed, factory marks, late
19th c. ...................................... **575.00**

**Plates,** 8" d., each decorated w/a
different berry, including

strawberries, grapes &
raspberries, pastel trim & ornate
openwork edge, artist-signed,
set of 6 ...................................... **285.00**

**Vase,** 14½" h., footed tall slender
ovoid body w/a slender squared
stick neck, long slender curved
handles from neck rim to
shoulder, decorated w/heavily
enameled colorful fuchsias &
green leaves on a pale yellow
ground, cobalt blue handles &
trim .......................................... **375.00**

**Wine jug w/stopper,** squatty
bulbous body w/short cylindrical
neck w/stopper & gold loop
handle, decorated
w/multicolored grapes & leaves
on a multicolored ground, ca.
1908, marked "P.H. Leonard
Importer," 7¼" h. to top of
stopper (wear on handle, cork
on stopper not original) ........... **275.00**

---

# BAUER

*The Bauer Pottery was moved to Los
Angeles, California from Paducah,
Kentucky, in 1909, in the hope that the
climate would prove beneficial to the
principal organizer, John Andrew
Bauer, who suffered from severe
asthma. Flowerpots, made of California
adobe clay, were the first production at
the new location, but soon they were
able to resume production of stoneware
crocks and jugs, the mainstay of the
Kentucky operation. In the early 1930s,
Bauer's colorfully glazed earthen
dinnerwares, especially the popular
Ring-Ware pattern, became an
immediate success. Sometimes confused
with its imitator, Fiesta Ware (first
registered by Homer Laughlin in 1937),
Bauer pottery is collectible in its own
right and is especially popular with
West Coast collectors. Bauer Pottery
ceased operation in 1962.*

*Bauer Marks*

**Baker,** individual, Ring-Ware
patt., green or yellow, 4" d.,
each ......................................... **$34.00**

**Batter bowl,** Ring-Ware patt.,
green, small ............................. **125.00**

**Beater pitcher,** Ring-Ware patt.,
red, 1 qt.................................... **110.00**

**Bowl,** berry, 5½" d., Ring-Ware
patt., yellow ............................. **55.00**

**Bowl,** soup, cov., 5½" d., lug
handles, Ring-Ware patt.,
orange, green, ivory or cobalt
blue, each ................................. **45.00**

**Bowl,** 8" d., Swirl patt., yellow....... **70.00**

**Bowl,** 13" d., Cal-Art line, green ... **30.00**

**Bowl,** 15" d., wide low sides,
white & brown speckled glaze,
No. 149 ..................................... **95.00**

**Butter dish,** cov., Ring-Ware
patt., delph blue (light blue) ...... **225.00**

**Butter dish,** cov., Ring-Ware
patt., red.................................... **145.00**

**Cake plate,** Monterey patt.,
yellow........................................ **185.00**

**Candleholders,** spool-shaped,
Ring-Ware patt., jade green,
pr. ............................................. **450.00**

**Carafe,** cov., Ring-Ware patt.,
copper handle, red.................... **125.00**

**Casserole,** cov., individual, Ring-
Ware patt., cobalt blue,
5½" d.......................................... **85.00**

**Casserole,** cov., individual, Ring-
Ware patt., ivory, 5½" d. ............. **95.00**

**Casserole,** cov., individual, Ring-
Ware patt., rust, 5½" d. ............... **85.00**

**Coffee carafe,** cov., copper
handle, Ring-Ware patt.,
delphinium ................................ **275.00**

**Console set:** console bowl & pr.
of three-light candlesticks; pink,
semi-matte finish, 3 pcs. ........... **245.00**

**Cookie jar,** cov., Monterey
Moderne patt., chartreuse........ **100.00**

**Cookie jar,** cov., Ring-Ware
patt., red.................................. **995.00**

**Creamer & cov. sugar bowl,**
Ring-Ware patt., ivory, pr......... **350.00**

**Creamer & cov. sugar bowl,**
Ring-Ware patt., orange, pr. ..... **125.00**

**Cup & saucer,** demitasse, Ring-
Ware patt., yellow .................... **225.00**

**Flowerpot,** Ring-Ware patt.,
cobalt blue ................................ **45.00**

**Flowerpot,** Speckleware, flesh
pink, 8¼" d., 6½" h..................... **40.00**

**Gravy boat,** Monterey Moderne
patt., pink ................................. **40.00**

**Gravy boat,** Ring-Ware patt.,
burgundy.................................. **145.00**

**Mixing bowl,** Atlanta line, No. 24,
cobalt blue .............................. **150.00**

**Mixing bowl,** nesting-type, Ring-
Ware patt., No. 18, chartreuse.... **75.00**

**Mixing bowl,** nesting-type, Ring-
Ware patt., No. 36, ivory, small... **55.00**

**Model of a swan,** chartreuse,
large.......................................... **85.00**

**Model of a swan,** yellow, large .. **135.00**

**Mug,** barrel-shaped, Ring-Ware
patt., jade or yellow, each ......... **300.00**

**Oil jars,** No. 100, white, 12" h.,
pr............................................ **3,000.00**

**Pie plate,** Ring-Ware patt., green ... **45.00**

**Pitcher,** cov., jug-type, ice water,
Monterey patt., turquoise ......... **325.00**

**Pitcher,** Ring-Ware patt., orange,
1 qt. ......................................... **85.00**

**Pitcher,** Ring-Ware patt.,
delphinium blue, 2 qt................ **250.00**

**Pitcher,** water w/ice lip, Monterey
patt., marigold .......................... **125.00**

**Planter,** model of a swan,
chartreuse, medium ................... **95.00**

**Plate,** dinner, 10½" d., Ring-Ware
patt., cobalt, yellow, delph or
orange, each ............................. **95.00**

**Plate,** dinner, 10½" d., Ring-Ware
patt., jade green ........................ **85.00**

**Plate,** chop, Monterey Moderne
patt., yellow............................... **45.00**

**Plate,** chop, 12" d., Ring-Ware
patt., burgundy......................... **250.00**

**Plate,** chop, 12" d., Ring-Ware
patt., white ............................... **295.00**

**Plate,** chop, 14" d., Ring-Ware
patt., yellow............................. **125.00**

**Plate,** chop, Monterey Moderne
patt, yellow................................ **45.00**

**Plate,** grill, Monterey Moderne
patt., chartreuse......................... **35.00**

**Punch bowl,** three footed, Ring-
Ware patt., jade green, 14" d. .... **550.00**

**Punch bowl,** three-footed, Ring-
Ware patt., cobalt blue,
14" d..................................... **1,295.00**

**Punch cup,** Ring-Ware patt., light
blue, cobalt blue, green, yellow
or burgundy, each ...................... **55.00**

**Relish dish,** divided, Ring-Ware
patt., cobalt blue ...................... **195.00**

**Salt & pepper shakers,** beehive-
shape, Ring-Ware patt., orange,
pr............................................... **60.00**

**Sugar bowl,** cov., demitasse,
Ring-Ware patt., burgundy.......... **45.00**

**Sugar shaker,** Ring-Ware patt.,
jade green ................................ **350.00**

**Syrup pitcher,** Ring-Ware patt.,
cobalt blue ............................... **285.00**

**Teapot,** cov., "Aladdin Lamp,"
Gloss Pastel Kitchenware line,
yellow, large ............................. **250.00**

**Teapot,** cov., Ring Ware patt.,
yellow...................................... **135.00**

**Teapot,** cov., Ring-Ware patt.,
burgundy, 2-cup size ............... **325.00**

**Teapot,** cov., Ring-Ware patt.,
yellow, 2-cup size (tiny nick) ..... **225.00**

**Vase,** 4¼" h., bulbous, hand-
thrown by Fred Johnson, jade
green.......................................... **50.00**

**Vase,** 8" h., deep trumpet-shaped
form w/widely flaring sides fluted
on the exterior, yellow.............. **250.00**

**Vase,** 10½" h., cylindrical, Ring-
Ware patt., delph blue................. **85.00**

**Vase,** 13" h., ovoid base w/widely
flared rim, shoulder handles,
jade, Matt Carlton ................. **1,200.00**

**Vase,** 22" h., Rebekah V, tall
slender baluster-form w/loop
handles near the short flaring
neck, turquoise ..................... **1,950.00**

# BAVARIAN

*Ceramics have been produced by various potteries in Bavaria, Germany for many years. Those appearing for sale in greatest frequency today were produced in the 19th and eary 20th centuries. Various company marks are indicated with some listings here.*

**Box,** cov., decorated w/grapes &
leaves, gold trim, artist-
signed .................................... **$195.00**

**Cup,** child's, Red Riding Hood &
wolf decoration........................... **39.00**

**Nut bowl,** scalloped baroque
blank, lavish gold trim, 8" d. ........ **43.00**

**Pitcher,** cider, large, Egyptian
motifs decoration, artist-signed. **120.00**

**Plate,** 8" d., h.p. pink & yellow
chrysanthemums, artist-signed... **38.00**

**Plate,** 9" d., transfer-printed
colored grape clusters, transfer-
printed signature "Koch,"
marked on back "Louise -
Bavaria" .................................... **28.00**

**Plate,** 10" d., h.p. portrait
decoration of woman w/long
hair, red & gold border ............. **175.00**

**Plates,** 12" d., decorated w/h.p.
birds on iridescent orange, pr. .. **325.00**

**Punch bowl & base,** interior &
exterior w/floral decoration,
marked "Bavaria," 13¾" d., 2
pcs. .......................................... **595.00**

# BELLEEK

*Belleek china has been made in Ireland's County Fermanagh for many years. It is exceedingly thin porcelain. Several marks were used, including a hound and harp (1865-1880), and a hound, harp and castle (1863-1891). A printed hound, harp and castle with the words "Co. Fermanagh Ireland" constitutes the mark from 1891. Belleek-type china also was made in the United States last century by several firms, including Ceramic Art Company, Columbian Art Pottery, Lenox Inc., Ott & Brewer and Willets Manufacturing Co. Also see LENOX.*

*Early Irish Belleek Mark*

### AMERICAN

**Book ends,** figural, modeled as
an elongated face & neck of a
lady w/cascading hair fashioned
to one side, green wreath mark,
9" h., pr. (Lenox - Belleek) ..... **$450.00**

**Bowl,** 4½" d., 2" h., decorated
w/gold florals & stems, pastel
sponge decoration around base,
gold ruffled edge (Ceramic Art
Company) ................................. **135.00**

*Ott & Brewer Cups & Saucers*

**Coffeepot,** cov., tall graceful shape decorated w/a portrait of Queen Louise highlighted by soft greens & heavy gold trim, 10½" h. (Lenox - Belleek) ........ **485.00**

**Coffee set:** pedestal-based cov. coffeepot, creamer & cov. sugar bowl; decorated w/yellow & pink roses w/gold trim, 3 pcs. (Ceramic Art Company) ........... **650.00**

**Creamer & cov. sugar bowl,** Shell patt., pr. (Willets)................ **65.00**

**Cup & saucer,** demitasse, shell-shaped, pink & blue w/gilt handle, rim & decoration (Ceramic Art Company) ............ **160.00**

**Cups & saucers,** rib-molded round shell-shaped cups & matching saucers, pearlized glaze w/gilded accents, red crown & dagger mark, cup 4" d., 2" h., set of 10, Ott & Brewer (ILLUS. above) ........................ **935.00**

**Mug,** cylindrical, decorated w/green holly leaves & red holly berries on light blue & pale lavender ground, gold band around base & rim & gold trim on handle, palette mark, 5¾" h. (Ceramic Art Company)............................. **200.00**

**Mugs,** waisted cylindrical, pale pink ground decorated w/h.p. purple & green grapes & leaves, base & C-scroll handle trimmed w/gold, marked "Belleek" in green on bottom, pr. (some wear to gold rim of one, small pinhead hole near base on one, very faint hairline on side of hole to other) ......... **250.00**

**Pitcher,** 6" h., 8" d. from handle to spout, decorated w/strawberries & leaves, gold trim, artist-signed (Ceramic Art Company) ........... **340.00**

**Salt dip,** h.p. decoration, 1¼" d. (Willets) ...................................... **30.00**

**Teapot,** cov., all-around floral border on mauve ground (Willets) ...................................... **95.00**

**Vase,** 8" h., purple & yellow irises on subtle satin iridescent salmon ground (Ceramic Art Company) ................................. **225.00**

## IRISH

**Basket,** three-strand, Shamrock patt., 4½ x 4½" ........................ **400.00**

**Bread plate,** Tridacna patt., molded ruffled side handles, large, 2nd black mark ............. **375.00**

**Butter plate,** Shamrock patt., green mark................................. **55.00**

**Cracker jar,** cov., barrel-shaped, Shamrock-Basketweave patt., 2nd black mark ....................... **150.00**

**Creamer,** Ivy patt., black mark...... **65.00**

**Creamer,** Neptune patt., pink trim, 2nd black mark .................. **65.00**

**Creamer,** Ribbon patt., green mark............................................ **40.00**

**Creamer,** Shamrock-Basketweave patt., 2nd black mark ......................................... **80.00**

**Creamer & open sugar bowl,** individual, Cleary patt., 3rd black mark, pr.................................... **140.00**

**Creamer & open sugar bowl,** Lotus patt., green mark, pr.......... **75.00**

*Neptune Pattern Cup & Saucer*

**Cup & saucer,** Neptune patt., pink trim, 3rd black mark on cup, 2nd black mark on saucer (ILLUS.) ....................................... **55.00**

**Cup & saucer,** Shamrock-Basketweave patt., pink tint, black mark (tiny chip on cup near handle)............................... **50.00**

**Dessert set:** 8" plate w/yellow center & cup & saucer; Tridacna patt., 2nd black mark, 3 pcs...... **250.00**

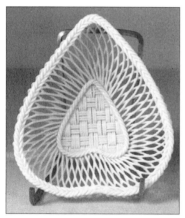

*Heart-shaped Belleek Dish*

**Dish,** heart-shaped, four-strand Basketware, 4⅛ x 4½", 1¾" h. (ILLUS.) ..................................... **335.00**

**Flowerpot,** bulbous swirled rib body w/scalloped rim, applied flowers, raised on three scroll feet, pink trim, 2nd black mark, 10½" h. ................................. **1,400.00**

**Model of a harp,** decorated w/shamrocks, 6½" h, 3rd green mark......................................... **165.00**

*Belleek Model of a Pig*

*Limpet Milk Pitcher*

**Model of a pig,** all-white, 2nd black mark, 4½" l., 2¾" h. (ILLUS. top) ............................. **325.00**

**Mug,** coffee, Thorn patt., green mark............................................. **75.00**

**Pitcher,** milk, jug-type, Limpet patt., 3rd black mark (ILLUS. bottom)...................................... **395.00**

**Plate,** 6" d., Neptune patt., green tint, 3rd black mark ................... **75.00**

**Plate,** 7¼" d., Institute patt., deep pink & gold trim, monogram in center, 1st black mark, also impressed mark (shallow chip at rim of underside)......................... **85.00**

**Plate,** 8" d., Tridacna patt., 2nd black mark ................................. **89.00**

**Salt dip,** Cleary patt., embossed shells decorated w/green shamrocks, 2nd black mark, 2 x 3",¼" 1" h. ............................ **65.00**

**Salt dip,** Shamrock-Basketweave patt., black mark ......................... **48.00**

*Belleek Sea Horse Vase*

**Sugar bowl,** open, Institute patt., pink trim, 2nd black mark ............ **85.00**

**Sugar bowl,** open, Shamrock-Basketweave patt., 2nd black mark .......................................... **80.00**

**Tea cup & saucer,** Hexagon patt., pink tint, 2nd black mark . **150.00**

**Tea set:** cov. teapot, creamer, open sugar bowl, 17½" l. tray & three cups & saucers: Shamrock-Basketweave patt., decorated w/green & brown enameled shamrocks, black mark, the set ............................ **770.00**

**Vase,** 3¾" h., 5" l., Sea horse patt., cornucopia-form, on a wave-molded rectangular base, beaded rim vase, all-white, 1st black mark (ILLUS. above) ....... **578.00**

**Vase,** 7" h., Sunflower patt., 2nd black mark .............................. **175.00**

**Vases,** spill, 6¾" h., Lily patt., tapering cylindrical body on narrow footring, sawtooth edge, decorated w/lily-of-the-valley, black mark, pr. .......................... **198.00**

# BENNINGTON

*Bennington wares, which ranged from stoneware to parian and porcelain, were made in Bennington, Vermont, primarily in two potteries, one in which Captain John Norton and his descendants were* principals, and the other in which Christopher Webber Fenton (also once associated with the Nortons) was a principal. Various marks are found on the wares made in the two major potteries, including J. & E. Norton, E. & L. P. Norton, L. Norton & Co., Norton & Fenton, Edward Norton, Lyman Fenton & Co. Fenton's Works, United States Pottery Co., U.S.P. and others.

*The popular pottery with the mottled brown on yellowware glaze was also produced in Bennington, but such wares should be referred to as "Rockingham" or "Bennington-type" unless they can be specifically attributed to a Bennington, Vermont factory.*

*Also see STONEWARE.*

*Bennington Marks*

**Baking dish,** eight-sided rectangular form, mottled brown Flint Enamel glaze, impressed "1849" mark, 8¾" l., 2" h. (three faint hairlines off the rim) ....... **$550.00**

**Book flask,** binding impressed "Bennington Battle," mottled Flint Enamel glaze, attributed to Lyman Fenton & Co., ca. 1850, 7¾" h. (one bottom corner chipped off, shallow chip on one top corner) .............................. **550.00**

**Book flask,** binding impressed "Bennington Battle," mottled Flint Enamel glaze, highly detailed pages & spine, 11" h. (invisible restoration along the upper rim) ............................ **4,950.00**

*Bennington Coachman Bottles*

*E. & L.P. Norton Crock*

**Book flask,** binding impressed "Ladies Companion," mottled Flint Enamel glaze, unmarked, 4 qt., 8¼" w., 11" h. (professional invisible repair & reglazing of a portion of edge of cover & one side) .................. **3,850.00**

**Bottle,** figural coachman wearing cloak & top hat, mottled dark brown Rockingham glaze, professional restoration to hat & base, 8½" h. (ILLUS. above left) .. **440.00**

**Bottle,** figural coachman wearing cloak & top hat, mottled brown Rockingham glaze, impressed "1849" mark, invisible restorations to hat & some base chips, 10½" h. (ILLUS. above right) ......................................... **523.00**

**Coffeepot,** cov., tall paneled baluster-form w/a flaring rim & inset high domed cover w/a pointed finial, swan's-neck spout & arched, angled handle, mottled Flint Enamel glaze, unmarked, 12¾" h. (excellent restoration to tip of spout & edges of three panels, underside of base w/invisible line restoration) ..................... **1,980.00**

**Crock,** stoneware, cylindrical w/eared handles & molded rim, slip-quilled cobalt blue long-tailed bird perched on a scrolling plume design, E. & L.P. Norton, Bennington, Vermont, ca. 1870, 3 gal., very minor surface chips on back rim, 10½" h. (ILLUS.) .. **963.00**

**Crock,** stoneware, cylindrical w/eared handles, slip-quilled cobalt blue foraging game birds, J. Norton & Co. mark, mid-19th c., 10⅝" h. (cracks, very minor chips, firing blemishes) ............. **403.00**

**Curtain tie-backs,** domed florette-form w/pointed petal tips, on a long cylindrical shaft w/a flaring base, mottled Flint Enamel glaze, hollow, unmarked, 4½" d., 4½" h., pr. .. **440.00**

**Cuspidor,** low paneled & waisted round sides w/side hole, mottled Flint Enamel glaze, impressed 1849 mark, 9" d., 4" h. ............. **220.00**

**Foot warmer,** ovoid tapering half-round form w/deeply indented foot impressions on top, small cylindrical neck, mottled brown Rockingham glaze, shell & scroll design on reverse, ca. 1847-58, 9" h. ......................................... **330.00**

**Jar,** stoneware, wide cylindrical body w/molded rim & eared handles, slip-quilled cobalt blue floral decoration, impressed

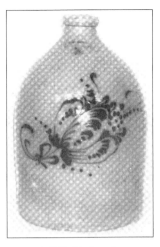

*J. & E. Norton Jug*

label "E. Norton & Co., Bennington, Vt." & "2," 2 gal., 11½" h. (small chip on one handle) ......................... **204.00**

**Jug,** stoneware, semi-ovoid w/a strap handle & molded rim, slip-quilled cobalt blue large stylized floral design, J. & E. Norton, Bennington, Vermont, ca. 1859, 3 gal., very minor stone & stack mark in front, 15" h. (ILLUS.) ... **605.00**

**Lamp,** table model, kerosene-type, the pottery base w/a square stepped base supporting a slender baluster-form standard w/a fine Flint Enamel glaze, a clear glass font engraved w/a band of leaves above a gilt connector & supporting a metal ring w/long prisms & a tall baluster-form free-blown clear diamond quilted shade w/a ruffled top, base 8⅞" h. (hole in side of glass font, tiny in-the-making firing separation in corner of base) ..................... **8,800.00**

**Model of a lion,** standing w/one paw resting on a ball, his tail over his back, facing right, coleslaw mane & tongue up, mottled Flint Enamel glaze, rare & exceptional coloring, 11¼" l., 7½" h. (professional restoration

to a hairline across the tail & to cracks across both rear legs, portion of one tooth missing) . **3,850.00**

**Mug,** footed baluster-form w/ornate C-scroll handle, mottled, spotty brown Rockingham glaze, 4¼" h. (three hard to find hairlines off the rim, a small chip) ........................................ **198.00**

**Paperweight,** domed rectangular form molded w/a small recumbent Spaniel on the top, overall dark mottled brown Rockingham glaze, impressed "Fenton" mark, 4½" l., 3" h. (few very minor base flakes) ........... **550.00**

**Pie plate,** wide flat bottom & low canted sides, mottled Flint Enamel glaze, impressed "1849" mark, 9⅞" d., 1½" h. ............... **825.00**

**Pitcher,** 6" h., toby-style, a bust of Benjamin Franklin wearing a tricorn hat, cloak & w/a molded "boot" handle, mottled brown Rockingham glaze, impressed "1849" mark (excellent hat brim restoration) ............................... **660.00**

**Pitcher,** 6¼" h., figural, a bust of General Stark, hero of the Battle of Bennington, wearing a tricorn hat forming the rim & epaulettes on his shoulders, mottled brown Rockingham glaze (invisible restoration to some small hat brim chips) ... **2,040.00**

**Pitcher,** 7" h., Alternate Rib patt., footed bulbous waisted body w/an arched spout & arched C-scroll handle, mottled Flint Enamel glaze, impressed "1849" mark ...................................... **1,320.00**

**Pitcher,** 9" h., hound-handled, the footed bulbous body below an angled shoulder to a cylindrical neck w/a high arched spout, relief-molded deer & dog hunting scene around the body & a vintage grape design around the shoulder & neck, mottled brown Rockingham glaze, small filled-in chip on spout (ILLUS. top next page)........................................ **935.00**

*Hound-handled Bennington Pitcher*

*Bennington Alternate Rib Pitcher*

**Pitcher,** 11¼" h., Alternate Rib patt., footed bulbous waisted body w/an arched scroll-molded spout & ribbed C-scroll handle, mottled Flint Enamel glaze, invisible restoration to spout rim, few small chips around base (ILLUS.) ................................ **1,320.00**

**Snuff jar,** cov., figural, seated Mr. Toby holding a pitcher in one hand & a glass in the other, his broad-brimmed hat forming the cover, mottled Flint Enamel glaze, impressed "1849" mark, 4¼" h. (hat broken & reglued, base rim chip restored) ............ **743.00**

**Tile,** square, relief-molded central diamond lattice design, molded shadowbox frame, Flint Enamel glaze, impressed "1849" mark, 7" w. ........................................ **660.00**

**Toilet box,** cov., Alternate Rib patt., narrow long oblong form w/flared rim & inset domed cover w/loop handle, mottled Flint Enamel glaze, 7⅞" l., 3¼" h. (corner of cover broken off & tightly reglued) ................ **495.00**

**Washbowl & pitcher,** Alternate Rib patt., tall slender finely ribbed waisted body w/a high scalloped rim & long arched spout, ornate C-scroll handle, deep matching bowl w/wide rolled rim & thick footring, Flint Enamel glaze on a pale cream ground w/yellow & brown predominant, bowl impressed "United States Pottery Company - Bennington, VT," bowl 13½" d., 4½" h., pitcher 12½" h., the set (few minor glaze rubs on edge of bowl) ................................... **4,290.00**

# BERLIN (KPM)

*The mark, KPM, was used at Meissen from 1723 to 1725, and was later adopted by the Royal Factory, Konigliche Porzellan Manufaktur, in Berlin. At various periods it has been incorporated with the Brandenburg sceptre, the Prussian eagle or the crowned globe. The same letters were also adopted by other factories in Germany in the late 19th and 20th centuries. With the end of the German monarchy in 1918, the name of the firm was changed to Staatliche Porzellan Manufaktur and though production was halted during World War II, the factory was rebuilt and is still in business. The exquisite paintings on porcelain were produced at the close of the 19th century and are eagerly sought by collectors today.*

*Ornate KPM Ewer*

*Fine KPM Figurines*

**Ewers,** a thick round foot supporting a swirled knopped standard below a swelled gadrooned band & a swelled ovoid body w/a wide gently sloping shoulder centered by a ringed & swirled short neck w/a scalloped rim & long spout, an ornate S-scroll handle from the rim to the shoulder & a serpent handle down one side of the body, the body decorated w/a continuous wide panel w/classical allegorical figures, colorful scroll decoration & embossed trim on the neck, shoulder & base, underglaze-blue sceptre mark & "KPM" in red, restorations, late 19th c., 23½" h., pr. (ILLUS. of one) . **$4,600.00**

**Figurines,** young man dressed in long coat, trousers & boots, holding cocked hat & young lady in Empire-style dress, fancy hat, holding a fan, both dressed in white w/much fine detailing in brown & gold trim, round bases w/gold trim, marked "K.P.M." in blue under glaze, 3½" d., 8½" h., pr. (ILLUS. top next column)..... **395.00**

**Luncheon service:** 6" h. cov. teapot (cover & spout repairs), 9" h. hot water pot (finial restored), creamer (handle damage), ten tea cups (one damaged), eleven saucers, ten coffee cups (one w/rim chip), eleven saucers, seven demitasse cups w/twelve saucers & eleven 8¾" d. plates; each piece w/molded basketweave borders, h.p. w/enameled floral designs & gilt edging, all w/factory marks, 19th c., the set ...................... **2,415.00**

**Plaque,** oval, a scene depicting the Penitent Magdalene shown recumbent & reading, impressed "KPM" marks, late 19th c., 4¾ x 6½" ................................. **633.00**

**Plaque,** rectangular, depicting a young dark haired woman wearing a loose robe fastened on one shoulder, daisies in her hair & holding three daisies in her hands, signed "Wagner" & "KPM" impressed on reverse, 6 x 9" (ILLUS. top next page)... **6,710.00**

**Plaque,** rectangular, decorated w/a mother & child, the reverse w/ink inscriptions & impressed marks, late 19th c., 6¼ x 9⅛" .. **978.00**

*KPM Plaque of Lovely Lady*

**Plaque,** rectangular, decorated w/a landscape scene w/a nude cupid seated on a stone step & playing w/butterflies, impressed "KPM" & sceptre mark & incised dimensions, late 19th c., 6¼ x 9¼".............................. **3,450.00**

**Plaque,** rectangular, painted w/the head of Christ wearing the crown of thorns, his eyes raised skyward, impressed "K.P.M." marks, 19th c., 7½ x 9¼" ...... **1,265.00**

**Plaque,** rectangular, painted w/a scene of the Three Fates, a standing central figure flanked by two seated figures, signed "R. Dittrich" & impressed w/the "KPM" & sceptre mark & dimensions, titled "Die Parzen," late 19th c., 6¼ x 9½" .......... **4,025.00**

**Plaque,** rectangular, decorated w/a scene of two peasant children carrying a third younger child across a stream on the joined arms, a wooded background, signed "Werner," impressed "KPM" & sceptre mark, "S" & incised dimensions & titled "A. Travers Le Ruisseau - Paris - Salon 1898," late 19th c., framed, 9 x 11" ................ **7,187.00**

**Plaque,** rectangular, depicting two youthful cavaliers in an interior scene, artist-signed, impressed "KPM" marks, ca. 1880, 9¾ x 12½" ................. **4,025.00**

*Decorative KPM Vases*

**Plaque,** rectangular, a scene depicting a gypsy water bearer in an Italianate landscape, artist-signed, impressed "KPM" marks, ca. 1880, 9½ x 13" ............... **4,600.00**

**Plaque,** rectangular, a scene of Hagar & Ishmael driven from the house of Abraham, artist-signed, impressed "KPM" marks, ca. 1880, 12 x 16" ...................... **8,050.00**

**Serving bowl,** oval, enamel-decorated w/a foliate design & gilt border, 19th c., 15" l. .......... **201.00**

**Vase,** cov., 5" h., 'jeweled' decoration, baluster-shape, raised floral decoration on a mottled brown & green ground, factory marks, 19th c. ............. **518.00**

**Vases,** cov., 13½" h., ovoid body w/lightly molded ribbing, the top fitted w/a ribbed domed cover w/a large spread-winged bird finial, the body w/two molded bands w/gold trim centering round reserve w/molded gilt wreath borders, the reserve w/courting couples in 18th c. dress in a landscape, scattered colored floral sprigs around the body & cover & molded & gilt-trimmed lappet band around the base, factory marks, late 19th c., pr. (ILLUS. bottom previous page) ............. **3,680.00**

# BING & GRONDAHL

*Founded in 1853 in Copenhagen Denmark, the firm of Bing and Grondahl combined the talents of Frederich Gronhahl, a former employee of the Royal Copenhagen factory, with the business expertise of brothers M.H. and J.H. Bing.*

*One of this firm's most enduring products has been their series of annual Christmas plates which have been produced in lovely shades of blue and white since their introduction in 1895. These charming plates continue to be issued each year and today collectors also* seek out their line of lovely figurines as well as the fine dinnerwares they produce. Following is a sampling of the figural pieces recently offered on the collectors' market. For a compilation of current Christmas plate values, see the COMMEMORATIVE PLATES section of our annual Antiques and Collectibles Price Guide.

**Figure of a boy holding a puppy,** No. 1747 BF, 6½" h.... **$117.00**

**Figure of a boy playing w/blocks,** No. 2306 BR, 4¼" h.. **124.00**

**Figure of a boy seated on book,** No. 1742 E ................................ **144.00**

**Figure of a girl w/tulips,** No. 2298 ......................................... **158.00**

**Figure group,** young boy standing by older lad seated on stool, No. 1648 TO, artist-signed, Ingebery Tlokro, 7½" h.. **187.00**

**Figure group,** Hans C. Anderson seated beside the standing figure of a girl, No. 2037, figures 8½" h. & 6¾" h. .......................... **325.00**

**Model of a cat,** seated, No. 2465 ......................................... **108.00**

# BISQUE

*Bisque is biscuit china, fired a single time but not glazed. Some bisque is decorated with delicate colors. Most abundant from the Victorian era are figures and groups, but other pieces from busts to vases were made by numerous potteries in the United States and abroad. Reproductions have been produced for many years so care must be taken when seeking antique originals.*

**Bust of a young girl,** wearing an 18th c. costume w/mobcap & kerchief around her neck, her eyes closed & head slightly tilted, raised on an associated parcel-gilt & cobalt blue socle, overall 26" h. ....................... **$1,495.00**

*Beautiful French Bisque Bust*

**Bust of a young man,** finely detailed w/a smiling expression & blue eyes, blond curly hair, wearing a green flower-trimmed hat, a high-collared flowered fabric jacket over a shirt front decorated w/overall delicate colored tiny flowers, on a paneled socle base w/blue & pink trim & a painted flower bouquet, impressed "M.B." mark, France, late 19th c., 6½" w., 11" h. (ILLUS.) ............ **295.00**

**Center bowl,** white pierced bowl raised on tripod feet modeled as figural cherubs, France, 19th c., 8¾" h. ...................................... **575.00**

**Figure,** boy standing by a fence, wearing 18th c. attire, tricorn hat, kneebreeches & coat w/tails, holding a basket filled w/small applied flowers, soft pink & blue pastels w/lavish gold trim, scrolled base, France, 5½" d., 7¼" h ............................ **125.00**

**Figure,** Dutch girl sitting w/hands clasped, signed "Heubach," 6" h............................................ **285.00**

*Bisque Figure of a Sailor*

**Figure,** nursery rhyme-type, "The Old Woman in a Shoe," Germany, 2" h............................. **78.00**

**Figure,** sailor standing at ship's wheel, Heubach, Germany, 11½" h. (ILLUS.) ...................... **450.00**

**Figure,** Scottish girl w/ball in her hands, dark curly hair w/a blue hat & wearing a red, white & blue plaid dress, pink & green pantalettes & lavender shoes, gold trim, on a gilt-trimmed socle base, France, late 19th c., 4" d., 9¼" h. (ILLUS. top next page) .. **165.00**

**Figure,** young boy carrying a basket, wearing a lavender short coat w/yellow bow, blue striped short pants, pale blue hat w/pink ribbons, blue band & yellow feather, France, late 19th c., 4¾" d., 13½" h. ......................... **195.00**

**Figures,** beautiful blonde lady in pink, white & blue ballgown standing holding a rose, man w/a powdered wig, standing dressed in blue, white & maroon w/yellow trim, both on round heavy bases w/blue trimming & highlights of yellow, France, late 19th c., 11" h., pr. (ILLUS. bottom left, next page) .............. **495.00**

*Scottish Girl Bisque Figure*

*An Ornate Couple in Renaissance Costume*

*Bisque Figures of an 18th c. Couple*

*Cute Bisque Dog*

**Figures,** a walking lady wearing an ornate flowered Renaissance costume & a matching male, each holding a book & posed on a round base, Villeroy & Boch, Germany, ca. 1890, 28½" & 31" h., pr. (ILLUS. top next column) ................................. **2,070.00**

**Model of a dog sitting up on his haunches,** all-white w/tan collar, tinted eyes, nose & mouth, hair falling over his eyes, printed & impressed mark "Heubach," 3⅝" d., 9" h. (ILLUS.) ................ **325.00**

**Nodding figure,** Chinese man
seated w/legs crossed, holding a
fan in one hand, decorated in
pinks, beige & beading, 4½" h. . **170.00**

**Piano baby,** lying on stomach,
foot raised, thumb raised to
mouth, pale blue gown w/sprigs
of flowers & ruffled collar,
unmarked, 8" l., 3¾" h............... **150.00**

**Piano baby,** w/pacifier in its
mouth, reclining on a pillow
beside a dog, 5½" h. ................... **85.00**

**Piano baby,** standing in a
"lookout" pose, 4" h. ................... **150.00**

**Snow baby,** girl on sled, arms
away, Germany, 1½" h. ............ **128.00**

**Snow baby,** on polar bear,
2½" h........................................ **85.00**

**Snow baby,** playing tuba,
saxophone or horn, Germany,
each ....................................... **150.00**

**Snow bear,** 1¾" h., Germany ....... **95.00**

# BLANC DE CHINE

*This ware is a fine white Chinese
porcelain with a rich clear glaze. It
became popular in France in the early
18th century and remained popular in
Europe and America through the 19th
century. Fine figural pieces are most often
found and the earlier examples bring the
highest prices.*

**Figure of Buddha,** the standing
figure well modeled on an oval
lotus plinth, his elegantly draped
robe tied at the waist, his right
hand pointing to the ground, his
left holding a 'jewel,' his face w/a
benign expression & tightly
curled hair, w/a cream colored
glaze, China, 17th c.,
9½" h. (tips of two fingers
restored) ........................... **$6,900.00**

**Figure of Guanyin,** the seated
lady crisply modeled wearing a
full-draped robe, one elbow

*Figure of Guanyin*

resting on a stand decorated w/a
prominent dragon-head-form leg
& claw foot, the other arm folded
to hold a *ruyi* sceptre, the head
bowed w/a serene expression
below a neatly combed coiffure,
the back molded w/a raised
square seal of the artisan, Lin
Hsiao-tsung, covered overall in a
creamy white glaze, China, 18th
c., 8¼" h. (ILLUS.) ................... **4,370.00**

**Vase,** 9¼" h., *gu*-form, a widely
flaring upper half & a flaring
lower half separated by a
rounded central band w/three
pierced raised flanges ............. **633.00**

# BLUE & WHITE POTTERY

*The category of blue and white or blue
and grey pottery includes a wide variety
of pottery, earthenware and stoneware
items widely produced in this country in
the late 19th century right through the
1920s. Originally marketed as
inexpensive wares, most pieces featured a
white or grey body molded with a fruit,
flower or geometric design and then*

*trimmed with bands or splashes of blue to highlight the molded pattern. Pitchers, butter crocks and salt boxes are among the numerous items produced but other kitchenwares and chamber sets are also found. Values vary depending on the rarity of the embossed pattern and the depth of color of the blue trim; the darker the blue, the better. The pattern names used with our listings are taken from two references,* Blue & White Stoneware, Pottery, Crockery *by Edith Harbin (Collector Books, 1977) and* Blue & White Stoneware *by Kathryn McNerney (Collector Books, 1981). For additional listings see* Antique Trader Books Country Americana Price Guide *and* Antique Trader's Antiques & Collectibles 1997 Price Guide.

*Eagle Pattern Butter Crock*

**Bean pot,** cov., bulbous spherical body on a narrow footring, a wide, short cylindrical neck w/an inset cover w/a flattened knob finial, C-scroll side handle, one side molded in high-relief w/two children, the other side embossed w/script wording "Boston Baked Beans" & a running leafy vine, 7½" h. ....... **$330.00**

**Bean pot,** cov., one side molded in high-relief w/man & woman eating at table, the other side embossed w/"Boston Baked Beans" ..................................... **450.00**

**Bowl,** 8½" d. , cov., embossed Chain Link patt. ........ **100.00 to 150.00**

**Butter crock,** cov., original bail handle, Eagle patt., 6" d., 6" h. (ILLUS. previous column) ......... **600.00**

**Butter dish,** cov., embossed Daisy patt., 4" h......................... **395.00**

**Canister,** cov., Blue Band patt., "Nutmeg".................................... **90.00**

**Cuspidor,** embossed Rose and Basketweave patt. .... **150.00 to 200.00**

**Meat tenderizer,** printed Wildflower patt. ........................ **675.00**

**Pitcher,** 5" h., embossed Chain Link patt. .................................. **135.00**

**Pitcher,** 7½" h., slightly swelled cylindrical textured tree-trunk form w/an angled branch handle, the sides molded in relief w/a cluster of blossoms & leaves & other scattered leaves & blossoms all trimmed in cobalt blue .......................................... **165.00**

**Pitcher,** 8½" h., embossed Cows patt.......................................... **295.00**

**Soap dish,** printed Wildflower patt. ......................................... **400.00**

# BLUE RIDGE DINNERWARES

*The small town of Erwin, Tennessee was the home of the Southern Potteries, Inc., originally founded by E.J. Owen in 1917 and first called the Clinchfield Pottery.*

*In the early 1920s Charles W. Foreman purchased the plant and he revolutionized the company's output, developing the popular line of hand-painted wares sold as "Blue Ridge" dinnerwares. Free-hand painted by women from the surrounding hills, these colorful dishes in many patterns, continued in production until the plant's closing in 1957.*

*Blue Ridge Marks*

Bowl, fruit, 5" d., Big Apple patt. ... **$8.00**

Bowl, fruit, 5" d., French Peasant
patt. .......................................... **25.00**

Bowl, fruit, 5" d., Poinsettia patt...... **4.00**

Bowl, cereal, 6" d., Poinsettia patt... **8.00**

Bowl, 6½" d., Chanticleer patt. ..... **20.00**

Bowl, 9" d., deep, Nocturne patt.,
Colonial shape ........................... **35.00**

Bowl, 13" d., Persian patt.,
depicts Sascha's two pet
Afghans.................................... **650.00**

Bowl, tab-handled, Coreopsis patt... **9.00**

Bowl, large berry, Big Apple patt... **17.00**

Bowl, large berry, Tropical patt....... **8.00**

Bowls, 8" d., Nocturne patt.,
Colonial shape, set of 7 ............. **84.00**

Box, cov., French Peasant patt. .. **268.00**

Box, cov., ships decoration........... **98.00**

Cake tray, leaf-shaped,
Chintz patt................................. **55.00**

Cake tray, leaf-shaped,
Verna patt. ................................ **48.00**

Candy box, cov., round, Hazel
patt., 6" d................................. **195.00**

Celery tray, leaf-shaped,
Chintz patt................................. **75.00**

Celery tray, French Peasant
patt...................................... **125.00**

Celery tray, leaf-shaped, Fruit
Punch patt................................. **68.00**

Celery tray, leaf-shaped,
Summertime patt. ...................... **68.00**

Celery tray, leaf-shaped, Verna
patt. .......................................... **75.00**

Character jug, Pioneer Woman,
6½" h..................................... **750.00**

Chocolate set: cov. chocolate
pot, creamer & cov. sugar; Rose
Marie patt., the set ................... **265.00**

Cigarette box, cov., Chintz patt. .. **89.00**

Cigarette box, cov., French
Peasant patt............................. **170.00**

Cigarette box, cov., Game Cock
patt........................................... **135.00**

Cigarette box, cov., Seaside
patt........................................... **145.00**

Creamer, Delicious patt. ................. **9.00**

Creamer, Mardi Gras patt............... **9.00**

Creamer, Rustic Plaid patt............. **6.00**

Creamer & sugar bowl,
demitasse, Nocturne patt.,
yellow, pr.................................... **65.00**

Cup & saucer, Normandy patt. .... **28.00**

Cup & saucer, Rustic Plaid patt. .... **7.00**

Dinner service: four each 6"
plates, cereal bowls, cups &
saucers; Shadow Fruit patt.,
16 pcs. ...................................... **45.00**

Pitcher, Antique Leaf patt........... **105.00**

Pitcher, figural Betsy patt., china,
green........................................ **165.00**

Pitcher, figural Betsy patt., china,
plaid w/flowers ......................... **155.00**

Pitcher, figural Betsy patt.,
earthenware, blue .................... **125.00**

Pitcher, figural Betsy patt.,
earthenware, red...................... **125.00**

Pitcher, Fruit Fantasy patt.,
Colonial shape ......................... **135.00**

Pitcher, Big Blossom patt., Grace
shape, ...................................... **70.00**

Pitcher, china, Milady shape,
8¼" h........................................ **135.00**

Pitcher, china, Sally shape......... **169.00**

Pitcher, Spiral shape ................... **89.00**

Pitcher, Suwanee patt., Grace
shape ...................................... **115.00**

Pitcher, Tralee Rose patt. ........... **69.00**

Pitcher, Virginia Gold patt. ......... **105.00**

Plate, 6" d., French Peasant patt. . **22.00**

Plate, 6" d., Roseanna patt. ........... **5.00**

**Plate,** 6¼" d., Normandy patt........ **23.00**

**Plate,** salad, 8½" d., County Fair patt............................................. **10.00**

**Plate,** 8½" d., Normandy patt........ **33.00**

**Plate,** 8½" d., Poinsettia patt., Colonial shape ............................. **4.00**

**Plate,** 8½" d., Roseanna patt........ **10.00**

**Plate,** 9" d., Beaded Apple patt....... **8.00**

**Plate,** luncheon, 9¼" d., French Peasant patt............................... **45.00**

*Green Briar Plate*

**Plate,** 9¼" d., Green Briar patt. (ILLUS.) ...................................... **8.00**

**Plate,** dinner, 9⅜" d., Rustic Plaid patt., Skyline shape ...................... **8.00**

**Plate,** 9½" d., Bamboo patt., Woodcrest shape .......................... **9.00**

**Plate,** dinner, Forest Fruit patt. ....... **7.00**

**Plate,** 10" d., Chanticleer patt., Skyline shape ............................. **55.00**

**Plate,** 10" d., Cock O' the Walk patt., Candlewick shape.............. **55.00**

**Plate,** dinner, 10" d., Normandy patt............................................. **39.00**

**Plate,** 10" d., Thanksgiving Turkey patt., Skyline shape ........ **58.00**

**Plate,** 11½" d., Grape Harvest patt............................................. **57.00**

**Plate,** 11½" d., Rock Rose patt..... **45.00**

**Plate,** dinner, Crab Apple patt., red border .................................. **10.00**

**Plates,** 6½" d., Nocturne patt., Colonial shape, set of 6 .............. **35.00**

**Platter,** 11½" l., Mardi Gras patt. .. **48.00**

**Platter,** 12½" l., Chanticleer patt., Skyline shape ............................. **65.00**

**Platter,** 12½" l., Forest Fruit patt. .............................. **12.00 to 18.00**

**Platter,** 17½" l., Thanksgiving Turkey patt., Clinchfield shape . **225.00**

**Platter,** 17½" l., Turkey with Acorns patt., Clinchfield shape . **225.00**

**Powder box,** cov., round, floral decoration, 5¼" d........................ **98.00**

**Salt & pepper shakers,** Blossom Top patt., pr. ............................... **68.00**

**Salt & pepper shakers,** Bud Top patt., pr........................................ **68.00**

**Salt & pepper shakers,** Charm House patt., 4" h., pr. ................ **229.00**

**Salt & pepper shakers,** figural black & white chickens, rooster 4¾" h., hen 4" h., pr. (repaired)... **85.00**

**Smoking set:** cov. cigarette box & four ashtrays; French Peasant patt., 5 pcs. ............................... **258.00**

**Snack tray,** Verna patt., Martha shape ......................................... **85.00**

**Teapot,** cov., Apple patt., Colonial shape ......................... **110.00**

**Teapot,** cov., Fantasy patt., Skyline shape ............................. **90.00**

**Teapot,** cov., Fruit Fantasy patt., Colonial shape ......................... **175.00**

**Toast dish,** cov., Roseanna patt. . **75.00**

**Tray,** snack, Martha patt. ........... **135.00**

**Vase,** 8" h., china, Mood Indigo patt.......................................... **125.00**

**Vase,** 9¼" h., ruffled rim, tapered body, Delphine patt.................. **120.00**

**Vegetable bowl,** open, French Peasant patt., 9¼" d. .................. **85.00**

**Vegetable bowl,** open, oval, Cock O' The Walk patt............... **60.00**

**Vegetable bowl,** open, oval, Poinsettia patt. ............................ **15.00**

# BOCH FRERES

*Boch Freres Mark*

The Belgian firm, founded in 1841 and still in production, first produced stoneware art pottery of mediocre quality, attempting to upgrade their wares through the years. In 1907, Charles Catteau became the art director of the pottery and slowly the influence of his work was absorbed by the artisans surrounding him. All through the 1920s wares were decorated in distinctive Art Deco designs and are now eagerly sought along with the hand-thrown gourd-form vessels coated with earthtone glazes that were produced during the same time. Almost all Boch Freres pottery is marked, but the finest wares also carry the signature of Charles Catteau in addition to the pottery mark.

**Centerpiece,** octagonal vessel raised on a conforming foot, decorated w/four panels, glazed in midnight blue, alternating w/panels decorated w/a geometric design in gold, yellow & ivory, marked, 9½" d., 6" h. . . **$805.00**

**Lamp,** table model, a large bulbous ovoid body tapering to a wide, short flared neck, carved & painted w/vertical bands in glossy decoration of stylized aqua blossoms w/vivid yellow centers among vivid dark blue leaves & berries w/black outlining against a cream crackle ground, w/tall pleated cloth shade, base 13" h., overall 35" h. ............................ **413.00**

**Lamp-vase,** double-gourd form, a bulbous ovoid lower section tapering to a narrow cylindrical waist below the small spherical upper section w/a short cylindrical neck, the lower section decorated w/a wide incised band of colorful Art Deco flowers & leaves in shades of rose, red, white, gold, green & blue, all against a slightly streaked green & blue

*Four Boch Freres Vases*

background on the rest of the body, Boch Freres blue inkstamp mark, incised "Gres Keramis," impressed "904" & "D 700" painted in black slip, hole in base for wiring, 8⅜" h. .............. **275.00**

**Vase,** 7⅞" h., 7¾" d., wide nearly spherical body raised on a small footring, the shoulder tapering to a short cylindrical neck, a wide shoulder band decorated w/two overlapping bands of oval 'cloud' designs, the body decorated w/zigzag upright branch stripes, enameled in matte black alternating w/a glossy cream crackle glaze, the shoulder band in shades of brown, designed by Charles Catteau, stamped "D.776," incised "Gres Keramis" & impressed "894C" (ILLUS. previous page, second from right) ........................................ **460.00**

**Vase,** 9" h., a small footring supports a wide bulbous ovoid body w/a rounded shoulder to the short, cylindrical neck, Art Deco design of incised & glossy-glazed deer in vivid royal blue, deep aqua & black, bordered at the top & base by a band of geometric rectangles & stylized grass & branches, all against a cream crackled ground, stamped company mark & artist mark ........................................ **880.00**

**Vase,** 10⅞" h., 5¼" d., slender ovoid body tapering to a short, gently flaring cylindrical neck, decorated w/long vertical bands of continuous scrolls in turquoise, yellow & black alternating w/bands in a creamy crackle glaze, impressed "806" (ILLUS. previous page, far left) .. **316.00**

**Vase,** 13½" h, 7⅞" d., wide ovoid body tapering toward the base, the curved shoulder centered by a wide short cylindrical neck, glossy enamel decoration of large stylized flowers & banding at the top & bottom in shades of

blue & rose w/a green on pale yellow ground, outlining in black, stamped mark "D.1755," inscribed "23" & impressed "914," minor base glaze chips (ILLUS. previous page, second from left) .................................. **431.00**

**Vase,** 13⅝" h., 5¾" d., swelled cylindrical body w/a wide rounded shoulder centered by a short cylindrical neck, a glossy enamel design w/long panels each filled w/large clusters of stylized flowers in shades of blue w/green & rust, all outlined in black, designed by Charles Catteau, stamped marks & impressed "723," drilled hole in base (ILLUS. previous page, far right) .................................. **173.00**

**Vases,** 11" h., baluster-form w/widely swelled shoulder tapering to a short cylindrical neck, the sides divided into three panels by long stripes, each panel w/a white crackled ground centered by a large oval bouquet of stylized turquoise, deep blue, greenish blue & red flowers & leaves, marked "Boch" & signed "Catteau," pr.............. **880.00**

*Boch Freres Striped Vases*

**Vases,** 11" h., slender ovoid body tapering to a narrow flat rim, the neck & shoulder incised w/entwined scrolling devices above the main body decorated w/alternating plain colored stripes & stripes topped by geometric crescent & ball clusters, in shades of turquoise blue, yellow & medium blue against a creamy white crackled ground, signed "Catteau," pr. (ILLUS. bottom previous page) .......................... **990.00**

**Vases,** 12" h., simple ovoid form w/a thin, flared flat rim, Art Deco design of three large deer in various poses, deer in medium light blue, green & black w/similarly colored florals & geometric top & base bands all against a white crackled ground, designed & signed by Charles Catteau, pr. ............................. **1,540.00**

# BRAYTON LAGUNA POTTERY

*Brayton Laguna Marks*

*In 1927 Durlin Brayton began an operation in Laguna Beach, California that would prove highly successful. However, it was not until he married Ellen (Webb) Webster Grieve and she became his partner that they were able to realize the fruits of their labor. The Braytons created numerous lines over the forty-one years the company operated. Among them were the very earliest hand-turned items; the African-American series; the Childrens' series; white crackle*

*that stood solely on its own merit or in combination with a high glaze green or a dark brown stain; Calasia, which was basically an art line of pots and vases; Gay Nineties figures; Circus series; and some kitchen items such as creamers and sugars, cookie jars and canisters. Brown-stained items were also made by Treasure Craft and sometimes their pieces are mistaken for Brayton. Treasure Craft items in most cases are a darker brown with a heavier stain application. Various*

*Brayton marks were used over the years making identification easier than with some other California companies. The items found without a mark can be readily identified with a little knowledge about the lines created. Durlin Brayton died in 1951 and Webb Brayton had died two years earlier. The business managed to survive until the late 1960s.*

*Provinical Line Cup with Holder*

**Bowl,** 10" d., 2" h., Calasia line, feather design in bottom, scalloped rim w/raised circles on inner rim, pale green .................. **$8.00**

**Candleholder,** figural, three choirboys ................................ **145.00**

**Candleholders,** figural Blackamoor, pr. ...................... **125.00**

**Cookie jar,** figural Mammy, burgundy base & turquoise bandanna, rare early version ................................. **1,300.00**

**Cookie jar,** figural Provincial Lady, textured woodtone stain w/high gloss white apron & scarf tied around head, red, green & yellow flowers & hearts motif on clothing, being reproduced so must be marked, "Brayton Laguna Calif. K-27," 13" h. ....... **455.00**

**Creamer,** figural cat ..................... **35.00**

**Cup w/tea bag holder,** Provincial line, brown bisque stain w/white & yellow flowers & green leaves outside, gloss yellow inside, marked "Brayton Laguna Calif. K31," 1¾" h. (ILLUS. above) ....... **16.00**

*African-American Boy & Girl*

**Figure,** African-American baby w/diaper, seated, green eyes, 3¾" h. .......................................... **95.00**

**Figure,** Blackamoor, walking & carrying a bowl in his hands, gloss gold earrings, white bowl & shoes, burgundy scarf, shirt & pantaloons, 8¼" h. .................... **125.00**

**Figure,** Blackamoor, kneeling & holding open cornucopia, heavily jeweled w/gold trim, 10" h. .......................................... **145.00**

**Figure,** Blackamoor, kneeling, jeweled trim, 15" h. ................... **275.00**

**Figure,** peasant woman w/basket at her front side & basket at her left back side, blue dress, yellow vest, incised mark "Brayton Laguna Pottery," 7½" h. .............. **90.00**

**Figure,** woman w/two wolfhounds, one on each side, woman w/red hair & wearing a long yellow dress, 9½" h. ............ **95.00**

**Figure group,** African-American boy & girl, boy holding basket of flowers in each hand, black shoes, yellow socks, barefoot girl, created by L.A. Dowd, early 1940s, paper label, 4¼" base, boy 7" h., girl 5½" h. (ILLUS. above) ...................................... **300.00**

**Figure group,** bride standing on left w/white dress w/pink flowers & green leaves, pink hat, bouquet in left hand, right hand on man's left shoulder, man seated w/striped trousers, black jacket, brown shoes & brown hat in left hand, black hair & mustache, stamp mark, 4¾" l., 8½" h. .......... **125.00**

**Figure group,** man & cat blended together in an abstract design on a base, marked in-mold, hard-to-find, mid-1950s, 21" h. . **300.00**

**Figure group,** "One Year Later," Mother seated on left w/green dress holding baby in white dress, man standing w/striped trousers, black hair, mustache, jacket & shoes, stamp mark, 4" l., 8¼" h. .............................. **120.00**

**Figures,** black jazz band musicians, set of 4 ................. **1,000.00**

**Flower holder,** figural, "Francis," girl standing & holding small planter in front, white crackle glossy glaze dress, yellow pot, brown hair w/blue ribbon, brown-stained face & arms, bluebird on right arm, 6½" h. ....................... **35.00**

**Model of a Carousel horse,** rearing position, 16" h. ............. **115.00**

**Model of a cat,** "Kiki," seated on oval base, tail wraps around to hide back legs & paws, socks on front paws, hat perched on head & tied at front, eyes closed, colorful sweater, assorted colors of pink, blue, black & white, marked on unglazed bottom, "Brayton Laguna" above a line & "Kiki" below the line, 6" l. base, 9¼" h. ...................................... **115.00**

**Model of a cat,** seated on oval base, socks on front paws w/left paw over right paw, head turned to left looking back, blue eyes open, hat perched on head between ears, bluebird on front of hat, colorful colors of blue, pink, white & black, unglazed bottom w/no marks, 6¼" l. base, 9" h. ......................................... **105.00**

*Brayton-Laguna Cat*

**Model of a cat,** lying down, head up, yellow body w/brown accents, green eyes, stamp mark, "Copyright 1941 by Brayton Laguna Pottery," 6½" l., 4¼" h. (ILLUS.) .......................... **55.00**

**Model of a dog,** sniffing, "Pluto," Walt Disney, 6" l., 3¼" h. ......... **165.00**

**Model of a duck,** standing w/head down, Provincial line, brown overall stain w/gloss yellow bill, 6½" h. ....................... **50.00**

**Model of a fawn,** standing, ears up, brown & white spots, unmarked, 6½" h. ....................... **75.00**

**Model of a fox,** seated, No. H-57 . **95.00**

**Model of an owl,** brown & white, 7" h............................................. **55.00**

**Model of a squirrel,** crouched w/tail behind & curving slightly upward on end, head & ears up, nondescript face, white crackle glaze, incised mark, "Brayton's Laguna Calif. T-15," 12¾" l., 6" h. (ILLUS. top next page) ..... **110.00**

**Model of a squirrel,** sitting on back feet w/tail up behind body & curved slightly on end, eating a nut, white crackle glaze, incised mark, "Brayton's Laguna Calif. T-14," 7¼" h. .................. **110.00**

**Models of a bull,** cow & calf, 3 pcs. ...................................... **285.00**

**Models of fawns,** woodtone w/white speckles, 5" h. & 7" h., pr................................................. **95.00**

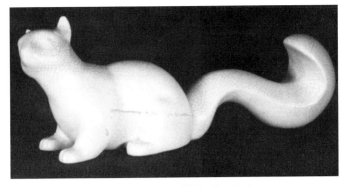

*Brayton-Laguna White Squirrel*

*Russian Lady Wall Plaque*

**Pitcher,** cream, model of a Calico kitten, high glaze white body w/pink, light blue & mauve flowers & brown stitching, pale blue ribbon around neck, black nose & eyes, stamp mark "Copyright 1942 by Brayton Laguna Pottery," 6½" h. ............. **55.00**

**Salt & pepper shakers,** figural Mammy & Chef, 5½" h., pr......... **85.00**

**Tile,** chartreuse & yellow bird, turquoise, yellow & white flowers, black background, incised mark, "Laguna Pottery," 7 x 7" ........................................ **115.00**

**Vase,** 7¼" h., 7" w., 7" l., pillow-shape w/feather design on each side & raised circles on recessed short base, fern green . **30.00**

**Wall plaque,** figural of woman, arms above head, Russian dress, Webton-ware mark, hard-to-find, 13½" h. (ILLUS. previous column) ..................................... **200.00**

**Wall pocket,** round & flared slightly at top, blue, mauve, flowers & buds & green leaves on front, two holes for hanging, Webton-ware mark on unglazed back, 2¾" w., 4¼" h. .................. **28.00**

# BUFFALO POTTERY

*Buffalo Pottery was established in 1902 in Buffalo, New York, to supply pottery for the Larkin Company. Most desirable today is Deldare Ware, introduced in 1908 in two patterns, "The Fallowfield Hunt" and "Ye Olden Days," which featured central English scenes and a continuous border. Emerald Deldare, introduced in 1911, was banded with stylized flowers and geometric designs and had varied central scenes, the most popular being from "The Tours of Dr. Syntax." Reorganized in 1940, the company now specializes in hotel china.*

*Buffalo Pottery Mark*

*Deldare Candlestick*

## DELDARE

**Bowl,** fruit, 9¼" d., Ye Village Tavern..................................... **$495.00**

**Candlesticks,** Ye Olden Days, 9½" h., pr. (ILLUS. of one, top next column) ........................... **400.00**

**Egg cup,** double, Ye Olden Days - Ye Village Street (couple of age marks in the glaze) ........... **250.00**

**Mug,** The Fallowfield Hunt - Breaking Cover, artist-signed, 1908, 3⅝" d., 3⅛" h. ................. **316.00**

**Mug,** The Fallowfield Hunt, 3¾" d., 4¼" .............................. **374.00**

**Mug,** Ye Olden Days - Ye Lion Inn, 3½" h................................. **295.00**

**Mugs,** Ye Olden Days - Ye Lion Inn, 3¾" d., 4½" h., set of six (ILLUS. below) .................... **1,265.00**

**Candleholder-match holder combination,** round chamberstick-form w/ring rim handle, cylindrical central socket

*A Set of Deldare Mugs*

& raised compartment for matches to one side, country village scene around dished base, stamped mark & incised artist's initials, M. Gerhardt, 1909, 5½" d., 1¾" h. ................ **518.00**

**Pitcher,** 6" h., octagonal, The Fallowfield Hunt, stamped marks & artist-signed, 1908 ................ **460.00**

*Deldare Octagonal Pitcher*

**Pitcher,** 6" h., octagonal, Their Manner of Telling Stories - Which He Returned with a Curtsey, stamped mark, artist-signed, 1908 (ILLUS.) ............... **345.00**

**Pitcher,** 7" h., octagonal, To Spare an Old, Broken Soldier - To Advise Me in a Whisper, artist-signed, 1908 .................... **374.00**

**Pitcher,** 7⅞" h., octagonal, To Spare an Old, Broken Soldier - To Advise Me in a Whisper, stamped mark, obscured artist's signature, 1909 ........................ **431.00**

**Pitcher,** 8½" h., The Fallowfield Hunt - The Return .................... **625.00**

**Pitcher,** tankard, 12¼" h., The Fallowfield Hunt - The Hunt Supper .................................. **1,375.00**

**Plate,** 7¼" d., Ye Village Street... **125.00**

**Plate,** 9½" d., The Fallowfield Hunt - The Start ........................ **175.00**

**Plate,** chop, 12" d., Ye Village Inn............................................. **550.00**

*Fallowfield Hunt Chop Plate*

**Plate,** chop,14" d., The Fallowfield Hunt - The Start (ILLUS. top) ............................. **795.00**

**Teapot,** cov., Ye Village Inn, artist-signed ............................. **495.00**

**Tea tile,** The Fallowfield Hunt - Breaking Cover, artist-signed, 6¼" d......................................... **374.00**

## EMERALD DELDARE

*Dr. Syntax Emerald Deldare Pitcher*

**Mug,** cylindrical w/gently tapering sides, Dr. Syntax in the Cellar with the Maid, artist-signed, 1911, 3⅛" d., 3⅝" h. ................. **546.00**

**Pitcher,** 8¾" h., octagonal, Dr. Syntax Setting Out to the Lakes (ILLUS.) ................................. **2,475.00**

Plate, 8½" d., Dr. Syntax -
Misfortune at Tulip Hall, artist-
signed & dated .......................... **550.00**

## MISCELLANEOUS

Bowl, 5" d., Blue Willow patt. ....... **12.00**

Bowl, 7¾" d., Blue Willow patt. .... **15.00**

Coffeepot, cov., Blue Willow patt.
(faint hairline) ........................... **150.00**

*Buffalo Blue Willow Cup*

Cup, Blue Willow patt.
(ILLUS.) ........................ **15.00 to 20.00**

Game plate, mallard duck
decoration .................................. **55.00**

Plate, 6" d., Blue Willow patt. ....... **12.00**

Plate, 7½" d., Niagara Falls
scenic decoration ....................... **65.00**

Plate, 8" d., Blue Willow patt. ....... **15.00**

Plate, 9" d., Blue Willow patt. ....... **20.00**

Plate, 9" d., center scene of "The
Gunner," deep blue-green
underglaze, gold trim on edge,
1907 ......................................... **85.00**

Plate, 9¼" d., American herring
gull decoration ........................... **65.00**

Plate, 9¼" d., dusky grouse
decoration .................................. **65.00**

Plate, 9¼" d., wild ducks
decoration .................................. **65.00**

Plate, 9¼" d., doe & stag
decoration .................................. **45.00**

Platter, 11 x 15", oval, doe & stag
decoration ................................. **110.00**

Platter, 11 x 14", oblong, gently
scalloped rim, American Indian
buffalo hunt scene in center,
wide dark bluish green
border ...................................... **300.00**

Wash bowl & pitcher,
Chrysanthemum patt., 2 pcs..... **295.00**

---

# CALIENTE POTTERY

*In 1979 the pottery world lost a man who used his talents to create satin matte glazes and blended colors. Virgil Haldeman's career got its start after he graduated from the University of Illinois in 1923. In 1927 he moved to Southern California and it was there that he and his partner opened the Haldeman Tile Manufacturing Company in Los Angeles. The business was sold just a few years later and Haldeman went to work for the Catalina Clay Products Company on Catalina Island. When Virgil quit his job as ceramics engineer and plant superintendent three years later he opened the Haldeman Pottery in Burbank, California.*

*Andrew Hazelhurst was the chief designer from the pottery's inception in 1933 to 1941 and Haldeman created the glazes. Virgil's wife, Anna, also worked closely with Haldeman at the pottery. In 1947 the business was moved to Calabasas, California and remained at that location until 1953. Items produced were shallow flower bowls called "floaters," with overlapped, irregular edges; baskets with hand-coiled handles; ewers; candleholders; planters; and miniature animals. Art Deco women, mostly in dancing positions, were also created.*

*In the early years, the word "Caliente" was used as a line name to designate flower frogs, figurines and flower bowls. Collectors now use the Caliente name almost exclusively to indicate all products made at the Haldeman pottery.*

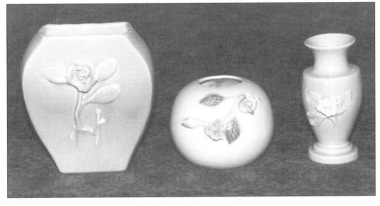

*Caliente Bowl & Vases*

At best, items were randomly marked and some simply bear a deeply impressed "Made In California" mark. However, in 1987 Wilbur Held wrote a privately printed book titled Collectable Caliente Pottery which aided tremendously in identifying Caliente products by a numbering system that the Haldeman company used. According to Held, molded pieces usually are numbered in the 100s; handmade pieces, 200s; mostly animals and fowl, 300s; dancing girls, 400s; continuation of handmade pieces, 500-549; and molded pieces with roses added, 550 and above. Stickers were also used and many are still firmly attached to the items.

*Caliente Marks*

**Basket,** round, footed rim w/rope handle, green, Model No. 222, incised "Handmade Calif.," 7" l. . **$25.00**

**Bowl,** 4¾" h., bulbous ivy-type, satin matte white gloss, two pink applied roses & one rosebud w/two green leaves, Model No. 560 (ILLUS. center) ................... **55.00**

**Candy dish,** figural, swan w/head bent at neck serving as handle, pink inside, white outside, Model No. 64, 9" l., 6" h. ...................... **32.00**

**Ewer,** handled, yellow gloss ground w/applied two white roses & three yellow leaves in-relief, incised mark "554 U.S.A." 5½" h. ......................................... **16.00**

**Ewer,** handled, ivory base & lower half of body darkening to pink w/overall pink inside, applied w/two ivory leaves, one pink rose & one white rose & white rosebud, marked "558 Handmade Cal.," 9½" h. ............ **27.00**

**Figure of a dancing girl,** arms outstretched w/each hand holding up tip of skirt, right foot visible, head bent far to the right touching right shoulder, pale green, impressed mark "Made in California," Model No. 408, 6½" h. (ILLUS. top left, next page) ........................................ **65.00**

*Caliente Dancing Girl Figures*

**Figure of dancing girl,** head bent w/right hand to shoulder, left hand holding dress up, kicking left leg, pale pink, impressed mark "Made in California," Model No. 407, 7" h. (ILLUS. top right) .............. **75.00**

**Figure of dancing girl in bloomers,** a scarf in each hand draping to the floor, head bent & slightly tilted, face features indistinct, left hand resting on waist, Model No. 406, very hard-to-find, 6½" h.............................. **85.00**

**Figure of a lady standing,** holding lower section of long dress away from body exposing legs, head tilted slightly w/hat on her head, Model No. 405, impressed "Made in California" in block letters, 6¼" h. (ILLUS. top center)................................... **45.00**

**Floater,** flat & shallow dish to float flowers, oval w/two overlapping rim cuts w/candle rings in two rose petals & four inward rim bends, script-incised mark, Model No. 509, 16" l. ................ **48.00**

**Flower frog,** model of a sailboat, satin matte white glaze, Model No. 73, 5" h. .............................. **30.00**

**Model of a hen,** standing on round base, unusual hand-decorated, brown body w/darker

*Caliente Hen & Rooster*

brown highlights, green & white base incised "336" & "USA," 3½" h. (ILLUS. right) ................. **45.00**

**Model of a pointer dog,** on oval base, walking position, tail & head up, white base & lower portion of dog's body, upper half caramel gloss, Model No. 360, 6¾" l., 4" h. ................................. **40.00**

**Model of a rooster,** seated on round base, unusual hand-decorated brown body w/darker brown highlights, green & white base, incised "306" & "USA," 3¾" h. (ILLUS. left) ................... **45.00**

**Planter,** model of a Dutch shoe w/one rose & leaves, green glaze w/pink, unmarked, Model No. 555, 5" l., 2½" h. ................. **12.00**

**Vase,** 7" h., urn-shaped w/three rings around base, pale pink body w/applied white rose & pink leaves, script incised mark, Model No. 581 (ILLUS. right w/bowl) ...................................... **25.00**

**Vase,** 8" h., flat front & back w/curved sides, slightly scalloped rectangular opening, one applied green rose & leaves blending to gold top w/two applied rosebuds, one rose & one leaf, "Model No. 570" & "Calif." etched into glazed bottom, a hard-to-find glaze combination (ILLUS. left w/bowl & vase) ...................................... **55.00**

**Wall pocket,** heart-shaped w/pie-crust edge & applied rose & leaves at center top, Model No. 7, 7" h. ............................... **30.00**

**Wall pocket,** three plumes w/bow near bottom, satin matte white glaze, incised mark, Model No. 6, 6½" h. .............................. **27.00**

---

# CALIFORNIA FAIENCE

*Chauncy R. Thomas and William V. Bragdon organized what was to become the California Faience Pottery in 1916, in Berkeley, California. Originally named after its owners, it later became The Tile Shop, finally adopting the California Faience name about 1924. Always a small operation whose output was a simple style of art pottery, primarily designed for the florist shop trade, it also made colorfully decorated tiles. During the mid-1920s, California Porcelain was produced by this firm for the West Coast Porcelain Manufacturers of Milbrae, California. The great Depression halted art pottery production and none was produced after 1930 although some tiles were made for the Chicago World's Fair about 1932. Collectors now seek out these somewhat scarce pieces that always bear the incised mark of California Faience.*

*California Faience Mark*

**Bowl,** 4¼" d., 2¾" h., squatty tapering bulbous form w/a closed rim, decorated in cuenca w/a band of violet, scarlet & lime green stylized flowers against blue on a yellow ground, incised company mark & ink marked "HOTEL PETALUMA" (ILLUS. left front) ................ **$1,540.00**

**Bowl-vase,** a wide squatty ovoid form w/a wide closed-in flat mouth above sharply tapering lower sides, the wide rounded shoulder decorated in cuenca w/a band of colorful stylized

*A Group of California Faience Pieces*

flowers against a dark blue ground, from the Eureka Inn, impressed "California Faience - Eureka Inn," 4" d., 2¼" h. ......... **990.00**

**Tile,** square, decorated in cuenca w/a galleon in matte ochre, brown & white against a matte, curdled dark blue ground, on glossy turquoise & dark blue waves, die-stamped "California Faience," 5¼" sq. ...................... **275.00**

**Tile,** square, decorated w/a stylized galleon under full sail in brown & blue on rough seas in two shades of blue below yellow skies, a dark blue border band, glossy & matte glazes, impressed mark, 5⅜" sq. (minor surface abrasions) ................... **275.00**

**Tile,** round w/raised rounded rim, decorated in cuenca w/a basket of colorful fruit in dark red, celadon green & yellow on a dark blue ground, impressed mark, 5½" d. ........................... **248.00**

**Tile,** square, decorated w/a raised pinwheel design in a dark matte blue glaze against a matte maroon ground, impressed company mark, 5½" sq. (ILLUS. back left, previous page) .......... **385.00**

**Tile,** square, decorated in cuenca w/a galleon under full sail on rough seas, the ship in a matte speckled brown w/light blue sails & light & dark blue seas against a yellow sky, minor surface scratches, impressed company mark, 5½" sq. (ILLUS. back right, previous page) ........ **495.00**

**Vase,** 2½" h., 4" d., bulbous ovoid body tapering to a cylindrical base, a wide closed rim, the shoulder decorated in cuenca w/a wide band of stylized polychrome flowers against a dark blue ground, impressed "California Faience - The Eureka Inn" (ILLUS. right front, previous page) ...................................... **660.00**

**Vase,** 4½" h., 6¼" d., a wide squatty bulbous body w/a wide rounded shoulder centered by a wide, short & slightly tapering neck w/a flat rim, glossy Persian blue glaze, incised mark .......... **165.00**

---

# CAMBRIDGE ART POTTERY

*The Cambridge Art Pottery was incorporated in Cambridge, Ohio in 1900 and began production of artwares in early 1901. Their earliest lines, Terrhea and Oakwood, were slip-decorated glossy-glazed wares similar to the products of other Ohio potteries of that era.*

*In 1902 they began production of an earthenware cooking ware line called Guernsey which featured a dark brown exterior and porcelain white lining. This eventually became their leading seller and in 1909 the name of the firm was changed to The Guernsey Earthenware Company to reflect this fact. In 1907 the company had introduced a matte green-glazed art line they called Otoe, but all production of their art pottery lines ceased in 1908. The company eventually became part of The Atlas Globe China Company which closed in 1933.*

**Ewer,** footed ovoid body w/tall cylindrical neck & widely flaring rim, C-scroll handle, brown & green mottled shiny glaze, impressed "Oakwood 228," 7" h. (in-the-making flakes on bottom edge)............................. **$22.00**

**Ewer,** footed bulbous body w/tall slender cylindrical neck, high arched spout & strap handle, decorated w/leaves & a yellow rose on green & dark brown glaze, impressed mark (professional repair).................... **50.00**

**Jug,** swelling cylindrical form w/molded rim & angled shoulder handle, decorated w/yellow cherries on green shaded to deep olive black shiny glaze, mpressed & incised marks, 5⅝" h................ **110.00**

**Pitcher**, tankard, 6" h., Arts & Crafts style, a tapering cylindrical body molded overall w/leaves & berries, an angular branch handle & small pinched spout, thick dark green matte glaze, unmarked (small flake on handle) ........................................ **88.00**

**Vase**, 5" h., cylindrical w/a wide squatty bulbous shoulder tapering to a narrow flat mouth, carved decoration of iris blossoms, leaves & stems, thick dark green matte glaze, unmarked (two glaze bubbles in the making) ................ **110.00**

**Vase**, 5" h., footed squatty bulbous body tapering to a narrow cylindrical neck w/flaring rim, mottled green, brown & white glaze, impressed "Oakwood 204" (crazed glaze) ... **28.00**

**Vase**, 5" h., bulbous body tapering to wide flat rim, decorated w/yellow & green vining flowers on a shiny shaded brown glaze, impressed "Cambridge" (small chips & interior lime deposits)....... **22.00**

**Vase**, 5½" h., bulbous body w/embossed berry decoration..... **90.00**

**Vase**, 6½" h., bulbous body, dark brown matte glaze ................... **110.00**

**Vase**, 8¾" h., inverted pear-shaped body on flared foot w/short narrow flared neck, mottled green & brown glaze, impressed "Oakwood 214".......... **33.00**

**Vase**, 11⅞" h., trumpet-form body w/flat rim, green matte glaze w/bubbles, probably Otoe line, impressed mark ........................ **220.00**

**Vase**, 12" h., ovoid body tapering to a wide cylindrical neck w/slightly flaring rim, shoulder handles, decorated w/berries on a green & dark brown glaze, impressed mark ........................ **149.00**

**Vase**, 12½" h., tapering cylindrical body w/flat rim on stepped flared foot, decorated w/leaves & a yellow rose on green glaze, impressed "Terrhea" ................. **138.00**

**Vase**, 15" h, slightly swelling cylindrical body tapering to a flat rim, donkey decoration on dark greenish brown glaze, impressed "Cambridge 226" (professional repair) .................. **165.00**

---

# CANTON

*This ware has been decorated for nearly two centuries in factories near Canton, China. Intended for export sale, much of it was originally inexpensive blue-and-white hand-decorated ware. Late 18th and early 19th century pieces are superior to later ones and fetch high prices.*

**Basket & undertray,** the deep oval basket w/reticulated sides & a rolled rim, on a conforming dished undertray, rain & cloud borders framing the landscape on undertray & around the basket rims, 19th c., undertray 11¼" l., 2 pcs. ........................ **$460.00**

*Canton Lobed Bowl*

**Bowl,** 9⅝" d., four-lobed rim, minor chips, 19th c. (ILLUS.) .... **863.00**

**Bowl,** 9¾" d., round, shallow sides, rain & cloud border around central landscape, 19th c. ..................................... **127.00**

**Coddle cup,** cov., footed swelled cylindrical sides flanked by shaped D-form handles, the low domed overhanging cover w/a berry finial, cover & body w/landscapes & rain & cloud borders, 19th c., 4¾" h. ........... **316.00**

*Canton Hot Water Plate*

*Canton Cider Pitcher*

*Large Canton Platter*

**Plate,** 7½" d. ................................. **50.00**

**Platter,** 9¼ x 11¾", oblong
w/gently canted corners, rain &
cloud border & central
mountainous landscape,
19th c. ...................................... **288.00**

**Platter,** 9¾ x 12½", shallow
dished oval form w/gently
canted corners, rain & cloud
borders around the central
landscape scene, 19th c. ......... **230.00**

**Platter,** 13½ x 16½", oval form
w/gently canted corners, rain &
cloud border, watery pagoda
landscape, 19th c.
(ILLUS. above) ...... **800.00 to 1,000.00**

**Sauce tureen, cover &
undertray,** the oblong squared
deep body w/boar's head
handles, the low domed cover
w/stem finial, on a conforming
dished undertray, 19th c., tureen
7½" l., the set (rim bruise) ......... **495.00**

**Teapot,** cov., baluster-shaped
w/berry finial on the domed
cover, entwined vine handle,
rain & cloud border & landscape
reserve, 19th c., 7" h. ............... **173.00**

**Teapot,** cov., footed, bulbous
body, domed lid w/berry finial, C-
form handle, 9⅛" h. (extensive
professional repair) ............... **1,045.00**

**Vegetable dish,** cov., rectangular
w/deep gently flaring sides &
rounded corners, the gently
sloping cover w/a pine cone

**Hot water plate,** paneled rim
w/small filling spout on one side
& tab handle on the opposite rim,
9¼" d., hairline (ILLUS. top) ......... **132.00**

**Pitcher,** jug-type, 6¾" h., ovoid
body tapering to a widely flaring
& shaped rim w/pointed spout,
arched D-form handle, diaper &
rain & cloud border above the
landscape scene, 19th c. ......... **518.00**

**Pitcher,** cov., cider, jug-type,
8½" h., wide body w/a domed
cover w/foo dog finial, an
entwined branch handle,
decorated w/diaper & rain &
cloud borders flanking the
central landscape, 19th c.
(ILLUS. bottom) .................... **1,250.00**

**Pitcher,** jug-type, 9½" h., washy
tones of underglaze-blue w/a
typical riverscape, 19th c. ........ **345.00**

finial, rain & cloud border & landscape on cover & base, 19th c., 8½ x 10" ...................... **127.00**

**Warming dish,** cov., a domed cover w/a pine cone finial decorated w/a pagoda landscape reserve within rain & cloud borders, the rectangular warming dish w/matching decoration, 19th c., 8½ x 13" ... **690.00**

---

# CAPO-DI-MONTE

*Production of porcelain and faience began in 1736 at the Capo-di-Monte factory in Naples. In 1743 King Charles of Naples established a factory there that made wares with relief decoration. In 1759 the factory was moved to Buen Retiro near Madrid, operating until 1808. Another Naples pottery was opened in 1771 and operated until 1806 when its molds were acquired by the Doccia factory of Florence, which has since made reproductions of original Capo-di-Monte pieces with the "N" mark beneath a crown. Some very early pieces are valued in the thousands of dollars but the subsequent productions are considerably lower.*

**Box w/domed cover,** rectangular, molded & decorated overall w/figural & foliate panels, 19th c., 4" h. ........................... **$690.00**

**Centerpiece,** figural, four allegorical figures representing the Four Seasons divided by four urn-form, four curved & four rectangular trough-form vases, figures 7" h. ............................. **690.00**

**Figurines,** allegorical, each representing one of the Four Seasons, each child shown w/the corresponding flora or fauna, late 19th c., 6¼" h., set of 4 (minor losses) ...................... **144.00**

**Figure group,** a detailed scene of a young woman seated beside a table plucking a goose while a seated older man eats dinner across from her, a hunting dog curled up beside him, all on an oval scroll-molded & gilt-trimmed base, delicate realistic coloring, artist-signed, ca. 1905, 12" l., 6¼" h. (ILLUS. below) ............. **275.00**

*Finely Detailed Capo-di-Monte Figure Group*

*Capo-di-Monte Jewel Casket*

*Ornate Capo-di-Monte Plate*

**Jewel casket,** cov., a long oblong box w/serpentine sides & raised on small scroll feet, the low domed cover molded in relief w/hand-colored classical figures & putti, further putti scenes & gilt scrolls around the sides, early 20th c. (ILLUS. top) ...................................... **358.00**

**Plaque,** pierced to hang, relief-molded h.p. cherubs, 12½" h. .... **250.00**

**Plates,** 9" d., each decorated around the scalloped border w/raised classical figures, the center w/a painted armorial crest surrounded by scrolls & floral sprigs, signed on the back "Palazzo Reale Napoli," slight surface wear, 19th c., set of 12 (ILLUS. of one bottom) .............................. **1,495.00**

# CARLTON WARE

*The Staffordshire firm of Wiltshaw & Robinson, Stoke-on-Trent, operated the Carlton Works from about 1890 until 1958, producing both earthenwares and porcelain. Specializing in decorative items like vases and teapots, they became well known for their lustre-finished wares, often decorated in the Oriental taste. The trademark Carlton Ware was incorporated into their printed mark. Since 1958, a new company, Carlton Ware Ltd., has operated the Carlton Works at Stoke.*

*Carlton Shell-shaped Bowl*

**Bowl,** 9¾" l., 3" h., shell-shaped w/incurved end handle, exterior & interior decorated w/multicolored coral bells, cobalt blue rim w/gold trim, pre-1921 (ILLUS.) ........................ **$270.00**

**Bowl,** 10" d., 3" h., Rouge Royale line, low gently flared sides w/three gilt pretzel-form open sections around the rim, raised on three small gold peg feet, the interior decorated w/an exotic bird & tall tree w/scattered butterflies within a black & colored floral border band, all against a deep red ground (ILLUS. top next page) ............ **485.00**

**Center bowl,** oval boat shape w/a pointed & scalloped rim & arching loop gold end handles,

*Rouge Royale Bowl*

*Carlton Ware Cookie Jar*

*Large Carlton Ware Ginger Jar*

**Cup & saucer,** demitasse, Rouge Royale line, finely enameled marsh scene w/storks, heavy gold trim ..................................... **75.00**

**Ginger jar,** cov., bulbous ovoid body w/domed fitted cover, overall 'Chinoiserie' decoration in multicolored enamel of Oriental homes, bridges, man in boat, trees, birds & people against a dark blue ground, lavish gold trim on base & rim of cover, 7¾" d., 10⅜" h. (ILLUS. above) ........................................ **895.00**

**Inkstand**, a narrow long rectangular pen tray centered by a raised central inkwell w/cap, a cobalt blue ground decorated w/the colorful Art Deco-style Egyptian Fan patt., 8" l., 2¼" h. . **600.00**

**Mantel garniture:** an 8¾" d., 4" h. bowl & a pair of 9¼" h., 4⅝" w. cov. paneled vases; "Kang Hsi" line, each piece w/a rich dark blue ground ornately decorated w/gold Oriental landscape scenes trimmed w/aqua, green & pink, the footed hexagonal vases w/conforming cover w/figural foo dog finial in gold, 3 pcs. (ILLUS. top next page) ........................ **1,200.00**

raised on a flaring base w/four knobbed gilt feet, decorated overall w/a black ground & painted inside & out w/clusters of pale purple irises & leaves & flying ducks, all w/gilt trim, 6½ x 13¼", 6½" h. .......... **920.00**

**Cookie jar,** cov., decorated w/embossed water lily blossoms & leaves in deep red & green against a soft golden yellow ground, relief-molded deep pink & green water lily bud on each side & finial, 5⅝" d., 6½" h. (ILLUS. bottom) ....................... **175.00**

*Carlton Ware Mantel Garniture*

*Persian Pattern Carlton Vase*

**Mug,** morbid scene of pilgrim hanging from a gallows, poem about drinking on reverse side.... **55.00**

**Vase,** cov., 7" h., 3¼" d., Persian patt., footed wide ovoid body tapering to a short molded rim supporting a low flaring cover w/a pointed gold finial, a dark blue ground decorated on the body w/a Persian scene including a mosque & figures in a garden all in color & heavily trimmed in gold, gold band trim on the cover & foot (ILLUS. above, this column) ...................**395.00**

*Handcraft Carlton Vase*

**Vase,** cov., 8½" h., 3¼" d., "Handcraft" line, temple jar-form, baluster-form w/cylindrical neck fitted w/a flaring domed cover w/a gold foo dog finial, a soft blue satin ground w/small spatters of darker blue & decorated w/a large stylized grey & black tree w/green leaves & large pink blossoms (ILLUS. above, this column) .... **450.00**

*Trumpet-form Carlton Vase*

*Tall Oriental-style Vase*

**Vase,** 5⅞" h., 3½" d., trumpet-form w/swelled foot, blue lustre ground w/multicolored exotic landscape of trees & bird, colorful decoration & heavy gold outlining & trim, mother-of-pearl lustre lining w/fancy gold interior top border (ILLUS.) .................. **450.00**

**Vase,** 6" h., slender cylindrical body w/narrow flared foot & widely flaring rim, pale orange ground decorated on the front & back w/oval reserves showing scenes of pixies blowing bubbles against a pearlized ground, matte black interior ..... **600.00**

**Vase,** 7½" h., Art Deco-style, bulbous ovoid footed body w/a short slightly incurved cylindrical neck, exotic circular flowerheads below a fan of yellow, green, orange & blue colored panels w/clouds of dots & gilding all on a dark red ground, No. 3558 patt. ......................................... **920.00**

**Vase,** 8" h., 9" d., wide bulbous ovoid body w/a short cylindrical neck, a bold Art Deco design of stylized large blossoms in blue & butterscotch on a pink & cream ground...................................... **220.00**

**Vases,** 11⅛" h., 4⅜" d., an Oriental form w/a wide baluster-form body w/a wide, tall cylindrical neck & widely flaring rim, the exterior w/a dark blue ground richly decorated w/an expansive Oriental landscape w/buildings & people in colored enamels highlighted overall w/gilt trim, a pearlized white lustre interior w/a gilt rim band, pr. (ILLUS. of one) ................... **895.00**

# CATALINA ISLAND POTTERY

*The Clay Products Division of the Santa Catalina Island Co. produced a variety of wares during their brief ten-year operation. The brainchild of chewing-gum magnate, William Wrigley, Jr., owner of Catalina Island at the time, and his business associate D.M. Retton, the plant was established at Pebbly Beach, near Avalon in 1927. Its two-fold goal was to provide year-round work for the island's residents and building material for Wrigley's ongoing development of a major tourist attraction at Avalon. Early production consisted of bricks and roof and patio tiles. Later, art pottery, including vases, flower bowls, lamps and home accessories, were made from a local brown-based clay and, about 1930, tablewares were introduced. These early wares carried vivid glazes but had a tendency to chip readily and a white-bodied, more chip-resistant clay, imported from the mainland, was used after 1932. The costs associated with importing clay eventually caused the Catalina pottery to be sold to a California mainland competitor in 1937. These wares were molded and are not hand-thrown but some pieces have hand-painted decoration.*

*Catalina Island Marks*

**Ashtray,** fish decoration, Model No. 550, Toyon red .................. **$95.00**

**Ashtray,** Model No. 657, green .... **95.00**

**Bowl,** fruit, 13" d., footed, blue.... **175.00**

**Bowl,** fruit, 13" d., footed, Toyon red............................................. **225.00**

**Bowl,** 9½ x 14", flared sides, white ........................................ **150.00**

**Carafe,** cov., handled, aqua........ **125.00**

**Carafe,** cov., handled, Toyon red............................................. **125.00**

**Charger,** Model No. 622, Toyon red, 17½" d. ............................. **225.00**

**Compote,** footed, Toyon red ...... **225.00**

**Model of a cowboy hat,** Descanso green........................ **195.00**

**Plate,** chop, 11" d., Descanso green............................................. **65.00**

**Plate,** chop, 12½" d., Toyon red ... **70.00**

**Plate,** chop, 17½" d., Model No. 622, Toyon red......................... **225.00**

**Salt & pepper shakers,** figural Senorita & Peon, Toyon red & yellow, pr.................................. **125.00**

**Salt & pepper shakers,** figural Senorita & Peon, Toyon red, early clay body, pr.................... **260.00**

**Salt & pepper shakers,** figural tulip, Catalina blue, pr. (small flakes on holes)......................... **55.00**

**Vase,** 5" h., Model No. 300, Descanso green........................ **50.00**

**Vase,** 5" h., handled, Model No. 612, Mandarin yellow................ **125.00**

**Vase,** 5½" h., Model No. 503, tan............................................. **100.00**

**Vase,** 5½" h., Model No. 600, tan... **95.00**

**Vase,** 7" h., Model No. 636, turquoise ................................... **145.00**

**Vase,** 7¼" h., sawtooth edge on each side, turquoise, Model No. 601 ............................................. **200.00**

**Vase,** 7½" h., trophy-form, handled, Toyon red.................. **350.00**

**Vase,** 7¾" h., blue, Model No. 627 ..................................... **135.00**

**Vase,** 8" h., Mandarin yellow....... **195.00**

**Water set:** old red clay handled pitcher & two tumblers; Toyon red, 3 pcs. (small nicks on the pitcher)...................................... **150.00**

# CAUGHLEY PORCELAIN

*Thomas Turner produced fine quality porcelain at the Caughley Works near Broseley, Shropshire, England, from 1775 until 1799, when the factory was taken over by the Coalport works. Much of the ware was impressed "salopian" in lower case letters, or marked "S" in underglaze-blue, indicating that it had been produced in Salop, another name for Shropshire county. While most of the porcelain was painted or printed in underglaze-blue, some was finely decorated in enamel and gilt. Turner's Salopian Warehouse in London was a great outlet for the wares.*

**Bowl,** 6¼" d., 2⅞" h., a deep footring supporting a deep rounded & gently flaring bowl, blue on white transfer-printed design of Oriental-style florals, "C" company mark, 18th c. (minor flakes on table ring) ..... **$253.00**

**Coffeepot,** cov., slender reeded baluster-form body w/a swan's-neck spout, ornate C-scroll handle & a domed cover w/button finial, blue transfer-printed decoration of fruit & floral reserves, third quarter 18th c., 9½" h. ...................................... **489.00**

**Tureen, cover & undertray,** deep rounded oval & slightly flaring body w/shell end handles, the stepped & domed cover w/a pod finial, on a dished oblong undertray w/shell end handles, all decorated overall w/blue transfer-printed floral clusters, third quarter 18th c., undertray 13" l., overall 9" h., the set .... **2,300.00**

# CELADON

*This ware is a highly-fired Oriental porcelain which features a glaze ranging in color from olive through tones of green, bluish green and grey. Such wares have been produced for centuries in China, Korea and Japan. Fine early celadon wares are costly while later examples can be found at more reasonable prices. Japanese celadon is called "Seiji."*

**Bowl,** 5¼" d., deep gently flaring sides, decorated to imitate carved stone, molded on the interior w/chrysanthemums on stylized leafy stems below a single line border, the similarly

*Early Celadon Bowl*

*Triple-Necked Celadon Vase*

molded exterior further carved w/ribs, resting on a short slightly waisted foot, overall olive green glaze, Northern Song Dynasty, China (ILLUS. top) .............. **$2,760.00**

**Dish,** round, Ch'ing Dynasty, crackled glaze, 10½" d. ........... **345.00**

**Vase,** 11" h., three baluster-form necks above a bulbous ovoid body resting on a narrow flaring foot, overall incised scrolling foliate designs, typical greenish blue glaze, Daoguang mark & period, China (ILLUS. bottom) ............................... **1,725.00**

# CERAMIC ARTS STUDIO OF MADISON

*Mrs. Blankety Blank Bank*

Founded in Madison, Wisconsin in 1941 by two young men, Lawrence Rabbitt and Reuben Sand, this company began as a "studio" pottery. In early 1942 they met an amateur clay sculptor, Betty Harrington and, recognizing her talent for modeling in clay, they eventually hired her as their chief designer. Over the next few years Betty designed over 460 different pieces for their production. Charming figurines of children and animals were a main focus of their output in addition to models of adults in varied costumes and poses, wall plaques, vases and figural salt and pepper shakers.

Business boomed during the years of World War II when foreign imports were cut off and, at its peak, the company employed some 100 people to produce the carefully hand-decorated pieces.

After World War II many poor-quality copies of Ceramic Arts Studio figurines appeared and when, in the early 1950s, foreign imported figurines began flooding the market, the company found they could no longer compete. They finally closed their doors in 1955.

*Since not all Ceramic Arts Studio pieces are marked, it takes careful study to determine which items are from their production.*

*Ceramic Arts Marks*

**Bank,** figural, Mrs. Blankety Blank, green striped dress, 4¼" h. (ILLUS.) ........................ **$90.00**

**Figurine,** Bali-Gong, 5¼" h. .......... 45.00

**Figurine,** Beth, 4¾" h. ................. 30.00

**Figurine,** Comedy, chartreuse, 10⅜" h. ....................................... 80.00

**Figurine,** Dance Moderne Man, 9⅞" h. .......................................... 60.00

**Figurine,** Dutch Love Girl, blue or yellow dress, 4⅞" h., each ............................. **30.00 to 35.00**

**Figurine,** Harmonica Boy, 4⅝" h. ......................................... 68.00

**Figurine,** Little Boy Blue, 5⅜" l. .... 25.00

**Figurine,** Mary, 6" h. ..................... 20.00

**Figurine,** Tragedy, dark green, 10" h. ............................................ 80.00

**Figurine,** Winter Bell, 5⅜" h. ........ 44.00

**Figurine,** shelf-sitter, Banjo Girl, 4¼" h. .......................................... 40.00

**Figurine,** shelf-sitter, Farmer Girl, 4½" h. .......................................... 40.00

**Figurine,** shelf-sitter, Sitting Boy w/Dog, 3⅝" h. ............................ 52.00

**Figurines,** shelf-sitters, Jack & Jill, 4⅞" h. & 4¾" h., pr ................. 40.00

**Figurines,** shelf-sitters, Maurice & Michelle, 7⅛" & 8¼" h., pr ......... 110.00

**Figurines,** shelf-sitters, Sun-Li & Su-Lin, 6¾" h. & 5½" h., pr. ........ 39.00

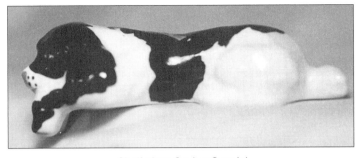

*Shelf-sitter Cocker Spaniel*

**Figurines,** shelf-sitters, Chinese Sitting Boy & Girl, 4" h., pr. ......... **48.00**

**Figurines,** Cinderella & her Prince, 6⅜" h. & 6¾" h., pr........ **145.00**

**Figurines,** Harry & Lillibeth, brown & yellow, pr. .................. **125.00**

**Figurines,** Mop-Pi & Smi-Li, 6" h. & 6¼" h., pr. ..................... **45.00**

**Figurines,** Peter Pan & Wendy, on bases w/tall leafy plants, pr.. **200.00**

**Figurines,** Promenade Man & Promenade Lady, 7¾" h & 8⅛" h., pr. ............................... **225.00**

**Figurines,** The Southern Couple, Lucindy & Colonel Jackson, browns & yellows, 6⅞" & 7¼", pr.............................................. **100.00**

**Figurines,** Swedish Lady & Swedish Man, 6½" h. & 7" h., pr.............................................. **125.00**

**Head vase,** Barbie, 7¼" h. .......... **150.00**

**Head vase,** Bonnie, 7¼" h. ......... **150.00**

**Model of a bunny,** 1⅞" h. ............ **38.00**

**Model of a canary** ........................ **15.00**

**Model of a chipmunk,** 2" h. ......... **45.00**

**Model of a dog,** poodle, FuFu, black, 2¾" h. .............................. **23.00**

**Model of a fawn,** 3¼" h. ............... **65.00**

**Model of a skunk,** Baby Girl (Dinky), 2" h. .............................. **25.00**

**Models of Mother & Baby Bear,** brown, pr. ................................... **55.00**

**Model of a dog,** shelf-sitter, Cocker Spaniel, black & white, 4¾" l., 1¼" h. (ILLUS. above) .... **65.00**

**Salt shaker,** figural crocodile, 4⅝" l............................................. **45.00**

**Salt & pepper shakers,** figural bear, brown, pr............................ **55.00**

**Salt & pepper shakers,** figural Chinese Girl & Boy, girl 4" h., boy 4¼" h., pr............................. **48.00**

**Salt & pepper shakers,** figural Clown & Clown Dog, 3½" h. & 2" h., pr. ................................... **150.00**

**Salt & pepper shakers,** figural Crocodile & Native Boy, 4⅝" l., 2½" h., pr. ................................ **160.00**

**Salt & pepper shakers,** figural Dokie on fall leaf, 2⅝" h. pr. ..... **165.00**

**Salt & pepper shakers,** figural Elephant & Boy, 5" h. & 2¾" h., pr.............................................. **225.00**

**Salt & pepper shakers,** figural Elf & Toadstool, 2" h & 2¼" h., pr. (ILLUS. top next page) .......... **50.00**

**Salt & pepper shakers,** figural Fish on Tail, pr. .......................... **75.00**

**Salt & pepper shakers,** figural Frog & Toadstool, 2" h. & 2⅜" h., pr. ................................... **53.00**

**Salt & pepper shakers,** figural girl in armchair, 2¼" h., pr........... **58.00**

**Salt & pepper shakers,** figural Gingham Dog & Calico Cat, dog, 2¾" h., cat 2⅞" h., pr. .............. **125.00**

**Salt & pepper shakers,** figural roosters, "fighting cocks," 3¼" h. & 3⅞" h., pr. ............................... **58.00**

**Salt & pepper shakers,** figural Mother & Baby Gorilla, 4" h & 2½" h., pr. ................................. **80.00**

*Elf & Toadstool Shakers*

**Salt & pepper shakers,** figural
Mouse & Cheese, 2" h.,
1½ x 2¾", pr................................ **24.00**

**Salt & pepper shakers,** figural
Mr. & Mrs. Penguin, 3¾" h., pr.... **55.00**

**Salt & pepper shakers,** figural
Oakie on Spring Leaf, 2¼" h.,
pr................................................ **80.00**

**Salt & pepper shakers,** figural
Siamese Cat & Kitten, pr. ........... **50.00**

**Salt & pepper shakers,** figural
Wee Piggy Girl & Wee Piggy
Boy, 3⅜" h. & 3¼" h., pr............. **70.00**

**Toby Jug,** seated man in tricorn
hat, 3¼" h.................................... **80.00**

**Vase,** bud, 7" h., figural, Wing-
Sang, Chinese man standing
playing a musical instrument in
front of a triple bamboo-form
vase .......................................... **45.00**

**Wall plaque,** pierced to hang,
figural Arabesque, 9½" h. ........... **35.00**

**Wall plaque,** pierced to hang,
figural Greg, 9¼" h. .................... **40.00**

**Wall plaque,** pierced to hang,
figural Lotus head, 7⅞" h. ........... **95.00**

**Wall plaque,** pierced to hang,
figural Manchu head, 7½" h. ....... **95.00**

**Wall plaque,** pierced to hang,
figural Zor, chartreuse ............... **40.00**

**Wall plaques,** pierced to hang,
figural Shadow Dancer A &
Shadow Dancer B, 7" h., pr. ..... **150.00**

---

# CHINESE EXPORT

*Large quantities of porcelain have been made in China for export to America from the 1780s, much of it shipped from the ports of Canton and Nanking. A major source of this porcelain was Ching-te-Chen in the Kiangsi province but the wares were also made elsewhere. The largest quantities were blue and white. Prices fluctuate considerably depending on age, condition, decoration, etc.*

*CANTON and ROSE MEDALLION export wares are listed separately.*

**Bowl,** fruit, 11⅛" d., blue
"Fitzhugh" patt., scalloped rim &
fluted sides, decorated on the
exterior & interior, ca. 1800 .... **$518.00**

**Fruit basket & undertray,** blue
Nanking patt., oval flaring basket
w/reticulated sides on a
matching undertray, 19th c.,
basket 8⅞" l., 2 pcs. (minor
chips, cracks) .......................... **518.00**

*Fitzhugh Pattern Platter*

*Famille Rose Punch Bowl*

**Platter,** 13¾" l., oval, in the Imari palette, 19th c. (minor chips, edge roughness, glaze & enamel wear) .......................... **259.00**

**Platter,** meat, 10 x 15", *famille rose* palette, ca. 1740-60 .......... **725.00**

**Platter,** 15¾" l., oval, blue "Fitzhugh" patt., very minor glaze chip, 19th c. (ILLUS. top) .. **460.00**

**Platter,** 18¾" l., oval, armorial-type, decorated w/a central sepia oval reserve featuring a mansion at the end of a tree-lined drive beneath a gilt monogram, the border bands of leaf scrolls or zigzag & dots in iron-red, salmon & brown w/gilt trim, early 19th c. .................. **1,495.00**

**Punch bowls,** *famille rose* palette, deep gently rounded sides on a thick footring, the exterior decorated w/an assortment of colorful tree peonies within rocky outcroppings, the interior w/trailing vines & blossoms & a scrolling border all on a white ground, w/associated hardwood stands, ca. 1740, one extensively restored, 15½" d., pr. (ILLUS. of one) ............... **5,750.00**

**Soup tureen,** cov., armorial-type, a deep bulbous oval body on a flaring foot & w/reeded entwined end strap handles, the high domed cover w/a large flowerhead knop above an

encircling border of molded leaves, the sides painted in sepia w/a small oval panel depicting a mansion at the end of a tree-lined winding drive all beneath a gilt monogram, the body & cover bordered by two encircling bands of leaf scrolls or zigzag & dots painted in iron-red, salmon & brown w/gilt highlights, early 19th c., 14" l., 11" h. ..................................... **4,025.00**

**Tea cup & saucer,** armorial-type, blue Nanking patt., 19th c., cup 4⅜" d., saucer 6¼" d. (minor chips, gilt & enamel wear) ........ **259.00**

**Tea service:** tall 'lighthouse'-form cov. coffeepot, cov. teapot, cov. sugar bowl, creamers, two tea bowls & saucers, two plates & a waste bowl; each piece in white decorated in the center w/an American Eagle w/shield, late 18th c., 11 pcs. (imperfections) ...................... **6,900.00**

**Vegetable dishes,** cov., deep oval sides w/flattened flanged rim, a low domed cover w/a pine cone finial, the cover decorated on one side w/a small oval sepia-painted panel of a mansion at the end of a tree-lined drive beneath a gilt monogram, the cover & bottom rim decorated w/border bands of leaf scrolls or zigzag & dots painted in iron-red, salmon & brown w/gilt trim, early 19th c., 11¼" l., pr. ............................. **1,840.00**

*Queen Anne Pattern Chintz Pieces*

## CHINTZ CHINA

There are over fifty flower patterns and myriad colors from which Chintz collectors can choose. That is not surprising considering companies in England began producing these showy, yet sometimes muted, patterns in the early part of this century. Public reception was so great that this production trend continued until the 1960s.

Chintz has managed somehow to go unnoticed by many researchers but is becoming one of the most sought after products on the collectibles market today. Collectors will pay top dollar for items such as breakfast pieces or sets, teapots, stackers, baskets, lamps and jugs. Also, compotes are gaining in popularity. Unusual items such as wall pockets, flower rings, cruet sets and biscuit jars are not easy to find. Patterns that are highly collectible are Welbeck, Hazel, Julia and Sweet Pea. However, Summertime remains the all-time favorite.

Chintz, a catch-all name for items covered with flowers via a transfer pattern, was produced mostly in Staffordshire, England. Companies such as Crown Ducal, Shelley, James Kent and the well-known Royal Winton (Grimwades), knew Chintz was a winner almost from the beginning. Transfer patterns were applied by hand and in some instances were also hand-painted.

Caution should be used by novice collectors when looking for Chintz; reproductions have been made. Chintz purists are not fooled but, there are collectors who do not seem to mind if the item is a reproduction or not. So great is the attraction to Chintz that there are clubs, seminars and a newsletter devoted entirely to collecting Chintz.

**Basket,** "Pekin" patt., black, 5" h. ...................................... **$115.00**

**Bonbon,** "Summertime" patt., Royal Winton ............................ **55.00**

**Box,** cov., rectangular, "Queen Anne" patt., Royal Winton, 3⅜ x 5", 2¼" h. (ILLUS. top left) ......... **95.00**

**Butter dish,** cov., "Hazel" patt., Royal Winton .......................... **325.00**

**Cake plate,** "Anemone" patt., Ascot, Royal Winton ............... **175.00**

**Cake plate,** "Queen Anne" patt., Ascot, Royal Winton ............... **175.00**

**Charger,** "Queen Anne" patt., Royal Winton, 12" d. ................. **190.00**

**Cheese dish,** "Briar Rose" pattern, marked "Lord Nelson Ware Made In England," base 4¾" w., 6" l., lid 4¾" l., 2½" h. (ILLUS. top next page) ............ **325.00**

**Chocolate compote,** open, "Old Cottage Chintz" patt., Royal Winton ...................................... **185.00**

*Briar Rose Cheese Dish*

*Crown Ducal Creamer & Sugar*

*Carnation Pattern Compote*

**Compote,** 6¼" l., 2¾" h., pedestalled, "Carnation" pattern by Royal Winton, deep blue ground w/red & pink flowers & light & dark green leaves, scalloped rim, ca. 1934-1950 (ILLUS. bottom) ....................... **165.00**

**Compote,** open, 6½" d., 2½" h., low foot, "Queen Anne" patt., Royal Winton (ILLUS. previous page, right) ................................. **69.00**

**Compote,** open, 9¼ x 10", 3¼" h., low foot, "Queen Anne" patt., Royal Winton (ILLUS. previous page, center) ............... **95.00**

**Creamer & sugar bowl,** "Spring Glory" patt., Royal Winton, pr. .. **195.00**

**Creamer & sugar bowl,** "Summertime" patt., Royal Winton, pr. ................................. **200.00**

**Creamer & cov. sugar,** unknown pattern, marked w/crown & below it, "Crown Ducal Ware England," production began ca. 1921, creamer 2¾" h., sugar w/cov. 2¼" h., set (ILLUS. center, above) ......................... **145.00**

**Cruet set,** "Cheadle" patt., Royal Winton, 4 pcs. .......................... **325.00**

**Cup & saucer,** demitasse, "Royalty" patt., Royal Winton ... **195.00**

*Summertime Cup & Saucer*

**Cup & saucer,** "Summertime" pattern by Royal Winton, (ILLUS.) .................................... **100.00**

**Cup & saucer,** straight sides, "Skylark" pattern, blue ground w/small yellow flowers & green leaves, gold trim on handle & rims, Lord Nelson mark, 4" d., 4" h. ............................... **100.00**

**Egg cup,** single, "Lynton" pattern, marked "Royal Winton Grimwades, England," produced ca. 1930-1950, 2½" h. (ILLUS. top, next column) ........................ **65.00**

**Jam jar w/metal lid,** "Summertime" pattern, marked "Royal Winton" in a circle w/"Grimwades England" in center, 3" h. ............................ **110.00**

**Pepper shaker,** "Pekin" patt., black, Royal Winton ................... **28.00**

**Pitcher,** milk, "Royalty" patt., Royal Winton .......................... **110.00**

**Plate,** 8½" d., octagonal, plain yellow 1½" rim w/assorted pink, blue & lilac flowers in center, marked w/crown & below it "Crown Ducal Ware England" ... **125.00**

**Plate,** 8¾" sq., "Orient" pattern, marked "Royal Winton Grimwades Made in England Orient 1953 Can. Rd. 1952," production began ca. 1951 (ILLUS. bottom, next column) ... **130.00**

**Relish dish,** cov., "Old Cottage" patt., Royal Winton, 2¼" h. ........ **50.00**

**Salt & pepper shakers,** egg-shaped on round base, "Summertime" pattern by Royal Winton, 2" h., pr. ..................... **140.00**

*Lynton Pattern Egg Cup*

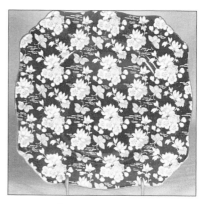

*Orient Pattern Plate*

**Sandwich tray,** "Eleanor" patt., Royal Winton .......................... **150.00**

**Sandwich tray,** "Old Cottage Chintz" patt., Royal Winton ....... **150.00**

**Teapot,** cov., stacking-type, "English Rose" pattern, production began ca. 1951, 6" h., 1-cup size, 4 pcs. ............ **500.00**

**Teapot,** cov., stacking-type, "Marina" patt. .......................... **595.00**

**Trivet,** "Summertime patt.," Royal Winton ..................................... **120.00**

**Vase,** 5" h., bulbous bottom rising to a long stick neck w/slightly flaring rim, "Anemone" pattern, muted blue, white & yellow flowers w/pale green leaves, gold trim on rim, Lord Nelson product ...................................... **115.00**

*A Variety of Clarice Cliff Patterns*

# CLARICE CLIFF DESIGNS

*Clarice Cliff was a designer for A.J. Wilkinson, Ltd., Royal Staffordshire Pottery, Burslem, England when they acquired the adjoining Newport Pottery Company whose warehouses were filled with undecorated bowls and vases. About 1925 her flair with the Art Deco style was incorporated into designs appropriately named "Bizarre" and "Fantasque" and the warehouse stockpile was decorated in vivid colors. These hand-painted earthenwares, all bearing the printed signature of designer Clarice Cliff, were produced until World War II and are now finding enormous favor with collectors.*

*Note: Reproductions of the Clarice Cliff "Bizarre" marking have been appearing on the market recently.*

*Clarice Cliff Mark*

**Bowl,** 5" d., Tonquin patt. ............. **$5.00**

**Butter dish,** cov., "Bizarre" ware, short, wide cylindrical body w/an inset cover w/large button finial, Secrets patt., decorated w/a stylized landscape in shades of green, yellow & brown w/red-roofed houses on a cream ground, marked, 4" d., 2⅝" h. (ILLUS. above left) ................... **259.00**

**Cracker jar,** cov., "Bizarre" ware, bulbous barrel shape w/large side knobs to support the arched woven wicker bail handle, wide flat mouth w/a slightly domed cover centered by a large ball finial, Gayday patt., decorated w/a wide band of large stylized flowers in orange, rust, amethyst, blue & green above a lower band in orange on a cream ground, the cover w/an orange finial & yellow band, 5⅞" d., 6¼" h. (ILLUS. above right) ........................................ **690.00**

**Jar,** cov., "Bizarre" ware, a sharply tapering conical base supported on four squared buttress feet & w/a sharply inward tapering shoulder supporting the conical cover

*Canterberry Bells Pattern Jar*

w/four small buttress tabs at the top, Canterberry Bells patt., decorated in mottled brown on the jar base w/a mottled brown rim & shoulder over a stylized floral band in orange, shades of green, blue amethyst & mottled yellow on a cream ground, 6" d., 8⅛" h. (ILLUS.) ........................ **690.00**

**Pitcher,** 6⅞" h., "Bizarre" ware, flaring cylindrical body w/a wide rim & wide arched spout opposite an angled handle, Secrets patt., decorated w/a stylized landscape in shades of green, yellow & brown w/a red-roofed house on a cream ground, stamped mark .............. **690.00**

**Plate,** 9¾" d., "Bizarre" ware, Viscaria patt., decorated in the center w/a landscape w/cottage in green, pale blue, orange, brown & black under a marbleized streaky sky in shades of red, brown & grey on a cream ground, impressed "10/35" (ILLUS. previous page, center) .................................... **345.00**

**Plate,** 10" d., "Bizarre" ware, Pansies Delicia patt., decorated w/vivid blue, yellow & rose pansies w/yellow, rose & purple centers on pale & dark green leaves against a blue, green, cocoa, brown & yellow opaque

drip glaze background, marked "Pansies - Bizarre by Clarice Cliff - Hand painted - England" & impressed "83" (minor wear)..... **121.00**

**Vase,** 8" h., "Bizarre" ware, Nasturtium patt., footed ovoid body w/a flaring rolled rim, decorated w/vivid orange, red & yellow blossoms w/black, red, yellow & green centers on rounded green leaves atop a mottled caramel & tan ground against a white background, marked "Nasturtium - Bizarre by Clarice Cliff - Hand painted - England" .................................... **770.00**

**Vase,** 10⅞" h., "Bizarre" ware, My Garden patt., cylindrical form tapering to flared foot decorated w/h.p. relief-molded orange & yellow flowers & black leaves on golden mushroom ground, shape No. 664, Wilkinson, Ltd. . **650.00**

**Vase,** 12¼" h., gently flaring conical body on a wide round foot, molded in bold relief w/green & yellow budgie birds on a leafy branch against a light blue shaded to cream ground ... **410.00**

# CLEMINSON CLAY

*Galagray Line Bowl*

*Betty Cleminson, a hobbyist living in Monterey Park, California, began using her garage during World War II to form what would later become known as*

*Cleminson Clay, one of the most successful companies in the United States.*

*Betty and George, her husband who took care of the business of running the small operation, started with only a few items such as the now-sought-after pie bird and many other kitchen-related items. Most of these early pieces were simply marked with a lower case "b" in an upper case "C," but new collectors sometimes mistake the mark for a copyright symbol. Later pieces would bear a stamp mark with a girl on one side, a boy on the other side of what resembles a plate and inside it are the words, "The California Cleminsons" and the older "b" inside a "C." Below the mark is "Hand Painted." Sometimes this mark will not include the boy and girl.*

*A line known as Galagray features an overall grey background with deep red accents or designs. Most often found are the man and woman salt and pepper shakers. At this time, the line is not a priority for collectors. Only time will prove whether or not the line becomes more popular with other generations.*

*Another line which is more popular is the Distlefink. It was a large group of items with either a white or light brown glazed bird with brown and green accents. This line, made two years after the opening of Cleminsons in 1941, was created in a new facility in El Monte, California. After the move the firm expanded eventually having up to 150 employees which enabled the Cleminsons to expand their lines. Included were butter dishes, canisters, cups and saucers, cookie jars, cleanser shakers, ring holders, recipe holders, wall plaques, and decorative plates, to name but a few.*

*In the late 1950s business was still prospering due, in part, to the free-lancing Hedi Schoop did at the Cleminson plant when Schoop's operation was destroyed by fire. However, by 1961 and facing, as did so many other businesses, the importation of cheaper gift and housewares, George and Betty decided to close the operation.*

*Most commonly found stamped mark with or without boy & girl on the sides.*

*Early Betty Cleminson incised mark with here initials. Sometimes confused with the copyright symbol.*

**Bowl,** 3" d., 2¾" h., straight ¼" base rising to a lightly flared rim, Galagray line, grey ground w/red gloss inside & red abstract leaves around the outside center (ILLUS. bottom previous page) ........................ **$19.00**

**Butter dish,** cov., figural, round model of a pudgy woman w/her skirt forming the lid & her upper body forming the handle, green dish w/cover in white gloss w/dark & light green, dark brown & black glazes, 7" h. .................. **95.00**

**Butter dish,** cov., figural, model of a Distlefink sitting on an oblong base, bird's head turned toward back, brown glossy glaze w/dark brown & rust accents, 7½" l., 5¾" h. .............................. **30.00**

**Cleanser shaker,** figure of a woman standing, yellow hair, pink scarf over head, pink & white dress w/grey trim, five holes in top of head, originally included a card around her neck w/a poem to explain she was a cleanser shaker, marked w/copyright symbol & the plate w/a girl & boy on each side, 6½" h. (ILLUS. top next page) .... **24.00**

*Cleminson Cleanser Shaker*

*Cleminson Sock Darner*

**Cleanser shaker,** figure of woman standing, yellow hair, brown scarf, white & brown apron over yellow dress, blue accents, very common, 6½" h..... **18.00**

**Salt & pepper shakers,** figural man & woman on square bases, Galagray line, red & grey colors, 6" h., pr. ..................................... **32.00**

**Pie bird,** figural, model of a bird, white body decorated in pink, blue & green, early mark, 1941, 4½" h.......................................... **40.00**

**Pitcher,** 10½" h., figural, model of a Distlefink, beak forms spout, tail is handle, white body w/brown & green accents ........... **45.00**

**Plate,** 6½" d., pale blue background w/white & black silhouette, woman standing & churning butter ........................... **23.00**

**Plate,** 7" d., ecru ground w/stylized fruit in center w/green leaves, blue rectangles around verge, two factory-drilled holes for hanging ................................. **18.00**

**Recipe holder,** small footed oblong base rising to scalloped sides & rim, hearts & flowers motif, words in brown & black show "Recipe holder," 4" l., 3" h.. **30.00**

**Ring holder,** figural, model of a dog w/tail straight up to hold jewelry, white body w/tan & dark brown accents, marked w/copyright symbol & plate w/a boy & girl on either side, 3" l., 2¾" h. ........................................ **32.00**

**Salt box w/hinged wooden lid,** figural bucket, white ground w/word "Salt" in maroon & green & maroon leaves, cherry fruit & leaves at top near drilled hole for hanging, 8" h. .............................. **55.00**

**Sock darner,** white ground w/h.p. woman's face & brown hair w/blue & maroon accents, words, "darn it" on front near bottom, feet on bottom unseen from standing position, 5" h. (ILLUS. above)........................... **70.00**

**Spoon rest,** elongated quatrefoil w/gloss grey & orange, dark grey & tan leaves & blossoms, 8½" l........................................... **25.00**

**String holder,** heart-shaped........ **65.00**

**Vase,** model of a watering can...... **30.00**

**Wall plaque,** oval w/scalloped rim trimmed in brown on inside edge, applied flowers & leaves in center w/h.p. background flowers, green gloss leaves,

*Cleminson Wall Plaque with Flowers*

pink flower bud & two pink flowers w/yellow centers, two factory holes for hanging, boy & girl mark, 6¾" h. (ILLUS.) ... **45.00**

**Wall pocket,** model of a teapot, wire & wood handle painted w/flowers, blue & brown glazes w/heart shaped motif w/words, "Kitchen bright & a singing kettle make home the place you want to settle," marked w/boy & girl, 9" d., 6" h. ................................... **35.00**

**Wall pocket,** slightly flared top & bottom w/top showing, "Let's pay off the Mortgage" & bottom showing a house & trees, gloss rose, 7" h.................................... **30.00**

**Wall pocket,** white ground w/scalloped blue edge, "Once burned," at top, "Twice shy," at bottom w/woman holding spoon facing away from a black wood-burning kitchen stove, ink stamp mark, 5¼" sq............................. **38.00**

**Wall pocket,** model of a frying pan w/design on bottom, "Them that works hard eats hearty," hole in handle for hanging, ink-stamp mark, 11⅜" l. including handle ...... **30.00**

# CLEWELL WARES

*Though Charles W. Clewell of Canton, Ohio, didn't operate a pottery, he is responsible for a category of fine art pottery through his development of a unique metal coating placed on pottery blanks obtained from Owens, Weller and others. By encasing objects in a thin metal shell, he produced copper- and bronze-finished ceramics. Later experiments led him to chemically treat the metal coating to attain the bluish green patinated effect associated with copper and bronze. Although he produced metal-coated pottery from 1902 until the mid-1950s, Clewell's production was quite limited for he felt no one else could competently recreate his artwork and, therefore, operated a small shop with little help.*

*Clewell Wares Mark*

**Vase,** 5" h., bottle-form, a small foot supports a bulbous body below a slender 'stick' neck w/molded rim, decorated w/stylized leaves & stems, original brown patina, obscured mark ....................................... **$413.00**

**Vase,** 5¼" h., 6¼" d., a footed wide bulbous ovoid body w/a wide flaring flat rim, fine reddish & verdigris patina, incised "Clewell - 418-2-6" ................... **605.00**

**Vase,** 5½" h., simple ovoid body w/the rounded shoulder tapering to a tiny cylindrical neck, rich light green, aqua, orange & brown patina, incised signature, No. 369 (some flaking to patina)...................................... **413.00**

**Vase,** 5½" h., wide bulbous ovoid body w/a narrow shoulder to the wide, short cylindrical neck, rich original dark orange, brown & pale green patina, incised "Clewell - 440-419" ................... **605.00**

**Vase,** 6½" h., original dark orange, green & brown patina, incised "Clewell - 444-224" ....... **605.00**

**Vase,** 6½" h., slender ovoid body tapering to a small, short neck, original brown, pale green, aqua & pale blue patina, incised "Clewell - 368-2-6" .................... **495.00**

**Vase,** 6⅝" h., footed bulbous ovoid body w/a narrow shoulder to the wide, rolled mouth, mottled turquoise & green patina over the brown copper ground, base engraved "Clewell 441," accompanied by an early company brochure, 2 pcs. ........ **550.00**

**Vase,** 7¼" h., plain ovoid body w/a rounded shoulder to a small, short neck w/a widely flaring rim, overall black & green patina, base marked "Clewell - 351-2-6"......... **605.00**

**Vase,** 7½" h., original green & orange patina, incised "Clewell - 290-211" .................................. **715.00**

**Vase,** 9" h., tall slender classical urn-form w/a flaring round foot & an angular shoulder centered by a short widely flaring neck flanked by angular handles, original vivid green & brown patina, incised "Clewell - 502-220"....................................... **1,320.00**

**Vase,** 9¼" h., 4" d., slender baluster-form w/a flaring rim, warm brown to verdigris finish, etched on the base "Clewell #305-2-6" ................................ **715.00**

**Vase,** 9¾" h., 5" w., squared Oriental-style double-gourd form w/a tall square tapering upper section above a widely flaring & rounded lower section w/upright squared handles at each side, the base raised on a platform base w/four short square legs, probably a Norse blank, fine original patina, unmarked ........ **550.00**

**Vase,** 10" h., tall slender swelled cylindrical body w/a flared flat rim, original dark green & brown patina, unmarked ..................... **523.00**

**Vase,** 12½" h., figural, tall slender baluster-form w/an Art Nouveau design, a broad twisting base tapering to the swelled shoulder w/a clinging nude female w/flowing hair, dramatic crimped & folded rim, original nut brown

*Ornate Clewell Vases*

patina w/dark green highlights, impressed "395," some copper missing inside the rim (ILLUS. right, bottom previous page) .... **880.00**

**Vase,** 13" h., wide ovoid body w/a rounded shoulder tapering to a short rolled neck, bold relief decoration of Cleopatra in a long flowing gown reclining atop a platform w/decoration of a stylized lion & wings between two tapered columns supported by a band of stylized stems & leaves around the base, flanked by a helmeted slave w/a long-handled fan, all backed by a stylized sun w/long pointed rays, restoration to drill hole in base (ILLUS. left, bottom previous page) ........................................ **825.00**

**Vase,** 13½" h., gently swelled cylindrical body tapering slightly to the flared rim, reticulation at the shoulder, decorated in bold relief w/three large poppy pods at one side of the rim atop narrow vertical stems, the stems backed by a large single poppy blossom w/curling petals & prominent center, two large poppy pods atop vertical stems on the reverse, rich original deep golden & brown patina, paper label reads "Clewell, Canton, O. #47" .................... **2,860.00**

**Vases,** bud-type, 7½" h., slender trumpet-form body on a widely flaring foot, each w/a crusty green patina on the applied copper ground, each engraved "Clewell 338-2-6," pr. ............... **523.00**

---

# COALPORT

*Coalport Porcelain Works operated at Coalport, Shropshire, England, from about 1795 to 1926 and has operated at Stoke-on-Trent as Coalport China, Ltd., making bone china since then.*

*Coalport Mark*

**Cup & saucer,** fluted, Indian Tree patt. .......................................... **$12.00**

**Ewer,** miniature, slender baluster-form, the gilt-ringed pedestal base supporting an ovoid body tapering to a slender neck w/a scrolled rim & high arched spout, an ornate gold scroll forked handle from rim to shoulder, the center of the side decorated w/a small oval reserve showing a river landscape against a turquoise blue jeweled background, marked, ca. 1885, 7¼" h. (ILLUS. below) ......................... **978.00**

**Platter,** two-handled, Indian Tree patt. ............................................ **35.00**

*Miniature Coalport Ewer*

*Early Coalport Teapot*

**Teapot,** cov., footed swelled oval body w/a waisted, flaring neck, a swan's-neck spout & C-scroll handle, the inset conical cover w/a pointed disc finial, decorated in the Imari style w/underglaze-blue, iron-red & gilt floral designs, patt. No. 819, ca. 1810, gilt wear, 6¼" h. (ILLUS.) ......... **575.00**

# COOKIE JARS

## AMERICAN BISQUE

*Casper the Friendly Ghost*

**Animal Crackers,**
"USA" ......................... **$30.00 to 50.00**

**Baby Elephant** .......................... **130.00**

**Bear,** flasher-type ...................... **495.00**

**Bear with Hat** ........................... **135.00**

**Bear with Honey,** "Corner Cookie Jar, 804 USA," flasher-type ...... **585.00**

**Blackboard Clown** (some paint off blackboard) .......................... **250.00**

**Blackboard Hobo** ...................... **300.00**

**Boots,** "USA 742" ...................... **120.00**

**Boy Bear,** blue shirt ..................... **45.00**

**Boy Bear,** green shirt .................. **40.00**

**Candy Baby** ............................. **145.00**

**Casper the Friendly Ghost** (ILLUS. bottom previous column) .................... **850.00 to 950.00**

**Cat,** paws in pockets, blue & yellow, bank head, 10½" h. (crazing) ................................... **150.00**

*Cheerleaders Cookie Jar*

**Cheerleaders,** flasher-type (ILLUS.) ..................................... **470.00**

**Chef,** standing ........................... **100.00**

**Chick** ......................................... **100.00**

**Churn,** "USA" .............................. **15.00**

**Churn Boy** ................................. **155.00**

**Collegiate Owl** .......................... **60.00**

**Cookie Sack** ............................... **45.00**

**Cow Jumped Over the Moon (The),** flasher-type ................... **975.00**

**Dog,** on quilted base ................ **135.00**

**Elephant w/Baseball Cap** ......... **110.00**

Elephant w/Beanie ...................... 60.00

Elephant w/Hands in Pocket ...... 80.00

French Poodle, maroon
decoration ................................... 85.00

French Poodle, pink................... 150.00

Girl Bear ....................................... 60.00

Granny......................................... 125.00

Hen with Chick, 9½" h. .............. 225.00

Jack-in-the-Box ......................... 125.00

Kids Watching TV, "Sandman
Cookies," flasher-type (inner rim
chip) ........................................... 295.00

Lamb with Flower....................... 160.00

Milk Wagon, w/"Cookies & Milk"
(some crazing) ............................ 70.00

Mrs. Rabbit................................. 220.00

Peasant Girl ............................... 875.00

Poodle, blue ................................. 80.00

Popeye ....................................... 775.00

Rabbit ......................................... 130.00

Rooster, multicolored (minor
crazing) ....................................... 70.00

Saddle, light colored lid, no
blackboard.................................. 300.00

Saddle Blackboard, "Musn't
Forget" ....................................... 280.00

Saddle Blackboard,
"Remember!".............................. 280.00

Sailor Elephant ........................... 85.00

Sea Bag ...................................... 275.00

Seal on Igloo ............. 330.00 to 350.00

Soldier ........................................ 120.00

Spaceship, "Cookies Out of the
World" ......................................... 325.00

Spool of Thread, w/thimble
finial ........................................... 250.00

Toothache Dog, brown .............. 550.00

Umbrella Kids ............................ 315.00

Yarn Doll, yellow dress & maroon
collar .......................................... 145.00

## BRUSH - MC COY

Antique Touring Car .............. 1,400.00

Cinderella Pumpkin (ILLUS.) .... 495.00

*Cinderella Pumpkin by Brush-McCoy*

*Formal Pig Cookie Jar*

Clown, standing, full figure,
brown pants .............................. 465.00

Clown Bust ................................ 450.00

Cookie House ............................ 175.00

Cow, w/cat finial, black & white. 1,200.00

Crock with duck finial ................. 50.00

Crock with praying angel finial .. 75.00

Davy Crockett, gold trim ........... 995.00

Dog w/Basket ............ 350.00 to 450.00

Donkey w/Cart, grey.. 450.00 to 500.00

Elephant w/Ice Cream Cone,
wearing baby hat ...................... 675.00

**Formal Pig** (ILLUS. bottom previous page) ......................... 375.00

**Granny** ........................................ 475.00

**Happy Bunny,** white .................. 210.00

**Humpty Dumpty with Peaked Hat** ........................................... 180.00

**Lantern** ........................................ 65.00

**Little Boy Blue,** large ................ 925.00

**Little Red Riding Hood** ............. 495.00

**Old Shoe** .................................... 95.00

**Panda Bear** ............................... 395.00

**Peter Pan,** large ......................... 725.00

**Puppy Police** ............................. 625.00

**Smiling Bear** .............................. 310.00

**Squirrel on Log** .......................... 120.00

**Squirrel w/Top Hat** .................... 495.00

**Teddy Bear,** feet apart .............. 220.00

**Teddy Bear,** feet apart, green apron, heavy gold trim ............. 875.00

## CALIFORNIA ORIGINALS

**Bear,** "G-405" .............................. 10.00

**Cookie Monster,** "copyright MUPPETS INC., 970" (ILLUS.)... 40.00

*Cookie Monster Cookie Jar*

**Count (The),** "975" ...................... 395.00

**Crawling Turtle** ........................... 20.00

**Elephant** ...................................... 40.00

**Elf School House** ........................ 30.00

**Ernie,** "copyright MUPPETS INC., 973" .......................................... 100.00

**Ernie and Bert Fine Cookies** .... 475.00

**Humpty Dumpty** ......................... 100.00

**Juggler** ........................................ 55.00

**Koala Bear** ................................. 200.00

**Oscar the Grouch,** "copyright MUPPETS INC., 972" .............. 100.00

**Santa Claus** ............................... 175.00

**Scarecrow** .................................. 365.00

**Sheriff,** w/hole in hat .................... 20.00

**Snowman** .................................... 375.00

**Squirrel on Stump** ...................... 90.00

**Superman,** w/phone booth, brown, w/original box ............... 395.00

**Superman,** w/phone booth, silver ......................................... 595.00

**Tigger** ......................................... 195.00

**Woody Woodpecker in Stump** .. 875.00

## REGAL CHINA

**Baby Pig w/diaper** ..................... 795.00

**Barn,** Old MacDonald Line ......... 250.00

**Cat,** tan ...................................... 260.00

**Cat,** white ................................... 470.00

**Dutch Girl,** peach dress (rare) ... 995.00

**French Chef** ............................... 475.00

*Regal Goldilocks Jar*

**Goldilocks** (ILLUS.) ................... 290.00

**Jim Beam,** cylinder ...................... 89.00

**Majorette,** bust ........................... 595.00

**Peek-a-Boo** ............................. 1,200.00

## ROBINSON RANSBOTTOM

*Cow Jumped Over Moon Jar*

**Cow Jumped Over Moon**
**(Hi Diddle Diddle)**
(ILLUS.) .................. 200.00 to 250.00

**Dutch Girl** .................................... 140.00

**Frosty the Snowman** (some
damage) ................................... 400.00

**Hootie Owl** ..................... 50.00 to 75.00

**Sailor Jack** ................ 175.00 to 200.00

**Peter Pumpkin Eater** ................ 475.00

**Whale** ......................................... 925.00

## TREASURE CRAFT

**Baseball Boy** .............................. 30.00

**Bear** ............................................ 20.00

**Cat with Mouse** ........................... 30.00

**Chef** ............................................ 45.00

**Famous Amos** ............................ 75.00

**Farmer Pig** .................................. 60.00

**Katrina** ...................................... 425.00

**Kitten with Goldfish Bowl** .......... 90.00

**Monk** ........................................... 35.00

**Rocking Horse** ............................ 50.00

**Spice** ........................................... 45.00

**Stagecoach** ................................ 40.00

**Sugar** .......................................... 60.00

**Truck,** red ................................... 385.00

## TWIN WINTON

**Bambi,** beside stump ................... 45.00

**Castle** ........................................ 225.00

*Ole King Cole Cookie Jar*

**Chipmunk** ..................................... 20.00

**Cop** .............................................. 95.00

**Dog on Drum** ............................ 100.00

**Duck with Drum** ........................ 110.00

**Fire Engine** .................................. 60.00

**Friar Tuck** .................................... 58.00

**Noah's Ark** ................................. 145.00

**Ole King Cole** (ILLUS. above) ... 350.00

**Sailor Elephant** ........................... 80.00

**Sailor Mouse** ............................... 30.00

## VANDOR

**Betty Boop,** head w/top hat ....... 145.00

**Betty Boop,** standing ................ 650.00

**Cowboy,** head ............................. 70.00

**Cowmen Mooranda**... 350.00 to 375.00

**Juke Box,** auxiliary wall box ....... 195.00

**Popeye Head** ............................. 425.00

## WISECARVER

**Hill Folk,** 12½" h. ...................... 170.00

**Indian Chief,** blue decoration ..... 170.00

**Indian Chief,** tan decoration ....... 170.00

**Mammy with Child** ..................... 130.00

**Pig,** 10¾" h. .............................. 150.00

**Raccoons,** 10" h. ........................ 110.00

# COORS

*It was in 1908 that John J. Herold, formerly of the Owens and Roseville potteries, relocated to Golden, Colorado and, together with the Adolph Coors family, founded the Herold Pottery Company. Mr. Herold remained with the company for just two years but the firm's name didn't change until 1920 when it became the Coors Porcelain Company. One of Coors' most popular patterns, Rosebud, is widely sought by collectors today and there are several variations available but generally collectors seek them all. Original glaze colors included green, orange, rose, white (ivory), yellow and blue and today the ivory glaze seems hardest to find.*

*Still operating today, the Coors Ceramic Division produces items for use in chemical laboratories.*

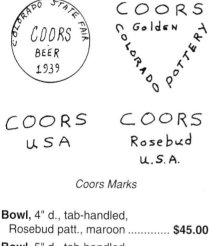

*Coors Marks*

**Bowl,** 4" d., tab-handled,
Rosebud patt., maroon ............ **$45.00**

**Bowl,** 5" d., tab-handled,
Rosebud patt., yellow or
turquoise, each .......................... **50.00**

**Cake plate,** Rosebud patt,
orange, 11" d. ........................... **65.00**

**Custard cup,** Rosebud patt.,
maroon...................................... **15.00**

**Honey pot,** cov., Rosebud patt.,
yellow...................................... **200.00**

**Pie plate,** Rosebud patt., red ........ **80.00**

**Pitcher,** cov., Rosebud patt.,
blue ...................................... **275.00**

**Plate,** 6" d., Rosebud patt., blue,
maroon, yellow or turquoise,
each ........................................ **10.00**

**Plate,** 9" d., scalloped gold
border, h.p. fruits decoration,
artist-signed ............................ **150.00**

**Plate,** 9" d., Rosebud patt., blue,
yellow or turquoise, each ........... **20.00**

**Platter,** 12" l., oval, Rosebud
patt., cobalt blue ........................ **45.00**

**Saucer,** Rosebud patt., blue,
maroon, yellow or turquoise,
each .......................................... **5.00**

**Shaker,** Rosebud patt., straight-
sided, cobalt blue, 4½" h. ........... **25.00**

**Sugar shaker,** green ................. **135.00**

**Teapot,** cov., Rosebud patt.,
green, large, 6-cup size .......... **190.00**

**Vase,** 8" h., footed form
w/protruding handles, russet
matte glaze w/matte green
interior, triangle mark ................ **85.00**

---

# COPELAND & SPODE

*W.T. Copeland & Sons, Ltd., have operated the Spode Works at Stoke, England, from 1847 to the present. The name Spode was used on some of its productions. Its predecessor, Spode, was founded by Josiah Spode about 1784 and became Copeland & Garrett in 1843, continuing under that name until 1847. Listings dated prior to 1843 should be attributed to Spode.*

*Copeland & Spode Mark*

*Copeland Pancake Server*

*Copeland Turkey Platter*

**Berry set:** handled serving bowl w/recessed wells for separate creamer & cov. sugar bowl; decorated w/life-size strawberries, leaves & stems, all trimmed in gold, on cream ground, impressed mark, bowl 8¾ x 10¼", 3½" h., the set...... **$210.00**

**Bowl,** 10¼" d., Italian patt., blue transfer-printed design w/landscape vignettes & a classical rim reserve, Spode, 19th c. ..................................... **196.00**

**Creamer,** Rose Bud Chintz patt.... **30.00**

**Cup & saucer,** Rose Bud Chintz patt............................................. **25.00**

**Dinner service:** eight each dinner plates, soup plates, crescent-shaped plates, side plates in three sizes, five bowls in three sizes, four platters, two sauceboats, two pitchers, two cov. cylindrical jars, a small basin, two cov. vegetable dishes, cov. cheese plate & tureen, cover & undertray; Italian Garden patt., blue & white transfer, late 19th c., the set (lines, restorations) ................ **1,265.00**

**Pancake server,** cov., footed dished base w/molded side handles, the wide domed cover w/a scrolled loop handle, blue on white geometric & floral bands on the base & cover w/gold trim on handles, registry mark dated June 4, 1852, 11¼" d., 7" h. (ILLUS. above) ... **290.00**

**Plate,** 9" d., Bermuda Flowers patt............................................. **20.00**

**Plate,** bread & butter, Rose Bud Chintz patt.................................. **10.00**

**Plate,** dinner, Rose Bud Chintz patt............................................. **20.00**

**Plate,** luncheon, Rose Bud Chintz patt............................................. **20.00**

**Plate,** salad, Rose Bud Chintz patt............................................. **15.00**

**Plates,** service, 10" d., cobalt blue ground borders w/raised gold & floral designs & white enamel beadwork, Copeland, ca. 1900, set of 6 ..................................... **920.00**

**Platter,** turkey-size, 16 x 20¾" oval, decorated in the center w/a large brightly colored turkey in a landscape w/greenery, the wide border band w/stylized scrolling floral designs in dark red & blue alternating w/greyish blue speckled panels, 1891 design registration (ILLUS. above) ...... **400.00**

**Sugar bowl,** cov., Rose Bud Chintz patt.................................. **45.00**

**Vase,** 5⅛" h., 5½" w., relief-molded Apple Blossom patt., soft blue & white ....................... **125.00**

**Warming dishes,** each w/polychrome-decorated blue transfer-printed Oriental foliate landscapes, impressed "Spode's New Stone China" marks, ca. 1810, 9⅜" d., pr. (light glaze wear)....................................... **201.00**

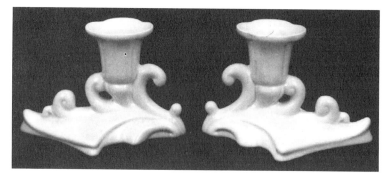

*Cowan Candlesticks*

# COWAN POTTERY

*R. Guy Cowan first opened a studio pottery in 1913 in Cleveland, Ohio. The pottery continued to operate almost continuously, at various locations in the Cleveland area, until it was forced to close in 1931 due to financial problems. This fine art pottery, which was gradually expanded into a full line of commercial productions, is now sought out by collectors.*

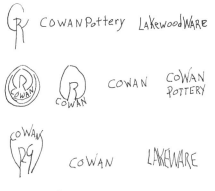

*Cowan Pottery Marks*

**Ashtray,** figural duck, light green glaze, mark No. 8, shape No. 774, 4" l., 2¾" h......................... **$50.00**

**Ashtray/nut dish,** pink or blue glaze, mark No. 8, Shape No. 769, ca. 1928, 2¼ x 3", 1" h., each ......................................... **30.00**

**Candlestick,** two-light, shape No. 745, large figural nude standing w/head tilted & holding a swirling drapery, flanked by blossom-form candle sockets supported by scrolled leaves at the base, ivory glaze, 9½" h. ................... **975.00**

**Candlesticks,** shape No. 625 A, round foot below flaring pointed ribs supporting a tall spiral-twist standard & a flaring socket w/a scalloped rim, blue iridescent glaze, mark No. 8, 8½" h., pr. ..... **90.00**

**Candlesticks,** shape No. 681, a wide flaring paneled foot supporting a short bulbous paneled standard below the short flaring candle socket, ivory glaze, ca. 1925, 3¾" h., pr. ......... **50.00**

**Candlesticks,** shapes Nos. 744-L & 744-R, a semi-nude standing female w/one arm down in front & one arm above head, w/legs crossed & posed on a round foot & scroll-molded base before gently curved open tree-form supports joining behind the figure & supporting the lobed, flaring socket, mark No. 2, ivory glaze, ca. 1928, 12¼" h., pr. ... **1,400.00**

**Candlesticks,** shape No. 782, a scallop-rimmed pointed base molded w/upright scrolls supporting the lobed blossom-form socket, ivory glaze, ca. 1928, 3¾ x 5", 3" h., pr. (ILLUS. above) ......................... **50.00**

*Cowan Golfing Scene Charger*

**Charger,** round, embossed stylized Art Deco golfing scene in brown on a rich celadon green ground, designed by Viktor Schreckengost & embossed "VS" on the front, back die-stamped "Cowan," 11¼" d. (ILLUS.) .................................... **550.00**

**Charger,** octagonal w/a recessed center w/a molded decoration of three nude females w/long hair among large birds w/broad wing spans, a wide border in geometric decoration, all covered in a deep mustard yellow crackle glossy glaze, designed by Thelma Frazier Winter, winner of a first place award at the 1930 Cleveland Museum May Show, impressed mark, paper label, ca. 1930, 13" d........................................ **880.00**

**Cigarette/match holder,** flared foot w/relief-molded sea horse decoration, shape No. 726, 3½ x 4"..................................... **35.00**

**Console set:** bowl & pr. of matching candlesticks; Etruscan patt., Oriental Red glaze, 3 pcs.. **395.00**

**Decanter set:** tall slender ovoid ribbed 10½" h. decanter w/stopper & six 2¼" h. pedestaled bell-shaped cups; Oriental Red glaze, decanter & top mark No. 8 & 9, shape No. X-16, cups, unmarked, shape No. X-17, ca. 1930, 7 pcs. ........ **400.00**

**Decanters,** figural King of Hearts & Queen of Hearts, shapes No. X-12 & X-13, Oriental Red glaze, 11" h. pr...................... **2,995.00**

**Figure,** Art Deco stylized figure of a seated Russian peasant playing a tambourine, beige crackled glaze, artist-signed on the side, die-stamped "COWAN," 7" w., 9½" h. ........... **660.00**

**Flower frog,** figural, Art Deco style, a nude female holding a flowing scarf, standing bent forward on one leg w/the other leg raised & one arm holding the end of the scarf above her lowered head, on an oblong wave-molded base w/flower holes, glossy white glaze, designed by Walter Sinz, 1920s, unmarked, 6" h.......................... **176.00**

**Flower frog,** figural, Art Deco style, two nude females partially draped in flowing scarves, each bending backward away from the other w/one hand holding the scarf behind each figure & their other hand joined, on an oval base w/flower holes, glossy white glaze, designed by R. Guy Cowan, 1920s, unmarked, 7½" l., 6½" h.............................. **198.00**

**Flower frog,** figural, Art Deco style, a nude female partially draped w/a flowing scarf standing & leaning backward w/one hand on her hip & the other raising the scarf above her head, on an oblong serpentine-molded wave base w/flower holes, glossy white glaze, 1920s, unmarked, 8" h. ............. **176.00**

**Flower frog,** figural, Art Deco style, a semi-nude sinewy lady standing & slightly curved backward, her arms away from her sides holding trailing drapery, in a cupped blossom-form base, glossy ivory glaze, impressed lozenge mark & paper label, 4½" d., 10" h. ........ **468.00**

**Flower frog,** figural, Art Deco
style, a semi-nude dancing lady
w/one leg raised & one arm
holding the end of a drapery that
trails behind her, her other arm
raised above her head, on an
oval platform base w/flower
holes, glazed in white,
impressed Cowan mark & "66,"
designed by R. Guy Cowan,
11⅞" h...................................... **440.00**

**Flower frog,** figural, Art Deco
style, tall sinewy nude lady
seated on a tall tree stump, one
arm bent out away from her
body, overall white crackled
semi-matte glaze, impressed
marks, 6" w., 14½" h. ........... **2,970.00**

**Strawberry pot & saucer,** shape
No. SJ-1, bulbous ovoid form
tapering to a wide slightly rolled
rim, four large spout-form
openings around the shoulder,
on a deep dished saucer base,
Oriental Red Glaze, 7½" h. ....... **295.00**

**Tobacco jar,** cov., shape No. X-
7, tapering wide melon-lobed
body w/a stepped & lobed cover
w/a large knob finial, dark
orange glaze, 6" h. .................... **325.00**

**Trivet,** round, glossy decoration
of pink, yellow, green & black
fish among seaweed &
blossoms of yellow & green
against a teal blue ground,
impressed mark, 6" d. .............. **176.00**

**Vase,** 4¼" h., shape No. 609,
wide ovoid body w/a narrow
shoulder tapering up to a flat
molded rim, Arabian Night
glaze ....................................... **100.00**

**Vase,** bud, 7¼" h., shape No.
725, figural seahorse base
supporting a tall slender lobed &
slightly flaring body, creamy
white glaze, ca. 1926 ................. **70.00**

**Vase,** 8" h., 6" w., Art Deco-style,
a fan-shaped folded & pleated
trumpet-form body raised on a
stepped notched base, gunmetal & silver lustre glaze, die-
stamped mark ......................... **605.00**

**Vase,** 11" h., bulbous body
w/wide cylindrical neck, short
molded buttressed shoulder
handles, shape No. V-63, deep
teal green w/indigo overspray,
marks No. 8 & 9 ........................ **425.00**

**Vase,** 11½" h., 8½" d., a deep
flaring foot supporting a tall ovoid
body w/a thin rolled rim, molded
w/narrow vertical braided ribs
alternating w/wider plain panels,
mottled purple satin glaze, die-
stamped circular floral mark ...... **413.00**

**Vase,** 12¼" h., shape No. 592,
Larkspur Blue glaze ................. **150.00**

# CUP PLATES
# (Earthenware)

*Like their glass counterparts, these
small plates were designed to hold a cup
while the tea or coffee was allowed to cool
in a saucer before it was sipped from the
saucer, a practice that would now be
considered in poor taste. The forerunner
of the glass cup plates, those listed below
were produced in various Staffordshire
potteries in England. Their popularity
waned after the introduction of the glass
cup plate in the 1820s.*

**Staffordshire,** dark blue, an
Oriental landscape scene
w/palm trees (double view),
impressed Clews mark, 3½" d.
(glaze rub on edge of base) ...... **$77.00**

**Staffordshire,** dark blue transfer-
printed design of flowers,
impressed Riley mark, 3⅞" d. ... **138.00**

**Staffordshire,** embossed blue
'feather-edge' border, central
red transfer-printed scene of a
woman w/a feathered headdress
& a tambourine, usually titled
"America," impressed "Wood,"
4⅛" d. (tiny rim flake) .............. **330.00**

**Staffordshire,** earthenware,
stylized eight-petaled
flowerhead in center w/leafy

sprigs & lines around the
flanged rim, design in red, black,
green, yellow & blue, early
19th c. 3¾" d. (stains) .............. **165.00**

# CYBIS

*Though not antique, fine Cybis
porcelain figures are included here because
of the great collector interest. They are
produced in both limited edition and non-
numbered series and thus there can be a
wide range available to the collector.*

*Cybis Marks*

**Alice,** No. 4006, 1978, 7¾" h. .... **$350.00**

**American Bullfrog,** "Enchanted
Prince," No. 654, 1971-72,
6½" h......................................... **480.00**

**Apple Blossoms,** No. 510, 1977,
5 x 8½", 4" h.............................. **475.00**

**Baby Bust,** No. 456, 1968-74,
11" h......................................... **600.00**

**Ballerina,** "Little Princess," No.
457, 1968-70, 10" h. ................. **450.00**

**Beagle Puppies,** "Branigan" &
"Clancy," 6 x 9½" ..................... **395.00**

**Bear,** No. 638, 1968-69, 6" h. ..... **150.00**

**Bear Cub,** No. 6026, 1983-84,
5¾" h......................................... **250.00**

**Berengaria,** No. 4015, 1979-81,
15" h...................................... **2,450.00**

**Blue Grey Gnatcatchers,** No.
349, 1961-70, 6 x 10"............. **1,275.00**

**Burro,** "Benjamin," No. 6031,
1983, 5¼" h.............................. **195.00**

**Carousel Pony,** "Sugarplum," No.
651, 1981, 12" h..................... **1,050.00**

**Christmas Rose,** No. 514, 1965-
70, 7½" h.................................. **450.00**

**Cinderella,** No. 429, 1960-68,
7½" h......................................... **750.00**

*Clematis with House Wren*

**Cinderella at the Ball,** No. 4033,
1980-83, 8½" h. ........................ **450.00**

**Clara,** ballerina, 8½" h. .............. **495.00**

**Clematis (White),** No. 533W,
6 x 8"........................................ **375.00**

**Clematis with House Wren,** No.
517, 1969-76, 12" h. (ILLUS.). **1,800.00**

**Colts,** "Darby and Joan," No.
648, 1969-73, 9" l., 9½" h. ........ **350.00**

**Columbine,** No. 4045, 1981-83,
15½" h.................................... **1,600.00**

**Dahlia,** No. 508, 1964-68, 12" h. . **900.00**

**David,** No. 4078, 1983, 8½" h..... **395.00**

**Duckling,** "Baby Brother," No.
361, 1962-79, 4½" h. ................ **125.00**

**Dutch Crocus "Blue
Enchantress" or "Golden
Goblet,"** No. 520, 1970-74,
8½ x 10", each ......................... **850.00**

**Edith,** No. 4007, 1978, 9¾" h. .... **325.00**

**Edward and Victoria,** Nos. 4027
& 4032, 1981-83, 10½" h., pr.... **950.00**

**First Flight,** No. 410, 1966-73,
4½" h......................................... **86.00**

**Fleurette,** 1981, 8¼" h............. **1,200.00**

**Flower Basket,** Constancy, No.
529, 1976-77, 5½ x 6".............. **595.00**

**Flower Basket,** Devotion, No.
526, 1976-78, 5½ x 6"............... **595.00**

**Flower Basket,** Felicity, No. 530,
1976-78, 5½ x 6"...................... **595.00**

**Flower Basket,** Majesty, No. 449,
1967-74, 5½ x 6"...................... **595.00**

**George Washington Bust,**
(w/official seal) No. 482, 1980,
12" h..................................... **1,500.00**

**Good Queen Anne,** 1978,
14" h..................................... **1,400.00**

**Great White Heron,** No. 359,
1964-73, 19" h. ..................... **1,800.00**

**Guinevere,** No. 448, 1967-71,
12" h..................................... **650.00**

**Heidi,** No. 432, 1966-73, 7½" h. . **175.00**

**Hermit Thrush,** No. 380, 1977,
9 x 15½"................................ **1,250.00**

**Jack in the Beanstalk,** 1984,
8" h....................................... **525.00**

**Jeanie with the Light Brown
Hair,** No. 4012, 1979, 9½" h. .... **495.00**

**Kestral (Sparrow Hawk),** No.
379, 1977, 14 x 18"............... **1,750.00**

**Kinglets on Pyrcantha (fire
thorn),** No. 384, 1978, 7½" h.... **950.00**

**Kitri,** ballerina, 6" h. ................... **575.00**

**Kitten,** "Topaz," No. 684R, russet,
1975-77, 3 x 5½"...................... **155.00**

**Kittens,** "Ruffles" & "Truffles," No.
6022, 1983-84, 5¾" h. (ILLUS.
top next column) ...................... **450.00**

**Kristina,** ballerina, No. 4074,
1982, 6¾" h............................. **575.00**

**Kwan Yin,** 13½" h.................... **1,750.00**

**Lady Bug,** "Duchess of Seven
Rosettes," No. 821, 1975-77 ....... **185.00**

**Lady Macbeth,** No. 483, 1975,
13" h..................................... **1,250.00**

**Lisa and Lynette,** 1978, 9 x 11".. **375.00**

**Little Blue Heron,** No. 347, 1960-
71, 8½ x 9½"......................... **1,200.00**

**Little Bo Peep,** No. 498, 1977-
Present, 10½" h. ...................... **450.00**

**Madonna with Bird,** white, No.
2148, 1953-62, 11" h. .............. **395.00**

**Magnolia,** No. 504, 7" l., 4" h...... **350.00**

**Mushroom "Jack-O-Lantern,"**
No. 521, 1970-72, 7" h............. **400.00**

*Kitttens "Ruffles" & "Truffles"*

**Narcissus,** No. 516, 1968-73,
11" h...................................... **325.00**

**Oriental Boy,** "Cheerful Dragon,"
No. 4029, 1979, 10" h. ............. **395.00**

**Otters,** "Baxter" & "Doyle,"
5½ x 10½"............................... **395.00**

**Pandora,** No. 454, 1967, 5" h. .... **175.00**

**Pegasus,** No. 667, 1971-76,
13 x 13½".............................. **2,000.00**

**Peter Pan,** No. 430, 1958-70...... **628.00**

**Pinto Colt,** No. 670, 1972-75,
5½ x 9" ..................... **350.00 to 450.00**

**Pollyanna,** No. 465, 1971-75,
7" h........................................ **275.00**

**Portia,** No. 472, 1973-76,
13½" h................................... **1,800.00**

**Raccoon,** "Raffles," No. 636,
1965, 7½ x 9".......................... **250.00**

**Rebecca,** No. 443, 1964-67,
6½" h..................................... **325.00**

**Sleeping Beauty,** No. 4060,
1982, 7½" h. (ILLUS. top next
page)...................................... **1,000.00**

**Solitary Sandpipers,** No. 362,
1965-71, 7½" h., pr. ................. **850.00**

**Stallion,** brown, No. 643, 1968-
74, 10 x 12"............................. **750.00**

**Thumbelina,** No. 437, 1957-72 .. **178.00**

**Tranquility Base "Apollo II
Moon Mission,"** No. 374, 1970-
71, 7½ x 18".......................... **1,700.00**

**Unicorn,** No. 664, 1969-74,
10 x 13"................................. **1,800.00**

**Unicorns,** "Gambol" & "Frolic,"
No. 693, 1977-79, 8 x 12½" ... **1,000.00**

*Sleeping Beauty*

was changed to *Chelsea Keramic Art Works and in 1891 to Chelsea Pottery, U.S.A. About 1895, the pottery was moved to Dedham, Massachusetts, and was renamed Dedham Pottery. Production ceased in 1943. High-fired colored wares and crackle ware were specialties. The rabbit is said to have been the most popular decoration on crackle ware in blue.*

*Since 1977, the Potting Shed, Concord, Massachusetts, has produced quality reproductions of early Dedham wares. These pieces are carefully marked to avoid confusion with original examples.*

*"Wellington" Walrus*

*Dedham & Chelsea Keramic Art Works Marks*

**Walrus,** "Wellington," No. 6033, 1983, 4½" h. (ILLUS.) .............. **275.00**

**Wendy,** No. 433, 1957-Present, 6½" h. ....................................... **325.00**

**Windflower,** No. 506, 8" h. ......... **350.00**

**Wood Duck,** No. 368, 1968-72, 10" h. ........................................ **550.00**

**Yankee Doodle Dandy,** No. 484, 1975-77, 9" h. ........................... **265.00**

---

# DEDHAM & CHELSEA KERAMIC ART WORKS

*This pottery was organized in 1866 by Alexander W. Robertson in Chelsea, Massachusetts, and became A. W. & H. Robertson in 1868. In 1872, the name*

**Bowl,** ½" h., a small footring supporting a deep rounded bowl, decorated w/a band of "cavorting turtles," marked ...... **$770.00**

**Bowl,** 5" d., deep upright sides, Lotus patt., marked .................. **440.00**

**Butter pat,** five-petal blossom-form, Crackle Ware, marked, 3½" d. ..................................... **220.00**

**Charger,** round, depicting a monkey w/a man's face seated on a dolphin w/a bestial face amid waves, decorated in a teal blue glaze, designed by Hugh Roberts & signed w/the artist's monogram & the words "Affer Dove" on the front, the back signed "CHELSEA KERAMIC WORKS ROBERTSON & SONS," 11" d. (ILLUS. top next page) ..................................... **1,495.00**

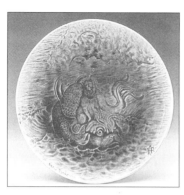

*Chelsea Keramic Charger*

*Dedham Turkey Pattern Plate*

**Knife rest,** model of a rabbit at rest, crackle glaze & blue trim, signed, 2½" l., 1½" h. ................ **275.00**

**Model of a rabbit,** posed at rest, cream crackle glossy glaze w/blue highlights, ink mark, 3½" l., 2½" h............................. **286.00**

**Pitcher,** 5" h., "Morning & Night" patt., a flattened ovoid body w/thick branch handle, molded in relief on each side & decorated w/blue trim, one side w/a spread-winged owl & its prey w/a crescent moon, the opposite side w/a crowing rooster, three hens & the sun, ink mark ................................... **550.00**

**Pitcher,** jug-type, 5" h., 6" d., Rabbit patt., marked (restoration to spout) ................................... **165.00**

**Plate,** 6" d., Magnolia patt........... **200.00**

**Plate,** 7½" d., Crab patt., impressed "Double Rabbit" mark, "Registered" logo & the "1931" Fairbanks Memorial ink stamp mark .............................. **440.00**

**Plate,** 7½" d., Lobster patt., impressed "Double Rabbit" mark...................................... **440.00**

**Plate,** 8" d., Turkey patt. (ILLUS. top next column) .......... **325.00**

**Plate,** 8½" d., Crab patt., ink mark...................................... **523.00**

**Plate,** luncheon, 8½" d., Duck patt., marked ........................... **165.00**

**Plate,** luncheon, 8½" d., Grape patt., decorated by Maud Davenport, marked .................. **165.00**

**Plate,** luncheon, 8½" d., Lobster patt., marked ......................... **1,100.00**

**Plate,** luncheon, 8½" d., Rabbit patt., initials "KF" for the Fairbanks estate also in the border ...................................... **990.00**

**Plate,** luncheon, 8½" d., Snow Tree patt., decorated by Maud Davenport, marked .................. **193.00**

**Plate,** 9" d., Duck patt. ................ **375.00**

**Plate,** 10" d., Duck patt. ............. **400.00**

**Plate,** 10" d., Horse Chestnut patt......................................... **275.00**

**Plate,** 11⅞" d., Rabbit patt. (small rim chip & chips on table ring) .. **138.00**

**Plates,** bread, 6" d., Lotus patt., marked, set of 6 ...................... **715.00**

**Vase,** 4½" h., 4½" d., footed spherical body w/a short, wide cylindrical neck, covered in a volcanic pink & grey glaze, Chelsea Keramic Art Works, mark hidden by glaze .............. **605.00**

**Vase,** 7" h., 3¼" w., Oriental-style, a squared baluster-form w/a tall gently tapering neck w/a molded rim, figural elephant head handles on the neck, mottled brown & olive green glaze, die-stamped "CHELSEA KERAMIC ART WORKS" .......................... **523.00**

*Chelsea Keramic Arts Vase*

**Vase,** 7¼" h., blue floral decoration on white crackle ground, early impressed mark, dated " '99" ....... **900.00**

**Vase,** 7½" h., 3¾" d., slender double-gourd form w/a *sang-de-boeuf* glaze in rich candy apple reddish orange textured & w/a light gold overlustre, Chelsea Keramic Arts impressed lozenge mark (ILLUS. top) ................. **1,320.00**

**Vase,** 9" h. simple ovoid body w/a narrow shoulder to the short, wide tapering neck, thick glossy drip glaze of mottled green, grey & teal blue over tan w/brown & green highlights, incised "Dedham Pottery - BW - VP 13A," early 20th c...................... **825.00**

# DELEE ART

*Delores and Lee Mitchell, owners of DeLee Art based in Los Angeles, California, seem to have quite accidentally enveloped themselves and their products in obscurity. While the Mitchells seemed to do everything possible to make DeLee a household name, little is known about this company except that the products created are popular with collectors today. Almost all pieces are marked in some fashion. The Mitchell's even gave names to their figurines, animals and so forth. Stickers with a silver background and black lettering have been found often with the proper names of many items.*

*Perhaps realizing that the stickers might be destroyed, the same pieces can be identified with an underglaze mark with the name DeLee Art, and might also include the name of the figurine and the date it was produced. Adding to this you can also find a DeLee Art sticker. However, collectors do find DeLee pieces void of any permanent mark and if the DeLee sticker has been destroyed, there is no mark to indicate the maker. Knowing the products made by the Mitchell's along with glazes helps immensely in indentifying their unmarked products.*

*Today their skunk line is probably the least desirable among collectors. This could be because so many, in varied positions, were created. Two exceptions to this are the boy skunk figurine with blue hat and the matching girl skunk with her large, wide-brimmed blue hat. These skunks were produced in the late 1940s. Many DeLee pieces bear a 1935 or 1938 mark and some have been found marked with a 1944 date so researchers have speculated that DeLee was in business from the early to mid-1930s through the 1940s.*

*de Lee Art © 1938          delee Art*

*Delee Art Marks*

**Bank,** figural rabbit, ears up, pink w/blue purse w/flower on purse, "Money Bunny" silver w/black lettering sticker, "DeLee" sticker & incised underglaze "DeLee," 9" h........................................... **$80.00**

**Cookie jar,** model of boy chef, head down, eyes closed, arms folded over chest w/spoon in hands, colorful flowers on sleeves, apron forms bulbous bottom, marked "DeLee Art 1944," 12½" h. ........................... **295.00**

**Figure of an angel,** standing, head tilted slightly to right, eyes closed, arms together in front at waist, overall glossy white glaze w/brown & blue tiny flowers & scallops on dress front & at wrist & neck, 6½" h.............................. **28.00**

*DeLee Girl Planter*

*DeLee Skunk Figure*

**Figure of a boy lying on his stomach,** head up, arms folded under his chest, 2¾" l. ................ **40.00**

**Figure of a girl holding up apron to form a small planter in front,** gloss white ground w/blue polka-dots, brown piping at edge of apron & collar of dress, large blue bow at waist in back, eyes closed w/brown eyelashes, incised underglaze mark, "Delee Art, 1938, Irene," 6" h. (ILLUS. above) .................. **28.00**

**Figures of a boy & girl lying on their backs w/legs crossed,** boy w/dark green short pants, white shirt w/green buttons, brown hair, soles & straps of shoes, girl w/brown hair, blue eyes, white dress w/blue polka-dots, bare-foot, both pieces marked w/a black & silver paper label, "DeLee Art, California, Hand decorated," 2½" l., pr. ......... **85.00**

**Model of a bunny,** name "Bunny Hug" on sticker, ears up, white ground w/tan on ears, colorful small flowers on top of head and chest, marked "DeLee," 6" h. ...... **35.00**

**Model of a camel,** seated w/front hoofs crossed over one another, head up & slightly tilted to right, pale pink gloss w/caramel glaze highlights on hoofs, mouth & ears, flowers between neck, open hump forms small planter, "Sahara Sue," 5½" h. .................. **50.00**

**Model of an elephant,** seated on back legs, trunk up, head bent to right touching shoulder, white ground w/small pink & blue flowers w/green leaves, 4¾" h. .... **38.00**

**Model of a skunk,** "Phew," standing w/tail up, black gloss glaze w/white, wide stripe from top of head to middle of tail, white & black eyes, pink nose, paper label, 4½" l. ...................... **16.00**

**Model of a skunk,** "Mr. Skunk," on sticker, black body w/white tail upright & against back forming a tiny planter, pink mouth & nose, white eyes & hair, blue derby hat, marked "DeLee Art 1940" & a copyright symbol, 6" h. (ILLUS. above) ...... **28.00**

**Wall pocket,** model of a skunk, "Mr. Stinkie," gloss black w/white, colorful flowers at left shoulder, small opening near stomach for matches, marked "DeLee Art," 7¼" h. ..................... **20.00**

# DELFT

*English Delft Charger*

*In the early 17th century Italian potters settled in Holland and began producing tin-glazed earthenwares, often decorated with pseudo-Oriental designs based on Chinese porcelain wares. The city of Delft became the center of this pottery production and several firms produced the wares throughout the 17th and early 18th century. A majority of the pieces featured blue on white designs, but polychrome wares were also made. The Dutch Delftwares were also shipped to England and eventually the English copied them at potteries in such cities as Bristol, Lambeth and Liverpool. Although still produced today, Delft peaked in popularity by the mid-18th century.*

**Bowl,** 10½" d., 4" h., deep flaring sides on thick footring, overall blue stylized floral decoration w/small leaf sprig alternating w/lines decoration on inside rim edge (chips & crazing) ............ **$385.00**

**Bowl,** 11⅞" d., 2¼" h., shallow w/wide flanged rim w/chain design border, center decoration of stylized flowers, blue on white (edge chips) ............................. **220.00**

**Charger,** the center decorated w/a stylized twisted blossoming tree above grasses, the wide flanged rim decorated w/alternating panels of double blossoms & leafy berried vines, blue on white, Bristol, England, ca. 1770, rim glaze wear & chips, 12" d. (ILLUS. top previous column) ..................... **460.00**

**Charger,** decorated w/a central Oriental landscape scene w/a stylized pagoda & blossom sprigs, the wide border band composed of oblong reserves w/scroll designs alternating w/diaper design sections, polychrome-decorated in blue, red & green, 13⅛" d. (edge chips) ....................................... **660.00**

**Charger,** decorated in the center w/a stylized Oriental landscape w/rockwork & flowers, a border band of swags & leaf sprigs, in polychrome colors of blue, red, yellow, green & purple, 13¾" d. (old chips) ................................ **440.00**

**Charger,** purple & white scene of two figures w/turkey, floral rim w/yellow tulip, back initialed "G.N.S." in underglaze blue, 13¾" d. (small rim chips & wear)......................................... **935.00**

**Clock,** tall case-style, an arched scalloped & scroll-molded crest above the round dial w/Roman numerals & metal bezel framed by scrolls above further scrolls & a platform raised on a waisted case decorated w/leafy scrolls flanking architectural landscape panels, the high rectangular base w/further scrolls framing narrow landscape panels & raised on flaring scroll feet, decorated in blue on white, Holland, 19th c., slight glaze wear, 17½" h. (ILLUS. top next page) ....................................... **316.00**

**Flower bricks,** upright rectangular form, decorated in blue on white w/landscape scene of homes & trees, raised on short bracket feet, 4½" l. pr. (damage & yellowed repair)...... **550.00**

*Dutch Delft Tall Case Clock*

*Dutch Delft Tall Jug*

**Jar,** a bulbous ovoid body raised on a slightly flaring tall octagonal base & tapering to a short octagonal neck, the main body decorated w/large oblong floral reserves between wide bands w/floral & bird medallions, the tall base w/a band of floral panels & the neck decorated w/a band of scrolls, decorated in blue on white, bottom marked "3," 13½" h. (edge chips) ........................... **550.00**

**Jar w/brass cover,** wide baluster-form body decorated w/a wide band of Oriental landscape scenes w/figures between a narrow scrolling upper border band & a wide lower leaftip band, decorated in blue & purple on a pale blue ground, 11½" h. (chips, hairlines) ................................ **605.00**

**Jug w/hinged pewter cover,** a flaring short pedestal base supporting a bulbous nearly spherical body w/a tall slender & slightly flaring neck w/a wide cupped rim w/pinched spout, a ropetwist handle from rim to shoulder, a hinged flat pewter cover w/large ball thumbrest, the body decorated in blue w/a continuous landscape of chinoiserie figures in a hilly countryside, the neck w/floral sprays on each side, the cover inscribed "JEREMIAS - OTTO - 1703," the pedestal base w/a band of leaftips & w/a pewter-mounted edge, Holland, late 17th - early 18th c., 11¾" h. (ILLUS.)........... **6,325.00**

**Picture,** composed of blue & white decorated tiles forming a scene of a covered wagon in a snowy landscape, after L. Apol, w/factory marks, late 19th - early 20th c., 25 × 31" (lines) .......... **1,265.00**

**Plate,** 8⅞" d., decorated in blue on white, large center floral design surrounded by oval reserves of stylized floral buds, triangle w/dot design background w/a chain border (ILLUS. top row, far left next page)......................................... **149.00**

Photo Courtesy of Garth's Auctions

*Large Group of Delft Plates*

**Plate,** 8⅞" d., center design of tree w/large feathery leaves & stylized flowers in blue on white, floral & scrolled border, hairline & chips (ILLUS. top row, second from left).................................... **116.00**

**Plate,** 8⅞" d., a center w/a small roundel framed by a large sunburst design, the outer border band w/a narrow checkered center band, blue, black & white, edge chips (ILLUS. top row, second from right) ........................... **25.00 to 50.00**

**Plate,** 9" d., decorated w/floral design in center and around border, blue on white (edge chips) ...................................... **165.00**

**Plate,** 9" d., blue on white center decoration of large flower surrounded by leaves, floral design border (edge chips) ....... **143.00**

**Plate,** 9" d., blue & white center decoration of stylized flower blossoms, geometric design border (edge chips).................... **50.00**

**Plate,** 9¼" d., a central design of dense florals, the flanged rim w/geometric scroll panels, blue & white w/a yellow rim band, edge chips (ILLUS. bottom row, far left) ..................................... **193.00**

**Plate,** 9⅜" d., octagonal, blue & white center decoration of stylized Oriental floral design, four floral clusters decorate border (edge chips).................. **275.00**

**Soup plate w/flanged rim,** a central decoration of bold stylized florals, the border w/alternating leaf swags & scalloped sections, blue on white, edge chips, 9" d. (ILLUS. top row, far right) ........................ **94.00**

**Soup plate w/flanged rim,** a central design of an urn issuing large stylized leafy blossoms, the flanged rim w/large round dots alternating w/scroll panels, blue & white w/a yellow rim band, small edge chips, 9" d. (ILLUS. bottom row, far right) .. **165.00**

**Soup plate w/flanged rim,** the center w/an overall design of large stylized florals, the flanged rim decorated w/leaf sprigs & blossoms, blue & white w/a yellow rim band, small edge chips, 9¼" d. (ILLUS. bottom row, second from left) ................................................. **160.00**

**Soup plate w/flanged rim,** a center design of a floral medallion issuing large stylized leafy blossoms, the flanged rim w/leafy swags & blossoms, yellow rim band, small edge chips, 9¼" d. (ILLUS. previous page, bottom row, second from right) ............... **193.00**

**Vase,** 4½" h., blue floral decoration on white (chips & yellowed & worn repair) .............. **94.00**

**Vase,** cov., 20" h., Oriental-style octagonal baluster-form w/a flanged, domed cover w/figural foo dog finial, decorated in blue on white w/a scene of an amorous couple in a coastal landscape w/scroll & lappet border bands at top & base & a landscape scene on the cover, Holland, 18th c. (rim chips on restored cover & on foot rim).... **1,035.00**

*A Large Assortment of Delftware*

**Plate,** 5¼" d., center polychrome decoration of floral fan in vase, Oriental cloud border design, edge chips & drilled hole above fan (ILLUS. top row, second from right) .............................................. **165.00**

**Plate,** 8¾" d., center decoration of standing figure surrounded by large flower blossoms, sgraffito border, attributed to Bristol or Lambeth, England, edge chips (ILLUS. bottom row, far right) .... **275.00**

**Plate,** 10½" d., decorated in blue on white, center decoration of floral fan in vase w/Oriental cloud design on border, yellow edge, initial mark, small chips & hairline (ILLUS. top row, second from left) .................................... **303.00**

**Plate,** 11½" d., blue on white central scene of tree & birds, border decorated w/alternating wide & narrow panels of stylized flowers & feathery leaf branches, edge chips (ILLUS. bottom row, center) ......... **385.00**

**Plates,** 8⅞" d., blue Oriental landscape scene on white, house & stylized trees & bushes w/boat on water, attributed to Bristol, England, edge chips, pr. (ILLUS. top row, far right, one of two) ........................................... **440.00**

**Plates,** 9" d., center polychrome decoration of stylized flowers & leaves in flowerpot, buds & leafy branches on border, edge flakes, pr. (ILLUS. previous page, top row, far left, one of two) ......................................... **605.00**

**Plates,** 9½" d., blue & white center Oriental landscape design w/pagoda & mountains & "A.M." beneath the scene, oval reserves w/stylized scenes of buildings & trees & purple marbling in border, edge chips, pr. (ILLUS. previous page, bottom row, far left) .................. **880.00**

**Tea caddy,** cov., rectangular w/angled corners, blue on white center design of trees & Oriental figure w/parasol, corner panels w/diamond lattice design, mismatched pewter lid, "Art Institute of Chicago" exhibition sticker, chips & yellowed repair along bottom edge, 5" h. (ILLUS. previous page, bottom row, second from left) ....................... **468.00**

**Tray,** 4⅞ × 7¼", oblong, blue on white center Oriental landscape scene of trees & homes & bridge, floral & diamond lattice design border, edge chips (ILLUS. previous page, bottom row, second from right) ............. **193.00**

# DERBY & ROYAL CROWN DERBY

*William Duesbury, in partnership with John and Christopher Heath, established the Derby Porcelain Works in Derby, England, about 1750. Duesbury soon bought out his partners and in 1770 purchased the Chelsea factory and six years later, the Bow works. Duesbury was succeeded by his son and grandson. Robert Bloor purchased the business about 1814 and managed it successfully until illness in 1828 left him unable to exercise control. The "Bloor" Period, however, extends from 1814 until 1848, when the factory closed. Former Derby workmen then resumed porcelain manufacture in another factory and this nucleus eventually united with a new and distinct venture in 1878 which, after 1890, was known as Royal Crown Derby.*

*A variety of anchor and crown marks have been used since the 18th century.*

*Derby & Royal Derby Crown Marks*

**Cup & saucer,** demitasse, Vine patt. ......................................... **$24.00**

*Royal Crown Derby Dinner Service*

*Figurine of Dr. Syntax*

**Dinner service:** cov. teapot, one open footed bowl, twelve dinner plates, twelve salad plates, eight bread & butter plates, four coffee cups & six saucers, four demitasse cups (one cracked) & three saucers (one w/scalloped rim), eight bouillon soup cups (one cracked) & six saucers, together w/four Aynsley bread & butter plates & two demitasse cups & three saucers; Imari patt., brightly decorated in tones of cobalt blue & rust on a white ground w/gilt trim, late 19th c., dinner plates 10¼" d., the set (ILLUS. bottom previous page) ......................................... **3,163.00**

**Figurine,** Dr. Syntax Sketching, the seated elderly gentleman wearing a tricorn hat, long jacket & kneebreeches, enamel & gilt decoration, puce painted mark, ca. 1865, small chips, line in base, 5" h. (ILLUS. top) ............ **690.00**

**Ewer,** mottled blue ground w/raised gilt & iron red-decorated bird & foliate designs, pierced handle, shape No. 409, printed mark, ca. 1888, 12½" h... **69.00**

**Tea set:** 9¼" l. cov. teapot, 3¼" h. creamer & 6" l. cov. sugar bowl; oval forms decorated in an Imari-style pattern, ca. 1883, 3 pcs. (rim repair, gilt wear) ..... **259.00**

**Tray,** Imari patt., 8 × 11", 2" h...... **275.00**

**Urns,** ovoid body w/elongated flaring neck, decorated w/floral reserves against a cobalt blue ground w/gilt highlights, 19th c., now fitted as table lamps, 16" h., pr. ............................. **1,380.00**

**Vase,** 7¾" h., decorated w/a mottled blue ground & an iron-red-enhanced gilt bird & foliage design, 1889, Royal Crown Derby (gilt wear) ...................... **575.00**

**Vase,** 8½" h., three-handled, enameled gold flowers & leaves on a pink ground ....................... **350.00**

**Vase,** 9½" h., footed bulbous bottle-form base w/ringed stick neck flanked by scalloped flattened handles, decorated w/ornate h.p. large florals & leaves, ca. 1885, Tiffany & Co., New York ............................... **1,100.00**

# DOULTON & ROYAL DOULTON

*Doulton & Co., Ltd., was founded in Lambeth, London, about 1858. It was operated there till 1956 and often incorporated the words "Doulton" and "Lambeth" in its marks. Pinder Bourne & Co., Burslem was purchased by the Doultons in 1878 and in 1882 became Doulton & Co., Ltd. It added porcelain to its earthenware production in 1884. The "Royal Doulton" mark has been used since 1902 by this factory, which is still in production. Character jugs and figurines are commanding great attention from collectors at the present time.*

*Royal Doulton Mark*

## ANIMALS

**Cat,** Persian, seated, black & white, HN 999, 1930-85, 5" h.... **$78.00**

**Dog,** Airedale Terrier Ch. "Cotsford Topsail," Rouge Flambé, HN 1023, 1931-85, 5¼" h........................................ **155.00**

**Dog,** Airedale Terrier, lying down, dark brown coat, light brown head & underbody, K 5, 1931-59, 1¼ × 2¼" ............................ **295.00**

**Dog,** Alsatian Ch. "Benign of Picardy," dark brown coat w/light brown underbody, black highlights, HN 1116, 1937-85, 6" h........................................... **155.00**

**Dog,** Bull Terrier, lying down, white, K 14, 1940-59, 1¼ × 2¾" .................................. **350.00**

**Dog,** Cocker Spaniel, K 9 ............. **80.00**

**Dog,** Cocker Spaniel, seated, golden brown w/black highlights, K 9A, 1931-77, 2½" h................ **100.00**

**Dog,** Cocker Spaniel, white w/light brown ears & eyes, brown patches on back, HN 1036, 1931-85, 5¼" h. .............. **155.00**

**Dog,** Cocker Spaniel with Pheasant, white coat w/dark brown markings, red brown & green pheasant, HN 1028, 1931-85, 5¼" h. ........................ **190.00**

**Dog,** Dachshund, standing, Ch. "Shrewd Saint," dark brown, light brown feet & nose, No. HN 1128, 1937-85, 4" h. ................ **145.00**

**Dog,** Dalmatian Ch. "Goworth Victor," white w/black spots, black ears, HN 1113, 1937-85, 5½" h........................................ **215.00**

**Dog,** French Poodle, HN 2631, medium.................... **150.00 to 200.00**

**Dog,** Irish Setter Ch. "Pat O'Moy," reddish-brown, HN 1055, 1931-85, 5" h.................................... **160.00**

**Dog,** Labrador, "Bumblikite of Mansergh," black, HN 2667, 1967-85, 5¼" h. ........ **100.00 to 150.00**

**Dog,** Pointer, white w/dark brown markings, yellow & green leaves & brown tree stump on base, HN 2624, 5½" h., 11½" l.................. **380.00**

**Dog,** St. Bernard, lying down, brown & cream, black highlights, K 19, 1940-77, 1½ × 2½" ........... **90.00**

**Dog,** Scottish Terrier, begging, grey w/black highlights, 1931-77, 2¾" h................................. **110.00**

**Dog,** Sealyham, lying down, white w/light brown patches over eyes & ears, K 4, 1931-59, 1½ × 3¼" .................................. **295.00**

**Dogs,** Terrier Puppies in a Basket, white w/light & dark brown markings, brown basket, HN 2588, 1941-85, 3" h. ........... **100.00**

**Monkeys (Mother and Baby),** No. 52, Rouge Flambé, 1912-62, 3" h. .......................... **350.00**

**Penguin,** grey & white w/black tips, K 22, 1940-68, 1¾" h. ....... **185.00**

**Rhinoceros,** lying down, No. 615, Rouge Flambé, 1973-present ... **875.00**

## CHARACTER JUGS

**Airman,** small, 4½" h. .................. **39.00**

**Anne Boleyn,** small, 3½" h........... **79.00**

**Anne of Cleeves,** horse's ears up, 1980-81, large, 6" h. ........... **295.00**

**Aramis,** small, 3½" h. ..... **50.00 to 75.00**

**Aramis,** large, 7¼" h.................... **79.00**

**'Arriet,** tiny, 1¼" h. ..... **125.00 to 150.00**

**'Arry,** tiny, 1¼" h......... **125.00 to 150.00**

**'Arry,** miniature, 2½" h.................. **70.00**

**Athos,** large, 7¼" h...................... **79.00**

**Beefeater,** miniature, 2½" h.......... **99.00**

**Blacksmith,** miniature, 2¼" h. ...... **75.00**

**Capt. Ahab,** large, 7" h. ......................... **100.00 to 125.00**

**Cardinal (The),** miniature, 2¼" h. .. **79.00**

**Cardinal (The),** "A" mark, large, 6½" h........................................ **145.00**

**Catherine Howard,** miniature, 2½" h........................................ **175.00**

*Drake with Hat Jug*

*John Barleycorn Jug*

*Mr. Pickwick Jug*

**Catherine Parr,** miniature,
2½" h............................................. **195.00**

**Charles Dickens,** tiny, 1½" h. .... **105.00**

**City Gent,** large, 7" h. ................... **89.00**

**Dick Turpin,** mask on hat, gun
handle, miniature, 2¼" h............. **62.00**

**Dick Turpin,** mask on hat, gun
handle, small, 3½" h. ................. **68.00**

**Dick Turpin,** mask covering eyes,
horse neck & head handle,
small, 3¾" h. .............................. **50.00**

**Dick Turpin,** mask covering eyes,
horse neck & head handle,
large, 7" h................................. **100.00**

**Drake with Hat,** small, 3¼" h.
(ILLUS. above) ............. **60.00 to 80.00**

**Falconer (The),** miniature, 2¼" h.. **57.00**

**Falstaff,** miniature, 2½" h. ............ **70.00**

**Falstaff,** large, 6" h. ................... **165.00**

**Fat Boy,** tiny, 1½" h. ..................... **60.00**

**Fat Boy,** miniature, 2¼" h. ............ **75.00**

**Fortune Teller,** small, 3¾" h....... **400.00**

**Friar Tuck,** large, 7" h................. **295.00**

**Genie,** large, 7" h. ...................... **285.00**

**Gone Away,** miniature, 2¼" h....... **65.00**

**Granny,** large, 6¼" h.. **100.00 to 125.00**

**Guardsman,** large, 8" h. ............. **110.00**

**Gulliver,** miniature, 2½" h. .......... **375.00**

**Jockey,** large, 7¾" h. ................. **330.00**

**John Barleycorn,** large, signed,
6½" h. (ILLUS. top next
column) ..................................... **185.00**

**John Peel,** small, 3½" h............... **59.00**

**Juggler (The),** large, 6½" h. ......... **95.00**

**King Arthur & Guinevere,** (two-
faced), large, 6½" h.................. **195.00**

**Little Mester Museum Piece,**
large, 6¾" h.............................. **225.00**

**London "Bobby" (The),**
miniature, 2½" h. ........................ **55.00**

**London "Bobby" (The),** large,
7½" h......................................... **110.00**

**Mephistopheles,** large, 7" h.... **1,775.00**

**Merlin,** miniature, 2½" h............... **70.00**

**Michael Doulton,** small, 4¼" h..... **45.00**

**Mine Host,** miniature, 2½" h. ........ **95.00**

**Mine Host,** large, 7" h. ................. **95.00**

**Mr. Micawber,** miniature, 2¼" h. .. **70.00**

**Mr. Pickwick,** miniature, 2¼" h.
(ILLUS. bottom this column) ....... **70.00**

**Napoleon,** large, 7" h.................. **160.00**

**Neptune,** miniature, 2½" h........... **55.00**

**Old Charley,** tiny, 1¼" h. ........... **100.00**

**Paddy,** miniature, 2¼" h. ............. **70.00**

**Pearly King,** large, 6¾" h. .......... **100.00**

**Pearly Queen,** large,
7" h. ........................ **125.00 to 150.00**

**Piper (The),** large, 8¼" h. .......... **255.00**

**Poacher (The),** miniature, 2½" h. . **55.00**

*Dickensware David Copperfield Tray*

**Porthos,** miniature ........................ **70.00**

**Rip Van Winkle,** miniature, 2½" h.. **70.00**

**Rip Van Winkle,** small, 4" h.......... **50.00**

**Robin Hood,** small, 4" h. .............. **65.00**

**Sairey Gamp,** large, 6¼" h. ....... **175.00**

**Sam Weller,** miniature, 2¼" h....... **79.00**

**Santa Claus,** reindeer handle,
1982, large, 7¼" h..................... **189.00**

**Scaramouche,** large, curtain
handle, 6¾" h............................. **65.00**

**Scaramouche,** guitar handle,
large, 7" h................................. **725.00**

**Sir Thomas More,** large, 6¾" h.. **110.00**

**Sleuth (The),** miniature, 2¾" h. .... **70.00**

**Smuggler (The),** large, 7¼" h..... **110.00**

**Snooker Player (The),** small,
4" h............................................. **45.00**

**Soldier (The),** small, 4½" h........... **39.00**

**Tam O'Shanter,** large, 7" h. ....... **110.00**

**Uncle Tom Cobbleigh,** large,
7" h........................................... **399.00**

**Veteran Motorist,** small, 3¼" h. ... **59.00**

**Viking,** large, 7½" h. ................... **210.00**

**Walrus and Carpenter (The),**
miniature, 2½" h......................... **60.00**

**Walrus and Carpenter (The),**
small, 3¼" h. .............................. **65.00**

**William Shakespeare,** large,
7¾" h......................................... **155.00**

**Winston Churchill,** Union Jack &
bulldog handle, large, 7" h. ....... **145.00**

## DICKENSWARE

**Plate,** 10" d., Cap'n Cuttle scene .. **125.00**

**Teapot,** cov., Sairey Gamp...... **1,500.00**

**Teapot,** cov., Tony
Weller ................ **1,400.00 to 1,500.00**

**Tray,** oblong, decorated w/a
scene of slightly embossed
figures of a grey-haired woman
wearing green dress & pink &
white bonnet, arms outstretched
to young boy wearing brown hat,
white shirt & blue vest, titled
"David & His Aunt" from "David
Copperfield," cream & light
brown ground, 4½ × 8⅝"
(ILLUS. above)........................... **85.00**

**Tray,** Cap'n Cuttle scene,
5⅝ × 10½" ................................ **125.00**

## FIGURINES

**Amy,** HN 3316, blue & rose,
1991........................................ **725.00**

**A Penny's Worth,** HN 2408, pale
blue, yellow & white, 1986-90 ... **125.00**

**As Good As New,** HN 2971,
blue, green & tan, 1982-85 ....... **119.00**

**Auctioneer (The),** HN 2988,
black, grey & brown, 1986 ........ **195.00**

**Ballerina,** HN 2116, lavender
dress, 1953-73.......................... **325.00**

**Balloon Seller (The),** HN 583,
green & cream, 1923-49 .......... **695.00**

**Beachcomber,** HN 2487, purple
& grey, 1973-76 ....................... **190.00**

*Bo-Peep*

**Belle,** HN 2340, green dress,
1968-88...................................... **65.00**

**Belle o' the Ball,** HN 1997, red &
white, 1947-79 .......................... **249.00**

**Blithe Morning,** HN 2021, mauve
& pink, 1949-71 ......................... **250.00**

**Bluebeard,** HN 2105, dark cloak,
orange & green costume,
1953-92..................................... **325.00**

**Bo-Peep,** M 82, pink dress,
1939-49 (ILLUS. above) .......... **500.00**

**Bride (The),** HN 1600, pale pink,
1933-49..................................... **950.00**

**Bride (The),** HN 2873, white
w/gold trim, 1980-89 ................ **149.00**

**Bridget,** HN 2070, green, brown
& lavender, 1951-73 ................ **275.00**

**Bumble,** M 76, green & red,
1939-82..................................... **76.00**

**Captain (The),** HN 2260,
1965-82..................................... **195.00**

**Captain Cuttle,** M 77, yellow &
black, 1939-82 ........................... **76.00**

**Carpenter (The),** HN 2678, blue,
white & brown, 1986-92 ........... **195.00**

**Carpet Seller (The),** HN 1464,
hand open, green & orange,
1929-?...................................... **240.00**

**Centurian (The),** HN 2726, grey
& purple, 1982-84 .................... **125.00**

**Chelsea Pensioner (A),** HN 689,
red, 1924-38 ............................ **900.00**

**Cherie,** HN 2341, bluish grey
dress, 1966-92 .......................... **135.00**

**Chief (The),** HN 2892, gold,
1979-88..................................... **175.00**

**China Repairer (The),** HN 2943,
blue, white & tan, 1983-88 ........ **149.00**

**Chinese Dancer,** HN 2840, red,
green, purple & lavender, 1980... **595.00**

**Clarinda,** HN 2724, blue & white
dress, 1975-81 .......................... **155.00**

**Clarissa,** HN 2345, green dress,
1968-81..................................... **180.00**

**Clockmaker (The),** HN 2279,
green & brown, 1961-75 .......... **275.00**

**Coachman (The),** HN 2282,
purple, grey & blue, 1963-71 .... **425.00**

**Country Lass,** HN 1991,
1975-81..................................... **110.00**

**Daisy,** HN 1961, pink, 1941-49... **329.00**

**Darby,** HN 2024, pink & blue,
1949-59..................................... **225.00**

**Debbie,** HN 2385, blue & white,
1969-82..................................... **110.00**

**Discovery,** HN 3428, matte
white, 1992 ............................... **80.00**

**Elegance,** HN 2264, green dress,
1961-85..................................... **125.00**

**Eleanor of Provence,** HN 2009,
purple & red, 1948-53 .............. **798.00**

**Embroidering,** HN 2855, grey,
1980-90..................................... **195.00**

**Enchantment,** HN 2178, blue
dress w/yellow sleeves, 1957-62
(ILLUS. top next page).............. **165.00**

**Ermine Coat (The),** No. 1981,
red & white, 1945-67................ **280.00**

**Estelle,** HN 1802, pink,
1937-49................................... **1,595.00**

**Eventide,** HN 2814, blue, white,
red, yellow & green, 1977-91.... **129.00**

**Fagin,** M 49, brown, 1932-83........ **76.00**

**Fagin,** HN 534, dark brown,
1922-32..................................... **76.00**

**Fat Boy,** M 44, blue & white,
1932-83..................................... **76.00**

**First Dance,** HN 2803, pale blue
dress, 1977-92.......................... **195.00**

**First Steps,** HN 2242, 1959-65 .. **450.00**

**First Waltz,** HN 2862, red dress,
1979-83..................................... **225.00**

*Enchantment*

*Forty Winks*

**Foaming Quart (The),** HN 2162, orange & brown costume, 1955-92 .................................... **129.00**

**Fortune Teller,** HN 2159, green & brown, 1955-67 ..................... **395.00**

**Forty Winks,** HN 1974, green & tan, 1945-73 (ILLUS. bottom) ... **225.00**

**Fragrance,** HN 3311, 1991 ......... **165.00**

**Francine,** HN 2422, green & white, 1972-81 .......................... **125.00**

*Granny's Heritage*

**Friar Tuck,** HN 2143, 1954-65 ... **475.00**

**Gay Morning,** HN 2135, pink dress, 1954-67 .......................... **229.00**

**Giselle,** HN 2139, blue & white, 1954-69 .................................... **345.00**

**Grandma,** HN 2052, blue shawl w/red & cream dress, 1950-59 .. **250.00**

**Granny's Heritage,** HN 2031, green skirt, light multicolored shawl, 1949-69 (ILLUS. above) .. **450.00**

**Granny's Shawl,** HN 1642, cream dress, red shawl, 1934-49 .................................... **525.00**

**Gwynneth,** HN 1980, red dress, 1945-52 .................................... **285.00**

**Heidi,** HN 2975, green & white, 1983-85 .................................... **129.00**

**Hilary,** HN 2335, 1967-80 ........... **175.00**

**Honey,** HN 1909, pink dress, 1939-49 .................................... **495.00**

**I'm Nearly Ready,** HN 2976, black, white & brown, 1984-85 .. **119.00**

**Indian Temple Dancer,** HN 2830, 1977 ........................................ **995.00**

**Invitation,** HN 2170, pink dress, 1956-75 .................................... **160.00**

**Janet,** M 75, white skirt, shaded rose overdress, 1936-49 ........... **485.00**

**Janice,** HN 2022, green & cream, 1949-55 .................................... **395.00**

**Jean,** HN 2032, 1949-59 ............. **325.00**

*Lady April*

**Jennifer,** HN 2392, blue,
1982-92 ..................................... **225.00**

**Joan,** HN 2023, blue dress,
1949-59 .................................... **205.00**

**Just One More,** HN 2980,
1984-85 .................................... **119.00**

**Katrina,** HN 2327, red, 1965-69 ... **275.00**

**Kerry,** HN 3036, white & pale
green, 1986-92 .......................... **35.00**

**Lady Anne Nevill (The),** HN
2006, purple & white, 1948-53 .. **795.00**

**Lady April,** HN 1958, red & purple,
1940-59 (ILLUS. above) ............. **248.00**

**Lady Betty,** HN 1967, red dress,
1941-51 .................................... **395.00**

**Lady Charmian,** HN 1948, green
dress w/red shawl, 1940-73 ...... **195.00**

**Lady Diana Spencer,** HN 2885,
blue & white, 1992 ................... **295.00**

**Last Waltz,** HN 2316, pink &
cream dress, 1987 ................... **195.00**

**Little Nell,** M 51, pink, 1932-83 .... **76.00**

**Lizzie,** HN 2749, green, white &
red, 1988-91 ........................... **119.00**

**Lyric,** No. 2757, cream dress,
1983-85 .................................... **80.00**

**Maisie,** HN 1618, yellow & blue,
1934-49 .................................... **795.00**

**Margaret of Anjou,** HN 2012,
1948-53 .................................... **798.00**

**Marie,** HN 1370, shaded purple
gown, 1930-88 .......................... **79.00**

*Minuet*

**Marigold,** HN 1447, white &
purple dress, 1931-49 .............. **550.00**

**Master (The),** HN 2325, greyish
green jacket, 1967-92 .............. **195.00**

**Maxine,** HN 3199, pink & purple,
1989-90 .................................... **110.00**

**Mayor (The),** HN 2280, red &
white, 1963-71 ......................... **395.00**

**Meditation,** HN 2330, peach &
cream, 1971-83 ........................ **225.00**

**Minuet,** HN 2019, patterned white
dress, 1949-71 (ILLUS. above)... **279.00**

**Mr. Macawber,** M 42, yellow &
black, 1932-83 .......................... **76.00**

**Mr. Pecksniff,** M 43, black,
1932-82 .................................... **76.00**

**Mother's Help,** HN 2151, black &
white, 1962-69 ......................... **165.00**

**My Teddy,** HN 2177, turquoise &
brown, 1962-67 ........................ **525.00**

**Nanny,** HN 2221, blue & white,
1958-91 .................................... **225.00**

**New Bonnet (The),** HN 1728,
pink dress, 1935-49 ................. **550.00**

**New Companions,** HN 2770,
purple, white & black, 1982-85 ... **175.00**

**Nicola,** HN 2804, red & lilac,
1987 ......................................... **280.00**

*Owd Willum*

**Noelle,** HN 2179, orange, white & black, 1957-67 .......................... **475.00**

**Old Meg,** HN 2494, blue & grey (matte), 1974-76 ....................... **250.00**

**Old Mother Hubbard,** HN 2314, green dress, polka dot apron, 1964-75.................................... **325.00**

**Olga,** HN 2463, 1972-75............. **195.00**

**Once Upon a Time,** HN 2047, pink dress w/white spots, 1949-55.................................... **275.00**

**Orange Lady,** HN 1953, light green dress, dark green shawl, 1940-75.................................... **230.00**

**Owd Willum,** HN 2042, brown jacket, 1949-73 (ILLUS. above) ......... **225.00 to 250.00**

**Paisley Shawl,** HN 1988, red & pink, 1946-75 .......................... **168.00**

**Parisian,** HN 2445, 1972-75 .................... **200.00 to 225.00**

**Parson's Daughter,** HN 564, multicolored skirt, 1923-49........ **515.00**

**Penny's Worth (A),** No. 2408, pale blue, yellow & white, 1986-1990.................................. **90.00**

**Pillow Fight,** HN 2270, pink nightgown, 1965-69 .................. **350.00**

**Poacher (The),** HN 2043, black & brown, 1949-59........................ **350.00**

**Polish Dancer,** HN 2840, red, green, purple & lavender, 1980.. **595.00**

**Polka (The),** HN 2156, pink, 1955-69.................................... **325.00**

**Premiere,** HN 2343, green cloak, 1969-79.................................... **195.00**

**Pride and Joy,** HN 2945, brown, gold & green, 1984 .................. **250.00**

**Prized Possessions,** HN 2942, cream, purple & green, Collector's Club edition ............. **475.00**

**Professor (The),** HN 2281, brown & black, 1955-81 ...................... **175.00**

**Prue,** HN 1996, red, white & black, 1947-55 .......................... **425.00**

**Punch & Judy Man,** HN 2765, green & yellow, 1981-90 ........... **260.00**

**Regal Lady,** HN 2709, turquoise & cream, 1975-83 .................... **195.00**

**River Boy,** HN 2128, blue trousers, white shirt, 1962-75 ... **165.00**

**Romance,** HN 2430, gold & green dress, 1972-81................ **175.00**

**Rosebud,** HN 1983, pink dress, red shawl, 1945-52 .................. **350.00**

**Sairey Gamp,** M 46, green, 1932-83...................................... **76.00**

**Sarah in Winter,** HN 3005, pale green & white, 1986................. **270.00**

**Scottish Highland Dancer,** HN 2436, red, black & white, 1978 ... **875.00**

**Silversmith of Williamsburg,** HN 2208, blue, white & brown, 1960-83.................................... **155.00**

**Sleepy Darling,** HN 293, blue & pink, Collector's Club edition, 1981 ...................................... **195.00**

**Spanish Flamenco Dancer,** HN 2831, red & white, 1977......... **1,500.00**

**Spring Flowers,** HN 1807, green & blue, 1937-59 ........................ **400.00**

**Statesman (The),** HN 2859, black & grey, 1988-1990 .................... **119.00**

**Stick 'em Up,** HN 2981, blue & tan, 1984-85.............................. **119.00**

**Stitch in Time (A),** HN 2352, purple, brown, turquoise, 1966-81.................................... **175.00**

**Summertime,** HN 3137, white & blue, 1987 ................................ **139.00**

*Doulton Flowing Blue Willow Bowl*

**Sweet Dreams,** HN 2380,
multicolored, 1971-90 .............. **155.00**

**Tinkle Bell,** HN 1677, pink dress,
1935-88..................................... **85.00**

**Uncle Ned,** HN 2094, brown,
1952-65..................................... **475.00**

**Uriah Heep,** M 45, black, 1932-83.. **76.00**

**West Indian Dancer,** HN 2384,
yellow & white, 1981 ................ **595.00**

## MISCELLANEOUS

**Bowl,** 7¾" d., 1½" h., Coaching
Days series ................................ **95.00**

**Bowl,** 8½" d., 3⅞" h., stoneware,
flow blue, Willow patt.,
decorated w/scene of Oriental
house, trees & flying birds
(ILLUS. top) .............................. **145.00**

**Cracker jar,** cov., stoneware,
cylindrical body decorated
w/alternating bands of
flowerheads & dots in diamonds
on a lattice ground colored in
dark blues & browns, silver plate
rim & inset flat cover w/etched
design & pointed finial, by
Elizabeth Adams, 1879, Doulton
- Lambeth mark, 4¾" d., 7" h. .. **400.00**

**Decanter without stopper,** Arts
& Crafts style, tall slender ovoid
body w/a slender cylindrical
neck w/molded rim & an applied
handle from the neck to the
shoulder, a pale green neck &

*Kingsware "Churchwarden" Flask*

shoulder above a brown
shoulder band decorated
w/large clusters of red, green &
dark blue fruit & leaves, the
lower body in a dark mottled
blue, impressed Royal Doulton
logo, notation "9000 × 8876 B" &
incised artist's monogram,
9⅛" h......................................... **110.00**

**Flask,** "Kingsware," tapering
ovoid body w/a slender slightly
flaring rim, small loop handle on
the shoulder, slip decoration of
the "Churchwarden," embossed
on the reverse "Dewar's Scotch
Whisky," ca. 1906, 9¼" h.
(ILLUS. bottom, this column) ... **489.00**

*Three Musketeers Loving Cup*

*Bunnykins Mug*

**Flask,** figural Uncle Sam, "Kingsware," early 20th c. ......... **500.00**

**Lamp,** table model, kerosene-type, squatty bulbous pottery font & ringed & domed pottery foot joined by a turned brass pedestal, the font & base in pale yellow w/greenish blue, steel blue & yellow bands of incised florette & other geometric designs, w/a brass ring supporting a domed milk glass shade w/a tall flaring top opening & an apparently original clear chimney, Doulton - Lambeth mark, overall 12½" h. (shade & ring may be newer) ... **585.00**

**Loving cup,** two-handled, a bulbous ovoid body tapering to a wide slightly flaring neck flanked by long handles down the sides, decorated w/a scene of The Three Musketeers, limited edition, signed by Noke & H. Fenton, w/original certificate, numbered 406 of 600, printed marks, early 20th c., 9¾" h. (ILLUS. above) ......................... **920.00**

**Loving cup,** "Kingsware," footed tall cylindrical body, flanked by long pointed loop handles, "Here's A Health," 13" h. ........... **500.00**

**Mug,** child's, "Bunnykins" line, tapering bulbous body decorated w/a colorful scene of bunnies in a swing & a girl bunny jumping rope on the reverse, a band of running bunnies around the top, on a creamy white ground, marked w/Barbara Vernon's name, 3⅛" d., 3" h. (ILLUS.) ................. **45.00**

**Pitcher,** 6¼" h., figural, brown salt-glazed stoneware, shoulder-length bust of Admiral Nelson wearing hat & uniform jacket, impressed mark of Doulton & Watts, ca. 1825 (rim line, firing line to the face) ........................ **288.00**

*Doulton Stoneware Pitcher*

**Pitcher,** 6½" h., jug-type, stoneware, wide cylindrical body tapering slightly to wide cylindrical neck w/pinched spout, applied strap handle, upper half dark brown w/band of incised design around base of neck, lower half w/Blue Willow decoration on tan ground, ca. 1891-1910, Doulton - Lambeth mark (ILLUS.) ........................... **395.00**

*Babes in the Woods Plaque*

**Pitcher,** 10½" h., earthenware, wide ovoid lobed body tapering to a short neck w/shaped rim, C-scroll handle, decorated on the front & back w/flowing cobalt blue irises & a wide cobalt blue band around the neck, shoulder & handle, all highlighted w/gilding, Doulton - Burslem mark ......................................... **415.00**

**Pitcher,** 13" h., figural, brown salt-glazed stoneware, half-length model of Admiral Nelson realistically modeled wearing a hat & decorated uniform w/various medals, incised inscriptions across the front of the oval base, impressed marks "Doulton & Watts," ca. 1825 (hairline in body) ...................... **316.00**

**Plaque,** pierced to hang, oval, flow blue, Babes in Woods series, young girl standing on a stony path & holding a basket, artist-signed, 7¾ × 9¾" (ILLUS. above) ..................... **1,525.00**

**Plaques,** pierced to hang, flow blue, Babes in Woods series, one w/scene of girl w/doll talking to frog & one w/scene of two girls talking to a pixie man, 7½ × 9½", pr. ......................... **3,075.00**

**Plate,** 8" d., Old English Coaching Scenes ..................................... **45.00**

**Plate,** 9" d., Historic England series, "Francis Drake at Plymouth Hoe," artist-signed, A mark, No. D 5940 ................... **85.00**

**Plate,** 9½" d., center portrait of George Washington, deep blue w/beautiful wide garland border, ca. 1910 ................................... **125.00**

**Plate,** 10" d., rack-type, Old English Coaching Scenes, Jock of the Bushveld ........................ **110.00**

**Plate,** 10" d., rack-type, The Doctor ................................. **95.00**

**Plate,** 10" d., Old English Coaching Scenes, Roger Solem El Cobler .................................. **110.00**

**Plate,** 10" d., Queen Elizabeth at Old Moreton ............................. **110.00**

**Plate,** 10½" d., scene of "Falstaff to Bardolph," checkered border ... **65.00**

**Plate,** 10½" d., motto-type, "He who won't be counseled can't be helped" ....................................... **65.00**

**Plates,** luncheon, 8" w., squared form decorated w/foliate scroll borders, printed marks, early 20th c., set of 12 .................. **1,265.00**

**Plates,** each w/a blue ground w/gilded foliate & trelliswork borders, 20th c., set of 12 ........ **805.00**

**Porridge set:** child's, plate, bowl & pitcher; decorated w/girls in long dresses, No. D3119, the set ..................................... **220.00**

**Soup tureen,** cov., Temple Garden patt. ............................. **175.00**

**Toby jug,** brown salt-glazed stoneware, seated Mr. Toby wearing a tricorn hat & holding cup & a bottle, on a rounded mound base, blue coat w/brown vest & hat, modeled by Harry Simeon, impressed mark, 20th c., 8½" h. (ILLUS. right, top left next page) ........................ **345.00**

**Toby jug,** salt-glazed stoneware, large figural Mr. Toby wearing a tricorn hat, seated astride an upright barrel & holding a pitcher

*Doulton Toby Jugs*

of ale, brown-glazed upper half & footring, impressed Doulton - Lambeth mark, late 19th c., brim restored, 13⅞" h. (ILLUS. above left) ............................................. **431.00**

**Umbrella stand,** pottery, a bulbous base below gently flaring cylindrical sides, decorated w/wide brown bands at the rim & near the base & overall scattered yellow leaves on a mottled blue ground, die-stamped "Doulton Lambeth," late 19th c., 13½" d., 25" h. ... **1,100.00**

**Vase,** 2¼ × 3¼", ovoid, Coaching Ways series ............................... **85.00**

**Vase,** 5¼" h., 3⅛" d., stoneware, ovoid body tapering to wide cylindrical neck w/molded rim, decorated w/shield-shaped panels of leafy designs in brown, green & light blue, artist-signed, dated "1887," Doulton - Lambeth marks ...................................... **195.00**

**Vase,** 5¼" h., footed tall slender ovoid body tapering to a widely flaring mouth, slender angled long handles down the sides, dark brown ground decorated w/a golden yellow witch standing beside a cauldron w/a crescent moon above, marked w/the Doulton logo.............................. **193.00**

**Vase,** 5½" h., flow blue, Babes in Woods series, scene of girl picking flowers ......................... **695.00**

*"The Twins" Stoneware Vase*

**Vase,** 5½" h., 2½" d., stoneware, footed slender waisted form w/a widely flaring rim, decorated w/a pair of standing twin boys dressed in red, blue & black against a tan ground, wide black rim band, marked on the side "The Twins" (ILLUS.) ............... **145.00**

**Vase,** 5¾" h., Flambé Ware, footed slender ovoid body tapering to a short rolled neck, a deep red ground decorated w/a black landscape view of a rural church surrounded by a field of flowers, base marked w/the Royal Doulton Flambé transfer logo, impressed "910" & the letters "OGM" & what appears to be a "B" (minor scratches on the back) ........................................ **220.00**

**Vase,** 6¾" h., flow blue, Babes in Woods, scene of woman sheltering child w/her cloak....... **665.00**

**Vase,** 8⅞" h., Flambé Ware, wide bulbous ovoid body w/a wide shoulder to a very small, slightly tapering short neck, rich red glaze on the upper half above swirling mottled dark blue to grey on the lower half, marked w/Royal Doulton trade-mark & notation "Flambé Veined 1616" ............... **495.00**

**Vase,** 9¼" h., Sung Ware, wide bulbous ovoid body w/a wide closed rim, decorated w/a range of colors including Flambé reds & blues to black & silver, marked w/Royal Doulton "Flambé" inkstamp & impressed numbers "7680" & "1-29," painted "Noke," "Sung" & "F.Allen," ca. 1920s .............. **2,420.00**

**Vase,** 9⅝" h., Chang Ware, wide bulbous ovoid body w/the wide shoulder centered by a small slightly molded mouth, thick congealed white glaze w/rust & yellow highlights flowing down over an iridescent bluish black glaze, marked "Chang Royal Doulton" & impressed "7826," painted signature of Charles Noke & monogram of Harry Nixon, ca. 1920s ................... **3,520.00**

**Vase,** 10½" h., flow blue, "Babes in the Woods" series, four children playing around a tree, artist-signed ........................... **595.00**

**Vase,** 10½" h., 4¾" d., Sung Ware, slender baluster form, overall fine red & cobalt blue lustered flambé glossy glaze, die-stamped "ROYAL DOULTON - MADE IN ENGLAND - NOKE - FM - SUNG," early 20th c. ............... **660.00**

**Vase,** 11½" h., flow blue, "Babes in the Wood" series, tall ovoid body w/an angled shoulder to the short, wide rolled neck, decorated w/a scene of a woman sheltering a young girl w/her cloak during a snowstorm .......................... **1,575.00**

**Vase,** 13" h., 8½" d., Moorish Sung Ware, wide ovoid body tapering to a short flaring neck, an Arabian city scene outlined in black under a ruby red glossy glaze, die-stamped "Royal Doulton - Made in England - Flambé - Moorish," early 20th c. .......................... **1,210.00**

*Doulton Hannah Barlow Vase*

**Vase,** 16¼" h., stoneware, gently tapering cylindrical body w/a narrow angled shoulder to the wide, tall gently flaring neck w/flattened rim, the body decorated w/a wide central band of incised cows grazing framed by flowerhead & scrolling foliate borders, signed by Hannah Barlow, impressed company marks, Doulton - Lambeth, 19thc., glaze flake on interior edge (ILLUS.) ......................... **633.00**

**Vase,** cov., 50½" h., exhibit-type, the ovoid body framed by two opposing fabulous monsters & two devilish gargoyles, the short neck & trumpet-form mouth molded w/grotesque cartouches, alternating w/bosses, all surmounted by a cover modeled w/the figure of a seated warrior maiden, a wolf pelt covering her long hair & a greyhound at her side, the sides each painted w/a large oval panel in color, the obverse depicting a man in traditional costume wearing a tam-o'-shanter, tweed jacket, waistcoat, kilt & sporran, he stands on a plateau gazing out over a highland valley accompanied by a pair of Irish wolfhounds & two Highland terriers, the reverse w/a stag & five doe standing among the heather w/grouse nearby all in a mountainous landscape, raised on a waisted plinth molded w/a female, gargoyle & devil masks w/four pierced cartouche scroll feet, mark printed in brown w/a crown over a circle inscribed "DOULTON, BURSLEM,

ENGLAND" & also marked on the cover rim in black "WORLD'S CHICAGO FAIR 1893," artist-signed ........................... **10,350.00**

**Vases,** 10½" h., stoneware, slightly tapering cylindrical form, decorated w/raised stylized leaf & floral decoration, impressed marks, ca. 1900, pr. .................. **259.00**

**Vegetable bowl,** open, Temple Garden patt. ............................. **175.00**

*Doulton Flambé Wares*

Photo Courtesy of Skinner, Inc.

**Model of a tiger,** the walking striped animal w/a Flambé glaze, printed mark, early 20th c., 14" l. (ILLUS. front) ..................................... **374.00**

**Vase,** 9½" h., Veined Flambé glaze, a wide bulbous nearly spherical body tapering to a short cylindrical stick neck, textured & mottled red, blue,

green & yellow glazes, printed mark, mid-20th c. (ILLUS. upper right) ............................. **173.00**

**Vase,** 11¼" h., Sung Ware, tall gently swelled cylindrical body tapering to a wide flat rim, mottled blue & red glazes, signed "Noke" & "F. Allen," printed company mark, 20th c. (ILLUS. top left) ........................ **403.00**

*Doulton Stoneware Vases*

Photo Courtesy of Christies

**Vase,** 11¼" h., stoneware, footed bulbous ovoid body tapering to a short cylindrical neck, incised w/a band of grazing cattle, horses & a dog & molded w/bands of stylized flowerheads, the shoulder & base incised w/a band of stylized leaves, in shades of royal blue, moss green & white against a buff ground, inscribed w/the monograms of artists Hannah Barlow & Arthur Barlow, impressed Doulton - Lambeth mark & "1879" (ILLUS. top row, left) .................................. **690.00**

**Vase,** 13⅓" h., stoneware, a slender baluster-form body w/a small flaring foot & a widely flaring trumpet-form neck, incised w/a band of grazing horses, enclosed by bands of stylized stars in shades of pale blue, midnight blue, rust, green & white, impressed monogram of artist Hannah Barlow & Doulton - Lambeth mark (ILLUS. bottom row, far right) ................ **633.00**

**Vase,** 17" h., stoneware, tall slender trumpet-form body w/a rounded shoulder tapering to a short cylindrical neck w/a flaring molded rim, incised w/a central band of grazing lions & cubs, further decorated w/swags & stylized floral & leaftip designs, in royal blue, slate blue & black, dated 1878 & inscribed artist's monogram of Hannah Barlow & impressed Doulton - Lambeth mark, repair to rim (ILLUS. top row, right) ................................ **633.00**

**Vases,** 12" h., stoneware, ovoid baluster-form body w/flaring foot & trumpet-form neck, the body incised w/a band of grazing deer enclosed by bands of flowerheads, in shades of moss green, caramel, sky blue & white on a buff ground, impressed monogram of Hannah Barlow & Doulton - Lambeth mark, pr. (ILLUS. bottom row, far left & center) ........................... **1,093.00**

# DRESDEN

*Ornate Dresden Clock*

Dresden-type porcelain evolved from wares made at the nearby Meissen Porcelain Works early in the 18th century. "Dresden" and "Meissen" are often used interchangeably for later wares. "Dresden" has become a generic name for the kind of porcelains produced in Dresden and certain other areas of Germany but perhaps should be confined to the wares made in the city of Dresden.

**Clock,** shelf or mantel, the round enameled dial w/Arabic numerals & a metal bezel set in an ornate rococo-style porcelain case encrusted w/flowers & pierced scrolls & painted w/a landscape scene on the lower front behind applied full-figure models of a standing lady & seated gentleman in 18th c. attire, 19th c., 20½" h. (ILLUS. previous column) .... **$1,760.00**

**Cups & saucers,** helmet-form cups decorated w/red & gilt enamels, shaped saucers w/similar decoration, Germany, late 19th c., 5¾" l., set of 6 ....... **805.00**

**Figure,** barefoot boy w/blond hair, blue jacket & pink knee pants holding basket w/applied greens under one arm & feeding geese & ducks, round base w/gold trim, 2⅞" d., 5⅛" h. ........ **145.00**

**Figures,** putti figures, one blowing a trumpet, the other at rest, printed marks, early 20th c., 5" h., pr. ........................ **259.00**

**Figure group,** two women seated at a table, a woman & two men standing, all wearing 18th c. costumes, giving a toast, scrolled gold-trimmed base, ca. 1910, 19" h. ........................ **895.00**

**Figure group,** "Voiture de mariage de Napoleon 1er," a man & woman, in period

*Figure Group of Napoleon's Marriage Coach*

costumes, seated in a golden carriage pulled by four white horses, two uniformed coachmen, a footman & a man standing near the lead horse, mounted on a narrow oblong base, marked "Germany" (ILLUS. bottom previous page)...................................... **3,100.00**

**Lamps,** banquet-type, round ball shade decorated w/h.p. cherubs framed by pink rose clusters, metal fittings to squatty onion-form font ornately embossed w/scrolls, decorated in colors & gilt trim, raised on a tall slender standard applied w/two full-figure winged cupids above a scroll-footed base w/applied pink flower blossoms & green leaves, overall 24" h., pr. (ILLUS. of one, top next column) ........ **3,500.00**

**Model of a dog,** a standing small Spaniel w/black & grey painted accents, ca. 1900, 13½" l. (ILLUS. bottom right) ................ **575.00**

**Nodder figure,** a rotund Oriental man seated cross-legged & laughing, "nodder" head & hands, decorated w/enamel trim & floral sprigs on his costume, Germany, ca. 1900, 10¼" h. (ILLUS. bottom left)................... **920.00**

**Plates,** 8¼" d., each decorated w/various floral designs in color, ca. 1900, set of 12 .................... **518.00**

*Ornate Dresden Banquet Lamp*

**Potpourri urn,** cov., tall baluster-form ornately decorated, the domed cover w/a heraldic shield flanked by two putti above the ovoid body decorated w/pairs of putti at each side above wide loop straps & surrounded by abundant applied flower blossoms all above a painted figural panel above a relief-molded heraldic shield below, raised on a spiral-twist pedestal

*A Dresden Nodder & Dog*

*Very Ornate Potpourri Urn*

w/further applied putti & flowers above the domed flaring scroll-molded footed base w/applied & painted flowers, losses & restorations, third quarter 19th c., 41½" h. (ILLUS.) ....... **6,325.00**

**Serving bowl,** 9 x 16", scalloped rim, decorated w/h.p. flowers, ca. 1887 ................................... **325.00**

**Urn,** cov., rococo-style, a waisted baluster-form w/a domed cover surmounted by an armorial cartouche supported by two putti, the shoulders w/pairs of opposing putti seated holding baskets & wreaths of flowers above the branch-form handles, the body painted w/a mythological scene depicting maidens attending a returning soldier in a landscape setting, the reverse w/sprays of *deutsche blumen*, applied on the waist w/a double armorial cartouche w/garland-holding putti acting as supporters, all raised on a socle & circular waisted plinth on four scroll feet,

the whole applied w/a profusion of garden flowers & fruit, blue crossed swords & "T" mark of Carl Thieme, late 19th c., 41½" h. (losses & restoration) .. **4,600.00**

**Vase,** 6½" h., footed, reticulated neck, h.p. scenic decoration & flowers in green ........................ **375.00**

---

# FIESTA

*Fiesta dinnerware was made by the Homer Laughlin China Company of Newell, West Virginia, from the 1930s until the early 1970s. The brilliant colors of this inexpensive pottery have attracted numerous collectors. On February 18, 1986, Laughlin reintroduced the popular Fiesta line with minor changes in the shapes of a few pieces and a contemporary color range. The effect of this new production on the Fiesta collecting market is yet to be determined.*

*fiesta*
*H L O  USA*

*Fiesta Mark*

**Ashtray**
  cobalt blue .............................. **$55.00**
  grey........................................... **83.00**
  medium green.......................... **196.00**
**Bowl,** individual fruit, 4¾" d.
  chartreuse................................. **27.00**
  medium green ........ **500.00 to 550.00**
  red ............................................ **30.00**
  turquoise................................... **21.00**
**Bowl,** individual fruit, 5½" d.
  grey........................................... **32.00**
  ivory ......................................... **28.00**
  rose........................................... **29.00**
**Bowl,** dessert, 6" d.
  light green................................. **30.00**
  rose........................................... **40.00**
  turquoise................................... **30.00**

**Bowl,** individual salad, 7½" d.
  medium green........................... **110.00**
  red ............................... **70.00 to 75.00**
**Bowl,** nappy, 8½" d.
  chartreuse................................. **46.00**
  cobalt blue ................................ **34.00**
  ivory ........................................ **32.00**
  light green................................. **28.00**
  rose ........................... **45.00 to 50.00**
  turquoise................................... **31.00**
**Bowl,** nappy, 9½" d.
  rose......................................... **57.00**
  turquoise................................... **52.00**
**Bowl,** fruit, 11¾" d.
  light green............................... **220.00**
  yellow ..................... **240.00 to 250.00**
**Bowl,** cream soup
  chartreuse .................. **65.00 to 75.00**
  ivory ........................................ **53.00**
  light green................................. **42.00**
  turquoise................................... **36.00**
**Bowl,** salad, large, footed
  light green .............. **260.00 to 270.00**
  red ........................................ **278.00**
**Candleholders,** bulb-type, pr.
  cobalt blue.............. **100.00 to 115.00**
  ivory ........................................ **90.00**
  turquoise................................... **88.00**
  yellow....................................... **59.00**
**Candleholders,** tripod-type, pr.
  ivory....................... **600.00 to 700.00**
  red .......................... **750.00 to 800.00**
  turquoise ................ **720.00 to 800.00**
**Casserole,** cov., two-handled,
  10" d.
  cobalt blue ............................. **224.00**
  grey ........................ **320.00 to 350.00**
  light green .............. **100.00 to 145.00**
  rose ........................ **245.00 to 275.00**
  yellow..................................... **159.00**
**Coffeepot,** cov., demitasse, stick
  handle
  turquoise................................. **355.00**
**Coffeepot,** cov.
  light green............................... **210.00**
  red .......................... **200.00 to 225.00**
  rose ........................ **400.00 to 425.00**
  turquoise (ILLUS. top next
    column)................................. **206.00**

*Fiesta Tall Coffeepot*

**Compote,** 12" d., low, footed
  ivory ....................................... **164.00**
  light green .............. **100.00 to 125.00**
  yellow...................................... **118.00**
**Compote,** sweetmeat, high stand
  cobalt blue ................................ **75.00**
  ivory ........................................ **81.00**
  turquoise................................... **91.00**
**Creamer,** stick handle
  light green................................. **36.00**
  red ........................................... **44.00**
**Creamer**
  light green................................. **20.00**
  medium green........................... **81.00**
  red ........................................... **31.00**
  yellow....................................... **20.00**
**Creamer & cov. sugar bowl,**
  individual size
  yellow on cobalt blue tray,
    3 pcs..................... **250.00 to 300.00**
**Cup & saucer,** demitasse, stick
  handle
  chartreuse............................... **384.00**
  red .............................. **60.00 to 70.00**
  rose ........................ **400.00 to 425.00**
**Cup & saucer,** ring handle
  forest green .............................. **35.00**
  turquoise................................... **26.00**
**Egg cup**
  chartreuse .............. **135.00 to 145.00**
  forest green ............................ **141.00**
  red ........................................... **70.00**

**Fork** (Kitchen Kraft)
yellow (ILLUS. w/mixing bowl) .. **162.00**
**Gravy boat**
cobalt blue.................. **50.00 to 60.00**
grey ........................... **60.00 to 70.00**
rose............................ **68.00**
**Lid for mixing bowl,** size No. 1
red .......................... **900.00 to 950.00**
**Lid for mixing bowl,** size No. 3
yellow...................................... **758.00**
**Lid for mixing bowl,** size No. 4
light green............................... **761.00**
**Marmalade jar,** cov.
yellow...................................... **285.00**
**Mixing bowl,** nest-type, size
No. 1, 5" d.
ivory.......................... **55.00 to 75.00**
red .......................... **200.00 to 210.00**
yellow...................................... **152.00**
**Mixing bowl,** nest-type, size
No. 2, 6" d.
light green ................................ **92.00**
turquoise ................. **100.00 to 150.00**
**Mixing bowl,** nest-type, size
No. 3, 7" d.
ivory........................ **125.00 to 150.00**
turquoise ................... **75.00 to 100.00**
**Mixing bowl,** nest-type, size
No. 4, 8" d.
ivory ....................................... **161.00**
red .......................... **125.00 to 155.00**
yellow (ILLUS. top next
column) ................................ **118.00**
**Mixing bowl,** nest-type, size
No. 5, 9" d.
cobalt blue.............. **175.00 to 185.00**
ivory ....................................... **160.00**
**Mixing bowl,** nest-type, size
No. 6, 10" d.
ivory ....................................... **200.00**
yellow...................................... **160.00**
**Mixing bowl,** nest-type, size
No. 7, 11½" d.
cobalt blue.............. **300.00 to 350.00**
**Mug**
forest green ............................. **77.00**
ivory........................... **50.00 to 55.00**
light green................................ **44.00**
rose ........................... **75.00 to 80.00**
turquoise.................................. **44.00**

*Mixing Bowl & Spoon & Fork*

*Fiesta Two-Pint Pitcher*

**Mug,** Tom & Jerry style
ivory/gold.................... **55.00 to 60.00**
yellow........................................ **39.00**
**Mustard jar,** cov.
yellow ...................... **175.00 to 180.00**
**Onion soup bowl,** cov.
light green .............. **400.00 to 425.00**
**Pie server** (Kitchen Kraft)
yellow........................................ **64.00**
**Pitcher,** jug-type, 2 pt.
chartreuse .............. **100.00 to 125.00**
turquoise (ILLUS. bottom, this
column) ..................... **50.00 to 60.00**
**Pitcher,** water, disc-type
chartreuse............................... **220.00**
turquoise................................... **86.00**
yellow ........................ **75.00 to 100.00**
**Pitcher,** w/ice lip, globular
light green................................. **90.00**
red ......................................... **145.00**
**Plate,** 6" d.
cobalt blue ................................. **6.00**
red ............................................. **6.00**
rose............................................ **8.00**
**Plate,** 7" d.
forest green ............................. **12.00**

turquoise ..................................... **9.00**
yellow.......................................... **8.00**
**Plate,** 9" d.
cobalt blue ............................... **15.00**
forest green ............................. **20.00**
medium green ............ **40.00 to 50.00**
red .......................................... **15.00**
yellow....................................... **12.00**
**Plate,** 10" d.
grey ........................... **45.00 to 50.00**
rose........................................... **40.00**
**Plate,** grill, 10½" d.
ivory ......................................... **30.00**
rose ........................... **50.00 to 75.00**
**Plate,** chop, 13" d.
cobalt blue ............................... **33.00**
forest green ............................. **76.00**
red .......................................... **58.00**
turquoise ................... **25.00 to 30.00**
**Plate,** chop, 15" d.
chartreuse............................... **121.00**
cobalt blue ............................... **56.00**
red .......................................... **61.00**
rose......................................... **116.00**
**Platter,** 12" oval
ivory ......................................... **28.00**
red ........................................... **60.00**
yellow....................................... **20.00**
**Relish tray w/five inserts**
ivory ....................................... **100.00**
turquoise................................. **185.00**
**Salt & pepper shakers,** pr.
light green................................. **16.00**
rose........................................... **32.00**
**Soup plate w/flanged rim,** 8" d.
ivory ......................................... **38.00**
rose........................................... **51.00**
turquoise................................... **34.00**
**Spoon** (Kitchen Kraft)
cobalt blue (ILLUS. w/mixing
bowl)..................... **150.00 to 175.00**
light green............................... **110.00**
yellow....................................... **80.00**
**Sugar bowl,** cov., individual size
yellow ....................... **90.00 to 100.00**
**Sugar bowl,** cov.
chartreuse................................. **51.00**
ivory ......................................... **33.00**
turquoise (ILLUS. top next
column) ............................... **34.00**

*Fiesta Sugar Bowl*

**Syrup pitcher w/original lid**
yellow....................................... **300.00**
**Teapot,** cov., medium size (6 cup)
chartreuse .............. **200.00 to 250.00**
ivory........................ **155.00 to 165.00**
medium green.......................... **689.00**
yellow ...................... **130.00 to 135.00**
**Teapot,** cov., large size (8 cup)
cobalt blue .............................. **244.00**
yellow ...................... **100.00 to 125.00**
**Tumbler,** juice, 5 oz.
light green................................. **29.00**
ivory ......................................... **40.00**
red ........................................... **43.00**
**Tumbler,** water, 10 oz.
red ........................................... **64.00**
yellow....................................... **50.00**
**Utility tray**
ivory ........................... **45.00 to 50.00**
turquoise................................... **50.00**
**Vase,** bud, 6½" h.
cobalt blue................. **95.00 to 100.00**
red ........................................... **85.00**
**Vase,** 8" h.
cobalt blue .............................. **550.00**
turquoise ................ **475.00 to 500.00**
**Vase,** 10" h.
ivory........................ **750.00 to 795.00**
red .......................... **800.00 to 810.00**
turquoise................................. **625.00**
**Vase,** 12" h.
cobalt blue.............. **725.00 to 800.00**
red .......................... **750.00 to 775.00**
yellow....................................... **860.00**

# FLORENCE CERAMICS

*Florence Ceramics Dog Bank*

*Florence Ward, devastated by the death of one of her sons in 1939, turned to the creation of clay products as therapy. She began working in her home garage and some of the first pieces she produced were of children, which are popular today and not easily found. In 1946 she expanded her business into a small plant in Pasadena, California but after only about three years Mrs. Ward realized that she needed an even larger facility. Once again, Mrs. Ward moved to larger quarters although the operation was still in Pasadena.*

*While she worked with birds and animals, it was her figurines that gave her the most pleasure and were the foundation of her business. To date, over 200 figurines have been documented. Florence Ward also used real lace for many of her figurines, dipping the lace in slip and applying it to many of her cast pieces before they were decorated. Godey figurines were extremely popular and Mrs. Ward used the Godey Ladies' Book to get her inspiration. Those figurines are just as popular today as they were then.*

*The Lefton Company copied the Florence Ceramics figurines resulting in several court battles and loss of revenue. The Wards won their cases but Lefton simply altered small details (size, color, position of hand, hat, leg and so on) and continued with the infringement. All values shown are for the authentic Florence products.*

*In the mid-1950s, well-known sculptor Betty Davenport Ford created a line the company called "stylized sculptures from the Florence wonderland of birds and animals." There were cats, doves, foxes, dogs, rabbits and so on in a bisque-finished treatment. Since this line was produced only two years, it is much in demand for collectors and the values reflect this. Collectors can find pieces marked with a script "Floraline," but this mark indicates a late-line of floral containers and collectors seem not to seek out these pieces, therefore, values are low.*

*In 1964 when Clifford Ward, Sr. died, the Scripto Corporation purchased Florence Ceramics. Scripto produced mostly advertising memorabilia and the operation closed completely in 1977.*

*Florence Ceramics Marks*

*There were variations on these two marks and sometimes the name of the figurine was included in-mold.*

Floraline
BY
FLORENCE CERAMKS INC
PASADENA, CALIFORNIA

*This mark was used on the floral container line.*

**Bank,** figural, model of a dog standing w/left paw across body w/"Ford" advertising under left paw & right paw on top of his head, head turned slightly to the left, glossy grey w/black highlights, in mold mark "Florence Ceramics Pasadena, Calif." & a copyright symbol, Scripto era, 6¾" h. (ILLUS.)...... **$90.00**

*Leaf-Shaped Florence Ceramics Dish*

**Clock,** electric, French w/Dresden flowers, footed case w/clock in center, nude baby sitting at top, white w/pink flowers, green leaves & gold tracing, working condition, 11½" h. ..................... **650.00**

**Dish,** model of two leaves, pale green, marked "Leaf twin by Florence Ceramics Inc. Pasadena, California," 9" l. (ILLUS. top) .............................. **15.00**

**Figure of an angel,** marked "Dude Corral Loveland, Colo.," 7" h. ......................................... **145.00**

**Figure of an angel w/yellow hair,** all white except gold-trimmed rope sash, cuffs & collar on robe, arms bent across upper body, part of angel's wings showing, gold & brown Florence Ceramics ribbon sticker, 7" h. ............................. **110.00**

**Figure of a boy,** "Mike," standing w/head thrown back & arms straight up & back, palms up, 6½" h. ....................................... **145.00**

**Figure of a boy,** standing w/dog seated at his left leg, Colonial white clothes w/gold trim, black shoes w/gold buckles, early years, 6" h. (ILLUS. bottom) .... **105.00**

**Figure of a boy,** standing w/legs apart & right leg slightly bent, holding a package in right hand, white shoes, jacket & shirt, pale blue socks, pants & hat, brown hair, 6¼" h. ............................. **105.00**

*Florence Colonial Boy & Dog*

**Figure of a choir boy,** head down & tilted slightly to the left, eyes lowered looking at song book, left hand under book, right hand near edge of book, white & black choir attire, ink stamp, 5½" h. ........................................ **100.00**

**Figure of a choir boy,** head raised, eyes looking upward, hair parted in middle, hands positioned under song book at spine, white & deep red choir attire, 6¼" h. .............................. **100.00**

**Figure of a girl,** "Blondie," standing w/feet slightly apart, sand pail in right hand & left arm bent at elbow holding shovel to shoulder, black bathing suit w/yellow polka dots, matching scarf tied around short blond hair w/bow at top, 7½" h. .......... **110.00**

**Figure of a girl holding container,** white dress w/pink flower trim & sash, early garage piece, 8½" h. .............................. **75.00**

**Figure of a girl w/bird,** young blonde girl seated, holding a bird in her hands, white dress & shoes w/grey trim & grey hat (early version) .......................... **110.00**

**Figure of a Godey woman,** "Camille," standing, w/glossy white dress & hair, trimmed in dipped lace, shawl over both arms made entirely of hand-dipped lace, white scarf tied at neck, 8½" h. .............................. **175.00**

**Figure of a Godey woman,** "Genevieve," standing w/head bent slightly, dark green hat, purse & dress (which shows only at middle base), pink coat w/heart shaped buttons & white trim, 8" h..................................... **160.00**

**Figure of a grandmother,** sitting in chair reading, "Memories," white w/22k gold trim, 6½" h. .... **650.00**

**Figure of a man,** "Blue Boy," standing on base, blue coat & knee pants, white stockings, collar & cuffs, right hand holding hat w/plume, 12" h. ................... **350.00**

**Figure of a man,** "Leading Man," 10½" h..................................... **275.00**

**Figure of a man,** "Louis XIV," knee britches, boots, shirt w/ruffled lace trim, knee-length coat, scroll-molded base, white w/22k gold trim, 10" h. (some lace damage) .......................... **125.00**

**Figure of a man,** "Martin," standing, right hand on hip, left hand resting on a walking stick, white trousers & tie, rose & royal knee-length coat w/cape & top hat, 10½" h............................... **175.00**

**Figure of a man,** "Victor," white trousers & shirt, royal red jacket

w/tails & long swirling white cape, holding white top hat in right hand, 9¼" h....................... **175.00**

**Figure of a Spanish dancer,** "Carmen," head slightly turned & tilted to left, right arm bent at elbow w/fingers touching black hair, left arm across body at waist, ruffled lace short sleeved, long dress w/lace underslip showing near bottom just below knee, white dress w/red trim & gold accents, 12½" h. .............. **875.00**

**Figure of a woman,** "Abigail," standing, wearing full-skirted dress, cape & bonnet, tan, 8½" h......................................... **155.00**

**Figure of a woman,** "Adeline, " standing, wearing full pleated skirt & holding a shawl wrapped around her lower arms, 9" h...... **265.00**

**Figure of a woman,** "Anita," standing w/right arm bent at elbow, palm extended near waist, left arm almost straight down at side, gold brocade long dress w/short sleeves & fitted waist, 15" h. .............................. **700.00**

**Figure of a woman,** "Ann," grey or teal dress, bonnet tied beneath chin, holding basket on left arm, 6" h., each..................... **75.00**

**Figure of a woman,** "Ann," blue dress, white hat, carrying white basket of flowers, 6" h................. **60.00**

**Figure of a woman,** "Ava," wearing green skirt w/brown dirndl waist & beige peasant blouse, all w/gold trim, left hand on hip & right arm raised & holding a large green basket on her head, 10½" h. ..................... **299.00**

**Figure of a woman,** "Betsy," standing, wearing green skirt & long full jacket w/tight bodice & long sleeves, hands in muff, ruffled floral trim on jacket, bonnet & muff, 7½" h. ................. **75.00**

**Figure of a woman,** "Charmaine," ruffled green dress, large hat w/flowers & holding a parasol, 8½" h......................................... **459.00**

**Figure of a woman,** "Clarissa,"
one hand on her shoulder, the
other holding a muff, wearing a
bonnet, full-sleeved jacket & a
long swirled & pleated skirt,
7¾" h........................................ **125.00**

**Figure of a woman,** "Claudia,"
ruffled dress, lace trim, large
hat, 8¼" h................................ **300.00**

**Figure of a woman,** "Colleen,"
8" h.......................................... **300.00**

**Figure of a woman,** "Delores,"
yellow dress w/tan collar & hat
w/floral trim, holding a parasol,
8" h.......................................... **499.00**

**Figure of a woman,** "Diane," pink
dress, white coat & hat
w/flowers, holding handbag ...... **299.00**

**Figure of a woman,** "Elaine,"
green, white, pink or grey dress,
6" h............................................. **75.00**

**Figure of a woman,** "Gibson
Girl," white dress w/gold trim,
lace & gold trim at cuffs &
bodice, large white hat w/gold &
floral trim, 10" h........................ **100.00**

**Figure of a woman,** "Her
Majesty," long dress w/long
sleeves, fitted bodice w/stand-up
collar, white w/gold trim, 7" h.
(ILLUS. top next column) .......... **170.00**

**Figure of a woman,** "Irene,"
standing, grey dress w/gold trim,
flower in upswept hair, right
hand holding muff near face,
6" h............................................. **70.00**

**Figure of a woman,** "Jenette," full
skirted dress w/peplum, white
collar & flower at neck, pink hat
w/flower, 7¾" h. ....................... **200.00**

**Figure of a woman,** "Julie," pink
dress, 7¼" h............................. **125.00**

**Figure of a woman,** "Laura,"
green dress, 7½" h.................... **100.00**

**Figure of a woman,** "Laura," grey
& pink dress, 7½" h.................. **140.00**

**Figure of a woman,** "Lillian,"
7¼" h......................................... **110.00**

**Figure of a woman,** "Linda Lou,"
green skirt & hat, dark green top
& peplum, white & gold trim,
7¾" h......................................... **125.00**

*Florence "Her Majesty" Figure*

**Figure of a woman,** "Louise,"
blue dress, 7¼" h. ..................... **135.00**

**Figure of a woman,** "Louise,"
grey dress, 7¼" h. ..................... **125.00**

**Figure of a woman,** "Mary," grey
dress, lacy jabot at neck & hat,
seated in a chair w/one foot on a
small footstool, 7½" h............... **499.00**

**Figure of a woman,** "Mathilda,"
grey dress, 8½" h...................... **135.00**

**Figure of a woman,** "Melanie,"
green or tan dress, 7½" h. ........ **110.00**

**Figure of a woman,** "Musette,"
royal red dress w/white lace &
gold trim, large white flower
trimmed hat, 8¾" h.................... **175.00**

**Figure of a woman,** "Rita,"
standing, dress w/ruffled skirt &
laced bodice, holding the skirt
out at both sides, 9½" h. .......... **160.00**

**Figure of a woman,** "Sarah,"
blue, grey or pink dress, 7½" h.,
each ........................................ **110.00**

**Figure of a woman,** "Scarlett,"
standing, violet dress & bonnet,
right hand holding muff near
face, left hand holding handbag,
8¾" h........................................ **249.00**

**Figure of a woman,** "Sue Ellen,"
8¼" h........................................ **110.00**

**Figure of a woman,** "Tess," light green dress w/ruffled off-the-shoulder neckline, large hat, holding the edge of skirt up over shoe .......................................... **429.00**

**Figure of a woman,** "Victoria," sitting on a couch, wearing very full ruffled dress, bonnet w/bow under chin, 7 x 8½" ................... **285.00**

**Figures,** "Blue Boy" & "Pinkie," figure of man standing on base, blue pants & coat w/white trim, white stockings, holding plumed hat in right hand & woman standing on base, wearing white dress w/rose trim & hat w/loose ribbon, right arm behind back, left arm held in front of body, 12" h., pr. .................................. **729.00**

**Figures of Chinese Boy & Girl,** 7¾" h., pr. ................................ **165.00**

**Figures of John Alden & Priscilla,** he dressed in dark grey knee britches, light grey coat, shoes & large brim hat & holds a gun, she dressed in a light grey skirt & cap, white apron, gloves & bonnet tied under the chin, both w/gold trim, 7¼" h. & 9¼" h., pr. ................... **375.00**

**Flower holder,** figural woman in flower trimmed dress, hat, basket on her arm ....................... **85.00**

**Head vase,** "Violet," girl w/brunette hair, moss green bodice & hat, 7" h. ...................... **150.00**

**Lamp base,** figural Oriental man & woman ................................. **125.00**

**Model of a fox on base,** running position, back legs & tail up, front legs down, face & ears turned to side, porcelain bisque, brown w/white, designed by Betty Davenport Ford, Model No. B-13, 16" l., 9" h. ................ **410.00**

**Model of a swan,** neck up & head bent downward, feathers form planter, stamped w/"Pasadena California" in a semi-circle w/"copyright" at bottom & "Florence Ceramics" in script in center, 12" l., 7" w., 7" h. ............................................ **275.00**

**Powder box,** cov., model of a girl, "Diane," w/full three-tiered ruffled lace skirt & fitted bodice, brown hair, white w/gold trim, Model No. F71, same mold as child figurine, 6" l., 6" h. ..................... **250.00**

**Wall plaque,** cameo, Model No. P7, irregular dark grey edge fading gradually to a light grey at center, man w/black hat, two factory holes at center below the verge, marked w/standard Florence mark, 7¼" h. ............... **125.00**

---

# FLOW BLUE

*Flowing Blue wares, usually shortened to Flow Blue, were made at numerous potteries in Staffordshire, England and elsewhere. They are decorated with a blue that smudged lightly or ran in the firing. The same type of color flow is also found in certain wares decorated in green, purple and sepia. Patterns were given specific names, which accompany the listings here.*

**ACME (Probably Sampson Hancock & Sons, ca. 1900)**
**Chocolate pot,** cov. .................. **$375.00**

**ADAMS (Wood & Sons, ca. 1907)**
**Sugar bowl,** open ....................... **100.00**

**AGRA (F. Winkle & Co., ca. 1891)**
**Bone dishes,** set of 8 ................. **325.00**

**ALASKA (W. H. Grindley, ca. 1891)**
**Plate** ............................................. **120.00**

**ALBANY (W. H. Grindley, ca. 1899)**
**Sugar bowl,** cov. ........................ **175.00**

**ALBANY (Johnson Bros., ca. 1900)**
**Creamer** ..................................... **235.00**
**Vegetable bowl,** cov. ................. **250.00**

**ALTON (W. H. Grindley, ca. 1891)**
**Sauce tureen, cover, undertray & ladle,** 4 pcs. .......................... **495.00**

*Amoy Plate*

### AMOY (Davenport, dated 1844)
Plate, 9" d. (ILLUS.) .................... 135.00
Platter, 20" l. ............................ 1,195.00
Sauce dish, 5" d. .......................... 70.00
Soup plate w/flanged rim.......... 200.00
Wash bowl & pitcher, the set ... 3,195.00

### ANGLESEA (J. & G. Meakin, ca. 1912)
Plate, 9" d. ................................... 55.00

### ANTIQUE BOTTLE (John Meir & Son, probably early-or mid-Victorian)
Bowl, 10" d. ................................. 99.00

### ARCADIA (Arthur Wilkinson, ca. 1907)
Plate, 10" d. ................................. 70.00

### ARGYLE (W.H. Grindley, ca. 1896)
Butter pat ..................................... 30.00
Platter, 15" l. (ILLUS. below) ...... 225.00

### ARGYLE (Myott, Son & Co., ca. 1898)
Teapot, cov. ............................... 525.00

### ASHBURTON (NORWICH) - W.H. Grindley, ca. 1891
Butter pat ..................................... 22.00
Ladle .......................................... 165.00

### ASTRAL (W. H. Grindley, ca. 1891)
Plate, 9" d. ................................... 50.00
Platter, 11½" l. ............................. 85.00

### ATHENS (Wm. Adams & Son, ca. 1849)
Plate ........................................... 115.00

### ATHOL (Burgess & Leigh, ca. 1910)
Egg cup ...................................... 125.00
Plate ............................................ 75.00

### AYR (W. & E. Corn, ca. 1900)
Platter, 10½" l. ............................ 120.00

### AZALEA (John Leigh (possibly), ca. 1885)
Cracker jar, cov., 9" h. ............... 225.00

### ASTORIA (New Wharf Pottery, ca. 1891)
Bowl, 9½" d. .............................. 150.00

*Argyle Platter*

**BAMBOO (Samuel Alcock & Co., ca. 1845)**
Creamer, large............................ 350.00
Soup tureen, cov.................... 1,550.00

**BEATRICE (J. Maddock & Son., ca. 1896)**
Vegetable bowl, cov., 11" d. ...... 105.00

**BELMONT (Alfred Meakin, ca. 1891)**
Ewer-vase, square-footed,
   decorated w/floral sprays, gold
   trim, 8¾" h............................... 120.00
Plate, 8" d. ................................. 65.00

**BLEEDING HEART (Unknown, early, brush-stroke painted)**
Platter, 12 x 15¾", twelve-sided... 180.00

**BLUE DANUBE, THE (Johnson Bros., ca. 1900)**
Vegetable bowl, cov. ................. 195.00

**BRIAR ROSE (Royal Doulton, ca. 1905)**
Posset bowl ............................ 1,100.00
Vase, 7" h., polychrome, Oriental
   scene decoration ..................... 160.00

**BRUNSWICK (Wood & Sons, ca. 1891)**
Cup & saucer .............................. 75.00
Plate, 9" d. .................................. 25.00

**BURLEIGH (Burgess & Leigh, ca. 1903)**
Coffeepot, cov............................ 250.00
Platter, 16" l................................ 250.00

**BURLINGTON (Ridgways)**
Soup tureen w/ladle, 2 pcs........ 475.00

**CAMBRIDGE (Hollinshead & Kirkham, ca. 1910)**
Vegetable bowl, cov., acorn
   finial ........................................ 125.00

**CAMBRIDGE (Alfred Meakin, ca. 1891)**
Plate, 10½" d. ............................. 85.00

**CARLTON (Henry Alcock, ca. 1900)**
Teapot, cov.............................. 1,095.00

**CARLTON (Samuel Alcock, 1850)**
Soup plate w/flanged rim,
   10¼" d...................................... 150.00

**CASHMERE (Ridgway & Morley, 1842-44)**
Hot plate .................................. 1,210.00
Pitcher, 7" h............................. 1,980.00
Sauce tureen, cov. ..................... 750.00
Sauce tureen, cover & underplate,
   3 pcs. ................................... 1,320.00
Teapot, cov., unmarked
   (hairline) ................................ 1,430.00

**CAVENDISH (Keeling & Co., ca. 1910)**
Chamber pot, vertical flutes,
   carnations decoration, 9¼" d.,
   5⅜" h........................................ 135.00
Ewer, bulbous base tapering to
   tall slender neck, 5" d., 9½" h. .. 275.00

**CHAPOO (John Wedge Wood, ca. 1850)**
Plate, 9½" d. (professional repair
   to rim)..................................... 140.00
Teapot, cov............................... 695.00

**CHATSWORTH (Myott, Son & Co., ca. 1900)**
Teapot, cov............................... 650.00

**CHRYSANTHEMUM (Probably F. & R. Pratt & Co., ca. 1855)**
Chocolate pot, cov.................... 350.00

**CHUSAN (Podmore, Walker & Co., ca. 1845)**
Plate, 8¼" d. ............................... 60.00
Wash pitcher, 11" h. (flaws)....... 675.00

**CLARENCE (W.H. Grindley, ca. 1891)**
Plate, 9" d. .................................. 85.00
Plate, 10" d. ................................ 85.00

**CLAREMONT (Johnson Bros., ca. 1891)**
Creamer ..................................... 125.00

**CLARENCE (W. H. Grindley, ca. 1900)**
Cup & saucer ............................. 70.00
Egg cup .................................... 125.00

**CLAYTON (Johnson Bros., ca. 1902)**
Platter, 14½" l. ........................... 145.00

**CLIFTON (Ford & Son, ca. 1900)**
Plate, 10½" d. .............................. 40.00

**CLIFTON (W.H. Grindley, ca. 1891)**
Cake plate, 9¾" d. ...................... 125.00
Plate, 10½" d. .............................. 50.00

**CLUNY (Furnivals, Ltd., ca. 1910)**
Soup tureen, cover &
    underplate, 3 pcs. .................... 695.00

**COBURG (John Edwards, ca. 1860)**
Gravy boat ................................ 275.00

**COLONIAL (J. & G. Meakin, ca. 1891)**
Creamer ...................................... 50.00
Cup & saucer ............................. 65.00
Gravy boat ................................. 85.00
Plate, 8⅞" d. ................................ 80.00
Platter, 11 x 14" ......................... 250.00
Platter ..................................... 185.00
Soup plate w/flanged rim, 9" d. .. 35.00
Sugar bowl, cov. ......................... 50.00
Vegetable bowl, cov. ................. 250.00

**CONWAY (New Wharf Pottery, ca. 1891)**
Plate, 10" d. ................................ 75.00

**COREY HILL (Unknown, ca. 1845)**
Plate, 8½" d., polychrome ............ 65.00

**COUNTESS (W. H. Grindley, ca. 1891)**
Cup & saucer ............................. 65.00

**COWS (Wedgwood & Co., Ltd., ca. 1906)**
Plates, 10" d., pr. ...................... 150.00
Platter, 13½ x 17" ...................... 400.00

**CYPRUS (Davenport, ca. 1850)**
Teapot, cov. .............................. 995.00

**DAISY (Burgess & Leigh, ca. 1897)**
Platter, 16" l. ............................. 198.00

**DAINTY (John Maddock & Son, ca. 1896)**
Platter, 17" l. (back chip) ........... 225.00

**DELFT (Mintons, ca. 1871)**
Dinner service, including eleven
    serving pieces, 54 pcs. .......... 2,200.00
Plate, 9" d. ................................. 43.00

**DEL MONTE (Johnson Bros., ca. 1900)**
Pitcher, milk, 4" h. ....................... 75.00

**DELPH (F. Winkle & Co., ca. 1897)**
Platter, 16" l. ............................. 250.00
Platter, 18" l. ............................. 295.00

**DIAMOND LEAF CROSS (Unknown, early, brush-stroke painted)**
Creamer ................................... 395.00

**DOROTHY (Johnson Bros., ca. 1900)**
Vegetable tureen, cov. .............. 275.00

**DOVER (W.H. Grindley, ca. 1891)**
Cup & saucer ............................. 75.00

**DUCHESS (W.H. Grindley, ca. 1891)**
Bowl, 6½" d. ............................... 25.00
Cup & saucer, demitasse ............ 28.00

**DUNDEE (Ridgways, ca. 1910)**
Bowls, cereal, pr. ........................ 90.00
Plate, 9" d. ................................. 50.00

**ECLIPSE (Johnson Bros., ca. 1891)**
Platter, 10½ x 14" ...................... 185.00

**FAIRY VILLAS II (W. Adams Co., ca. 1891)**
Plate, 8¼" d. ................................. 65.00
Plate, 10½" d. ............................. 75.00

**FASAN (Villeroy & Boch, ca. 1856)**
Bowl, 9" d. ................................... 89.00

**FESTOON (W.H. Grindley, ca. 1891)**
Toothbrush holder ................... 110.00

**FLORAL (Thomas Hughes & Son, ca. 1895)**
Shaving mug............................. 100.00

**FLORENTINE (Thomas Furnival & Sons, ca. 1871)**
Butter pat .................................... 35.00

**FLORIDA (Johnson Bros., ca. 1900)**
Vegetable bowl, cov., footed,
  open-handled (minor flake repair
  on lid) ...................................... 195.00

**GAINSBOROUGH (Ridgways, ca. 1905)**
Vegetable bowl, cov. ................. 350.00

**GEISHA (Ford & Sons, ca. 1893)**
Cake set, 10¼" handled cake
  plate & four matching 6¾"
  scalloped individual plates,
  5 pcs. (small flake under one
  small plate) .............................. 550.00

**GEISHA (Upper Hanley Potteries Ltd., ca. 1901)**
Platter ......................................... 95.00

**GENEVA (Royal Doulton, 1906, 1907)**
Sauce tureen, cover, ladle &
  undertray, 4 pcs....................... 700.00

**GENEVA (New Wharf Pottery, ca. 1891)**
Plate, 10" d. ................................ 85.00

**GIRONDE (W. H. Grindley, ca. 1891)**
Butter pat .................................... 35.00

**GLOIRE DE DIJON (Doulton, ca. 1897)**
Foot bath bowl & pitcher,
  2 pcs. ................................... 1,500.00
Vase, 24" h.............................. 1,950.00

**GOTHIC (Jacob Furnival, ca. 1850)**
Platter, 18" l. ............................. 895.00

**GRANADA (Alcock)**
Gravy boat w/underplate .......... 175.00

**HADDON (W. H. Grindley, ca. 1891)**
Pitcher, 5" h.............................. 395.00
Pitcher, 8" h.............................. 298.00

**HAMILTON (John Maddock & Sons, ca. 1896)**
Butter pat .................................... 45.00
Creamer..................................... 130.00
Plate, 10" d. ................................ 80.00

**HADDON (W.H. Grindley, ca. 1891)**
Plate, 10" d. ................................ 60.00

**HAWKSLEY (Sampson Hancock & Son, ca. 1910)**
Platter, 14" l. .............................. 79.00

**HAWTHORN (Mercer Pottery Co., ca. 1890)**
Platter, 13¼" l. ........................... 110.00
Vegetable bowl, cov. ................. 200.00

**HINDUSTAN (John Maddock, ca. 1855)**
Creamer..................................... 300.00
Platter, 18" l. .............................. 398.00

**HOFBURG (W.H. Grindley, ca. 1891)**
Butter pat .................................... 35.00

**HOLLAND (THE) (Alfred Meakin, ca. 1891)**
Bowl, cereal, 6¼" d....................... 45.00

**HONG KONG (Charles Meigh, ca. 1845)**
Sauce tureen, cov. (hairline) ...... 275.00

**HUDSON (J. & G. Meakin, ca. 1890)**
Bone dishes, set of 6 ................ 225.00

**IDRIS (W.H. Grindley, ca. 1910)**
Pitcher ......................................... 95.00
Vegetable bowl, cov. ................. 200.00

**INDIAN (possibly F & R. Pratt, ca. 1840)**
Pitcher ....................................... 350.00

**INDIAN JAR (Jacob & Thos. Furnival, ca. 1843)**
Creamer, 5½" h. ........................ 750.00
Plate, 8⅞" d. ............................... 75.00

**INDIAN STONE (E. Walley, ca. 1850)**
Plate, 10½" d. ........................... 125.00
Sugar bowl, cov. ........................ 395.00

**INDIANA (Wedgwood & Co., ca. 1870)**
Platter, 16" l. ............................. 475.00

**IRIS (Arthur Wilkinson/Royal Staffordshire Potteries, ca. 1907)**
Butter pat ................................... 13.00
Gravy boat ................................ 165.00
Plate, dinner.............................. 90.00
Platter, 14½" l. .......................... 210.00
Platter, 12 x 16½" ...................... 195.00
Vegetable bowl, cov., 7½" ......... 310.00

**IVANHOE (Wedgwood, ca. 1901)**
Plate............................................. 95.00
Teapot, cov............................... 125.00

**IVY (Unknown, ca. 1880)**
Cheese dish, cov.
   (Utzschneider) ......................... 250.00

**JAPAN (Thos. Fell & Co., ca. 1860)**
Platter, 14¼ x 18" (professional
   restoration)............................. 445.00

**JEDDO (W. Adams & Son, ca. 1845)**
Vegetable bowl, cov. ................. 260.00
Wash bowl & pitcher, 2 pcs. .. 3,495.00

**JENNY LIND (Arthur Wilkinson Ltd., Royal Staffordshire Pottery, ca. 1895)**
Vegetable bowl, 7½" d. .............. 195.00

**JEWEL (Johnson Bros., ca. 1900)**
Vegetable bowl, cov., oval ........ 250.00

**KAOLIN (Podmore & Walker, ca. 1850)**
Teapot, cov. (minor professional
   restoration to spout tip) ............ 795.00

**KELMSCOTT (Unknown, ca. 1900 English)**
Platter, 18" l. ............................. 295.00

**KELVIN (Alfred Meakin, ca. 1891)**
Plate, 9" d. .................................. 45.00

**KENSINGTON (Keeling & Co., Ltd., ca. 1909)**
Cheese dish, cov. ...................... 475.00
Pitcher w/pewter lid, 6¾" h. ...... 375.00
Syrup pitcher, cov. .................... 225.00

**KENWORTH (Johnson Bros., ca. 1900)**
Bowl, 5½" d. ................................ 19.00
Plate, 6¼" d. ............................... 21.00

**KIRKEE (John Meir & Son, ca. 1861)**
Platter, 13¾ x 17½" ................... 695.00

**KYBER (W. Adams & Co., ca. 1891)**
Plates, 9¼" d., pr. (ILLUS. of
   one, top next page) .. 125.00 to 150.00

**LA BELLE (W.H. Grindley, ca. 1893)**
Candy dish, leaf-shaped, 6¼".... 110.00
Celery dish................................ 295.00
Cup & saucer (hairline in
   saucer)..................................... 120.00
Plate, 9½" d. ............................... 85.00
Relish dish ................................ 295.00
Syrup pitcher w/hinged metal
   lid, 4½" h. ................................ 395.00

*Kyber Plate*

## LA FRANCAIS (French China Co., ca. 1890)
Butter pat ..................................... 22.00
Plate, 7" octagonal ....................... 45.00

## LAHORE (Thos. Phillips & Son, ca. 1840)
Plate, 9¾" d. .............................. 110.00
Plate, 10" d. ............................... 125.00

## LAKEWOOD (Wood & Sons, ca. 1900)
Plate, 8" d. .................................. 50.00
Vegetable bowl, cov., oval ........ 250.00

## LANCASTER (W. & E. Corn, ca. 1900)
Cup & saucer ............................ 110.00

## LANCASTER (New Wharf Pottery, ca. 1891)
Creamer.................................... 185.00
Cup & saucer ............................ 115.00

## LEICESTER (Sampson Hancock, ca. 1906)
Plate, 9" d. ................................ 100.00

## LE PAVOT (W.H. Grindley, ca. 1896)
Platter, 11 x 16" ......................... 285.00

## LILY (W. Adams & Sons, ca. 1860)
Plate ............................................. 75.00
Sauce tureen, cover & underplate, 3 pcs. ................... 150.00

## LINDA (John Maddock & Sons, Ltd., ca. 1896)
Butter pat ................................... 55.00
Egg cup ..................................... 125.00
Plate, 8" d. ................................. 40.00

## LOIS (New Wharf Pottery, ca. 1891)
Vegetable bowl, open, 9" d. ....... 100.00

## LONSDALE (Ridgways, ca. 1910)

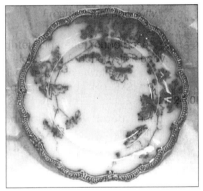

*Lonsdale Plate*

Plate, 8" d. (ILLUS.) ..................... 65.00

## LORNE (W.H. Grindley, ca. 1900)
Butter pat ................................... 60.00
Plate, 10" d. ............................... 95.00
Platter, 14" l. ............................. 275.00
Vegetable bowl, cov. ................ 295.00

## LOTUS (W.H. Grindley, ca. 1910)
Bone dish ................................... 50.00

## LUCERNE (New Wharf Pottery, ca. 1891)
Bowl, soup ................................... 80.00

## LUSITANIA (Alfred Colley & Co., Ltd., ca. 1910)
Cup & saucer .............................. 50.00
Plate, 10" d. ............................... 55.00

**MADRAS (Samuel Alcock & Co., ca. 1845)**
Cup & saucer, oversize............. 175.00

**MADRAS (New Wharf Pottery, ca. 1891)**
Butter pat .................................... 20.00

**MANHATTAN (Henry Alcock, ca. 1900)**
Sauce dish ................................... 30.00

**MANILLA (Podmore, Walker & Co., ca. 1845)**
Plate, 9" d. ................................. 100.00

**MARECHAL NIEL (W.H. Grindley, ca. 1895)**
Bone dish..................................... 55.00
Butter pat .................................... 55.00
Vegetable bowl, cov. ................. 235.00

**MARGUERITE (W.H. Grindley, ca. 1891)**
Platter, 13 x 18" ......................... 200.00
Vegetable bowl, cov. ................. 250.00

**MARIE (W.H. Grindley, ca. 1891)**
Gravy undertray ........................... 70.00
Vegetable bowl, cov. ................. 250.00

**MARLBOROUGH (Wood & Sons, ca. 1900)**
Shaving mug............................... 125.00

**MELBOURNE (W.H. Grindley, ca. 1900)**
Butter pat .................................... 37.00
Gravy boat w/attached
  undertray ................................. 195.00
Platter, 16" l. ............................. 235.00
Sauce tureen, cover &
  undertray, 3 pcs. (chip)............ 395.00

**MELTON (Sampson Hancock, ca. 1910)**
Pitcher, 7" h............................... 135.00

**MESSINA (Cauldon Ltd., ca. 1905)**
Bowl, large................................. 145.00
Cup & saucer .............................. 65.00

*Non Pareil Plate*

**MESSINA (Alfred Meakin, ca. 1891)**
Platter, 13" l. ............................. 145.00

**MILAN (W.H. Grindley, ca. 1893)**
Pitcher, 5½" h............................. 145.00

**MINWOOD (Henry Alcock & Co., ca. 1891)**
Platter, 19½" l. ........................... 150.00

**MOREA (J. Goodwin, ca. 1878)**
Bowl, 9" d. ................................. 295.00

**MONGOLIA (Johnson Bros., ca. 1900)**
Plate, 9" d. ................................... 80.00

**NANKIN (Ashworth, ca. 1865)**
Creamer...................................... 275.00
Platter, 21½" l., well & tree
  (professional restoration) ......... 850.00

**NAVY (Thos. Till & Son, ca. 1891)**
Plate, 8" d. ................................... 80.00

**NEOPOLITAN (Johnson Bros., ca. 1900)**
Butter pat .................................... 35.00

**NING PO (R. Hall & Co., ca. 1845)**
Soup tureen, cov.................... 1,485.00

**NON PAREIL (Burgess & Leigh, ca. 1891)**
Plate, 6" d. ................................... 75.00
Plate, 9⅞" d. (ILLUS. above) ...... 100.00

**NONPAREIL (J. & G. Meakin, ca. 1907)**
Teapot, cov. ............................... 450.00

**NORFOLK (Royal Doulton, ca. 1891)**
Plate, 10" d. ................................ 65.00

**NORMANDY (Johnson Bros., ca. 1900)**
Fish sauce dish ......................... 375.00
Plate, 6¼" d. ................................ 27.00
Plate, 10" d. ................................ 85.00

**OPHIR (E. Bourne & J. E. Leigh, ca. 1891)**
Soup plate w/flanged rim,
  9¼" d. ........................................... 98.00

**ORCHID (John Maddock & Sons, Ltd., ca. 1896)**
Chocolate pot, cov., 10½" h. ..... 235.00

**OREGON (T.J. & J. Mayer, ca. 1845)**
Plate, 9½" d. .............................. 150.00

**ORIENTAL (Samuel Alcock, ca. 1840)**
Platter, 17 x 20½", w/well &
  tree ........................................ 1,100.00

**ORIENTAL (New Wharf Pottery, ca. 189)**
Plate, 9" d. .................................. 80.00

**ORIENTAL (Ridgways, ca. 1891)**
Pitcher, 1½ qt. ........................... 375.00
Soup plate w/flanged rim, 9" d. .. 75.00
Vegetable bowl, cov., footed,
  tab-handled (tiny imperfections).. 195.00

**ORMONDE (Alfred Meakin , ca. 1891)**
Pitcher ....................................... 200.00

**OSBORNE (W.H. Grindley, ca. 1900)**
Plate, 7" d. .................................. 80.00
Platter, 13⅜ x 18¼" ................... 500.00

**OSBORNE (T. Rathbone & Co., ca. 1910)**
Platter, oval, 13½" (some
  staining) ................................... 170.00

**OVANDO (Alfred Meakin, ca. 1891)**
Vegetable bowl, cov., large ....... 265.00

**OXFORD (Johnson Bros.)**
Vegetable bowl, open, 7 x 9½" .... 95.00

**PAISLEY (Mercer, ca. 1890)**
Plate, 9¾" d. ................................ 75.00
Soup plate w/flanged rim, 9" d. .. 65.00

**PARIS (New Wharf Pottery)**
Bowl, 8" d. ................................... 50.00
Platter, 14½" d. .......................... 150.00

**PEACH (Johnson Bros., ca. 1891)**
Soup plate w/flanged rim, 7½" d.. 60.00

**PEKIN (Arthur J. Wilkinson, ca. 1909)**
Soup plate w/flanged rim .......... 115.00

**PEKING (Podmore, Walker & Co., ca. 1850)**
Plate, 10" d. .............................. 125.00
Platter, 18" l. ............................. 550.00
Platter, oval, 19¼" l. (minor
  crazing) .................................... 319.00

**PELEW (E. Challinor, ca. 1840)**
Platter, 13⅜" l. ........................... 303.00

**PENANG (W. Ridgway, ca. 1840)**
Cup plate (hairline) ...................... 30.00

**PERSIAN (Johnson Bros., ca. 1902)**
Butter pat .................................... 35.00
Platter, 12 x 16" ......................... 295.00

**PERSIAN SPRAY (Doulton & Company, ca. 1885)**
Plates, set of 8 .......................... 200.00
Soup plate w/flanged rim ........... 50.00

**POPPY (W.H. Grindley, ca. 1891)**
Butter dish, cov. ......................... 200.00
Creamer & cov. sugar bowl,
  2 pcs. ...................................... 200.00
Gravy boat w/undertray ............ 150.00
Plate, 10" d. ................................ 55.00
Relish tray, 8½" l. ........................ 40.00

**QUEEN (Alfred Meakin)**
Soup plate w/flanged rim, 9" d. .. **60.00**

**RALEIGH (Burgess & Leigh, ca. 1906)**
Relish dish ................................. **48.00**

**REGENT (Alfred Meakin Ltd., ca. 1897)**
Plate, 6½" d. ............................... **48.00**
Soup plate w/flanged rim,
  8¾" d.......................................... **85.00**

**RHINE (Thomas Dimmock, dated May 7, 1844)**
Cup & saucer, handleless .......... **145.00**

**RHODA (William Adams & Son, ca. 1891)**
Butter pat ................................... **45.00**

**RHONE (Thomas Furnival, ca. 1845)**
Pitcher, 2 qt. .............................. **500.00**
Plate, 10½" d. ............................ **100.00**

**RICHMOND (Burgess & Leigh, ca. 1904)**
Bread plate, 11½" h. .................. **250.00**

**ROCK (Challinor, ca. 1850)**
Platter, 12½" l. ........................... **365.00**

**ROMEO (Wedgwood & Co., ca. 1908)**
Butter pat ................................... **35.00**

**ROSE (W.H. Grindley, ca. 1893)**
Plate, 7" d. ................................. **80.00**

**ROSE (Myott Son & Co.)**
Jardiniere, 10" d., 7" h............... **385.00**

**ROSEVILLE (John Maddock & Sons, ca. 1891)**
Butter pat ................................... **45.00**

**ROWENA (Fleming, ca. 1900)**
Soup plate w/flanged rim, 10" d.. **50.00**

**ST. LOUIS (Johnson Bros., ca. 1900)**
Plate, 7" d. ................................. **42.00**

**SAVOY (Johnson Bros., ca. 1900)**
Vegetable bowl, cov., round ...... **235.00**

**SCINDE (J. & G. Alcock, ca. 1840 & Thomas Walker, ca. 1847))**
Butter dish, cover & drainer.. **1,100.00**
Cup plate.................................. **195.00**
Gravy boat ............................... **475.00**
Pitcher, water .......................... **1,100.00**

*Scinde Dinner Plate*

Plate, 10½" d. (ILLUS.) .............. **170.00**
Plates, 9½" d., set of 4............... **380.00**
Platter, 10½ x 13" ...................... **285.00**
Platter, 13½" l. ........................... **575.00**
Platter, 16" l. ............................. **485.00**
Platter, 18" l. ............................. **795.00**
Platter, 20¼" l. ........................ **1,150.00**
Sauce dishes, 5" d., pr.............. **110.00**
Sauce tureen, cover &
  underplate, 3 pcs.................. **1,050.00**
Teapot, cov., large (hairline in
  teapot & chip on lid) ................. **695.00**
Vegetable bowl, cov. ................ **750.00**
Vegetable bowl, open, oblong,
  6 x 8" (ILLUS. top next
  page ......................... **450.00 to 550.00**
Washbowl & pitcher set,
  2 pcs. ..................................... **2,250.00**
Waste bowl ................................ **500.00**

*Scinde Vegetable Bowl*

### SENATOR (J. Dimmock, ca. 1900)
**Butter dish,** cov. (spider inside
lid does not go through) ............ **150.00**

### SEVILLE (New Wharf Pottery, ca. 1891)
**Bowl,** cereal ................................. **45.00**
**Bowl,** soup, gold trim .................... **75.00**
**Creamer & cov. sugar bowl,** pr.
(sugar w/small chip to top) ........ **290.00**

### SEVRES (Wood & Sons, ca. 1900)
**Soup plate w/flanged rim,** 9" d. .. **45.00**

### SHANGHAI (W. & T. Adams, ca. 1870)
**Plate,** 9¾" d. ............................... **83.00**

### SHANGHAI (W.H. Grindley, ca. 1891)
**Plate,** 9½" d. ............................... **59.00**

### SHELL (Wood & Challinor, ca. 1840)
**Cup & saucer,** handleless .......... **145.00**

### SOBRAON (unknown, probably English, ca. 1850)
**Platter,** 20" l. ............................. **700.00**
**Vegetable bowl,** cov. ................. **495.00**

### SPINACH (Libertas, ca. 1900 & Maastricht, Holland)
**Cup & saucer** .............................. **85.00**

### SYRIAN (W.H. Grindley, ca. 1891)
**Toothbrush holder** .................... **220.00**

### TEMPLES (Whittingham, Ford & Co., ca. 1868)
**Vegetable bowl,** open, 9" d. ....... **150.00**

### TOGO (F. Winkle, ca. 1900)
**Butter pat** ................................... **24.00**
**Wash bowl & pitcher,** the set .... **950.00**

### TOKIO (Keeling & Co., ca. 1886)
**Teapot,** cov., gaudy decoration .... **85.00**

### TONQUIN (W. Adams & Son, ca. 1845)
**Pitcher,** water (professional
repair) ..................................... **1,540.00**
**Plate,** 9½" d. .............................. **150.00**
**Plate,** 10" d. ............................... **185.00**
**Platter,** 13" l .............................. **550.00**
**Soup plate w/flanged rim** .......... **125.00**

### TOURAINE (Henry Alcock, ca. 1898 & Stanley Pottery, ca. 1898)

*Touraine Plate*

**Creamer** .................... 250.00 to 275.00
**Cup & saucer** ........................... 110.00
**Pitcher,** 7" h. .............................. 625.00
**Pitcher,** milk............................. 1,095.00
**Plate,** 8¼" d. ............................... 60.00
**Plate,** 9" d. ................................. 80.00
**Plate,** 10" d. (ILLUS.) .................. 125.00
**Platter,** 10¼" l. ........................... 159.00
**Platter,** 16" l. .............................. 375.00
**Sugar bowl,** cov. ........ 300.00 to 350.00
**Vegetable bowl,** cov., oval,
10½" l. ..................................... 395.00

*Touraine Vegetable Bowl*

**Vegetable bowl,** open, oval,
   9¾" (ILLUS.) ............................ **125.00**
**Waste bowl** ................ **200.00 to 230.00**

**TRENT (New Wharf Pottery, ca. 1891)**
**Cup & saucer** ............................... **65.00**

**TRILBY (Wood & Son, ca. 1891)**
**Hot water pitcher** ....................... **175.00**
**Toothbrush holder** .................... **165.00**

**TROY (Charles Meigh, ca. 1840)**
**Plate,** 10¼" d. ............................. **145.00**

**TURIN (Johnson Bros., ca. not given)**
**Casserole,** cov., pedestal base,
   flower finial, ca. 1913 ................ **300.00**

**VALENCIA (Sampson Hancock & Sons, ca. 1910)**
**Cup & saucer** .............................. **25.00**
**Vegetable bowl,** cov. ................. **145.00**

**VENETIAN SCENERY (W. Adams & Co., ca. 1900)**
**Cup & saucer** .............................. **35.00**
**Plate**............................................. **94.00**

**VERONA (Wood & Son, ca. 1891)**
**Plate,** 10" d. ................................. **85.00**
**Waste bowl,** 3 x 5¼" ................. **125.00**

**VERMONT (Burgess & Leigh, ca. 1895)**
**Butter pat** ..................................... **55.00**

**VIRGINIA (John Maddock & Sons, ca. 1891)**
**Vegetable bowl,** open ................ **175.00**

**VIRGINIA (J. & G. Meakin, ca. 1891)**
**Plate,** 10" d. ................................. **75.00**

**WALDORF (New Wharf Pottery, 1892)**

*Waldorf Cup & Saucer*

**Cup & saucer** (ILLUS.)............... **110.00**
**Plate,** 9" d. ................................... **65.00**
**Plate,** 9¾" d. ................................ **80.00**

**WARWICK (Podmore Walker & Co., ca. 1850)**
**Molasses pitcher** w/metal top &
   gold trim .................................... **375.00**

**WARWICK PANSY (Warwick Co., ca. 1900)**
**Chocolate pot,** cov..................... **695.00**
**Creamer**...................................... **135.00**
**Gravy boat & underplate,** 2 pcs.. **95.00**

**WATTEAU (Doulton & Co., ca. 1900)**
**Cup & saucer** ............................... **65.00**

**WATTEAU (New Wharf Pottery)**
**Bowl,** 8¾" d. ................................ **80.00**
**Bowl,** 9" d. ................................. **125.00**
**Dessert server,** open-handled ... **275.00**
**Pitcher** ........................................ **150.00**
**Vegetable bowl,** cov., oval......... **275.00**

**WAVERLY (John Maddock & Son, ca. 1891)**
Soup tureen, cov......................... 675.00

**WENTWORTH (J. & G. Meakin, ca. 1907)**
Plate, 8" d. .................................... 50.00

**WHAMPOA (Samuel Keeling & Co., ca. 1845)**
Relish dish ................................. 295.00

**WHEEL (Unknown)**
Plate, 8" d. .................................... 50.00

Tea set, child's, 15 pcs. ........... **1,155.00**

**WILD TURKEY (Cauldon, ca. 1905)**
Platter, 18½ x 22" ....................... 595.00

**WILLOW (Doulton & Co., ca. 1891)**
Pitcher, water, 8½" h. ................. 280.00

**WIND FLOWER (Burgess & Leigh, ca. 1895)**
Vegetable dish, cov., 11½" l. ..... 140.00

**YEDDO (Arthur Wilkinson, ca. 1907)**
Platter, 9¼ x 12¾" ..................... 195.00

*A Variety of Fine Flow Blue Pieces*

***Top row - left to right:***

**Manilla patt.,** water pitcher, Podmore, Walker & Co., 9" h.... **550.00**
**Ning-Po patt.,** soup tureen & cover, R. Hall, 14½" h. ........... **1,485.00**
**Tonquin patt.,** water pitcher, J. Heath, 11½" h. .......................... **825.00**

***Center row - left to right:***

**Scinde patt.,** saucer tureen & cover, footed, scrolled loop handles, 6" h. ........................... **990.00**
**Coburg patt.,** cup, by Edwards 4" h........................................... **303.00**

**Beauties of China patt.,** sauce tureen & cover, 8" h. (professional cover repair) ........ **385.00**

***Bottom row - left to right:***

**Chapoo patt., cov.** sugar bowl, Wedgwood & Co., 8¼" h........... **770.00**
**Horticultural patt.,** handled chestnut basket & undertray, Wedgwood Ware, 12" l., 2 pcs. ....................................... **715.00**
**Chapoo patt., cov.** sugar bowl, Wedgwood & Co., chip on base ......................................... **770.00**

# FRANCISCAN WARE

*Desert Rose Butter Dish*

A product of Gladding, McBean &
Company of Glendale and Los Angeles,
California, Franciscan Ware was one of a
number of lines produced by that firm
over its long history. Introduced in 1934
as a pottery dinnerware, Franciscan Ware
was produced in many patterns including
"Desert Rose," introduced in 1941 and
reportedly the most popular dinnerware
pattern ever made in this country.
Beginning in 1942 some vitrified china
patterns were produced under the
Franciscan name also.

After a merger in 1963 the company
name was changed to Interpace
Corporation and in 1979 Josiah
Wedgwood & Sons purchased the
Gladding, McBean & Co. plant from
Interpace. American production ceased in
1984.

*Franciscan Mark*

**Ashtray,** individual, apple-
shaped, Apple patt., 4 × 4½" ..... **$22.00**

**Ashtray,** individual, California
Poppy patt., 3¼ × 4¼" ................. **90.00**

**Ashtray,** individual, rose-shaped,
Desert Rose patt., ca. 1941,
3½" d.......................................... **12.00**

**Ashtray,** individual, leaf-shaped,
Ivy patt. ..................................... **22.00**

**Ashtray,** individual, poppy-
shaped, Wildflower patt.,
3½" d........................................... **75.00**

**Baking dish,** shaped like half an
apple, Apple patt., ca. 1940,
4¾" w., 5¼" l. ............................ **225.00**

**Baking dish,** Apple patt., 1 qt.,
8¾" w., 9½" l., 2" h.................... **150.00**

**Baking dish,** Desert Rose patt.,
1 qt., 8¾" w., 9½" l., 2" h........... **175.00**

**Baking dish,** Meadow Rose patt.,
1½ qt., 9 × 14", 2¼" h. ............... **165.00**

**Batter pitcher,** handled, Apple
patt., ca. 1940, 7" l.,
3½" h. ....................... **200.00 to 300.00**

**Bone dish,** Apple patt., 4¾ × 8".... **22.00**

**Bowl,** cov., bouillon, Desert Rose
patt., 4½" d., 2" h. ..... **200.00 to 300.00**

**Bowl,** fruit, 5¼" d., Apple patt. ...... **12.00**

**Bowl,** fruit, 5¼" d., Desert Rose
patt............................................. **10.00**

**Bowl,** cereal or soup, 5¼" d.,
footed, Fruit patt.......................... **65.00**

**Bowl,** cereal or soup, 6" d., Apple
patt............................................. **12.00**

**Bowl,** cereal or soup, 6" d., Fresh
Fruits patt., ca. 1979 ................... **18.00**

**Bowl,** cereal or soup, 6¼" d.
footed, California Poppy patt. ..... **35.00**

**Bowl,** cereal or soup, 6" d.,
Meadow Rose patt., ca. 1977 ..... **18.00**

**Bowl,** coupe soup, Desert Rose
patt............................................. **16.00**

**Bowl,** soup, footed, 5½" d.,
2¼" h., Desert Rose patt............. **27.00**

**Bowl,** soup, footed, 5½" d., 2" h.,
Ivy patt., ca. 1948 ...................... **45.00**

**Bowl,** soup, footed, 5½" d.,
2¼" h., Meadow Rose patt.,
ca. 1977 ..................................... **28.00**

**Bowl,** salad, 10" d., Apple patt...... **80.00**

**Bowl,** salad, 10" d., Desert Rose
patt............................................. **72.00**

**Bowl,** salad, 11¼" d., Ivy patt. .... **165.00**

**Box,** cov., heart-shaped, Cafe
Royal patt., ca. 1981,
approximately 5 × 5", 2¼" h. ....... **55.00**

**Box,** cov., heart-shaped, Desert
Rose patt., 4½" l., 2½" h. .......... **145.00**

**Butter dish,** cov., Coronado
patt., coral ................................. **60.00**

**Butter dish,** cov., Desert Rose
patt., ¼ lb. (ILLUS. top previous
page)......................................... **50.00**

**Butter dish,** cov., Ivy patt., ¼ lb. .. **65.00**

**Butter dish,** cov., Meadow Rose
patt., ca. 1977 ........................... **65.00**

**Candleholders,** apple-shaped,
Apple patt., 3" h., pr. ................ **125.00**

**Candleholders,** Coronado patt.,
turquoise glossy glaze, pr. .......... **60.00**

**Casserole,** cov., individual,
single-handled, Apple patt.,
3¼" h.......................................... **48.00**

**Casserole,** cov., Desert Rose
patt., ca. 1941, 1½ qt., 4¾" h. ..... **95.00**

**Casserole,** cov., Fruit patt., ca.
1949, 1½ qt. ............................. **395.00**

**Casserole,** cov., Starburst patt.,
large........................................... **95.00**

**Cigarette box,** cov., Apple patt. . **145.00**

**Cigarette box,** cov., Coronado
patt., turquoise glossy glaze ..... **150.00**

**Cigarette box,** cov., Desert Rose
patt., 3½ × 4½", 2" h. .................. **115.00**

**Coffeepot,** cov., Metropolitan
Service, ivory, ca. 1940 ............. **75.00**

**Coffee set, demitasse:** cov.
coffeepot & six demitasse cups
& saucers, Coronado patt.,
turquoise glaze, 13 pcs. ............ **200.00**

**Compote,** open, Apple patt.,
8" h., 4" h. ................................ **125.00**

**Compote,** open, footed,
Coronado patt., coral, 7½" h. ...... **70.00**

**Compote,** open, Desert Rose
patt., 8" d., 4" h. .......................... **95.00**

**Compote,** open, Ivy patt., green
trim, 8" d., 3¾" h. ...................... **155.00**

**Creamer,** individual, Apple patt.,
2¾" h........................................... **12.00**

**Creamer,** individual, Desert Rose
patt.............................................. **30.00**

**Creamer,** Ivy patt., 4" h. .............. **18.00**

**Creamer,** footed, Coronado patt.,
turquoise glossy glaze ............... **75.00**

**Creamer & cov. sugar bowl,**
demitasse, El Patio line, apple
green glossy glaze, pr................ **65.00**

**Creamer & cov. sugar bowl,**
demitasse, El Patio line,
Mexican blue glossy glaze, pr..... **65.00**

**Creamer & open sugar bowl,**
individual, Desert Rose patt., pr. **160.00**

**Creamer & cov. sugar bowl,**
Apple patt, pr. ............................ **40.00**

**Creamer & cov. sugar bowl,**
California Poppy patt., pr. ......... **145.00**

**Creamer & cov. sugar bowl,**
Desert Rose patt., pr................... **50.00**

**Creamer & cov. sugar bowl,**
Fruit patt., pr. ........................... **125.00**

**Cup & saucer,** demitasse, Apple
patt.............................................. **45.00**

**Cup & saucer,** demitasse, Desert
Rose patt., ca. 1941.................... **42.00**

**Cup & saucer,** coffee, Desert
Rose patt., cup 3½" d., 3" h.,
saucer 5¾" d. ............................. **65.00**

**Cup & saucer,** Apple patt.
(ILLUS. front, top next page) ...... **12.00**

**Cup & saucer,** Apple patt., extra
large............................................ **65.00**

**Cup & saucer,** California Poppy
patt.............................................. **35.00**

**Cup & saucer,** Fruit patt., ca.
1940............................................ **40.00**

**Cup & saucer,** Indigo patt., ca.
1970............................................ **15.00**

**Cup & saucer,** Mesa patt. ............. **5.00**

**Cup & saucer,** October patt. ........ **14.00**

**Cup & saucer,** Wildflower patt.,
ca. 1942 ................................... **100.00**

**Dinner set for four,** Starburst
patt., ca. 1954, the set ............. **125.00**

**Dinner service:** nine 10" d.
dinner plates, eleven 8" d. salad
plates, seven 6¼" d. bread &
butter plates, fourteen cups &
twelve saucers; Poppy patt.,
53 pcs. ................................... **1,250.00**

*Apple Pattern Plate & Cup & Saucer*

**Goblet,** Meadow Rose patt.,
6½" h., 1977.............................. **125.00**

**Gravy boat,** California Poppy
patt., ca. 1950 ............................. **85.00**

**Gravy boat w/attached
undertray,** Apple patt.,
ca. 1940 .................................... **45.00**

**Gravy boat w/attached
undertray,** Daisy patt. ................ **45.00**

**Gravy boat w/attached
undertray,** Meadow Rose
patt. ............................................. **90.00**

**Gravy boat w/ladle,** Starburst
patt., 2 pcs. ................................ **75.00**

**Gravy boat, cover & undertray,**
Madeira patt., 3 pcs. .................. **45.00**

**Gurnsey jug,** cov., El Patio patt.,
turquoise glaze, 5½" h. ............... **60.00**

**Jam jar,** cov., apple-shaped,
redesigned, Apple patt., 4¼" h.. **245.00**

**Jam jar,** cov., apple-shaped,
Apple patt., 5" h. ....................... **125.00**

**Ladle,** undecorated, Apple patt.,
10" l.......................................... **600.00**

**Ladle,** undecorated, Desert Rose
patt., 10½" h.............................. **600.00**

**Mixing bowl set,** Apple patt.,
3 pcs. ....................................... **365.00**

**Mixing bowl set,** Desert Rose
patt., 3 pcs. .............................. **365.00**

**Mug,** Apple patt., 7 oz. .................. **25.00**

**Mug,** Desert Rose patt., 7 oz. ....... **25.00**

**Mug,** Fresh Fruit patt., ca. 1979,
7 oz., 3" d., 2¾" h.,.................... **25.00**

**Mug,** Madeira patt., 12 oz. ............ **12.00**

**Mugs,** Starburst patt., ca. 1954,
set of 4 ..................................... **125.00**

**Napkin rings,** Apple patt., set
of 4 in original box..................... **185.00**

**Onion soup bowl,** cov., w/tab
handles, Coronado patt.,
maroon glossy glaze ................... **45.00**

**Pepper mill,** Starburst patt. ........ **185.00**

**Piggy bank,** Desert Rose patt. ... **350.00**

**Pitcher,** jug-type, 4" h., Apple
patt., w/label............................. **225.00**

**Pitcher,** milk, 6¼" h., Apple patt.,
1 qt. ............................................ **95.00**

**Pitcher,** milk, 6½" h., Desert
Rose patt., 1 qt. .......................... **69.00**

**Pitcher,** Madeira patt., 1 qt. .......... **22.00**

**Pitcher w/ice lip,** water, 8¾" h.,
Apple patt., 2 qt......................... **125.00**

**Pitcher,** water, Coronado patt.,
coral glossy glaze ....................... **70.00**

**Pitcher,** water, 10" h., Daisy patt. .. **125.00**

**Pitcher,** water, El Patio line, restyled, redwood glossy glaze, ca. 1934, 2½ qt. ........................ **125.00**

**Pitcher,** water, 8" h., Ivy patt., 2½ qt. ......................................... **185.00**

**Pitcher,** Starburst patt., large ..... **125.00**

**Plate,** heart-shaped, Desert Rose patt., 5½ × 5¾" .......................... **170.00**

**Plate,** side salad, 4½" w., 8" l., crescent-shaped, Desert Rose patt. ............................................ **40.00**

**Plate,** side salad, 4½ × 8", crescent-shaped, Meadow Rose patt., ca. 1977 ............................ **45.00**

**Plate,** side salad, 4½ × 8", crescent-shaped, Starburst patt.. **35.00**

**Plate,** bread & butter, 6¼" d., California Poppy patt. ................. **15.00**

**Plate,** bread & butter, 6½" d., Apple patt. (ILLUS. back, w/cup & saucer) ...................................... **9.00**

**Plate,** bread & butter, 6½" d., Desert Rose patt. .......................... **6.00**

**Plate,** bread & butter, 6½" d., Fruit patt., ca. 1949 ..................... **15.00**

**Plate,** bread & butter, 6½" d., Meadow Rose patt., ca. 1977 ..... **12.00**

**Plate,** bread & butter, Mesa patt. ..... **3.00**

**Plate,** bread & butter, 6½" d., October patt. ................................. **6.00**

**Plate,** bread & butter, 6½" d., Wildflower patt. ........................... **40.00**

**Plate,** child's, divided, 7¼ × 9", Apple patt., ca. 1940 ................. **175.00**

**Plate,** child's, divided, 7¼ × 9", Desert Rose patt. ..... **100.00 to 125.00**

**Plate,** child's, divided, Starburst patt. ............................................ **55.00**

**Plate,** T.V. w/cup well, 8¼" w., 14" l., Apple patt., ca. 1940 ....... **195.00**

**Plate,** T.V. w/cup well, 8¼" w., 14" l., Ivy patt., ca. 1948 ........... **195.00**

**Plate,** salad, 8½" d., Desert Rose patt. ............................................ **16.00**

**Plate,** salad, 8½" d., Fruit patt. ....... **50.00**

**Plate,** salad, 8½" d., Meadow Rose patt. ................................... **20.00**

**Plate,** salad, Mesa patt. ................. **5.00**

**Plate,** salad, 8½" d., Wildflower patt. ............................................ **75.00**

**Plate,** luncheon, 9½" d., Fruit patt., ca. 1949 ........................... **40.00**

**Plate,** dinner, 10" d., California Poppy patt. ................................. **35.00**

**Plate,** dinner, 10¼" d., Ivy patt. ...... **25.00**

**Plate,** dinner, 10½" d., Fruit patt., ca. 1949 ...................................... **45.00**

**Plate,** dinner, 10½" d., Wildflower patt. ............................................ **110.00**

**Plate,** coupe, party w/cup well, 10½" d., Apple patt. ................... **65.00**

**Plate,** coupe, steak, 8½ × 11", Apple patt. ................................. **175.00**

**Plate,** grill, 11" d., Desert Rose patt. ............................................ **95.00**

**Plate,** chop, 12" d., California Poppy patt. ............................... **150.00**

**Plate,** chop, 12" d., Desert Rose patt., ca. 1941 ............................ **45.00**

**Plate,** chop, 12" d., Ivy patt., ca. 1948 .................... **100.00 to 150.00**

**Plate,** chop, 14" d., Desert Rose patt. ............................................ **125.00**

**Plate,** chop, 14" d., Ivy patt. ........ **125.00**

**Plate,** chop, 14" d., Wildflower patt. ............................................ **275.00**

**Platter,** 12" l., Mesa patt. ............. **20.00**

**Platter,** 12" l., Twilight Rose patt. . **28.00**

**Platter,** 12¾" l., Desert Rose patt. ............................................. **30.00**

**Platter,** 12¾" l., Apple patt. ........... **30.00**

**Platter,** 13" l., California Poppy patt. ............................................ **120.00**

**Platter,** 13" l., Ivy patt., ca. 1948... **65.00**

**Platter,** 13" l., Madeira patt. .......... **20.00**

**Platter,** 14" l., Desert Rose patt. .... **49.00**

**Platter,** 14" l., October patt. .......... **45.00**

**Platter,** 19" l., Desert Rose patt.. **265.00**

**Relish dish,** Apple patt., 10" l....... **35.00**

**Relish dish,** divided, Desert Rose patt., ca. 1948, 12" l. ................... **48.00**

**Relish dish,** divided, Ivy patt., 12" l., 7½" w. .............................. **95.00**

**Salt & pepper shakers,** Apple
patt. 2¼" h., pr. ........................... **28.00**

**Salt & pepper shakers,**
California Poppy patt., 2¾" h.,
pr. ............................................... **85.00**

**Salt & pepper shakers,** Starburst
patt., tall, pr. ............................... **60.00**

**Salt & pepper shakers,** Twilight
Rose patt., ca. 1983, 6¼" h., pr. . **95.00**

**Salt shaker & pepper mill,** Apple
patt., wooden top & base,
5½" h., pr. ................................. **340.00**

**Salt shaker & pepper mill,** Apple
patt., bulbous base, 6" h., pr. ..... **205.00**

**Salt shaker & pepper mill,** Apple
patt., cylindrical base, 6" h., pr... **295.00**

**Salt shaker & pepper mill,**
Desert Rose patt., bulbous
base, 6" h., pr. ........................... **195.00**

**Salt shaker & pepper mill,**
Desert Rose patt., cylindrical
base, 6" h. pr. ........................... **300.00**

**Sherbet,** footed, Apple patt.,
4" d., 2½" h. ............................... **20.00**

**Snack plate,** Meadow Rose patt.,
ca. 1977, 8" sq. ......................... **165.00**

**Soup plate w/flanged rim,**
Desert Rose patt., ca. 1941,
8½" d., ......................................... **20.00**

**Soup tureen,** cov., footed,
handled, Apple patt.,
9¼" h. ........................................ **550.00**

**Soup tureen,** cov., flat bottom,
Desert Rose patt., 8" h. ............. **650.00**

**Soup tureen,** cov., footed,
Desert Rose patt., 9½" h. .......... **475.00**

**Soup tureen,** cov., Ivy patt.,
8¾" d., 5" h. ............................... **995.00**

**Sugar bowl,** cov., California
Poppy patt. ................................. **75.00**

**Sugar bowl,** cov., Desert Rose
patt. ............................................ **25.00**

**Sugar bowl,** cov., Meadow Rose
patt., ca. 1977 ........................... **35.00**

**Sugar bowl,** cov., Wildflower
patt. .......................................... **245.00**

**Syrup pitcher,** Apple patt., ca.
1940, 6¼" h., 1 pt. ...................... **95.00**

**Syrup pitcher,** Desert Rose patt.,
6¼" h., 1 pt. ................................ **50.00**

**Teapot,** cov., individual, El Patio line,
coral glossy glaze, 1-cup size ..... **45.00**

**Teapot,** cov., California Poppy
patt., 5¼" h. .............. **100.00 to 150.00**

**Teapot,** cov., Coronado patt.,
coral glossy glaze ...................... **60.00**

**Teapot,** cov., Coronado patt.,
maroon glossy glaze .................. **70.00**

**Teapot,** cov., Desert Rose patt.,
6½" h. ...................... **100.00 to 125.00**

**Teapot,** cov., El Patio line, coral
glossy glaze ............................... **65.00**

**Teapot,** cov., El Patio line,
redwood glossy glaze ................. **65.00**

**Teapot,** cov., El Patio line,
turquoise glossy glaze ............... **65.00**

**Teapot,** cov., Ivy patt., 6½" h. ..... **225.00**

**Teapot,** cov., Meadow Rose
patt. .......................................... **125.00**

**Teapot,** cov., Starburst patt., ca.
1954 .......................................... **250.00**

**Teapot,** cov., Wildflower patt ...... **825.00**

**Tidbit tray,** two-tier, Desert Rose
patt. ............................................ **90.00**

**Thimble,** Apple patt., 1 × 1" ........ **145.00**

**Toast cover,** Desert Rose patt.,
5½" d., 3" h. ............................... **168.00**

**Trivet,** fluted, Apple patt., 6" d. ... **265.00**

**Trivet,** El Patio patt., turquoise
glossy glaze ............................... **40.00**

**Tumbler,** juice, Apple patt., 6 oz.,
3¼" h. ........................................ **45.00**

**Tumbler,** El Patio line, coral or
turquoise glossy glaze, each ...... **25.00**

**Tumbler,** El Patio line, white satin
glaze .......................................... **25.00**

**Tumbler,** Fruit patt., 10 oz.,
5¼" h. ........................................ **100.00**

**Tumbler,** Ivy patt., 10 oz., 5" h. .... **45.00**

**Tumbler,** Meadow Rose patt.,
10 oz., 5" h. ............................... **45.00**

**Vegetable bowl,** open, round,
California Poppy patt., 8" d. ...... **150.00**

**Vegetable bowl,** open, round,
Meadow Rose patt., ca. 1977,
8" d.............................................. **38.00**

**Vegetable bowl,** open, round,
October patt., 8¾" d., 2½" h........ **25.00**

**Vegetable bowl,** open, round,
California Poppy patt., 9" d. ...... **150.00**

**Vegetable bowl,** open, round,
Meadow Rose patt., ca. 1977,
9" d.............................................. **45.00**

**Vegetable bowl,** open, round,
Mesa patt., 9" d........................... **20.00**

**Vegetable bowl,** open, round,
October patt., 8¾" d., 2½" h........ **25.00**

**Vegetable bowl,** open, round,
Madeira patt., ca. 1967, 9¼" d.... **20.00**

**Vegetable bowl,** open, oval, Fruit
patt., 10½" l............................... **145.00**

**Vegetable bowl,** open, oval,
divided, Apple patt., 7 × 10¾" ..... **60.00**

**Vegetable bowl,** open, oval,
divided, Daisy patt., 9" l. ............. **35.00**

**Vegetable bowl,** open, oval,
divided, Ivy patt., 8 × 12¼" .......... **65.00**

**Vegetable bowl,** open, round,
divided, Starburst patt., ca. 1954.. **20.00**

# FRANKOMA POTTERY

*While Mr. John Frank's Frankoma Potteries had its start in 1933 in Norman, Oklahoma, it was not until he moved the company to Sapulpa, Oklahoma in 1938, that he felt he was home. With that wisdom came a*

*dedication and drive to weather even some of the worst storms imaginable for any business. Shortly after the 1938 move, on November 11, 1938 a fire destroyed the entire operation; everything was lost including the pot and leopard mark that John Frank had used since 1935. Also, in 1942, Frankoma was out of business due to the war effort which created a lack of materials and men. However, in 1943, John & Grace Lee Frank bought the plant as junk salvage and started over. The time spent in Norman produced some of John's finest artware and most of the items were marked either "Frank Potteries" or "Frank Pottery" and these are marks sought avidly by collectors today.*

*By far, one of the most popular, yet elusive, marks shows "First Kiln Sapulpa 6-7-38" denoting this was the mark used by Mr. Frank for one day only and signifies the first firing in Sapulpa. Based on that information, it has been estimated that perhaps 50 to 75 pieces were fired on June 7, 1938. A creamy beige clay known as "Ada" clay was in use until 1953. After that date a red brick shale was found in Sapulpa and used until just a decade or so ago when, by the addition of an additive, the clay became a reddish-pink. Rutile glazes were used early in Frankoma's history. It is this very glaze that causes collectors to believe they have a "two-tone" or two unrelated colors on an item. However, it is the rutile that caused the clay to show through. For example, White Sand is white but it also has brown on it; however, the brown is*

*Frankoma Ocelot Book Ends*

*simply the rutile allowing that color to come through into the recesses, designs, folds, etc. This makes for a striking, eye-pleasing appeal and one that was never duplicated by any other companies.*

*In 1970 the U.S. government closed the rutile mines in America and Frankoma had to buy it from Australia. It was not the same and the results were different. Each glaze where rutile was used has its following, some preferring the pre-1970 version and some the post-1970 version. Values are higher for the pre-1970 rutile.*

*John Frank died in 1973 and his daughter, Joniece Frank, who had been a ceramic designer at the pottery, became president of the company. In 1983, Frankoma was once again destroyed by fire. They rebuilt but in 1990, after the IRS had shut the doors for non-payment, Joniece, true to the Frank legacy, filed for Chapter 11 (instead of bankruptcy) so she could reopen and continue with the work she loved best. In 1991, Richard Bernstein purchased the pottery and the name was changed to Frankoma Industries.*

*Frankoma Mark*

**Baker,** Westwind patt., Model No. 6vs, Peach Glow glaze, 1½ qt. . **$24.00**

**Book ends,** Bucking Bronco, Model No. 423, Prairie Green glaze, 5½" h., pr. ...................... **295.00**

**Book ends,** Walking Ocelot on a two-tiered oblong base, black high glaze, Model No. 424, signed on reverse of tiered base "Taylor" denoting designer Joseph Taylor, pot & leopard mark on bottom, 7" l., 3" h., pr. (ILLUS. bottom previous page) .. **925.00**

*1960 Frankoma Christmas Card*

**Bottle-vase,** V-1, 1969, limited edition, 4,000 created, small black foot w/Prairie Green body, 15" h.......................................... **125.00**

**Bowl,** 11" l., divided, Lazybones patt., Brown Satin glaze, Model No. 4qd ...................................... **18.00**

**Broach,** four-leaf clover-shape, Desert Gold glaze, 1¼" h. ........... **30.00**

with original card....................... **40.00**

**Catalog,** 1953, unnumbered sixteen pages, dated July 1, 1953, two versions for color cover, one w/photograph of Donna Frank or one w/photograph of Grace Lee Frank........................................... **45.00**

**Christmas card,** figural fish tray, Woodland Moss glaze, marked, "1960 The Franks, Frankoma Christmas Frankoma," 4" l. (ILLUS. above)........................... **60.00**

**Christmas card,** "Statue of Liberty Torch," White Sand glaze, created by Grace Lee Frank Smith for her & Dr. A. Milton Smith's friends, 1986, 3½" l. .......................................... **75.00**

**Cigarette box,** cov., oblong, cover w/single raised & hard-to-find curved leaf handle, Bronze Green glaze, Ada clay, marked "Frankoma," 6¾" l., 4" w., 3½" h. (ILLUS. top next page)............... **95.00**

**Figure of a Fan Dancer,** seated, No. 113, Ivory glaze, Ada clay, 14" l, 9" h................................. **600.00**

**Figure of a farmer boy,** wearing dark blue overalls, light blue short sleeved shirt, black scarf

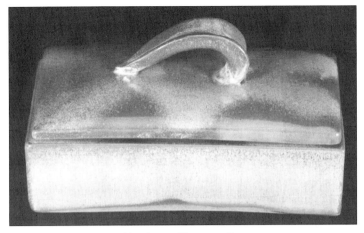

*Frankoma Cigarette Box*

tied around neck, yellow hair &
ivory wide-brim hat w/only brim
showing from front, black shoes,
bisque arms, hands, face &
neck, marked "Frankoma 702,"
6¾" h........................................ **115.00**

**Figure of a gardener girl,** holding
pale green apron to form a basket
in front of her, light blue dress
w/short puffed sleeves & scooped
neckline, long yellow hair w/dark
blue bow on top, bisque face,
neck, arms & hands, marked
"Frankoma 701," 5¾" h............... **115.00**

**Figure,** Indian Chief, No. 142,
Desert Gold glaze, Ada clay,
7" h. (ILLUS. bottom next
column) .................................... **125.00**

**Mug,** 1968, (Republican)
elephant, white........................... **75.00**

**Mug,** 1970 (Republican) elephant. **20.00**

**Mug,** 1971 (Republican) elephant. **20.00**

**Mug,** 1973 (Republican) elephant. **20.00**

**Mug,** 1974 (Republican) elephant. **20.00**

**Pitcher,** Wagon Wheel patt.,
Model No. 94d, Prairie Green
glaze, Ada clay, 2 qt. ................. **30.00**

**Plate,** 8½" d , Bicentennial Series,
Limited Edition No. 1,
"Provocations," eleven signers
of the Declaration of
Independence, White Sand
glaze, 1972 ............................... **75.00**

*Frankoma Indian Chief Figure*

Same plate w/wrong spelling in
United States of America; it
shows "Staits" .......................... **125.00**

**Plate,** 8½" d., Christmas, 1968,
"Flight into Egypt"...................... **35.00**

**Plate,** 7½" d., Easter, 1972,
"JESUS IS NOT HERE...HE IS
RISEN," scene of Jesus' tomb.... **25.00**

**Plate,** 10" d., Mayan Aztec patt.,
Woodland Moss glaze, Model
No. 7fl ......................................... **6.00**

**Plate,** 7" d., Wildlife Series, Limited Edition No. 1, Bobwhite quail, Prairie Green glaze, 1,000 produced .................................... **115.00**

**Political chip,** John Frank's profile on front surrounded by the words, "Honest. Fair.Capable." & at bottom, "Elect John Frank Representative 1962," obverse w/outline of Oklahoma state in center w/"One Frank" inside it, around edge, "Oklahomans deserve outstanding leadership" & "For statesmanship vote Republican," unglazed red brick color, ⅛" h., 1¾" d...................... **25.00**

**Postcard,** color photograph of Joniece Frank sitting w/various Frankoma products used to show the current Frankoma glazes, 5½ × 6½".......................... **10.00**

**Salt & pepper shakers,** model of an elephant, Desert Gold glaze, No. 160h, produced in 1942 only, Ada clay, 3" h., pr. ............. **80.00**

**Teapot,** cov., Wagon Wheel patt., Model No. 94j, Desert Gold glaze, Ada clay, 2 cup................. **35.00**

**Trivet,** Eagle sitting on branch, large wings fill up most of the trivet, Peach Glow glaze, Model No. 2tr, 6" sq. .............................. **60.00**

**Trivet,** Eagle, undated, Woodland Moss glaze, Model No. AETR, 6" d............................................... **12.00**

**Trivet,** Lazybones patt., Model No. 4tr, produced in 1957 only, hard-to-find, 6" d. ........................ **65.00**

**Trivet,** Spanish Iron patt., created by Joniece Frank, Woodland Moss glaze, produced 1966-1989, 6" sq.................................. **18.00**

**Tumbler,** juice, Plainsman patt., Model No. 5lc, Autumn Yellow glaze, 6 oz. .................................. **5.00**

**Vase,** 3½" h., round foot rising to bulbous body w/short neck & rolled lip, unusual high gloss deep blue, marked "Frank Potteries" .................................. **375.00**

**Vase,** 4" h., small foot rising to a flat, narrow body w/tab handle on each side, Ivory glaze, marked "Frankoma" .................... **70.00**

**Vase,** 4" h., small foot rising to a flat, narrow body w/tab handle on each side, Ivory glaze, pot & leopard mark............................. **125.00**

**Vase,** 6" h., square-shaped w/relief-molded flying goose, relief-molded reed decoration on reverse, No 60B ......................... **18.00**

**Vase,** 7" h., Art Deco-style w/round foot w/panel on each side at base, rising to a plain, flat body w/stepped small, elongated handles, Jade Green glaze, Model No. 41, pot & leopard mark............................. **195.00**

**Wall masks,** bust of Oriental man, No. 134 & Oriental woman, No. 133, Jade Green glaze, pot & leopard mark, Ada clay, man 5½" h., woman 4¾" h. pr........... **290.00**

# FREEMAN-MCFARLIN

*While McFarlin Potteries had been in business in El Monte, California since 1927, the brainchild of Gerald McFarlin, it was not until the early 1950s that the operation flourished. Many collectors and researchers believe this is because Maynard Anthony Freeman joined forces with McFarlin, becoming the chief designer and partner. Freeman created earthenware sculpture items including animals, birds, human figures, nodders and a variety of other everyday household pieces. When the company favored a particular item in their line, it was copyrighted and that symbol was included in the mark. Major department stores across the country carried Freeman's line (simply incised "Anthony").*

*After Kay Finch closed her business in 1963, Freeman-McFarlin purchased her molds. Later, Finch created a series of pieces which were mostly dogs. Her*

*Freeman-McFarlin items were marked with that company's name and generally a three digit number in the 800s; however, not all 800 numbers were of Finch's creations.*

*Freeman-McFarlin used several glaze treatments throughout its history. There were porcelain white glaze finishes including a high gloss bright white; Florentine white glaze finish, a dull white with a light brown flowing into the crevices, recessed lines and folds of a piece; and beige or yellow glaze finishes sometimes used in combination with white gloss. The fine arts finish was usually a mixing of glazes such as woodtone (dark brown) with white which was mostly reserved for human figurines and birds and animals; and the stoneware finish sandstone (light brown) and stoneware finish moonstone (dark brown) were reserved primarily for planters and figurines.*

*Another plant was opened in 1968 in San Marcos (San Diego County) and the El Monte plant closed in 1975. In the early 1970s, Multifoods purchased the company but by 1980, Hagen-Renaker had bought everything connected with Freeman-McFarlin—molds, glazes, land, buildings, and so on.*

**Ashtray,** rectangular w/four cigarette rests, silver leaf finish w/bright glossy blue in raised center, Model No. 283, 6½" w., 2" h............................................ **$15.00**

**Figure of a mermaid,** holding shell-shaped soap dish, open back, pink tinge on unglazed face & body, blonde hair in a ponytail, some high gloss gold on mermaid's fish tail, marked "Freeman-McFarlin Potteries 1958 USA" & a copyright symbol, 8" h. ............................ **100.00**

**Ginger jar,** cov., narrow base rising to bulbous body w/tapering short neck, bell-shaped lid w/round knob, porcelain white glaze finish, Model No. 747, 6" d., 12" h. ........ **95.00**

*Freeman-McFarlin Kitty*

**Lighter,** cigarette, round base w/elongated & ribbed stick body, silver leaf finish w/blue highlights, Model No. 272, 12½" h........................................ **24.00**

**Model of a "Baby Hippo,"** head up, eyes open, porcelain white glaze finish, unmarked, Model No. 903, 4" l., 3½" h. ................... **15.00**

**Model of a kitty,** seated w/front legs together & between back legs, tail up, head up looking skyward & legs pointed & up, gold leaf finish, marked "133 USA," 3¼" l., 3¾" h. (ILLUS. above)........................................ **10.00**

**Model of a "Ma Hippo,"** standing, head slightly down, porcelain white glaze finish, impressed mark, "Anthony 902," 11½" l., 5½" h............................. **45.00**

**Model of "Mr. Fox,"** a modernistic fox seated on back legs w/front legs joined & between back paws, ears up, eyes open, silver leaf finish, impressed mark "Anthony 144," 6¾" w., 9¾" h............................. **35.00**

**Model of "Mrs. Fox,"** a modernistic fox seated, front legs between back legs w/right front paw slightly behind left paw, tail wrapped around to front, head down, eyes closed, gold leaf finish, impressed mark, "Anthony 145," 6" w., 9" h. .......... **38.00**

**Model of "Mr. Rabbit,"** seated on back legs, front legs together, ears almost straight up, beige glaze finish, Model No. 114, 6½" l., 10½" h............................ **50.00**

**Model of "Mrs. Rabbit,"** lying down, legs under body, ears back over body, beige glaze finish, Model No. 115, 8" l., 6½" h......................................... **50.00**

**Model of praying hands,** w/fingers & thumbs touching, robe cuffs on both wrists serve as base w/left hand slightly higher than right hand, Florentine white glaze finish, Model No. 148, 6½" l., 6¾" h. ..................................... **17.00**

**Planter,** figural, baby elephant, standing on short legs, large ears cover most of elephant's height, open back, head down w/trunk up, Model No. 401, stoneware finish, sandstone color, 9" l., 7" h............................ **19.00**

**Planter,** figural dog "Bow Wow," standing on short legs, tail down & out, big eyes, ears down, top of dog's back open for plants, introduced 1977, stoneware finish, moonstone color, Model No. 490, 5" h., 12" l. .................... **28.00**

**Tray,** model of a leaf, porcelain white glaze finish, in-mold mark, "Anthony 766 USA," 10½" l., 1" h. (ILLUS. top next column).... **11.00**

**Vase,** 7½" h., 9" d., squatty bulbous body w/lobed sides, silver leaf finish w/glossy turquoise glaze inside, Model No. 752 ..................................... **35.00**

**Vase,** 20" h., 6" d., round ringed pedestal base rising to an elongated fluted body w/a tapering neck & flaring at the scalloped rim, porcelain white glaze finish, Model No. 719 ........ **32.00**

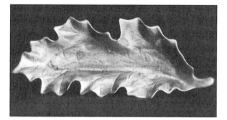

*Leaf-shaped Tray*

**Wall pocket,** model of a fish, pink body w/green fins & tail, black eye & eyelashes, label, "McFarlin Potteries El Monte, Calif." & copyright symbol, 7½" h.......................................... **45.00**

**Wall shelf,** kidney-shaped w/leaf & scrollwork attached below, woodtone finish, Model No. 968, 11" l., 7½" h................................ **25.00**

---

# FULPER POTTERY

*The Fulper Pottery was founded in Flemington, New Jersey, in 1805 and operated until 1935, although operations were curtailed in 1929 when its main plant was destroyed by fire. The name was changed in 1929 to Stangl Pottery, which continued in operation until July of 1978, when Pfaltzgraff, a division of Susquehanna Broadcasting Company of York, Pennsylvania, purchased the assets of the Stangl Pottery, including the name.*

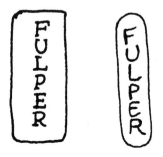

*Fulper Marks*

**Bowl,** 10" d., 6" h., deep sides w/a rounded wide base below a flattened medial paneled band molded in relief w/stylized peacock feathers, the wide, slightly rounded shoulder tapering to a wide, flat molded mouth, bluish green & yellow flambé glaze, vertical ink mark. **$770.00**

**Bowl,** 12⅝" d., 2¾" h., low rounded sides, glossy glaze w/blue of the sky flambé interior & the exterior in beige streaked over green, a raised band rim, vertical stamped box mark, No. 17L .................................... **230.00**

**Bowl w/flower frog,** 11" l., 3¼" h., deep lobed shell-shaped form w/one section of the rear pulled in & attached to the front rim & pierced w/holes to form the flower frog, covered in a Flemington green & elephant's breath flambé glaze, vertical rectangular ink mark ................ **330.00**

**Bowl-vase,** a footring below a wide round compressed body w/the wide shoulder tapering slightly up to the wide short cylindrical neck, a green & cream flambé glaze over a mustard yellow matte ground, early ink mark, 9¾" d., 4" h. ...... **935.00**

**Bowl-vase,** a wide low cushion-form body centered by a wide, short cylindrical neck, a streaked blue, green & cream flambé glaze over a mustard yellow matte glaze, vertical rectangular inkstamp mark, 10⅛" d., 3⅞" h.. **440.00**

**Candleholder,** two-handled, brown glaze, base 5" d., 3½" h. .. **90.00**

**Candleholder,** shield back-style, a tall coved & rounded shield back above a dished circular base centered by a short cylindrical candle socket, green crystalline glaze, vertical ink racetrack mark, 5" d., 7½" h...... **110.00**

**Candlesticks,** a domed, stepped foot below the tall slender & slightly tapering standard below the lily-form candle socket

w/widely flared rim, caramel brown to a flowing green crystalline flambé glaze, oval ink mark, 5" d., 15" h., pr. ........... **1,760.00**

**Center bowl,** a wide disc foot centered by a short pedestal supporting a wide flattened bowl w/low incurved sides, fine mahogany flambé glaze ending over a mustard yellow matte glaze, early vertical ink stamp mark, 8" d., 3¼" h. ................... **138.00**

**Center bowl,** Effigy-type, a wide shallow bowl w/incurved sides raised on three molded seated figures on a stepped disc base, caramel flambé glaze on bowl interior, mustard yellow matte over matte mouse grey glazes on the exterior, vertical inkstamp mark, 10¼" d., 7⅜" h. ............ **1,210.00**

**Center bowl,** Effigy-type, a wide shallow bowl w/incurved sides raised on three molded seated figures on a stepped disc base, stippled sky blue, midnight blue & slate grey glazes, marked, ca. 1910-12, 10¼" d., 7¾" h. .......... **403.00**

**Compote,** 6⅛" h., a wide deep rounded & widely lobed body w/a wide flattened & slightly paneled rim, raised on a short pedestal & domed, lobed round foot, crystalline snowflake flambé glaze, vertical oval inkstamp mark ......................... **220.00**

**Doorstop,** figural, model of a sitting bulldog covered in Chinese blue flambé glaze dripping lightly on a mustard matte ground, unmarked, 7½ × 11" (small nick on face & ⅛" clay separation on ear) ........ **880.00**

**Lamp,** table model, a 17½" d. low widely flaring mushroom-shaped pottery shade w/small oblong red leaded glass inserts, raised above the very wide bulbous, nearly spherical base w/small squared shoulder handles, each covered w/a soft, silvery cat's eye lustre flambé glaze, early ink mark, 19" h. (two repaired cracks in shade).................. **16,500.00**

*Fulper "Mushroom" Lamp*

**Lamp,** table model, a wide low domed mushroom-shaped pottery shade w/a pointed center, inset around the sides w/geometric panels of blue & green slag glass, raised on a tall slender waisted cylindrical base w/a widely flaring base, shade & base w/a flowing Chinese blue flambé glaze, one short line from one piece of glass to shade rim, black ink mark (ILLUS.) ......... **7,150.00**

**Moon flask,** a footed flattened round form w/the sides tapering to a short cylindrical neck w/a flared mouth flanked by S-scroll handles to the shoulder, fine gunmetal glaze w/flowing silver stars, oval ink mark, 7½" w., 10¼" h. ...................................... **468.00**

**Perfume lamp,** cov., figural, modeled in the form of a young Art Deco lady standing wearing a high yellow turban w/tiny red sprigs & a matching spherical gown w/numerous folds above a separate cylindrical section forming the base, the lady w/her arms folded in front & holding a black open fan, perfume escapes through holes in the turban, curving oval mark, 6½" h. ......................................... **605.00**

**Pitcher,** 9" h., 5" d., musical, plays "How Dry I Am," cat's-eye flambé glaze ............................. **175.00**

**Pitcher,** 10" h., 8½" d., bulbous body on slightly flared foot w/braided handle, mottled wisteria matte glaze, incised vertical mark ............................. **330.00**

**Powder box,** cov., figural Art Deco lady cover, her gown forming the lower box ............... **225.00**

**Vase,** 4⅛" h., baluster-form w/a wide, flat molded mouth, overall fine Copper Dust crystalline glaze, vertical oval ink stamp mark, shape No. 826 ............... **358.00**

**Vase,** 4½" h., wide bulbous half-round base below a wide angled shoulder tapering to a wide flat mouth flanked by angular handles from rim to shoulder, cat's eye flambé glaze in streaked shades of dark brown, bluish green & yellow ............... **275.00**

**Vase,** 4⅞" h., footed spherical body w/a short, wide cylindrical neck, overall mirrored black glaze w/small silver crystal throughout, vertical oval inkstamp mark .......................... **275.00**

**Vase,** 5" h., thin footring supporting a narrow cushion-form lower body centered by a tall, slender cylindrical neck, vivid tan, yellow, brown, blue & cocoa glossy to matte glaze, vertical ink mark ....................... **187.00**

**Vase,** 5½" h., 2¾" d., slightly swelled cylindrical body tapering to slightly swelled cylindrical neck w/closed rim, covered in elephant's breath flambé glaze, early ink mark ........................... **358.00**

**Vase,** 6" h., footed wide bulbous ovoid body tapering to a short neck flanked by curved loop handles from the rim to the shoulder, streaked cat's-eye flambé glaze in black browns & bluish greens, impressed vertical oval mark ..................... **330.00**

**Vase,** 6¼" h., wide bulbous & nearly spherical body tapering to a low incurved neck w/closed mouth flanked by small angled loop handles from the rim to the shoulder, blue snowflake crystalline glaze, vertical oval inkstamp mark .......................... **770.00**

**Vase,** 6⅜" h., footed very wide nearly spherical body w/a wide, low cylindrical neck flanked by three applied small loop handles to the shoulder, overall slightly glossy crystalline matte over wisteria glaze, raised vertical oval mark ................................. **330.00**

**Vase,** 6½" h., 6¼" d., footed squatty bulbous onion-form tapering to a slightly rolled rim, the shoulders mounted w/three curving 'horn' handles, ivory to Chinese blue to mirrored black flambé glaze, early ink mark .. **1,210.00**

**Vase,** 6½" h., 7¼" d., wide tapering ovoid body w/the wide rounded shoulder centering a short rolled neck, fine leopard skin crystalline glaze, incised racetrack mark ....................... **1,045.00**

**Vase,** 6⅞" h., ovoid body tapering to a short neck w/a widely flaring rolled neck, overall mirrored black glaze w/a profusion of small silver crystals, marked w/vertical oval inkstamp mark ... **385.00**

**Vase,** 7" h., ovoid body w/an angular shoulder to the wide, short rolled neck flanked by three short buttress handles to the shoulder rim, gunmetal, tan, brown & blue cat's-eye glossy glaze, vertical mark .................. **275.00**

**Vase,** 7⅞" h., bullet-shaped w/a rounded shoulder centered by a small slightly molded flat mouth, dark grey elephant's breath glaze, vertical rectangular inkstamp mark ........................... **413.00**

**Vase,** 8" h., bulbous ovoid base w/a rounded shoulder to a tall cylindrical neck w/flared rim, tan, caramel & gunmetal cat's-eye flambé glaze, vertical mark ....... **330.00**

**Vase,** 8" h., 5¼" d., slightly ovoid body w/a wide rounded shoulder centered by a tiny mouth, elephant's breath grey flambé glaze, early ink mark ................ **880.00**

**Vase,** bud, 8¼" h., 2¼" w., a slender slightly tapering square form raised on a low angled square foot, metallic Flemington green glaze dripping over a matte mustard yellow ground, early vertical box mark .............. **275.00**

**Vase,** 8¼" h., 5¾" d., a squatty cushion-form base w/the wide angled shoulder centered by a wide cylindrical body w/four double-rib buttresses from the base to near the rim, cat's-eye flambé glaze, ink racetrack mark ......................................... **358.00**

**Vase,** 8½" h., 5½" d., tapering wide cylindrical body w/a wide rounded shoulder centered by a small closed-in mouth, fine Flemington green glaze w/silver threading, ink racetrack mark ... **220.00**

**Vase,** 9" h., wide bulbous ovoid body below a wide cylindrical neck flanked by T-form squared Chinese-style handles, the neck w/a fine oatmeal flambé glaze streaking down over a mirrored black glaze, raised vertical oval mark ....................................... **1,320.00**

**Vase,** 9½" h., wide bulbous half-round base below an angled shoulder w/a tall tapering neck flanked by downswept angled handles from the rim to the shoulder, copper dust over Flemington green glazes, raised vertical oval mark ..................... **413.00**

**Vase,** 10" h., 4½" d., tall cylindrical body pierced on the upper body on two sides w/large rectangular openings w/rounded corners, molded in bold relief around the base w/a continuous band of various mushrooms, Flemington green flambé glaze, early ink mark & Jordan-Volpe Gallery label ........................... **1,210.00**

**Vase,** 10" h., 5½" d., seven-sided ovoid body w/flat rim, covered in brownish green, blue, mahogany & cat's-eye flambé glaze, incised vertical racetrack mark .......................................... **413.00**

**Vase,** 11" h., wide bulbous ovoid body tapering to a short cylindrical neck, rust-colored crystalline matte glaze over a cream glossy glaze, early rectangular vertical ink stamp (small professionally repaired rim chip, several small grinding chips on base) ......................... **715.00**

**Vase,** 11" h., 7¾" d., very squatty base tapering to slightly swelled buttressed cylindrical neck, cat's-eye flambé glaze, early ink mark ......................................... **660.00**

**Vase,** 11½" h., 5" w., tall slender slightly tapering paneled body w/a flat mouth flanked by squared & pierced wing-like handles extending halfway down the sides, silvery cucumber crystalline glaze, early ink mark. **550.00**

**Vase,** 11½" h., 11" d., a wide bulbous baluster-form w/a short stepped neck, hammered surface covered in a mirrored black & turquoise blue flambé crystalline glaze, raised racetrack mark ....................... **2,970.00**

**Vase,** 12" h., tall slender baluster-form body w/disc foot & short flaring neck, vibrant pale blue, rose & violet matte glaze, vertical mark (flake at rim)......... **385.00**

**Vase,** 12½" h., 5" d., Germanic rocket-shaped body w/four small buttresses below the swelled & tapering top, fine curdled mirrored blue glaze, unmarked .............................. **1,320.00**

**Vase,** 12½" h., 11¾" d., wide baluster-form w/molded rim & horizontal loop handles at the shoulders, hammered surface covered in a cat's-eye flambé glaze, ink racetrack mark .......... **770.00**

*Fulper "Cattails" Vase*

**Vase,** 13" h., slightly tapering slender cylindrical body deeply molded w/dense cattails on narrow stems w/long, narrow leaves, medium & dark olive green matte glaze, ink mark, minor bruise on top rim (ILLUS.) ................................ **1,540.00**

**Vase,** 13" h., 7¼" d., tall slender ovoid body w/two heavy ring handles near the top, metallic trailing blue snowflake crystalline base w/undertones of rust & mahogany, vertical ink racetrack mark ....................... **1,320.00**

**Vase,** 13¼" h., baluster-form w/a widely flaring rim, a caramel flambé glaze on the neck & upper shoulder streaked down over a mirrored black glaze, impressed vertical oval mark .... **935.00**

**Vase,** 16" h., 5½" h., tall slender cylindrical body w/a narrow rounded shoulder to a flat molded mouth, cat's-eye flambé glaze, incised vertical racetrack mark ....................................... **1,320.00**

*A Variety of Fulper Pieces*

**Beer set:** 13" h., 6½" d. tankard pitcher & six conical beer mugs; Nurenberg-type, the pitcher w/a tall slender cylindrical neck w/a pinched spout above the conical base, a long squared handle down the side, each conical mug w/a short cylindrical neck & square handle, all w/a cat's-eye flambé glaze, all w/the vertical rectangular ink mark, one mug cracked, the set (ILLUS. far right & front left) .................... **550.00**

**Book ends,** figural, seated Buddha on a round platform base, matte blue & bluish green glaze, vertical rectangular ink mark, one restored, 3¾" d., 6" h., pr. (ILLUS. front, center).............. **165.00**

**Book ends,** figural, Ramses-type, figure of the kneeling early Egyptian king at a table w/an open book & an urn, fine matte green crystalline glaze w/the clay showing through, vertical rectangular ink mark, 5¼" w., 7½" h., pr. (ILLUS. back row, second from left) .... **385.00**

**Book ends,** figural, Sleepy Reader-type, a young lad sitting cross-legged w/a large book on his lap, his head nodding forward, matte crystalline green glaze, vertical racetrack ink mark, restored chip to back of one collar, 5" w., 5¾" h., pr. (ILLUS. second from right)............................... **358.00**

**Book ends,** figural, Temple Gate-type, models of tall Oriental angular gates w/curved top crossbars, a pair of small foo dogs flank the steps at the bases, mustard against a cafe-au-lait ground, vertical rectangular ink mark, restoration to corner of one, 5¼" w., 7½" h., pr. (ILLUS. far left)........................................ **440.00**

**Centerpiece w/flower frog,** the widely flaring bowl raised on a high flaring foot pierced w/geometric openings, a figural fish on waves flower frog in the center, flowing matte blue flambé glaze, vertical ink racetrack mark, 17" d., 6¼" h. (ILLUS. back center)................ **330.00**

# GOLDSCHEIDER

*Goldscheider Figural Planter*

*The Goldscheider firm, manufacturers of porcelain and faience in Austria between 1885 and the present, was founded by Friedrich Goldscheider and carried on by his widow. The firm came under the control of his sons, Walter and Marcell, in 1920. Fleeing their native Austria at the time of World War II, the Goldscheiders set up an operation in the United States. They were listed in the Trenton, New Jersey, City Directory from 1943 through 1950 and their main production seems to have been art pottery figurines.*

*Goldscheider Marks*

**Figure of an Art Deco dancer,** a young woman standing wearing a long floral blue evening dress & stepping forward & holding up the ends of her skirt, on an octagonal black base, after a model by Dakon, printed factory marks & impressed "6553 -224 - 19," 7⅞" h. (restoration) ......... **$380.00**

**Figure of an Art Deco dancer,** the striding lady w/head tilted back & her arms extended holding up the ends of her long center-split gown, also wearing a halter top & high heeled shoes, on an oval base, decorated in rose & black on a white ground, designed by Dakon, impressed designer's name, stamped marks, incised "7826 - 266 - 19 - X11B - S," Austria, 8⅞" h. .......................... **489.00**

**Figure of Columbine,** shown seated on a green & floral chair w/her legs crossed over a large guitar, from a model by Podany, printed factory marks & impressed "4996 - 72 - 8," 9¼" h. (restoration) .................. **380.00**

**Figure of a female nude,** terra cotta, the woman kneeling on one leg w/arms raised over her head, on a rectangular base, under a brown glaze, impressed factory mark, numbered "8495 - 13," 15¼" h. (minor chips) ....................................... **380.00**

**Figure of a Southern Belle,** blue ruffled dress & hat, No. 800-438, 8" h., Everlast Corp. mark .......... **70.00**

**Figure of White Christmas Lady,** Everlast Corp. mark ......... **90.00**

**Planter,** figural, terra cotta, modeled as two young girls on a rocky outcrop, looking down into a pool forming the planter opening, impressed factory marks, numbered "3531 - 141 - 14," overpainting, restoration to wrist, 24½" h. (ILLUS. top previous column) ...... **400.00 to 600.00**

**Plaque,** rectangular, molded w/the bust of a young woman gathering cherries from a tree & facing a young boy holding a bowl to receive them, slender trees in the right background & a mountainous landscape in the distance, glazed in matte shades of brown against a gilded ground, back stamped "FABRIQUE AN AUSTRICHE - GOLDSCHEIDER - WIEN," factory mark & numerals, ca. 1900, 9¼ × 20" (very minor chip) .......................... **805.00**

**Powder dish,** cov., figural lady forms the cover, her skirt forms the base, Everlast Corp. mark (base repaired) ........................... **115.00**

# GONDER

*Lawton Gonder founded Gonder Ceramic Arts in Zanesville, Ohio in 1941 and it continued in operation until 1957.*

*The firm produced a higher priced and better quality of commercial art potteries than many firms of the time and employed Jamie Matchet and Chester Kirk, both of whom were outstanding ceramic designers. Several special glazes were developed during the company's history and Gonder even duplicated some museum pieces of Chinese ceramic. In 1955 the firm converted to the production of tile due to increased foreign competition and by 1957 their years of finest production were over.*

**Candleholders,** E-14, pr. ........... **$25.00**

**Console bowl,** figural dolphins on each side, No. 556, 12" d........... **75.00**

**Figures,** Chinese man & woman, flanked by baskets hanging from bar across shoulders, dark green, pr. ................................... **95.00**

**Lamp,** TV-type, model of a ship, green, 14" h. .............................. **85.00**

**Model of a cat,** modern design, No. 521, yellow & red mottling, 12" h.......................................... **475.00**

**Model of a panther,** green & yellow mottling, No. 210, 19" l... **175.00**

**Vase,** 8½" h., trumpet form w/molded scrolls on front, angled handle at top right & lower left, gold crackle finish, H-56 ........................................... **25.00**

# GOUDA

*Gouda Chamberstick*

*While tin-enameled earthenware has been made in Gouda, Holland since the early 1600s, the productions of modern factories are attracting increasing collector attention. The art pottery of Gouda is easily recognized by its brightly colored peasant-style decoration with some types having achieved a "cloisonne" effect. Pottery workshops located in, or near, Gouda include Regina, Zenith, Plazuid, Schoonhoven, Arnhem and others. Their wide range of production included utilitarian wares, as well as vases, miniatures and large outdoor garden ornaments.*

*Gouda Marks*

**Bowl,** 6½" d. bulbous body, tapering to 4½" d. base & mouth, 4¾" h., 1" w. collar, floral decoration, artist-signed ........ **$295.00**

**Chamberstick w/ring handle,** triangular-shape, decorated w/rich blue Art Deco stylized flowers outlined in gold & surrounded by brown & rust leaves, satin finished brown ground & handle, black & gold exterior, 6½" d., 2¼" h. (ILLUS. previous page) .............. **110.00**

*Small Gouda Pitcher*

**Pitcher,** 3⅝" h., 2⅝" d., bulbous body tapering to a flaring molded rim w/a pinched spout, C-form handle, decorated w/multicolored Art Deco stylized flowers, black ground & black interior (ILLUS.) ......................... **50.00**

**Plate,** 7⅜" d., footed, multicolored center decoration of large flowerhead, border of oval reserves w/Art Deco flowers, black ground .............................. **28.00**

**Vase,** 6⅝" h., footed ovoid body tapering to flaring rim, decorated w/polychrome geometric design on black ground, underglaze blue label & paper label ............. **83.00**

**Vase,** 12" h., footed bottle-form w/a bulbous body tapering to a tall slender & slightly flaring stick neck, decorated w/abstract lobes & scrolls in olive green, blue, rust & brown, inscribed & impressed marks of the Yssel Pottery (ILLUS. top next column).................... **400.00 to 450.00**

*Tall Gouda Vase*

# GRUEBY POTTERY

*Some fine art pottery was produced by the Grueby Faience and Tile Company, established in Boston in 1891. Choice pieces were created with molded designs on a semi-porcelain body. The ware is marked and often bears the initials of the decorators. The pottery closed in 1907.*

# GRUEBY

*Grueby Pottery Mark*

**Bowl,** 4⅜" d., 3" h., a short footring supporting upright cylindrical sides w/a rounded base & flat rim, mottled matte green glaze, impressed mark ........................................ **$345.00**

**Bowl,** 5" d., 4" h., wide flat slightly incurved mouth above tapering ovoid sides, the exterior w/a thick curdled matte bluish green glaze, the interior in yellow, impressed circular mark ........... **605.00**

**Bowl,** 6¼" d., 3¼" h., a wide squatty bulbous body w/a wide shoulder to the wide, short slightly flaring neck, the body molded in low-relief w/wide shaped overlapping leaves, matte green glaze, impressed marks, artist's initials "ER" & "10/30" ................................... **1,380.00**

**Bowl-vase,** wide squatty bulbous form w/incurved wide mouth, opaque pale blue matte glaze, 4" d., 1½" h. ............................. **275.00**

**Bowl-vase,** squatty bulbous form w/a flat closed rim, prominent finger rings, covered in a thick yellow matte glaze, impressed mark, 4" d., 2" h. ....................... **715.00**

**Bowl-vase,** squatty bulbous form w/a flat closed rim, molded w/wide rounded leaves w/curled tips alternating w/tall stems w/yellow buds, organic matte green glaze, marked on the ground base, 5¼" d., 3" h. (restored) .............................. **1,210.00**

**Bowl-vase,** wide bulbous body w/a wide rounded shoulder centered by a low flat wide mouth, the sides molded in relief w/bands of wide pointed overlapping leaves, rich organic matte green glaze, impressed pottery mark & "91," 6½" d., 4¾" h...................................... **3,190.00**

**Bowl-vase,** squatty bulbous form w/a short slightly flaring mouth, w/rows of tooled & applied rounded leaves w/curly edges, under a fine veined matte dark green glaze, impressed "Faience" mark, artist's cipher & "48A," 8" d., 5¾" h. (small flakes beneath rim & glaze bubbles) .. **2,090.00**

**Lamp,** table model, a wide bulbous ovoid base w/a wide shoulder to a short wide flaring neck, decorated w/three crisply tooled & applied jonquils, one each in blue, red & yellow, surrounded by light green leaves on a smooth dark matte green ground, w/original three-arm fittings supporting a domed slag glass shade composed of radiating small rectangles of mottled green & white glass, probably by Duffner & Kimberly, raised on a low round Oriental-style carved wood foot, impressed pottery mark, base only 8" d., 10" h. (neat base drill hole, rim restoration) .............. **7,150.00**

**Lamp,** table model, the bulbous ovoid base w/a rounded shoulder tapering to a short flaring neck, decorated w/yellow jonquils & green leaves against a green ground, w/a domical leaded glass Tiffany shade w/a band of yellow leaves on a green & white slag glass ground, base marked "GRUEBY POTTERY," the shade impressed "TIFFANY STUDIOS NEW YORK," original fittings, shade 18" d., overall 22" h. (minor resoldering to shade, some color run on base flowers) ................................ **13,200.00**

**Paperweight,** figural, model of a scarab beetle, matte green & gunmetal glaze, two original paper labels, 4" l., 1¼" h. (small nick)................................ **880.00**

**Tile,** square, a geometric design in thick crackled ivory matte glaze against a reddish brown clay ground, in a wide flat oak frame, tile 4" w. ........................ **193.00**

**Tile,** square, molded bunny w/long ears in red terra cotta clay, in a wide flat oak frame, tile 4" w. .................................... **330.00**

**Tile,** square, a molded elephant in red terra cotta clay, in a wide flat oak frame, tile 4" w. .................. **193.00**

**Tile,** square, an incised scene of a galleon ship under full sail w/clouds in the sky beyond, matte glazed in yellow, cream, green & blue outlined in blackish mauve, raised mark, inscribed "MD" in glaze, 4¼" w................. **259.00**

**Tile,** square, a landscape scene w/low hills & two tall green & brown trees in the foreground, shades of green & blue in the background, matte glaze, slip-signed on the back "M.D.," 6" w. (minor surface glaze nicks) ....... **990.00**

**Tile,** square, a stylized design of a walking winged mythological beast seeming to hold the sun before itself, rich cream matte glaze w/blue highlights backed by a thick glossy black glaze, in an early wide flat oak frame, tile 6" w. ................................... **413.00**

**Tile,** square, decorated in cuenca w/a sailing boat in ivory, brown & caramel against a green sky & rolling ocean, die-stamped "GRUEBY - BOSTON," signed "MK," in old Art & Crafts-style frame, tile 8" w. ...................... **2,530.00**

**Tile,** square, a scene of a large brown & yellow Spanish galleon w/billowing cream sails being tossed on a swirled sea in shades of green, dark blue sky w/greyish blue clouds, matte glaze, back marked "MTC - O," two paper labels, in older narrow oak frame, 9" w. (cracked across the face, reglued & professionally repaired) ......... **1,045.00**

**Tiles,** square, each w/a geometric four-petal design in rich cream w/brown highlights on a mint green ground, in a period wide flat oak frame, each 4" w., set of 4 ...................................... **319.00**

**Tiles,** square, a geometric design w/thick ivory matte glaze on a dark brown clay against a mint green ground, in a flat wide oak frame, each 8" w., set of 4 ........ **275.00**

**Vase,** 3" h., short foot supports a miniature broad-shouldered form w/a short, wide rim, dark green mottled matte glaze, original paper label ................................ **523.00**

**Vase,** 3" h., 3½" d., simple spherical body tapering to a tiny rolled mouth, matte ochre glaze, unsigned ................................... **460.00**

**Vase,** 4" h., cylindrical body rounded at the base & shoulder, w/a short, wide molded mouth, unusual pale green & chalk white matte glaze, impressed mark .......................................... **385.00**

**Vase,** 4" h., 4" d., bulbous ovoid body w/a molded mouth, molded w/crisply molded broad rounded leaves & tight yellow buds, fine matte cucumber green glaze, obscured marks ..................... **3,360.00**

**Vase,** 4½" h., 5" d., footed squatty bulbous wide body tapering to a short, waisted cylindrical neck, tooled & applied wide slightly pointed leaves alternating w/crisply molded quatrefoil blossoms in yellow around the neck, decorated by W. Post, impressed "Pottery" mark & "WP-3-7," 1907 ..................... **4,290.00**

**Vase,** 4¾" h., 3" d., bulbous vase w/slightly flared lip, w/tooled & applied leaves on the rounded part of the vase, under a cucumber matte glaze, mark obscured by glaze (three glaze nicks at top rim) ..................... **2,640.00**

**Vase,** 6⅞" h., 3⅝" d., sharply tapering cylindrical form w/a tall neck, matte green glaze, impressed mark ........................ **546.00**

**Vase,** 7" h., 8" d., a wide squatty bulbous base w/a wide rounded shoulder to the wide slightly flaring neck w/flat rim, the lower model molded in low-relief w/wide overlapping leaves w/a matte green glaze, impressed mark & incised artist's initials, Wilhelmina Post ..................... **1,725.00**

**Vase,** 7½" h., 4½" d., a squatty bulbous base tapering to a tall wide cylindrical neck, carved w/long round-tipped leaves extending down from the rim to the base, the base w/incised grooves between rounded lobes, thick rich organic matte green glaze, impressed circular "Faience" mark ....................... **1,430.00**

*Grueby Pottery Vases*

**Vase,** 7⅞" h., 4½" h., tall baluster-form body w/a flaring rim, decorated w/widely spaced lightly molded ribbing, matte pale blue glaze, impressed mark & partial incised artist's initials, Wilhelmina Post ........................ **920.00**

**Vase,** 8" h., tall simple cylindrical form, thick textured dark green matte glaze, large unglazed area to side reveals rich caramel & dark brown clay, impressed mark ...................................... **1,100.00**

**Vase,** 9¼" h., 8" d., gourd-shaped form tapering to slightly flaring cylindrical neck w/flat mouth, w/modeled & applied leaves under a feathered matte green glaze, impressed (roughness to leaf edges) ............................ **2,970.00**

**Vase,** 9½" h., 4½" d., slender ovoid form ending in flaring five-sided rim, w/five tooled & applied tall leaves alternating w/buds on long stems, under a fine, rich, leathery matte green glaze, die-stamped "GRUEBY FAIENCE," by Anna Lingley (glaze scrape at base) ........... **2,090.00**

**Vase,** 10¼" h., 8¾" d., footed wide tapering ovoid body w/a wide low rolled neck, decorated w/alternating wide pointed leaves & buds on slender stems in low-relief, matte green glaze, modeled by Ruth Erickson, impressed mark, "160" & incised artist's initials (ILLUS. above left) ....................................... **2,645.00**

**Vase,** 11" h., gently swelled cylindrical body tapering to a short ruffled six-sided rim, carved & applied w/three daffodil blossoms in profile, one each in white, yellow & dark brown, delicately carved vertical leaves around each blossom, rich medium green matte glaze, impressed "147," artist's initials "AB," professional repair at lip (ILLUS. top next page) ........... **6,600.00**

**Vase,** 11" h., 8" d., wide footed ovoid body w/a narrow shoulder to the wide rolled rim, molded w/tall wide overlapping leaves around the sides, under an ochre matte glaze, impressed mark (repair to circular glaze chip on the side of the base) .. **3,080.00**

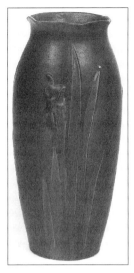

*Grueby Vase with Daffodils*

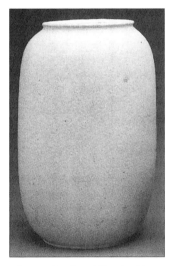

*Oatmeal-colored Grueby Vase*

**Vase,** 12" h., bulbous cylindrical form on a thin footring & w/a thin rim, oatmeal-colored glaze, impressed factory mark & "86" (ILLUS.) ........................ **2,530.00**

**Vase,** 12½" h., 8½" d., tall wide ovoid body tapering to a molded flat mouth, the sides molded w/high-relief alternating rows of tall tapering overlapping rounded leaves & stems

w/molded yellow trefoil blossoms, all on a green ground, die-stamped marked & "MS," decorated by Margaret Seaman (small chip to one leaf edge, some color run to flowers) ... **13,200.00**

*Leaf & Blossom Grueby Vase*

**Vase,** 12⅝" h., wide ovoid body carved w/tall, wide leaves alternating w/small blossoms around the shoulder, a short waisted cylindrical neck, dark matte green glaze w/yellow blossoms, decorated by Ruth Erickson, stamped company mark & incised artist's initials, original company paper label & paper price tag (ILLUS.) ...... **10,350.00**

**Vase,** 12¾" h., 8" d., squatty bulbous base molded w/bands of wide, short overlapping leaves w/curled tips, the shoulder tapering to a tall, wide cylindrical neck w/molded rim, matte green glaze, modeled by Ruth Erickson, impressed marks & artist's initials, ca. 1904 (ILLUS. right top previous page) ........................ **2,760.00**

**Vase,** 13" h., 8½" d., footed tapering ovoid body w/a molded flaring rim, decorated w/three crisply tooled yellow irises & stacked light green leaves, on a

*Fine Large Grueby Vases*

rich dark green matte ground,
impressed factory mark &
illegible artist's initials, one minor
glaze chip to a small bud
(ILLUS. top, left).................. **22,000.00**

**Vase,** 17¾" h., 8½" d., a wide
squatty bulbous base centered
by a very tall slender cylindrical
neck w/a flaring rim, the rim
molded w/a band of small
quatrefoils, the lower body
molded w/a band of wide
pointed leaves, fine matte green
glaze, impressed pottery mark &
"133 - A," original paper label
(restoration to three small rim
chips) ..................................... **5,775.00**

**Vase,** 20" h., 11½" d., a narrow
footring below a wide bulbous
body tapering to a tall cylindrical
neck w/a flaring rim, carved &
applied staggered rows of
pointed leaves around the base,
rare matte French blue glaze,
impressed Faience mark & "120"
(ILLUS. above right).............. **8,800.00**

**Vase,** 23½" h., slender ovoid
body tapering to a tall cylindrical
neck, high-relief tall pointed

*Rare Tall Grueby Vase*

leaves alternating w/seven
ridged buds around the neck,
matte green glaze w/yellow
buds, modeled by Kiichi
Yamada, ca. 1901, impressed
company mark, incised artist's
initials & paper labels, trace of
red paint (ILLUS.) ................ **10,925.00**

*A Varied Grouping of Grueby Pieces*

Photo Courtesy of David Rago

**Tile,** salesman's, rectangular, decorated w/a light green chamberstick & yellow candle below the words "GRUEBY TILE," against a fine matte green ground, used by M. Seaman, restoration to one corner, 4½ × 6" (ILLUS. front, second from right) .................. **1,430.00**

**Vase,** 5½" h., 7" d., squatty bulbous body w/a wide shoulder centered by a short cylindrical neck, the sides tooled w/vertical ribbing, curdled matte green glaze, impressed Faience mark & "155" (ILLUS. front, second from left) ................................ **3,190.00**

**Vase,** 5¾" h., 6½" d., squatty bulbous body w/a wide shoulder centered by a short rolled neck, the sides modeled w/wide overlapping pointed leaves, dark matte green glaze, impressed company mark & "WP - 155," decorated by W. Post (ILLUS. front, center) .......................... **3,960.00**

**Vase,** 8¼" h., 4½" w., ovoid three-sided body w/a gently flaring three-lobed rim, molded w/full-

length broad rounded leaves alternating w/tooled buds, fine matte green glaze, by W. Post, impressed pottery mark & artist's initials (ILLUS. far right) ......... **3,300.00**

**Vase,** 9½" h., 7¼" d., tall footed barrel-shaped body w/a molded rim, decorated w/tooled & applied alternating tall & short pointed leaves, green matte glaze, impressed Faience mark, invisible repair to small base chips (ILLUS. back, second from right) ...................................... **3,740.00**

**Vase,** 9¾" h., 6½" d., ovoid body w/a molded rolled rim, molded w/tall broad leaves, fine mottled green matte glaze, by Ellen Farrington, impressed company mark & artist's initials (ILLUS. far left) ........................................ **6,600.00**

**Vase,** 13" h., 8" d., a bulbous base tapering to a tall, wide cylindrical neck w/a molded rim, fine curdled ochre brown matte glaze, probably intended as a lamp base, impressed company mark (ILLUS. back, second from left) ........................................ **2,090.00**

# HALL

*Royal Rose Casserole*

Founded in 1903 in East Liverpool, Ohio, this still-operating company at first produced mostly utilitarian wares. It was in 1911 that Robert T. Hall, son of the company founder, developed a special single-fire, lead-free glaze which proved to be strong, hard and non-porous. In the 1920s the firm became well known for their extensive line of teapots (still a major product) and in 1932 they introduced kitchenwares followed by dinnerwares in 1936 and refrigerator wares in 1938.

The imaginative designs and wide range of glaze colors and decal decorations have led to the growing appeal of Hall wares with collectors, especially people who like Art Deco and Art Moderne design. One of the firm's most famous patterns was the "Autumn Leaf" line, produced as premiums for the Jewel Tea Company. For listings of this ware see "Jewel Tea Autumn Leaf."

Helpful books on Hall include, The Collector's Guide to Hall China by Margaret & Kenn Whitmyer, and Superior Quality Hall China—A Guide for Collectors by Harvey Duke (An ELO Book, 1977).

*Hall Marks*

**Batter bowl,** Five Band line, Chinese red .............................. **$60.00**

**Batter jug,** Sundial line ................ **45.00**

**Bean pot,** cov., New England #4 shape, Orange Poppy patt ......... **105.00**

**Bean pot,** cov., Orange Poppy patt. ........................................... **120.00**

**Bean pot,** cov., Pert shape, blue .. **50.00**

**Bowl,** salad, 7" d., Crocus patt. .... **10.00**

**Bowl,** salad, 9" d., Royal Rose patt. ............................................. **25.00**

**Bowl,** 10" d., Orange Poppy patt. . **21.00**

**Canister,** cov., Pert shape, Chinese red ................................. **45.00**

**Casserole,** cov., individual, Blue Blossom patt. ............................. **90.00**

**Casserole,** cov., Pastel Morning Glory patt. ................................... **45.00**

**Casserole,** cov., Royal Rose patt., thick rim (ILLUS. top previous column) ......... **30.00 to 40.00**

**Casserole,** cov., Radiance shape, Shaggy Tulip patt. ........... **30.00**

**Casserole,** cov., Radiance shape, Yellow Rose patt. ............ **30.00**

**Coffeepot,** cov., Drip-o-later, all-china, Springtime patt., nine cup .............................................. **60.00**

**Coffeepot,** cov., Drip-o-later, Waverly shape, Crocus patt........ **50.00**

**Coffeepot,** cov., individual, Sundial shape, Chinese red........ **90.00**

**Coffeepot,** cov., Drip-o-later, all-china, Kadota shape, Homewood patt........................... **75.00**

**Coffeepot,** cov., percolator-type, game birds decoration ............... **95.00**

**Coffeepot,** cov., Washington shape, Wild Poppy patt............. **125.00**

**Cookie jar,** cov., Orange Poppy patt., gold label .......................... **85.00**

**Creamer,** breakfast size, Blue Blossom patt. ............................. **50.00**

**Creamer & cov. sugar bowl,** Moderne shape, Blue Bouquet patt., pr....................................... **45.00**

**Creamer & cov. sugar bowl,** Pert shape, Rose Parade patt., pr. ..... **36.00**

**Creamer & cov. sugar bowl,**
Pert shape, Wildfire patt., pr. ...... **50.00**

**Creamer & cov. sugar bowl,**
Cameo Rose patt., pr.................. **25.00**

**Custard cup,** Orange Poppy patt. ... **8.00**

**Custard cups,** Rose Parade
patt., pr....................................... **40.00**

**Dinner service for eight,**
Monticello patt.......................... **200.00**

**Drip jar,** open, Crocus patt. .......... **42.00**

**Gravy boat,** Red Poppy patt......... **50.00**

**Leftover dish,** cov., Hotpoint
line, grey ..................................... **25.00**

**Leftover dish,** cov., rectangular,
Silhouette patt. ............................ **45.00**

**Leftover dish,** cov., rectangular,
Westinghouse line, Hercules
patt., Sunset red ......................... **20.00**

**Leftover dish,** cov., rectangular,
Westinghouse line, Phoenix
patt., blue ................................... **15.00**

**Mixing bowl,** Crocus patt., large .. **40.00**

**Mixing bowls,** nesting-type, Rose
Parade patt., set of 3 ................. **75.00**

**Pie baker,** Crocus patt................. **50.00**

**Pie baker,** Heather Rose patt. ...... **34.00**

**Pie baker,** Taverne patt. .............. **45.00**

**Pitcher,** ball-type, Chinese red,
No. 1, small............................. **145.00**

**Pitcher,** ball-type, Royal Rose
patt.......................................... **110.00**

**Pitcher,** ball-type, Springtime
patt............................................. **80.00**

**Pitcher,** jug-type, Heather Rose
patt............................................. **22.00**

**Pitcher,** jug-type, Radiance
shape, Wild Poppy patt.............. **75.00**

**Plate,** dinner, 9" d., Crocus patt. ... **16.00**

**Plate,** dinner, 9" d., Springtime
patt............................................... **8.00**

**Plate,** dinner, 9" d., Wildfire patt. .... **9.00**

**Pretzel jar,** cov., Orange Poppy
patt........................................... **115.00**

**Sauce dish,** Crocus patt.............. **10.00**

**Salt & pepper shakers,** Blue
Blossom patt., pr........................ **89.00**

**Salt & pepper shakers,** handled,
Pert shape, Rose Parade patt.,
pr................................................ **25.00**

**Salt & pepper shakers,** handled,
Pert shape, Royal Rose patt., pr.. **25.00**

**Salt & pepper shakers,** handled,
Pert shape, Wildfire patt., pr. ...... **50.00**

**Soup plate w/flanged rim,**
Springtime patt............................. **9.00**

**Sugar bowl,** cov., Sundial line,
yellow......................................... **30.00**

**Teapot,** cov., Airflow shape,
cobalt blue w/gold trim ............... **95.00**

**Teapot,** cov., Aladdin shape,
Blue Bouquet patt. .................... **250.00**

**Teapot,** cov., Aladdin shape, oval
opening, Chinese red................ **145.00**

**Teapot,** cov., Aladdin shape, Red
Poppy patt.................................. **45.00**

**Teapot,** cov., Aladdin shape,
yellow w/gold trim ...................... **69.00**

**Teapot,** cov., Albany shape,
brown w/gold trim....................... **50.00**

**Teapot,** cov., Automobile shape,
canary ...................................... **425.00**

**Teapot,** cov., Automobile shape,
Chinese red ............................. **600.00**

**Teapot,** cov., Baltimore shape,
warm yellow ............................... **40.00**

**Teapot,** cov., Basket shape,
canary w/silver trim ................... **110.00**

**Teapot,** cov., Blue Bouquet patt.
w/infuser .................................. **120.00**

**Teapot,** cov., Boston shape,
Crocus patt. ............................. **350.00**

**Teapot,** cov., Boston shape, light
green w/gold trim ....................... **45.00**

**Teapot,** cov., Boston shape,
Wildfire patt............................... **200.00**

**Teapot,** cov., Boston shape,
yellow w/gold trim ...................... **40.00**

**Teapot,** cov., Cameo Rose patt.... **70.00**

**Teapot,** cov., Cleveland shape,
Emerald green w/gold trim.......... **60.00**

**Teapot,** cov., Doughnut shape,
Chinese red .............................. **320.00**

**Teapot,** cov., Doughnut shape,
delphinium ................................ **375.00**

**Teapot,** cov., French shape, ivory w/gold .......................................... **45.00**

**Teapot,** cov., French shape, ivory w/gold, "lace" band decoration.. **279.00**

**Teapot,** cov., Grape shape by Thorley, white & gold w/jewel encrusted grapes ...................... **135.00**

**Teapot,** cov., Hollywood shape, Gold Label line, yellow ................ **45.00**

**Teapot,** cov., Hook Cover, Chinese red, six-cup ................. **150.00**

**Teapot,** cov., Hook Cover, yellow w/gold ......................................... **40.00**

**Teapot,** cov., Los Angeles shape, Gold Label line, celadon ............. **45.00**

**Teapot,** cov., Los Angeles shape, Stock green & gold, 1920s backstamp .................................. **75.00**

**Teapot,** cov., Manhattan shape, yellow .......................................... **85.00**

**Teapot,** cov., McCormick shape, brown w/gold trim......................... **50.00**

**Teapot,** cov., McCormick shape, turquoise ..................................... **45.00**

**Teapot,** cov., Medallion shape, Taverne patt............................... **65.00**

**Teapot,** cov., Melody shape, Chinese red & white.................. **350.00**

**Teapot,** cov., Moderne shape, ivory w/gold spout & trim............. **25.00**

**Teapot,** cov., Nautilus shape, yellow ........................................ **175.00**

**Teapot,** cov., New York shape, Crocus patt. ............................ **245.00**

**Teapot,** cov., New York shape, yellow w/gold trim ...................... **39.00**

**Teapot,** cov., Pert shape, Rose White patt.................................... **43.00**

**Teapot,** cov., Philadelphia shape, Gold Label line, pink ................... **60.00**

**Teapot,** cov., Plume patt., pink ..... **45.00**

**Teapot,** cov., Rose Parade patt.... **68.00**

**Teapot,** cov., Rose White patt. ..... **70.00**

**Teapot,** cov., Star patt., turquoise w/gold trim ................................... **35.00**

**Teapot,** cov., Streamline shape, blue w/gold trim.......................... **75.00**

**Teapot,** cov., Surfside shape, Emerald green w/gold trim........ **130.00**

**Teapot,** cov., T-Ball, canary yellow, round............................... **75.00**

**Teapot,** cov., T-Ball, silver, round........................................ **150.00**

**Teapot,** cov., Twinspout, Chinese red............................................. **175.00**

**Teapot,** cov., Twinspout, ivory ...... **95.00**

**Teapot,** cov., Wildfire patt. w/infuser ................................... **125.00**

**Teapot,** cov., Windshield shape, game birds decoration ............. **195.00**

**Teapot,** cov., Windshield shape, Gold Label line, ivory w/gold dot. **50.00**

**Teapot,** cov., Windshield shape, yellow.......................................... **75.00**

**Tea set:** cov. teapot, creamer & cov. sugar bowl; Philadelphia shape, black w/gold trim, 3 pcs... **69.00**

**Tea set:** cov. teapot, creamer & cov. sugar bowl; Philadelphia shape, light blue w/floral decal & red trim, 3 pcs. ........................... **65.00**

**Water server,** cov., Westinghouse line, Phoenix patt., blue ................................... **75.00**

# HAMPSHIRE POTTERY

*Hampshire Pottery Urn*

*Hampshire Pottery was made in Keene, New Hampshire, where several potteries operated as far back as the late 18th century. The pottery now known as Hampshire Pottery was established by*

*J.S. Taft shortly after 1870. Various types of wares, including Art Pottery, were produced through the years. Taft's brother-in-law, Cadmon Robertson, joined the firm in 1904 and was responsible for developing over 900 glaze formulas while in charge of all manufacturing. His death in 1914 created problems for the firm and Taft sold out to George Morton in 1916. Closed during part of World War I, the pottery was later reopened by Morton for a short time and manufactured white hotel china. From 1919 to 1921, mosaic floor tiles became the main production. All production ceased in 1923.*

*Hampshire Marks*

**Bowl,** 8¼" d., 3¾" h., matte green glaze on recessed & repeating decoration, unsigned .............. **$230.00**

**Lamp base,** wide squatty bulbous form w/a wide shoulder tapering to a wide flat molded mouth, matte green glaze, designed by Cadmon Robertson, No. 001, impressed marks & paper label, 5⅛" d., 5¾" h. .......................... **633.00**

**Lamp base,** tall baluster-form body w/a flaring foot & short flaring neck, mottled matte green over brown glaze, factory drilled, impressed "151," 15¾" h. .......... **201.00**

**Urn,** cov., wide bulbous ovoid body w/the wide shoulder w/upright loop handles & tapering to a short cylindrical neck w/molded rim, a flat inset cover, rich green matte glaze, incised marks, 8" d., 8" h. (ILLUS.) .................................... **715.00**

**Vase,** 7" h., simple ovoid body w/a gently angled shoulder to the flat mouth, green & brown matte glaze, marked ................. **413.00**

**Vase,** 14" h., 5¼" d., slender baluster-form body w/a slender neck widely flared & ruffled at the top, matte green glaze, glaze-obscured impressed mark ......... **173.00**

# HARKER POTTERY COMPANY

*The original Harker Pottery was established in East Liverpool, Ohio in 1840 by Benjamin Harker, Sr. Fifty years later, in 1890, the firm was incorporated as the Harker Pottery Company. The former plant of the National China Company was acquired by 1911 and the closed Edwin M. Knowles pottery of Chester, West Virginia was purchased in 1931.*

*The earliest products from Harker were utilitarian yellowware and Rockingham-glazed wares made from local clays. Whiteware was introduced after 1900 but produced with imported materials. The company's well-known Cameoware line was introduced in the 1930s and became one of their best sellers and is widely sought by collectors today. The line features solid color glazes with white "cameo" style designs in a silhouette fashion.*

*A wide range of patterns and body styles came from the Harker Pottery over the years and all are growing in collectibility, however, production ceased in 1972 after the firm had been purchased by the Jeanette Glass Company.*

*Harker Pottery Marks*

**Ashtray,** Antique Auto ............... **$25.00**

**Ashtray,** Cameoware, Dainty
Flower patt., pink ........................ **15.00**

**Batter pitcher,** Calico Tulip patt. .. **40.00**

**Cake lifter,** Mallow patt................ **28.00**

**Cake lifter,** Modern Tulip patt. ...... **30.00**

**Cake plate,** Cactus patt. .............. **30.00**

**Cake plate,** Carnivale patt. ........... **25.00**

**Cake plate,** Deco Dahlia patt........ **28.00**

**Casserole,** cov., Red Apple patt.,
9" d.............................................. **75.00**

**Casserole,** cov., stacking-type,
Petit Point I patt. ......................... **55.00**

**Condiment set in rack,** Deco
Dahlia patt., the set ..................... **75.00**

**Cookie jar,** cov., Cameoware,
Dainty Flower patt., blue ............. **58.00**

**Cookie jar,** cov., Modern Tulip
patt., Modern Age shape ........... **60.00**

**Creamer & cov. sugar bowl,**
Cameoware, Dainty Flower
patt., pr...................................... **15.00**

**Creamer & cov. sugar bowl,**
Stone China line, pink engobe,
pr................................................. **20.00**

**Custard cup,** Deco Dahlia patt..... **30.00**

**Custard cup,** Mallow patt. ............ **30.00**

**Mixing bowl,** Ivy Vine patt. ........... **30.00**

**Mixing bowl,** Modern Tulip patt.,
Modern Age shape ..................... **19.00**

**Mug,** child's, Cameoware,
decorated w/elephant & toy
soldier, pink & white.................... **30.00**

**Pie baker,** Calico Tulip patt. ......... **25.00**

**Pie baker,** Modern Tulip patt.,
Modern Age shape ..................... **30.00**

**Pie baker,** Petit Point II patt......... **35.00**

**Pie baker,** Red Apple patt. ........... **35.00**

**Pie plate,** Modern Tulip patt. ......... **8.00**

**Plate,** 7" d., Peacock patt............... **8.00**

**Plate,** 7½" d., Spanish Gold patt... **15.00**

**Plate,** 10" d., Ivy Vine patt............. **18.00**

**Plate,** 10" d., Provincial Tulip
patt., celadon ............................. **12.00**

**Plate,** 10" d., Red Apple patt......... **18.00**

**Plate,** child's, Cameoware, blue
sailboat decoration...................... **10.00**

**Platter,** Coronet patt., blue
engobe........................................ **25.00**

**Platter,** Modern Tulip patt.,
Modern Age shape ..................... **30.00**

**Platter,** Springtime (Magnolia)
patt.............................................. **25.00**

**Range set:** cov. lard jar, salt &
pepper shakers; Deco Dahlia
patt., Skyscraper shape, the set . **70.00**

**Rolling pin,** Cameoware, Dainty
Flower, blue ................................ **80.00**

**Rolling pin,** Modern Tulip patt...... **80.00**

**Rolling pin,** Petit Point Rose patt.. **95.00**

**Serving fork,** Modern Tulip patt. .. **45.00**

**Serving fork,** Swirl shape............. **45.00**

**Serving spoon,** Calico Tulip patt.. **35.00**

**Serving spoon,** Ivy Vine patt. ...... **35.00**

**Serving spoon,** Mallow patt. ........ **35.00**

**Serving spoon,** Petit Point II patt.. **35.00**

**Serving spoon,** Swirl shape......... **40.00**

**Syrup pitcher,** cov., Calico Tulip
patt.............................................. **36.00**

**Syrup pitcher,** cov., Modern
Tulip patt., Modern Age shape.... **30.00**

---

# HARLEQUIN

*The Homer Laughlin China Company,
makers of the popular "Fiesta" pottery
line, also introduced in 1938 a less
expensive and thinner ware which was
sold under the "Harlequin" name. It did
not carry the maker's trade-mark and was
marketed exclusively through F.W.*

*Woolworth Company. It was produced in a wide range of dinnerwares in assorted colors until 1964. Out of production for a number of years, in 1979 Woolworth requested the line be reintroduced using an ironstone body and with a limited range of pieces and colors offered. Collectors also seek out a series of miniature animal figures produced in the Harlequin line in the 1930s and 1940s.*

**Ashtray,** regular style, blue ........ **$40.00**

**Ashtray,** saucer-type, red ............. **90.00**

**Ashtray,** saucer-type, rose ........... **60.00**

**Ashtray,** saucer-type, spruce
green............................................ **45.00**

**Bowl,** 36s, 4½" d., chartreuse....... **25.00**

**Bowl,** 36s, 4½" d., light green....... **33.00**

**Bowl,** 36s, 4½" d., medium green. **50.00**

**Bowl,** 36s, 4½" d., turquoise......... **25.00**

**Bowl,** 5½" d., maroon ................... **10.00**

**Bowl,** oatmeal, 6½" d., light green. **22.00**

**Bowl,** oatmeal, 6½" d., medium
green............................................ **45.00**

**Bowl,** oatmeal, 6½" d., red ........... **25.00**

**Bowl,** oatmeal, 6½" d., yellow....... **20.00**

**Bowl,** individual salad, 7" d.,
chartreuse ................................... **10.00**

**Bowl,** individual salad, 7" d.,
turquoise ..................................... **15.00**

**Bowl,** 9" d., turquoise.................... **15.00**

**Butter dish,** cov., cobalt blue,
½ lb. .......................................... **300.00**

**Butter dish,** cov., ivory, red,
turquoise, or yellow, ½ lb.,
each .......................................... **165.00**

**Butter dish,** cov., light green or
rose, ½ lb., each ....................... **225.00**

**Casserole,** cov., maroon ........... **215.00**

**Casserole,** cov., red ................... **130.00**

**Casserole,** cov., spruce green ... **215.00**

**Casserole,** cov., turquoise............ **55.00**

**Creamer,** individual size, blue ...... **19.00**

**Creamer,** individual size, light
green......................................... **125.00**

**Creamer,** individual size, rose ...... **19.00**

**Creamer,** individual size, spruce
green............................................ **25.00**

**Creamer,** individual size,
turquoise ..................................... **16.00**

**Creamer,** individual size, yellow ... **16.00**

**Creamer,** high lip, blue ............... **375.00**

**Creamer,** novelty, ball-shaped,
light green ................................... **45.00**

**Creamer,** novelty, ball-shaped,
grey............................................. **95.00**

**Cream soup,** handled, light green. **40.00**

**Cream soup,** handled, spruce
green............................................ **40.00**

**Cup,** demitasse, spruce green...... **95.00**

**Cup,** demitasse, turquoise ............ **55.00**

**Cup,** turquoise or yellow, each ....... **8.00**

**Cup & saucer,** demitasse, blue.. **150.00**

**Cup & saucer,** demitasse, light
green............................................ **75.00**

**Cup & saucer,** demitasse,
maroon...................................... **110.00**

**Cup & saucer,** demitasse, red ... **130.00**

**Cup & saucer,** turquoise or
yellow, each ............................... **10.00**

**Egg cup,** single, spruce green...... **35.00**

**Egg cup,** double, blue ................. **16.00**

**Egg cup,** double, grey ................. **25.00**

**Egg cup,** double, turquoise .......... **15.00**

**Egg cup,** double, yellow .............. **15.00**

**Gravy boat,** chartreuse ............... **10.00**

**Gravy boat,** forest green ............. **35.00**

**Marmalade jar,** cov., turquoise... **300.00**

**Nut dish,** individual size,
basketweave interior, light
green......................................... **125.00**

**Nut dish,** individual size,
basketweave interior, rose........ **125.00**

**Pitcher,** 9" h., ball-shaped w/ice
lip, grey ..................................... **100.00**

**Pitcher,** 9" h., ball-shaped w/ice
lip, blue ....................................... **75.00**

**Pitcher,** cylindrical, 22 oz.,
chartreuse ................................... **49.00**

**Pitcher,** cylindrical, 22 oz., grey ... **95.00**

**Pitcher,** cylindrical, 22 oz., spruce
green............................................ **65.00**

Plate, 6" d., grey .............................. 5.00

Plate, 6" d., turquoise or yellow,
each .............................................. 4.00

Plate, 7" d., turquoise...................... 4.00

Plate, 9" d., green ........................... 8.00

Plate, 9" d., maroon ........................ 8.00

Plate, 10" d., grey ......................... 45.00

Plate, 10" d., maroon ................... 55.00

Relish tray, red, yellow & maroon
inserts, blue sides .................... 430.00

Salt & pepper shakers,
chartreuse or spruce green,
each pr......................................... 8.00

Salt & pepper shakers, grey or
maroon, each pr........................... 9.00

Soup plate w/flanged rim,
maroon, 8" d. .............................. 35.00

Soup plate w/flanged rim,
medium green, 8" d..................... 75.00

Spoon rest, turquoise................. 265.00

Sugar bowl, cov., grey ................ 45.00

Sugar bowl, cov., maroon ............ 45.00

Teapot, cov., grey...................... 185.00

Teapot, cov., red........................ 125.00

Tumbler, blue, or spruce green .... 35.00

Tumbler, red................................ 50.00

Tumbler, rose .............................. 75.00

Tumbler, yellow ........................... 32.00

## HARLEQUIN ANIMALS

Model of a cat, maroon ............. 225.00

Model of a cat, yellow ............... 225.00

Model of a duck, maroon........... 145.00

Model of a duck, yellow ............ 195.00

Model of a fish, blue ................. 175.00

Model of a fish, blue inside,
overall gold ................................ 85.00

Model of a fish, yellow .............. 225.00

Model of a lamb, maroon........... 175.00

Model of a lamb, yellow ............ 225.00

Model of a penguin, maroon ..... 145.00

Model of a penguin, yellow ....... 165.00

Salt & pepper shakers, model of
a duck & a penguin, iridescent
blue, pr....................................... 75.00

# HAVILAND

*A Cat-decorated Haviland Plate*

*Haviland porcelain was originated by Americans in Limoges, France, shortly before the mid-19th century and continues in production. Some Haviland was made by Theodore Haviland in the United States during the last World War. Numerous other factories also made china in the city of Limoges. Also see LIMOGES.*

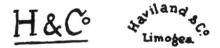

*Haviland Marks*

Bowls, 7⅜" d., 1¼" h., Drop Rose patt., made for Bailey, Banks & Biddle Co., Philadelphia, Pennsylvania, set of 10 (five w/a small nick) ............................... **$875.00**

Butter pats, scalloped round shape, pink floral decoration, set of 6 ............................................. 45.00

Cake plate, open handled, Blank No. 705 ...................................... 45.00

Chocolate set: 8½" h. scallop-based cov. chocolate pot & five cups & saucers; decorated w/h.p. pink, white & yellow roses, 11 pcs. .......................... 450.00

**Chocolate set:** 8¾" h. slender lobed cylindrical cov. chocolate pot w/a scalloped base & six tall gently ribbed flaring cups w/saucers; all decorated w/a soft pastel green shading to ivory ground w/pink touches & highlighted w/tiny pink roses & green leaves around the rims & cover, gold handles, late 19th c., the set ........................................ **650.00**

**Coffeepot,** cov., Moss Rose patt., gold trim ........................... **135.00**

**Dinner service:** eight dinner plates, eight cups & saucers, five bread & butter plates, four soup plates w/flanged rim, creamer & sugar bowl, gravy boat & cov. casserole; Apple Blossom patt., Theodore Haviland, New York, 37 pcs...... **600.00**

**Dinner service:** thirty-six 10¼" d. dinner plates, eighteen 7⅝" d. salad plates, sixteen 6⅝" d. bread & butter plates, eighteen bouillon cups & sixteen underplates, eighteen tea cups & saucers, eighteen coffee cups & seventeen saucers, two cov. sugar bowls, two creamers, two cov. vegetable dishes, two oval 16" l. platters, four 9" l. oval dishes, & two 12⅝" d. round chop plates; all decorated w/a jade green soufflé enamel border between tooled or tracery gilt bands, centered by a gilt monogram, underglaze-brown printed mark "Haviland Limoges, France" beneath a castle emblem, second half 20th c., 189 pcs. ................................... **2,185.00**

**Oyster plate,** five-section, blue & muted colored flowers................ **79.00**

**Pitcher,** tankard, corseted cylindrical body w/scalloped feet, gold rim, feet & handle, decorated w/large white & deep pink roses .................................. **79.00**

**Plate,** 8½" d., h.p. center decoration of white cat w/green eyes, soft blue & beige ground, finely scalloped gold edge (ILLUS. top previous page) ......... **85.00**

**Plate,** 9" d., bird decoration, cobalt ground, gold border & green center, artist-signed ......... **80.00**

**Plates,** dinner, 9½" d., decorated w/roses & embossing, gold trim, No. 350J, set of 12 (three chipped) ..................................... **90.00**

**Plates,** 9¾" d., w/juice well, Drop Rose patt., American Beauty roses around scalloped border of gold, green & gold trim, made expressly for Bailey, Banks & Biddle Co., Philadelphia, Pennsylvania, set of 12......... **2,700.00**

**Platter,** 12¾" l., Moss Rose patt.... **35.00**

**Platter,** 10¼ × 15", oval, w/juice well at each end, Drop Rose patt., made expressly for Bailey, Banks & Biddle Co., Philadelphia, Pennsylvania....... **800.00**

**Soup tureen,** cov., decorated w/pink rose garlands, No. 145 on No. 131 gold blank, 8¼" d., 12" l......................................... **150.00**

*Haviland Vase with Ladies*

**Vase,** 5½" h., 3¾" d., a cylindrical footring supports the wide cylindrical body w/a flattened shoulder to the short rolled neck, decorated around the sides w/oval medallions each featuring a lady in a large hat, tan leaf & red berry swags around the top & base, deep red, tan & black figures & tan bands at the shoulder & base, Charles Field Haviland mark (ILLUS. bottom previous page) .......................... **295.00**

**Vegetable bowl,** cov., oval, white ground decorated w/clusters of small red roses, ribbon finial & handles ..................................... **145.00**

# HEAD VASES

*Baby with Bonnet Head Vase*

*Generally, novice head vase collectors feel all head vases were imported from Japan. There were, however, numerous companies in the United States creating these charming collectibles. Ceramic Arts Studio, Cleminson Clay, DeLee Art, Florence, Royal Haeger, Hull, Morton, Shawnee, Royal Copley, Reliable Glassware and Pottery Company (RELPO), Nelson McCoy, Betty Lou Nichols, National Potteries Corporation (NAPCO) were a few of the USA companies. Of course, there were companies that got their start in the United States and then branched out to Canada, Japan and other countries. There is a wealth of differing head vases from which to choose and printed catalogs and brochures from the companies are not too difficult to locate.*

*A wide range of prices exists for collectors. Mini head vases can be* purchased *sometimes as low as $25, but a Jacqueline Kennedy might sell for $300 and a Marilyn Monroe look-alike could go as high as $1,500. Children carrying open umbrellas or holding telephones are a specialty of their own and many collectors will seek only those particular novelties. The same is true of the animal vases. Some head vases, while identical in clothing, accessories, and features may come in as many as seven or eight different sizes.*

**Baby w/bonnet,** bonnet tied in bow at shoulder on right side, blonde curly hair w/large curl in middle & dropping onto forehead, blue eyes, rosy cheeks, red lips, pale pink bonnet & dress, marked, "Japan," 5¼" h. (ILLUS. previous column) ........................ **$85.00**

**Girl w/blonde hair,** head down, eyes closed, hands in praying position, red long sleeve nightgown, marked "Inarco Cleve. Ohio," Model No. E 778, 5½" h........................................... **75.00**

**Girl w/brown hair in ringlets,** green & white flowers in her hair & green & white dress to match, double strand of pearls, unmarked, 5½" h......................... **70.00**

**Girl w/flower in her brown hair,** one side pulled behind ear & other side curled upward hiding the left ear, brown eyes open, mouth closed, light blue dress, marked "Inarco," 5½" h. .............. **55.00**

*Blonde Girl Head Vase*

*Girl with Scarf Head Vase*

*Lady with Jewelry Head Vase*

**Girl w/hat,** blonde hair, hands up w/palms turned toward face, "P" mark, 3" h. (ILLUS. bottom previous page) ........................... **40.00**

**Girl w/scarf around head & tied at neck,** large descriptive black eyes w/red lips, marked "Japan" underneath a wreath, 4" d., 7¾" h. (ILLUS. above) ............. **180.00**

**Island girl,** hibiscus fastened in black hair over right ear, eyes closed, green sarong draped over left shoulder, marked "Shawnee U.S.A., 896," hard-to-find, 6" h. .................................. **85.00**

**Lady w/blonde hair,** arched eyebrows, eyes open w/a black pancake hat trimmed w/a group of white & gold roses, pearl earrings, & necklace, black dress w/white & gold trim w/a bow in the middle of the trim, Relpo production, 5¾" h. ............ **95.00**

**Lady w/blonde hair,** pearl earrings & necklace, ring on finger, hand near face w/thumb resting on chin, green dress, produced by Rubens Originals, marked "R 482" (ILLUS. top next column) ...................................... **65.00**

*Lady with Hair Bow Head Vase*

**Lady w/blonde hair,** long bangs, eyes closed w/heavy brown eyelashes, single strand pearl necklace, lilac double bow in middle of hair & lilac dress w/narrow ruffled edge, marked "Japan 4127," 5½" h. (ILLUS. bottom above) ............................ **55.00**

*Brown-haired Lady Head Vase*

**Lady w/brown hair,** blue eyes, black earrings, black & white dress w/puffed short sleeves (earrings & dress colors can be green & yellow), marked "P," 6¼" h. (ILLUS.) ........................... **60.00**

**Lady w/heart-shaped blue & white bonnet tied at chin,** head turned slightly, blonde hair, rosy cheeks, blue ruffled off-the-shoulder dress w/one shoulder higher than the other, "Barbie," marked by Ceramic Arts Studio, 7½" h......................................... **165.00**

*Gentleman Head Vase*

**Man w/brown hair,** handlebar mustache, comma eyebrows & eyes, black & white jacket, white shirt, green & white tie (white flower in lapel & yellow tie can be found), marked "P," 6½" h. (ILLUS. bottom previous column) ....................................... **65.00**

# HISTORICAL & COMMEMORATIVE WARES

*Battle of Bunker Hill Plate*

*Numerous potteries, especially in England and the United States, made various porcelain and earthenware pieces to commemorate people, places and events. Scarce English historical wares with American views command highest prices. Objects are listed here alphabetically by title of view.*

*Most pieces listed here will date between about 1820 and 1850. The maker's name is noted in parentheses at the end of each entry.*

**All Souls College - St. Mary's Church & C - Oxford (England) well-and-tree platter,** florals & classical figure vignettes border, dark blue, 20¾" l. (Ridgway)... **$990.00**

**Alms House in the City of New York plate,** floral scroll border, dark blue, 10" d. (Andrew Stevenson)............................... **468.00**

**American Eagle on an Urn pepper pot,** floral border, dark blue, urn-shaped on pedestal foot, 4½" h., Clews (unseen chip on underside of top flange, 'bite' out of rim)................................. **550.00**

**American Poets plate,** round vignette bust portraits of seven American poets in center, dark blue, ca. 1890s, 10" d. (Rowland & Marsellus)............................... **55.00**

**Arms of New York soup plate,** flowers & vines border, spoked wheels equidistant around border, dark blue, impressed "Mayer," 9½" d. (wear, shallow rim flakes & pinpoints on table ring)........................................ **633.00**

**Arms of South Carolina cup plate,** floral border, dark blue, 4" d. (Mayer) ............................ **770.00**

**Ascent to the Capitol - Boston From the Dorchester Heights soup tureen,** cov. w/The Gothic Church, New Haven - Utica, small flowers & moss border, light blue, 15" l., 9½" h., C. Meigh (short hairline off cover ladle hole, shallow chip on finial side, hint of spiders under base)........................................ **825.00**

**Baltimore & Ohio Railroad (Incline) (The) plate,** shell border, dark blue, 9" d., E. Wood (slight wear & few scratches).... **605.00**

**Bank of the United States, Philadelphia plate,** spreadwinged eagles amid flowers & scrolls border, dark blue, 10⅛" d. (Joseph Stubbs).. **605.00**

**Battle of Bunker Hill plate,** battle scene in center, fruit & flowers border, dark blue, ca. 1890s, 10" d., Rowland & Marsellus (ILLUS. bottom previous page)........................ **66.00**

*Castle Garden, Battery Platter*

**Battle of Lake Erie plate,** battle scene in center, fruit & flowers border, dark blue, ca. 1890s, 10" d., (Rowland & Marsellus) .... **66.00**

**Boston From the Dorchester Heights platter,** light blue, small flowers & moss border, 17⅞" l., C. Meigh (faint hairline off the rim)............................................ **413.00**

**Boston State House plate,** floral border, medium blue, 8½" d., Wood (faint scratching) ............. **115.00**

**Boston State House sauce tureen undertray,** floral border, dark blue, 8⅛" l. oval (Rogers) . **825.00**

**Cadmus (so-called) plate,** diorama border, dark blue, 9⅛" d. (unknown maker) ........... **385.00**

**Capitol at Washington (The) plate,** shell border, circular center, dark blue, mismarked "Mount Vernon" on reverse, 6½" d. (E. Wood) ...................... **468.00**

**Castle Garden, Battery, New York platter,** shell border, dark blue, 18⅞" l., Wood (ILLUS. bottom previous page ............ **3,300.00**

**Catholic Cathedral, N.Y. plate,** floral scroll border, dark blue, 6⅜" d., Andrews Stevenson (slight scratching, tiny nick on footring).................................... **660.00**

**Catskill Mountain House, U.S. plate,** flowers & scrolls border, brown, 10⅛" d. (Adams) ........... **330.00**

**Charles Dickens plate,** bust portrait in center, vignette scenes border w/rolled rim, dark blue, ca. 1890s, 10" d. (Rowland & Marsellus)............................... **99.00**

**City Hall, New York plate,** flowers within medallions border, medium blue, Ridgway, minor scratches, 9¾" d. (ILLUS. top next column) ............................ **149.00**

**City Hotel, New York, New York plate,** acorn & oak leaves border, dark blue, 8½" d., Ralph Stevenson................................ **375.00**

*City Hall, New York Plate*

*Commodore MacDonnough's Victory Dish*

**City of Albany, State of New York plate,** shell border, dark blue, 10¼" d., Wood (trace of mellowing on reverse, slight scratching) ................................ **550.00**

**Columbia College, New York plate,** oak leaves & acorns border, dark blue, 6½" d. (Ralph Stevenson and Williams) .......... **385.00**

**Commodore Bainbridge - Commodore Lawrence pitcher,** black transfer-printed bust portrait on each side flanked by warships & name of the officer, pink lustre highlights & borders, 4⅝" h. (some lustre wear)..................................... **1,760.00**

**Commodore MacDonnough's Victory leaf-shaped dish,** shell border, irregular center scene, dark blue, two very small flakes on tips of rim, 6¼" l., E. Wood (ILLUS. bottom this column) .. **2,200.00**

**Commodore MacDonnough's Victory plate,** shell border, irregular center, dark blue, impressed "Wood," 10" d. (rim glaze flakes)............................ **358.00**

**Discovery of America pitcher,** 7½" h., light blue, ca. 1900 (Rowland & Marsellus)............. **275.00**

**Dr. Syntax punch bowl,** pearlware, seven different brown transfer-printed views of Dr. Syntax inside & outside including "Dr. Syntax Returned From His Tour," "Dr. Syntax Bound to a Tree by Highwaymen" & more, floral border, all highlighted in polychrome colors, ca. 1820-40, 10¼" d., 4⅝" h. (invisible restoration to several small rim chips & hairlines off the rim) ..... **935.00**

**Erie Canal Inscription...DeWitt Clinton Eulogy plate,** views of the canalboats & locks border, dark blue, 6⅝" d., unknown maker (light scratching) ............ **440.00**

**Fairmount Near Philadelphia plate,** spreadwing eagle border, dark blue, 10¼" d., Stubbs (some facial scratching & overall mellowing)................................ **176.00**

**Fairmount Near Philadelphia platter,** spreadwing eagle border, dark blue, 20½" l., Stubbs (ILLUS. top next column) ...................... **2,070.00**

**Fairmount Near Philadelphia soup tureen undertray,** spreadwing eagle border, dark blue, 14½" l. oval, Stubbs (old repair on one handle needs reworking) ............................. **1,210.00**

**Famous Musicians & Composers plate,** depiction of nine bust portraits, dark blue, 10" d. (Rowland & Marsellus)....... **85.00**

**Fulton's Steamboat on the Hudson - Cadmus teapot,** cov., boat-shaped w/black transfer-printed oblong ship vignettes on each side, pink lustre line border, 6" h., probably Wood (light flaking at end of spout)........................... **385.00**

*Fairmont Near Philadelphia Platter*

**Great Fire - City of New York - Exchange, New York plate,** fire engines & eagles border, light blue, 10¼" d. (rim chip)............. **248.00**

**Gyrn, Flintshire, Wales (Britain) platter,** fruit & flowers border, dark blue, 17" l., Hall (some severe glaze rubbing on edge) . **605.00**

**Hartford, Connecticut plate,** floral border, brown, 10⅜" d. (Jackson) .................................. **138.00**

**Hospital, Boston plate,** entwined vine border, dark blue, 9" d., R. Stevenson (minor chips, edge roughness, knife marks, staining) .................................... **288.00**

**Lafayette at Franklin's Tomb wash bowl,** floral border, dark blue, 10⅞" d., 4" h., Wood (three large under rim chips, faint 'spider' in base)........................ **605.00**

**Landing of General Lafayette at Castle Garden, New York, 16 August, 1824 cup plate,** floral & vine border, dark blue, 3½" d. (Clews)..................................... **413.00**

**Landing of General Lafayette at Castle Garden, New York, 16 August, 1824 plate,** floral & vine border, dark blue, 6¾" d., impressed "Clews" (short rim hairlines & very minor glaze flakes on edge of rim) ............... **220.00**

**Landing of General Lafayette at Castle Garden, New York, 16 August, 1824 plate,** floral & vine border, dark blue, 10⅛" d., Clews (ILLUS. top next page) ... **330.00**

*Landing of Lafayette Plate*

*Newburgh, Hudson River Platter*

*Landing of the Fathers Plate*

**Landing of General Lafayette at Castle Garden, New York, 16 August, 1824 well & tree platter,** floral & vine border, dark blue, 18¼" l., Clews (few light facial scratches, minute glaze rim flake) ............................... **2,090.00**

**Landing of the Fathers at Plymouth, Dec. 22, 1620 plate,** pairs of birds & scrolls w/four medallions w/ships & inscriptions border, medium dark blue, 6½" d., Wood (light mellowing on reverse).............. **121.00**

**Landing of the Fathers at Plymouth, Dec. 22, 1620 plate,** pairs of birds & scrolls w/four medallions w/ships & inscriptions border, medium blue, light scratching, 10⅛" d., Wood (ILLUS. bottom this column) .................................... **143.00**

**Log Cabin cup & saucer,** handleless, medallions of Maj. Gen'l W. H. Harrison between medallions of urns border, for 1840 presidential campaign, pink, Adams (small chip on rim & base of cup, chip & hairline on saucer) .................................... **1,375.00**

**Marine Hospital, Louisville, Kentucky plate,** shell border, dark blue, 9" d., Enoch Wood (two unseen back rim chips, wear on the face) ..................... **413.00**

**Mitchel & Freeman's China and Glass Warehouse, Chatham Street, Boston plate,** foliage border, dark blue, 10⅛" d. (Adams) .................................... **605.00**

**Mount Vernon, the Seat of the Late General Washington pitcher,** floral border, dark blue, unknown maker, 6¾" h. ................. **1,500.00 to 2,000.00**

**Newburgh, Hudson River platter,** floral border, black, trace of inner rim wear, faint scratching, 15¾" l., Clews (ILLUS. top this column) .......... **413.00**

**Niagara From the American Side soup tureen undertray,** shell border, dark blue, 14⅛" l., Wood (stains, facial scratches). **825.00**

**Octagon Church, Boston (interior) open footed compote,** Exchange, Charleston - Bank Savannah (exterior), flowers within medallions borders, deep rounded & flaring sides w/attached scroll handles, dark blue, 10¼" d., 5" h., Ridgway (areas of light mellowing) ....... **1,980.00**

**Passaic Falls, State of New York sauce tureen,** Hudson River View cover, shell border, dark blue, 8" l., 6⅜" h., Wood (faint line off edge of foot, shallow flake on handles) ...... **1,045.00**

**Pass in The Catskills sauce tureen undertray,** oval, shell border, dark blue, 8" l. (Wood).. **935.00**

**Patrick Henry Addressing the Virginia Assembly plate,** center interior scene, fruit & flowers border, dark blue, ca. 1890s, 10" d. (Rowland & Marsellus) ................................... **66.00**

**Pine Orchard House, Catskill Mountains soup plate,** shell border, circular center, impressed "Wood," 9⅜" d. (minor wear & light scratches) .. **523.00**

**Pittsfield Elm (double transfer) cup plate,** dark blue, impressed mark, 3⅞" d. (Clews) ................ **220.00**

**Residence of the Late Richard Jordan, New Jersey (The) cup & saucer,** handleless, floral border, black, J. Heath & Co. (minor stains & pinpoint flakes). **275.00**

**Residence of the Late Richard Jordan, New Jersey (The) soup plate,** floral border, red, 10¼" d., J.H. & Co. ................... **248.00**

**Sancho Panza at the Boar Hunt soup plate,** six point star w/birds & flowers border, dark blue, 10" d. (Clews).................. **350.00**

**Schuylkill Water Works, Philadelphia teapot,** cov., octagonal, small flowers & moss border, light blue, 8" h., Meigh (trace of interior mellowing) ...... **523.00**

**Seal of the United States pitcher,** flowers & scrolls series w/floral border, seal under the spout, dark blue, 6½" h., Adams (faint hairline across the body)...................................... **1,540.00**

*Table Rock Plate*

**Shannondale Springs, Virginia , U.S. plate,** flowers, shells & scrolls border, red, 8" d., Adams (some reverse crazing) .............. **88.00**

**Skenectady On The Mohawk River soup tureen, cover & undertray,** cover w/"Newport, Rhode Island," & undertray w/"Yale College and State House, New Haven," floral borders, light blue, tureen 13" l., 10" h., undertray 15¾" l., Jackson, the set (minute flake along cover ladle hole)........... **1,430.00**

**State House, Boston leaf-shaped dish,** flowers in medallions border, dark blue, 5" l., Ridgway (chip, few flakes & glaze rubs around rim) ............. **550.00**

**States series cup plate,** three story mansion, small extension, names of the fifteen states in festoons on border, separated by five- or eight-point stars, dark blue, 4⅝" d., Clews (overall light mellowing)................................ **358.00**

**States series platter,** castle w/flag, names of the fifteen states in festoon on border, separated by five- or eight-point stars, dark blue, 12⅞" l., Clews (unseen back chip) ................ **1,210.00**

**Table Rock, Niagara plate,** shell border, dark blue, 10¼" d., Wood (ILLUS. above) .............. **523.00**

*Upper Ferry Bridge Platter*

**Tappen Zee From Greensburg vegetable dish,** open, shell border, dark blue, 8⅞" l. oval (Wood) .................................. **1,650.00**

**Texan Campaign - Battle of Buena Vista sauce tureen,** cov., symbols of war "goddess-type" seated border, light blue, 5¾" h., Anthony Shaw (fine restoration to small rim chip, line off the chip) .............................. **550.00**

**Transylvania University, Lexington plate,** 9" d., shell border, circular center, dark blue, impressed "Wood" (wear & light scratches)......................... **358.00**

**Tunbridge Castle, Surrey (England) basket,** openwork, wild rose border, dark blue, impressed mark, 11½" l. (Andrew Stevenson) .............. **1,320.00**

**Two Sailboats cup plate,** irregular shell border, dark blue, 4¼" d. (Wood)........................... **413.00**

**Union Line plate,** shell border, irregular center, dark blue, 10¼" d. (Enoch Wood & Sons) ... **550.00**

**Upper Ferry Bridge Over the River Schuylkill well-&-tree platter,** spread eagle & floral scrolls border, dark blue, in-the-making shoulder glaze rub, 18¾" l., Stubbs (ILLUS.)........ **1,100.00**

**Upper Ferry Bridge Over the River Schuylkill sauce tureen,** cov., spread eagle & floral scrolls border, dark blue, acanthus leaf handles, floral finial, 8¼" l., 5¾" h., Stubbs (cover w/excellent restoration to chip & crack) ............................ **990.00**

**Valentine (The) plate,** large flowers & scrolls border, dark blue, 9" d. (Clews).................... **350.00**

**View Near Philadelphia (A) soup plate,** floral border, dark blue, underglaze title, 9¾" d. (Davenport) .............................. **424.00**

**View of the Catskill Mountain House, N.Y. plate,** floral border, light blue, 10½" d. (Jackson)..... **440.00**

**Wadsworth Tower cup & saucer,** shell border, dark blue, pr. (Wood) ................................. **605.00**

*Welcome Lafayette Pitcher*

**Washington Standing at His Tomb, Scroll in Hand teapot,** cov., floral border, dark blue, 8" h., Wood (minor chips) ......... **633.00**

**Welcome Lafayette The Nations Guest pitcher,** floral border, bulbous ovoid footed shape w/C-scroll handle, dark blue, transfer a bit blotchy, good restoration to a few cracks off the rim & section of the base, 6¼" h., Clews (ILLUS. above)... **715.00**

**West Point, Military Academy basket,** openwork sides, shell border, dark blue, 11" l. (Wood) ................................... **2,475.00**

**Wilkes Barre, Vale of the Wyoming cup plates,** bunches of moss on a network of moss border, light blue, 4" d., Ridgway, set of 4 ..................... **220.00**

---

# HULL

*This pottery was made by the Hull Pottery Company, Crooksville, Ohio, beginning in 1905. Art Pottery was made until 1950 when the company was converted to utilitarian wares. All production ceased in 1986.*

*Reference books for collectors include* Roberts' Ultimate Encyclopedia of Hull Pottery *by Brenda Roberts (Walsworth Publishing Company, 1992), and* Collector's Guide to Hull Pottery—The Dinnerware Lines *by Barbara Loveless Gick-Burke (Collector Books, 1993).*

*Hull Marks*

**Ashtray,** Butterfly patt., No. B3-7", 7" w. ..................................... **$55.00**

**Bank,** figural pig, pink & blue ........ **95.00**

**Bank,** figural sitting pig, House 'N Garden Line, Mirror Brown glaze **50.00**

**Basket,** Blossom Flite patt., No. T-8", 8¼ × 9½" .......................... **115.00**

**Basket,** Dogwood patt., No. 501-7½", cream & blue, 7½" h. ........ **250.00**

**Basket,** Magnolia Matte patt., No. 10-10½", 10½" h. ...................... **325.00**

**Basket,** Morning Glory patt., No. 62-8", 8" h. ................................. **250.00**

**Basket,** Tokay patt., No. 6-8", 8" h. .............................................. **75.00**

**Basket,** Woodland Gloss patt., No. 9-8¾", 8¾" h. (ILLUS. below).. **80.00**

**Basket,** hanging-type, Woodland Matte patt., pink, No. W12-7½", 7½" h. (manufacturing flaw) ...... **300.00**

**Basket,** Woodland Matte patt., pink, No. W-22-10½", 10½" h. .. **795.00**

*Woodland Gloss Basket*

**Bottle,** liquor, figural, seated elephant, pink, white & yellow, neck for stopper at the top of the head, marked "Leeds, USA," ca. 1939-44, 7¾" h. .......................... **50.00**

**Coaster/spoon rest,** figural Gingerbread Man, grey, 5" h....... **25.00**

**Coaster/spoon rest,** figural Gingerbread Man, tan, 5" h......... **25.00**

**Console set:** 14" d. bowl & pr. of 3½" h. candleholders; Woodland Gloss patt., 3 pcs. .................... **100.00**

**Cookie jar,** cov., House 'N Garden Line, Mirror Brown, 8" h. **125.00**

**Cookie jar,** cov., Little Red Riding Hood patt., round closed basket, floral decals, 13" h. (ILLUS. top next column) ............................ **300.00**

**Cookie jar,** cov., Little Red Riding Hood patt., gold stars on apron, 13" h. ............................ **475.00**

**Cookie jar,** cov., Little Red Riding Hood patt., maroon shoes, gold stars, unusual flowers, 13" h. ......................... **525.00**

**Cornucopia-vase,** Bow-Knot patt., B-5-7½", 7½" h................. **135.00**

**Cornucopia-vase,** Magnolia Gloss patt., No. H-10-8½", 8½" h. (ILLUS. bottom next column) ...................................... **60.00**

**Cornucopia-vase,** Wildflower patt., No. W-7-7½", 7½" h. .......... **65.00**

**Cornucopia-vase,** Woodland Matte patt., pink, No. W2-5½", 5½" h........................................... **75.00**

**Cornucopia-vase,** double, Woodland Matte patt., pink, No. W-23-14", 14" h........................ **525.00**

**Cracker jar,** cov., Little Red Riding Hood patt., 8½" h........... **470.00**

**Creamer,** head pour, Little Red Riding Hood patt. ...................... **625.00**

**Creamer,** tab-handled, Little Red Riding Hood patt. ...................... **500.00**

**Creamer & cov. sugar bowl,** Bow-Knot patt., turquoise & blue, B-21-4" & B-22-4", pr. ...... **400.00**

*Red Riding Hood Cookie Jar*

*Magnolia Gloss Cornucopia-Vase*

**Creamer & cov. sugar bowl,** side-pour, Little Red Riding Hood patt., pr. .......................... **295.00**

**Ewer,** Blossom Flite patt., No. T-13, 13½" ................................ **165.00**

**Ewer,** Bow-Knot patt., No. B-1-5½", 5½" h. ............................... **145.00**

**Ewer,** Butterfly patt., No. B-15, 13½" h....................................... **125.00**

**Ewer,** Ebb Tide patt., No. E-10, 14" h.......................................... **225.00**

*Woodland Gloss Flowerpot*

*Hull Swan Planter*

**Ewer,** Iris patt., No. 401-8", 8" h.. **145.00**

**Ewer,** Magnolia Gloss patt., No.
H-3-5½", 5½" h. ........................... **42.00**

**Ewer,** Magnolia Matte patt., No.
14-4½", 4½" h. ............................ **58.00**

**Ewer,** Rosella patt., No. R-11-
7" R, 7" h. .................................... **50.00**

**Ewer,** Sueno Tulip patt., pink, No.
109-33-8", 8" h. .......................... **225.00**

**Ewer,** Sueno Tulip patt., pink, No.
109-33-13", 13" h. ...................... **400.00**

**Ewer,** Woodland patt., No. W-6,
6½" h. .......................................... **75.00**

**Flower frog,** figural, model of a
hippopotamus, Novelty Line,
green .......................................... **60.00**

**Flowerpot w/attached saucer,**
Woodland Gloss patt., pink, No.
W-11- 5¾", 5¾" h.
(ILLUS. above) ......... **100.00 to 130.00**

**Jardiniere,** Woodland Matte patt.,
pink, No. W7-5½", 5½" h........... **150.00**

**Jardiniere,** Sueno Tulip patt.,
pink, No. 115-33-7", 7" h. .......... **325.00**

**Lavabo & base,** Butterfly patt.,
No. B-24 B-25, w/original
hanger, 16" h. ........................... **150.00**

**Lamp,** table model, Little Red
Riding Hood patt. ................... **2,350.00**

**Lamps,** Orchid patt., matte finish,
10" h., pr. .............................. **1,200.00**

**Match box,** wall-type, Little Red
Riding Hood patt. ...................... **400.00**

**Mustard jar, cover & spoon,**
Little Red Riding Hood patt.,
the set ...................................... **425.00**

**Pitcher,** 8" h., Little Red Riding
Hood patt. ................. **275.00 to 300.00**

**Pitcher,** milk, Little Red Riding
Hood patt. ................................. **375.00**

**Planter,** figural, model of a frog,
Imperial Line .............................. **60.00**

**Planter,** figural, model of a kitten,
No. 61, 7½" ................................. **30.00**

**Planter,** figural, model of a kitten
with spool, No. 89, 6" h. .............. **50.00**

**Planter,** figural, model of a
monkey, crouching position,
Novelty Line, 5½" h. .................... **50.00**

**Planter,** model of a swan w/head
up, No. 80, 1951, 6" l. (ILLUS.
above) ........................................ **26.00**

**Planter,** Woodland Matte patt.,
pink, No. W19-10½", 10½" l. ...... **140.00**

**Salt & pepper shakers,** Little Red
Riding Hood patt., 3½" h., pr. ....... **125.00**

**Salt & pepper shakers,** Little
Red Riding Hood patt., 5" h., pr. **195.00**

**Serving plate,** figural
Gingerbread Man, House 'N
Garden Line, Mirror Brown,
10 × 10" ..................................... **35.00**

**Serving tray,** three-compartment,
Butterfly patt., B23-11½",
11½" l. ....................................... **125.00**

**Sugar bowl,** cov., standing figure,
Little Red Riding Hood
patt. ........................................... **675.00**

*Hull Bow-Knot Tea Set*

*Red Riding Hood Crawling Sugar*

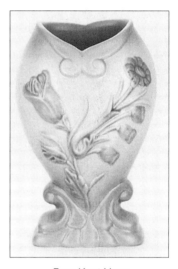

*Bow-Knot Vase*

**Sugar bowl,** cov., crawling-style, Little Red Riding Hood patt., w/floral decals (ILLUS.)............. **475.00**

**Teapot,** cov., Bow-Knot patt., turquoise & blue, B-20-6", 6" h.. **300.00**

**Teapot,** cov., Little Red Riding Hood patt. ................................. **375.00**

**Teapot,** cov., Serenade patt., No. T-14 ........................................ **100.00**

**Teapot,** cov., Waterlily patt., No. L-18-6", pink & green, 6" h........ **200.00**

**Tea set:** cov. teapot, open sugar bowl & creamer; Bow-Knot patt., 3 pcs. (ILLUS. top).................... **700.00**

**Tea set:** cov., teapot, creamer & cov. sugar bowl; Magnolia Gloss patt., Nos. H-20-6½", H-21-3¾" & H-22-3¾", 3 pcs.................... **150.00**

**Vase,** 4¼" h., Open Rose patt., No. 127-4¼"............................... **60.00**

**Vase,** 4¾" h., Magnolia patt., No. 13-4¾" ...................................... **48.00**

**Vase,** 4¾" h., Open Rose patt., No. 130-4¾"............................... **65.00**

**Vase,** 6" h., Sueno Tulip patt., pink, No. 103-33-6" ................... **200.00**

**Vase,** 6" h., Sueno Tulip patt., pink, No. 106-33-6½" ............... **110.00**

**Vase,** 6¼" h., Camellia patt., No. 122-6¼" ..................................... **45.00**

**Vase,** 6¼" h., Magnolia Gloss patt., No. H-4-6¼" ...................... **40.00**

**Vase,** 6¼" h., Wildflower patt., No. 11-6¼"................................. **75.00**

**Vase,** 6½" h., Bow-Knot, blue & cream, No. B-3-6½" (ILLUS. bottom this column) ................. **180.00**

**Vase,** 6½" h., Poppy patt., pink & blue, No. 607-6½" .................... **150.00**

**Vase,** 6½" h., Rosella patt., No.
R6-6½"........................................ **35.00**

**Vase,** 6½" h., Woodland Gloss
patt., No. W-4-6½"....................... **30.00**

**Vase,** 7" h., Crab Apple patt.,
yellow....................................... **125.00**

**Vase,** 7½" h., Wildflower patt.,
No. 8-7½".................................... **65.00**

**Vase,** 7½" h., Woodland Matte
patt., pink, No. W17-7½"........... **250.00**

**Vase,** 8" h., Sueno Tulip patt.,
pink, No. 105-33-8".................. **185.00**

**Vase,** 8½" h., Bow-Knot patt., No.
B7-8½"..................................... **210.00**

**Vase,** 8½" h., Dogwood patt., No.
515-8½".................................... **125.00**

**Vase,** 8½" h., Magnolia Gloss
patt., two-handled, No. H-9-
8½".............................................. **95.00**

**Vase,** double bud, 8½" h.,
Woodland Matte patt., pink, No.
W15-8½".................................... **150.00**

**Vase,** 9" h., Mardi Gras patt......... **95.00**

**Vase,** 9½" h., Wildflower patt.,
No. W-12-9½"............................ **175.00**

**Vase,** 10" h., Sueno Tulip patt.,
pink, No. 100-33-10"................. **300.00**

**Vase,** 10½" h., Poppy patt., blue,
No. 607-10½" (ILLUS. top next
column)..................................... **325.00**

**Vase,** 10½" h., Wildflower patt.,
pink & blue, No. W-14-10½"..... **185.00**

**Vase,** 11" h., Ebb Tide patt.,
figural fish base, No. E-7-11".... **100.00**

**Vase,** 12" h., Tokay patt., pink &
green, No. 12.............................. **70.00**

**Wall plaque,** pierced to hang,
round, Bow-Knot patt., blue, No.
B28-10", 10" d.......................... **985.00**

**Wall plaque,** pierced to hang,
round, Bow-Knot patt., pink,
yellow & blue, No. B28-10",
10" d...................................... **1,375.00**

**Wall pocket,** model of a duck,
No. 540...................................... **45.00**

**Wall pocket,** model of a pitcher,
Bow-Knot patt., blue & green,
No. B-26-6", 6" h....................... **230.00**

*Hull Poppy Vase*

**Wall pocket,** Woodland Matte
patt., pink, No. W13-7½",
7½" h........................................ **175.00**

**Window box,** Woodland Matte
patt., pink, No. W14-10", 10" l... **125.00**

# HUMMEL FIGURINES

*Auf Wiedersehen with Cap*

The Goebel Company of Oeslau,
Germany, first produced these porcelain
figurines in 1934 having obtained the
rights to adapt the beautiful pastel

*sketches of children by Sister Maria Innocentia (Berta) Hummel. Every design by the Goebel artisans was approved by the nun until her death in 1946. Though not antique, these figurines with the "M.I. Hummel" signature, especially those bearing the Goebel Company factory mark used from 1934 and into the early 1940s, are being sought by collectors though interest may have peaked some years ago.*

*Crown Mark*

*Full Bee Mark*

*Last Bee Mark*

**Accordion Boy,** 1972-79, 5¼" . **$130.00**

**Adoration,** 1940-57, 6¼" h......... **220.00**

**Adoration,** 1956-68, 6¼" h......... **270.00**

**Angelic Sleep candleholder,**
1940-56, 3½ × 5"...................... **200.00**

**Angel Serenade,** part of Nativity
set, 1963-71, 3" h........................ **55.00**

**Angel with Accordion,** 1963-71,
2½" h........................................... **30.00**

**Angel with Bird font,** 1934-49,
2¾ x 3½".................................. **160.00**

**Angel with Lute,** 1963-71,
2½" h. .......................................... **42.00**

**Apple Tree Boy,** 1956-68, 4" h. ... **85.00**

**Apple Tree Boy,** 1956-68, 6" h. . **175.00**

**Apple Tree Boy,** 1972-79, 6" h. . **135.00**

**Apple Tree Boy table lamp,**
1940-56, 7½" h. ........................ **595.00**

**Apple Tree Boy & Apple Tree
Girl book ends,** 1956-68,
5¼" h., pr. ................................. **250.00**

**Apple Tree Girl,** 1956-68, 4" h. ... **105.00**

**Apple Tree Girl,** 1963-71, 4" h. ..... **70.00**

**Apple Tree Girl,** 1956-68, 6" h. ... **178.00**

**Apple Tree Girl table lamp,**
1972-79, 7½" h. ........................ **210.00**

**Auf Wiedersehen,** w/cap, 1940-
57, 5¼" h. (ILLUS. bottom
previous page) ....................... **1,800.00**

**Auf Wiedersehen,** 1956-68,
5¼" h........................................... **125.00**

**Auf Wiedersehen,** 1979-90,
5¼" h........................................... **162.00**

**Baker,** 1940-57, 4¾" h. ............... **150.00**

**Baker,** 1956-68, 4¾" h. ............... **125.00**

**Band Leader,** 1940-57, 5¼" h. .... **220.00**

**Band Leader,** 1972-79, 5¼" h. .... **110.00**

**Barnyard Hero,** 1963-71, 4" h. ...... **95.00**

**Barnyard Hero,** 1972-79, 4" h. ...... **90.00**

**Barnyard Hero,** 1963-71,
5¾" h........................................... **163.00**

**Begging His Share,** 1940-57,
5½" h........................................... **500.00**

**Begging His Share,** 1956-68,
5½" h........................................... **190.00**

**Be Patient,** 1956-68, 4¼" h. ....... **120.00**

**Be Patient,** 1963-71, 4¼" h. ....... **100.00**

**Be Patient,** 1979-90, 6¼" h. ....... **195.00**

**Big Housecleaning,** 1972-79,
3¹⁵⁄₁₆" h. .................................... **189.00**

**Bird Duet,** 1940-57, 4" h............. **165.00**

**Bird Duet,** 1972-79, 4" h............... **91.00**

**Bird Watcher,** 1979-90, 5" h. ..... **144.00**

**Birthday Serenade,** old mold,
1956-68, 4¼" h. ........................ **295.00**

**Birthday Serenade,** 1963-71,
4¼" h........................................... **125.00**

**Birthday Serenade,** old mold,
1963-71, 4¼" h. ........................ **250.00**

*Boots*

*Chick Girl*

**Birthday Serenade,** 1979-90,
4¼" h......................................... **114.00**

**Blessed Event,** 1963-71, 5½" h.. **220.00**

**Bookworm,** 1956-68, 4" h. ......... **175.00**

**Bookworm,** 1972-79, 4" h. ......... **140.00**

**Bookworm book ends,** 1956-68,
5½" h., pr. ................................. **325.00**

**Boots,** 1940-57, 5¼" h.
(ILLUS. above) ......... **200.00 to 225.00**

**Boots,** 1972-79, 5¼" h................ **132.00**

**Boy with Horse candleholder,**
1956-68, 3½" h. ........................... **38.00**

**Boy with Toothache,** 1972-79,
5½" h......................................... **105.00**

**Brother,** 1956-68, 5½" h............. **125.00**

**Brother,** 1972-79, 5½" h............. **100.00**

**Builder,** 1963-71, 5½" h. ............ **125.00**

**Busy Student,** 1963-71, 4¼" h..... **88.00**

**Busy Student,** 1979-90, 4¼" h... **104.00**

**Candlelight candleholder,** 1963-
71, 6¾" h................................. **120.00**

**Chick Girl,** 1940-57,
3½" h. (ILLUS. top next
column)..................... **175.00 to 200.00**

**Chick Girl,** 1956-68, 3½" h......... **110.00**

**Chimney Sweep,** 1956-68, 4" h. .. **83.00**

**Chimney Sweep,** 1940-57,
5½" h......................................... **250.00**

**Chimney Sweep,** 1972-79,
5½" h.......................................... **85.00**

*Close Harmony*

**Close Harmony,** 1963-71, 5½" h.
(ILLUS. bottom) ........................ **150.00**

**Confidentially,** 1972-79, 5½" h. .. **145.00**

**Congratulations,** 1956-68, no
socks, 6" h. ............................... **148.00**

**Congratulations,** 1956-68,
socks, 6" h. ............................... **132.00**

**Coquettes,** 1956-68, 5¼" h. ....... **175.00**

**Crossroads,** 1972-79, 6¾" h...... **264.00**

**Culprits,** 1934-49, 6¼" h. ........... **550.00**

**Culprits,** 1940-57, 6¼" h. ........... **195.00**

**Culprits,** 1940-57, eyes open,
6¼" h. ........................................ **325.00**

**Culprits,** 1979-90, 6¼" h. ........... **189.00**

**Dealer display plaque,** 1972-79,
4 × 5½" ..................................... **113.00**

**Doctor,** 1956-68, 4¾" h. ............. **100.00**

**Doll Mother,** 1940-57, 4¾" h. ..... **425.00**

**Doll Mother,** 1956-68, 4¾" h. ..... **170.00**

**Easter Greetings,** 1972-79,
5½" h. ....................................... **132.00**

**Eventide,** 1940-57, 4¾" h. ........... **360.00**

**Eventide,** 1956-68, 4¾" h. ........... **300.00**

**Farm Boy,** 1972-79, 5" h. ........... **115.00**

**Farm Boy & Goose Girl book
ends,** 1956-68, 6" h., pr. ........... **300.00**

**Favorite Pet,** 1972-79, 4¼" h. .... **158.00**

**Feeding Time,** 1934-49, 4¼" h... **700.00**

**Feeding Time,** 1956-68, 4¼" h... **120.00**

**Feeding Time,** 1940-57, 5¾" ...... **225.00**

**Feeding Time,** 1963-71, 5¾" h... **138.00**

**Festival Harmony,** 1940-57,
8" h. ....................................... **1,000.00**

**Festival Harmony,** 1956-68,
10¾" h. ..................................... **695.00**

**Flower Madonna,** colored, 1956-
68, 8¼" h. ................................. **158.00**

**Flower Vender,** 1972-79, 5¼" h.. **150.00**

**For Father,** 1940-57, 5½" h. ....... **230.00**

**For Mother,** 1963-71, 5¼" h. ...... **100.00**

**For Mother,** 1972-79, 5¼" h. ...... **105.00**

**Friends,** 1972-79, 10¾" h. ........... **725.00**

**Girl with Doll,** 1963-71, 3½" h...... **42.00**

**Globe Trotter,** 1956-68, 5" h. ..... **138.00**

**Globe Trotter,** 1972-79, 5" h. ..... **124.00**

**Going to Grandma's,** 1979-90,
4¾" h. ....................................... **174.00**

**Going to Grandma's,** 1972-79,
6" h. ......................................... **280.00**

**Going to Grandma's,** 1979-90,
6" h. ......................................... **259.00**

**Good Friends,** 1956-68, 4" h. .... **140.00**

**Good Friends,** 1972-79, 4" h. .... **129.00**

*Happiness*

**Good Friends table lamp,** 1956-
68, 7½" ..................................... **495.00**

**Good Hunting,** 1963-71, 5¼" h.. **190.00**

**Good Hunting,** 1972-79, 5¼" h.. **162.00**

**Good Shepherd,** 1956-68,
6¼" h. ....................................... **150.00**

**Good Shepherd,** 1972-79,
6¼" h. ....................................... **135.00**

**Goose Girl,** 1934-49,
4" h. ......................... **225.00 to 250.00**

**Goose Girl,** 1956-68, 4" h. ......... **140.00**

**Goose Girl,** 1956-68, 4¾" h. ...... **150.00**

**Goose Girl,** 1972-79, 7½" h. ...... **250.00**

**Happiness,** 1940-57, 4¾" h.
(ILLUS. above) ......................... **145.00**

**Happiness,** 1979-90, 4¾" h. ......... **85.00**

**Happy Birthday,** 1956-68,
5½" h. ....................................... **138.00**

**Happy Days,** 1956-68, 4¼" h. .... **113.00**

**Happy Days,** 1940-57, 5¼" h. .... **250.00**

**Happy Days,** 1979-90, 5¼" h. .... **195.00**

**Happy Pastime,** 1940-57,
3¼" h. ....................................... **265.00**

**Happy Pastime,** 1956-68,
3¼" h. ....................................... **100.00**

**Happy Traveler,** 1956-68, 8" h... **265.00**

**Hear Ye, Hear Ye,** 1940-57, 5" h. **200.00**

**Hear Ye, Hear Ye,** 1972-79, 5" h. **100.00**

**Hear Ye, Hear Ye,** 1934-49, 6" h. **365.00**

**Hear Ye, Hear Ye,** 1972-79, 6" h. **165.00**

**Hear Ye, Hear Ye,** 1979-90,
7½" h.......................................... **240.00**

**Heavenly Angel,** 1940-57,
4¼" h.......................................... **145.00**

**Heavenly Angel,** 1956-68, 4¼" h. **75.00**

**Heavenly Angel,** 1972-79, 6" h. . **125.00**

**Heavenly Angel,** 1956-68,
8¾" h.......................................... **350.00**

**Hello,** 1940-57, 6¼" h. ................ **240.00**

**Hello,** 1956-68, 6¼" h. ................ **138.00**

**Hello,** 1979-90, 6¼" h. ................ **110.00**

**Herald Angels candleholder,**
1956-68, 2¼ × 4"........................ **159.00**

**Home From Market,** 1940-57,
4¾" h.......................................... **160.00**

**Home From Market,** 1972-79,
4¾" h.......................................... **96.00**

**Homeward Bound,** 1963-71,
5" h............................................. **215.00**

**Joyful,** 1940-57, 4" h. ................. **130.00**

**Joyful,** 1956-68, 4" h. ................... **90.00**

**Joyful,** 1972-79, 4" h. ................... **77.00**

**Joyful candy box,** 1972-79,
6¼" h.......................................... **120.00**

**Joyous News,** 1934-49, w/white
face, 4¼ × 4¾" ........................ **1,800.00**

**Joyous News candleholder,**
angel w/lute, 1956-68, 2¾" h. ..... **42.00**

**Just Resting,** 1940-57,
3¾" h. ...................... **125.00 to 150.00**

**Just Resting,** 1972-79, 3¾" h. ... **150.00**

**Just Resting,** 1956-68, 5" h. ...... **275.00**

**Just Resting,** 1963-71, 5" h. ...... **170.00**

**Kiss Me,** without socks, 1963-71,
6" h............................................. **140.00**

**Kiss Me,** with socks, 1963-71,
6" h............................................. **425.00**

**Kiss Me,** without socks, 1972-79,
6" h............................................. **195.00**

**Latest News,** 1940-57, 5¼" h..... **290.00**

**Latest News,** 1972-79, 5¼" h..... **195.00**

**Let's Sing,** 1940-57, 3¼" h......... **125.00**

**Let's Sing,** 1963-71, 3¼" h........... **65.00**

**Let's Sing,** 1972-79, 3¼" h.......... **70.00**

**Let's Sing,** 1963-71, 3⅞" h......... **108.00**

**Let's Sing,** 1979-90, 3⅞" h.......... **98.00**

**Letter to Santa Claus,** 1963-71,
7" h............................................. **350.00**

**Letter to Santa Claus,** 1972-79,
7" h............................................. **158.00**

**Little Band,** 1963-71, 3 × 4¾"..... **188.00**

**Little Band music box,** 1963-71,
4¾ × 5"...................................... **350.00**

**Little Bookkeeper,** 1963-71,
4¾" h. ...................... **300.00 to 350.00**

**Little Cellist,** 1956-68, 6" h. ....... **138.00**

**Little Cellist,** 1979-90, 6" h. ....... **138.00**

**Little Cellist,** 1956-68, 8" h. ....... **315.00**

**Little Cellist,** 1972-79, 8" h. ....... **180.00**

**Little Drummer,** 1963-71, 4¼" h. . **75.00**

**Little Fiddler,** 1956-68, 4¾" h. ... **130.00**

**Little Fiddler,** 1972-79, 4¾" h. ... **105.00**

**Little Fiddler,** 1956-68, 6" h. ...... **150.00**

**Little Fiddler,** 1972-79, 6" h. ...... **115.00**

**Little Fiddler,** 1934-49, 11" h. . **1,900.00**

**Little Gardener,** 1956-68, 4¼" h. . **75.00**

**Little Gardener,** oval base, 1956-
68, 4¼" h.................................... **95.00**

**Little Goat Herder,** 1956-68,
4¾" h.......................................... **120.00**

**Little Goat Herder,** 1963-71,
4¾" h.......................................... **100.00**

**Little Helper,** 1956-68, 4¼" h ....... **80.00**

**Little Helper,** 1972-79, 4¼" h. ...... **72.00**

**Little Hiker,** 1979-90, 4¼" h. ........ **72.00**

**Little Hiker,** 1934-49, 5½" h. ...... **475.00**

**Little Hiker,** 1940-57, 5½" h. ...... **225.00**

**Little Hiker,** 1979-90, 5½" h. ...... **115.00**

**Little Pharmacist,** 1963-71, 6" h. **125.00**

**Little Pharmacist,** "Rizinusol,"
1963-71, 6" h. .......................... **225.00**

**Little Scholar,** 1956-68, 5½" h... **100.00**

**Little Scholar,** 1972-79, 5½" h... **115.00**

**Little Sweeper,** 1940-57, 4½" h. **135.00**

**Little Sweeper,** 1956-68, 4½" h. .. **88.00**

**Little Tailor,** 1972-79, 5½" h. ..... **130.00**

**Little Tailor,** 1979-90, 5½" h. ..... **125.00**

**Lost Sheep,** 1963-71, 4½" h. ....... **75.00**

*Lullaby Candleholder*

**Lost Sheep,** 1940-57, 5½" h. ..... **215.00**

**Lost Sheep,** 1956-68, 5½" h. ....... **90.00**

**Lullaby candleholder,** 1972-79,
3¼ × 5" ...................................... **80.00**

**Lullaby candleholder,** 1972-79,
6 × 8" (ILLUS. above) ............... **235.00**

**Madonna,** praying, standing, no
halo, w/color, 1956-68 ............... **40.00**

**Mail Coach plaque,** 1956-68,
4½ × 6¼" ................................. **150.00**

**Mail is Here (The),** 1940-57,
4¼ × 6¼" ................................. **660.00**

**March Winds,** 1940-57, 5" h. .... **300.00**

**March Winds,** 1956-68, 5" h. ..... **100.00**

**March Winds,** 1979-90, 5" h. ....... **94.00**

**Max & Moritz,** 1963-71, 5¼" h.... **120.00**

**Meditation,** 1979-90, 4¼" h. ......... **91.00**

**Meditation,** 1972-79, 5" h. .......... **129.00**

**Meditation,** 1934-49, 5¼" h. ....... **425.00**

**Meditation,** 1956-68, 5¼" h.
(ILLUS. bottom next column) .... **168.00**

**Merry Wanderer,** 1956-68,
4¼" h. ......................................... **95.00**

**Merry Wanderer,** 1979-90,
4¼" h. ......................................... **81.00**

*Meditation*

**Merry Wanderer,** 1956-68,
4¾" h. ......................................... **130.00**

**Merry Wanderer,** 1972-79,
6½" h. ......................................... **165.00**

**Merry Wanderer,** 1972-79,
30" h. ...................................... **8,000.00**

*Out of Danger*

*School Girls*

**Merry Wanderer plaque,** 1963-
71, 4¾ × 5⅛" .............................. **83.00**

**Mother's Darling,** 1940-57,
5½" h...................................... **425.00**

**Mother's Helper,** 1956-68, 5" h.. **125.00**

**Mountaineer,** 1963-71, 5¼" h. ... **125.00**

**Mountaineer,** 1972-79, 5¼" h. ... **100.00**

**Not For You,** 1963-71, 6" h. ....... **125.00**

**Out of Danger,** 1956-68, 6¼" h.
(ILLUS. above).......................... **188.00**

**Out of Danger,** 1979-90, 6¼" h.. **174.00**

**Photographer,** 1940-57, 4¾" h. . **315.00**

**Photographer,** 1963-71, 4¾" h. . **145.00**

**Playmates,** 1956-68, 4" h. .......... **115.00**

**Playmates,** 1979-90, 4" h. .......... **100.00**

**Playmates,** 1956-68, 4½" h. ....... **165.00**

**Postman,** 1956-68, 5¼" h........... **210.00**

**Postman,** 1979-90, 5¼" h........... **132.00**

**Prayer Before Battle,** 1940-57,
4¼" h...................................... **120.00**

**Prayer Before Battle,** 1956-68,
4¼" h...................................... **110.00**

**Puppy Love,** 1956-68, 5" h. ....... **239.00**

**Puppy Love,** 1972-79, 5" h. ....... **150.00**

**Retreat to Safety,** 1940-57,
4" h......................................... **200.00**

**Retreat to Safety,** 1956-68,
4" h......................................... **113.00**

**Retreat to Safety,** 1956-68,
5½" h...................................... **220.00**

**Retreat to Safety,** 1972-79,
5½" h...................................... **165.00**

**Run-A-Way,** 1972-79, 5¼" h. ..... **138.00**

**School Boy,** 1934-49. 4" h. ........ **160.00**

**School Boy,** 1956-68, 4" h. .......... **95.00**

**School Boy,** 1940-57, 5½" h. ..... **215.00**

**School Boy,** 1956-68, 5½" h. ..... **115.00**

**School Boy,** 1972-79, 5½" h. ..... **100.00**

**School Boys,** 1963-71, 7½" h. ... **675.00**

**School Girl,** 1972-79, 4¼" h......... **90.00**

**School Girl,** 1979-90, 4¼" h......... **84.00**

**School Girl,** 1940-57,
5¼" h. ...................... **150.00 to 175.00**

**School Girl,** 1956-68, 5¼" h....... **129.00**

**School Girls,** 1963-71, 7½" h.
(ILLUS. above).......................... **800.00**

**Sensitive Hunter,** 1956-68,
4¾" h...................................... **126.00**

**Sensitive Hunter,** 1956-68,
5½" h...................................... **196.00**

**Sensitive Hunter,** 1956-68,
7½" h...................................... **285.00**

**Serenade,** 1956-68, 4¾" h............ **85.00**

**She Loves Me,** 1940-57, 4¼" h.. **210.00**

**She Loves Me,** 1979-90, 4¼" h.. **126.00**

**Shepherd's Boy,** 1940-57, w/two
lambs, 5½" h. ............................ **325.00**

*Spring Dance*

**Shepherd's Boy,** 1956-68,
5½" h........................................ **138.00**

**Signs of Spring,** 1940-57, 4" h. . **247.00**

**Signs of Spring,** 1963-71, 4" h. . **123.00**

**Signs of Spring,** 1956-68, 5" h. . **182.00**

**Silent Night candleholder,** 1956-
68, 4¾ × 5½" ........................... **188.00**

**Singing Lesson,** 1956-68,
2¾" h........................................ **90.00**

**Singing Lesson ashtray,** 1940-
57, 3½ × 6¼" ........................... **175.00**

**Singing Lesson ashtray,** 1972-
79, 3½ × 6¼" ............................ **85.00**

**Sister,** 1963-71, 4¾" h................. **75.00**

**Sister,** 1956-68, 5¾" h............... **125.00**

**Skier,** 1940-57, 5¼" h. **150.00 to 200.00**

**Skier,** 1956-68, 5¼" h. (wooden
poles) ..................................... **160.00**

**Smart Little Sister,** 1963-71,
4¾" h........................................ **180.00**

**Soldier Boy,** 1963-71, 6" h......... **113.00**

**Soloist,** 1956-68, 4¾" h............... **85.00**

**Spring Cheer,** 1940-57, 5" h. ..... **210.00**

**Spring Cheer,** yellow dress,
1956-68, 5" h. .......................... **150.00**

**Spring Dance,** 1972-79, 6½" h.
(ILLUS. above)......................... **350.00**

**Stitch in Time,** 1972-79,
6¾" h........................................ **173.00**

**Stormy Weather,** 1934-49,
6¼" h........................................ **695.00**

**Stormy Weather,** 1972-79,
6¼" h........................................ **295.00**

**Street Singer,** 1940-57,
5" h........................................... **210.00**

**Street Singer,** 1956-68,
5" h........................................... **126.00**

**Strolling Along,** 1934-49,
4¾" h........................................ **495.00**

**Strolling Along,** 1956-68,
4¾" h. ...................................... **175.00**

**Supreme Protection,** 1979-90,
9" h........................................... **250.00**

**Surprise,** 1934-49, 5½" h. .......... **595.00**

**Surprise,** 1956-68, 5½" h. .......... **220.00**

**Telling Her Secret,** 1940-56,
5¼" h........................................ **450.00**

**Telling Her Secret,** 1956-68,
5¼" h........................................ **197.00**

**Telling Her Secret,** 1963-71,
5¼" h........................................ **150.00**

**Telling Her Secret,** 1940-57,
6¾" h........................................ **450.00**

**To Market,** 1956-68, 4" h. ........... **105.00**

**To Market,** 1956-68, 5½" h. ........ **165.00**

**Trumpet Boy,** 1956-68, 4¾" h...... **85.00**

**Umbrella Boy,** 1963-71, 5" h.
(ILLUS. left, top next page) ....... **325.00**

**Umbrella Boy,** 1956-68,
8" h. ......................... **825.00 to 875.00**

**Umbrella Girl,** 1940-57, 4¾" h. .. **630.00**

**Umbrella Girl,** 1956-68, 4¾" h.
(ILLUS. right, top next page) ..... **381.00**

**Umbrella Girl,** 1963-71, 8" h. ..... **795.00**

**Valentine Gift,** 1972-79, 5½" h.
(Special Club Edition No. 1)...... **248.00**

**Village Boy,** 1956-68, 4" h. ......... **75.00**

**Village Boy,** 1972-79, 4" h. ......... **60.00**

**Village Boy,** 1972-79, 5" h. ......... **70.00**

**Village Boy,** 1940-57,
6" h. ......................... **225.00 to 250.00**

**Village Boy,** 1972-79, 6" h. ........ **110.00**

**Volunteers,** 1940-57, 5" h. ......... **260.00**

**Volunteers,** 1956-68, 5" h. ......... **143.00**

**Waiter,** 1956-68, 6" h................. **138.00**

*Umbrella Boy & Umbrella Girl*

*Wash Day*

**Waiter,** Rhine Wine label, 1956-
68, 7" h..................................... **195.00**

**Wall vase Boy,** 1956-68, 4½ ×
6¼"......................................... **400.00**

**Wall vase Girl,** 1956-68,
4½ × 6¼" ................................. **400.00**

**Wash Day,** 1963-71, 5¾" h.
(ILLUS. bottom) ........ **150.00 to 200.00**

**Wayside Devotion,** 1940-57,
7½" h....................................... **435.00**

**Wayside Devotion,** 1972-79,
7½" h....................................... **270.00**

**Wayside Harmony,** 1956-68,
3¾" h....................................... **100.00**

**Wayside Harmony,** 1940-57,
5" h.......................................... **295.00**

**Wayside Harmony lamp,** 1956-
68, 9½" h.................................. **160.00**

**Weary Wanderer,** 1963-71, 6" h.. **125.00**

**Whitsuntide,** 1979-90, 7¼" h. .... **198.00**

**Worship,** 1940-57, 5" h. ............. **135.00**

**Worship,** 1956-68, 13" h. ........... **950.00**

# IMARI

*This is a multicolor ware that originated in Japan, was copied by the Chinese, and imitated by the English and European potteries. It was decorated in overglaze enamel and underglaze-blue. Made in Hizen Province and Arita, much of it was exported through the port of Imari in Japan. Imari often has brocade patterns. Since contemporary Imari-type wares are available on today's market, a collector must take care when purchasing to assure the piece is not modern.*

**Bowl,** 5"d., twelve-sided, deep
upright sides decorated on the
interior w/alternating oblong
cartouches w/scroll & floral
designs in orange & green on

white & framed by dark blue alternating w/narrow rectangular panels in dark orange w/white scroll designs, seal mark, ca. 1860 ......................................... **$88.00**

**Bowl,** 7⅜" d., 'Black Ship' patt., cartouches of figures & ships in the typical palette, late 19th c. .. **575.00**

**Bowl,** 8¾" d., geometric designs alternating w/figural panels in a typical palette, 19th c. ............... **374.00**

**Charger,** round, the center decorated w/a large round reserve decorated w/a large orange Phoenix bird perched on a fence corner w/green & orange blossoms & leaf sprigs scattered behind, the wide outer border composed of alternating orange triangular panels w/white scroll decoration & rectangular bordered dark blue panels w/scrolled border bands & centering small four-lobed scenic reserves, ca. 1865, 14½" d........ **275.00**

**Charger,** round, cartouches of figures between a seashell field, central foliate decoration, typical palette, 19th c., 18½" d. ............ **460.00**

**Plate,** 9" d., round w/lightly scalloped rim, decorated w/a large shaped triangular reserve across the center in orange leafy scrolls on white centered by a blue & orange pot holding orange blossoms w/green leaves, the border w/dark blue segments decorated w/small white blossoms & scrolling gold vines, ca. 1830......................... **110.00**

**Plate,** 10" d., scalloped & fluted rim, alternating wide panels decorated w/orange leafy scrolls & Oriental cartouches & narrow panels w/blue grounds & orange geometric & floral designs, ca. 1840 ................................... **165.00**

**Plates,** 10" d., fluted internally & externally, the center w/a round reserve of stylized dark blue & orange designs bordered by a white scalloped band within wide

border bands, the inner band w/three long panels w/stylized tree landscapes on a white ground & divided by double blue bars, the narrow outer border band in alternating bands of dark orange & blue w/various geometric designs, ca. 1825, pr.................................................. **550.00**

**Platter,** 15½" l., oval, scalloped sides, the center w/a scalloped oval reserve w/a stylized floral arrangement beside a bouquet of flowers, the wide outer border composed of alternating panels of orange, white & green blossoms on a white ground & dark blue & orange panels w/stylized white blossom decoration, underglaze-blue seal mark, ca. 1835 ......................... **275.00**

**Platter,** 18" d., decorated w/alternating panels of figures & foliage on a trelliswork ground, late 19th c. ............................... **431.00**

**Temple jar,** cov., a high-shouldered body w/vertical ribbing, the domed cover w/a foo dog finial, decorated overall w/panels of birds among flowers in underglaze-blue & iron-red enamel, 19th c., 19" h. .............. **805.00**

**Umbrella stand,** cylindrical, decorated w/the typical palette of iron-red & blue w/bird & floral designs, late 19th c., 24" h........ **690.00**

**Vase,** 8" h., ovoid body w/a short flaring neck, the body decorated overall w/large orange blossoms & blue vining leaves, geometric border bands at the neck & base, ca. 1830 ......................... **138.00**

**Vase,** 10" h., pear-shaped, a continuous scene of a pheasant among flowering prunus & chrysanthemums, in underglaze-blue, iron-red, green & blue enamels w/traces of gilt, a lappet border below, 19th c. ..... **690.00**

**Vase,** 10" h., trumpet-shaped w/a widely flared rim, oblong scenic panels & lobed floral panels

*Handsome 19th Century Imari Vases*

against a dark blue ground w/a wide orange band w/stylized white florals up one side, top & base bands in orange w/white Oriental designs & the top rim band w/alternating dark blue & orange & white & orange panels, early 19th c. ............................. **264.00**

**Vase,** 12½" h., tall baluster-form body w/a slender neck & a widely flaring fluted neck, the sides w/figural panels framed by a dark blue ground w/colorful stylized florals, ca. 1860 .......... **220.00**

**Vases,** 9" h., handled, paneled decoration in typical color palette, ca. 1835, pr. ................. **605.00**

**Vases,** 27½" h., a bulbous ovoid lower body tapering to a tall cylindrical neck w/a widely flaring & flattened serrated rim, molded S-scroll handles flanking the neck, the neck painted w/a tall oblong floral panel & the body w/a cartouche-shaped figural panel in typical colors against an ivory white ground, late 19th c., pr. (ILLUS. above) ................. **1,725.00**

# IRONSTONE

*The first successful ironstone was patented in 1813 by C.J. Mason in England. The body contained iron slag incorporated with the clay. Other potters imitated Mason's ware and today much hard, thick ware is lumped under the term ironstone. Earlier it was called by various names, including graniteware. Both plain white and decorated wares were made throughout the 19th century. Tea Leaf Lustre ironstone was made by several firms in England and America.*

## GENERAL

**Cheese keeper,** cov., a triangular base w/a tall conforming cover, decorated w/blue transfer-printed floral designs, 19th c... **$219.00**

**Cheese keeper,** cov., round base w/molded rim, cylindrical domed cover & button finial, Imari style design, impressed "Ironstone," 12" d., overall 10" h. (stains, crazing & wear w/old glaze flakes around finial)................... **770.00**

*An Early Ironstone Dinner Service*

**Creamer,** "gaudy" decoration, cobalt blue, red & green, serpent handle, "Mason's" mark ............ **260.00**

**Cup & saucer,** handleless, paneled sides, "gaudy" Urn patt., mid-19th c. (minor flaking & small rim chip on saucer) .......... **105.00**

**Cup & saucer,** handleless, "gaudy" strawberry decoration w/flowers on saucer (mismatched, stains & cup w/hairline) ................................ **165.00**

**Cups & saucers,** handleless, decorated w/black transfer-printed Vincennes patt., marked "John Alcock, Cobridge," 6 sets (minor damage) ........................ **253.00**

**Dinner service:** eleven 9¼" d. soup plates, nine 10¼" d. soup plates, twenty-five 10¾" d. plates, seven 9¼" d. plates, eight oval platters ranging from 10¾" to 20¾" l., cov. soup tureen, cov. sauce tureen w/underplate, two cov. vegetable dishes, footed fruit compote, two 10¼" l. oval vegetable bowls, six shaped serving dishes ranging from 10" to 11" l., one 7" l. gravy boat, two 5¾" l. shaped dishes & four coffee cups; each piece decorated w/puce floral transfer-printed designs w/orange & blue enamel trim, by Hicks & Meigh,

ca. 1830, various damages & some light staining, the set (ILLUS. of part) ...................... **4,025.00**

**Pitcher,** 5¼" h., octagonal w/a bulbous base below a gently flaring wide neck w/scalloped rim, serpent-form handle, black transfer-printed design of a fierce flying dragon around the lower body & neck both highlighted in green enamel, green & black on the handle, black "Mason's" mark, mid-19th c. ................................. **176.00**

**Pitcher,** 10" h. including hound-handle, relief-molded scene of woman sitting, flanked by four dogs, section of house in background, white ground w/dark flowing blue at top rim & base & top & bottom half of figural hound dog handle, Burleigh, Staffordshire, England ...................................... **425.00**

**Pitcher,** 12½" h., footed ovoid body tapering to tall cylindrical neck w/long arched handle from mid-section of body to rim, decorated w/brown transfer-printed Yeddo patt. ...................... **61.00**

**Plaques,** pierced to hang, rectangular, black transfer-printed scenes of boxers "Langan" & "Spring" w/black self-frames, 6" w., 7⅜" h., pr.

(damage w/stains, chips, hairlines & old repair) ............... **330.00**

**Plate,** 9⅞" d., "gaudy" strawberries & flowers decoration, impressed "Thos Walker" (minor stains) .............. **275.00**

**Plate,** 10¼" d., "gaudy" elaborate floral decoration .......................... **75.00**

**Plates,** 10¼" d. & 9½" d., decorated w/black transfer-printed Vincennes patt., marked "John Alcock, Cobridge," four 10¼" & eight 9½"d., 12 pcs....... **413.00**

**Platter,** 15⅜" l., oblong w/wide notched corners, the deep-welled center transfer-printed w/a design of a large Oriental landscape w/a temple, lake & trees, stylized Oriental designs around the rim, blue & white, 19th c. ...................................... **248.00**

**Platter,** 18½" l., octagonal, cobalt blue Oriental decoration, marked "Batavia, Imperial Stone" & impressed "Oriental Stone," 19th c. ...................................... **165.00**

**Platter,** 25" l., "gaudy" floral border w/gold trim (minor wear & gold touch-up repair) ................ **385.00**

**Sauce tureen,** cov., blue transfer-printed Oriental scene, molded handles & figural finial, Mason's, 6½" l ........................................ **138.00**

**Sauce tureens,** cov., a round tapering double-pedestal base supporting a wide half-round lobed bowl w/molded scroll handles, the high domed & lobed cover w/a pointed florette finial, decorated in the Oriental style w/the famille rose palette depicting trelliswork, Chinese figures & gilded foliage, England, mid-19th c., restorations, 8" h., pr. (ILLUS. of one, top next column) .......... **431.00**

**Soup tureen,** cov., blue transfer-printed Oriental scene, molded in handles & figural finial, marked "Nanking, Stone China," 13" l. (wear, stains & hairlines, lid repair) ................................. **138.00**

*Ornate Ironstone Sauce Tureen*

**Soup tureen,** cov., oval, footed, flaring sides w/molded handles, domed cover w/molded finial, brown transfer-printed floral decoration, impressed crescent mark w/monogram & "& Sons" & impressed English registry mark, 14" l ........................................... **83.00**

**Soup tureen set:** tureen, cover & 13¾" l. undertray & six soup bowls; black transfer-printed floral decoration, impressed "Copeland," the set (bowls w/minor stains & one w/hairline) ................................. **468.00**

**Sugar bowl,** cov., Gothic-style footed octagonal body w/scroll handles & florette finial, "gaudy" feathered scroll design around base & cover, ca. 1850, 8" h. (very minor chips & hairline on underside of finial) ................... **314.00**

## TEA LEAF IRONSTONE

**Apple bowl,** scalloped rim, Alfred Meakin ...................................... **650.00**

**Baker,** oval, Chinese Shape, Anthony Shaw.......................... **160.00**

**Baker,** oval, 1856 Fan Shape, Anthony Shaw, 6 x 7½"............ **130.00**

**Boston egg cup,** Alfred Meakin (professionally repaired small rim chip) ................................... **275.00**

**Bowl,** fruit, 9" d., scalloped rim, Anthony Shaw.......................... **220.00**

**Bowl,** 10" d., Chelsea patt., J. Wedgwood (some surface wear) .......................................... **225.00**

**Brush box,** cov., long rectangular form, Pagoda Shape, Burgess (professional small rim chip repair) ........................................ **275.00**

**Butter dish,** cov. & liner, Cable patt., Anthony Shaw .................. **270.00**

**Butter dish, cover & liner,** Favorite Shape, Grindley .......... **160.00**

**Butter dish,** cover & liner, Simple Square patt., J. Wedgwood (rim roughness on cover, base pitted) ........................................ **120.00**

**Cake plate,** open-handled, Bamboo patt., Alfred Meakin ...... **70.00**

**Chamber pot,** cov., Lily of the Valley patt., Anthony Shaw ....... **625.00**

**Chamber pot,** Maidenhair Fern patt., Wilkinson (no cover) ........ **175.00**

**Compote,** open, Simple Square patt., Red Cliff, ca. 1960s ......... **120.00**

**Creamer,** child's, Rondeau patt., Davenport (professionally repaired inside spout chip)........ **600.00**

**Creamer,** Simple Pear Shape, Alfred Meakin (slight potting roughness) ................................ **185.00**

**Creamer & cov. sugar bowl,** Chinese Shape, Red Cliff, ca. 1960s, pr. ................................. **210.00**

**Cup & saucer,** handleless, Lily of the Valley patt., Anthony Shaw . **100.00**

**Cup & saucer,** handled, cone-shaped, Thomas Furnival (lightweight, potting flaw in saucer) ........................................ **40.00**

**Cup & saucer,** handled, Square Ridged shape, Red Cliff, ca. 1960s ......................................... **35.00**

**Cup & saucer,** handleless, squatty shape, Alfred Meakin ..... **70.00**

**Cup plate,** Rondeau patt., Davenport ................................ **110.00**

**Dish,** side, oval, Mellor, Taylor, 4¾ x 6¾" ..................................... **35.00**

**Dish,** square, Scalloped Rim Shape, Alfred Meakin, 7" w......... **65.00**

**Gravy boat,** Cable patt., Thomas Furnival ...................................... **70.00**

**Gravy boat,** Cable patt., unmarked .................................... **50.00**

**Gravy boat,** Crewel patt., Alfred Meakin ..................................... **140.00**

**Gravy boat,** Simple Square patt., J. Wedgwood .............................. **50.00**

**Mixing bowl,** Kitchen Kraft line by Homer Laughlin, gold lustre, ca. 1930s, 10⅜" d., 5½" h. (some interior design wear) .................. **55.00**

**Mug,** child's, Anthony Shaw........ **400.00**

**Mush bowl,** Alfred Meakin............ **90.00**

**Mustache cup & saucer,** Cable patt., Anthony Shaw (glaze & lustre wear) ................. **950.00**

**Pie plate,** Kitchen Kraft line, Home Laughlin, gold lustre, ca. 1930s ................................... **40.00**

**Pitcher,** 7" h., gold Tea Leaf decoration, Wick China Co. ........ **50.00**

**Pitcher,** milk, 7½" h., Hanging Leaves Shape, Anthony Shaw.. **475.00**

**Pitcher,** wash-type, 12½" h., Niagara Fan Shape, Anthony Shaw (tight medium hairline near lip) ...................................... **425.00**

**Plates,** 9" d., Acanthus patt., Johnson Bros., set of 4 .............. **75.00**

**Plates,** 9½" d., Chinese Shape, Anthony Shaw, set of 6 (some glaze wear) .............................. **150.00**

**Platter,** 8 x 10¾", rectangular w/rounded corners, Alfred Meakin ........................................ **35.00**

**Posset cup,** footed, Tea Leaf inside the cup, attributed to Davenport ................................. **105.00**

**Relish dish,** Peerless patt., Edwards .................................... **110.00**

**Sauce tureen, cover, ladle & undertray,** Empress patt., Micratex by Adams, ca. 1960s, the set (small nick on ladle, finial repaired) ................................... **340.00**

**Sauce tureen, cover, ladle & undertray,** Square Ridged patt., Red Cliff, ca. 1960s, the set...... **170.00**

**Service tray,** Bullet patt., Anthony Shaw, 6¼ x 9¾".......................... **70.00**

**Service tray,** oval, Cable patt., Anthony Shaw, 12" l.................. **105.00**

*Cable Pattern Tea Leaf Vegetable Dish*

*Chinese Shape Tea Leaf Shaving Mug*

**Shaving mug,** Basketweave patt., Anthony Shaw (two small base chips) .............................. **450.00**

**Shaving mug,** Cable patt., Anthony Shaw .......................... **170.00**

**Shaving mug,** Chinese Shape, Anthony Shaw (ILLUS. bottom) .. **95.00**

**Shaving mug,** Erie Shape, gold lustre, Wick China Co. (worn lustre, two tiny pinpoint marks) . **150.00**

**Shaving mug,** Fish Hook patt., Alfred Meakin (two glaze cracks in base) ..................................... **135.00**

**Shaving mug,** Plain Round patt., Anthony Shaw .......................... **210.00**

**Shaving mug,** Scroll patt., Alfred Meakin ..................................... **180.00**

**Shaving mug,** Square Ridged patt., attributed to J. Wedgwood ........................... **250.00**

**Sugar bowl,** cov., child's, gold Tea Leaf, Mellor, Taylor ........... **160.00**

**Sugar bowl,** cov., Bamboo patt., Alfred Meakin ............................. **40.00**

**Sugar bowl,** cov., Cable patt., Anthony Shaw ............................. **90.00**

**Teapot,** cov., Acanthus patt., Johnson Bros. (glaze crack) ..... **325.00**

**Teapot,** cov., Beaded Handle patt., East End Pottery ............. **180.00**

**Teapot,** cov., Fig Cousin patt., pink & copper lustre, Davenport (minor spout roughness) ............................... **500.00**

**Tea set,** child's, gold lustre, Mellor, Taylor, 12 pcs. ............. **800.00**

**Toothbrush vase,** Fish Hook patt., Alfred Meakin .................. **275.00**

**Toothbrush vase,** w/drain hole, Anthony Shaw .......................... **220.00**

**Toothbrush vase,** cov., Polonaise Shape, Edge Malkin (¼" base rim flake) ................... **400.00**

**Vegetable dish,** cov., rectangular, Bamboo patt., Alfred Meakin, 6 x 9" ................ **100.00**

**Vegetable dish,** cov., rectangular, Basketweave patt., Anthony Shaw, 6¾ x 11¼"........ **200.00**

**Vegetable dish,** cov., oval, Cable patt., Anthony Shaw, 7 x 10" (ILLUS. top previous page)....... **175.00**

**Vegetable dish,** cov., rectangular, Favorite Shape, Grindley, 11" l. (bottom wear) ... **150.00**

**Washbowl & pitcher,** Lion's Head patt., Mellor, Taylor, 2 pcs. (small handle chip, rim roughness on bowl) ................. **325.00**

**Waste bowl,** Chinese Shape, Anthony Shaw (tiny interior bull's-eye) ................................... **80.00**

## TEA LEAF VARIANTS

**Coffeepot,** cov., Fanfare Shape, Tobacco Leaf patt., Elsmore & Forster ..................................... **550.00**

**Creamer,** child's, Paneled Grape Shape, Chelsea Grape lustre decoration, unmarked, 3½" h.... **220.00**

**Creamer,** Embroidered Chelsea patt., copper lustre band, Burgess...................................... **80.00**

**Creamer,** Fanfare Shape, Tobacco Leaf patt., Elsmore & Forster (small spout chip) ......... **230.00**

**Cup & saucer,** handleless, Ceres Shape, lustre trim, Elsmore & Forster (lightweight) .................... **80.00**

**Cup & saucer,** handleless, Laurel Wreath patt., lustre decoration, Elsmore & Forster ..................... **115.00**

**Cup & saucer,** handleless, Portland Shape, Morning Glory patt., Elsmore & Forster (some crazing) ...................................... **80.00**

**Cuspidor,** round w/lion head side openings, Tobacco Leaf patt., attributed to Elsmore & Forster . **650.00**

**Gravy boat,** Gothic Shape, lustre band, E. Walley.......................... **60.00**

**Gravy boat,** Wrapped Sydenham Shape, Lustre Scallops patt., E. Walley.................................. **160.00**

**Pitcher,** 6¼" h., Wheat-in-the-Meadow Shape, Lustre Rose patt., Powell & Bishop (small rim chip) ................................... **350.00**

**Pitcher,** 8" h., Grape Octagon Shape, Pinwheel patt., unmarked................................... **230.00**

**Pitcher,** 9¾" h., Gothic Shape, greenish lustre band, E. Walley .. **60.00**

**Platter,** 9" l., oval, Oak Leaf patt., Mayer......................................... **55.00**

**Platter,** 9¼ x 12⅞", rectangular, Heavy Square Shape, Teaberry patt., Clementson (lustre & glaze wear) ........................................ **150.00**

**Platter,** 14" l., oval, Fanfare Shape, Tobacco Leaf patt., Elsmore & Forster...................... **80.00**

**Platter,** 14" l., rectangular, Gothic Shape, lustre band decoration, E. Walley................................... **40.00**

**Platter,** 14" l., Portland Shape, Morning Glory patt., Elsmore & Forster ..................................... **120.00**

**Platter,** 12 x 15½", rectangular, Classic Gothic Shape, Livesley & Powell, lustre band decoration . **43.00**

**Soup plate w/flanged rim,** Laurel Wreath patt., lustre trim, Elsmore & Forster, 6⅞" d......... **200.00**

**Sugar bowl,** cov., Embroidered Chelsea patt., copper lustre band, Burgess............................ **90.00**

**Sugar bowl,** cov., Fanfare Shape, Tobacco Leaf patt., Elsmore & Forster..................... **240.00**

**Sugar bowl,** cov., Golden Scroll patt., Powell & Bishop, gold lustre .......................................... **95.00**

**Sugar bowl,** cov., Portland Shape, Morning Glory patt., Elsmore & Forster..................... **225.00**

**Teapot, cov.,** Embroidered Chelsea patt., copper lustre band, Burgess.......................... **150.00**

**Teapot,** cov., Gothic Full Paneled Shape, Teaberry patt., attributed to Jacob Furnival (professional rim chip repair on cover) .......... **470.00**

**Teapot,** cov., Niagara Shape, Pomegranate patt., E. Walley ... **400.00**

**Waste bowl,** Gothic Shape, lustre band decoration, E. Walley......... **70.00**

**Waste bowl,** Plain Round Shape, Teaberry patt., Clementson (rim roughness, surface wear) ......... **125.00**

# JASPER WARE
## (Non-Wedgwood)

*Adams Cracker Jar*

*Schafer & Vater Jam Pot*

*Jasper ware is fine-grained exceedingly hard stoneware made by including barium sulphate in the clay and was first devised by Josiah Wedgwood, who utilized it for the body of many of his fine cameo blue-and-white and green-and-white pieces. It was subsequently produced by other potters in England and Germany, notably William Adams & Sons, and is in production at the present. Also see WEDGWOOD - JASPER and SCHAFER & VATER.*

**Cracker jar,** cov., bulbous barrel-shaped, white relief dancing classical figures w/scarves around the body below deep white relief floral swags on a dark blue ground, silver plate rim, cover & twisted bail handle, marked by Adams, 19th c., 5" d., 7" h. (ILLUS. above) ............... **$175.00**

**Jam pot,** cov., scalloped rim on a waisted cylindrical body, inset domed cover w/spoon notch & button finial, white relief classical figures of two ladies on front & back, medium blue ground, white floral & scroll design on cover & white finial, marked by Schafer & Vater, 3¾" d., 5¼" h. (ILLUS. top next column) ............ **95.00**

*Cupid & Target Plaque*

**Plaque,** pierced to hang, round, white relief figures of Venus & Cupid on green ground, 4" d. ....... **40.00**

**Plaque,** pierced to hang, round, white relief figure of Cupid holding bow & hat in outstretched hands, a target on a tree in the background has a heart bull's-eye w/an arrow through it, floral & leafy scroll border on green ground, Germany, late 19th c., 5⅜" d. (ILLUS. bottom this column) ....... **65.00**

*Autumn Leaf French Baker*

## JEWEL TEA AUTUMN LEAF

*Though not antique this ware has a devoted following. The Hall China Company of East Liverpool, Ohio, made the first pieces of Autumn Leaf pattern ware to be given as premiums by the Jewel Tea Company in 1933. The premiums were an immediate success and thousands of new customers, all eager to acquire a piece of the durable Autumn Leaf pattern ware, began purchasing Jewel Tea products. Though the pattern was eventually used to decorate linens, glasswares and tinware, we include only the Hall China Company items in our listing.*

*Jewel Tea Autumn Leaf Mark*

*Autumn Leaf Gravy & Undertray*

*Autumn Leaf Aladdin Teapot*

**Bean pot,** one-handled, 2¼ qt. . **$600.00**

**Bowl,** fruit, 5½" d. .......................... **6.00**

**Cake plate,** 9½" d. .......... **15.00 to 25.00**

**Creamer** ........................................ **8.00**

**Drip jar,** cov. ............................... **18.00**

**French baker,** swirled soufflé-
style, 2 pt. (ILLUS. top) .............. **85.00**

**Gravy boat & undertray,** 2 pcs.
(ILLUS. middle) .......................... **35.00**

**Mixing (or utility) bowl,** nest-
type, "Radiance," 3 qt. ............... **25.00**

**Mug,** conical, 10 oz. ...................... **55.00**

**Pitcher w/ice lip,** ball-type,
5½ pt. ......................................... **85.00**

**Sugar bowl,** cov. .......................... **12.00**

**Teapot,** cov., w/tea strainer,
Aladdin shape, complete
(ILLUS. bottom previous
page)........................................... **65.00**

**Vegetable bowl,** open, round,
9" d............................................. **110.00**

**Warmer,** teapot-type, oval upright
form w/pierced holes................. **195.00**

---

# KAY FINCH CERAMICS

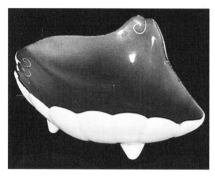

*Kay Finch Shell-shaped Bowl*

Kay Finch along with her husband,
Braden, opened Kay Finch Ceramics in
1939 in Corona del Mar, California. An
extremely talented and dedicated artist,
Finch is more well known for her animals
than any of her other creations. Dogs
were a favorite of hers and can be found
as figurines, decorating trays, trinket
boxes, ashtrays, planters, plates and other
pieces. Ideas seemed endless for Finch's
creativity. Even in the early days, Kay's
ceramics were expensive and have
continued to be so today. During a period
of production, Kay personally trained
twenty-five decorators who assisted her.
Braden died in 1963 and the business
ceased. Kay used her energies for the good
of dog breeding shows.

In the mid-1970s, Freeman-McFarlin,
another California company, hired Kay to
create a set of dog figurines which was
later followed with other Finch animal
designs. These were done in a gold-leaf
treatment and marked in block letters
with the Kay Finch name and model
numbers in the 800s. However, not all
Freeman-McFarlin 800 numbers indicate
a Finch creation. Freeman-McFarlin had
previously purchased Kay's molds and
the working relationship lasted until
about 1980. Kay Finch died on June 21,
1993 at the age of 89.

*Kay Finch Marks*

**Bowl,** 4" l., 2¾" h., shell-shaped,
three feet, scalloped rim, ivory
exterior, dark green interior, ca.
1939-1945, stamp mark "Kay
Finch California," Model No. 510
(ILLUS.) .................................... **$75.00**

**Bowl,** swan-shaped, chartreuse
glaze, No. 4956........................ **190.00**

**Candleholder,** figure of "Scandie"
girl w/round candle support on
her head, pale pink body, light
blue accents & trim, 5¼" h. ....... **150.00**

**Cup,** child's, figural cat's head ...... **75.00**

**Figure of a bride,** black hair
w/pink flower, head bent
downward, white swirling long
dress w/pink accents, blue &
pink flowers bouquet w/three
blue ribbons trailing down the
gown, elbow length white
gloves, Model No. 201, 6½" h.
(ILLUS. right, top next page)..... **245.00**

*Kay Finch Bride & Groom Figures*

**Figure of a child,** "P.J.," standing, brown hair in pigtails tied w/big bows, head slightly tilted to left, white ground w/blue accents, Model No. 5002, 5" h.. **165.00**

**Figure of a "Godey" woman,** standing, head w/hat slightly turned & lowered to left, cape across shoulders, hands just below waist & in a muff, basic glazes of white, green, pink, rose & grey, Model No. 122, 9½" h......... **135.00**

**Figure of a groom,** standing w/legs slightly apart, black hair, mustache, shoes & jacket w/flower in lapel, grey trousers, Model No. 204, 6½" h. (ILLUS. left, above) .................. **245.00**

**Figure of a "Scandie" girl,** standing in long white dress w/blue apron & scarf tied around her blonde hair, Model No. 126, 5¼" h......... **125.00**

**Figures of Sage & Maiden,** each on a base, No. 4852-55, pr. ...... **275.00**

**Model of a bear,** No. 4847, 5" h. .. **175.00**

**Model of a bird,** "Mrs. Dove," gold-leaf treatment, Freeman-McFarlin item introduced in 1977, Model No. 804, 8½" l., 5½" h......... **55.00**

**Model of a cat,** "Hannibal," 10¼" h......... **625.00**

**Model of a dog,** Shih Tzu, gold-leaf treatment, marked w/block letters, Freeman-McFarlin piece, Model No. 837, 10" h. .............. **385.00**

**Model of an elephant,** seated, white w/pink inside ears, Model No. 4804, 4½" h. ....... **140.00**

**Model of an elephant,** "Popcorn," Model No. 192, 6¾" h. ............. **325.00**

**Model of a hen,** yellow & green ... **90.00**

**Model of a hippo,** standing w/head up & mouth open, bow tied around neck, pink body w/polka dots & pastel accents, Model No. 5019, 5¾" h. ........... **400.00**

**Model of a lamb,** kneeling, ears out, pink body, white & dark pink accents, Model No. 136, 2½" l., 2¼" h......... **85.00**

**Model of an owl,** "Hoot,"
standing, ears up, ruffled
feathers, pastel green & lilac on
pink body, black eyes & nose,
Model No. 187, 8½" h. .............. **125.00**

**Model of an owl,** "Toot,"
standing, ears up, ruffled
feathers, pastel green & tan over
white body, Model No. 188,
companion piece to "Hoot,"
6¾" h......................................... **100.00**

**Model of a penguin,** "Polly,"
white body w/pastel blue, green
& yellow w/darker green, Model
No. 467, 4¾" h. ......................... **200.00**

**Model of a pig,** "Winkie," pink
w/blossom decoration, Model
No. 185, 3¾" h. ......................... **125.00**

**Model of Mr. Bird,** matte
teakwood, Model No. 454 .......... **95.00**

**Model of Mrs. Bird,** matte
teakwood, Model No. 453 .......... **75.00**

**Model of a rabbit,** "Cottontail,"
Model No. 152 ........................... **95.00**

**Models of lambs,** kneeling,
Model No. 136, 2¼" h., pr. ........ **125.00**

**Models of a rooster & a hen,**
Butch & Biddy, Model Nos. 176
& 177, pr. .................................. **225.00**

**Mug,** figural Missouri Mule, yellow
glaze, 5" h. ................................. **55.00**

**Nativity group,** iridescent barn
w/gold trim outside, green gloss
on inside bottom, brown gloss
straw, & blue sky, Model No.
4952, can also be hung as a
wall display, marked underglaze,
"Kay Finch California," iridescent
white w/gold trim, Jesus in a
manger w/gold trim on top of
manger, iridescent kneeling
angel in prayer, iridescent
standing white angel w/gold trim,
barn, 6" l., 6½" h., Jesus in
manger, 1¼" h., kneeling angel,
1½" h., standing angel, 2¼" h.,
set of 4 (ILLUS. top next
column) ..................................... **150.00**

**Planter,** baby's block, Baby's
First from California line,
6½" h......................................... **165.00**

*Kay Finch Nativity Set*

*Kay Finch Bear Planter*

**Planter,** "Baby book," pink baby
in diaper w/left leg & arm raised
& leaning against an open book,
in relief flower decoration on
book, marked "Baby's First from
California," Model No. B5143,
6½" h......................................... **115.00**

**Planter,** model of a bear seated,
white gloss w/pink ears, eyes &
paws, Model No. 4906, 5¾" h.
(ILLUS. bottom) ........................ **285.00**

**Trinket box,** heart-shaped, bird
perched on lid, deep green box
w/royal blue bird, Model No.
B5051, 2½" h. ........................... **135.00**

**Vase,** 7¼" h., 5¼" w., straight
sides, light & dark green & light

& dark brown leaves overall except plain green on recessed ¾" base, marked "Kay Finch California" .................................. **75.00**

**Wall plaque,** figural, boxer dog, rounded corners, one of many from the Parade of Champions set, Model No. 4955, 4¾" sq....... **55.00**

**Wall pocket,** Santa face, white beard, red mouth, pink cheeks, black eyes & red cap on right side extending to tip of beard, holly sprig on forehead at edge of cap, Model No. 5373, 9½" h......................................... **375.00**

Same wall pocket w/"Merry Xmas" in gold script at bottom center of beard.......................... **400.00**

---

# KEELER, BRAD

*Keeler Kitten in Basket*

*In 1952 Brad Keeler, a talented creator and modeler working in the field of art (particularly ceramics), died at the age of 39. He has left a legacy for future collectors who are beginning to recognize his enormous talents. At first, the Keeler family used their home garage in Glendale, California to open a small studio and it was there that Brad, at the age of 26, created hand-decorated birds. Riding on the success of his bird line, Brad Keeler leased a small amount*

*of space from Evan Shaw who had taken special interest in Keeler's birds, so much so that he included them in his American Pottery Company line. In 1946, Keeler struck out on his own with Shaw continuing to help him. Among the lines Brad Keeler produced over the years, his bird line is a favorite among collectors today. This is understandable because they were done in a variety of sizes, shapes and glazes. Many joined soft muted tones of green, pink or tan with more vibrant glazes. Pheasants, flamingos, herons, blue jays, ducks, peacocks and others were quick sellers.*

*He also created a well-known lobster dinnerware using the Ming Dragon Blood glaze which he and Andrew Malinovsky, Jr. developed. The lobster line is a large one including chip and dip sets, serving bowls, large divided bowls with a full-bodied lobster serving as the divider, and soup bowls with lids. Many collectors like Keeler's whimsical, cute figurines and animals. It must have also been true when Keeler created his Pryde & Joy line. A trait of this line is the 'stitching' scattered in various places over the pieces as if they are being held together with string or thread.*

*When Brad Keeler had his fatal heart attack he was building a large factory in San Juan Capistrano and there was every reason to believe that, with his talent and the success he had already achieved, his products could out-perform even the imports that were streaming into the United States. Almost all Keeler products are marked in some fashion. There was a Brad Keeler label and an American Pottery label; in-mold mark with "Brad Keeler" and a model number; a harder-to-find copyright symbol with "B.B.K. made in U.S.A." stamp on small items or on outside designers' work. (Each designer used their initials to designate their decorating talents).*

BRAD KEELER
MADE IN U.S.A.
87

*In-Mold Mark*

Brad Keeler
W     25

*Incised Mark*

269
© CMK
MADE IN
U.S.A.

*Stamped Mark*

HANDDECORATED
Brad Keeler
ART WARES
LOS ANGELES CALIF

*All-Gold Sticker*

**Bowl,** 6½" d., 4½" h., white gloss bowl & lid w/Ming Dragon Blood glaze, lobster handle ................. **$55.00**

**Bowl,** 9¼" d., 2½" h., chip & dip-type, pale green gloss w/full-bodied Ming Dragon Blood glaze, lobster serving as divider & handle ..................................... **70.00**

**Bowl,** 7" l., 4¼" h., cauliflower shape w/pale green shading to darker green & Ming Dragon Blood glaze, lobster on each end serving as handle, marked "Brad Keeler" ............................. **75.00**

**Model of a canary w/tail down,** female, yellow w/grey blends & grey tree stump w/branches, 6" h............................................. **40.00**

**Model of a cat,** seated on a dark brown square, fluffy pillow, cat w/large eyes looking upward, marked "Brad Keeler," 4" h. ........ **38.00**

**Model of a cockatoo,** sitting on a branch, 8¾" h.............................. **75.00**

*Keeler Bird of Paradise*

**Model of a Cocker Spaniel puppy,** seated in a begging position, light brown & off-white gloss glaze, marked "Brad Keeler 735," 6¼" h. .................... **70.00**

**Model of a flamingo,** standing on oval base, head bent, leaves rising from base hide most of the bird's legs, in-mold mark "Brad Keeler 3," 7½" h. ......................... **95.00**

**Model of a flamingo,** standing on round base, pink & white gloss body w/grey base, dark grey tipping on wings & beak, wings raised, head down, inkstamp mark, "Brad Keeler 47," 10¼" h. . **80.00**

**Model of a kitten,** seated in a yellow wicker basket w/two loop handles turned slightly upward, head up, grey & white kitten w/pink mouth & ears, blue & black eyes, stamp mark, "Brad Keeler 942 H," 4¼" d., 3¼" h. (ILLUS. previous page) .............. **45.00**

**Model of a male bird-of-paradise,** standing on round base w/one leg resting on tree stump, shaded & muted rose, tan, beige & green gloss, inkstamp mark, Brad Keeler 717," 11" h. (ILLUS. above) ........ **80.00**

**Model of a rooster,** standing on round yellow base, colorful details in green, brown, red, yellow & rose, marked "Brad Keeler 935," 5½" h. (ILLUS. below) ........................................ **55.00**

**Planter,** model of a chicken, standing w/large pink plaid hat tied w/big pink bow at neck, brown body, yellow beak, toes peeping out from long pink plaid skirt, inkstamp mark, "B.B.K. Made in U.S.A. 517, " 7" h. ...................................... **35.00**

**Planter,** model of a dog, front section of dog w/head atop two front legs, left ear pointed upward & out to the side w/right ear down, back legs straight, tail up & hole in top of back to form small planter, pink paws & one pink inner ear, black eyes & nose, green & yellow thin stripes & brown 'stitching,' ink-stamp mark w/copyright symbol & "B.B.K. Made in U.S.A. 520," & also a Pryde & Joy paper label, 4½" h.......................................... **40.00**

**Salt & pepper shakers,** model of a lobster, Ming Dragon Blood glaze, stamp mark "Brad Keeler Made in U.S.A.," 3¼" h., pr. ........ **30.00**

*Brad Keeler Rooster*

# KUTANI

*An Ornate Kutani Jar*

*This is a Japanese ware from the area of Kutani, a name meaning "nine valleys" where porcelain was made as early as about 1675. The early wares are referred to as "Ko-Kutani" and "Ao-Ko Kutani."*

**Cups,** handleless, each decorated w/a continual design of a phoenix surrounded by a floral scroll, *ruyi* lappet borders around the interior rim & foot, w/an underglaze-blue, iron-red & gilt Fukagawa mark on base, 19th c., 3¼" d., set of 6 .......... **$345.00**

**Jar,** cov., wide ovoid body w/a fitted domed cover w/a peach-form finial, the body enameled on one side w/a scene of children playing w/butterflies & on the other side w/three figures, each wearing a draped robe & loose pants, centered by birds amid blossoming branches within shaped panels, on an iron-red ground decorated w/gilt wrigglework & scrolling clouds, 19th c., 11½" h. (ILLUS. above) ...................................... **517.00**

**Vase,** 11" h., ovoid form, decorated w/a procession of deities, now mounted as a lamp, late 19th c. ............................... **259.00**

**Vase,** 18" h., bottle-form, bulbous body on a raised foot & tapering to a tall slender neck, decorated w/patterned stripes swirling around the body, signed on the base, 20th c. ............................. **575.00**

# LAUGHLIN (Homer) CHINA COMPANY

*It was after the Civil War that Homer Laughlin journeyed to East Liverpool, Ohio and set up his first short-lived stoneware pottery. In 1870 Homer and his brother Shakespeare opened another pottery which produced yellowwares and Rockingham-glazed utilitarian pieces. Some years later the firm added whiteware to the production as well as fine white ironstone china.*

*By the early 20th century the firm had grown tremendously and although Homer Laughlin sold out his interest in the company to the W.E. Wells family in 1898, the company name continued as the Homer Laughlin China Company. During the 1920s numerous additional production factories were opened and a wide range of dinnerwares became the main focus of their output. In the 1930s the famous Fiesta, Harlequin and Riviera lines were produced and met with great public success. Today the Homer Laughlin firm continues in operation as one of this country's longest continually running potteries*

*The products of Homer Laughlin are well marked and often carry a dating code as well as the trademark. A wide range of factory-named dinnerware shapes were made by the company, however, many of the patterns they used were only given numbers, which makes collecting by pattern a little more difficult today. The following is a brief listing of Homer Laughlin dinnerware lines and patterns. We list the widely collected Fiesta Ware and Harlequin lines separately.*

*Helpful references in this field are The Collector's Encyclopedia of Homer Laughlin China by Joanne Jasper (Collector Books, 1993) and The Collector's Encyclopedia of Fiesta, Plus Harlequin, Riviera and Kitchen Kraft, by Bob & Sharon Huxford (Collector Books, 1992).*

*Laughlin Marks*

**Bowl,** fruit, 6" d., Serenade line, late 1930s ................................ **$12.00**

**Bowl,** soup w/lug handles, Serenade line.............................. **18.00**

**Casserole,** cov., handled Serenade line.............................. **65.00**

**Coffeepot,** cov., china, Suntone patt., Debutante shape, ca. 1940s .................................... **75.00**

**Cup & saucer,** Serenade line......... **9.00**

**Gravy boat,** Serenade line .......... **30.00**

**Mixing bowl,** Kitchen Kraft line, Petit Point Rose patt., 10" d........ **25.00**

**Mixing bowls,** nesting-type, molded Orange Tree patt., set of 4........................................... **135.00**

**Nappy,** Serenade line ................... **25.00**

**Plate,** bread & butter, 6" d., Serenade line................................ **8.00**

**Plate,** 6" d., Virginia Rose shape .... **8.00**

**Plate,** 9" d., Serenade line ............ **14.00**

**Plate,** 10" d., Serenade line .......... **25.00**

**Plate,** chop, 13" d., Serenade
line...................................... **45.00**

**Platter,** 12" l., oval, Virginia Rose
shape ........................................ **25.00**

**Platter,** 12½" l., oval, Serenade
line ........................................... **45.00**

**Soup plate w/flanged rim,**
Serenade line, pink ..................... **22.00**

# LEEDS

*Leeds Creamware Tureen*

*The Leeds Pottery in Yorkshire, England, began production about 1758. It made, among other things, creamware that was highly competitive with Wedgwood's. In the 1780s it began production of reticulated and punched wares. Little of its production was marked. Most readily available Leeds ware is that of the 19th century during which time the pottery was operated by several firms.*

**Basket & undertray,** basket
w/oval w/flaring reticulated sides
in a basketweave design,
matching undertray, ca. 1800,
11½" l., 2 pcs. (very minor chips,
staining) .................................. **$345.00**

**Cup & saucer,** handleless,
pearlware, "gaudy" floral
decoration in blue, green &
ochre (minor wear & cup w/old
bruise on foot).......................... **110.00**

**Figure of Andromache,**
pearlware, a classical lady
standing wearing a red & black
polka dot dress w/a pink & red
shawl & black sandals, holding a
floral garland of pink, red & green
in one hand & leaning on a large
floral-trimmed urn w/lion head
handles at the sides raised on a
square plinth w/embossed round
medallions in a wreath w/swords
& arrows & set on paw feet, all
raised on a raised rectangular
platform w/arch-molded sides,
impressed under the hollow base
"LEEDS POTTERY," ca. 1790-
1810, 12" h. (light flaking, small
chips, broken & reglued piece on
back of base) ........................ **1,210.00**

**Plate,** 7⅝" d., pearlware, "gaudy"
floral decoration in yellowish-
ochre, blue, green & greenish
brown, green feather edge
design (worn w/chips &
hairlines) .................................. **105.00**

**Plate,** 8" d., pearlware, green
feather-edge design w/center
decoration of large eagle in
brown, blue, yellow & green
(pinpoint rim flakes) .................. **495.00**

**Plate,** 9⅞" d., pearlware, green
feather-edge design w/eagle &
shield center decoration in
brown, blue & yellowish ochre
(pinpoint flakes) .................... **1,045.00**

**Sugar bowl,** cov., pearlware,
flaring cylindrical foot, round flared
sides w/molded lion head handles
& low-domed cover w/blossom
finial, "gaudy" floral decoration in
blue, green & ochre, 4½" h. (small
edge chips)................................. **193.00**

**Tureen,** cov., creamware, flaring
shell-molded foot supporting a
deep half round body molded
w/wide scrolling leaves & shell-
molded end handles, the domed
cover w/upturned scroll-molded
ends & finely ribbed sides
topped w/pine cone & leaf finial,
ca. 1800, 13½" from handle to
handle (ILLUS. previous
column) ..................................... **489.00**

*A Variety of Leeds Pearlware Pieces*

**Charger,** pearlware, center decoration of large stylized flower within a circle & surrounded by four similar flowers, all in green, blue, brown & yellow w/blue feather-edge, wear, small flakes & rim hairline w/old yellowed repair, 13¼" d. (ILLUS. center) ......................... **330.00**

**Loving cup,** pearlware, decorated w/yellowish ochre, green, blue & brown flowers & leaves in flowerpot, small edge chips, hairline in rim & in-the-making hairline in stem, 5⅜" h. (ILLUS. top right) ..................... **303.00**

**Mug,** pearlware, cylindrical w/C-form handle, Oriental decoration w/pagoda & stylized trees in yellowish-ochre, blue, brown & green, very minor edge flakes & crazing, glazed over small indentation in bottom rim, 6⅛" h. (ILLUS. bottom left) .................. **605.00**

**Potpourri jar,** cov., footed flaring urn-form w/low domed cover pierced w/holes, button finial, floral decoration in blue, green, brown & yellowish ochre w/similar decoration on cover, very minor pinpoint flakes on finial & small flake on under edge of foot, 8¼" h. (ILLUS. bottom right) .......................... **1,980.00**

**Teapot,** cov., pearlware, octagonal paneled body w/paneled swan's-neck spout & angular C-form handle, floral decoration in yellow, green, blue, brown & orange w/band of flower buds around shoulder, flattened inset cover w/figural swan finial, small chips on tip of spout & rim, swan finial professionally repaired, 6¾" h. (ILLUS. top left) ........................ **330.00**

---

# LEFTON CHINA

*Lefton China is one of the most desirable and sought-after collectibles on today's market. The company was founded in the early 1940s by Mr. George Zolton Lefton who had immigrated to the United States from Hungary. In the 1930s he was involved in the designing and manufacturing of sportswear, and his hobby of collecting fine china and porcelain led him to the creation of his own ceramics business.*

*When the bombing of Pearl Harbor occurred in December of 1941, Mr. Lefton befriended and helped a Japanese-American protect his property from being destroyed. Through this friendship after the war Mr. Lefton learned of the Japanese porcelain factory owned by Kowa Toki K.K. From that point until 1980 this factory produced thousands of pieces that were sold by the Lefton Company and bore the initials of "KW" before the item number. These items and the many whimsical pieces such as Bluebirds, Dainty Miss, Miss Priss, Cabbage Cutie, Mr. Toodles and the Dutch Girl line are eagerly collected today. As with most antiques and collectibles, prices vary depending on location, condition and availability. For additional information on the history of Lefton China, its factories, marks and products, readers should consult the* Collector's Encyclopedia of Lefton China *by Loretta DeZozier (Collector Books, 1995).*

**Ashtray,** small four-lobed form in white w/applied purple violets w/rhinestones at the gold-trimmed rim, No. 194, set of 4, each (ILLUS. top next column) ... **$20.00**

**Bowl,** model of a sleigh, white w/large pink roses, trimmed in sponged gold, 8" l., 4½" h. ........ **125.00**

**Box,** cov., oblong, the low domed cover centered by applied pink roses & green leaves, a border band of inset rhinestones, gold rim band & gilt bands on base, No. 90254, 2½ x 3" (ILLUS. below) ........................................ **35.00**

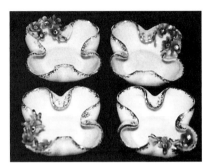

*Lefton Decorated Ashtrays*

*Delicate Lefton Box*

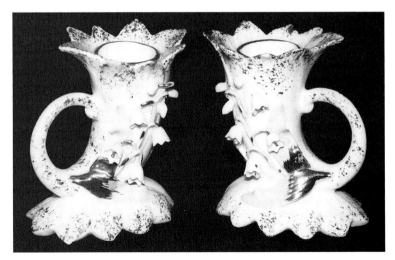

*Lefton Cornucopia Candleholders*

*Lefton Condiment Set*

*Fluted Lefton Dish*

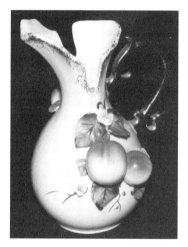

*Lefton Ewer with Fruit*

**Candleholders,** cornucopia-form w/loop handle & scalloped foot, applied w/lily-of-the-valley blossoms, trimmed in sponged gold, No. 285, pr. (ILLUS. bottom previous page) ............... **75.00**

**Condiment set,** stack-type, a teapot-form jam pot base w/spoon hole, center cup-form sugar bowl & top cov. creamer, all decorated w/painted pansies, w/a spoon, No. 3529, the set (ILLUS. above) ............................. **38.00**

**Cookie jar,** cov., figural Young Lady Head, w/flowered hat ....... **195.00**

**Cookie jar,** cov., figural Miss Priss, cat head wearing hat ...... **100.00**

**Creamer,** figural Miss Priss .......... **45.00**

**Creamer & cov. sugar bowl,** figural Bluebird, pr. ...................... **65.00**

**Creamer & cov. sugar bowl,** figural Girl Head, No. 1708, pr. ... **75.00**

**Cup & saucer,** footed, each decorated w/an unusual & colorful assortment of roses ........ **55.00**

**Dish,** rounded w/deeply fluted & pointed scalloped edge tapering to a round foot w/applied "coleslaw" & flowers above a gilt looped lattice-trimmed base, a colorful bouquet of flowers on the interior, trimmed in sponged gold, No. 8242, 5" d. (ILLUS. top next column) ............................... **75.00**

**Ewer,** footed bulbous body tapering to a flaring forked rim, ornate scrolling gilt handle, the base applied w/large applied fruit, leaves & tiny blossoms, trimmed in sponged gold, No. 7363, 6½" h. (ILLUS.) ............... **60.00**

**Figurine,** angel of the month, bisque, 4" h., each .................... **24.00**

**Figurine,** angel of the week, "Tuesday's Child" ..................... **30.00**

**Figurine,** Bloomer Girl, variety of poses, No. 576, 4" h., each ...... **45.00**

**Figurine,** Colonial woman, "Old Masters," No. 341, 10" h. .......... **85.00**

**Figurines,** a dancing girl & boy, each holding a flower, fine pastel painting & applied flowers, round base, No. 4140, 7" h., pr. ........................................ **95.00**

*Lefton Colonial Couple*

*Lefton Donkey Planter*

**Figurines,** a Colonial-style man wearing a long coat & dancing & playing a gold violin & a matching dancing lady wearing a low-cut gown & carrying a basket of flowers, No. 1705, 10½" h., pr. (ILLUS.)................ **300.00**

**Jam jar, cover, spoon & undertray,** Cabbie Cutie, the set. **46.00**

**Mug,** figural Bluebird, No. 284 ...... **65.00**

**Mug,** figural Miss Priss.................. **75.00**

**Perfume set,** pineapple-shaped containers applied overall w/small pink blossoms & gold trim on the top leaf cluster, No. 9567, set of 3 (ILLUS. bottom).. **185.00**

**Planter,** figural, Calico donkey, brightly painted w/floral sprigs on a white body w/yellow trim on the head, ears & legs, No. 5897, 5½" l. (ILLUS.) ........................... **45.00**

**Planter,** figural, model of a pheasant, 5½" l. ......................... **35.00**

**Salt & pepper shakers,** figural Mr. Tootles, No. 3235, 3¾" h., pr.................................................. **25.00**

**Sugar bowl,** cov., figural Bluebird. **30.00**

**Teapot,** cov., figural Cabbage Cutie, model of a cabbage w/a little girl on the cover, 4-cup size.............................................. **100.00**

**Teapot,** cov., figural Miss Priss... **125.00**

**Teapot,** cov., figural Young Lady Head, wearing hat, No. 321 ...... **150.00**

*Lefton Pineapple-form Perfume Set*

*Lefton Elegant Rose Tea Set*

**Tea set:** cov. teapot, cov. sugar bowl & creamer; Elegant Rose patt., oval cylindrical bodies w/narrow fluting, each decorated w/large pink rose clusters & sponged gold trim, Nos. 2275 & 2276, 3 pcs. (ILLUS. top) .......... **200.00**

**Vase,** 5" h., head-type, a girl wearing a green plaid dress & hat, "Dainty Miss" ...................... **110.00**

**Vase,** 6" h., a small round foot supporting three slender leaf-form curved legs holding a tall ruffled & crimped flora-form base trimmed w/small pink ribbons & painted w/tiny red roses & sponged gold, roses & gold trim on the legs & base, No. 70039 (ILLUS. middle next column) ...................................... **95.00**

**Wall plaque,** pierced to hang, oval, a gold-trimmed scroll-molded border frames a romantic Colonial couple molded in full-relief & carefully hand-decorated & trimmed w/applied flowers, he dressed in a dark green suit & she wearing a pale pink & cream gown, No. 3438, 9½" h. (ILLUS. bottom next column) ................... **110.00**

**Wall plaque set,** a large bird & two small birds, each decorated in pink & green, 3 pcs. ................ **85.00**

*Small Lefton Vase*

*Ornate Lefton Wall Plaque*

# LENOX

*Lenox Swan Nut Dish*

*The Ceramic Art Company was established at Trenton, New Jersey, in 1889 by Jonathan Coxon and Walter Scott Lenox. In addition to true porcelain, it also made a Belleek-type ware. Renamed Lenox Company in 1906, it is still in operation today.*

*Lenox Mark*

**Cup & saucer,** Gadroon patt., ivory ......................................... **$20.00**

**Cup & saucer,** Springdale patt, platinum trim .............................. **20.00**

**Dish,** footed, fan-shaped, pink.... **110.00**

**Dish,** leaf-shaped, white w/heavy gold trim, No. 3005, gold wreath mark, 10½" l., 2" h....................... **75.00**

**Lamp,** Art Deco-style, figural "Leda," a nude w/a swan, No. 3154, 10" h. ........................ **339.00**

**Luncheon service:** fourteen 10½" d. plates, fourteen 8¼" d. plates, twelve 8⅜" d. soup plates, twelve 6¼" d. plates & twenty-four cups & saucers; each w/a burgundy red border w/gilt acanthus leaves, 20th c., the set................ **748.00**

**Mustard pot,** cov., glossy brown glaze overlaid in silver ......................... **150.00 to 175.00**

**Nut dish,** model of a swan in plain white, green wreath mark, 5" l., 3¾" h. (ILLUS.) ................... **30.00**

**Plate,** dinner, Springdale patt., platinum trim ............................... **20.00**

**Platter,** Springdale patt., platinum trim............................................. **20.00**

**Vase,** 4⅜" h., 1⅝ x 4", embossed lilies on the front & back, 24k gold-decorated handle, gold wreath mark ............................... **50.00**

# LIMOGES

*Numerous factories produced china in Limoges, France, with major production in the 19th century. Some pieces listed below are identified by the name of the maker or are identified by the name of the maker or the mark of the factory. Although the famed Haviland Company was located in Limoges, wares bearing their marks are not included in this listing. Also see HAVILAND.*

*An excellent reference is* The Collector's Encyclopedia of Limoges Porcelain, Second Edition, *by Mary Frank Gaston (Collector Books, 1992).*

**Bowl,** 10" d., 4" h., interior & exterior decoration of h.p. seashells, T & V - Limoges - France (Tresseman & Vogt) ... **$225.00**

**Box,** cov., Art Nouveau free-form design, decorated w/relief-molded scrolls, violet sprays & brushed gold, 5½ x 9", 3½" h.... **165.00**

**Box,** cov., four-footed, decorated w/enameled white forget-me-nots & green foliage on semi-matte pink ground, 4¾ x 13", 3¾" h. (T & V - Limoges, France) ..................................... **395.00**

**Cake plate,** open-handled, decorated w/florals, 12" d. (T & V - Limoges)........................ **66.00**

*French Limoges Dresser Set*

**Chamberstick,** h.p. pale blue floral decoration w/gold trim, applied molded handle, 4" d., 5" h............................................. **150.00**

**Cracker jar,** cov., decorated w/blue & gold flowers, relief-molded scrolls, leaf & scroll loop handles, 5½" d., 7½" h. (Wm. Guerin)..................................... **145.00**

**Dinner service for eight,** including serving pieces, Cornflower decoration w/embossed gold accents, the set (Limoges - France - Deposé)........................ **650.00**

**Dresser set:** footed, 5¾" d., 3½" h. handled & cov. hair receiver & matching powder box on a palette-form 9½ x 12⅞" tray; each piece decorated w/a blue & cream pastel background decorated w/lovely pink flowers, gold handles, legs & rim bands, marked, the set (ILLUS. top)..... **195.00**

**Dresser tray,** h.p. scene of windmill, cottage & water w/fisherman on boulder-strewn shore in foreground, last quarter 19th c. ...................................... **165.00**

**Fish set:** 12 x 17¼" platter & ten 8½" d. plates; platter decorated w/h.p. fish on green, yellow & orange ground w/brushed gold trim, plates each show different scene, artist-signed, 11 pcs. ..... **650.00**

*Limoges Game Plate*

**Game plate,** h.p. scene of two brown & white grouse-like birds in flowers & grasses, scroll-molded gilt rim band, artist-signed, marked, 10⅝" d. (ILLUS.) ................................... **155.00**

**Game set:** 12 x 18" open-handled platter & twelve 9" d. plates; h.p. birds, relief-molded scrolls, sponged gold, 13 pcs............. **1,600.00**

**Gravy boat & underplate,** soft peach color fading to off-white, gold trim w/interior decoration of nine fish swimming in bottom, tiny delicate branches & flowers ................................... **85.00**

*Two Limoges Plaques with Deer*

**Ice cream set:** 9¼ x 16¼" tray & ten 6½ x 8" dishes; each piece w/ornate scroll & scalloped gilt borders w/blue forget-me-nots & pink rosebuds around the borders, molded end handles on the tray & small central oval gilt & floral medallion, the set ........ **425.00**

**Mush bowl, cover & underplate,** two-handled bowl, h.p. decoration of white & blue flowers w/yellow centers, dark blue to lavender ground, signed "E. M. Townsend Christmas 1908 to Grandma," marked "GDA Limoges, France" the set (Gerard, Dufraissex, and Abbot) . **49.00**

**Oyster plates,** gilt trim scrolled foliate borders on an ivory ground, ca. 1900, 9½" d., Tresseman & Vogt, set of 12 .... **633.00**

**Pitcher,** 7¾" h., footed bulbous body w/arched spout & ornate C-scroll handle, decorated w/h.p. roses (T & V - Limoges - France) .................................. **193.00**

**Pitcher,** 8" h., ribbed cylindrical body w/scalloped base & rim, C-scroll handle, h.p. floral decoration (G.D.A., France)...... **300.00**

**Pitcher,** tankard, 15½" h., slender cylindrical body w/arched spout, decorated w/grapes of various colors, leaves in shades of green on multi-hued

background, applied leaf & curling vine decorated handle, ca. 1893, artist-signed (T & V - Limoges, France)...................... **475.00**

**Plaque,** rectangular, decorated w/h.p. scene of two cows grazing by a pond, mountains in background, framed, 7 x 9½" (T & V, Limoges, France).......... **295.00**

**Plaques,** round w/ornate scroll-molded gold border, each h.p. w/detailed woodland scene, one w/two large stags, the other w/two running doe, artist-signed, 13¼" d., pr. (ILLUS. above) ...... **845.00**

**Plate,** 9¾" d., pierced to hang, gold rococo border, center scene of young lady being serenaded by young nobleman (Limoges, France)...................... **78.00**

**Plate,** 9¾" d., a center h.p. scene of an older bearded man sitting by a window, wearing a work apron & examining an artwork or music, the wide border w/a gently scalloped rim in dark cobalt blue w/delicate gilt scrolls & three oval reserves w/a white ground decorated w/a bar of music or flowers & scrolls, artist-signed..... **165.00**

**Plate,** 10" d., pierced to hang, gold rococo border, center decoration of large pink floral flowers & leaves, artist-signed (Limoges, France)...................... **75.00**

*Romantic Limoges Plate*

*Large Limoges Plate with Fruits*

**Plate,** 10¼" d., pierced to hang, round w/ornate molded scroll gilt border band, h.p. w/a large cluster of fruits & leaves including purple grapes, peaches & berries, artist-signed, marked ..................................... **135.00**

**Plate,** 10⅜" d., pierced to hang, gold rococo border, center landscape scene of a shepherdess, seated & petting a lamb w/a young nobleman suitor seated beside her & talking to her, artist-signed, marked (ILLUS. top) .............................. **135.00**

**Plate,** 10½" d., pierced to hang, rococo gilt border surrounding colorful Victorian courting scene, artist-signed ............................. **150.00**

**Plate,** 12¼" d., pierced to hang, heavy gold rococo border, decorated w/purple plums & a large pomegranate & leaves against a shaded pastel ground, artist-signed, unmarked (ILLUS. bottom previous column) ........... **245.00**

**Plate,** chop, 13⅛" d., scrolled border, decorated w/h.p. fish, artist-signed, marked "L. R. L. Limoges" (Lazeyras, Rosenfeld and Lehman)............................. **248.00**

**Plates,** 9½" d., game-type, each w/a scroll-molded & beaded wide gold border, one h.p. w/two pheasants near berry bushes, the other w/two grouse in a similar setting, facing pr. .......... **225.00**

**Potpourri jar,** cov., decorated w/h.p. florals w/heavy gold outlining, openwork on lid, gold handles & finial, D & C - France, 7½ x 8½" (R. Deliniéres)........... **295.00**

**Punch set:** 13" d. pedestal-based punch bowl on a 16" d. tray w/five matching pedestal-based punch cups; all decorated w/h.p. grape clusters & berries, bottom-marked "Limoges," the set ........ **750.00**

**Punch set:** punch bowl, base & six cups; each decorated w/h.p. pink & red roses, 8 pcs. ............ **800.00**

**Salt dish,** light shading to dark pink pearlized enamel interior, edge trimmed w/gold & white pearlized swirls, made for Saks Fifth Avenue, probably designed & made by G. Faure, ca. 1920, France, 4¼" d. ............................ **65.00**

**Seafood set:** 9½ x 13¾" platter & six 8¾" d. plates; h.p. shellfish w/raised enamel touches, each a different design, 7 pcs............ **485.00**

**Toothpick holder,** black base w/floral decoration on upper one third, gold collar & handle ........... **35.00**

**Vase,** 10" h., baluster-form, decorated w/the profile portrait of a woman wearing flowers in her hair, reserved on a red ground decorated w/gilt foliate scrolls, 19th c. ........................... **770.00**

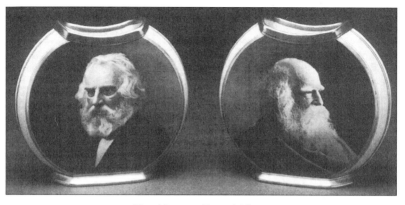

*Fine Limoges Portrait Vases*

**Vase,** 12½" h., footed ovoid body tapering to wide cylindrical neck w/flared rim trimmed w/brownish band, ornate gold handles from mid-section to rim, h.p. deep red roses, green leaves on shaded blue & green ground (wear & some crazing on interior) .......... **125.00**

**Vase,** 12½" h., 6½" d., decorated w/a frieze of five Art Nouveau large pink hibiscus w/trailing stems & buds, gold bands on cream ground, artist-signed ...... **350.00**

**Vase,** 14" h., baluster-form, decorated w/a portrait of an elegant young woman by rose bushes & a continuous riverscape, artist-signed, printed factory marks, late 19th - early 20th c. ..................................... **805.00**

**Vases,** 8½" h., pillow-form, a narrow oblong foot supports flat-sided body w/curved edges & incurved opening, each decorated *en grisaille* w/a bust portrait & quote, one w/Longfellow & the other w/W. Cullen Bryant, impressed marks, ca. 1885, pr. (ILLUS. above) ..... **805.00**

**Wastebasket,** four large gold feet, two large loop handles, Pickard-type decoration of red & orange poppies & lavish gold, artist-signed, 9" d. at widest, 12½" h. ..................................... **500.00**

# LIVERPOOL

*Liverpool is most often used as a generic term for fine earthenware products, usually of creamware or pearlware, produced at numerous potteries in this English city during the late 18th and early 19th centuries. Many examples, especially pitchers, were decorated with transfer-printed patriotic designs aimed specifically at the American buying public.*

**Bowl,** 9¼" d., 4⅜" h., creamware, a wide footring below deep rounded & gently flaring sides, decorated w/black transfer-printed designs, one side of the exterior w/a bust profile of Washington & banners reading "His Excellency General Washington," the opposite side w/a bust portrait of Benjamin Franklin wearing a fur cap & banners reading "Benjm Franklin, LLD, FRS..Born at Boston in New England 17 Jan 1706," the interior w/a border band of martial symbols & the bottom w/a scene of a maiden & a departing sailor w/a ship in the background & a banner above titled "Poor Jack," two generic English country scenes also on the exterior (over-restoration to a crack running off the rim, across the Franklin bust & across the base) ................. **$1,100.00**

**Mug,** tall cylindrical form w/D-form handle, black transfer-printed title & design w/polychrome trim, "An East View of Liverpool Light House & Signal on Bidston Hill...," w/a view of the lighthouse flanked by numerous flags, decorated in yellow, red, green, blue & black, late 18th - early 19th c., 4⅞" h. (light stain, small rim & base chip) ........................................ **660.00**

**Pitcher,** jug-type, 6¼" h., creamware, bulbous ovoid body w/an angled handle, one side w/a black transfer-printed scene of two battling ships titled "The CONSTITUTION in close action with the GUERRIERE," the reverse w/another scene of battling ships titled "THE WASP BOARDING THE FROLIC," pink lustre rim & handle lines, ca. 1812 (few minor flakes on the rim, trace of a small rim hairline) ................................. **1,650.00**

**Pitcher,** jug-type, 9" h., creamware, one side transfer-printed in black w/a portrait of George Washington, the other side printed w/an allegorical scene representing "Peace, Plenty and Independence," early 19th c. (spout repaired, hairlines) .................................. **748.00**

**Pitcher,** jug-type, 9¼" h., creamware, one side transfer-printed in black w/a three-masted sailing ship flying the American flag, the other side decorated w/an oblong vine-trimmed panel filled w/Masonic emblems, polychrome trim, an American Eagle under the spout, early 19th c. (hairline from rim, crazing) ................... **1,495.00**

**Pitcher,** 9½" h., a tapering cylindrical body w/a molded base rim & a long angular rim spout, a D-form handle, one side

transfer-printed in black w/the American eagle & shield & on the other w/a three-masted sailing ship, early 19th c., spout repair........................................ **489.00**

**Pitcher,** jug-type, 9½" h., creamware, black transfer-printed decorations, one side w/a three-masted ship flying the American flag & decorated in red, blue, yellow & green, the opposite side w/an oval series of rings each naming a state encircling an allegorical grouping of figures representing Peace, Plenty & Liberty under the Latin quote "Deus Nobis Haec Otia Fecit," under the spout an oval reserve around the name "B. Leffingwell" (two networks of internal hairlines around the handle attachments, hairline off the rim near the spout, hints of tiny 'spiders' on the base) ............................... **3,025.00**

**Pitcher,** jug-type, 9¾" h., creamware, one side transfer-printed in black w/an allegorical scene within a circular band representing Virtue & Valor, the other side w/a portrait of George Washington, an American Eagle under the spout, early 19th c. (some imperfections)............ **1,725.00**

**Pitcher,** jug-type, 10½" h., creamware, one side w/a black transfer-printed scene titled "Washington in His Glory" showing him standing holding a telescope next to his horse being held by a black groom, decorated w/blue, yellow, green, black & brown enamels, the reverse w/another transfer-printed scene of a the American eagle & figure of Liberty weeping at Washington's tomb & titled "America in Tears," under the spout is a transfer-printed foliate monogram & inscription "A Man without example - A Patriot without

*Rare Washington Liverpool Pitcher*

reproach," early 19th c., cracks along spout, darkening, some handle glaze wear (ILLUS. above, front & back)............. **10,350.00**

**Pitcher,** jug-type, 11¼" h., creamware, one side transfer-printed in black w/a round medallion showing an officer leading troops w/a ship in the background all encircled by banners readings "By Virtue and Valour, We Have Freed Our Country, Extended Our Commerce and Laid the Foundation of a Great Empire," the opposite side w/a scalloped star-trimmed oval border around a small bust portrait of George Washington surrounded by emblems of Liberty, the outer border w/the names of the fifteen states, under the spout a floral wreath surrounding the name "Benjamin Butler" (tiny flake on tip of spout) ............. **2,090.00**

**Pitcher,** jug-type, 11¼" h., creamware, black transfers w/polychrome trim, one side w/a large oval reserve showing a military officer, flags, cannons, etc., w/a caption reading "Success to America Whose Militia is Better Than Standing Armies," the reverse w/a similar oval reserve w/bust portraits of Samuel Adams & John Hancock beneath a memorial monument, w/the inscription "Washington and the Proscribed Patriots," under the spout the spread-winged eagle Seal of the United States w/a quote from Jefferson dated 1802, the back under the handle w/Fame w/a trumpet, decorated in yellow, blue, red & green, applied band of maroon around the lip (small chip on side of spout, some slight flaking to maroon band, three small 'spiders' along the side of the base)....................................... **3,025.00**

**Pitcher,** jug-type, creamware, one side w/a black transfer-printed oval reserve w/a bust portrait of Thomas Jefferson above his name & a brief inscription all within a floral & scroll wreath below the top inscription "Jefferson And Liberty" & another floral swag, early 19th c. (ILLUS. top next page)....................................... **9,350.00**

**Plate,** 10" d., creamware, flanged rim, the center transfer-printed in black w/a three-masted sailing ship, floral sprigs around the rim, early 19th c. (a few small base chips) ........................................ **288.00**

*Rare Jefferson Pitcher*

*Rare Liverpool Tureen*

**Punch bowl,** creamware, footed, deep rounded sides, the exterior transfer-printed w/a harbor & fishing scenes, the interior w/a three-masted sailing ship & a foliate monogram, early 19th c., 12¼" d. (hairlines) .................. **2,415.00**

**Soup tureen, cover & ladle,** creamware, a deep bulbous oval body tapering toward the flaring foot & wide, flaring rim, loop end handles, the low domed overhanging cover w/loop handle & ladle hole, decorated on one side w/a black transfer-printed scene of a three-masted sailing ship trimmed w/yellow & green enamel, the other side w/a castle view, scattered floral clusters on the sides & landscape scenes & florals on the cover, an obelisk on the interior, early 19th c., chips, ladle repaired, 14¼" l., the set (ILLUS. bottom, this column) .. **1,610.00**

# LLADRO

*Spain's famed Lladro porcelain manufactory creates both limited and non-limited edition figurines as well as other porcelains. The classic simple beauty of the figures and their subdued coloring makes them readily recognizable and they have an enthusiastic following of collectors.*

*Lladró Mark*

**Admiration,** No. 4907, 6½" h. .. **$490.00**

**Attentive Bear,** No. 1204, 4" h. ..... **75.00**

**At the Ball,** No. 5398, 13¾" h..... **675.00**

**Bird in Nest,** No. 1299, 6¼" h., w/original box .......................... **475.00**

**Boy with Goat,** No. 4506, 10½" h...................................... **350.00**

**Cart (The),** No. 1245, 8½" h. ...... **550.00**

**Chinese Noblewoman,** No. 4916, 13" h............................ **1,750.00**

**Clean Up Time,** No. 4838, 7½" h....................................... **135.00**

**Clown with Concertina,** No. 1027, 17¾" h............................ **695.00**

**Cutting Flowers,** No. 5088, 10½" h.................................... **1,450.00**

**Dancing Partner (A),** No. 5093, 10½" h.................................... **450.00**

**Daughters,** No. 5013, 12½" h..... **545.00**

**Doctor,** No. 4602, 15¾" h.......... **350.00**

**Dog,** Lhasa Apso, No. 4642, 5½" h..................................... **295.00**

**Dog Playing Bongos,** No. 1156, 7½" h...................................... **400.00**

**Dressmaker,** No. 4700, 14¼" h.. **325.00**

**Dutch Boy,** No. 4811, 8½" h. (ILLUS. top next page)............. **295.00**

**Dutch Girl with Braids,** No. 5063, 9¾" h............................. **425.00**

**Eskimo Girl,** No. 2008.30, 11½" h...................................... **225.00**

*Lladro Dutch Boy*

**Feeding Her Son,** No. 5140,
9" h................................ **325.00**
**First Date,** No. 1393, 16¼" h... **5,300.00**
**Flowers of the Season,** No.
1454, 11" h............................ **1,975.00**
**Girl with Bonnet,** No. 1147,
8½" h........................................ **200.00**
**Girl with Flowers,** No. 1172,
8¼" h........................................ **250.00**
**Girl with Goose and Dog,** No.
4866, 10½" h............................ **190.00**
**Girl with Parasol and Geese,**
No. 4510, 10½" h. ..................... **245.00**
**Girl with Turkey,** No. 4569,
5½" h........................................ **215.00**
**Hang On!,** No. 5665, 6" h. .......... **285.00**
**Julia,** No. 1361, 9" h. ................. **120.00**
**Lady at Dressing Table,** No.
1242, 11¾" h......................... **2,995.00**
**Land of the Giants,** No. 5716,
8½" h........................................ **225.00**
**Little Girl with Goat,** No. 4812,
9" h.......................................... **350.00**
**Little Unicorn,** No 5826, 6½" h. . **177.00**
**Lolo,** No. 7605, 8¼" h. ............... **125.00**
**Lovers in the Park,** No. 1274,
11¾" h...................................... **725.00**
**Madonna,** No. 4586, 13¾" h....... **275.00**
**Man of La Mancha,** No. 1269,
15" h...................................... **3,600.00**
**Marketing Day,** No. 4502,
13¾" h...................................... **295.00**
**Medieval Lady,** No. 5126,
11½" h...................................... **495.00**

**Motoring in Style,** No. 5884,
7¾" h................................ **2,700.00**
**Nurse,** No. 4603, 15¾" h. .......... **350.00**
**On the Lake,** No. 5216,
13¾" h................................ **1,075.00**
**Pilar,** No. 5410, 6" h., matte
finish ........................................ **275.00**
**Platero an Marcelino,** No. 1181,
7¾" h........................................ **235.00**
**Pretty Posies,** No. 5548,
6½" h........................................ **495.00**
**Quiet Evening,** No. 5606,
7¾" h........................................ **165.00**
**Sad Note,** No. 5586, 7" h. .......... **275.00**
**Sealore Pipe,** No. 5613, 3½" h... **160.00**
**Shelley,** No. 1357, 6¼" h. .......... **130.00**
**Snowman (The),** No. 5713,
8¼" h........................................ **210.00**
**Summer Soiree,** No. 5597,
8¼" h........................................ **108.00**
**Taylor (The),** No. 5326, 12¼" h.. **895.00**
**Teacher (The),** No. 4801, 15" h.. **175.00**
**Tenderness,** No. 2094, 8¼" h. ... **115.00**
**This One's Mine,** No. 5376,
6½" h........................................ **495.00**
**Traveling in Style,** No. 5680,
6½" h........................................ **495.00**
**Wandering Minstrel,** No. 5676,
9½" h........................................ **310.00**
**Yachtsman,** No. 5206, 13¼" h. .. **210.00**

# LUSTRE WARES

*Lustred wares in imitation of copper, gold, silver and other colors were produced in England in the early 19th century and onward. Gold, copper or platinum oxides were painted on glazed objects which were then fired, giving them a lustred effect. Various forms of lustre wares include plain lustre with the entire object coated to obtain a metallic effect, bands of lustre decoration and painted lustre designs. Particularly appealing is the pink or purple "splash lustre" sometimes referred to as "Sunderland" lustre in the mistaken belief it was confined to the production of*

*Sunderland area potteries. Objects decorated in silver lustre by the "resist" process, wherein parts of the objects to be left free from lustre decoration were treated with wax, are referred to as "silver resist."*

*Wares formerly called "Canary Yellow Lustre" are now referred to as "Yellow-Glazed Earthenwares." Also see YELLOW-GLAZED EARTHEN-WARES.*

## SUNDERLAND PINK & OTHERS

*Two Pink Lustre Pitchers*

## COPPER

*Early Copper Lustre Sugar Bowl*

**Pitcher,** 6½" h., relief-molded scene of couple dancing ........... **$75.00**

**Plaque,** pierced to hang, round, wide copper lustre border band, the center w/lengthy black transfer-printed religious inscriptions in small letters below an all-seeing eye at the top & the words "Thou God Seest Me" in large capital letters, 19th c., 7" d........................................... **281.00**

**Sugar bowl,** cov., deep oblong body w/an angled shoulder & flaring rim, inset stepped & domed cover w/a blossom finial, decorated w/a continuous enameled band of blossoms, leaves & berries in pink, green, yellow & white, ca. 1840 (ILLUS. above) ........ **275.00 to 325.00**

**Bowl,** 4¾" d., 3" h., raised on a flaring low pedestal base, one side decorated w/a black transfer-printed scene of a man giving two children food, trimmed w/pink lustre banding, the other side w/a pink lustre-trimmed scroll cartouche enclosing the religious quotation "He that refuseth instruction despiseth his own soul," 19th c. (old restoration to tiny rim chip) .. **72.00**

**Cup & saucer,** handleless, overall pink lustre finish over a black transfer-printed landscape scene w/a city & cathedral in the center of the saucer framed by a wide floral border, the footed cup w/a landscape scene w/city & titled on one side "DURHAM," marked by Davenport, early 19th c. ...................................... **105.00**

**Loving cup,** small model of a frog in the bottom, transfer-printed clipper ship decoration w/printed verses from "The Sailor's Farewell," 19th c. ...................... **395.00**

**Pitcher,** jug-type, 5¾" h., pearlware, ovoid body w/flat rim & rim spout, C-scroll handle, the body relief-molded w/a grapevine border around the neck above a scene of two pointers w/a bird on one side & a setter w/a bird on the opposite side, the molded design heavily trimmed in pink lustre & green enamel, first half 19th c............. **770.00**

**Pitcher,** jug-type, 7" h., 6½" d., a footed tapering ovoid body w/a short cylindrical neck & long spout, one side w/a large transfer-printed scene showing Masonic emblems, the other side w/a transfer-printed Carpe Diem poem, the background in Sunderland pink splash lustre on white, early 19th c. (ILLUS. right, top previous page) .......... **275.00**

**Pitcher,** jug-type, 7¼" h., 6¾" d., footed wide bulbous ovoid body w/a short cylindrical neck & long spout, decorated on one side w/a color-trimmed transfer-printed scene of "The Sailor's Farewell" & on the other w/a tribute to the Crimean War, a poem in an oval wreath under the spout, pink lustre "squiggles" in the background & pink lustre banding at the neck & foot, hairline crack, mid-19th c. (ILLUS. left, top previous page)... **275.00**

**Pitcher,** jug-type, 8½" h., 8" d., footed bulbous ovoid body tapering to a short cylindrical neck w/a long spout, D-form handle, black transfer-printed designs w/a large Mariner's Compass on one side & a sailor's poem on the other & a large sailing ship under the spout, each reserve outlined w/yellow & brown bands & green leaves w/bands of pink lustre at the top, shoulder & neck, first half 19th c. (ILLUS. left, top next column) .................................... **358.00**

**Pitcher,** jug-type, 9½" h., 8½" d., footed bulbous body w/a short cylindrical neck & long spout, D-form handle, decorated w/three black transfer-printed reserves, on one side w/a large Mariner's Compass, on the other side a poem titled "To A Friend," & under the spout a scene of the Iron Bridge, each reserve outlined in yellow & brown bands & green leaves, pink lustre bands at the base, shoulder & neck, first half 19th c. (ILLUS. right, top next column) .................................... **358.00**

*Two Large Pink Lustre Pitchers*

*Rare Sunderland Lustre Pitcher*

**Pitcher,** jug-type, ovoid body w/wide rim spout & D-form handle, each side w/a large black transfer-printed portrait reserve, one showing "Captain Jones of the Macedonian" w/cannon & ship masts & the other showing "Captain Hill of the Constitution" w/similar trim, overall background of Sunderland pink splash lustre, ca. 1812 (ILLUS.)................... **5,500.00**

**Plaque,** pierced to hang, rectangular w/slightly scalloped flaring edges, the center decorated w/a black transfer-printed wreath surrounding "Thou GOD Seest Me," Sunderland pink splash lustre border, indistinct impressed mark, probably Dixon, ca. 1830, 7½ x 8½" ................................... **270.00**

**Plaque,** pierced to hang, round w/lightly scalloped & scroll-molded rim, the center decorated w/a black transfer-printed wreath around the inscription "Behold GOD will not cast away a perfect man, neither will HE help the evil doers. Job 8.20.," Sunderland pink splash wide border band w/copper lustre rim band, indistinct impressed mark, probably Dixon, England, ca. 1830, 8½" d. ......... **550.00**

**Tea set:** cov. teapot, creamer, urn-shaped cov. sugar bowl & eight handleless cups & saucers; decorated w/h.p. house scenes, one saucer impressed "Dawson," the set (minor damage).................................. **550.00**

**Toddy plates,** decorated w/a h.p. house scene, embossed floral rims, 5⅜" d., set of 5 (stains & hairlines) ................................. **363.00**

**Vase,** 6¾" h., baluster-form w/a wide trumpet neck, decorated overall w/a pink lustre finish over black transfer-printed vignettes of hunting scenes, one side showing a hunter & dog titled "Snipe Shooting," on the reverse two whippets chasing rabbits, the title smeared but probably "Coursing," a band of green enamel leaves around the neck, 19th c. ..................................... **220.00**

# MAJOLICA

*Majolica, a tin-enameled glazed pottery, has been produced for centuries. It originally took its name from the island of Majorca, a source of figuline (potter's clay). Subsequently it was widely produced in England, Europe and the United States. Etruscan majolica, now avidly sought, was made by Griffen, Smith & Hill, Phoenixville, Pennsylvania, in the last quarter of the 19th century. Most majolica advertised today is 19th or 20th century. Once scorned by most collectors, interest in this colorful ware so popular during the Victorian era has now revived and prices have risen dramatically in the past few years.*

## ETRUSCAN

*Etruscan Mark*

**Bowl,** 7¾" d., Shell & Seaweed patt. ...........................................**$275.00**

**Butter pat,** Geranium patt. ...........**95.00**

**Cup & saucer,** Classical series .....**90.00**

**Humidor,** cov., Shell & Seaweed patt., cobalt blue glaze............**4,000.00**

**Pitcher,** 6¾" h., Shell & Seaweed patt. ...........................................**445.00**

**Plate,** 8" d., Classical series ..........**75.00**

**Syrup pitcher w/hinged metal lid,** hexagonal, Bamboo patt., impressed mark, 7½" h. .............**201.00**

**Tea set:** cov. teapot, cov. sugar bowl, creamer & 8" d. plate; Cauliflower patt., small chips, the set .......................................**578.00**

## GENERAL

**Basket,** figural, a basket w/molded sides resembling crudely woven wicker folded together at the center w/the figure of a young boy playing the clarinet forming the handle, polychrome colors, Europe, late 19th - early 20th c., 11" l., 11" h..................................**275.00**

**Bouquet holder,** figural, fish standing on tail, polychrome, George Morley, Wellsville, Ohio, 13" h.........................................**385.00**

**Cake set:** 13" d. handled serving plate & six 6" d. plates; decorated w/red & green florals on basketweave ground, 7 pcs...**175.00**

**Centerpiece,** colorful figural lobster on footed white basketweave base unmarked, 11" d., 10¾" h. ..........................**350.00**

**Charger,** pierced to hang, decorated w/large white flowers

*Wedgwood Tremblay Dessert Service*

w/deep purple & green centers, large green leaves, pale green & yellow matte ground, Villeroy & Boch, 11¾" d. ...........................**200.00**

**Compote,** open, reticulated floral bowl, scene of young woman singing & man playing lute on floral pedestal next to tree trunk standard, 16½" d., 11" h. ...........**875.00**

**Dessert service:** twelve 8¾" d. plates, four 2¾" h. low tazzas & two 5¾" h. tall tazzas; Wedgwood "Tremblay" wares, green centers w/classical scenes w/polychrome borders, modeled by Thomas Greatbach for Thomas Goode, ca. 1871, small chips, marks on base altered, the set (ILLUS. top)..........................................**1,380.00**

**Ewer,** Art Nouveau design, a tall slender ovoid body molded in the form of a calla lily blossom in white w/long pointed green leaves & ornate scrolling leaf handle, scrolled four-footed base w/small white blossom (ILLUS. bottom next column) .....**770.00**

**Humidor,** cov., figural Irish jockey head, 5¼" h...............................**225.00**

**Humidor,** cov., figural Scotsman head, blue coat, incised numbers on base, 6½" h. (minor nicks on shoulder)......................**235.00**

*Calla Lily Ewer*

**Match holder,** oblong angled base w/match striking bands along the sides, the tapering oval body molded at one end w/a mask of Tragedy & at the other w/a mask of Comedy, decorated w/pale blue & golden yellow....................**770.00**

**Oyster plate,** alternating pink & blue wells (chip on back) ...........**200.00**

**Pedestal,** the tripartite top decorated around the bottom edge w/leaftips & beading above a conforming body w/rectangular panels, the canted sides headed by rams' head masks joined by foliate swags & ending in cloven hoof feet, impressed "Minton 790," 19th c., restorations, 35½" h. (ILLUS. top next page)............**3,162.00**

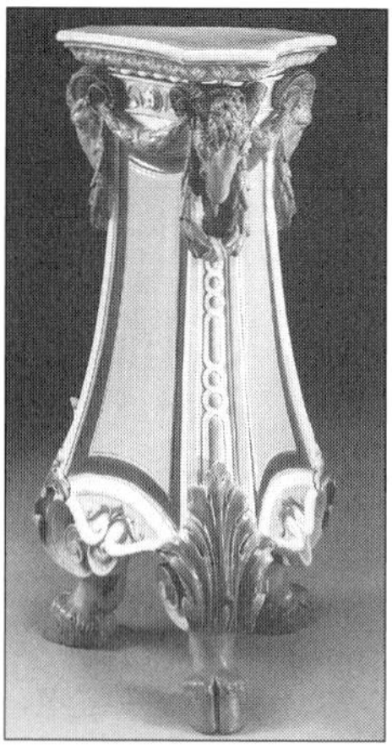

*Fine Minton Pedestal*

**Pitcher,** 6" h., blackberry
decoration ...................................**100.00**

**Pitcher,** 6" h., footed, bulbous
body tapering to cylindrical neck
w/pinched spout, branch handle,
water lily decoration,
polychrome w/blue & brown
ground (chips) ...........................**165.00**

**Pitcher,** jug-type, 7½" h., figural
owl .............................................**210.00**

**Pitcher,** 7¾" h., 5½" d., fruit
decoration on front & back,
brown textured ground & pink
interior (very minor nicks).............**85.00**

**Pitcher,** 8¼" h., footed tapering
paneled body w/angled branch
handle, decorated w/polychrome
birds & flowers, English registry
mark .........................................**358.00**

**Pitcher,** 8½" h., decorated
w/large multicolored flowers
w/green stems trailing around
the sides, green handle & base
band on a tan ground, France ...**250.00**

**Pitcher,** 9¼" h., model of a duck
in shades of green & yellow
(small chips)................................**55.00**

**Plaques,** pierced to hang, round,
each molded in full-relief w/fruit,
one w/red & yellow pears on a
brown branch w/green leaves,
the other w/clusters of red
cherries on a brown branch
w/green leaves, each on a
shaded dark brown to mottled
pale blue ground, France,
19th c., 12½" d., pr. (ILLUS.
bottom)......................................**450.00**

**Plate,** 5½" d., center multicolored
leaf design on basketweave
ground........................................**39.00**

**Plate,** 8" d., blackberry decoration
on basketweave ground.............**135.00**

**Plate,** 8⅜" d., leaves & flowers in
green & pink on yellow ground
(small rim flakes).......................**116.00**

**Plate,** 9" d., floral decoration on
olive green ground, Imperial
Bonn mark .................................**45.00**

**Plate,** the center h.p. w/a large
brown horse head among green
leaves against a shaded dark
green to cream ground, a wide
pierced looping rim band,
Wedgwood (ILLUS. top next
page)......................................**1,210.00**

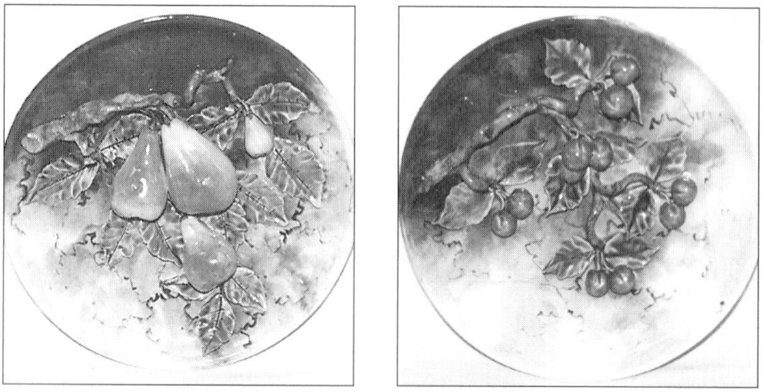

*Two French Majolica Plaques*

*Wedgwood Horse Plate*

*Holdcroft Sardine Box*

**Platter,** 12" l., decorated w/leaves & ferns ......................................**180.00**

**Platter,** 13" l., blackberry decoration, marked "Clifton Decor" .......................................**200.00**

**Sardine box,** cov., a domed rectangular cover w/rounded corners, a molded crab & fish on the top & a brown seaweed top border band above small molded fish around the sides, the conforming rectangular base molded at each corner w/white blossoms & green leaves, cover & base w/a pale blue ground, Holdcroft, England, 19th c., rim chip (ILLUS. top next column)...**2,200.00**

**Strawberry plates,** individual, rounded form w/a narrow brown vine border band, the dark blue wide border band w/clusters of white blossoms & green leaves on two sides & oblong slightly indented wells on the other two sides, the center in plain pale blue, George Jones, England, pr............................................**2,640.00**

**Sugar bowl,** cov., Wild Rose patt...**90.00**

**Teapot,** cov., Bamboo patt., James S. Taft, Keene, New Hampshire, 19th c.....................**125.00**

**Toothbrush holder,** Maple Leaf patt. ...........................................**175.00**

**Tray,** rectangular w/irregular scalloped edge, brown w/light blue vining border, 8¼ x 11¼" (minor flakes on table ring) ........**116.00**

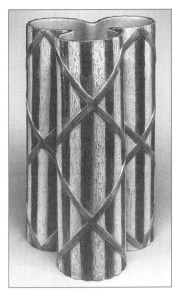

*Bamboo-form Umbrella Stand*

**Umbrella stand,** modeled as a cluster of three large striped bamboo stalks tied together w/crisscrossed straps, indistinctly stamped, 19th c., 21" h. (ILLUS.) .......................**1,610.00**

**Vase,** 12⅞" h., 5⅞" d. at neck & base, cylindrical, relief-molded applied hot pink & orange flowers & green leaves, Barbotine-style icing-type glaze freely trailed on, black ground shading to smoky grey at base, by Massier's, Golfe Juan, France (piece of large leaf on back missing, some very small nicks) ......................................**1,200.00**

**Vase & stand,** overall 4' 5" h., the bulbous baluster-form vase raised on a slender pedestal base, the wide shoulders tapering to a tall trumpet-form neck w/a rolled rim flanked by long coiling green snake handles continuing down to the shoulder, the body decorated w/a colorful riverside landscape w/peasant figures, the base of the vase resting on a raised disc on a pedestal platform w/a ringed base & paneled foot decorated in dark blue & grey, Italy, late 19th c. (base of vase damaged)...............................**2,875.00**

**Vases,** 13" h., circular body w/applied winged griffin handles, decorated w/cranes on flowering branches, the opposite side w/insects & leaves, marked "S.T.," late 19th c., pr. ................**770.00**

Photo Courtesy of Michael Strawser Auctions

*Figural Majolica Pitchers & Teapots*

### Top row, left to right:
**Pitcher,** figural bear .....................**413.00**
**Pitcher,** figural cat .......................**770.00**
**Pitcher,** bust of bearded man w/name at bottom, by Frie Onnaing ...................................**523.00**
**Pitcher,** figural seated bulldog, by Frie Onnaing ............................**770.00**
**Pitcher,** figural seated brown dog...........................................**605.00**

### Bottom row, left to right:
**Pitcher,** figural white pelican w/green leaves...........................**605.00**
**Pitcher,** figural monkey seated in front of & grasping a tree w/branch handle .......................**385.00**
**Teapot,** cov., figural begging hound in black & brown .............**138.00**
**Teapot,** cov., figural fish on a round melon...............................**770.00**

# MARBLEHEAD POTTERY

*Marblehead Bowl-Vase*

*This pottery was organized in 1904 by Dr. Herbert J. Hall as a therapeutic aid to patients in a sanitarium he ran in Marblehead, Massachusetts. It was later separated from the sanitarium and directed by Arthur E. Baggs, a fine artist and designer, who bought out the factory in 1916 and operated it until its closing in 1936. Most wares were hand-thrown and decorated and carry the company mark of a stylized sailing vessel flanked by the letters "M" and "P."*

*Marblehead Pottery Mark*

**Bowl,** 8½" d., 2" h., wide shallow incurved sides, smooth speckled dark blue matte exterior & a light blue interior, ship mark .......... **$330.00**

**Bowl,** 9¾" d., 5½" h., a small footring supporting a deep trumpet-form bowl w/a widely flaring & flattened rim, smooth matte green glaze, satin finish interior, mark obscured by glaze ....................................... **495.00**

**Bowl-vase,** squatty bulbous body tapering to a flat mouth, pale pink matte glaze, impressed mark obscured by glaze, 3½" d., 1½" h....................................... **143.00**

**Bowl-vase,** squatty bulbous body tapering to a closed flat mouth, the top carved w/a repeated design of caramel & black fruit among brown leaves w/prominent spines against an olive green matte ground, impressed mark & incised "HT," 4½" d., 3" h. (ILLUS. top previous column) .................. **1,650.00**

**Tile,** square, painted w/a scene of a Spanish galleon in brown, white & green on a green & blue sea, impressed mark & original paper label, 4½" w. ................... **303.00**

**Tile,** square, decorated w/a tall waisted yellow latticework central basket overflowing w/yellow & green flowers & blue fruit, a pair of facing blue & yellow parrots perched on the arched handle, against a cream-colored crackle glaze ground w/a narrow blue border band, impressed company logo, partial paper label, incised "X" & painted "BT," 6" sq. (several edge chips) ......... **770.00**

**Vase,** 3" h., 3½" d., squatty wide bulbous body tapering to a wide flaring rim, decorated w/stylized incised seaweed in brown on a striated periwinkle blue ground, decorated by A.E. Baggs, die-stamped ship mark & "AEB" ................................... **605.00**

**Vase,** 3½" h., 4¼" d., squatty bulbous ovoid body tapering to a rolled rim, decorated w/stylized blue flowers on green stems on a matte mauve ground, impressed ship mark & paper label (rim hairline) .................. **1,320.00**

**Vase,** 3¾" h., 4½" d., squatty spherical body w/a closed-in rim, incised black dots & lines around the mouth, smooth matte speckled green ground, impressed ship mark & "H.T.," by Hannah Tutt ...................... **1,430.00**

**Vase,** 4½" h., 3½" d., simple ovoid body tapering slightly to a flat rim, surface-decorated w/a band of stylized green leaves, blueberries & brown stems on a mustard yellow matte ground, impressed mark ................... **2,530.00**

**Vase,** 5" h., simple baluster-form body w/a wide, short cylindrical neck, rich dark green matte glaze, impressed mark.............. **358.00**

**Vase,** 6" h., 3" d., simple cylindrical form, an incised Greek key band around the rim in dark purplish blue against a grey speckled matte ground, ship mark & "M.T." ................. **1,320.00**

**Vase,** 7" h., wide ovoid body tapering to a small rolled mouth above a delicate incised geometric rim band, medium blue flecked matte glaze, impressed mark & incised artist's mark (small base chip) .. **440.00**

**Vase,** 7⅛" h., simple slightly tapering cylindrical body w/a

rounded base & flat, wide mouth, an overall dark moss green ground w/a carved band of slinking black panthers around the top, each in front of rectangular panels forming a window into a forest setting, by Hannah Tutt, marked ............. **3,850.00**

**Vase,** 7½" h., 10" d., broad-shouldered ovoid body w/a short, wide rim, carved w/a repeated decoration of three large stylized blossoms & long, narrow overlapping vertical leaves, muted brown against an olive green matte ground, impressed marks & incised artist's mark. **17,600.00**

**Vase,** 8" h., 4½" d., slender tapering ovoid body w/a flared mouth, even pebbly dark blue matte glaze, die-stamped ship mark ......................................... **495.00**

*Incised Marblehead Vases*

Photo Courtesy of Skinner, Inc.

**Vase,** 3⅝" h., 4⅝" d., squatty bulbous tapering ovoid body w/a rolled rim, matte blue ground incised w/a repeating design of stylized bud-forms in a pale green, impressed mark, by Hannah Tutt w/incised artist's initials & paper label, ca. 1909 (ILLUS. right) ........................ **1,150.00**

**Vase,** 3¾" h., 4⅜" d., squatty bulbous tapering ovoid body w/a rolled rim, matte blue ground

incised w/flowers & leaves in dark blue, green & red, impressed mark (ILLUS. center).................................... **1,093.00**

**Vase,** 6" h., 5½" d., bulbous tapering ovoid body w/a flared mouth, matte grey glaze w/blue speckling, decorated w/a wide incised stylized floral band in blue, impressed mark, minor rim nick, two rim hairlines (ILLUS. left) ......................................... **1,035.00**

# MARTIN BROTHERS POTTERY

*Martin Brothers Pitchers*

*Martinware, the term used for this pottery, dates from 1873 and is the product of the Martin brothers—Robert, Wallace, Edwin, Walter and Charles— often considered the first British studio potters. From first to final stages, their hand-thrown pottery was completely the work of the team. The early wares may be simple and conventional, but the Martin brothers built up their reputation by producing ornately engraved, incised or carved designs as well as rather bizarre figural wares. The amusing face-jugs are considered some of their finest work. After 1910, the work of the pottery declined and can be considered finished by 1915, though some attempts were made to fire pottery as late as the 1920s.*

*RW Martin & Brothers
London & Southall*

*Martin Brothers Mark*

**Jar,** cov., modeled as a grotesque bird w/a large brown beak & blue feathers, inscribed "Martin Brothers - London & Southall - 9-1890," w/a round wooden stand, 4½" w., 8½" h. ......... **$11,000.00**

**Pitcher,** jug-type, 6¼" h., globular form w/loop handle from shoulder to rim w/short spout, molded in relief on each side w/a smiling face, glaze in cream & chocolate brown, incised "R.W. Martin & Bros. London & Southall" (ILLUS. right) .......... **2,760.00**

**Pitcher,** jug-type, 6½" h., globular form w/loop handle from shoulder to rim w/short spout, molded in relief on each side w/a smiling face, glazed in slate grey & mustard yellow, incised "B37 - R.W. Martin & Bros. London & Southall" (ILLUS. left top previous column) ............ **2,990.00**

*Martin Bros. Face Pitcher*

**Pitcher,** jug-type, 7¼" h., globular w/a loop handle from shoulder to rim w/short spout, molded in relief on each side w/a humorous smiling face, brown glaze, incised mark & dated 1898, restored rim chips (ILLUS.) ......................... **1,495.00**

**Pitcher,** 8¾" h., 5¾" w., slender squared ovoid form w/a conforming rim w/one end tapering & curving down to form the handle, each side etched w/grotesque fish in green on a light blue ground between stripes of reddish brown, 1903, inscribed "6-1903 - Martin Bros - London & Southall" (hairlines, restoration to rim & handle base).................... **880.00**

**Tile,** square, incised stylized rounded flowers on curved stems w/scrolled leaves in black on a brown ground, unmarked, 5¾" w. ...................................... **110.00**

**Vase,** miniature, 3½" h., 2¼" w., a squared ovoid form w/a small flat mouth, each side incised w/grotesque fish outlined in blue against a grey ground, incised "2-1901 - Martin Bros. - London - Southall," 1901 ....................... **825.00**

# MASSIER (Clement)

*Large Massier Jardiniere*

Clement Massier was a French artist potter who worked in the late 19th and early 20th centuries creating exquisite earthenware items with lustre decoration.

*Clement-Massier*
*Sdk Juan AM*

*Massier Mark*

**Charger,** round, decorated w/a southern French scene of pines by a body of water, in a lustre glaze w/gold on a burgundy ground, die-stamped "Clement Massier - Golfe Juan - AK," w/the same mark painted on, 12½" d.................................... **$1,540.00**

**Jardiniere & pedestal,** the columnar base & footed bulbous jardiniere w/a widely flaring rim, each molded in low-relief w/an overall design of delicate interlacing foliate & scroll designs, the pedestal divided into arched panels, both w/a sea green glaze, impressed marks, overall 4' 11½" h., 2 pcs. (ILLUS.) .................................. **1,527.00**

**Plate,** 10" d., iridescent poppy decoration ................................. **625.00**

**Vase,** 4⅛" h., cylindrical body tapering to a quatrefoil rim, decorated w/a continuous panorama of bamboo canes before a lake, purple lustre glaze, impressed & painted factory marks (restoration) ........ **191.00**

**Vase,** 11⅞" h., Limoges-style, tall gently tapering cylindrical form w/a squared mouth, decorated w/small scallop shells in ivory, gold & dark red against a stylized deep sea background in bronze & green iridized ground, impressed "Clement Massier - Golfe Juan (A.M.)," & inscribed "Clement Massier - Golfe. Juan - A.M.," ca. 1900 ........................ **345.00**

# MC COY

*Chipmunk Cookie Jar*

Collectors are now seeking the art wares of two McCoy potteries. One was founded in Roseville, Ohio, in the late 19th century as the J.W. McCoy Pottery, subsequently becoming Brush-McCoy Pottery Co., later Brush Pottery. The other was founded also in Roseville in 1910 as Nelson McCoy Sanitary Stoneware Co., later becoming Nelson

*McCoy Pottery. In 1967 the pottery was sold to D.T. Chase of the Mount Clemens Pottery Co. who sold his interest to the Lancaster Colony Corp. in 1974. The pottery shop closed in 1985. Cookie jars are especially collectible today.*

Some helpful reference books are The Collector's Encyclopedia of McCoy Pottery, *by the Huxfords (Collector Books),* McCoy Cookie Jars From the First to the Latest, *by Harold Nichols (Nichols Publishing, 1987), and* McCoy Pottery Collector's Reference & Value Guide *by Bob Hanson, Craig Nissen and Margaret Hanson (Collector Books).*

*McCoy Mammy Cookie Jar*

*McCoy Mark*

**Basket,** hanging-type, squatty bulbous form w/relief-molded clusters of berries & large leaves on each side w/undulating molded ribs between them, pierced hanging holes around the incurved rim, dark brick red w/dark green on the leaves & berries, Nelson McCoy Sanitary Stoneware Company, ca. 1926 .................................... **$45.00**

**Bowl,** 6½" d., yellow basketweave design .................. **16.00**

**Coffee set:** cov. coffee server & four mugs; El Rancho Bar-B-Que line, ca. 1960s, the set ..... **220.00**

**Cookie jar,** Bananas, 1948-52 (crazing) ................................... **160.00**

**Cookie jar,** Bear and Beehive, No. 143, w/box ........................... **45.00**

**Cookie jar,** Chilly Willy, 1986-89, w/box ......................................... **45.00**

**Cookie jar,** Chipmunk, 1960-61 (ILLUS. bottom previous page) . **110.00**

**Cookie jar,** Circus Horse, black, 1961 ......................................... **195.00**

**Cookie jar,** Coalby Cat, 1967-68.................................... **240.00**

**Cookie jar,** Cow, reclining, black & white, No. 8166, w/box ........... **50.00**

**Cookie jar,** Happy Face, 1972-79..................................... **35.00**

**Cookie jar,** Hocus Rabbit, 1978-79 ...................... **40.00 to 50.00**

**Cookie jar,** Mammy, "Cookies" only, yellow dress (ILLUS. above) ...................................... **550.00**

**Cookie jar,** Penguin, yellow, 1940-43.................................... **185.00**

**Cookie jar,** Puppy with Sign, 1961-62..................................... **70.00**

**Cookie jar,** Raggedy Ann, 1972-75..................................... **60.00**

**Cookie jar,** Upside-down Panda, 1978-79..................................... **50.00**

**Decanter,** figural len, marked "Apollo" ..................................... **50.00**

**Decanter set,** figural, train engine, coal car & two additional cars, marked "Jupiter 60," 1969, made for McCormick, the set .... **240.00**

**Flowerpot w/attached saucer,** embossed white roses ............... **35.00**

**Food warmer,** cov., El Rancho Bar-B-Que line, model of a Chuck Wagon w/rack, ca. 1960s ................. **175.00 to 200.00**

*Ivy Pattern Tea Set*

*McCoy Quails Planter*

**Jardiniere,** embossed holly decoration, green glaze, small, ca. 1935, 4½" h. ........................... **50.00**

**Lamp base,** model of a pair of brown cowboy boots w/electric fittings ........................................ **50.00**

**Mugs,** coffee, El Rancho Bar-B-Que line, ca. 1960s, set of 6 ..... **120.00**

**Planter & saucer,** figural Happy Face, yellow & black, 4" h. .......... **12.00**

**Planter,** figural, model of a bird dog, brown & white, standing holding bird in its mouth, in front of a rail fence on a rockwork base, 1954, 12½" l., 8½" h. ........ **145.00**

**Planter,** figural, model of a frog w/umbrella, 1954 ...................... **85.00**

**Planter,** figural, rodeo cowboy design, rectangular w/front embossed w/a cowboy on horseback roping a calf, brown & ivory, 1956, 4 x 7¾" .............. **155.00**

**Planter,** figural, spinning wheel w/dog & cat, grey, 1953, 7½" h. ...................................... **40.00**

**Planter,** figural, two quail & baby quail on base w/foliage background, natural colors, ca. 1955, 4 x 8½", 7" h. (ILLUS. bottom previous column) ........... **45.00**

**Planter,** figural Wishing Well, ca. 1950 ............................................ **19.00**

**Planter,** figural, pussy at the well, 1957, 7 x 7" ................................. **85.00**

**Serving plate,** El Rancho Bar-B-Que line, model of a Sombrero, ca. 1960s ................................. **250.00**

**Soup tureen w/sombrero cover,** El Rancho Bar-B-Que line, ca. 1960s, 2 pcs...................... **300.00**

**Stein,** model of a seven league boot, brown & black glossy glaze, 1971, 8¼" h. ..................... **25.00**

**Tea set:** cov. teapot, creamer & open sugar bowl; Ivy patt., twig handles, tan w/brown relief-molded ivy leaf decoration, 1950, 3 pcs. (ILLUS. top) ........... **58.00**

**Vase,** 7" h., cylindrical, Butterfly line, yellow ................................. **35.00**

**Vase,** 7¼" h., figural lily, Flower Form line, w/original label .......... **60.00**

**Vase,** 9" h., lobed ovoid body
w/flaring foot & rim, loop handles
from shoulder to rim, yellow
glaze, ca. 1950 .......................... **45.00**

**Vase,** 10" h., black ground
w/embossed plant design in
mottled brown, glossy glaze,
marked "Olympia," 1905 .......... **245.00**

**Wall pocket,** Blossomtime line,
white glaze & white & yellow
blossoms ................... **75.00 to 100.00**

**Wall pocket,** figural, a cluster of
white grapes against a ground of
green leaves, ca. 1953 .............. **75.00**

---

# MEISSEN

*The secret of true hard paste porcelain,
known long before to the Chinese, was
"discovered" accidentally in Meissen,
Germany, by J.F. Bottger, an alchemist
working with E.W. Tschirnhausen. The
first European true porcelain was made in
the Meissen Porcelain Works, organized
about 1709. Meissen marks have been
widely copied by other factories. Some
pieces listed here are recent.*

*Meissen Mark*

**Bottle,** small double-gourd form,
painted w/alternating figural &
foliate panels on a turquoise
ground, factory marks, late
19th c., 7½" h. (wear).............. **$374.00**

**Candelabra,** figural, one molded
in the form of a young man, the
other in the form of a young
woman, both holding a flower,
seated on the edge of two
baskets at the base of a branch-

Meissen Figural Clock

form standard issuing two
foliate-molded & floral-encrusted
finials, ca. 1900, underglaze-
blue crossed swords mark &
incised "2034," w/a pair of
Meissen bobeches also marked,
8¾" h., pr. (restored).............. **1,955.00**

**Clock,** shelf or mantel, figural, a
round clock dial w/Roman
numerals enclosed at one end of
a porcelain case, the bezel
surrounded by a ropetwist band
& the rounded top surmounted
by a spread-winged crowing
rooster, a young boy seated &
reading while leaning against
the clock case, all mounted on a
rectangular molded base
w/ropetwist bands, molded
center shells & corner blocks on
short, square tapering legs, h.p.
detailing, 19th c., 10½" h.
(ILLUS. top) .......................... **1,430.00**

**Cruet w/original stopper,** Indian
Flower patt., magenta, blue
crossed swords mark ............... **175.00**

**Dessert set:** cup & saucer
w/matching 8" d. plate; red,
white & gold decoration, blue
crossed sword mark, the set..... **325.00**

**Egg cup,** Blue Onion patt. .......... **100.00**

**Figure,** allegorical, a
representation of Astronomy, a
partially clad female looking
through a telescope & holding a
compass in her other hand, a
globe w/the stars beside her,
incised "369," underglaze-blue

*Meissen Allegorical Figure*

*Meissen Figure Group*

crossed swords mark, late
19th c., one seconds mark,
16½" h. (ILLUS.) .................... **3,575.00**

**Figure of a gallant,** a gentleman
wearing a 18th c. courtly
costume, holding his tricorn hat
& standing before a tree stump
looking down at his greyhound
seated by his side, underglaze-
blue crossed swords mark,
incised model number "L.162,"
painted numerals, early 20th c.,
8⅞" h. (some restoration
to extremities) ........................ **2,185.00**

**Figure of a vintager,** a man
standing wearing a tricorn black
hat, light blue coat, checkered
waistcoat, cream kneebreeches,
grey knee socks & black clogs,
carrying a basket of grapes on
one arm, raised on a scroll-
molded mound base, from the
Cris de Paris Series, modeled
by J.J. Kaendler & P. Reinicke,
18th c., underglaze-blue crossed
swords mark & "3," 5¾" h. ........ **920.00**

**Figure group,** allegorical, a nude
lady reclining against two small
leafy trees & holding a long
cornucopia w/flowers spilling out
of the end, a putto to each side,
on an oval base, polychrome
decoration, 19th c., 6¾" h. ..... **1,265.00**

**Figure group,** a baby girl stooping
over to pick up her doll, she
wearing a floral-decorated slip,
factory marks, early 20th c.,
4½" h. (ILLUS.)............................ **920.00**

**Figure group,** two children & a
dog, the boy standing to the
right in front of a small leafy tree
& wearing a tricorn hat, jacket &
kneebreeches, the seated girl
beside him wearing a cap & a
floral-sprigged dress, a small
dog to her left, on a molded oval
base, polychrome decoration,
19th c., 6½" h. ........................ **1,035.00**

**Figure group,** Europa and the Bull,
polychrome decoration, impressed
& painted factory marks, late 19th
c., 8¼" w., 9¾" h. ...................... **863.00**

**Model of a bird,** the long-billed
bird perched on a leafy tree
stump w/its head turned, 20th c.,
8¾" h......................................... **863.00**

**Model of a cockatoo,** the white
bird painted w/orange accents,
perched atop a tree trunk
w/blossoming flowers, on a
shaped base, underglaze-blue
crossed swords mark, ca. 1900,
9½" h......................................... **748.00**

**Plates,** 9½" d., enamel-decorated
w/bird & insect decorations,
gilded border, 19th c., set of 11
(gilt wear) ................................ **1,150.00**

*Ornate Potpourri Urns*

*Meissen Serving Dish*

**Plates,** fruit, 9¾" d., reticulated border, each painted w/a still life of fruit w/elaborate openwork pierced borders & gilded edge, marked, late 19th c., pr. ............ **690.00**

**Potpourri urns,** cov., each ovoid body w/a horizontal gilt band molded on the front w/a raised panel painted in colors w/cherub figures at play among clouds & on the reverse w/a floral wreath, bow & quiver of arrows, the band suspending swags of acanthus leaves & berries & flanked by lovebird figural handles, raised on a slender foliate-molded pedestal stem chamfered square foot, the high domed covers molded w/graduated bands of foliate medallions beneath a gilt floral wreath & quiver of arrows knop, underglaze-blue crossed swords marks, incised & impressed numbers, late 19th c., numerous chips & losses, 14" h., pr. (ILLUS. above) .................... **12,075.00**

**Salt dip,** figural, figure of putto sitting next to seashell, on a scroll-molded oval base, factory marks, late 19th c. ................... **489.00**

**Serving dishes,** round w/gently scalloped rims & sections of molded S-scrolls around the wide rim alternating w/plain panels all w/a latticework border band, h.p. overall w/scattered floral sprays, factory marks, late 19th c., 15" d., set of 4 (ILLUS. of one, above) ...................... **1,495.00**

**Tureen,** cov., oval, magenta & pink floral design w/cherub finial, crossed swords mark, 14½" l. (minor edge damage on flowers around cherub) ........................ **275.00**

**Vases,** cov., 16" h., *pate-sur-pate*, tall baluster-form body raised on a ringed flaring pedestal base, a tall waisted neck w/cobalt blue ground & ornate gilt lattice trim supports a high domed matching cover w/fruit cluster finial, the shoulders of the body mounted w/tall scroll-molded handles reaching to the rim & topped by grotesque animal heads, the sides of the body decorated on each side w/a cobalt blue ground w/a large oval reserve framing white slip scenes of classical figures & reveling bacchanalian putti within a scrolled border, late 19th c., pr. (restorations) ...................... **20,700.00**

# MERRIMAC POTTERY

*The Merrimac Ceramic Company of Newburyport, Massachusetts, was initially organized in 1897 by Thomas S. Nickerson for the production of* inexpensive garden pottery and decorated tile. Within the year, production was expanded to include decorative art pottery and this change was reflected in a new name, Merrimac Pottery Company, adopted in 1902. Early glazes were limited to primarily matte green and yellow but by 1903, a variety of hues, including iridescent and metallic lustres, were used. Marked only with a paper label until after 1901, it then bore an impressed mark incorporating a fish beneath "Merrimac." Fire destroyed the pottery in 1908 and this relatively short span of production makes the ware scarce and expensive.

Merrimac Mark

**Vase,** 3" h., 6" d., an angled widely flaring lower half below the upwardly slanted wide shoulder to a wide, short cylindrical neck, a rounded arch handle on one side of the neck to the shoulder, rich dark green mottled glaze ........................... **$66.00**

**Vase,** 6½" h., 6½" d., a wide bulbous base below a wide angled shoulder tapering to a thick cylindrical neck flanked by squared loop handles from the rim to the shoulder, fine satin deep green & gunmetal glaze, die-stamped mark .................... **495.00**

**Vase,** 14" h., 7" d., footed tall slightly tapering cylindrical body w/a flared mouth, glossy metallic dark green & gunmetal flambé glaze, unmarked ...................... **550.00**

**Vase,** floor-type, 24" h., 12" d., a tall slender ovoid body w/a short rolled neck, matte green & gunmetal crystalline glaze, die-stamped mark & paper label (hairline at base goes slightly up the side) ............................... **3,300.00**

# METLOX POTTERIES

*Metlox Drummer Boy Cookie Jar*

California, particularly southern California, was a Mecca for studio potters and production pottery companies in the early part of this century. Metlox Potteries, one of the largest production businesses, opened in 1927 in Manhattan Beach, California. T.C. and Willis Prouty, a father and son team, were the owners. Before Metlox, the Prouty family owned a tile business which, when sold in 1926, ended up being a part of the western division of American Encaustic Tiling Company. Within five years dinnerware was a large part of the Metlox operation and two years later a complete line of Poppytrail dinnerware came on the market. Today Poppytrail is a favorite among collectors.

When designer Carl Romanelli came on board in the late 1930s, figural products were put into production. However, during World War II, the figurals were drastically curtailed as was dinnerware. After the war, Evan K. Shaw bought Metlox when Shaw's American Pottery Company was destroyed by fire. Romanelli animals and figures, especially those of women, were well received by the buying public. Poppets by Poppytrail are also popular with collectors today. There are many poppets *from which to choose, even a complete set of a Salvation Army band. Helen Slater was responsible for these doll-like flower holders, figurines and shelf sitters. Cookie jars were a continuing part of the Metlox business throughout the years. Evan Shaw ran the business until his death in 1980 and the family continued its operation until 1989 when the business closed.*

METLOX
MADE IN
U.S.A.

*Incised or stamped mark*

C Romanelli

*Carl Romanelli's name found on the base rim of nudes and certain vases.*

Miniatures
by METLOX
MANHATTAN BEACH
CALIFORNIA

*Paper label in blue on silver.*

**Ashtray,** Sombrero patt.,
2¾ x 6"..................................... **$30.00**

**Ashtray,** Homestead Provincial
patt., 8¼" d................................. **60.00**

**Bowl,** soup, 5" d., lug handle,
Red Rooster patt......................... **12.00**

**Bowl,** soup, 8⅛" d., Sculptured
Grape patt................................. **11.00**

**Butter dish,** cov., Sculptured
Grape patt................................. **40.00**

**Candlestick,** Homestead
Provincial patt. ........................... **30.00**

**Canister,** cov., model of broccoli
stalks, "Vegetable" line, green
glaze w/darker green cover,
1½ qt. ..................................... **120.00**

**Casserole,** cov., hen on nest,
California Provincial patt., 1 qt.,
10 oz. ..................................... **195.00**

**Cookie jar,** Ballerina Bear .......... **110.00**

**Cookie jar,** Bear w/Blue Sweater . **95.00**

**Cookie jar,** Chef Pierre. **75.00 to 100.00**

**Cookie jar,** Drummer Boy
(ILLUS. top previous page)....... **750.00**

**Cookie jar,** Parrot, seated on a
short brown tree stump, green &
yellow, Model No. 555 .............. **400.00**

**Cookie jar,** Pine Cone w/grey
squirrel finial, Model No. 509,
11" h............................................ **85.00**

**Cookie jar,** Rex, dinosaur, white . **110.00**

**Cookie jar,** Rose Blossom, pale
pink w/green leaves at bottom,
Model No. 513, 2¾ qt. (ILLUS.
right below) ............................... **380.00**

**Cookie jar,** Tulip, yellow & green
(ILLUS. left below) ..................... **425.00**

**Cup & saucer,** Pintoria patt.,
rectangular shape saucer

*Tulip & Rose Cookie Jars*

*Metlox Surrey with Man & Woman Figures*

w/round depression for round cup, Poppy Orange gloss, scarce pattern, set ...................... **95.00**

**Cup & saucer,** Sculptured Grape patt., blue fruit w/green leaves & brown twigs, set .......................... **19.00**

**Figure of a man,** seated, shelf-sitter, "Papa," Model No. 653, 5¼" h. (ILLUS. right in surrey) .... **65.00**

**Figure of a woman,** seated, shelf sitter, "Mama," Model No. 652, 5" h. (ILLUS. left in surrey).......... **60.00**

**Figure,** Poppets series, "Cigar Store Indian," w/basket without handles attached to body from left foot to below waist, full headdress, blanket around shoulders, white & brown, 8¾" h........................................ **105.00**

**Figure,** Poppets series, "Grover," bass drum man, blue coat & hat, black shoes, drum w/white front & "Rejoice" in blue, 6¾" h. (ILLUS.) ...................................... **75.00**

**Gravy boat,** California Provincial patt., 1 pt. ..................................... **65.00**

**Gravy bowl w/attached underplate,** Sculptured Grape patt............................................. **30.00**

*Poppets "Grover" Figure*

**Jam/mustard jar,** cov., Homestead patt. ......................... **65.00**

**Match box,** hanging-type, Homestead Provincial patt.......... **75.00**

**Model of a surrey w/metal fringe,** pale green, Nostalgia Line, 10½" l., 9" h. (ILLUS.) ........ **95.00**

**Planter,** model of three owls seated on a log w/mama on left, papa on right & baby in front, blue & white w/black accents & yellow eyes, 5¾" h. ..................... **50.00**

**Plate,** bread & butter, 6½" d.,
Sculptured Grape pattern,
muted brown leaves, blue fruit.... **10.00**

**Plate,** salad, 7½" d., Red Rooster
patt. ............................................... **6.00**

**Plate,** dinner, 10" d., Red Rooster
patt. ............................................. **10.00**

**Plate,** dinner, 10¼" d., California
Ivy patt. ...................................... **10.00**

**Plate,** chop, 12¼" d., Homestead
patt. ............................................. **65.00**

**Platter,** oval, 13½" l., Red
Rooster patt. .............................. **30.00**

**Platter,** 14" d., "Cabbage" line,
green........................................... **40.00**

**Platter,** 19" l., oval, "Holstein
Herd" late line pattern, black
splotches on a white ground ....... **70.00**

**Salt & pepper shakers,** model of
an owl, brown & gold glaze, salt,
5¼" h., pepper, 5" h., pr. ............. **55.00**

**Sugar bowl,** cov., California
Strawberry patt. ......................... **18.00**

**Teapot,** cov., California Provincial
patt. ........................................... **115.00**

**Teapot,** cov., Red Rooster patt..... **85.00**

**Tureen,** cov., "Cabbage" line,
green cabbage, 3 qt. ................. **110.00**

**Vase,** 9¼" h., model of a sea
horse upright on a deeply
scalloped, oblong base, white
gloss, Model No. 1809 .............. **165.00**

**Vegetable bowl,** cov., Provincial
Blue patt., 10" d., 1 qt. ............. **125.00**

**Vegetable bowl,** open, divided,
Sculptured Daisy patt., 8" d. ....... **45.00**

---

# METTLACH

*Ceramics with the name Mettlach were
produced by Villeroy & Boch and other
potteries in the Mettlach area of Germany.
Villeroy and Boch's finest years of
production are thought to be from about
1890 to 1910. An important reference to
this collecting field is* The Mettlach Book
*by Gary Kirsner (Glentiques, Ltd., Coral
Springs, Florida).*

*Mettlach Mark*

**Jardinere,** phanolith, footed oval
wide bowl w/a gadrooned base
band & incurved flaring rim,
decorated w/a continuous band
of white relief cameo figures of
Grecian men & women riding in
a chariot or sitting at a table &
drinking, green ground, No.
7000 & No. 17 marked on base,
8¾ x 10", 5½" h. .................... **$495.00**

**Pitcher,** 8¾" h., 6½" d., paneled
ovoid base below cylindrical
neck w/angular handle & flared
lip, incised w/stylized berries &
leaves in mustard & dark blue
on a white ground, impressed
mark......................................... **358.00**

**Plaque,** pierced to hang, etched
scene of waiter serving wine,
No. 2623, 7½" d. ...................... **200.00**

*Charming Mettlach Plaque*

**Plaque,** pierced to hang,
Phanolith, oval, white relief
figures of two young boys
playing musical instruments &
serenading a young girl holding
a fan in a garden setting, on a
green ground, No. 2445,
7¼ x 10¼" (ILLUS.) .................. **640.00**

*A Pair of Mettlach Cameo Plaques*

**Plaque,** pierced to hang, rectangular, etched scene of woman picking flowers, signed "Warth," No. 1473, 11 x 17" ... **1,470.00**

**Plaques,** round, Cameo, one w/white relief figures of Trojan warriors disembarking from a boat, the mate w/white relief figures of a Trojan lady seated among her servants, each on a green ground, No. 2442 & No. 2443, each signed "Stahl," 18⅛" d., pr. (ILLUS. top) ........ **1,495.00**

## STEINS

*Mettlach Master Stein*

**No. 6,** covered, master-size, the baluster-form body w/a wide spout decorated overall w/relief-molded tan grapevines against a grey ground, arched blue panels around the bottom each w/a white relief figure of the Avenging Angel w/sword, Noah & the Ark or a man playing a harp, the hinged metal lid inset w/a pottery plaque w/molded grapes on a blue & grey ground, tall metal thumbrest, 1½ liter, 11¾" h. (ILLUS. bottom previous column) ......... **450.00**

**No. 1947,** etched design of a man & a verse in German, inlaid lid, ½ liter ...................... **350.00**

**No. 2001C,** modeled as a shelf of books for scholar philosophers, hand-painted, inlaid lid, ½ liter ...................... **675.00**

**No. 2001K,** modeled as a shelf of books for banking or commerce, hand-painted, inlaid lid, ½ liter **650.00**

**No. 2002,** Munich stein, etched on the upper half w/a townscape below a shield w/the Munich Child & a banner w/the city name, the lower half etched w/a lengthy inscription, inlaid lid, ½ liter ................................ **650.00**

# MINTON

*Fine Minton Pate-Sur-Pate Compote*

*The Minton factory in England was established by Thomas Minton in 1793. The factory made earthenware, especially the blue-printed variety and Thomas Minton is sometimes credited with invention of the blue "Willow" pattern. For a time majolica and tiles were also an important part of production, but bone china soon became the principal ware. Mintons, Ltd., continues in operation today.*

*Minton Marks*

**Compote,** cov., *pate-sur-pate*, a tall bell-form domed foot below a large knopped stem supporting a wide shallow bowl w/a flanged rim supporting the wide, low domed cover w/a pointed knob finial, the black ground w/teal blue trim & panels w/white slip depicting reclining maidens

*Minton Majolica Toby Jugs*

w/putti, scrollwork borders & base, artist monogram of Albione Birks, printed & impressed factory marks, restored chip to foot rim of bowl, light gilt wear, 10½" d., 14" h. (ILLUS. top previous column) ............................. **$5,463.00**

**Demitasse set:** cov. coffeepot, creamer, cov. sugar bowl & six cups & saucers; Birds of Paradise patt., ca. 1863, artist-signed, 15 pcs.................. **300.00**

**Ewer,** pewter-mounted, the baluster form molded w/a relief depicting frolicking swag-draped putti above a vining border, 19th c., 9½" h............................ **316.00**

**Toby jugs,** majolica, a standing Quaker-style Mr. & Mrs. Toby, each wearing a tricorn hat & dressed in 18th c. costume, polychrome enamel decoration, ca. 1868, impressed marks, 11¼" h., pr. (ILLUS. top this column) ................................... **4,600.00**

**Vase,** 20⅝" h., *pate-sur-pate*, classical baluster-form raised on a bell-form foot, the tall slender neck w/a ringed rim joined to the shoulders by straight handles centered by fanned scallops, the body in dark blue decorated in white slip w/"The Creation of the

Earth," one side w/putti playing w/orbs, the reverse w/a female figure bearing torches w/orbs below, the neck & foot w/wide gilt-decorated borders, artist-signed by Louis Solon, printed & impressed marks, ca. 1889.. **20,700.00**

**Vases,** 8¾" h., *pate-sur-pate*, classical urn-form w/a flattened shoulder tapering to a short cylindrical neck w/a flaring rim flanked by pointed arched gilt handles, raised on a ringed pedestal w/a round gilt-trimmed base & square foot, one side decorated w/a white slip classical female allegorical figure, the reverse w/a white slip putto, dark ground, gilt geometric designs around the neck, signed "L. Solon" & printed globe marks, late 19th c., pr. ................................ **3,737.00**

---

# MOCHA

*Mocha decoration is found on basically utilitarian creamware or yellowware articles and is achieved by a simple chemical reaction. A color pigment of brown, blue, green or black is given an acid nature by infusion of tobacco or hops. When this acid nature colorant is applied in blobs to an alkaline ground color, it reacts by spreading in feathery seaweed designs. This type of decoration is usually accompanied by horizontal bands of light color slip. Produced in numerous Staffordshire potteries from the late 18th until the late 19th centuries, its name is derived from the similar markings found on mocha quartz. In addition to the seaweed decoration, mocha wares are also seen with Earthworm and Cat's Eye patterns or a marbleized effect.*

**Bowl,** 4⅜" d., 3⅛" h., footed, slightly tapering cylindrical body, white band w/blue seaweed decoration, blue stripes (stains & small rim flakes) ..................... **$275.00**

**Bowl,** 6¼" d., 4⅜" h., white band w/blue seaweed decoration & brown stripes (hairlines) ............ **149.00**

**Bowl,** 8½" d., 4¼" h., footed, tapering sides, wide blue band w/Earthworm patt. in blue, white & dark brown (wear & interior flakes & hairline in bottom of bowl) ........................................ **385.00**

**Bowl,** 11½" d., bulbous cylindrical body on a thin footring, the sides tapering to flaring rim, white band w/blue seaweed decoration, dark brown stripes, East Liverpool, Ohio (wear, stains & interior scratches & surface flakes) ....... **275.00**

**Chamber pot,** miniature, footed bulbous body w/a flattened flaring rim, yellowware w/a wide white center band decorated w/blue seaweed design & flanked by dark brown stripes, 2⅛" h......................................... **385.00**

**Creamer,** baluster-form w/pinched spout, leaftip handle, tan band w/black seaweed decoration, 3¾" h. (wear, small flakes & handle w/professional repair) ....................................... **358.00**

**Egg cup,** waisted cylindrical form w/blue bands, black stripes & black seaweed decoration on brown ground, 2⅞" h. ............... **330.00**

**Jar,** cov., cylindrical w/molded footring, low-domed cover w/button finial, yellowware w/wide white band w/blue seaweed decoration, blue stripes, 4½" d., 4⅛" h. (cover very chipped, base w/pinpoints)............................... **523.00**

**Mug,** cylindrical w/wide yellowish-ochre bands w/black seaweed decoration, brown stripes, leaftip handle, 2⅝" h. (professional repair, hairlines & pinpoint rim flakes) ........................................ **330.00**

**Mug,** cylindrical, D-form leaftip handle, a wide blue center band w/Earthworm patt., a narrow leaf

*A Variety of Mocha Wares*

Photo Courtesy of Skinner, Inc.

band around the rim,
imperfections, 3½" h. (ILLUS.
second from left, front row) ....... **690.00**

**Mug,** cylindrical w/leaftip handle,
decorated w/thin stripes in tan &
dark brown w/a tooled green rim
& green at handle, 4¾" h.
(strains, small rim flakes, crow's-
foot in base) .............................. **385.00**

**Mug,** cylindrical w/D-form leaftip
handle, three wide greyish blue
bands separated by pairs of thin
blackish brown stripes, the two
wide bands decorated w/brown
Earthworm patt., 5" h. (ILLUS.
far left, front row)....................... **403.00**

**Mug,** cylindrical w/D-form leaftip
handle, a wide pumpkin orange
center band w/brown seaweed
decoration, wide plain brown
bands at rim & base, hairlines &
chips, 6" h. (ILLUS. left,
top row) ..................................... **633.00**

**Mustard pot,** cov., cylindrical
w/flat rim & low-domed cover
w/button finial, leaftip handle,
olive grey central band w/black
seaweed design & dark brown
stripes, 2⅞" d., 2⅛" h. (rim chip
& bruise, lid chipped & slightly
oversize) ................................... **385.00**

**Mustard pot,** cov., bulbous
baluster-form w/a D-form leaftip
handle, low domed cover

w/knob finial, a wide blue center
band decorated w/brown & white
Cat's-Eye patt., narrow blue &
brown stripes around top, base
& cover, imperfections, 3¾" h.
(ILLUS. right, top row).............. **431.00**

**Mustard pot,** cov., bulbous
baluster-form w/a D-form
leaftip handle, low domed
cover w/knob finial, a wide
center pumpkin orange band
decorated w/brown seaweed
design, narrow stripes of
brown & pumpkin around base,
rim & cover, 4" h. (ILLUS.
second from right, front row) .. **690.00**

**Pitcher,** cov., 6¼" h., ribbed
handle, white band w/black
seaweed decoration, white &
blue stripes (chips on spout, lid
chips & hairline) ........................ **935.00**

**Pitcher,** 8¾" h., barrel-shaped
w/arched spout & large C-form
handle, white w/bands & stripes
of blue, teal & black (minor edge
wear)......................................... **358.00**

**Salt dip,** wide squatty bulbous
bowl raised on a short flaring
foot, yellowware decorated w/a
wide white band w/blue
seaweed decoration, blue
stripes, 3" d., 2¼" h. (wear,
stains & rim chips) .................... **440.00**

**Shaker,** cov., footed baluster-form fitted w/a pierced domed top, embossed green band, dark brown stripes & orange bands w/black seaweed decoration, 4¼" h. (chips) ............................ **605.00**

**Shaker,** footed baluster-form w/domed cover, wide blue center band w/Earthworm patt., narrow brown & blue bands at top & base, chips, 4¾" h. (ILLUS. far right, top previous page) ........................................ **690.00**

**Wash bowl & pitcher,** miniature, yellowware w/white band decorated w/blue seaweed design, flanked by blue stripes, 4½" d., 3¼" h. ......................... **2,310.00**

**Waste bowl,** deep flaring sides above a thick footring, white band w/blue seaweed decoration, flanked by blue stripes, 5½" d., 3" h. (wear & small flakes on table ring) ......... **358.00**

---

# MOORCROFT

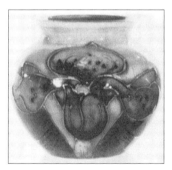

*Small Moorcroft Vase*

*William Moorcroft became a designer for James Macintyre & Co. in 1897 and was put in charge of their art pottery production. Moorcroft developed a number of popular designs, including Florian Ware while with Macintyre and continued with that firm until 1913 when they discontinued the production of art pottery.*

*After leaving Macintyre in 1913, Moorcroft set up his own pottery in Burslem and continued producing the art wares he had designed earlier as well as introducing new patterns. After William's death in 1945, the pottery was operated by his son, Walter.*

**MOORCROFT**

*Moorcraft Marks*

**Bowl,** 6" d., footed, Poppy patt., red poppies on a cobalt blue ground..................................... **$250.00**

**Bowl,** 7⅜" d., Orchid patt., widely flaring shallow sides, the interior decorated w/dark blue, pink, yellow & green blossoms alternating w/clusters of small blue blossoms on a mottled cobalt blue ground, impressed factory mark & facsimile signature w/"Potter to H.M. the Queen - Made in England" & the painted initials of Walter Moorcroft................................... **220.00**

**Candlesticks,** a wide flattened & flaring hammered pewter foot supporting a slightly tapering slender cylindrical ceramic shaft in the Pomagranate patt. & topped by a hammered pewter candle socket w/flattened bobeche, the shaft painted w/red, ochre & pink fruit against a cobalt blue ground, impressed marks "H - TUDRIC - MOORCROFT - 01362 - MADE BY LIBERTY & CO.," early 20th c., 5¼" d., 7¾" h., pr. ..... **1,870.00**

**Jar,** cov., wide ovoid body w/a rounded shoulder to the short cylindrical neck fitted w/a domed cover, Pomegranate patt., decorated w/large red pomegranates, dark yellowish brown leaves & red & purple berries, impressed "Moorcroft - Made in England - 769" & green script signature, 10" h. .............. **715.00**

**Lamp-vase,** Orchid patt., footed bottle-form, ovoid body tapering to a tall slender slightly flaring neck, a dark bluish green shading up to a yellowish green ground, decorated around the body w/large stylized blossoms in mottled blue & white w/yellow & red leaves & green stems, base impressed w/factory logo & facsimile signature & "Pottery to H.M. the Queen - Made in England," painted initials of Walter Moorcroft, 10½" h. ......... **330.00**

**Mug,** cov., Caribbean patt., waisted cylindrical body w/a C-form applied handle & flattened domed cover w/a round knob finial, decorated in shades of blue, green, rose & yellow w/sailboats & flying fish, impressed "Moorcroft - Made in England," 6¼" h. ....................... **385.00**

**Tea tile,** Florian Ware, round, the center decorated w/a ring of small golden brown & blue poppy blossoms on stems & leaves against a bright yellow ground, a thin blue border band within an outer border of small scrolled green leaves, designed by William Moorcroft, Macintyre period, marked "Gesso Faience" & notation "M 1454 N," 6⅜" d. .. **550.00**

**Vase,** 2¾" h., Orchid patt., squatty bulbous ovoid body tapering to a short cylindrical neck w/a molded rim, in shades of deep purple, dark red, cobalt blue & pale green (ILLUS.) ....... **350.00**

**Vase,** 3½" h., Wisteria patt., footed squatty bulbous body tapering to a flaring trumpet neck, decorated w/large fruits in dark blue, red & yellow w/green leaves, on a cobalt blue ground, impressed "Moorcroft - C - Made in England," painted initials of William Moorcroft ...................... **165.00**

**Vase,** 4¾" h., Florian Ware, bulbous ovoid body tapering to a cylindrical neck flanked by curved strap handles, decorated w/stylized daisies in shades of blue, yellow & green, made for Liberty & Company, ca. 1903-13, marked w/green signature "W. Moorcroft des.," registration number 360576 & the notation "Made for Liberty & Co." ........... **935.00**

**Vase,** 6" h., Aurelian Ware, footed bottle-form w/a spherical body & tall, slender ringed neck w/flared rim, decorated w/red poppy sprigs on dark blue scrolling stems between smeary dark blue leafy branches, vertical bands of small red blossoms w/gold leaves alternating w/blue bands up the neck, further blue & gold trim on the neck, shoulder & foot, marked w/"Macintyre Burslem" logo & the notation "Rd No 314901" .... **413.00**

**Vase,** 6⅛" h., Cornflower patt., baluster-shaped w/a short flaring neck, Powder Blue glaze, a medium blue speckled ground decorated w/tall swirled stems & leaves supporting clusters of small blue blossoms tinged w/purple, marked "Moorcroft - Made in England," impressed Wm. Moorcroft initials, incised circle & slightly obscured shape number, ca. 1920 ...................... **715.00**

**Vase,** 9¾" h., 6" d., Pomegranate patt., large ovoid body tapering to a thick molded & rolled rim, decorated in the squeezebag technique w/orange & purple fruit on a dark blue flambé ground, die-stamped "MOORCROFT - MADE IN ENGLAND" & ink signature (some crazing) .......................... **935.00**

**Vase,** 13" h., 9½" d., large wide bulbous body tapering to a wide slightly flaring cylindrical neck, decorated w/red orchids, blue iris & white blossoms on a cobalt blue ground, die-stamped "MOORCROFT - MADE IN ENGLAND" ........................... **1,210.00**

*Large Moorcroft Orchid Vase*

**Vase,** 15⅞" h., Orchid patt., wide ovoid body tapering to a short rolled neck, decorated w/a continuous band of colorful orchids & other blossoms under a flambé glaze, impressed marks, signed & dated "1939" (ILLUS.) ................................. **4,025.00**

**Vases,** 3¾" h., 4¼" d., bulbous ovoid body tapering to a wide, short rolled neck, Landscape patt., mottled yellowish green trees against an orange & cobalt blue ground, die-stamped "MOORCROFT - MADE IN ENGLAND - 55," pr. ............... **1,045.00**

---

# MULBERRY

*Jeddo Mulberry Plate*

Mulberry or Flow Mulberry wares were produced in the Staffordshire district of England in the period between 1835 and 1855 at many of the same factories which produced its close "cousin," Flow Blue china. In fact, some of the early Flow Blue patterns were also decorated with the purplish mulberry coloration and feature the same heavy smearing or "flown" effect. Produced on sturdy ironstone bodies, quite a bit of this ware is still to be found and it is becoming increasingly sought-after by collectors although presently its values lag somewhat behind similar Flow Blue pieces. The important references to Mulberry wares is Petra Williams' book, Flow Blue China and Mulberry Ware, Similarity and Value Guide *and Ellen R. Hill's comprehensive guide,* Mulberry Ironstone—Flow Blue's Best Kept Little Secret.

**Chamber pot,** cov., Seaweed patt. ........................................ **$325.00**

**Creamer,** Corean patt., Podmore, Walker & Co. ............................ **175.00**

**Creamer,** Cyprus patt., Davenport ................................ **225.00**

**Creamer,** Flora patt., Hulme & Booth ........................................ **150.00**

**Creamer,** Moss Rose patt., Jacob Furnival & Co. .......................... **205.00**

**Creamer,** Nankin patt., Davenport ................................ **225.00**

**Creamer,** Panama patt., Edward Challinor & Co. .......................... **215.00**

**Creamer,** Rose patt., Thomas Walker ...................................... **215.00**

**Creamer,** Venture patt., Ralph Hammersley .............................. **95.00**

**Creamer,** Vincennes patt., Samuel Alcock ......................... **225.00**

**Creamer,** Washington Vase patt., Podmore, Walker & Co. ............ **215.00**

**Cup & saucer,** handleless, Washington Vase patt., Podmore, Walker & Co. .............. **95.00**

**Cup plate,** Corean patt., Podmore, Walker & Co. .............. **95.00**

**Gravy boat,** Corean patt.,
Podmore, Walker & Co. ............. **55.00**

**Pitcher,** 8" h., Corean patt.,
Podmore, Walker & Co. ........... **295.00**

**Pitcher,** 10" h., Corean patt.,
Podmore, Walker & Co. ........... **300.00**

**Pitcher,** Jeddo patt., Wm. Adams
& Sons, 2 qt. ............................ **425.00**

**Pitcher,** Rose patt., Thomas
Walker., 2 qt. ............................. **375.00**

**Plate,** 7½" d., Scinde patt.,
Thomas Walker .......................... **40.00**

**Plate,** 8" d., Washington Vase
patt., Podmore, Walker & Co. ..... **35.00**

**Plate,** 9" d., Corean patt.,
Podmore, Walker & Co. ............. **40.00**

**Plate,** 9" d., Washington Vase
patt., Podmore, Walker & Co. ..... **50.00**

**Plate,** 9¼" d., Jeddo patt., Wm.
Adams & Sons (ILLUS. bottom
previous page ............................ **65.00**

**Plate,** 10" d., Rhone Scenery, T.J.
& J. Mayer ................................. **45.00**

**Plate,** 11" d., Cyprus patt.,
Davenport ................................. **55.00**

**Plate,** 11" d., Pelew patt., Edward
Challinor & Co. ........................... **50.00**

**Platter,** 8 x 11", Washington Vase
patt, Podmore, Walker & Co. ..... **150.00**

**Platter,** 14" l., Heath's Flower
patt., T. Heath .......................... **275.00**

**Platter,** 15" l., Tavoy, Thomas
Walker ...................................... **130.00**

**Platter,** 12 x 16", Corean patt.,
Podmore, Walker & Co. ........... **225.00**

**Platter,** 14 x 18", Corean patt.,
Podmore, Walker & Co. ........... **325.00**

**Platter,** 14 x 18", Vincennes patt.,
Samuel Alcock .......................... **300.00**

**Sauce tureen,** cov., Vincennes
pat., Samuel Alcock .................. **295.00**

**Sauce tureen, cover &**
**underplate,** Bochara patt., John
Edwards, the set ...................... **495.00**

**Soup plate w/flanged rim,** Nin-
Po patt., R. Hall & Co. ................ **95.00**

**Teapot,** cov., Alleghany patt., T.
Goodfellow ............................... **295.00**

**Teapot,** cov., Calcutta patt.,
Edward Challinor ..................... **275.00**

**Teapot,** cov., Corean patt.,
Podmore, Walker & Co. ........... **300.00**

**Teapot,** cov., Cyprus patt.,
Davenport ................................ **275.00**

**Vegetable bowl,** cov., Bochara
patt., John Edwards ................. **375.00**

**Vegetable bowl,** cov., Corean
patt., Podmore, Walker & Co. ... **325.00**

**Vegetable bowl,** cov., Cyprus
patt., Davenport ....................... **375.00**

**Vegetable bowl,** cov., Jeddo
patt., Wm. Adams & Sons ......... **395.00**

**Vegetable bowl,** cov., Pelew
patt., Edward Challinor
& Co. ........................ **350.00 to 400.00**

**Waste bowl,** Corean patt.,
Podmore, Walker & Co. ........... **250.00**

# NEWCOMB COLLEGE POTTERY

*This pottery was established in the art department of Newcomb College, New Orleans, Louisiana, in 1897. Each piece was hand-thrown and bore the potter's mark & decorator's monogram on the base. It was always a studio business and never operated as a factory and its pieces are therefore scarce, with the early wares being eagerly sought. The pottery closed in 1940.*

*Newcomb College Pottery Mark*

**Ashtray set:** match holder & ashtray; short cylindrical ashtray & cylindrical match holder w/closed rim, both decorated w/white flowers & green leaves on a deep blue ground, ashtray marked "NC - JM - A.M. - 101 - GX4," by A.F. Mason, 1914, ashtray 3½" d., match holder 2¾" h., the set ..................... **$1,650.00**

*Rare Newcomb Lemonade Set*

**Bowl,** 6" d., 2½" h., deep slightly tapering rounded sides w/a wide flat rim, a rim band carved & painted w/a floral decoration in purple, yellow & green against a blue to green ground, marked "S. Irvine - #KA50" .................... **770.00**

**Jar,** cov., squatty bulbous body on rounded foot, decorated w/trellis design of white blossoms within green diamond pattern on a cobalt blue ground, w/paper label & impressed "NC - SI - SF7 - 242," decorated by Sadie Irvine, 1930, 5¾" h., 5½" d. (minor chip repair on lid edge).................................... **2,750.00**

**Lemonade set:** tall tapering cylindrical cov. pitcher & six tall tapering cylindrical mugs on underplates; each piece decorated around the upper half w/an incised wide band of stylized cherries suspended on stems & a leaf band on the pitcher & enclosed in a blocked band on the mugs, each piece w/a long squared handle, decorated by Maria De Hoa Le Blanc, 1906, the set (ILLUS. above).................... **13,750.00**

**Plaque,** rectangular, a scene of large live oak trees hung w/Spanish moss & a full moon above, in shades of dark & light purplish blue, by Anna F. Simpson, impressed "NC - AFS - SG15," in quartered oak Arts & Crafts frame, 5¾ x 7¾" .......... **7,425.00**

**Plate w/flanged rim,** 8½" d., mottled medium green center, the rim w/a continuous repeating band of carved & painted chrysanthemums in white, yellow & green on a dark blue ground, potted by Joseph Meyer, decorated by Anna Frances Simpson, 1910 (dark age lines on the back, minor scratches, small burst bubble on face, minor warpage) ................ **660.00**

**Syrup pitcher,** cov., cylindrical w/small rim spout & D-form handle, flattened cover w/knob finial, the upper half w/a wide band of incised & painted stylized flowers in cream & green on a light green ground, by E. H. P., 1907, marked "NC - JM - E.H.P. - BV10" (small flat chip to cover retaining rim, nick to pitcher's retaining rim) ....... **1,540.00**

*Small Handled Newcomb Vase*

**Vase,** 3" h., footed ovoid body tapering to a thick flaring rim, mint green matte glaze, impressed "NC," thrown by Joseph Meyer ........................... **220.00**

**Vase,** 4" h., 4½" d., wide ovoid body tapering to a wide flat mouth, green swirling design on a blue ground, matte glaze, Sadie Irvine, 1933, impressed NC - SI - UD8" ......................... **825.00**

**Vase,** 4¼" h., 4⅜" d., wide bulbous ovoid body w/the rounded shoulder tapering to a short cylindrical neck flanked by loop handles to the shoulder, a raised thorn branch band at the rim & shoulder in green w/stylized flower clusters in pale blue over cream & pale yellow on a blue body, glossy glaze, by May S. Morel, impressed "NC - JM," incised "M Morel -S," inscribed "cx-16," ca. 1911 (ILLUS. above)....................... **1,495.00**

**Vase,** 4½" h., 5¼" d., wide squatty ovoid body w/a flat closed rim, decorated around the mouth & shoulder w/hanging Spanish moss above a moonlit bayou scene in dark blue & feathered green on a light blue ground, by Henrietta Bailey, 1933, impressed "NC - UN91 - HB - F" ................................... **2,420.00**

**Vase,** 5½" h., 5½" d., bulbous ovoid vase tapering to short cylindrical neck w/flat rim, decorated w/white flowers & green leaves on a deep blue matte ground, incised "NC - JM - AFS - 72 - OT21," A.F. Simpson ................................. **1,320.00**

**Vase,** 6¼" h., 2½" d., tall slender corseted cylindrical body, incised & painted w/white & yellow flowers around the top on tall, slender green leaves & stems on a cobalt blue ground, glossy glaze, by Sadie Irvine, 1908, impressed "NC - JM - SI - W - CM86" ............................ **2,200.00**

**Vase,** 6½" h., 3½" d., ovoid form w/bulbous shoulder tapering to cylindrical neck w/rolled rim, decoration w/incised & painted blue & red squash blossoms on a yellow ground, under high-glaze ox blood finish, incised "NC - LN - Q - AT68," by Leona Nicholson, 1902 ..................... **5,060.00**

**Vase,** 7" h., slender cylindrical form w/a widely flaring foot, carved w/glossy glazed decoration of delicate white blossoms w/yellow centers atop bluish green leaves & stems against a dark blue & white background, bands in dark blue & white above & below decoration at the rim, by Marie De Hoa LeBlanc, thrown by Joseph Meyer ........................ **4,125.00**

**Vase,** 8½" h., 4" d., slender ovoid body w/a rounded shoulder to the short cylindrical neck, a landscape w/large live oak trees & Spanish moss in celadon green & dark blue on a pale blue ground, 1923, impressed "NC - ? - 250 - MZ - 86" .................. **2,640.00**

**Vase,** 8¾" h., 3¼" d., slender gently swelled cylindrical body tapering above a shoulder to a flat molded rim, carved decoration of white narcissus & green leaves on a blue ground, matte glaze, Anna Simpson, 1923, impressed "NC - AFS - JM - MX46 - 97" ........................... **2,200.00**

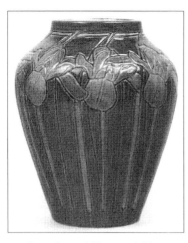

*Rare Carved Newcomb Vase*

**Vase,** 9" h., wide ovoid body tapering to a flat mouth, deeply carved & painted decoration of large overlapping iris blossoms atop vertical narrow stems in medium blue, the stems separated by dark green & blue vertical leaves w/prominent spines extending into the rim & backed by a rich dark blue background, glossy glaze, impressed "NC - JM," signed by Henrietta Bailey & "CT-83" (ILLUS.) .............................. **20,900.00**

**Vase,** 10" h., 4½" d., tall cylindrical body w/a slightly flared foot & a widely flared rim, carved & decorated bayou scene w/oak trees & dripping Spanish moss in blue & green on a pink, blue & green ground, by Anna Simpson, 1927, impressed "NC - ARS 229 - JM - Q038" ............................ **4,400.00**

**Vase,** 11¼" h., broad ovoid body tapering to a wide slightly tapering cylindrical neck w/a molded rim, a band of upright berry cluster-form blossoms above a band of tall, wide & pointed overlapping leaves around the lower two-thirds, dark mottled green against a black ground on the neck, potted

by Joseph Meyer, decorated by Harriet Coulter Joor, 1902 (semicircular firing crack on the side, spider cracks in base & side, rim w/several small chips) .................................... **2,200.00**

# NILOAK POTTERY

*Mission Ware Cylindrical Vase*

*This pottery was made in Benton, Arkansas and featured hand-thrown varicolored swirled clay decoration in objects of classic forms. Designated Mission Ware, this line is the most desirable of Niloak's production which was begun early in this century. Mission Ware pieces were generally produced in simple, classic forms. Included were such items as candlesticks, covered jars, jardinieres and, most abundantly, vases in all shapes and sizes. Less expensive to produce, the cast Hywood Line, finished with either high gloss or semi-matte glazes, was introduced during the economic depression of the 1930s. The pottery ceased operation about 1946.*

**NiᴄᴏAʜ**

*Niloak Pottery Mark*

**Candlesticks,** Mission Ware, widely flaring round base tapering to a stepped, tapering cylindrical shaft supporting a cupped candle socket, swirled brown, cocoa, terra cotta & blue clays, impressed "Niloak," 8" h., pr. ................................. **$132.00**

**Cigarette humidor,** cov., Mission Ware, tall slightly tapering cylindrical body w/a wide molded rim, inset flattened cover w/knob finial, swirled, brown, tan, red, cream & blue clays, impressed second mark, 4⅜" h......................................... **275.00**

**Hatpin holder,** Mission Ware, swirled multicolored clays, 6" h.. **700.00**

**Planter,** Hywood Line, model of a deer, tan glaze, 5" h.................... **30.00**

**Vase,** 6½" h., Mission Ware, baluster-form w/flattened flaring rim, swirled cocoa & dark brown & mutted orange clays, marked. **110.00**

**Vase,** 8½" h., Mission Ware, ovoid body tapering to a molded, rounded rolled mouth, swirled dark brown, cocoa, cream & blue clays, impressed mark ...... **176.00**

**Vase,** 10" h., 4¾" d., Mission Ware, slender ovoid body w/a closed-in mouth, swirled brown, rust, white & blue clays, impressed mark ........................ **495.00**

**Vase,** 10½" h. tall cylindrical body w/a flaring foot, swirled blue, cream, rust & cocoa brown clays, marked (ILLUS. previous page).. **413.00**

**Wall pocket,** Mission Ware, swirled multicolored clays, 6¼" h......................................... **350.00**

# NIPPON

"Nippon" is a term which is used to describe a wide range of porcelain wares produced in Japan from the late 19th century until about 1921. It was in 1891 that the U.S. implemented the McKinley Tariff Act which required that all wares exported to the United States carry a marking indicating the country of origin. The Japanese chose to use "Nippon," their name for Japan. In 1921 the import laws were revised and the words "Made in" had to be added to the markings. Japan was also required to replace the "Nippon" with the English name "Japan" on all wares sent to the United States.

Many Japanese factories produced Nippon porcelains and much of it was hand-painted with ornate floral or landscape decoration and heavy gold decoration, applied beading and slip-trailed designs referred to as "moriage." We indicate the specific marking used on a piece, when known, at the end of each listing below. Be aware that a number of Nippon markings have been reproduced and used on new porcelain wares.

Important reference books on Nippon include: The Collector's Encyclopedia of Nippon Porcelain, Series One through Three, by Joan F. Van Patten (Collector Books, Paducah, Kentucky) and The Wonderful World of Nippon Porcelain, 1891-1921 by Kathy Wojciechowski (Schiffer Publishing, Ltd., Atglen, Pennsylvania).

**Ashtray,** round, thick flat-topped sides w/four cigarette indentations, each top panel decorated w/stylized florals, the interior decorated w/a sailboat seascape at sunset, 5" d. (green "M" in Wreath mark)................ **$193.00**

**Ashtray-match holder,** a rectangular dished base w/incurved sides centered w/a upright rectangular box for holding a small box of matches, the upright section painted w/a continuous autumnal lakeside landscape at sunset on a shaded yellow ground continuing down to the base interior, 3½" h. (green "M" in Wreath mark) ............................. **94.00**

**Basket,** "moon" form, a gold-footed flattened round disc w/a pierced oblong inverted heart-shaped handle opening, the fine linen tapestry ground decorated w/a landscape scene w/swans swimming on a large pond surrounded by a wooded landscape, 9" h. (blue Maple Leaf mark).............................. **1,870.00**

**Bowl,** 7½" d., footed shallow rounded body w/angled gold loop side handles, the interior decorated in rust red, white, tan & pale yellow w/a geometric border band above a continuous wide band of ancient Egyptian symbols & figures on a pale yellow ground w/a ringed design in the bottom center (green "M" in Wreath mark) ....................... **275.00**

**Bowl,** 8" w., deep curved squared sides gently rounded & notched at the corners, upturned gold handles at each side, the center decorated w/large clusters of light & dark purple wisteria blossoms & green leaves against a shaded violet to white ground, the exterior decorated w/a mottled brown & black finish (green "M" in Wreath mark)........ **61.00**

**Celery tray,** decorated w/leaves & grapes, gold on white ground, lavish gold trim, 5½ x 12" (green "M" in Wreath mark)................... **40.00**

**Center bowl,** Wedgwood-style, a wide shallow round bowl w/a wide interior border band in Wedgwood blue w/white moriage scrolls around a white center decorated w/colorful roses & green leaves, the bowl raised on the backs of three figural blue & white winged griffins resting on a triangular platform base w/a blue & white border band, 8" d. (green "M" in Wreath mark) ........................... **605.00**

**Charger,** round, fine linen tapestry ground decorated w/a raised gold edge band around large clusters of pink open roses & buds & green leaves on a

shaded rosey tan to cream ground, 12" d. (blue Maple Leaf mark)...................................... **2,640.00**

**Chocolate pot,** cov., tankard-type, the tall slightly waisted cylindrical body w/a deeply ruffled base & gently flared & scalloped rim w/short arched spout, an ornate looping angular handle & an inset conical cover w/a florette finial, the cover, handle & body decorated overall in heavy gold in a grape cluster & grapevine design w/a central oval reverse decorated w/yellow, white & pink florals & green leaves on a white ground, 10½" h. (blue Maple Leaf mark) ................................ **330.00**

**Chocolate set:** cov. chocolate pot & four cups & saucers; h.p. sunset scene of sailboat on lake, 9 pcs. (blue RS mark) .............. **245.00**

**Chocolate set:** cov. chocolate pot & six cups & saucers; soft green clover decoration, outlined in gold on white ground, gold handles & gold trim, 13 pcs. ..... **195.00**

**Cigarette box,** cov., rectangular w/a flat cover, the base & cover w/wide brown border bands w/stylized decoration, the top of the cover w/a quarter-round corner vignette of a h.p. horse head, the rest of the cover w/a grey ground decorated w/a small horseshoe & other details, plain grey side panels, 3½ x 4½", 2½" h. (green "M" in Wreath mark)........................................ **468.00**

**Condensed milk can holder, cover & underplate,** the holder w/a cylindrical body flanked by angled gilt handles, the low domed cover w/a pointed gilt handle, the body w/a wide top rim band of purple wisteria blossoms & gold-trimmed green leaves, a matching border band on the cover, the matching undertray w/similar trim, all on a white ground, 6" h., the set (blue "M" in Wreath mark).................. **110.00**

**Condensed milk can holder, cover & underplate,** the holder w/a waisted & lightly lobed cylindrical body flanked by long pointed loop gold handles, the gently flared rim supporting a domed cover w/a florette finial, the cover & the upper half of the body decorated w/very ornate gold lattice designs & scrolls against a pale green ground w/small oval reserves of pink roses & green leaves, the lower body in white w/gold spearhead drops, the scalloped & dished underplate w/a wide gold border, 6½" h., the set ("RC Noritake" mark)........................................ **303.00**

**Cracker jar,** cov., three-footed, lobed body w/h.p. roses decoration on cobalt ground w/gold trim, unmarked, 6" d., 7" h.......................................... **165.00**

**Creamer & cov. sugar bowl,** tapering cylindrical body w/angled handle, the low domed sugar cover w/a pointed ball finial, each piece decorated w/rim & base bands w/geometric devices, the body decorated w/a cartoon-type continuous landscape w/trees & hills, 4" h., pr. (blue "M" in Wreath mark).... **275.00**

**Cup & saucer,** white w/pearlized iridescence (blue Maple Leaf mark)........................................ **12.00**

**Demitasse pot, cover & matching trivet,** the gently tapering cylindrical pot w/a long side handle in brown & a straight angled spout, the domed cover w/a button finial, the body decorated w/a continuous lakeside landscape at sunset w/similar trim on the cover & matching round trivet, pot 6½" h., the set (blue Maple Leaf mark)........................................ **330.00**

**Dresser set:** tall footed hair receiver, compote & open-top hatpin holder; pink, blue & gold, the set (green "M" in Wreath mark)........................................ **120.00**

**Egg cup,** handled, trophy-form, the deep rounded bowl flanked by angular handles & raised on a short pedestal w/a square foot, decorated w/a continuous sailboat scene, 2½" h................. **83.00**

**Ewer,** a small flaring foot supports a wide bulbous body tapering to a slender neck ending in a widely flaring trumpet neck w/a slanted rim, a hook-ended straight handle extending from the upper neck rim to the lower part of the body, decorated w/a long undulating moriage dragon in dark grey & white w/yellow glass eyes against a pale yellow ground trimmed w/mottled brown clouds, 10½" h. (Paulownia Flower & Leaves mark)............. **495.00**

**Ferner,** round, raised on four short gilt tab feet & w/angled gilt handles at each side, a narrow gilt rim band & gilt stripes down the sides dividing it into Nile River scenes at sunset, w/original tin liner, 3" h. (green "M" in Wreath mark)................. **385.00**

**Ginger jar,** cov., ovoid body w/a fitted, domed cover, large moriage phoenix or bird of paradise around the sides in shades of purple & white w/heavy gold outlining against a black ground, 6½" h. (Nippon "circle" mark)........................... **110.00**

**Humidor,** cov., footed barrel-shaped, inset domed cover w/a large knob finial, decorated w/a relief-molded black & white recumbent collie in a yellow, orange & brown sunset landscape above the black lower half, green "M" in Wreath mark (ILLUS. center, top next page).. **425.00 to 475.00**

**Humidor,** cov., bulbous ovoid body tapering to a wide low domed cover, decorated w/a relief-molded scene of a Native American w/headdress & rifle on a running horse against a mottled black & brown background (ILLUS. right, top next page) ....... **850.00**

*Three Nippon Humidors*

**Humidor,** cov., footed, tapering cylindrical body decorated w/a relief-molded woodland scene of an elk being chased by dogs, low domed cover w/large knob finial & scrolled decoration (ILLUS. left above) .................... **700.00**

**Lamp,** table-type, tall ovoid body tapering at the shoulders to a short, slender neck w/flaring rim, arched gold handles from rim to shoulder, the body decorated overall w/large shaded yellow & orange fruits among green leaves against a shaded brown & yellow ground, w/original tall slender brass two-light electric fittings w/a spearpoint-shaped green glass finial, the body fitted on a carved walnut round base, overall 22" h. ............................ **220.00**

**Match holder,** hanging-type, a rectangular scallop-edged backplate w/raised enamel border trim & an outset rectangular box w/enamel trim around a front landscape medallion, 5" h. (blue Maple Leaf mark) ................................ **160.00**

**Mug,** tall tapering cylindrical body w/narrow decorated top & base bands & a bead-trimmed C-scroll handle, the body decorated w/a wide continuous scene of an ancient Egyptian warship sailing past a large temple at sunset, 6" h. (green "M" in Wreath mark) .................. **385.00**

**Nut set:** 8½" oval four-lobed master bowl & six matching 3¾" bowls; decorated w/a sunset scene & swans, 7 pcs. .............. **150.00**

**Pancake server,** cov., the dished plate base w/scalloped rim decorated w/ornate scrolling gold on pale yellow, the high domed cover w/a button finial in gold & pale yellow above a band of gold-trimmed white pierced w/air holes, the sides of the cover w/a pale yellow ground ornately decorated overall w/feathery gilt scrolls & lattice & molded rococo designs, 10" d. (blue Maple Leaf mark) .............. **83.00**

**Pitcher,** tankard, 10" h., moriage, slightly flaring cylindrical body w/a flared base & a pointed rim spout, long C-scroll handle, overall green & white vines applied to lavender, green & purple wisteria blossoms (blue Maple Leaf mark) ..................... **375.00**

**Pitcher,** tankard, 16" h., a gently swelled squatty base tapering gently to a wide cylindrical body topped by a low, wide spout & bead-trimmed rim, ornate C-scroll handle, overall ornate moriage florals blossoms outlined in greenish white w/petals in gold & shades of pink on a overall gold ground, unmarked .................................. **715.00**

**Plaque,** pierced to hang, decorated w/relief-molded Boston Bulldog, 10" d. (green "M" in Wreath mark) .................. **865.00**

**Plaque,** pierced to hang, round, a wide gold border band around a large bouquet of white & golden yellow roses & pale green leaves overflowing a wide wickerwork basket against a shaded yellow ground, 10" d. (green "M" in Wreath mark) ....... **248.00**

**Plate,** 8½" d., wide border w/beading & ornate scrolling, decorated w/gristmill pastoral scene & twelve reserves of various shapes & sizes enclosing colorful enamel designs (green "M" in Wreath mark) ......................................... **125.00**

**Plate,** 8½" d., souvenir-type, the round six-lobed dished rim decorated w/purple violet clusters against a pale green ground all heavily trimmed in gilt w/a heavy gold inner back around large pendent clusters of purple violets & green leaves on a pale green ground, at the bottom center is a small oval gilt-bordered reserve painted w/a scene of a large mountain & lake titled "Mt. Rainier & Lake Washington" (SNB mark) .......... **248.00**

**Powder jar,** cov., three-footed, decorated w/floral medallions, cobalt ground, gold trim, unmarked, 5" d., 3½" h. ............ **130.00**

**Ring tree,** a small round shallow dish centered by an uplifted open small gold hand, the base trimmed around the border w/blue florals, 3½" h. (green "M" in Wreath mark) ......................... **33.00**

**Salt set:** master salt dip & six individual salt dips; h.p. gold, pink, green & peach flowers, artist-signed, 7 pcs. ................... **110.00**

**Shaving mug,** a gently flaring cylindrical body on a flared foot, looped ring handle, a rim & base band of stylized geometric devices, the body w/a band of American Indian-style designs centered by a shaped panel w/a cartoon-style half-length portrait of a Native American brave, overall raised enamel decoration, 3½" h. (green "M" in Wreath mark) ........................... **275.00**

**Spoon holder,** horizontal table-type, narrow oblong upright sides w/a deep central indentation & squared gold end handles, the sides decorated w/a lakeside landscape scene, 8" l. (green "M" in Wreath mark) ........................................ **110.00**

**Sugar shaker,** floral border on white ground w/gold handle, 3¾" h. ........................................ **125.00**

**Syrup pitcher, cover & underplate,** the diamond-shaped underplate w/deep flaring edges supports a conforming diamond-form pitcher w/incurved sides & an arched angled gold handle, the squared domed cover w/an angular loop gold finial, the border of the cover & the sides of the pitcher decorated w/a continuous cartoon-style autumn landscape w/tall slender trees w/small tufts of leaves, overall 5" h., the set (green "M" in Wreath mark) ........................... **193.00**

**Tea set,** child's: cov. teapot, creamer & cov. sugar bowl; decorated w/a scene of a boy & girl in a cart being pulled by a goat, 3 pcs. .............................. **220.00**

**Tea strainer,** a round shallow dish w/a wide flattened rim & tiny rim spout, the bottom pierced w/fine holes, a slightly scalloped rim & a rounded scroll-molded tab side handle w/a hanging hole, decorated overall w/a heavy gold & burgundy decoration, 4½" d. (blue Maple Leaf mark) ............. **176.00**

**Toothpick holder,** three-handled, simple cylindrical body w/three D-form handles, decorated w/a continuous Nile River landscape scene w/moriage-painted trees, 2" h. (green "M" in Wreath mark) ........................................ **143.00**

**Trivet,** octagonal, a wide panel-painted border band featuring stylized lotus designs alternating w/light & dark blocks, the center decorated w/the bust profile portrait of an ancient Egyptian princess, 7" w. (green "M" in Wreath mark) ........................... **275.00**

**Urn,** cov., tall baluster-form body on a ringed pedestal foot bolted to a waisted round platform base w/three scroll-molded feet, the ovoid body tapering to a short waisted neck fitted w/a high domed cover w/a pointed knob finial & flanked by ornate C-scroll handles down the shoulders, ornate h.p. rococo overall decoration, the body w/large white blossoms & scrolls on a deep purplish red ground centered by an oval floral reserve within a scrolled gilt border & a gilt band joining it to other reserves, the neck & lower body w/dark green borders around creamy bands highlighted w/gilt scrolling, the domed cover in deep red w/white scrolls & radiating creamy white, green & gold-trimmed leaves, the pedestal & lower base w/bands of deep red & green w/floral reserves & gilt trim, marked "J.M.D.S. - Crown Nippon," 18½" h. (ILLUS. top next column) ..................... **7,700.00**

**Vase,** 5" h., nearly spherical bulbous body on a narrow footring, the sides tapering to a short cylindrical neck flanked by two small loop handles, heavy ornate swag & beaded gold decoration framing & separating large & smaller squared panels decorated w/lakeside landscape scenes (blue Maple Leaf mark).. **358.00**

*Rare Ornate Nippon Urn*

**Vase,** 6" h., wide squatty bulbous body w/the wide rounded shoulder tapering to a short, rolled neck, a fine linen tapestry ground decorated w/large peaches on leafy stems against a brown shaded to pale yellow background (blue Maple Leaf mark) ........................................ **990.00**

**Vase,** 7" h., bulbous ovoid body raised on three small gold peg feet, the shoulders tapering to a short flaring gold neck, three figural gold elephant head handles around the shoulders, decorated w/a continuous cartoon-style seascape w/galleons under full sail on a dark purplish blue sea below a pale blue sky w/puffy white clouds (green "M" in Wreath mark) ........................................ **468.00**

**Vase,** 7¾" h., pillow-form, decorated w/giant h.p. roses, gold beading & trim on a cobalt blue ground, late 19th c. ........... **275.00**

**Vase,** 9" h., coralene-type, a tall slender cylindrical form rounded at the foot shoulder w/a short, molded gold rim, decorated w/modernistic stylized yellow blossoms around the upper half on slender branched green stems all outlined in gold against a shaded azure blue ground (burgundy Kinran mark w/patent date)......................................... **908.00**

**Vase,** 9½" h., wide ovoid body on a low scalloped gold foot, the shoulders tapering to a short neck w/a deeply scalloped flaring rim, large looped gold "pretzel-style" shoulder handles, the body decorated w/heavy gold-painted chrysanthemum blossoms w/gilt band & scroll trim, delicate gold trim on the shoulder & neck (blue "M" Wreath mark) ............................ **193.00**

**Vase,** 9¾" h., footed square based baluster-form w/short flaring rim & shoulder handles, scenic decoration of ship on water, cottage & trees near the shoreline, flanked by raised red cherries, green enameled leaves & much raised gold work, cobalt ground (green "M" in Wreath mark)......... **395.00**

**Vase,** 10" h., wide ovoid body raised on a flaring gilt foot, the wide shoulders centered by a short gold neck w/an incurved four-lobed rim flanked by undulating, whiplash gold handles continuing down the sides, the body decorated w/a large cluster of full-blown white, deep red & yellow roses & green leaves against a shaded yellow ground (green Maple Leaf mark) ............. **550.00**

**Vase,** 12½" h., slender gently flaring cylindrical body w/a bulbous shoulder tapering up to a short flaring neck flanked by arched shoulder handles, the body decorated w/a long continuous seascape w/tall trees in the foreground & a fishing boat on the sea w/Mt. Fuji in the far background, cobalt blue w/gold trim borders (red S & K mark)........................................ **440.00**

**Whiskey jug w/stopper,** a slightly swelled cylindrical body w/a wide flattened shoulder centered by a short cylindrical neck w/rim spout & angled gold handle to shoulder rim, fitted w/a mushroom-capped gold stopper, the body decorated w/an upper paneled band filled w/Egyptian designs over gold swags & tassels, a narrow gold & black base band & a paneled neck design, w/advertising for E.M. Higgins Old Velvet, 6½" h. (green "M" in Wreath mark)..................................... **825.00**

# NORITAKE

*Azalea Pattern Demitasse Pot*

*Noritake china, still in production in Japan, has been exported in large quantities to this country since early in this century. Though the Noritake Company first registered in 1904, it did not use "Noritake" as part of its backstamp until 1918. Interest in Noritake has escalated as collectors now seek out pieces made between the "Nippon" era and World War II (1921-41). The Azalea pattern is also popular with collectors.*

*Noritake Mark*

**Bouillon cup & saucer,** Azalea
patt., No. 124, the set .............. **$22.00**

**Bowl,** cream soup w/underplate,
Alvin patt., the set ...................... **10.00**

**Bowl,** shell-shaped, on three ball
feet, Azalea patt., No. 188,
7¾" l. ........................................ **325.00**

**Bread tray,** decorated w/blue
flowers, gilt rim ........................... **75.00**

**Butter tub w/insert,** Azalea patt.,
No. 54, 2 pcs. ............................. **45.00**

**Casserole,** cov., round, Azalea
patt., No. 372, 10¾" d. .............. **315.00**

**Coffeepot,** cov., demitasse,
Azalea patt., No. 182 (ILLUS.
bottom previous page) ............. **550.00**

**Creamer & cov. sugar bowl,**
Azalea patt., No. 122, pr. .......... **130.00**

**Cup & saucer,** Alvin patt. ............. **15.00**

**Cup & saucer,** Azalea patt.,
No. 2 (ILLUS. top next column) .. **12.00**

**Cup & saucer,** Chelsea patt. ........ **30.00**

**Dresser tray,** decorated w/an Art
Deco lady wearing a large,
floppy hat, lustre finish,
7" l. ........................................... **175.00**

**Egg cup,** Azalea patt., No. 120 .... **55.00**

**Gravy boat,** Alvin patt. .................. **25.00**

**Jam jar,** cov., Azalea patt.,
No. 125 ..................................... **110.00**

**Mayonnaise set:** three-footed
bowl, ladle & underplate;
decorated w/an Art Deco style
swan & kingfisher scene w/a
lustre finish, 3 pcs. ...................... **75.00**

**Plate,** bread & butter, Patt.
No. 175 ......................................... **7.00**

**Plate,** salad, Patt. No. 175 ............ **12.00**

Plate, dinner, Patt. No. 175 ......... **30.00**

**Plate,** 7½" d., Alvin patt. ................. **5.00**

**Plate,** 10" d., Alvin patt. ................ **10.00**

*Azalea Pattern Cup & Saucer*

**Plates,** luncheon, landscape
scene w/a russet background
decorated w/an Arab astride a
camel amid palm trees done in
black w/gold tracery, black &
gold borders, set of 6 .................. **98.00**

**Powder box,** cov., footed, blue
lustre, black trim, figural red rose
w/green leaves finial, 4" d.
(green "M" in Wreath mark) ......... **65.00**

**Relish dish,** oval, Azalea patt.,
No. 18 ........................................ **18.00**

**Relish dish,** divided, four-
compartment, Azalea patt.,
No. 119 ..................................... **115.00**

**Salt dip,** basket-type w/spoon,
floral decoration, 2 pcs. .............. **24.00**

**Salt dip & matching pepper
shaker,** blue & orange lustre
w/black trim, 1¼" h., pr. ............. **18.00**

**Soup plate w/flanged rim,** Alvin
patt. ............................................... **8.00**

**Spoon holder,** long horizontal
table-type w/end handles &
center indentation, Azalea patt.,
No. 189, overall 8" l. .................... **95.00**

**Sugar bowl,** cov., Alvin patt. ........ **12.00**

**Syrup pitcher,** cov., Azalea patt.,
No. 97, 4½" h. ............................. **95.00**

**Teapot,** cov., Azalea patt., No. 15 . **95.00**

**Tray,** lemon, scrolled handle on
top near the rim, Azalea patt.,
No. 121, 5½" d. ........................... **24.00**

**Vase,** 5½" h., fan-shaped, Azalea
patt., No. 187 ........................ **1,100.00**

**Vegetable bowl,** open, oval,
handled, Azalea patt. No. 101,
10½" l. ........................................ **50.00**

# NORSE POTTERY

*Norse Pottery Bowl-Vase*

*The Norse Pottery was founded in Edgerton, Wisconsin in 1903 by Thorwald P.A. Samson and Louis Ipson, both of whom had previous pottery-making experience. In 1904 A.W. Wheelock of Rockford, Illinois purchased the pottery and moved the founders to a new pottery facility in Rockford. Among the pottery's unique products were ceramic renditions of ancient bronze relics which had been excavated in Denmark, Norway and Sweden. These wares often featured a dull metallic glaze. Until its final closing in 1913 the pottery also produced a range of items including candlesticks, vases, cigar humidors, bowls and other utilitarian wares.*

*The mark on Norse pottery is the word "Norse" impressed vertically on the base of pieces with the oversized "N" surrounding the other letters.*

**Bowl-vase,** a squatty bulbous
wide body raised on small feet,
the wide flattened shoulder
centering a wide, short flat
cylindrical neck flanked by
stylized figural salamander
handles, stylized incised Nordic
scroll designs on the shoulder &
a ring band around the body, the
interior w/a snugly fitted metal
insert probably for a lamp font,
pale greenish highlights in
incised designs, company logo
& shape No. 70, 3⅞" h.
(ILLUS. previous column) ....... **$550.00**

**Bowl-vase,** a broad tapering
ovoid body raised on three
pointed flaring feet molded
w/stylized human faces, a wide
gently angled shoulder to the
wide flat mouth, the lower body
incised w/a design of chain links
& snake-like conjoined birds, the
shoulder w/a band of wave-like
bird design, golden bronze finish
w/pale green highlighting the
incised decoration, impressed
company mark & shape No. 61,
6⅛" h. ........................................ **495.00**

**Vase,** 9¼" h., simple cylindrical
form incised w/wide upper &
lower hammered-looking bands
& a wide center band of incised
ducklings around the body,
black w/greenish highlights,
impressed company logo &
shape No. 99 (two professionally
repaired base chips) ................ **660.00**

# NORTH DAKOTA SCHOOL OF MINES

*All pottery produced at the University of North Dakota School of Mines was made from North Dakota clay. In 1910, the University hired Margaret Kelly Cable to teach pottery making and she remained at the school until her retirement. Julia Mattson and Margaret Pachl were other instructors between 1923 and 1970. Designs and glazes varied through the years ranging from the Art Nouveau to modern styles. Pieces were marked "University of North Dakota - Grand Forks, N.D. - Made at School of Mines, N.D." within a circle*

*North Dakota School of Mines Vases*

*and also signed by the students until 1963. Since that time, the pieces bear only the students' signatures. Items signed "Huck" are by the artist Flora Huckfield and were made between 1923 and 1949. Pieces were marked with the University name until 1963.*

*North Dakota Mark*

**Bowl-vase,** "Prairie Rose" patt., squatty bulbous ovoid body w/a closed-in mouth, decorated around the shoulder w/a wide band of pink roses & green leaves against a grey band, the lower body w/a rose-colored ground, by Huckfield, circular mark & "WOLFF - Huck - 2837," 5½" d., 4¼" h. (ILLUS. above right) ......... **275.00**

**Lamp,** oil-type, footed squatty bulbous "Aladdin-lamp" style w/a wide rounded rim spout w/a flat top centered by a wick hole, the rim handle curving up to form a tall C-scroll above the rim embossed w/a band of mustard yellow prairie roses, the inset cover w/a prairie rose-embossed finial, the body in a dark reddish brown matte glaze, inscribed under the lid "Minot Art Club," probably a presentation piece, 4½" h. (small rim bruise on lid) . **413.00**

**Vase,** 3½" h., 3¾" d., bulbous ovoid body w/a closed-in mouth, decorated around the upper portion w/a band of greyish blue wolves against an ivory ground, circular ink mark, repair to a short rim line (ILLUS. above left) .......................................... **550.00**

**Vase,** 4" h., 7" d., wide squatty bulbous body w/the wide shoulder tapering to a flat mouth, pale yellow over peach matte glaze, circular ink mark, incised "Gooslaw - 3/10/44" ...... **385.00**

**Vase,** 4½" h., 5" d., squatty bulbous ovoid form tapering to short cylindrical form, decorated w/stylized birds in black & yellow against a brick red semi-matte ground, circular ink mark, incised "Armstrong" ................... **770.00**

**Vase,** 6" h., ovoid body w/a narrow base, the sides tapering gradually to a flat rim, the middle carved w/a wide band featuring a series of young girls holding hands against a textured ground, nut brown matte glaze, blue circular mark, incised "Summers" .............................. **319.00**

**Vase,** 7¾" h., 6" d., footed wide bulbous ovoid body tapering to a short cylindrical neck, molded rings up the shoulder & neck, overall metallic dark green matte glaze, by Julia Mattson, circular ink mark & "JM - 217" (ILLUS. center, top previous page) ........ **413.00**

**Vase,** 8½" h., 4¾" d., simple ovoid body molded around the upper neck & shoulder w/a continuous band of stylized serrated leaves under a matte dark reddish brown glaze, circular mark w/"D'Obrien" ........ **550.00**

---

# OHR (George) POTTERY

*Small Ohr Pitcher*

*George Ohr, the eccentric potter of Biloxi, Mississippi, worked from about 1883 to 1906. Some think him to be one of the most expert throwers the craft will ever see. The majority of his works were hand-thrown, exceedingly thin-walled items, some of which have a crushed or folded appearance. He considered himself the foremost potter in the world and declined to sell much of his production,* *instead accumulating a great horde to leave as a legacy to his children. In 1972 this collection was purchased for resale by an antiques dealer.*

GEO. E. OHR
BILOXI, MISS.

*Ohr Pottery Marks*

**Bowl,** 3¾" d., 2" h., upright crimped four-lobed form, fine speckled green glaze over orange clay, marked "GEO. E.OHR - BILOXI, MISS." ......... **$935.00**

**Bowl,** 5½" d., 1¾" h., low diamond-shaped form w/a folded & dimpled rim, mottled amber & gunmetal glaze, die-stamped "GEO. E. OHR, BILOXI, MISS." ........................ **990.00**

**Bowl,** 6" w., 1¾" h., a wide, shallow heavily manipulated crinkled & folded bowl, amber, olive green & gunmetal glaze, die-stamped "G.E. OHR, BILOXI" .................................. **1,540.00**

**Bowl-vase,** wide cylindrical form w/a heavily dimpled & scalloped rim above a rounded bottom band & narrow footring, speckled green & gunmetal glaze, die-stamped "G.E. OHR - Biloxi, Miss.," 4¾" d., 4¼" h. ... **1,320.00**

**Brothel coins,** bisque, each bearing a suggestive comment in rhebus form, the set ............. **485.00**

**Chamberstick,** bottle-shaped body w/ear-shaped handle, all above an in-body twist at base, covered in smooth even microcrystalline gunmetal glaze, hand incised "G E OHR," 4" d., 5½" h. ...................................... **825.00**

**Inkwell,** decorated w/Victorian arabesque pattern in relief under mottled green high glaze, die-stamped "GEO E OHR - BILOXI," 5¾" d., 1½" h. (two small glaze flakes at top) .......... **605.00**

**Mug,** Joe Jefferson-type, simple ringed baluster-form w/an inverted D-form handle, interior w/a mottled cobalt blue glaze, the exterior w/a raspberry glaze & the incised greeting beginning "Here's to your health...," dated 1896, the base impressed "GEOHR - BILOXI, MISS. - 8-18-96," 4½" d., 3½" h. ............ **1,045.00**

**Pitcher,** 4" h., 4¾" d., a flaring pedestal foot supports a wide pinched & dimpled body w/a wide incurved rim above a cut-out handle, decorated w/a fine mottled green & red glaze, die-stamped "G.E.OHR, Biloxi, Miss." (thin glaze scrape on edge)..................................... **6,050.00**

**Pitcher,** 4½" h., 8¼" d., footed pinched upright sides w/a widely flaring ruffled rim, long angular cut-out handle, covered in a semi-gloss raspberry glaze w/yellow froth at the top, a curdled blue & amber interior, script signature (ILLUS. previous page)..................................... **9,350.00**

**Vase,** 3¼" h., 3¼" d., footed trumpet-form body w/dimpled sides, rare orange, white & green marbleized glaze, die-stamped "G.E. OHR, Biloxi, Miss." ..................................... **2,750.00**

**Vase,** 3¾" h., 3½" d., squatty base tapering to cylindrical neck w/flat rim, sponge-decorated in green, dark blue & brown on a yellow ground, hand-incised "Biloxi" (minute glaze flake on top rim)..................................... **990.00**

**Vase,** 3⅞" h., footed flattened ovoid body tapering from the shoulder band to a tall twisted & crumpled neck, the lower body w/a sgraffito scenic panel depicting a bird in grass & plants, impressed mark "G.E.OHR - Biloxi, Mississippi," ca. 1895 ..................................... **805.00**

*Ohr Twisted & Compressed Vase*

**Vase,** 4" h., 5¼" d., a footring supports a wide squatty bulbous body w/a band of large dimples around the sides, the wide shoulder tapering to a short swirled & crimped neck, bisque-fired buff clay, incised "GE Ohr" ..................................... **770.00**

**Vase,** 5¼" h., 4½" d., footed gently tapering cylindrical form w/a wide mid-body in-body twist flanked by long scrolled & looped handles all below the wide, deep cupped rim, mottled brown glaze, die-stamped "G.E. OHR, Biloxi, Miss."................. **4,950.00**

**Vase,** 6¼" h., 3¾" d., a waisted cylindrical lower half below a medial in-body twisted band, the upper half a tapering conical form, covered in a rare matte mauve & green mottled glaze, script signature ..................... **2,750.00**

**Vase,** 6¾" h., 7" d., a twisted & compressed disc near the base below a swelled cylindrical wide body tapering to a wide flaring neck w/a pinched & twisted rim, the lower body w/a semi-matte speckled mustard yellow glaze, the upper portion w/a matte gunmetal glaze, impressed "BILOXI, MISS. - GEO. E. OHR" (ILLUS. above)....................... **5,225.00**

**Vase,** 7¾" h., 5½" d., footed spherical lower body below a tall trumpet neck flanked by long looping ribbon handles, glossy mottled dark green, amber & gunmetal glaze w/random red spots, marked "GEO. OHR, Biloxi, Miss." (minute glaze bruise on side) ...................... **4,125.00**

# OLD IVORY

*Old Ivory No. 16 Plate*

*Old Ivory china was produced in Silesia, Germany, in the late 1800s and takes its name from the soft white background coloring. A wide range of table pieces was made with the various patterns usually identified by a number rather than a name.*

**Bonbon,** round, handled, No. 76, 6½" d....................................... **$115.00**

**Bowl,** 6½" d., No. 84..................... **50.00**

**Bowl,** 9¼" d., No. 15................... **195.00**

**Bowl,** 9¼" d., No. 200................ **195.00**

**Bowl,** 9½" d., deep sides, Holly patt., No. 22 ............................. **225.00**

**Bowls,** berry, 5" d., No. 84, pr. ..... **40.00**

**Butter pat,** No. 16...................... **150.00**

**Cake plate,** open-handled, Holly patt., No. 22 ............................. **145.00**

**Celery bowl,** 5½ x 11", No. 84.... **150.00**

**Chocolate set:** cov. chocolate pot & five cups & saucers; No. 16, the set ................................. **625.00**

**Coffeepot,** cov., demitasse, No. 16 ..................................... **395.00**

**Creamer,** No. 16 ........................ **110.00**

**Cup & saucer,** No. 75 .................. **65.00**

**Cup & saucer,** No. 76 .................. **75.00**

**Ladle holder,** No. 84 .................... **95.00**

**Plate,** bread & butter, 6⅛" d., No. 16 (ILLUS. previous column).. **75.00**

**Plate,** bread & butter, 6⅛" d., No. 84 ........................................ **75.00**

**Plates,** luncheon, No. 76, set of 4 .......................................... **135.00**

**Teapot,** cov., No. 15 ................... **395.00**

**Toothpick holder,** No. 16 ......... **195.00**

**Tray,** self-handled, oval, No. 11, 8¼ x 11½".................................. **150.00**

# OLD SLEEPY EYE

*Old Sleepy Eye Quart Pitcher*

*Sleepy Eye, Minnesota, was named after an Indian chief. The Sleepy Eye Milling Co. had stoneware and pottery premiums made at the turn of the century first by the Weir Pottery Company and subsequently by Western Stoneware Co., Monmouth, Illinois. On these items the trademark Indian head was signed beneath "Old Sleepy Eye." The colors were Flemish blue on grey. Later pieces by Western Stoneware to 1937 were not made for Sleepy Eye Milling Co. but for other businesses. They bear the same Indian head but "Old Sleepy Eye" does not appear below. They have a reverse design of teepees and trees and may or may not be marked Western Stoneware on the base. These items are usually found in cobalt blue on cream and are rarer in other colors. In 1952, Western Stoneware made a 22 oz. and 40 oz. stein with a chestnut brown glaze. This mold was redesigned in 1968. From 1968 to 1973 a limited number of 40 oz. steins were produced for the Board of Directors of Western Stoneware. These were marked and dated and never sold as production items. Beginning with the first convention of the Old Sleepy Eye Club in 1976, Western Stoneware has made a souvenir which each person attending receives. These items are marked with the convention site and date. It should also be noted that there have been some reproduction items made in recent years.*

*Stoneware Sleepy Eye Vase*

**Pitcher,** 4" h., cobalt blue on white, w/small Indian head on handle, Western Stoneware Co., 1906-37, half pint (chip on bottom edge) .......................... **$200.00**

**Pitcher,** 6¼" h., cobalt blue on white, w/small Indian head on handle, Western Stoneware Co., 1906-37, quart (ILLUS. bottom previous page) .......... **325.00 to 350.00**

**Pitcher,** 7¾" h., cobalt blue on white, w/small Indian head on handle, Western Stoneware Co., 1906-37, half-gallon (discoloration & crazing) .......... **350.00**

**Vase,** 9" h., cylindrical, Flemish blue on grey stoneware, cattails on both sides, Weir Pottery Co., 1903 (ILLUS. above) ................. **475.00**

# OVERBECK

*Early Overbeck Vases*

*The four Overbeck sisters, Margaret, Hannah B., Elizabeth G. and Mary F., established their pottery in their old family home in Cambridge City, Indiana in 1911. Different areas of the house and yard were used for the varied production needs.*

*Their early production consisted mainly of artware before 1937 with most pieces being hand-thrown or hand-built in such forms as vases, bowls, candlesticks, flower frogs, tea sets and tiles. Pieces during this era were decorated generally either with glaze inlay or carving and several colors of subtle matte glazes were used first with brighter glazes added later.*

*After the death of Elizabeth G. in 1937 Mary F. became the driving force behind the pottery. The output became less varied, until mainly small molded figures of various sorts of humans, some humorous or grotesque, and animals and birds were the main products. Work was carried on alone by Mary F. until her death in 1955.*

*Marked pieces of Overbeck usually carry the "OBK" cipher and early wares may carry the initial or initials of the sister(s) who produced it.*

**Figurines,** stylized figures of a stylish Victorian man standing & holding a top hat & wearing a monocle, blue cravat, pink jacket & blue pants & hat, w/an equally stylish standing lady wearing a wide-brimmed hat in red, blue & green & a long mottled dark green gown trimmed w/a band of flowery trim, woman marked w/Overbeck logo, man 5¼" h., pr. (man w/broken & reattached leg & small nick off underside brim of his hat) ........................ **$413.00**

**Model of a rooster,** a stylized grotesque large-footed strutting bird in white w/red & brown trim, incised "OBK," 1¾" w., 3¼" h.... **275.00**

**Vase,** 5¾" h., bulbous ovoid body w/the rounded shoulder centered by a short, slightly flaring cylindrical neck, overall deep rose w/the upper half carved w/six dark brown lunettes, each a stylized wooded landscape & three larger lunettes w/the same settings w/the addition of a woman wearing a wide-brimmed hat & holding the hand of a small child, marked w/incised company logo & letters "E" & "F" for Elizabeth & Mary Frances Overbeck ............................... **2,420.00**

**Vase,** 6¼" h., 4" d., swelled cylindrical body w/an angled shoulder tapering to a short cylindrical neck, decorated w/large incised & painted medallions showing geese in flight, in pink, brown, green & violet on a raspberry ground, incised "OBK - E - H" (ILLUS. left, second column previous page) .................................... **3,080.00**

**Vase,** 6¾" h., two-color, ovoid body tapering to a wide & slightly flaring cylindrical neck, brick red ground decorated around the body w/a wide cream brick red ground decorated around the body w/a wide cream band carved w/a design of small stylized birds feeding in a vine & berry patch, marked w/Overbeck logo & initials of Elizabeth & Hannah Overbeck.................. **4,400.00**

*Paneled Overbeck Vase*

**Vase,** 8" h., 3¾" d., a tall cylindrical body w/a swelled shoulder angling in to a short, slightly flaring, cylindrical neck, carved w/three full-length stylized landscape panels, matte mustard yellow glaze against a brown ground, each panel shows a color change to indicate day, dusk & evening, by Elizabeth & Frances, marked "OBK - E.F." (ILLUS.)............................... **7,700.00**

**Vase,** 8" h., 4½" d., gently swelled cylindrical body tapering to a short gently flaring neck, carved & painted in three panels w/a pink & green stylized bird in a tree in red, green, brown & ivory on a mustard yellow body, modeled by Elizabeth & Hannah, incised "OBK - E - H" (ILLUS. right, second column, previous page) ..................... **14,300.00**

**Vase,** 11½" h., cylindrical body w/wide slightly tapering flat neck, decorated w/painted & lightly incised scene consisting of a repeating sequence of tall light tan trees in the background w/a single pale green leaf prominently overlaid in the foreground, mustard yellow ground, marked w/incised Overbeck logo & initials of Mary Frances & Elizabeth Overbeck ............................. **13,750.00**

# OWENS POTTERY

*Owens pottery was the product of the J.B. Owens Pottery Company, which operated in Ohio from 1890 to 1929. In 1891 it located in Zanesville and produced art pottery from 1896, introducing "Utopian" wares as its first art pottery. The company switched to tile after 1907. Efforts to rebuild after the factory burned in 1928 failed and the company closed in 1929.*

*Owens Pottery Mark*

**Creamer,** bulbous w/long pinched spout, C-shape handle, decorated w/purple grapes & green leaves on a black ground, glossy glaze, impressed "Owens Lotus" & "X 236," 3⅛" h. (ILLUS. below front, center) ................. **$220.00**

**Ewer,** Utopian line, floral decoration, 8" h. (hairline to handle)..................................... **200.00**

**Lamp base,** ovoid body w/a flat mouth, shaded black to dark brown ground decorated w/pansies, artist-initialed, impressed "SO" in large block letters, cast hole in base, 8" h. (ILLUS. back row, second from left, below) ............................... **220.00**

**Mug,** tankard-type, Utopian line, tapering cylindrical body w/angled handle, decorated w/red cherries & green leaves, dark brown shading to tan, artist-initialed, impressed "J.B. Owens Utopian" & "830," 6⅞" h. (ILLUS. back row, second from right, below) ............................. **193.00**

**Pitcher,** jug-type, Utopian line, h.p. corn decoration, artist-signed ....................................... **295.00**

**Pitcher,** tankard, 9½" h., Utopian line, cylindrical body w/a pinched rim spout below an arched opening, angled handle, shaded black to dark brown ground decorated w/red & yellow cherries & dark green leaves, artist-initialed, impressed "Owens - 1 - A 14" (ILLUS. back row, far left, below) ................... **165.00**

Photo Courtesy of David Rago
*Fine Grouping of Owens Pottery Pieces*

**Tile,** Arts & Crafts style, decorated w/scene of trees, grass, rock path & mountains in background, shades of green, white, mauve & orange matte glaze, minor edge chips & abrasions, impressed twice on back, "Owens" & embossed "285," 8¼ x 11¾" (ILLUS. back row, third from left, below) ..... **1,760.00**

**Vase,** 6½" h., an ovoid body on four tiny feet, the sides molded w/four vertical spines tapering to a narrow neck ending in a forked mouth, dark green matte glaze . **165.00**

**Vase,** 8" h., 3¾" d., bottle-form, a bulbous ovoid body tapering sharply to a small neck w/flared rim, matte slip-relief decoration of large leaves in brown, blue & grey against a shaded blue & brown ground, die-stamped "Owens - 817" (rim restoration) .................... **55.00**

**Vase,** 11¾" h., Utopian line (or possibly Lotus) footed bulbous body tapering to short cylindrical neck, decorated w/the profile of a woman surrounded by apple blossoms, tan matte finish, neat ⅜" hole drilled through the base & minor scuffs & glaze discoloration, artist-initialed in white slip, impressed "Owens Utopian," "S," "1025" & "1" (ILLUS. back row, third from right, below) .............................. **660.00**

**Vase,** 13" h., Utopian line, h.p. dogwood blossom decoration ... **300.00**

**Vase,** 13½" h., Utopian line, slender trumpet-form body flaring at the stepped base, a compressed knob at the top of the neck, h.p. red tulips & green leaves on a black shading to brown ground, artist-initialed in brown slip, impressed "Owens" & "123" (ILLUS. back row, far right, below) ............................ **220.00**

**Vase,** 15½" h., 7½" d., Utopian line, tall ovoid body tapering to a tiny flared neck, slip-decorated w/a cat portrait in gold & brown against a dark brown ground,

glossy glaze, decorated by Hester Pillsbury, impressed mark & artist-initialed ............. **2,200.00**

**Vase in stand,** 11" h., Mission line, the tapering ovoid body w/a wide rounded shoulder to the tiny molded mouth, decorated w/a design of red drips over a green ground, fitted in an Arts & Crafts oak cross-form holder w/short square legs, impressed mark, 2 pcs.(glaze wear, chips to rim)........................................ **468.00**

**Wall pocket,** shell-shaped, Verde Matte line, aqua glaze............... **295.00**

---

# OYSTER PLATES

*Limoges Oyster Plates*

*Oyster plates intrigue a few collectors. Oysters were shucked and the meat served in wells of these attractive plates specifically designed to serve oysters. During the late 19th century they were made of fine china and majolica. Some plates were decorated in the realistic "tromp l'oeil" technique while others simply matched the pattern of a dinner service. Following is a random sampling of oyster plates that were sold in the past eighteen months.*

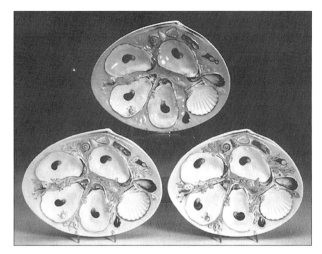

*Union Porcelain Works Oyster Plates*

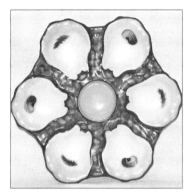

*Unmarked Oyster Plate*

**Limoges porcelain,** decorated w/dainty flowers, 7½" d. ............ **$80.00**

**Limoges porcelain,** six-well, squared shape w/cut-corners, six half-shell indentations & a rounded ribbed sauce well at one side, trimmed in yellow, blue, green, pink, white & peach-colored grounds, light surface & gilt rim wear, late 19th c., 7¾" w., set of 12 (ILLUS. of part w/intro) ..................................... **1,150.00**

**Limoges porcelain,** five-well, Seaweed patt., gold & green, Tresseman & Vogt, 8¼" d .......... **90.00**

**Porcelain,** relief-molded shell & leaf design on pink lustre ground w/gold trim, 8¾" d. ...................... **50.00**

**Porcelain,** six-well, white w/gold decoration & trim, 8½" d., unmarked, probably France ........ **75.00**

**Porcelain,** six-well, each well in shaded pink to pale yellow w/brown trim, mottled brown between each well & a pale blue round center well, unmarked, 9" d. (ILLUS. bottom, previous column) ...................................... **75.00**

**Royal Vienna china,** four-well, gold decoration on white, 8½" d.. **85.00**

**Union Porcelain Works,** four-well, oblong half-shell form w/four oyster shell indentations & a shell-shaped sauce indentation at one end, molded small shells & seaweed between the wells, ornate enamel decoration, Greenpoint, New York, late 19th c., printed marks, 8⅓" l., set of 12 (ILLUS. of part, top this page)...................................... **1,840.00**

# PARIAN

*Parian is unglazed porcelain in the biscuit stage, and takes its name from its resemblance to Parian marble used for statuary. Parian wares were made in this country and abroad through much of the last century and continue to be made.*

*Bust of King Edward VII*

**Bust of King Edward VII,** the bearded monarch w/an official uniform & medals of state, mounted on a round socle base, sculpted by W.C. Lawton, marked by Robinson & Leadbeater, incised factory marks & titles, late 19th c., overall 22¾" h. (ILLUS.)....... **$1,380.00**

**Bust of Shakespeare,** signed "J. & T.B.," James & Thomas Bevington, Staffordshire ............. **45.00**

**Figure of Canova,** classical maiden standing w/one hand near her mouth, the other arm holding a floral wreath, a short tree stump behind her, on a round base w/her name impressed, impressed Minton marks, ca. 1863, small chips to floral wreath, 15" h. (ILLUS. right, top next column) ............. **748.00**

**Figure of a farmer,** the young man shown seated on a rocky free-form base & holding bagpipes, wearing a long coat & a tall, tapering hat, impressed Copeland marks, ca. 1875, pipes & fingers restored, small chips to sheaf of wheat beside him, 11¾" h. (ILLUS. left, top next column) ............................ **173.00**

*Two English Parian Figures*

**Model of owls,** two birds snuggling up to each other on a branch by a tree stump-form match holder, rectangular base w/chamfered corners & the embossed title, "Match Making," embossed English registry mark for 1871, 5½" d., 7½" h. ............ **225.00**

---

# PARIS & OLD PARIS

*China known by the generic name of Paris and Old Paris was made by several Parisian factories from the 18th through the 19th century; some of it is marked and some is not. Much of it was handsomely decorated.*

**Dinner service:** nine dinner plates, eight luncheon plates, thirteen bread & butter plates, thirteen salad plates, twelve shallow bowls, nine rimmed soup bowls, two cov. vegetable dishes & underplates, four oval shaped platters, a footed open compote, a two-tiered server & a cov. sauce tureen on underplate; each piece painted w/sprays of multicolored flowers in a wide border band, mid-19th c., the set (wear, lines) ......................... **$1,150.00**

*Fine Paris Jardiniere*

**Figure of an artist,** dressed in a Cavalier outfit, modeled as a bearded young man wearing a feathered hat, cloak, jacket, kneebreeches & boots, seated among classical ruins & sketching in a book, an artist's palette & book on the ground by his feet, probably by Jacob Petit, taken from the top of a mantel clock, second half of the 19th c., 9¼" h. (minor gilt wear) ............. **460.00**

**Jardinieres,** a deep U-form bowl w/rolled rim, raised on a stepped round base, the sides reserved on the front w/a square panel finely painted w/ladies, one a fashionable young lady, the other her young maid, the other side showing four country women standing behind a fifth holding a straw hat, each against a dusky sky within a tooled gilt foliate framework interrupting beneath the gilt-edged flaring rim, a gold & platinum foliate border repeated around the lower body above matte-gold lady's masks issuing tall plumes forming the handles & the stands w/a narrow cobalt blue border between a matte-gold milled rim & fluted, beaded & foliate-molded borders above the burnished gold foot rim, minor wear & flaws & chips, 1815-25, 11" h., pr. (ILLUS. of one above) .......................... **18,400.00**

*Paris Pot-de-Creme Set*

*Decorated Paris Porcelain Vase*

**Pot-de-creme set:** a pair of two-tiered compotes & thirteen cov. *pot-de-creme* two-handled cups; each cup, cover & compote decorated w/wide pink bands around the center w/a gilt Greek key border all on white, the compotes w/top gilt ring handles & gilt pedestal bases, 19th c., overall 13" h., pr. (ILLUS. of one, top this column) ............ **990.00**

**Spill vase,** modeled as a seated woman wearing a white gown trimmed in gilt in front of the vase, 19th c., 10½" h. ............... **138.00**

**Vase,** 17" h., pedestal-footed tall slender baluster-form w/a tall flaring trumpet neck, ornate arched leafy scroll handles at the shoulders above Bacchic masks, each side h.p. w/a large rectangular panel on the white ground, one side w/an early 19th c. couple, the young man serenading the young lady seated on a bench, the reverse w/a mountainous landscape scene, first half 19th c. (ILLUS. bottom right, previous page) ..... **358.00**

---

# PATE-SUR-PATE

*Pate-sur-pate Neptune Plaque*

*This ware takes it name from the French term, "paste-on-paste," and pieces feature designs in relief, obtained by applying successive thin layers of pottery paste one upon the other. A white slip is generally used resulting in a cameo effect with white designs on a dark background. The majority of this specialized ceramic ware was produced in France and England in the second half of the 19th century. The Minton factory in England is especially noted for their fine examples.*

**Flask,** bottle-form, footed flattened round body tapering to a short, slender cylindrical neck flanked by small loop handles, the olive green ground decorated w/a white slip figure of a classical youth standing on one leg & pulling a legging on the other leg, gilt handles & gilt floral trim on the neck & shoulders, signed "L. Solon," late 19th c., 10¼" h. .............. **$1,725.00**

**Plaque,** rectangular, the brown ground decorated in white slip w/a bearded walking nude male figure representing the god Neptune holding an inverted vessel at each side & pouring a stream of water, a long drapery flowing down & over one shoulder, gilt-accented w/fish, artist-signed "M," France, 19th c., gilt wear, 3¾ x 6¾" (ILLUS.) .................................... **978.00**

**Plaque,** oval, dark brown ground decorated in white slip w/a figure of a standing cupid holding a chain, artist-signed by Louis Solon, dated 1907, England, in a beveled ebonized wood frame, 4½ x 6½" .............................. **2,645.00**

**Plaque,** rectangular, brown ground w/white slip decoration depicting five female classical figures armed w/shields, swords & helmets standing below a cupid figure reclining over a trellis, artist-signed by Louis Solon & dated 1880, England, mounted in an ebonized wood frame, 8½ x 15½" .................. **9,200.00**

**Vase,** cov., 16½" h., figural, flattened circular deep green panels on each side decorated in white slip w/a scene of Psyche being carried

*Ornate Pate-sur-pate Vase*

# PAUL REVERE POTTERY

*This pottery was established in Boston, Massachusetts, in 1906, by a group of philanthropists seeking to establish better conditions for underprivileged young girls of the area. Edith Brown served as supervisor of the small "Saturday Evening Girls Club" pottery operation which was moved, in 1912, to a house close to the Old North Church where Paul Revere's signal lanterns had been placed. The wares were mostly hand decorated in mineral colors and both sgraffito and molded decorations were employed. Although it became popular, it was never a profitable operation and always depended on financial contributions to operate. After the death of Edith Brown in 1932, the pottery floundered and finally closed in 1942.*

S.E.G.

*Paul Revere Pottery Marks*

heavenward by Cupid, each framed by a serrated border, full-figural classical maidens seated on each shoulder, the shoulder tapering to a ribbed knob below the flat & flaring neck fitted w/a domed cover w/a ribbed pointed knob finial, the body raised on heavy C-scroll supports, overall gold trim, artist-signed by Frederick Schenck, impressed factory mark of George Jones, England, cover damaged, hairlines in figures., gilt wear, ca. 1880 (ILLUS.) ... **3,565.00**

**Vases,** 10¾" h., footed baluster-form w/the stepped round foot supporting a tall ovoid body tapering to a short cylindrical neck w/a widely flaring mouth, arched gilt handles from the neck to the shoulder & ending in classical masks, the dark brown ground decorated in white slip w/a classical figure standing behind a small table set w/tiny figures of putti, gilt trim on the neck, handles & base, artist-signed by Louis Solon, printed Minton marks, late 19th c., corner of one handle repaired, pr. ......................................... **5,750.00**

**Bowl,** 6½" d., 2½" h., squatty bulbous form w/a wide incurved mouth, a band of carved landscape w/trees w/brown trunks & green leaves on a cocoa ground backed by a green tree line & blue sky, outlined in black & backed by a rich blue glaze, marked "S.E.G. - b-21 - FL" ............................ **$1,000.00**

**Dinner service:** six dinner plates, six luncheon plates, six bread & butter plates, six cups & eight saucers, five mugs, five small bowls, two larger bowls, jug-form pitcher, serving bowl, two chargers, creamer, sugar bowl & a cov. butter dish; each piece glazed in blue & white, decorated in the center w/a small round landscape medallion in green, blue, white & yellow w/black outlining, pieces

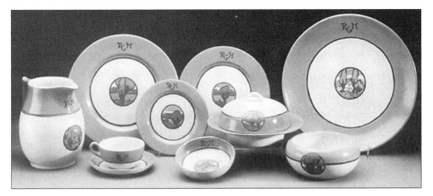

*Paul Revere Dinner Service*

monogrammed "RGH," dated 1921, charger 11¾" d., pitcher 7" h., the set (ILLUS. of part) . **4,600.00**

**Plate,** 8½" d., decorated around the rim w/blue & white bands & clusters of green trees, ivory ground, marked in black "S.E.G. 9-15" & artist's mark.................. **358.00**

**Tea set:** cov. teapot, creamer & six 6" d. plates; traditional blue glaze, teapot 9" w., 4" h., the set (minor chips) ............................ **154.00**

**Trivet,** round, molded & surface-painted w/a bucolic landscape of a quaint cottage w/trees by a river in shades of blues, brown & greens, marked "A.M. - 12-17 S.E.G.," 5¼" d........................ **1,760.00**

# PENNSBURY POTTERY

*Pennsbury Ashtray*

*Henry Below and his wife Lee founded the Pennsbury Pottery in Morrisville, Pennsylvania in 1950. The Belows chose the name because William Penn's home was nearby. Lee, a talented artist who designed the well-known Rooster pattern, almost the entire folk art designs and the Pennsylvania German blue and white hand-painted dinnerware, had been affiliated with Stangl Pottery of Trenton, New Jersey. Mr. Below had learned pottery making in Germany and became an expert in mold making and ceramic engineering. He, too, had been associated with Stangl Pottery and when he and Lee opened Pennsbury Pottery, several workers from Stangl joined the Belows. Mr. Below's death in 1959 was unexpected and Mrs. Below passed away in 1968 after a long illness. Pennsbury filed for bankruptcy in October, 1970. In 1971 the pottery was destroyed by fire.*

*During Pennsbury's production years, an earthenware with a high temperature firing was used. Most of the designs are a sgraffito-type similar to Stangl's products. The most popular coloring, a characteristic of Pennsbury, is the smear-type glaze of light brown after the sgraffito technique has been used. Birds are usually marked by hand and most often include the name of the bird. Dinnerware followed and then art pieces, ashtrays and teapots. The first dinnerware line was Black Rooster followed by Red Rooster. There was also a line known as Blue Dowry which had the same decorations as the brown folk art patterns but the decorations were done in cobalt.*

Pennsbury

Pottery

Pennsbury
Pottery

morrisville, Pa.

*Pennsbury Pottery Marks*

**Ashtray,** motto-type, Amish boy & girl under umbrella w/saying, "It's making down," 5½" d. (ILLUS. bottom previous page) .. **$38.00**

**Ashtray,** Hex patt., three cigarette rests, 5" d. .................... **35.00**

**Bank,** model of a Hershey Kisses candy, unmarked, hard-to-find, gloss dark brown, 4" h. .............. **55.00**

**Bowl,** 6½" d., Red Rooster patt. ... **15.00**

**Bowl,** 9" d., Dutch Talk patt., Pennsylvania Dutch emblems & ten Pennsylvania Dutch sayings arranged haphazardly around the piece, hard-to-find.............. **145.00**

**Cake stand,** pedestaled, Red Rooster patt., not easy to find, 11" d........................................ **125.00**

**Candleholder,** Tulip patt., stylized tulips on round base, 5" d............................................... **55.00**

**Cookie jar,** cov., Red Barn patt., 8" h............................................ **295.00**

**Cookie jar,** cov., Red Rooster patt., 8" h................................. **175.00**

**Creamer,** Red Rooster patt., 2½" h.......................................... **30.00**

**Cruets w/original stoppers,** oil & vinegar, Black Rooster patt., figural rooster stoppers, 7" h., pr. .................................... **265.00**

**Desk basket,** Two Women Under Tree patt., 5" h. ........................... **85.00**

**Egg Cup,** Red Rooster patt., 4" h.. **38.00**

**Lamp base,** jug-style, Black Rooster patt., large (hairline crack on side) ........................... **100.00**

**Model of a Blue Jay,** perched atop a tree stump w/a small leaf cluster, blue, white & black bird, pale green & white tree stump, Model No, 108, signed "D. Parker," 10½" h......................... **525.00**

**Model of a Cardinal,** Model No. 120, 6½" h................................. **225.00**

**Model of a chickadee-type bird w/tail pointed upward,** seated on a hollowed out gourd, "Slick Chick," unmarked, 5½" h. (ILLUS. right below) .................. **110.00**

*Pennsbury "Slick Chick" Models*

**Model of a chickadee-type bird w/tail pointed upward,** marked in block letters, "P.M.A.A. 1967" & in script "Pennsbury Pottery Morrisville, PA," 5½" h. (ILLUS. left, bottom previous page) ....... **115.00**

**Model of a Magnolia Warbler,** Model No. 112 .......................... **200.00**

**Model of a Redstart,** peach, Model No. 113, 3" h. ................... **65.00**

**Model of a Scarlet Tannager,** Model No. 105R or 105L, 5½" h., each ............................ **245.00**

**Mug,** beer-type, Barber Shop Quartet patt. ................................ **45.00**

**Mug,** beer-type, Gay Ninety patt... **45.00**

**Mug,** coffee, Red Barn patt. .......... **35.00**

**Mug,** Red Rooster patt., smear glaze w/dark brown inside, 5" h. . **60.00**

**Pie plate,** "Picking Apples," framed...................................... **125.00**

**Planter,** model of a Dutch Shoe, brown smear glaze, no decoration, 5" l. .......................... **55.00**

**Plaque,** Eagle patt., 21½" l. ........ **425.00**

**Plate,** 10" d., Blue Dowry patt., birds & hearts w/leaves on wide banded edge in blue glaze, center void of decoration ............ **60.00**

**Plate,** 10" d., Red Rooster patt. .... **35.00**

**Platter,** 11" h., oval, Red Rooster patt............................................ **60.00**

**Salt & pepper shakers,** Red Rooster patt., dark brown glazed tops, 2½" h., pr............................ **35.00**

**Sign,** dealer display-type, rectangular w/slightly flaring rim, yellow bird perched on top w/head & tail up, "Pennsbury Pottery" on two lines underneath bird, light brown smear glaze, 4½" l., 5" h................................ **250.00**

**Sugar bowl,** cov., Red Rooster patt., 4" h..................................... **30.00**

**Teapot,** cov., Red Rooster patt... **150.00**

**Vegetable bowl,** divided, Red Rooster patt., 6¼ x 9½" .............. **50.00**

**Wall plaque,** man rising out of his chair w/hand on head, pedestal table in front of him, saying

"Don't stand up while the room is in motion," common item, easily found, 6" d. ...................... **60.00**

---

# PETERS & REED

*In 1897 John D. Peters and Adam Reed formed a partnership to produce flowerpots in Zanesville, Ohio. Formally incorporated as Peters and Reed in 1901, this type of production was the mainstay until after 1907 when they gradually expanded into the art pottery field. Frank Ferrell, a former designer at the Weller Pottery, developed the "Moss Aztec" line while associated with Peters and Reed and other art lines followed. Though unmarked, attribution is not difficult once familiar with the various lines. In 1921, Peters and Reed became Zane Pottery which continued in production until 1941.*

*Peters & Reed Mark*

**Bowl,** 10" d., 3" h., Landsun line ......................................... **$100.00**

**Console bowl & flower frog,** Landsun line, 2 pcs. .................. **125.00**

**Ewer,** Moss Aztec line, decorated w/molded lion's head w/grapevine designs on a glossy ground, 11" h. .......................................... **160.00**

**Ivy bowl,** matte green glaze, 10" d............................................ **45.00**

**Jar,** bulbous ovoid body w/short cylindrical neck, Moss Aztec line, glossy brown glaze w/molded amber busts of George Washington, 5½" h......... **83.00**

**Vase,** 3½" h., Moss Aztec line, molded sprig design on glossy brown ground ............................. **65.00**

**Vase,** 6½" h., bulbous, handled, Moss Aztec line, molded floral decoration on glossy brown ground........................................ **40.00**

**Vase,** 7 x 7", footed pillow-form w/fluted rim, Moss Aztec line, molded floral decoration ............ **45.00**

**Vase,** 8" h., cylindrical body w/a flared rim, molded decoration of overlapping blossoms w/long, narrow petals against a textured ground covered in a terra cotta brown matte glaze, impressed "Ferrell" ...................................... **55.00**

**Vase,** 9" h., Shadow Ware, glossy glaze ........................................ **135.00**

**Vase,** 9¼" h., Landsun line ........... **75.00**

**Vase,** 9½" h., Moss Aztec line, slightly flaring cylindrical body deeply molded in relief w/pine cones, needles & limbs down the sides, deep brick red matte exterior glaze w/green tinting, glossy interior glaze, probably designed by Frank Ferrell, unmarked.................................. **330.00**

**Vase,** 10" h., Landsun line ............ **85.00**

**Vase,** 10" h., Moss Aztec line, molded wreath decoration, brown glossy-glazed ground..... **150.00**

---

# PEWABIC POTTERY

*Mary Chase Perry (Stratton) and Horace J. Caulkins were partners in this Detroit, Michigan pottery. Established in 1903, Pewabic Pottery evolved from their Revelation Pottery, "Pewabic" meaning "clay with copper color" in the language of Michigan's Chippewa Indians. Caulkins attended to the clay formulas and Mary Perry Stratton was artistic creator of forms & glaze formulas, eventually developing a wide range of colors for her finely textured glazes. The pottery's reputation for fine wares and architectural tiles enabled it to survive the depression years of the 1930s. After Caulkins died in 1923, Mrs. Stratton continued to be active in the pottery until*

*her death, at age 94, in 1961. Her contributions to the art pottery field are numerous.*

*Pewabic Mark*

**Bowl,** 2⅛" h., hand-thrown, ringed base below widely flaring cylindrical sides, covered w/a volcanic brown over yellow over cream glazes, base signed w/a large "P" in white slip .............. **$220.00**

**Bowl,** 5"d., 2¾" h., a small round foot below the deep flaring sides, lustered mottled green & purple glaze, paper label ......... **330.00**

**Figure of a young girl,** standing holding a small dog, wearing a long, pleated shift, iridescent grey & gold glazes, on a raised square foot, artist-signed on base "Gwen Lux," 4¼" w., 11¾" h...................................... **440.00**

**Vase,** 4" h., 5" d., squatty bulbous body w/rolled rim, covered in a fine dripping turquoise, gold lustered & apple green glaze, impressed circular stamp.......... **935.00**

**Vase,** 5" h., 5" d., footed bulbous ovoid body w/a rounded shoulder to the wide, short cylindrical neck, overall turquoise & purple lustre glaze, circular die-stamped mark "PEWABIC DETROIT".............. **495.00**

**Vase,** 6½" h., 6" d., footed vessel w/angular ovoid sides, tapering shoulder w/flaring neck, covered in a fine gold lustered glaze dripping over a matte cobalt blue base, w/circular stamp mark .. **1,760.00**

**Vase,** 7" h., 4½" d., ovoid body tapering to a short cylindrical neck, lustered glaze of concentric circles of purples, blues & greens, mark obscured by glaze ................................... **660.00**

*Ornate Pickard Short Pitchers*

# PICKARD

*Pickard, Inc., making fine hand-colored china today in Antioch, Illinois, was founded in Chicago in 1894 by Wilder A. Pickard. The company now makes its own blanks but once only decorated those bought from other potteries, primarily from the Havilands and others in Limoges, France.*

**Basket,** curved oval, gold floral decoration, 5 x 7¼" .................. **$65.00**

**Bonbon,** double-handled, decorated w/a Chinese pheasant, artist-signed, 8½" l. .. **235.00**

**Bowl,** 9" d., 4¾" h., pedestal base, Modern Conventional decoration, artist-signed ........... **285.00**

**Bowl,** 11" d., angled rim w/double pierced rim handles, vellum scenic "Yosemite," Nippon blank, artist-signed.................... **350.00**

**Bowl,** hexagonal, enameled grapes & pomegranates in blue, red & green on band of black, 1912 mark................................ **295.00**

**Coffee set:** 10¾" h. cov. coffeepot, creamer & sugar bowl; Aura Argenta Linear patt., artist-signed, the set ................. **660.00**

**Condensed milk container w/underplate,** violet panels & green leaves, artist-signed, 2 pcs. ...................................... **395.00**

**Dish,** hexagonal, handled, decorated w/grapes, plums & raspberries, heavy gold trim, ca. 1915, artist-signed, 4 x 8¼" ...... **175.00**

**Nappy,** finely h.p. w/a landscape scene within a gold rim, artist-signed, 7" l. ............................... **220.00**

**Pitcher,** cider, decorated w/h.p. poppies on gold ground, artist-signed ...................................... **275.00**

**Pitcher,** jug-type, 5½" h., squatty bulbous lower body w/an angled shoulder tapering to a flared mouth, pointed angular gold handle, Daisy Multiflora patt., white daisy blossoms against a black band w/tall gold daisy clusters down the white sides, 1905-10 mark (ILLUS. above left)........................................... **275.00**

**Pitcher,** jug-type, 5½" h., footed hexagonal body w/looped angular gold handle, Deserted Garden patt., a wide upper band of colored fruits on a pastel shaded ground w/fruit cluster suspended into the gold lower body, gold rim band, artist-signed, 1912-18 mark (ILLUS. above center)............................ **900.00**

**Pitcher,** jug-type, 5½" h., footed hexagonal body w/looped angular gold handle, Encrusted Linear patt., stylized blue & white floral panels & bands against a textured gold ground, 1912-18 mark (ILLUS. above right)......................................... **450.00**

**Pitcher,** jug-type, 5½" h., pastel ground w/apple blossoms decoration highlighted w/gold, artist-signed .............................. **530.00**

**Pitcher,** cider, decorated w/h.p. poppies on gold ground, artist-signed ...................................... **275.00**

*Rare Pickard Tobacco Jar*

**Plate,** 8½" d., Gooseberry
Conventional decoration, artist-
signed ...................................... **145.00**

**Plate,** 8½" d., decorated
w/strawberries & heavy gold
trim, artist-signed ...................... **185.00**

**Plate,** 12" d., decorated w/tulips,
lustre finish, artist-signed .......... **250.00**

**Plate,** open-handled, white violets
linear decoration, artist-signed.. **120.00**

**Salt shaker,** decorated w/purple
pansies, gold trim, 1910 mark..... **85.00**

**Salt & pepper shakers,** Lemon
Tree patt., lovely shape, artist-
signed, 1910-12 mark, pr. ......... **125.00**

**Tobacco jar, cov.,** bulbous ovoid
body w/a fitted low domed cover,
h.p. on the front w/a bust portrait
of a Native American chief
against a shaded dark brown to
orange ground, the reverse w/a
landscape w/teepees, birds &
mountains, a tomahawk & peace
pipe on the cover, artist-signed
(ILLUS. above)...................... **2,420.00**

**Trinket box,** cov., cream ground
w/gold scrolling & Tomascheko
Edelweiss border, unsigned, ca.
1905-10, D & G, France blank,
3" d., 2" h. ................................ **145.00**

**Vase,** 8½" h., ovoid w/slightly
flaring rim, small looped gold
shoulder handles, decorated
w/exotic, colorful flowers, birds &
butterflies on white ground,
etched gold band around base,
rim & shoulder (ILLUS. top next
column) .................................... **325.00**

*Ovoid Pickard Vase*

**Vase,** 8¾" h., Encrusted Linear
patt., blue & white stylized floral
bands extend to the base &
around the neck ........................ **650.00**

# PIERCE (Howard) PORCELAINS

*Pierce Owls in a Tree*

*Howard Pierce was born in Chicago,
Illinois in 1912. He attended the
university there and also the Chicago Art
Institute but by 1935 he wanted a change*

and went to California. That move would alter his life forever. He settled in Claremont and attended the Pomona College. William Manker, a well-known ceramist, hired Mr. Pierce in 1936 to work for him. That liaison lasted about three years. After leaving Manker's employment Howard opened a small studio in Laverne, California and, not wishing to be in competition with Manker, began by creating miniature animal figures, some of which he made into jewelry. In 1941, he married Ellen Voorhees who was living in National City, California. In the 1950s, Mr. Pierce had national representation through the N.S. Gustin Company.

Polyurethane animals are high on collectors lists as Howard, after creating in the early years only a few pieces using this material, realized he was allergic to it and had to discontinue its use. Pierce was a man of many talents and a great deal of curiosity. He experimented with various mediums such as a Wedgwood Jasper Ware-type body, then went into porcelain bisque animals and plants that he put close to or in open areas of high-gloss vases. When Mt. St. Helens volcano erupted, Pierce was one of the first to experiment with adding the ash to his silica which produced a rough-textured glaze. Lava, while volcano associated, was a glaze treatment unrelated to Mt. St. Helens. Howard described Lava as "...bubbling up from the bottom..."

Pierce also created some pieces in goldleaf which are harder to find than the gold treatment he formulated in the 1950s for Sears. They had ordered a large number of pieces and wanted all of them produced in the gold treatment. Many of these pieces are not marked. Howard also did what he termed 'tipping' in relation to glazes. A piece would be high-gloss overall but, then, the tops, bottoms, sides, etc. would be brushed, speckled or mottled with a different glaze, most often brown, black or grey. For example, a set of three fish made in the late 1950s or early 1960s were on individual bases that were 'tipped' as were the fins with the bodies

being a solid brown or black. Toward the late 1970s, Mr. Pierce began putting formula numbers on his pieces and recording the materials used to create certain glazes.

In November 1992, because of health problems, Howard and Ellen Pierce destroyed all the molds they had created over the years. Mr. Pierce began working on a limited basis producing miniature versions of past porcelain wares. These pieces are simply stamped "Pierce." Howard Pierce passed away in February, 1994.

*Howard Pierce Marks*

**Bowl,** 7¼" d., 4¼" h., fluted body flaring to a fluted rim, Manker influence, pale & deep blue w/black accents, incised mark, "Pierce 1983" in script .............. **$85.00**

**Figure group,** boy standing w/head bent & left arm extended to feed dog seated at his left side, nondescript, mottled brown glaze, marked "Howard Pierce," 5" h.............................................. **75.00**

**Figures of a Hawaiian boy & girl,** overall black bodies w/green mottled pants on boy, green mottled grass skirt on girl, both w/hands in Hula dance position, 1950s, boy, 7" h., girl, 6¾" h., pr. ................................. **175.00**

**Figure of a native woman,** w/long body, short legs, arms behind her back, dark brown glaze w/mottled brown skirt, hard-to-find, 3½" w., 16½" h. .... **285.00**

**Figure group,** three monkeys stacked on top of one another, black, one-piece, Model No. 300P, 15" h. ............................. **125.00**

**Figure group,** two owls in a tree, seated on branches, three open branches for small flowers, dull dark brown tree, light & dark brown owls, larger, unusual size for Pierce owls in tree, stamp mark "Howard Pierce," tree, 6" w., 13" h., large owl, 6" h., small owl, 3½" h. (ILLUS. w/intro) ...... **225.00**

**Jug,** bulbous body w/small pouring spout & small finger hold, brown mottled rough-textured glaze, stamp-mark "Howard Pierce," 5¾" h.............. **85.00**

**Magnet,** model of a dinosaur, gloss grey glaze, 3" l., 1½" h....... **30.00**

**Model of a bear,** brown, 7" l. ........ **85.00**

**Model of a circus horse,** head down, tail straight, leaping position w/middle of body supported by small, round center base, light blue w/cobalt accents, experimental glaze, 7½" l., 6½" h............................ **145.00**

**Model of a hippo,** standing, short tail, bulbous body, large nose & mouth, small ears & eyes, very distinct features, dark grey bottom, mottled grey top, 1950s, stamp marked "Howard Pierce Porcelain," 9¾" l., 3" h. (ILLUS. top next column) ............ **95.00**

**Model of a panther,** pacing position, brown glaze, 11½" l., 2¾" h....................................... **110.00**

**Models of birds,** seated, heads up, nondescript bodies except for eyes & beaks, black satin-matte glaze w/orangish red breasts, stamp mark "Howard Pierce," large, 4½" h., medium, 3" h., small, 1¾" h., the set ......... **65.00**

**Models of fish,** each on a half-circle base, dark brown bodies w/speckled bases & fins, large fish, 6" h., medium fish, 4¾" h. small fish, 3" h., the set ............ **125.00**

**Models of giraffes,** stylized, black, 10" h. & 12" h., pr. .......... **100.00**

**Models of monkeys,** grey, pr..... **165.00**

*Howard Pierce Hippopotamus*

**Pencil holder,** nude women in relief around outside, tan & brown glaze, one year limited production, 1980, 3½" d., 4¼" h. ... **65.00**

**Planter,** half-circle alcove in goldleaf w/white bisque angel holding songbook & standing in alcove, hard-to-find, 7" h. .......... **155.00**

**Vase,** 9" h., tapering body w/a flaring neck & stretched rim, brown bottom half of body & neck, yellow mid-section of body & interior, stamp mark, "Howard Pierce" & copyright symbol, hard-to-find color combination .... **75.00**

**Wall plaque,** rectangular, modernistic birds in-relief, pale green background w/darker green birds, cement, 19" l., ½" deep, 6¼" h................................. **75.00**

**Whistle,** bird-shaped w/hole at tail, grey w/white textured glaze, 3½" h.......................................... **35.00**

**Whistle,** snake crawling w/body forming an "M" shape, brown w/white glaze, 3¼" l., 2¾" h. ........ **25.00**

# PISGAH FOREST POTTERY

*Pisgah Forest Tea Set*

*Walter Stephen experimented with making pottery shortly after 1900 with his parents in Tennessee. After their deaths in 1910, he eventually moved to the foot of Mt. Pisgah in North Carolina where he became a partner of C.P. Ryman. Together they built a kiln and a shop but this partnership was dissolved in 1916. During 1920 Stephen again began to experiment with pottery and by 1926 had his own pottery and equipment. Pieces are usually marked and may also be signed "W. Stephen" and dated. Walter Stephen died in 1961 but work at the pottery still continues, although on a part-time basis.*

Pisgah Forest Marks

**Jar,** cov., mottled green & turquoise glaze exterior, pink interior, No. D1936 ................... **$65.00**

**Pitcher,** 4 x 8", maroon & blue glaze w/crystals ........................ **145.00**

**Tea set:** cov. teapot, cov. sugar bowl & creamer; Cameo Ware, each w/a squatty bulbous body, white relief decoration of an ox-drawn covered wagon & a horse on a matte olive green ground, embossed mark & signed on base "W. Steven," teapot 9" d., 4½" h., 3 pcs. (ILLUS. bottom previous page) ...................... **1,045.00**

**Vase,** 6" h., 3¾" d., simple baluster-form body, light metallic brown & cream flowing crystalline flambé glaze, embossed mark, 1943 .............. **110.00**

**Vase,** 9¾" h., 5" d., tall baluster-form body, covered in a good white, celadon green & golden crystalline glaze, 1940, raised potter's mark ............................ **770.00**

**Vase,** 12" h., Cameo Ware, baluster-form w/a molded, rolled

rim, a central white relief band showing a bearded mountain man wearing a wide-brimmed hat sitting outside a cabin w/a young dog on one side, the opposite side w/a team of oxen pulling a covered wagon followed by a horse w/two riders, all against a lavender blue matte ground, factory-drilled holes on the side & base, signed on the side "Stephen" ......................... **935.00**

---

# PRATT WARES

Pratt Ware Figure Group

*The earliest ware now classified as Pratt ware was made by Felix Pratt at his pottery in Fenton, England from about 1810. He made earthenware with bright glazes, relief sporting jugs, toby mugs and commercial pots and jars whose lids bore multicolored transfer prints. The F. & R. Pratt mark is mid-19th century. The name Pratt ware is also applied today to mid- and late 19th century English ware of the same general type as that made by Felix Pratt.*

Pratt Wares Mark

*Pratt Ware Sauceboat*

**Cup & saucer,** handleless, swirled embossed flute design, each decorated w/a yellow band border surrounding delicate floral sprigs & sprays in blue, light green & orangish ochre, early 19th c. (trace of spider crack in saucer) ........................ **$55.00**

**Figure of Winter,** allegorical figure of a standing figure wrapped in long spotted animal skins decorated w/early ochre, blue & orange enamels & clear & green glazes, ca. 1780-1800, 8½" h. (invisible restoration to lower portion of the base) ......... **430.00**

**Figure group,** a young cowherd standing beside a cow & small recumbent calf, raised on an oval base, blue sponge decoration on the cow & base, the cowherd w/a blue jacket, red sash & ochre pants, ca. 1800-20, cow horns missing, head of cowherd reglued, 7½" l., 5½" h. (ILLUS. previous page) ..................................... **605.00**

**Pitcher,** 7¼" h., pearlware, baluster-form w/C-scroll handle, molded floral & leaf band designs around the top & base w/large central heart reserves w/children, one side labeled "Mischievous Sport," the other "Sportive Innocence," highlighted in yellow, green, tan, blue & brown, early 19th c. (chips on handle & spout, short, minor hairline) .......................... **534.00**

**Sauceboat,** figural, in the form of a fox's head forming the body & spout & a swan forming the handle, the raised waisted base decorated w/a band of tall upright painted yellow & green acanthus leaves on a white ground, the fox in orangish ochre & the swan in white w/brown-sponged wings & a yellow bill, late 18th c., body reglazed over restoration, 7" l., 5" h. (ILLUS. top previous column) ..................................... **935.00**

# PURINTON POTTERY

*The Purinton Pottery Company was founded in Shippenville, Pennsylvania in 1941 by Bernard S. Purinton. Earlier, beginning in 1936, Mr. Purinton started a smaller pottery operation in Wellsville, Ohio, but by 1941 he wished to expand and chose the site near Shippenville where a large, new plant was constructed.*

*Most of Purinton's products were cast and then hand-painted with a variety of colorful patterns by local people trained at the factory. One of their best known and most popular designs was Peasant Ware, originally introduced at the Wellsville plant in the 1930s. Until the plant was finally closed in 1959, the company continued to produce a colorful, hand-decorated range of tablewares, kitchenwares, vases and novelty items.*

**Cookie jar,** Humpty Dumpty ..... **$425.00**

**Cookie jar w/wooden lid,** Pennsylvania Dutch patt. .......... **225.00**

**Creamer & cov. sugar bowl,** miniature, Fruit patt., 2" h............ **28.00**

**Decanter w/cork stopper,** miniature, Intaglio patt., 5" h. ...... **35.00**

**Honey jug,** long tapering spout joined to high arched handle ending at the side of the body, Petals patt., 6¼" h...................... **43.00**

**Pitcher,** 4½" h., Kent jug-type,
Fruit patt., 1 pt............................ **29.00**

**Pitcher,** 5¾" h., Dutch jug-type,
Apple patt., 2 pt.......................... **59.00**

**Platter,** 12¼" l., divided, Apple
patt.............................................. **55.00**

**Salt & pepper shakers,** miniature
jug-style, Pennsylvania Dutch
patt., 2½" h., pr. .......................... **75.00**

**Salt & pepper shakers,** range-
style, Fruit patt., 4" h., pr............. **45.00**

**Spaghetti bowl,** Apple series,
14½" l. (chip restoration)........... **130.00**

**Spaghetti bowl,** Normandy Plaid
patt., 14½" l............................... **195.00**

**Teapot,** cov., Mountain Rose
patt., 2-cup size, 4" h. ................. **39.00**

---

# QUIMPER

*Floral-decorated Quimper Plate*

*This French earthenware pottery has been made in France since the end of the 17th century and is still in production today. Because the colorful decoration on this ware, predominantly of Breton peasant figures, is all hand-painted and each piece is unique, it has become increasingly popular with collectors in recent years. Most pieces offered today date from about the mid-19th century to the present. Modern potteries continue to operate today and contemporary examples are available in gift shops.*

*Quimper Marks*

**Bell,** figural female, "Henriot
Quimper - France" mark,
3½" h...................................... **$235.00**

**Butter pat,** portrait decoration of
man in center, unmarked ............ **55.00**

**Cask set:** a yellow-glazed barrel-
shaped cask w/spigot mounted
on a wooden stand w/six small
matching cups, three hanging
along each side; yellow floral
decoration, the cask 5 x 8", the
set ........................................... **275.00**

**Menu holder,** rectangular, male
peasant decoration, "HR -
Quimper" mark, 3½" h.............. **390.00**

**Plate,** 7½" d., center floral
decoration w/sponged border
band, Henriot - Quimper, France
(ILLUS. bottom previous column).. **75.00**

**Plate,** 8" d., peasant man or lady
decoration, Henriot - Quimper,
France, each .............................. **55.00**

**Plate,** 9¼" d., decorated
w/peasant man wearing top hat
pushing wheelbarrow, "HB"
mark .......................................... **60.00**

**Plate,** 11" h., h.p. peasant girl
decoration (small rim
restoration)................................ **65.00**

**Salt dip,** double, figural shoes,
3" l............................................. **75.00**

**Teapot,** cov., h.p. bird decoration,
yellow glaze, 5½" h. .................. **450.00**

**Teapot,** cov., scalloped shape w/h.p.
peasant man & woman decoration,
7" h. (repaired spout).................... **395.00**

**Teapot,** cov., paneled shape, h.p.
Art Deco decoration of "Sailor &
his Girl," 9½" h. ........................ **450.00**

**Tray,** flattened oval bagpipe
shape w/ribbon trim, peasant
decoration, "HB - Quimper"
mark, 6" l................................... **135.00**

**Wall pocket,** bagpipe-shaped,
"HR - Quimper" mark, 8" h. ....... **495.00**

# REDWARE

*Redware Creamer*

Red earthenware pottery was made in the American colonies from the late 1600s. Bowls, crocks and all types of utilitarian wares were turned out in great abundance to supplement the pewter and handmade treenware. The ready availability of the clay, the same used in making bricks and roof tiles, accounted for the vast production. The lead-glazed redware retained its reddish color though a variety of colors could be obtained by adding various metals to the glaze. Interesting effects occurred accidentally through unsuspected impurities in the clay or uneven temperatures in the firing kiln which sometimes resulted in streaks or mottled splotches.

Redware pottery was seldom marked by the maker. Also see SHENANDOAH VALLEY POTTERY.

**Bottle,** figural, Toby-style, three-quarter portrait of Mr. Toby holding mug, brown running glaze, attributed to Solomon Bell, 7⅞" h.(wear, small glaze flakes on one cuff) .............. **$1,760.00**

**Creamer,** tall ovoid boat-shape w/wide arched spout & ornate C-scroll handle, the sides molded w/a spread-winged American eagle & shield flanked by foliage, overall dark brown glaze, possibly New Jersey, ca. 1820, small chips, 4¼" h. (ILLUS. above).......................... **316.00**

**Cup,** bell-shaped w/tooled lines & applied strap handle, mottled greenish brown glaze, attributed to Baecher, Winchester, Virginia, 3½" h. (edge chips)..... **440.00**

**Flowerpot w/attached saucer base,** crimped rim & tooled lines around top, clear glaze w/light peachy amber, brown & green, 5" h. (minor chips & wear)........ **248.00**

**Food mold,** Turk's turban-form, brown running glaze, impressed "John Bell," 6⅞" d. (professional repair) ...................................... **853.00**

**Jar,** cov., ovoid w/eared shoulder handles, flaring molded rim w/inset cover w/button finial, reddish amber glaze, 19th c., 12" h. (chips on lip & cover) ...... **110.00**

**Jar,** cov., bulbous ovoid w/eared shoulder handles, faint tooled design, flaring molded rim w/inset domed cover w/button finial, dark brown glaze w/black splotches 12" h. (wear & chips, lid good fit but color varies) ....... **220.00**

**Jar,** ovoid, well-defined brown & amber glaze, 19th c., 6" h. (minor flakes) ........................... **220.00**

**Jar,** bulbous ovoid w/wide flaring rim, rope twist handles, yellow amber glaze w/serpentine line of brown sponging, green dots & brown flecks, 7" h. (wear & small flakes, chip on base) ............. **1,815.00**

**Jar,** bulbous ovoid body tapering to a wide slightly flaring rim, eared handles, incised straight & wavy lines, dark patina w/simple brushed brown flower at shoulder, impressed "John Bell Waynesboro," interior glaze 13" h. (chips & hairlines & damage in base) ...................... **187.00**

**Jug,** footed, bulbous ovoid w/tooled lines at shoulder, ribbed strap handle, greenish amber glaze w/brown flecks, 6¾" h........................................ **374.00**

**Jug,** footed bulbous ovoid body w/ribbed strap handle, dark brown glaze, 10¾" h. ................ **110.00**

*Early Redware Mug & Porringer*

**Milk pan,** round w/deep, flaring sides, dark brown glaze, 18" d. (worn interior glaze) ................. **121.00**

**Mug,** tall cylindrical body w/applied C-form handle, brown manganese splotches on a greenish ground, New England, 1770-1810, 4¾" d., 5¾" h. (ILLUS. above right) .............. **4,025.00**

**Pitcher,** 5⅜" h., squatty ovoid body tapering to a slightly flared rim, ribbed strap handle, brown running glaze, impressed "John Bell" ...................................... **2,200.00**

**Porringer,** cup-shaped footed bowl w/a rolled rim & strap handle, brown manganese streaked splotches on a greenish ground, New England, 1780-1820, flakes, 5¾" d., 3⅛" h. (ILLUS. above left) ...... **2,415.00**

**Porringer,** cup-shaped bowl w/rolled rim & strap handle, dark glaze w/black splotches, 5½" d., 3½" h. (wear & chips on base) ...................................... **160.00**

**Preserving jar,** footed cylindrical tapering to wide flaring rim, orange glaze w/dark brown splotches, 8¼" h. (chips) ........... **347.00**

**Spill holder,** waisted cylindrical form, impressed "John Bell, Waynesboro," mottled brown glaze, 4⅛" h. (minor edge chips) .................................... **1,045.00**

**Teapot,** cov., footed bulbous body w/molded ribs, wide shoulder to high oval neck, branch handle & spout, inset domed cover w/pointed finial, clear glaze w/orange & dark brown splotches, 7⅛" h. (small chips, finial glued) .................... **385.00**

**Toothpick holder,** model of a lady's shoe on a conforming base w/a green, brown & ochre glaze, attributed to the George Wagner Pottery, Weissport, Carbon County, Pennsylvania, 19th c., 4⅛" h. ........................... **242.00**

---

# RED WING POTTERY

*The Red Wing Stoneware Company was organized in 1868 in Red Wing, Minnesota. Other potteries opened in the area during the following years and in 1894 a number of them merged to form the Red Wing Union Stoneware Company. A wide variety of stoneware utilitarian wares were produced during the following decades but when the need for such pottery waned the company introduced an art pottery line. In 1930 the name was changed to the Red Wing Potteries, Inc. to better reflect their changing product lines. Stoneware ceased to be made at the plant in 1947 but other artware and dinnerware lines continued in production until the closing of the plant in 1967.*

*Red Wing Marks*

## ART POTTERY
**Figures of a cowboy & cowgirl,** fully decorated, 11" h., pr. ....... **$500.00**

**Planter,** hanging-type, No. M-1487 ................................. **45.00**

**Vase,** 7" h., expanding cylinder w/squared handles rising from narrow shoulder to mouth, No. 163-7, grey & tan glaze ...... **100.00**

**Vase,** 7" h., No. 1509-7, black satin matte glaze ......................... **35.00**

**Vase,** 9" h., ribbed, No. 637 ........ **145.00**

**Vase,** 9½" h., No. M1442-9½, Colonial buff & salmon ................ **65.00**

**Vase,** 10" h., No. 902-10, lustre Dubonnet ................................. **100.00**

**Vase,** 11" h., No. 1377/11, green & yellow glaze ............................ **75.00**

**Vase,** No. 839, blue glaze ........... **100.00**

**Vase,** No. 1079, blue glaze ........... **55.00**

**Vase,** deer decoration, No. 1120 .. **45.00**

**Vase,** figural elephant handle, ivory ground, matte finish, Rum Rill mark ........................... **125.00**

**Wall pocket,** No. M 1630, brown glaze, 10" h. ............................... **80.00**

## BRUSHED & GLAZED WARES

**Vase,** 7" h., bulbous body tapering to a short cylindrical neck, angled handles, decorated w/acorn & oak leaf design, dark & light green, No. 149-7 ............ **150.00**

**Vase,** 8" h., flower design decoration, No. 1107, green & mauve (minor base flake) ........... **75.00**

**Vase,** 15" h., swelling cylindrical body tapering to a flat rim, angled shoulder handles, green & yellow, No. 186-15 ................ **125.00**

**Vase,** leaf decoration, No. 1166, buff & green ............................... **35.00**

## DINNERWARES & NOVELTIES

**Ash receiver,** figural, model of a seated donkey w/mouth wide open, green glaze ...................... **25.00**

**Beverage server w/stopper,** Bob White patt. ........................... **95.00**

**Beverage server w/stopper,** Smart Set patt. .......................... **195.00**

**Bowl,** berry, Bob White patt. ........... **8.00**

**Bowl,** berry, Capistrano patt. .......... **9.00**

**Bowl,** berry, Tampico patt. ............. **10.00**

**Bowl,** cereal, Bob White patt. ....... **25.00**

**Bowl,** cereal, Tampico patt. .......... **15.00**

**Bowl,** salad, 12" d., Capistrano patt. ............................................ **45.00**

**Bowl,** salad, 12" d., Tampico patt. ............................................ **85.00**

**Bowl,** salad, Random Harvest, large .............................................. **40.00**

**Bowl,** soup, Bob White patt. ......... **20.00**

**Bread tray,** rectangular, Bob White patt., 24" l. ...................... **100.00**

**Bread tray,** Round Up patt. ........ **150.00**

**Butter dish,** cov., Bob White patt., ¼ lb. ..................................... **75.00**

**Butter warmer,** Bob White patt. ... **95.00**

**Candlesticks,** Magnolia patt., pr. . **45.00**

**Carafe,** cov., Bob White patt. ...... **185.00**

**Casserole,** cov., Bob White patt., 2 qt. ............................................. **40.00**

**Casserole,** cov., Smart Set patt., 2 qt. ............................................. **68.00**

**Casserole,** cov., Bob White patt., 4 qt. ............................................. **50.00**

**Celery dish,** Flight patt. .............. **175.00**

**Cocktail tray,** Bob White patt. ...... **40.00**

**Cookie jar,** cov., Bob White patt... **60.00**

**Cookie jar,** cov., figural Katrina (or Dutch girl), yellow glaze ........ **80.00**

**Cookie jar,** cov., figural Monk, blue glaze .................................. **40.00**

**Cookie jar,** cov., side handle & side top, red glaze .................... **225.00**

**Coffeepot,** cov., Village Green Line ............................................. **22.00**

**Creamer,** Bob White patt. ............. **25.00**

**Cruets w/stoppers,** Bob White patt., pr. .................................... **200.00**

**Cruets w/stoppers in metal rack,** Bob White patt., the set ... **325.00**

**Cup & saucer,** Bob White patt. ...... **9.00**

**Cup & saucer,** Capistrano patt..... **13.00**

**French bread tray,** Bob White patt., 24" l. ..................................... **90.00**

**French casserole,** cov., w/stick handle, Town & Country patt., peach glaze ............................... **95.00**

**Gravy boat,** cov., Bob White patt. ............................................ **55.00**

**Gravy boat w/stand,** Tampico
patt., 2 pcs. ................... **60.00**

**Hors d'oeuvre holder,** Bob
White patt., model of a bird
pierced for picks.......................... **50.00**

**Mug,** Bob White patt. .................... **80.00**

**Pitcher,** Bob White patt., 60 oz..... **50.00**

**Pitcher,** 12" h., Round Up patt.... **185.00**

**Pitcher,** jug-type, Tampico patt.,
2 qt............................................. **65.00**

**Plate,** 6½" d., Bob White patt. ......... **6.00**

**Plate,** 6½" d., Capistrano patt. ........ **5.00**

**Plate,** 6½" d., Tampico patt............. **7.00**

**Plate,** 8" d., Bob White patt............. **8.00**

**Plate,** 8½" d., Tampico patt.......... **12.00**

**Plate,** 10½" d., Bob White patt..... **12.00**

**Plate,** 10½" d., Capistrano patt. .... **10.00**

**Plate,** 10½" d., Tampico patt......... **14.00**

**Plate,** salad, Flight patt. ............... **60.00**

**Platter,** 13" l., Bob White patt. ...... **80.00**

**Platter,** 20" l., Bob White patt. .... **100.00**

**Platter w/metal rack,** Bob White
patt., large, 2 pcs. ..................... **150.00**

**Relish tray,** Bob White patt.,
three-part ................................. **70.00**

**Relish tray,** Bob White patt.,
two-part...................................... **45.00**

**Relish tray,** Tampico patt., 13" l. ... **35.00**

**Salt & pepper shakers,** figural
bird, Bob White patt., pr. ............. **40.00**

**Salt & pepper shakers,** figural
pitcher, jug-type w/ice lip, red,
Rum Rill mark, pr. ....................... **20.00**

**Salt & pepper shakers,** figural
Shmoo, cinnamon glaze, Rum
Rill mark, pr................................. **65.00**

**Salt & pepper shakers,** figural
Shmoo, bronze glaze, pr............. **95.00**

**Syrup pitcher,** Town & Country
patt., blue glaze .......................... **75.00**

**Teapot,** cover & stand, Bob White
patt., the set .............................. **140.00**

**Teapot,** cov., Village Green Line .. **22.00**

**Tidbit tray,** Random Harvest
patt., original paper label ........... **27.00**

**Tray on warmer,** Smart Set patt.,
large, 2 pcs. ............................. **155.00**

**Vegetable bowl,** open, divided,
Capistrano patt. .......................... **24.00**

**Vegetable bowl,** open, divided,
Smart Set patt............................. **65.00**

**Vegetable bowl,** open, divided,
Tampico patt. ............................. **45.00**

## STONEWARE & UTILITY WARES

**Bean pot,** cov., white & brown
glazes, wire handles, marked
"Red Wing Union Stoneware" ..... **80.00**

**Beater jar,** cylindrical w/a molded
rim, white glazed w/blue bands
& advertising in a rectangle on
the front..................................... **145.00**

**Beater jar,** cylindrical, Sponge
Band line ................................... **265.00**

**Bowl,** 4" d., spongeware, paneled
deep rounded form ................... **350.00**

**Bowl,** Sponge Band line, South
Dakota advertising in bottom,
No. 7 ........................................ **235.00**

**Butter crock,** cylindrical, large
wing mark, 20 lbs...................... **875.00**

**Churn w/wooden cover &
dasher,** swelled cylindrical body
w/eared handles & a molded rim,
white-glazed, large wing mark
w/oval wing stamp below, 2 gal... **250.00**

**Churn w/wooden lid & dasher,**
swelled cylindrical body, Union
Stoneware Co., large wing mark,
3 gal. ........................................ **193.00**

**Churn w/wooden cover &
dasher,** swelled cylindrical body
w/eared handles & a molded
rim, white-glazed, blue birch
leaves over oval & slip-quilled
"4," Union Stoneware Co., Red
Wing, Minnesota, 4 gal., 20" h. .. **295.00**

**Cooler,** iced tea, white-glazed,
bail handles, no wing mark,
5 gal., 11¾" d............................ **385.00**

**Crock,** cylindrical, white-glazed,
big wing mark, 1 gal. ................. **350.00**

**Crock,** cylindrical w/molded rim,
white-glazed, large "2" over
double bird leaves & oval marks,
Red Wing Union Stoneware, 2
gal., 9¾" d. (ILLUS. top next
page)......................................... **65.00**

*Red Wing Union Stoneware Crock*

*Red Wing Fruit Jar*

**Crock,** cylindrical w/eared handles & molded rim, cobalt blue hand-decorated leaf below a "5," grey salt glaze, sidewall stamp, 5 gal. ............................ **425.00**

**Crock,** cylindrical w/eared handles, white-glazed, oval Red Wing stamp mark & 4" stamped wing mark, 6 gal., 13" d. ............. **55.00**

**Crock,** cylindrical, white-glazed, 6" l. wing mark, 40 gal................ **800.00**

**Crock,** cylindrical, white-glazed, large wing mark, 50 gal.......... **1,250.00**

**Fruit jar w/screw-on metal cover,** cylindrical w/tapering shoulder, white-glazed, blue or black stamp reads "Stone - Mason Fruit Jar - Union Stoneware Co. - Red Wing, Minn.," ½ gal. (ILLUS. top next column) ............................... **235.00**

**Jar,** cov., white-glazed, ball lock, 4" wing over Red Wing oval stamp mark, 5 gal. .................... **175.00**

**Jug,** cylindrical w/a salt glazed body & tapering rounded brown-glazed shoulder & neck, oval printed panel w/liquor advertising, ½ gal...................... **278.00**

**Jug,** beehive-shaped, small cylindrical neck, dark blue printed diamond w/Iowa advertising above the blue double birch leaf mark, 5 gal. (ILLUS. bottom next column) .. **2,860.00**

*Rare Red Wing Jug*

**Jug,** beehive-shaped, white-glazed, w/Portland, Oregon advertising, 5 gal...................... **950.00**

**Jug,** cylindrical w/white-glazed shoulder, 4" wing above Red Wing oval mark, 5 gal. ............... **85.00**

**Poultry drinking fount,** cylindrical w/end opening, "Eureka"-style, marked around opening "Patd. April 7, 1885," Red Wing marking on bottom ... **245.00**

**Refrigerator jar,** stacking-type, short cylindrical form w/a molded rim, white-glazed w/narrow blue bands & "Red Wing Refrigerator Jar" on the side, 5½" d. (ILLUS. top next page)............. **165.00**

**Salt box,** cov., hanging-type, Grey Line ............................... **1,950.00**

*Red Wing Refrigerator Jar*

**Water cooler,** cov., cylindrical, white-glazed, side handles, large wing mark, 5 gal............... **350.00**

# RIDGWAYS

*There were numerous Ridgways among English potters. The firm J. & W. Ridgway operated in Shelton from 1814 to 1930 and produced many pieces with scenes of historical interest. William Ridgway operated in Shelton from 1830 to 1865. Most wares marked Ridgway that have been offered in this country were made by one of these two firms, or by Ridgway Potteries, Ltd., still in operation. Also see HISTORICAL & COMMEMORATIVE WARES.*

*Ridgways Mark*

**Bowl,** 8½" d. handled, "Shepherd Pie" scene, Coaching Days & Ways series ............................. **$35.00**

**Mug,** Coaching Days & Ways series, 4½" h. ............................. **25.00**

**Plate,** 9" d., Coaching Days & Ways series ............................... **25.00**

**Tea set,** child's: cov. teapot, cov. sugar, creamer, waste bowl, six cups & saucers & two plates; Regent patt., flowers in blue &

brown w/gold trim on white, the set .............................................. **325.00**

**Vegetable dish,** cov., oval, Deak patt., flowing blue & white, 12" l., 6¼" h......................................... **210.00**

# ROCKINGHAM WARES

*The Marquis of Rockingham first established an earthenware pottery in the Yorkshire district of England in around 1745 and it was occupied afterwards by various potters. The well-known mottled brown Rockingham glaze was introduced about 1788 by the Brameld Brothers and became immediately popular. It was during the 1820s that the production of true porcelain began at the factory and continued to be made until the firm closed in 1842. Since that time the so-called Rockingham glaze has been used by various potters in England and the United States, including some famous wares produced in Bennington, Vermont. However, very similar glazes were also used by potteries in other areas of the United States including Ohio and Indiana and only wares specifically attributed to Bennington should use that name. The following listings will include mainly wares featuring the dark brown mottled glaze produced at various sites here and abroad.*

**Bottle,** figural, modeled as a mermaid w/a woman's bust attached to a long curled-up scaly fish tail, molded short neck at top of her head, mottled brown Rockingham glaze, 19th c., 7⅞" h......................... **$303.00**

**Flask,** model of a book, mottled brown glaze, 7¾" h. .................. **193.00**

**Pitcher,** 8¼" h., bulbous ovoid, flat rim w/pinched spout, angled handle, mottled dark brown glaze ......................................... **193.00**

**Pitcher,** 9" h., footed bulbous octagonal body w/incurved panels to short neck w/mask spout & angled handle, overall mottled & streaky brown & green glaze (kiln adhesion chips on bottom)...................................... **193.00**

**Tobacco jar,** cov., footed cylindrical body w/widely flaring rim, low domed cover w/button finial, mottled dark brown w/molded grapevine design, small chips, 7½" h..................... **220.00**

---

# ROOKWOOD

*Considered America's foremost art pottery, the Rookwood Pottery Company was established in Cincinnati, Ohio in 1880, by Mrs. Maria Nichols Longworth Storer. To accurately record its development, each piece carried the Rookwood insignia, or mark, was dated, and, if individually decorated, was usually signed by the artist. The pottery remained in Cincinnati until 1959 when it was sold to Herschede Hall Clock Company and moved to Starkville, Mississippi, where it continued in operation until 1967.*

*A private company is now producing a limited variety of pieces using original Rookwood molds.*

*Rookwood Mark*

**Ashtray,** figural, modeled w/a square tray featuring a seated clown w/his legs straddling two sides, yellow outfit w/dark blue spots & white cuffs & a blue pointed hat & boots, yellow face, interior in dark yellow w/a dark blue border, designed by Sallie Toohey, 1928, 4" h. (dark line by clown's right foot)................... **$385.00**

*Rookwood Union Terminal Book Ends*

**Basket,** a wide compressed & flaring cornucopia-form w/exterior wide ribbing, the narrow end curving up the side to form one end of the arched pointed handle which terminates on the opposite rim, medium mottled green on interior & upper half of the exterior, the lower half of the exterior decorated w/a maniacal-looking frog in green & yellow sitting at the edge of a large dark green scrolled & ruffled lily pad trailing up the handle, Standard glaze, No. 360, 1887, Albert Valentien, 7½" h................................... **6,600.00**

**Book ends,** figural, modeled as a Colonial lady w/a wide pleated dress & puffy sleeves, her head tilted back & w/a high hairdo, on a thin molded base, dark green Matte glaze, No. 2185, 1919, 5¾" h., pr. (very minor glaze misses) ..................................... **358.00**

**Book ends,** figural, model of a large, long rook perched on an open book w/back half folded up to form backplate, rich mottled brown Matte glaze, No. 2274, 1922, 6½" h., pr. ...................... **990.00**

**Book ends,** figural, modeled as the arched facade of Union Terminal w/a half-round base, light-colored matte glaze, pr. (ILLUS. above)...................... **4,510.00**

**Bowl,** 4½" d., 3" h., bulbous squatty form w/a wide flat molded rim, incised w/a geometric wave-like design in yellow & green over a brown ground, Matte glaze, No. 54, 1901, A.M. Valentien ............... **550.00**

**Bowl,** 12" d., a very wide nearly flat bottom w/rounded incurved low sides, the interior decorated w/an outer band of stylized dark rose red & dark blue blossoms w/yellow centers against an overall dark brownish green Matte glaze ground, No. 2573 C, Vera Tischler, 1923 (small glaze bubbles on underside, minor glaze discoloration).................. **303.00**

**Bowl-vase,** a wide & deep form rounded at the base & raised on a low footring, the exterior decorated around the upper half w/a wide creamy band decorated w/a continous band of long slender green leaves & dark pink berry clusters, the interior, rim band & lower body w/a dark pink ground, glossy glaze, No. 2465, 1921, Lorinda Epply, 7⅞" h.......................... **3,520.00**

**Box,** cov., deep nearly spherical body fitted w/a domed cover decorated w/a band of dark red blossoms & dark green leaves around a mottled red & purplish green center, the body in an overall dark purplish black Matte glaze, No. 622 C, 1908, Olga Geneva Reed, 3½" h. ............ **1,760.00**

**Breakfast set:** coffeepot, two sugars & two creamers, two teacups w/saucers, two demitasses, one 9½" d., bowl, two 8" bowls, five 6" bowls, four two-handled bowls, one 6½" bread plate, thirteen 8" plates; Jewel porcelain, faceted bodies slip-painted w/blue galleons, impressed mark, the set (hairline to smallest creamer, ¼" line to one creamer) ........................ **2,310.00**

**Chambersticks,** a dished & pointed ovoid saucer base w/an integral loop handle from the rim to the base of the central waisted shaft supporting a dished drip pan & short cylindrical socket, curdled violet over pale blue Matte glaze, No.1638, 1921, 5½" d., 3½" h., pr........................ **275.00**

**Doorstop,** figural, a model of a stout seated cat wearing a ruffled collar, overall very dark blackish cobalt blue glossy glaze, No. 2637, 1924, 7¾" h. (repaired ear, small chips on the collar) .................................... **2,420.00**

**Ewer,** squatty bulbous low wide base centered by a tall slender cylindrical neck w/a widely flaring tricorn rim, slender S-scroll handle from rim to shoulder, decorated w/red & yellow clover & green leaves around the lower body against a yellow shaded to tan shaded to dark brown ground, Standard glaze, No. 433, 1890, 7¼" h. .... **385.00**

**Ewer,** footed baluster-form w/a wide rounded spout & high arched loop handle, a blue ground shading from dark blue at the top & base to a pale blue in the middle, decorated up the sides w/long branches of pale bluish green prunus blossoms w/yellow centers on green leafy stems, Matte glaze, No. 6008 E, 1931, Kataro Shirayamadani, 10⅛" h.................................... **1,329.00**

**Flower frog,** figural, modeled as two stylized kneeling nudes facing each other w/heads turned & arms outstretched & entwined above the molded oblong rockwork base pierced w/holes, mottled brown Matte glaze, No. 2338, 1921, base marks & notation "Original Model by Chester Beach," 6⅛" h. (small glaze flake on one side of base) ............................ **385.00**

**Humidor,** cov., slightly swelled cylindrical body w/an inset flat cover w/a large knob finial, the body molded around the shoulder w/a wide band of triangles & rectangles, rich dark green Matte glaze, No. 812, 1908, 6" d., 7" h. ..................... **770.00**

**Jar,** cov., wide squatty bulbous body raised on four bun feet, fitted domed cover, the cover glazed in dark blue & the sides of the base decorated w/a continuous band of dark blue sea horses against a pale blue ground, Vellum glaze, No. 1349, 1911, E.T. Hurley, 3½" h. (small glazed-over chip on one foot) .. **1,100.00**

**Jug w/pointed stopper,** ovoid body tapering to a short cylindrical neck w/molded rim & small loop handle from rim to shoulder, original pointed stopper, decorated w/slip-painted ears of corn on a shaded brown ground, Standard glaze, No. 512B, 1903, Lenore Asbury...................................... **330.00**

**Match holder,** a narrow wide round disc foot tapering to a wide cylindrical body, decorated w/dark orange small flowers against a blackish brown ground, Standard glaze, No. 855, 1898, Ed Diers, 1⅞" h....... **220.00**

**Model of a cat,** seated animal on a rectangular base, looking back over its shoulder, brown Matte glaze, No. 1883, 1922, 5¼" h....................................... **605.00**

**Mug,** tapering cylindrical body w/heavy C-form handle, decorated w/large medium blue grape clusters w/pale green leaves & stem against a cobalt blue shaded to light blue ground, Iris glaze, No. 587 C, 1901, Ed Diers, 4¾" h. ............................ **770.00**

**Mug,** wide slightly tapering cylindrical body w/a long, thick angled handle, Arts & Crafts style w/the sides divided into long panels separated w/bands composed of three thin incised lines, mottled moss green shading to dark rose ground, Matte glaze, No. l587 B, 1909, Cecil Duell, 5¾" h. (glaze pooling on the base) ................. **275.00**

**Paperweight,** figural, model of a stylized Art Deco bluejay, the small free-standing bird w/pointed beak & webbed feet, overall medium blue Matte

glaze, designed by Louise Abel, No. 6277, 1931, 4⅜" h. ............. **605.00**

**Paperweight,** figural, model of a lamb, free-standing Art Deco stylized animal, gunmetal black glaze, No. 6665, 1954, 5⅛" h. .. **303.00**

**Perfume jug,** large ovoid body w/a small molded neck & applied strap handle, Limoges-style decoration w/buff at the top & handle above a shaded pale violet to violet to dark green ground, decorated w/a large yellow & black butterfly & Oriental grasses, trimmed w/fired-on gold, No. 123, 1883, Albert Valentien, 9" h. (professionaly repaired glaze skip on base) ............................ **413.00**

**Pitcher,** 4¼" h., gently flaring cylindrical sides w/a very wide triangular mouth w/a pinched spout at each corner, angular handle, the rim & handle cover w/Gorham silver overlay & over half of the body is covered w/an ornate pierced scrolling & lattice silver overlay design, decorated under the front w/bright orange wild roses & shaded green leaves against a dark brown ground, Standard glaze, No. 259 E, 1893, Sallie Coyne (two 1½" lines in the back corners) ......... **825.00**

**Pitcher,** 7¼" h., footed slightly ovoid body tapering to a gently rolled rim w/pinched spout & applied C-form handle, decorated w/an amusing profile busts of two rather bizarre ladies surrounded by fanciful flowers & scrolls all in shaded brown to cream against a mottled blue ground, glossy glaze, No. 6757, 1949, Jens Jensen................. **1,650.00**

**Plaque,** rectangular, a scenic winter landscape of tall trees w/white trunks backed by a pink & grey stream surrounded by icy banks & birch covered greyish brown land, snow-covered peaks in the distance in lavender & pale blue against an evening sky in shades of aqua, green, yellow & peach, Vellum glaze, Mary Grace Denzler, in original wide flat oak frame, 6 x 8"...................................... **3,850.00**

**Plaque,** rectangular, a large nocturnal Venetian canal scene w/a gondolier moving his vessel past buildings while other gondolas are tied up to a small wharf, done in shades of blues & white, Vellum glaze, 1919, in original brown & gilt molded frame w/original typed Rookwood label inscribed "A Venetian Night E.T. Hurley," E.T. Hurley, 9¼ x 14¾"......... **8,800.00**

**Plate,** 10¼" w., slightly squared rounded sides w/a wide flanged rim, a shaded dark & light brown ground decorated w/a curved branch of white & greenish white fruit blossoms & leaves, Cameo glaze, No. 317, 1886, M.A. Daly (minor glaze scratches) ............ **220.00**

**Potpourri jar w/inner & outer covers,** wide ovoid body tapering to a wide rounded shoulder centering a short cylindrical neck fitted w/an inner flat cover w/finial & high, domed outer cover w/a pointed finial & a wide pierced edge band, a decoration of small flowers mostly obscured by the rich flowing blue Black Opal glaze, interior of jar & covers in bright green, No. 2451, 1923, Sara Sax........................................ **1,045.00**

**Reliquary box,** decorated overall w/Moorish pattern of curlicues, acanthus leaves, birds & lions cut-back under a Matte mustard glaze, No. 2470, impressed w/flame mark & artists cipher, 1920, Arthur Conant, 7 x 9" ... **1,210.00**

**Stein w/hinged pewter cover,** tapering cylindrical body ringed at the rim & base, C-form handle, decorated w/a glossy yellow glaze, the front w/a spread-winged eagle above a large red initial "W," base

w/company marks & notation "The Geo. Wiedemann Brewing Co. Inc.," 1948, 5⅝" h. .............. **605.00**

**Tile,** rectangular, Arts & Crafts-style, "A Sandy Shore," decorated w/a mountainous landscape of tall green firs & a brown foreground against a blue lake & tall mountains, Vellum glaze, signed by artist on front, 1914, Sara Sax, w/original dark brown quartered oak frame & backing, tile 5¼ x 9¼" (some pitting) .................................... **2,750.00**

**Trivet,** square, the center molded w/a large black rook against a deeply incised latticework ground in dark blue lined w/white, dark blue border & edges, Matte glaze, No. 1794, 1925, 5⅝" w. (small glaze nick of back edge) ........................... **330.00**

**Vase,** 4" h., 3" d., bulbous ovoid body w/a tapering cylindrical neck, molded & painted holly leaves & berries in red & green on a burgundy ground, Matte glaze, No. 969, 1904, Sallie Toohey ..................................... **605.00**

**Vase,** 5¼" h., 3¼" d., ovoid body w/a rounded shoulder to a short flaring neck, decorated w/swallows in flight around the shoulder in shades of green on a green ground, Sea Green glaze, No.605, 1896, Bruce Horsfall.................................. **2,310.00**

**Vase,** 5½" h., 3½" d., ovoid body tapering to rolled rim, slip-painted w/ivory & yellow daffodils on green stems against a grey ground, Matte glaze, No. 4, 1901, A.R. Valentien, w/original paper label from Buffalo-Pan American Exhibition .............................. **3,080.00**

**Vase,** 5¾" h., 3" d., slender waisted cylindrical form, decorated w/abstract branches of red & blue flowers on a shaded ivory to purple ground, No. 1358F, 1923, Fred Rothenbusch............................ **935.00**

**Vase,** 6" h., 3½" d., simple ovoid body tapering to a flaring molded rim, decorated w/a landscape of trees in a meadow, in greens & dark blue against a shaded blue to ivory sky, Vellum glaze, No. 913E, 1923, Fred Rothenbush .......................... **1,430.00**

**Vase,** 6" h., 6" d., bulbous ovoid body tapering to a short, wide neck, decorated w/large pink dogwood blossoms & green leaves on a blue & pink feathered ground, Wax Matte glaze, No. 912, 1929, K. Jones ................................... **660.00**

**Vase,** 6¼" h., Limoges-style, simple swelled cylindrical body tapering slightly to a flaring short neck, decorated overglaze in blue w/undersea crabs in black & shades of brown, rough red clay ground around the upper half, No. 80B, 1884, Laura A. Fry (rim chip, rim glaze loss) ..... **460.00**

**Vase,** 6½" h., 3½" d., baluster-form tapering to a tall slightly flaring neck w/a rolled rim, decorated w/pink, white & yellow flowers on a butterfat blue & pink ground, Wax Matte glaze, No. 2966, 1927, Katharine Jones ........................................ **330.00**

**Vase,** 6½" h., 6½" d., bulbous ovoid form designed as a water lily in salmon, yellow & cream, against a fully articulated greenish grey lily leaf, Vellum glaze, No. 51, 1904, Kataro Shirayamadani ..................... **10,450.00**

**Vase,** 6½" h., 9½" d., squatty bulbous body w/short cylindrical neck, the shoulder decorated w/blue birds in flight against a cross-hatched green & burgundy ground, on a bluish green base, Carved Matte glaze, No. 158, 1914, W. Hentschel (tight in-body hairline crack) ............... **1,320.00**

**Vase,** 6⅝" h., swelled cylindrical body w/a low molded flat rim, decorated w/fish in shades of

*Sea Green Glazed Vase*

green, Sea Green glaze, No. 904E, 1906, E.T. Hurley (ILLUS.) ................................ **2,300.00**

**Vase,** 6¾" h., 6½" d., bulbous ovoid body tapering to slightly flared rim, decorated w/stylized organic pattern in brown & bluish green squeezebag against yellow ground, Matte glaze, No. 130, impressed w/flame mark & atrist's initals, 1928, Elizabeth Barrett (in-body line) ................. **413.00**

**Vase,** 7" h., slightly swelled cylindrical body w/a wide flattened shoulder centered by a short cylindrical neck w/a molded rim, dark golden yellow shaded to dark brown ground decorated on one side w/a large cluster of yellow jonquils & shaded dark green leaves & stems, the neck overlaid in Gorham sterling silver & issuing long bands of swirled clouds down the shoulder & sides, Standard glaze, No. 735 DD, 1898, Albert Valentien ........... **2,310.00**

**Vase,** 7" h., 4¼" d., ovoid form w/rounded rim, decorated w/a snow scene w/blue trees & a green horizon on a snowy field, Vellum glaze, No. 938D, 1917, E. McDermot (restoration to rim chip) ......................................... **800.00**

**Vase,** 7¼" h., flaring foot supporting a gently flaring cylindrical body w/an angled shoulder to a flat mouth, decorated around the upper half w/a landscape scene of four geese flying past a full moon toward a stand of leafy trees, all in shades of pale & dark green w/the shoulder & lower body in a dark moss green, Vellum glaze, No. 1356 E, 1911, Sallie Coyne ................................... **2,530.00**

**Vase,** 7½" h., 3½" d., slender ovoid form w/a flat rim, incised around the top half w/stylized peacock feathers in brown & yellow on a lighter brown ground, Carved Matte glaze, No. 939D, 1914, Charles Todd........ **880.00**

**Vase,** 7½" h., 6" d., bulbous body tapering to flaring rim, decorated w/orange & red jasmine blossoms w/green foliage against deep purple celadon butterfat ground, Matte glaze, No. 6206D, impressed w/flame mark & artist initials, 1931, K. Shirayamadani....................... **4,675.00**

**Vase,** 8" h., 4" d., slender ovoid body tapering to a short rolled neck, decorated w/pink & white apple blossoms & green leaves on a blue & brown ground, Vellum glaze, No. 1922D, 1917, C. Steinle ................................. **715.00**

**Vase,** 8" h., 4½" d., footed corseted cylindrical body w/flaring rim, Coramundel Aventurine flambé glaze, 1932 . **495.00**

**Vase,** 8" h., 4½" d., simple ovoid body tapering to a short cylindrical neck, decorated w/large purplish blue irises & celadon green leaves & stems on a shaded grey to pink ground, Iris glaze, No. 900C, 1900, Carl Schmidt ................ **5,775.00**

**Vase,** 8¼" h., 4" d., slightly ovoid body w/rounded shoulder & flared mouth, decorated w/a scene of birch trees by a lake in orange, pink, blue & green, Vellum glaze, No. 2441, impressed w/flame mark & artist's initials, 1948, E.T. Hurley .................................... **2,200.00**

**Vase,** 8½" h., 3¾" d., cylindrical ovoid body w/short cylindrical neck, decorated w/pink wild roses & dark green leaves on a shaded dark brownish green to celadon ground, Iris glaze, No. 907E, impressed w/flame mark & artist's initials, 1903, O.G. Reed ...................................... **1,540.00**

**Vase,** 8⅝" h., swelled cylindrical body on a narrow footring & w/a wide molded mouth, a black shaded to grey shaded to pale yellow ground decorated w/large white thistles on pale shaded green leafy stems, Iris glaze, No. 892, 1904, Fred Rothenbusch........................... **7,150.00**

**Vase,** 8¾" h., 3½" d., tall slender ovoid body tapering to a short cylindrical neck, decorated w/yellow & orange autumn leaves on a solid black ground, Black Iris glaze, No. 907A, 1903, Sara Sax (hairline on back, shallow glaze scratches)........ **2,090.00**

**Vase,** 9" h., 3¾" d., gently swelled cylindrical body w/a narrow rounded shoulder to the short cylindrical neck, decorated w/a marsh landscape w/white, grey & black egrets against palm leaves on a shaded grey to ivory sky, Vellum glaze, No. 907E, 1908, E.T. Hurley................... **3,575.00**

**Vase,** 9" h., 4" d., slightly swelled cylindrical form tapering to 'organic' rim, covered w/relief-molded daffodils, covered w/a fine raspberry & grey leathery Matte glaze, No. 1003, 1910..... **715.00**

**Vase,** 9¼" h., 7" d., wide ovoid body tapering to a flat mouth, molded in high-relief w/large undulating poppy stems, leaves & blossoms under a dark red & green glaze against a warm ochre brown ground, Matte glaze, No. 604C, 1907, Sallie Toohey ................................... **2,530.00**

**Vase,** 9½" h., 4" d., gently swelled cylindrical form w/a slightly flared flat mouth, decorated w/red & pink cyclamen on a shaded bluish black to raspberry ground, Matte glaze, No. 194CZ, 1902, Harriet Wilcox ............. **8,250.00**

**Vase,** 9½" h., 4½" d., a bulbous base tapering to a tall cylindrical body w/a gently flaring rim, decorated w/white & purple poppies on celadon green stems against a shaded yellow to greyish green ground, Iris glaze, No. 833W, 1904, Fred Rothenbush (ILLUS. left, top next column).... **4,290.00**

**Vase,** 10" h., 3¼" d., slender ovoid body tapering to a slender neck w/a widely flaring, flattened rim, decorated w/purple sweet peas & celadon green leaves on a shaded black to light green ground, Iris glaze, No. 482W, 1907, Carl Schmidt (ILLUS. right, top next column)............. **4,070.00**

**Vase,** 10" h., 4" d., slender tall ovoid body w/a short gently flaring neck, decorated w/blue jonquils w/yellow centers on a shaded deep green to celadon green ground, Sea Green glaze, No. 562, 1901, Sallie Coyne................................... **2,310.00**

**Vase,** 10" h., 5" d., Jewel Porcelain, bulbous ovoid body tapering to a wide slightly tapering cylindrical neck, decorated in the Jugenstil style w/vertical bands of pink flowers around the neck above a soft blue ground below, No. 989C, 1918, Sara Sax ...................... **4,290.00**

**Vase,** 10¼" h., 3½" d., tall swelled cylindrical body w/a closed-in rim & tapering down to a squared base, decorated w/dark amber poppies on a shaded brown ground, Standard glaze, No. 821C, 1900, Lenore Asbury...................................... **660.00**

*Two Iris Glazed Vases*

**Vase,** 10½" h., 5" d., slightly ovoid body w/flat ring mouth, painted w/winter forest scene in tones of blue & green against an ivory sky, surrounded by teal band, Vellum glaze, No. 977, impressed flame mark, 1913, Edward Diers ......................... **1,760.00**

**Vase,** 11" h., 4¾" sq., 'skyscraper'-type, rectangular stepped form, each side w/stepped panels in high-relief & incised linear patterns, Matte green turquoise glaze highlighted w/crystalline pooling over a white glossy ground, No. 6120, 1929 (minute base flakes) ...................................... **489.00**

**Vase,** 11½" h., 7¼" d., enititled "Four Bulls of the Assinaboines," bulbous ovoid form w/curled handle tapering to thin flared neck & rim, body shows three-quarter portrait of a young brave holding a spear, dressed in period garb, in muted tones on amber, green, copper & brown on a shaded dark to mahogany ground, Standard glaze, impressed w/flame mark & artists initials, No. 787C, 1899, Grace Young......................... **3,850.00**

**Vase,** 13¼" h., cylindrical lower body below a bulbous swelled shoulder tapering to a flat

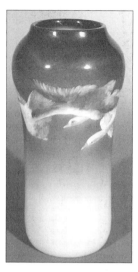

*Valentien Iris Glaze Vase*

mouth, decorated around the shoulder w/a band of flying geese against a dark shaded to light ground, Iris glaze, 1905, A. Valentien (ILLUS.) .............. **16,500.00**

**Vase,** 18" h., 9¼" d., floor-type, bisque, gently flaring cylindrical body w/a swelled shoulder & wide flat mouth, slip-painted w/blue gooseberries & brown & green leaves against a shaded grey ground, No. 30A, A. Valentien (small nick to base) ..................................... **2,860.00**

**Wall pocket,** figural, a light brown squirrel on a dark brown oak branch against green & blue leaves, Matte glaze, No. 2278, impressed w/flame mark, 1915, 7½" w., 13½" h. ..................... **2,090.00**

**Whiskey jug without stopper,** double-gourd form, the bulbous body tapering to a small short neck w/loop handle from rim to shoulder, decorated w/brownish green hops & leaves on a shaded brown ground & covered w/silver overlay on the neck, handle & forming lacy scrolls down one side, silver marked by Gorham, No. 674, 1896, Sallie Toohey ................................... **1,650.00**

# ROSELANE POTTERY

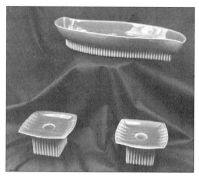

*Roselane Bowl & Candleholders*

*Many potteries in the 1930s started out as home-based operations. Roselane was no exception. William and Georgia Fields opened their pottery in 1938 and in 1940 they moved it to Pasadena, California. "Doc," as he was called, and Georgia produced varied items and treatments in myriad glazes. There were wall pockets, sculptured animals on wood bases, ashtrays, bowls, covered boxes, figurines and vases.*

*They created the Sparkler series in the 1950s. The original Sparklers had glass eyes but later plastic eyes were used. This line has been reproduced so novices would be wise to buy only the marked Sparklers or the ones with a paper label. With experience, it is easier to distinguish between the real thing and a reproduction.*

*In 1968 Roselane was moved again, this time to Baldwin Park, California where it operated for six years. When "Doc" died in 1973, Georgia sold Roselane and it was moved to Long Beach. In 1977 the business closed.*

Rose ła ne
U.S.A. ©

Roselane

*Roselane Marks*

*Roselane Goose*

*Bulbous Roselane Vase*

**Bowl,** 9" d., 2" h., gloss dark green outside, light & dark green inside w/sgraffito-type green "snowflakes" design, scroll mark, Model A-9 ................................. **$50.00**

**Bowl,** 13" l., 2½" h., Chinese influence w/a vertical ribbed base rising to a low rim w/ends slightly bending in opposite directions, gloss grey outside, rose gloss inside, incised "Roselane 213," (ILLUS. top, right column, previous page) ...... **58.00**

**Candleholders,** Chinese influence w/a vertical ribbed base rising to a thin, square-shaped single holder, gloss grey base w/gloss rose top, incised "C-1," 2½" h., pr. (ILLUS. bottom, right column, previous page) ....... **55.00**

**Figure of a girl,** kneeling, arms folded over chest w/hands together in prayer, head slightly raised, eyes closed, reverse of girl shows ponytail & bottoms of feet & toes, satin matte beige & brown, incised "Roselane U.S.A." w/a copyright symbol, 4½" h.......................................... **25.00**

**Model of a baby owl,** seated, plastic brown eyes w/dark green body, "Sparkler" series, 2¼" h. ... **10.00**

**Model of a horse,** standing on oval base, thin front legs together & back legs apart

w/right one positioned forward, head tucked into a stylized neck, short feathered tail, gloss grey w/tan accents, paper sticker, 8½" h............................................ **35.00**

**Model of a goose,** on round base, wings out w/neck & head turned to side, yellow gloss w/caramel highlights, incised "126 Roselane," 3½" w., 5" h. (ILLUS.) ..................................... **23.00**

**Model of a Scotty dog,** seated, ears up, black gloss w/blue Sparkler eyes, impressed mark, "Roselane U.S.A." & a copyright symbol, 4⅛" h. ........................... **25.00**

**Sign,** advertising, scroll design curving forward on left side & behind on right side, "Roselane" in-relief w/upper-case "R" in script & other letters in lower-case, teal gloss, 12½" l., 3" h. .. **175.00**

**Vase,** 4½" h., 5" d., small foot w/bulbous body tapering to a short flared neck, body decorated w/incised geometric shapes, light grey body w/darker grey designs, incised underglaze "Roselane 19 U.S.A." (ILLUS. above) .............. **22.00**

---

# ROSEMEADE

*Laura Taylor was a ceramic artist who supervised Federal Works Projects in her native North Dakota during the Depression era and later demonstrated at the potter's wheel during the 1939 New York World's Fair. In 1940, Laura Taylor and Rogert J. Hughes opened the Rosemead-Wahpeton Pottery, naming it after the North Dakota county and town of Wahpeton where it was located. Rosemeade Pottery was made on a small scale for only about twelve years with Laura Taylor designing the items and perfecting colors. Her animal and bird figures are popular among collectors. Hughes and Taylor married in 1943 and the pottery did a thriving business until her death in 1959. The pottery closed in 1961 but stock was sold from the factory salesroom until 1964.*

*Rosemeade Mark*

**Book ends,** figural Wolfhound,
pr. .............................................. **$250.00**

**Console bowl,** w/figural bird
flower frog, 2 pcs. ....................... **60.00**

**Creamer & sugar bowl,** model of
an ear of corn, pr. ....................... **55.00**

**Flower frog,** model of a frog ........ **48.00**

**Flower frog,** model of a pheasant. **75.00**

**Model of a chickadee,**
miniature ................................... **125.00**

**Model of a cock pheasant,**
11½" h. ...................................... **250.00**

**Model of a cowboy boot,** 5" h. ..... **55.00**

**Model of a coyote,** black glaze,
4¼" h. ........................................ **365.00**

**Salt & pepper shakers,** model of
a Bluebird, pr. ............................ **55.00**

**Salt & pepper shakers,** model of
a Bobwhite, pr. ........................... **50.00**

**Salt & pepper shakers,** model of
a cucumber, pr. ........................... **65.00**

**Salt & pepper shakers,** model of
a dog head, pr. ............................ **65.00**

**Salt & pepper shakers,** model of
an elephant, pink glaze, pr. ......... **85.00**

**Salt & pepper shakers,** model of
a flamingo, pr. ........................... **140.00**

**Salt & pepper shakers,** model of
a kangaroo, pr. .......................... **120.00**

**Salt & pepper shakers,** model of
a Mallard duck, pr. ...................... **30.00**

**Salt & pepper shakers,** model of
a pheasant, tail down, pr. ............ **68.00**

**Salt & pepper shakers,** model of
a running rabbit, pr. ..................... **95.00**

**Salt & pepper shakers,** model of
a Scottie dog head, black glaze,
pr. ............................................... **25.00**

**Salt & pepper shakers,** model of
a turkey, pr. ................................ **45.00**

**Spoon rest,** model of a Prairie
Rose ........................................... **50.00**

# ROSE MEDALLION & ROSE CANTON

*Rose Medallion Punch Bowl*

*The lovely Chinese ware known as Rose Medallion was made through the past century and into the present one. It features alternating panels of people and flowers or insects with most pieces having four medallions with a central rose or peony medallion. The ware is called Rose Canton if flowers and birds or insects fill all the panels. Unless otherwise noted, our listing is for Rose Medallion ware.*

**Bowl,** 11½" d., deep rounded
sides decorated w/typical panels
of figures alternating w/birds on
blossoming branches, all on a
gilt ground strewn w/fruits,
flowers & butterflies, 19th c.,
w/a wooden stand, 2 pcs. .... **$1,035.00**

**Bowl,** 10¼" d., scalloped rim ...... **275.00**

**Compote,** 10" d., 5" h. ................ **550.00**

**Fruit basket & undertray,** Rose
Canton palette, oval
w/reticulated basketweave sides
& a wide rolled rim w/small loop
end rim handles, matching
reticulated undertray, 19th c.,
basket 11" l., 2 pcs. (minor
chips, enamel wear).................. **633.00**

**Garden seat,** barrel-shaped
w/overall colorful decoration,
19th c., 18½" h. ...................... **2,530.00**

**Platter,** 14½" l., oval, Rose
Canton palette, 19th c.............. **690.00**

**Punch bowl,** deep gently
rounded & flaring sides,
alternating panels of figures &
landscapes, chips, minor gilt &
enamel wear, 19th c., 16¼" d.
(ILLUS. top previous page).... **1,495.00**

**Soup tureen,** cov., Rose Canton
palette, 19th c., 10½" l. .......... **1,955.00**

**Teapot,** Rose Canton palette,
Cadogan-type, puzzle-form
painted w/birds & foliage on a
light blue ground, late 19th c.,
6" h. (minor chips)..................... **144.00**

**Vase,** 16¼" h., gourd-form,
19th c. (minor gilt & enamel
wear)........................................ **690.00**

**Vegetable dish,** cov., oval, Rose
Canton palette, marked "Made
in China," 8 x 9", 5½" h. ............ **285.00**

---

# ROSENTHAL

*The Rosenthal porcelain manufactory
has been in operation since 1880 when it
was established by P. Rosenthal in Selb,
Bavaria. Tablewares and figure groups
are among its specialties.*

*Rosenthal Marks*

*Fine Rosenthal Lamp Base*

**Cups & saucers,** coffee-size, Art
Nouveau design, white porcelain
w/initial "M," in .800 grade silver
holder & saucer, set of 6 ......... **$750.00**

**Figure of a blackamoor,** dressed
in white carrying a tray laden
w/fruit, 7" h. ............................... **245.00**

**Figure of a boy w/lamb** ............. **145.00**

**Figures,** one man standing
playing a string bass, one man a
French horn w/a euphonian at
his feet & a third man playing a
woodwind instrument, possibly a
clarinet, w/a small brown dog
beside him, each 3" d. base,
8¼" h., set of 3 ....................... **1,000.00**

**Lamp base,** figural, a seated
nude female holding aloft a
conical torchere, seated on a
triangular base molded
w/geometric designs, clear
glazed all-white, probably
designed by Gerhard
Schliepstein, ca. 1925, w/conical
pleated shade, unsigned, base
24" h. (ILLUS. above) ............ **1,721.00**

**Model of a kitten,** seated, black
& white, 5" h.............................. **129.00**

**Model of a mouse,** begging
pose, 1¾" h. ............................... **89.00**

**Plate,** 7¾" d., Pompadour patt.,
gold trim ..................................... **10.00**

**Plates,** dinner, 11" d., gilt foliate
banding over a deep blue
ground border, 20th c., set
of 12 ...................................... **1,035.00**

**Tea set:** cov. teapot, creamer,
cov. sugar bowl & twelve salad
plates; Flowers patt., the set ..... **195.00**

# ROSEVILLE

*Roseville Pottery Company operated
in Zanesville, Ohio from 1898 to 1954
but originally began in business for six
years prior to that in Muskingum
County, Ohio. Art pottery wares, similar
to those of Owens and Weller Potteries,
were their original focus of production;
however, by the 1920s new and varied
lines of a more commercial nature became
the mainstay of their output. Items listed
here are by patterns or lines.*

$\mathcal{R}_{\alpha reville}$

*Roseville Mark*

## APPLE BLOSSOM (1948)

*White apple blossoms in relief on blue,
green or pink ground; brown tree branch
handles.*

**Basket,** hanging-type, pink
ground, 8" ............................. **$250.00**

**Basket w/low overhead handle,**
green ground, No. 310-10",
10" h. ....................... **195.00 to 225.00**

**Book ends,** blue ground,
No. 359, pr. ............................ **200.00**

**Bowl,** 6½" d., 2½" h., flat handles,
pink ground, No. 326-6" ........... **135.00**

**Bowl,** 10" d., pink ground, No.
329-10" .................... **140.00 to 175.00**

**Candleholders,** blue ground, No.
351-2", 2" h., pr. ........................ **85.00**

**Console bowl,** blue ground,
No. 333-14", 8 x 18" oval ......... **175.00**

*Apple Blossom Wall Pocket*

**Cornucopia-vase,** pink ground,
No. 321-6, 6" h. .......................... **95.00**

**Jardiniere,** pink ground, No.
302-8", 8" h. ............................. **495.00**

**Jardiniere & pedestal base,** blue
ground, No. 306-10", overall 31"
h., 2 pcs. (tiny chip
professionally repaired) ........ **1,200.00**

**Jardiniere & pedestal base,**
green ground, No. 306-10",
overall 31" h.,
2 pcs. ................. **1,190.00 to 1,225.00**

**Pedestal base,** green ground,
No. 305-8", 8" h. ...... **375.00 to 400.00**

**Teapot,** cov., pink ground, No.
371-P ...................................... **290.00**

**Vase,** 6" h., two-handled, squatty
base, long cylindrical neck, blue
ground, No. 381-6" ................... **115.00**

**Vase,** bud, 7" h., base handles,
flaring rim, pink ground, No.
379-7" ........................ **85.00 to 100.00**

**Vase,** 7" h., asymmetrical rim &
handles, pink ground, No.
382-7" ...................................... **125.00**

**Vase,** 8¼" h., pink ground, No.
385-8" ...................................... **185.00**

**Vase,** 9½" h., 5" d., asymmetrical
handles, cylindrical w/disc base,
pink ground, No. 387-9" .......... **200.00**

**Vase,** 10" h., base handles, blue
ground, No. 388-10" ................. **170.00**

**Vase,** 18" h., floor-type, blue
ground, No. 393-18" (restored
on base) ................................... **400.00**

**Wall pocket,** conical w/overhead handle, No. 366-8¼", 8¼" h. (ILLUS. top previous page) ...................... **275.00 to 300.00**

**Window box,** end handles, blue ground, No. 368-8", 2½ x 10½" ................ **80.00 to 100.00**

**Planter,** rectangular form on small knob feet, the bottom center pierced through w/an opening fitted w/a small curving twig, yellow ground, No. 1056-10", 6½ x 10"............................ **90.00**

## AZTEC (1915)

*Muted earthy tones of beige, grey, brown, teal, olive, azure blue or soft white with sliptrailed geometric decoration in contrasting colors.*

**Jardiniere,** bulbous form w/four buttressed handles, decorated w/heavy slip-trail work of yellow, brown & green flowers on a glossy mahogany ground, 7¾" d., 5¾" h. ......................... **400.00**

**Jardiniere,** spherical shape w/three feet & three buttressed handles, decorated w/white crocus blossoms w/bluish grey leaves against a curdled mustard ground, artist signed "CS," decorated by C. Steinle, 10" d., 7½" d. (two hairlines at rim)......................................... **495.00**

**Vase,** 10½" h., tall cylindrical base w/a flaring foot, the bulbous nearly spherical upper body centered by a short tapering neck w/flat rim, medium blue ground decorated w/slip trailing w/white swags w/yellow dashes between thin bands of dark blue w/scrolls on the upper body & similar designs around the foot, artist-initialed "E," unmarked (two small glaze nicks on edge of base)...................... **165.00**

**Vase,** 10¾" h., pyramid-shaped w/slip-trail work of stylized white & blue flowers on celadon ground.................................... **550.00**

**Vase,** 12" h., cylindrical body rising to a short projecting collar beneath a flaring rim, squeezebag decoration of stylized heart-shaped devices on thin stems around collar in white & sandy tan against a blue ground .................... **435.00 to 450.00**

## BANEDA (1933)

*Band of embossed pods, blossoms and leaves on green or raspberry pink ground.*

**Bowl-vase,** footed wide squatty bulbous body tapering to a wide flat molded mouth flanked by small scroll handles, pink ground w/blue band, 6½" d., 5¼" h. (ILLUS., No. 4) ........................ **990.00**

**Bowl-vase,** footed wide squatty bulbous body tapering to a wide flat molded mouth flanked by small scroll handles, green ground w/blue band, 7¼" d., 5½" h. (ILLUS., No. 7).............. **660.00**

**Candleholders,** hexagonal domed base tapering to support the tall paneled candle socket, green ground, No. 1086-4½", 4½" h...................................... **400.00**

**Console bowl,** footed oblong low-sided form w/small end handles, pink ground, No. 234-10", 10" l. ........................ **400.00**

**Jardiniere,** green ground, 9¼ x 14", unmarked (chip to base).................................... **1,045.00**

**Jardiniere & pedestal base,** raspberry pink ground, 14¼" d., overall 28¼" h., 2 pcs. (two underbase chips & a line in the base of jardiniere, curving line under the top of the pedestal on the side) ............................... **2,310.00**

**Vase,** 4¼" h., 5½" d., footed sharply tapering squatty bulbous body w/tiny neck flanked by tiny rim handles, green ground, No. 603-4" ............... **450.00 to 525.00**

**Vase,** 5¼" h., 4¼" d., rounded pear-shaped body tapering to a

1　　2　　3　　4　　5　　6　　7　　8　　9　　10　　11

*A Variety of Baneda Pieces*

small mouth flanked by two handles at rim, green ground (ILLUS., No. 2) ........................ **330.00**

**Vase,** 6" h., footed bulbous body w/a swelled neck tapering to a short cylindrical neck, low loop handles from the base of the neck to the lower body, green ground ..................................... **595.00**

**Vase,** 6½" h., 6½" d., footed bulbous body w/a wide shoulder tapering up to a short flaring neck flanked by curved shoulder handles, green ground ............. **440.00**

**Vase,** 7" h., 6¾" d., small round foot supports a wide cylindrical body rounded at the base & rim & tapering slightly to a wide short rolled neck flanked by small C-scroll handles, pink ground w/blue band, large silver foil label (ILLUS., No. 8) ........... **468.00**

**Vase,** 7½" h., 5½" d., footed swelled cylindrical body tapering to a short, wide cylindrical neck flanked by small down-curved loop handles, raspberry pink or green ground, each (ILLUS., No. 1, 10 & 11) ........................ **495.00**

**Vase,** 8¼" h., 5" d., tapering conical body w/loop handles at base, raspberry pink ground, No. 593-8" (ILLUS., No. 5) ....... **468.00**

**Vase,** 8½" h., 8" d., a small round foot supports a wide bulbous nearly spherical body tapering to a flat molded mouth flanked by C-scroll handles down the shoulder, raspberry pink ground (ILLUS., No. 3) ........................ **880.00**

**Vase,** 9¼" h., 7½" d., footed bulbous body tapering to a swelled shoulder band tapering to a short cylindrical neck, C-scroll handles from neck to lower body, raspberry pink ground (ILLUS., No. 9) .......... **1,320.00**

**Vase,** 12¼" h., 6½" d., a rounded domed foot supporting a tall slender trumpet-form body w/low loop handles from foot to side of body, green ground (ILLUS., No. 6) ................................... **1,540.00**

**Wall pocket,** flaring flattened fanned sides w/an angular backplate w/loop handles, green ground, 8" h. ........................ **1,540.00**

## BITTERSWEET (1940)

*Orange bittersweet pods and green leaves on a grey blending to rose, yellow with terra cotta, rose with green or solid green bark-textured ground; brown branch handles.*

**Basket,** w/pointed overhead handle & conforming rim, grey ground, No. 809-8"................... **148.00**

**Basket,** hanging-type, green ground..................................... **200.00**

**Cornucopia-Vase,** upright cornucopia w/a wide high arched rim, the body tapering to a slender scroll end resting on an oval base w/a twig handle to the side, grey ground, No. 882-6", 6" h.............. **110.00**

**Ewer,** yellow ground, No. 816-8", 8" h......................................... **210.00**

**Vase,** 8" h., tall ovoid body w/a slightly flared foot & gently undulating rim, asymmetrical twig handles, grey ground, No. 883-8" ................. **90.00 to 100.00**

**Vase,** 15½" h., floor-type, footed slender baluster form w/trumpet neck, No. 888-16", grey ground .. **523.00**

## BLACKBERRY (1933)

*Band of relief clusters of blackberries with vines and ivory leaves accented in green and terra cotta on a green textured ground.*

**Jardiniere,** bulbous nearly spherical body tapering to a wide molded mouth flanked by two tiny low handles, strong mold & color, 6" h. (ILLUS., No. 5) ....................................... **385.00**

**Urn-vase,** squatty bulbous body, tiny loop handles at rim, 6" h.... **468.00**

**Vase,** 6" h., 5" d., ovoid body w/an angled center band, the upper half tapering sharply to a wide flat mouth flanked by small loop handles, strong mold & color, each (ILLUS., No. 2) ...... **660.00**

**Vase,** 6" h., 7" d., nearly spherical body w/a short wide cylindrical neck flanked by small loop handles, each (ILLUS., Nos. 1 & 8) .............................. **385.00**

**Vase,** 6¼" h., 5¾" d., gently flaring cylindrical body w/a molded wide mouth, low curved handles from rim to center of the sides (ILLUS., No. 7) ............... **468.00**

**Vase,** 8" h., 5½" d., ovoid body tapering to a cylindrical neck flanked by small loop handles (ILLUS., No. 3)......................... **468.00**

**Vase,** 8" h., 5½" d., ovoid body tapering to a cylindrical neck flanked by small loop handles, sharp mold & color, black label (ILLUS., No. 6) ........................ **990.00**

1    3    4    6    8
  2      5      7

*A Varied Selection of the Blackberry Pattern*

**Vase,** 10¼" h., 7" d., waisted cylinder w/two handles at midsection (ILLUS., No. 4).... **1,320.00**

**Wall pocket,** fan-shaped body tapering sharply to a pointed base, small pointed hanging handle at the top back rim, large silver label, 6¾" w. at rim, 8¼" h. ...................................... **990.00**

## BLEEDING HEART (1938)

*Pink blossoms and green leaves on shaded blue, green or pink ground.*

*Bleeding Heart Vase*

**Basket,** hanging-type, two-handled, pink ground, No. 362-5", 8" w.............................. **275.00**

**Jardiniere & pedestal base,** green ground, jardiniere 8" h., 2 pcs. (small chip on jardiniere, repair to base)......................... **650.00**

**Vase,** 8" h., a small round foot supports a wide squatty base w/a sharply angled shoulder band tapering to a trumpet-form neck w/a gently fluted rim, angular open handles at the lower shoulder, blue ground, No. 969-8" (ILLUS.)... **200.00 to 225.00**

**Vase,** 15" h., two-handled, flaring hexagonal mouth, green ground, No. 976-15"............................ **425.00**

**Wall pocket,** conical w/pointed, angular handle arching across the top, No. 1287-8", 8" h. ....... **425.00**

## BUSHBERRY (1948)

*Berries and leaves on blue, green or russet bark-textured ground; brown or green branch handles.*

**Ashtray,** handled, blue ground, No. 26 .................................... **165.00**

**Basket w/asymmetrical overhead handle,** blue ground, No. 371-10", 10" h.................... **195.00**

**Beverage set:** pitcher & eight mugs; green ground, 9 pcs. ... **1,300.00**

**Bowl,** 6" d., russet ground, No. 412-6" .............. **130.00 to 150.00**

**Bowl,** 14" d., blue ground, No. 417-14"............................. **250.00**

**Cornucopia-vase,** double, blue ground, No. 155-8", 6" h. ......... **145.00**

**Jardiniere & pedestal base,** blue ground, No. 657-8", overall 25" h..................................... **1,320.00**

**Mug,** russet ground, No. 1-3½", 3½" h. ...................... **100.00 to 125.00**

**Urn-vase,** pedestal base w/round foot supports a squatty compressed body tapering to a wide cylindrical neck flanked by angular handles from neck to shoulder, green ground, No. 157-8", 8" h........................ **210.00**

**Vase,** 10" h., two-handled, russet ground, No. 37-10" .. **135.00 to 175.00**

**Vase,** 14½" h., a tall slender baluster-form body w/a flaring rim, asymmetrical handles near the top on each side, green ground, No. 39-14".................. **440.00**

**Wall pocket,** conical form fanned at the rim w/asymmetrical branch handles on each side, blue ground, No. 1291-8", 8" h. .... **215.00**

## CARNELIAN I (1910-15)

*Matte glaze with a combination of two colors or two shades of the same color with the darker dripping over the lighter tone or heavy and textured glaze with intermingled colors and some running.*

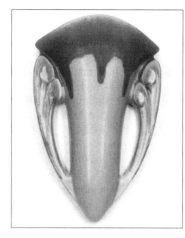

*Carnelian I Wall Pocket*

**Ewer,** a wide tapering round pedestal base below a tall slender ovoid body tapering to a low flaring neck w/a tall arched spout, a high arched double-scroll handle from the neck to near the foot, blue & pink glazes, 15" h. ........................... **525.00**

**Flower frog,** five-hole, low conical foot supports a flattened half-round vase w/a row of holes across the top, 4½" h. ................ **55.00**

**Vase,** 18" h., tall slender ovoid body raised on a flaring round foot, the rounded shoulder tapering to a short incurved neck, small rounded loop shoulder handles, bluish grey drip glaze w/cornflower highlights on a pale blue matte glaze ground, No. 340-18" ....... **286.00**

**Wall pocket,** trumpet-form body w/arched rim, long double-scroll open handles down the sides, dark blue & light blue, 8" h. (ILLUS. above) ........ **135.00 to 175.00**

### CARNELIAN II (1915)

*Intermingled colors, some with a drip effect.*

**Candleholders,** intermingled shades of rose & bronze, 3" h., pr. ................................... **185.00**

**Urn,** compressed globular form, short flaring rim, pierced curved handles, intermingled shades of blue, 5" h. ................................ **150.00**

**Urn,** footed wide gently flaring cylindrical body w/a wide angled shoulder tapering to a short molded mouth, curved handles rising from base to shoulder, green & red, 8" h. ..................... **413.00**

**Vase,** 10" h., footed, bulbous body w/wide flaring cylindrical neck, scrolled handles rising from shoulder to beneath rim, mottled greyish green & brown marbleized glaze...................... **440.00**

**Vase,** 16½" h., 10" d., floor-type, footed tall ovoid body tapering to a slightly flaring cylindrical neck, intermingled shades of turquoise blue................... **1,835.00 to 2,500.00**

### CHERRY BLOSSOM (1933)

*Sprigs of cherry blossoms, green leaves and twigs with pink fence against a combed bluish green ground or creamy ivory fence against a terra cotta ground shading to dark brown.*

**Jardiniere,** squatty bulbous body tapering to a wide flat rolled neck flanked by small loop handles, bluish green ground, match head sized glass skip on side, 5½" d., 4" h. (ILLUS., top next page, No. 2) .............. **385.00**

**Jardiniere,** bulbous nearly spherical body tapering to a wide slightly flaring mouth, small loop shoulder handles, terra cotta ground, 8" d., 6" h. (ILLUS., No. 4) ........................ **413.00**

**Jardiniere,** large bulbous body tapering slightly to wide flat & slightly flared rim, small loop shoulder handles, terra cotta ground, 10½" d., 8" h.(ILLUS., top next page, No. 5) .............. **605.00**

**Vase,** 4" h., compressed squatty bulbous body w/a short slightly flared neck flanked by small loop handles, bluish green ground .. **350.00**

```
        3              5          8
1                 4          7        9
   2                     6
```

*Various Cherry Blossom Pieces*

**Vase,** 5¼" h., footed nearly spherical body tapering to a flat molded mouth, small loop shoulder handles, bluish green ground (ILLUS., No. 9)............. **410.00**

**Vase,** 5½" h., 7" d., wide squatty bulbous body w/the wide shoulder tapering to a flat molded mouth flanked by small loop handles, bluish green ground (ILLUS., No. 1)............. **468.00**

**Vase,** 7½" h., footed ovoid body tapering to a small rolled neck, small loop shoulder handles, bluish green ground (ILLUS., No. 7) ...................................... **605.00**

**Vase,** 12" h., tall swelled cylindrical body tapering to a short rolled neck, small loop shoulder handles, terra cotta ground (ILLUS., No. 8)............. **825.00**

**Vase,** 15" h., 11" d., floor-type, bulbous ovoid body, small shoulder handles, terra cotta ground, repair to rim & handles, some flakes to body, No. 628-15" (ILLUS., No. 3) ........... **770.00**

**Wall pocket,** flaring conical form w/a pointed hanging tab at the top, terra cotta ground, 5½" w., 8¼" h. (ILLUS., No. 6)............. **1,760.00**

## CHLORON (1907)

*Molded in high-relief in the manner of early Roman and Greek artifacts. Solid matte green glaze, sometimes combined with ivory. Very similar in form of Egypto.*

*Chloron Vase*

**Vase,** 5½" h., 7½" d., squatty bulbous form, loop shoulder handles, decorated w/embossed leaves, green matte glaze (ILLUS.) ................................... **468.00**

**Vase,** 6½" h., 7" d., bulbous ovoid body w/fluted rim, shoulder loop handles, decorated w/embossed leaves & fruit, dark green matte glaze ....................................... **600.00**

**Wall pocket,** flattened rectangular form w/rounded corners, molded w/the figure of an Indian papoose on a carrying board, rich leathery matte green glaze, 4" w., 10½" h. ............. **1,320.00**

## CLEMATIS (1944)

*Clematis blossoms and heart-shaped green leaves against a vertically textured ground—white blossoms on blue, rose-pink blossoms on green and ivory blossoms on golden brown.*

*Clematis Fancy Basket*

**Basket,** hanging-type, green or brown ground, No. 466-5", 5" h., each ...................................... **235.00**

**Basket w/ornate circular handles,** blue ground, No. 387-7", 7" h. (ILLUS.).............. **250.00**

**Cookie jar,** cov., green ground, No. 3-8", 8" h. .......... **250.00 to 350.00**

**Vase,** 6" h., round pedestal supports an angular urn-form body w/pointed angular shoulder handles, green ground, No. 188-6" ........................ **65.00 to 80.00**

**Vase,** 7" h., blue ground, No. 105-7" ...................................... **125.00**

**Vase,** 9" h., green ground, No. 109-9" (small repair on base)..... **80.00**

**Vase,** 15" h., floor-type, footed tall slender baluster-form body w/a widely flaring mouth, long angular handles down the sides, terra-cotta ground, No. 114-15"............................. **330.00**

**Wall pocket,** angular side handles, No. 1295-8", 8½" h. (repair) .................................... **165.00**

## COLUMBINE (1940s)

*Columbine blossoms and foliage on shaded ground—yellow blossoms on blue, pink blossoms on pink shaded to green and blue blossoms on tan shaded to green.*

*Columbine Basket & Floor Vase*

**Basket,** hanging-type, squatty bulbous form w/a wide short neck pierced w/hanging holes, tan ground, No. 464-5", 8½" d., 5" h. ...................................... **325.00**

**Basket,** a thick disc base supports an ovoid section supporting a wide oblong deep rim w/stepped & fanned sides, a high pointed arch handle curves down & inward to connect at the disc base, blue ground, No. 368-12", 12" h. (ILLUS. front)... **495.00**

**Bowl,** 6" d., wide flat base below low angled sides to a wide flat & slightly shaped rim, small pointed end handles, brown ground, No. 401-6".................... **95.00**

**Jardiniere,** squatty bulbous body tapering to a wide slightly shaped flat mouth, small angular shoulder handles, tan ground, No. 655-6", 6" h. ...... **175.00 to 185.00**

**Vase,** 8" h., cylindrical w/a gently flaring base, small angular handles near the top, blue ground, No. 20-8" .................... **160.00**

**Vase,** 16" h., floor-type, footed slender ovoid body tapering to a slightly flared & shaped rim, pointed angular shoulder handles, blue ground, No. 27-16" (ILLUS. back, previous page) .................. **575.00**

## COSMOS (1940)

*Embossed blossoms against a wavy horizontal ridged band on a textured ground—ivory band with yellow and orchid blossoms on blue, blue band with white and orchid blossoms on green or tan.*

**Basket,** a low pedestal base supports a spherical body w/a closed rim, a high round handle arches from shoulder to shoulder, blue ground, No. 357-10", 10" h.......... **250.00 to 300.00**

**Console bowl,** footed oblong boat-shape w/an undulating and double-notched rim, blue ground, No. 374-14", 15½" l. ..................... **250.00 to 275.00**

**Jardiniere,** bulbous ovoid body tapering to a undulating notched rim, low arched handles down the sides, green ground, No. 649-4", 4" h........................ **125.00**

**Urn-vase,** a round short pedestal supports a tall classical urn-form body w/long curved handles from the shoulders to the center of the cylindrical neck, green ground, No. 135-8", 8" h. ........................ **225.00 to 250.00**

**Vase,** 7" h., footed baluster-form w/a bulbous base & tall slender neck w/four leaf-form rim lobes, large curved handles from sides of neck to shoulder, blue ground, No. 948-7" .................. **275.00**

**Vase,** 18" h., floor-type, trumpet-shaped w/scalloped rolled rim, long curved handles from below rim to mid-body, blue ground, No. 958-18" ............. **700.00 to 750.00**

## DAHLROSE

*Band of ivory daisy-like blossoms and green leaves against a mottled tan ground.*

*Dahlrose Wall Pocket*

**Basket,** hanging-type, squatty bulbous form tapering to a molded flat rim w/holes for hanging, 7½" d. ....... **180.00 to 200.00**

**Bowl,** 10" l., oval, footed squatty bulbous body tapering to a low molded rim w/angular end handles from rim to shoulder .. **260.00**

**Vase,** 5" h., 7" w., pillow-shaped, narrow rectangular footring below the deep gently rounded rectangular body w/a narrow molded rim flanked by tiny angular handles ...... **125.00 to 155.00**

**Vase,** triple bud, 6" h., a ringed domed base supports a central slender swelled cylindrical vase flanked by flared & curved slender squared vases joined by floral panels to the central vase ......................................... **295.00**

**Vase,** bud, 8" h., a ringed oblong domed base supports at one side a slender swelled cylindrical vase w/a flaring rim, a long, high arched handle runs from one side of vase down to a forked

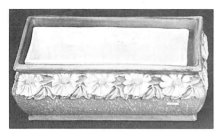

*Dahlrose Window Box*

juncture w/the base, a smaller down-curved angular handle joins the vase to the opposite side of the vase........................ **193.00**

**Wall pocket,** a pointed bullet-form body below a swelled neck w/a molded rim, long angled handles from rim to sides of the body, 10" h. (ILLUS. top previous page) ........................ **358.00**

**Window box w/original liner,** rectangular foot supports a deep curved rectangular body w/a rolled rim, roughness to edge, 16" l., 6¼" h. (ILLUS. above) ... **495.00**

## DELLA ROBBIA, ROZANE (1906)
*Incised designs with an overall high-gloss glaze in colors ranging from soft pastel tints to heavy earth tones and brilliant intense colors.*

**Coffeepot,** cov., cylindrical body w/large angular handle & flaring spout, cover w/ball finial, incised w/Japanese fans, tea cups & saucers, hearts & whiplash lines, marked w/wafer mark & "IW" on side, designed by Frederick Rhead (minor chip & tiny hairline inside cover, restoration to tip of spout) ........ **990.00**

**Vase,** 15¾" h., 5½" d., tall slender ovoid body w/a reticulated gently flaring rim, the sides decorated w/long panels of excised stylized flowers in browns & oranges w/green foliage on a textured pumpkin orange ground, celadon green body, wafer mark (excellent restoration to top & base) .................................... **7,150.00**

*Rare & Expensive Della Robbia Vase*

**Vase,** a tall trumpet-form body w/a wide rounded shoulder centered by a slender short trumpet-form neck, the neck & body decorated w/a continuous repeating design of incised pale cream & yellow blossoms & swirled pale & dark green leaves against a greyish blue ground on a white background, ca. 1906 (ILLUS.) .............................. **13,000.00**

## DONATELLO (1915)
*Deeply fluted ivory and green body with wide tan band embossed with cherubs at various pursuits in pastoral settings.*

*Donatello Wall Pocket*

**Basket,** hanging-type, deep
  bulbous body w/a wide flat rim,
  decorative figural panel around
  the middle, No. 327-6", 6" h. .... **265.00**

**Bowl,** 10" d., 3" h., wide squatty
  form w/the upper half tapering
  up to a closed rim ........ **75.00 to 90.00**

**Flowerpot w/saucer,** flaring
  cylindrical sides,
  5" h. ......................... **120.00 to 130.00**

**Jardiniere,** wide bulbous ovoid
  tapering form w/a wide flat
  mouth, 7" d., 6" h. ...... **85.00 to 100.00**

**Jardiniere & pedestal base,**
  overall 22½" h., 2 pcs. ............ **850.00**

**Umbrella stand,** No.
  183-10" ................... **375.00 to 425.00**

**Vase,** 12" h., tall slender baluster-
  form w/a flaring foot & a short
  flaring wide neck, No. 184-12" ... **225.00**

**Wall pocket,** bullet-shaped, wide
  center figural band, 11½" l.
  (ILLUS. bottom previous
  page)....................................... **200.00**

### EARLAM (1930)

*Mottled glaze on various simple
shapes. The line includes many crocus or
strawberry pots.*

**Bowl-vase,** two-handled globular
  body, No. 516-4½", 4½" h. ........ **195.00**

**Planter,** rectangular foot below
  the flattened long sides & curved
  ends, arched side rims, curved
  angular end handles, mottled
  green & blue glaze, No. 89-8",
  5 x 10½" .................. **195.00 to 250.00**

**Vase,** 18½" h., floor-type, bulbous
  ovoid body w/flaring foot &
  slightly flaring wide cylindrical
  neck, Carnelian blank, mottled
  orange & brown flambé glaze ..**1,210.00**

### EARLY EMBOSSED PITCHERS
### (pre-1916)

*Utility pitchers with various embossed
scenes; high gloss glaze.*

**The Bridge,** 6" h. ...................... **135.00**
**The Cow,** 6½" h........ **300.00 to 350.00**

*Roseville Tulip Pitcher*

**Holland,** No 1, 6½" h. ............... **225.00**
**Iris,** 9" h. .................... **130.00 to 150.00**
**Tulip,** 7½" h., professional repair
  to spout (ILLUS.)...................... **175.00**

### FALLINE (1933)

*Curving panels topped by a semi-
scallop separated by vertical peapod
decorations; blended backgrounds of tan
shading to green and blue or tan shading
to darker brown.*

**Urn,** footed slightly flaring
  cylindrical body w/a closed rim,
  large D-form handles from
  shoulder to center of sides, tan
  shading to blue & green, 6" h... **440.00**

**Vase,** 6¼" h., 4¾" d., ovoid body
  tapering to a small flat mouth, C-
  scroll handles from shoulder to
  center body, tan shading to
  brown ground (ILLUS. top next
  page, No. 7) ............................ **358.00**

**Vase,** 6½" h., 6½" d., spherical
  broad body w/a narrow swelled
  shoulder below the wide short
  cylindrical neck, C-scroll handles
  from the neck to the top of the
  body, mottled tan ground (ILLUS.
  top next page, No. 5) ................. **825.00**

**Vase,** 6½" h., 6½" d., spherical
  broad body w/a narrow swelled
  shoulder below the wide short
  cylindrical neck, C-scroll handles
  from the neck to the top of the
  body, mottled green, blue &
  brown ground (ILLUS. top next
  page, No. 3) ......................... **1,210.00**

2            4        6        8

1            3        5        7

*Fine Selection of Falline*

**Vase,** 7" h., 5½" d., slender ovoid body tapering to a short small cylindrical neck flanked by small C-scroll handles, tan shading to brown ground (ILLUS., No. 1).. **468.00**

**Vase,** 7¼" h., 6¾" d., wide spherical body tapering to a stepped shoulder & a short cylindrical neck, C-scroll handles from base of neck to top of the body, green pods on shaded brown ground (ILLUS., No. 8).. **605.00**

**Vase,** 8¼" h., 6" d., footed trumpet-form w/a widely flaring rim, low arched handles from under the rim to mid-body, tan shading to brown ground, gold label, No. 646-8" (ILLUS., No. 6) ..................................... **468.00**

**Vase,** 9" h., 7½" d., swelled horizontally-ringed lower section below a tall conical upper body w/a flat wide mouth, long C-scroll handles from rim to top of ringed section, tan shading to brown ground (ILLUS., No. 2).. **935.00**

**Vase,** 13¾" h., 7" d., floor-type, a tall wide cylindrical body w/a narrow rounded shoulder to the short rounded neck w/a molded flat rim, small C-scroll handles from the neck to the shoulder, green 'pods' on a tan shaded to blue ground, professional invisible repair to very small base chip & chip to inside of one handle, gold label (ILLUS., No. 4) ................................... **2,420.00**

## FERELLA (1930)

*Impressed shell design alternating with small cut-outs at top and base; mottled brown or turquoise and red glaze.*

**Bowl,** 12½" l., 5½" h., a small pierced & tapering round foot supports a deep & widely flaring bowl, brown ground, No. 212-12 x 7"............................. **770.00**

**Candlestick,** chalice-form w/a low pedestal base supporting a wide deep pierced rounded cup centered by a cylindrical candle socket, turquoise & red glaze, No. 1078-4", 4½" h.................. **185.00**

**Console bowl w/attached flower frog,** turquoise & red glaze, No. 87-8", 8" d......................... **650.00**

**Vase,** 4" h., small tapering foot supports a wide flaring & gently rounded body w/a short, wide waisted neck, low angular handles down the sides, No. 498-4" ......... **303.00**

**Vase,** 5½" h., 6½" d., tapering pierced foot supports a ringed bulbous ovoid body tapering slightly to a wide short cylindrical neck, inverted loop handles from shoulder to lower body, turquoise & red glaze, No. 504-5½" ........... **605.00**

**Vase,** 9" h., sharply compressed globular base, large handles rising from midsection to below rim, turquoise & red glaze (spider underneath) ................. **750.00**

**Wall pocket,** half-round basket-form w/widely flaring rim & high shaped & arched backplate w/hanging hole, brown ground, No. 1266-6½", 6½" h................ **900.00**

## FLORENTINE (1924-28)

*Bark-textured panels alternating with embossed garlands of cascading fruit and florals; ivory with tan and green, beige with brown and green or brown with beige and green glaze.*

**Basket,** hanging-type, squatty bulbous form w/a wide flat mouth, rim holes for hanging, 9" d. (no chain)........................ **175.00**

**Bowl,** 7" d., footed low rounded sides w/a wide flat molded rim w/small squared rim handles, brown ground............................ **98.00**

**Compote w/flower frog,** 10" d., footed low wide rounded bowl w/incurved rim, beige ground, 2 pcs. ....................................... **135.00**

**Umbrella stand,** footed tall cylindrical body w/a slightly inset short, wide cylindrical neck flanked by low squared handles, brown ground, No. 763-20", 11" d., 20¼" h. ........................ **495.00**

**Vase,** 18" h., floor-type, tall wide cylindrical footed body w/an indented band below the thick rolled rim, ivory ground, No. 298-18" ............................ **575.00**

**Wall pocket,** bullet-form w/closed rim, arched backplate w/hanging hole, brown ground, 12½" h. .................... **165.00 to 195.00**

## FOXGLOVE (1940s)

*Sprays of pink and white blossoms embossed against a shaded matte finish ground.*

*Foxglove Jardiniere & Pedestal*

**Basket,** hanging-type, deep half-round body w/small pointed rim handles, blue ground, No. 466-5", 6½" h........... **250.00 to 275.00**

**Console bowl,** green ground, No. 421-10", 10" l. ... **120.00 to 150.00**

**Cornucopia-vase,** blue ground, No. 164-8", 8" h........................ **325.00**

**Ewer,** pedestal foot supports a wide ovoid body tapering at the shoulder to a deeply forked neck w/a high upright squared spout, a high pointed arch handle from rim to shoulder, blue ground, No. 5-10", 10" h........................ **210.00**

**Jardiniere & pedestal base,** green ground, No. 659-10", overall 30½" h. (ILLUS. above) .............. **1,500.00 to 2,000.00**

**Model of a conch shell,** blue ground, No. 426-6", 6" l. ........................... **100.00 to 125.00**

**Rose bowl,** two-handled, pink ground, No. 418-6", 6" h. ......... **150.00**

**Tray,** flattened wide leaf shape
w/an open rim handle on one
side, blue ground,
8½" w....................... **100.00 to 140.00**

**Vase,** 9" h., pink ground, No.
49-9" ....................................... **225.00**

**Vase,** 14" h., tall conical body
w/flaring mouth, four short
curved handles rising from disc
base to lower body, green
ground, No. 53-14".................. **400.00**

**Vase,** 18" h., floor-type, blue
ground .................... **580.00 to 650.00**

## FREESIA (1945)

*Trumpet-shaped blossoms and long
slender green leaves against wavy
impressed lines—white and lavender
blossoms on blended green; white and
yellow blossoms on shaded blue or terra
cotta and brown.*

*Freesia Basket*

**Basket,** footed deep oblong body
w/an arched & notched rim below
a high arched handle w/pointed
ends, terra cotta ground,
No. 391-8", 8" h. (ILLUS.)........... **175.00**

**Book ends,** brown ground,
No. 15, pr. .............................. **350.00**

**Bowl,** 8½" d., footed wide squatty
rounded sides w/a wide flat rim,
terra cotta ground, No. 464-6" ... **60.00**

**Candlesticks,** disc base tapers to
a cylindrical candle socket,
angled loop handles at the base,
terra cotta ground, No.
1161-4½", 4½" h., pr. ............... **110.00**

*Freesia Footed Ewer*

**Ewer,** footed half-round wide
body w/a flat shoulder tapering
to a short forked neck w/a high
arched spout & an arched
handle from rim to shoulder
edge, terra cotta ground, No.
19-6", 6" h. (ILLUS.).................. **75.00**

**Jardiniere & pedestal base,**
green ground, No. 669-8",
2 pcs. ................................... **1,100.00**

**Pitcher,** tankard, 10" h., footed
slender ovoid body w/wide spout
& pointed arched handle,
No. 20-10".............................. **200.00**

**Urn-vase,** footed slender ovoid
body w/a narrow flattened
shoulder centered by a low
molded neck, small angular
handles from shoulder rim down
the sides, terra cotta ground,
No. 463-5", 5" h. ..................... **175.00**

**Vase,** 9½" h., a short ringed
pedestal base supporting a
flaring half-round base w/an
angled shoulder tapering slightly
to a tall, wide cylindrical neck,
down-curved angled loop
handles from center of neck to
rim of lower shoulder, blue
ground, No. 123-9".................. **165.00**

**Vase,** 18" h., 8¼" d., floor-type,
footed tall slender ovoid body
tapering to a flared rim, small
pointed angular shoulder
handles, green ground, No.
129-18" ................................. **660.00**

## FUCHSIA (1939)

*Coral pink fuchsia blossoms and green leaves against a background of blue shading to yellow, green shading to terra cotta or terra cotta shading to gold.*

*Fuchsia Vase*

**Basket & flower frog,** a short pedestal foot supports a wide squatty half-round body w/small half-round tabs on two sides of the incurved rim, a high round handle joins the two other edges, terra cotta ground, No. 350-8", 8" h. ...... **300.00 to 325.00**

**Bowl-Vase,** footed squatty bulbous body w/a short & wide cylindrical neck w/a molded rim flanked by tiny angled branch handles, blue ground, No. 645-3", 3" h. ............................ **140.00**

**Console bowl,** a low oval foot supports a long narrow oval boat-shaped bowl w/an undulating rim & C-form handles under the ends, green ground, No. 353-14", 14" l. .................... **290.00**

**Ewer,** footed wide half-round body w/a sharply angled flattened shoulder tapering to a tall slender deeply forked neck w/a wide upright spout, a long handle curves from the neck to the shoulder, blue ground, No. 902-10", 10" h. .................... **395.00**

**Vase,** 6" h., footed spherical body w/a ringed cylindrical neck w/a flaring rim, long C-form handles from center of the neck to the center of the body, terra cotta ground, No. 891-6" .................. **170.00**

**Vase,** 8" h., footed ovoid body w/a flattened narrow shoulder w/a short four-lobed neck, long low handles from the shoulder to the base of the body, blue ground, No. 897-8" ............... **200.00 to 250.00**

**Vase,** 8" h., footed bulbous body tapering slightly to a wide gently tapering cylindrical neck w/a rolled rim, long curved handles from just under the rim to the mid-body, green ground, No. 898-8" (ILLUS. previous column) ..................................... **155.00**

**Vase,** 18" h., 10" d., floor-type, a disc foot supports a tall baluster-form body w/long low C-form handles down the sides, blue ground, No. 905-18" ............. **1,100.00**

**Wall pocket,** flattened bullet-form body w/an arched & fanned rim, small C-form handles at the sides, green ground, No. 1282-8", 8½" h. ........................ **450.00**

## FUTURA (1928

*Varied line with shapes ranging from Art Deco geometrics to futuristic. Matte glaze is typical although an occasional piece may be high gloss.*

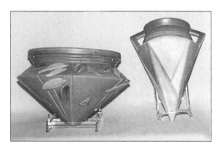

*Futura Basket & Wall Pocket*

**Basket,** hanging-type, a thick flat molded rim above a short ringed neck above the narrow sharply sloping shoulders above sharply angled lower sides coming to a point, embossed w/stylized pastel foliage, terra cotta, blue & brown No. 344-5", 5" (ILLUS. left, bottom previous page) ...... **325.00**

**Candlesticks,** tall slender cylindrical tiered "Christmas tree" style on round flat foot, No. 390-10", 10" h., pr. (small flat chips off bases of both pieces) **523.00**

**Jardiniere & pedestal base,** footed jardiniere w/widely flaring lower sides below a sharply angled shoulder tapering to a wide thick molded rim flanked by small square handles, the slightly tapering cylindrical pedestal w/a flaring, stepped foot, pink & lavender leaves on grey ground, jardiniere 13½" d., 9½" h., overall 28" h., 2 pcs. . **1,650.00**

**Vase,** 5" h., squared flaring shape raised on four square feet, blue w/yellow interior & green feet, No. 198-5" ............................... **880.00**

**Vase,** 7" h., 5½" d., high domed & stepped beehive-form body below a wide & flaring neck joined by two short strap handles to the shoulder, shaded cream to blue body w/green leaves around the body, unmarked, No. 403-7" .............. **715.00**

**Vase,** 8" h., a raised flaring foot supports a rounded-base cylindrical body w/a wide flat mouth flanked by thin buttresses from the rim halfway down the sides, decorated w/stylized rounded blossoms & scrolling tendrils, No. 427-8" ................ **465.00**

**Vase,** 9" h., a wide low domed foot below four short, narrow side buttresses flanking the tall gently flaring trumpet-form body decorated w/crocuses, purple, No. 429-9" ............................... **875.00**

**Wall pocket,** a heavy molded round ringed neck above a sharply tapering paneled body coming to a point, small angular rim handles, geometric design in

blue, yellow, green & lavender on brown ground, No. 1261-8", 6" w., 8¼" h. (ILLUS. right, bottom previous page) ............ **350.00**

## GARDENIA (1940s)

*Large white gardenia blossoms and green leaves over a textured impressed band on a shaded green, grey or tan ground.*

**Basket,** small round foot supports deep widely flaring sides w/a three-scalloped rim joined from end to end by a high arched handle, No. 608-8", 8" h. .......... **185.00**

**Book end,** model of a half-open book w/a blossom in the center, grey ground, No. 659 .............. **100.00**

**Ewer,** footed tall slender baluster-form w/high arched spout & loop shoulder handle, green ground, No. 617-10", 10" h. .................. **230.00**

**Jardiniere,** wide deep cylindrical sides rounded at the base & w/a molded low neck flanked by tiny loop handles, tan ground, No. 600-4", 4" h. ......................... **85.00**

**Vase,** 8" h., stepped disc foot below the slightly swelled cylindrical body w/a narrow shoulder tapering to a low scalloped & flaring neck, long low curved handles from the shoulder to the base, tan ground, No. 683-8" .... **80.00 to 100.00**

**Wall pocket,** bullet-shaped body w/a widely fanned arched rim, thick curved handles from under the rim to the center body, grey ground, No. 666-8", 9½" h. ...................... **175.00 to 200.00**

## IMPERIAL II (1924)

*Varied line with no common characteristics. Many of the pieces are heavily glazed with colors that run and blend.*

**Vase,** 5¼" h., 4" d., ovoid inverted-beehive ringed form, mottled green over yellow

2       4       5       7

1       3       6

*A Selection of Imperial II Pieces*

flambé glaze, No. 467-5"
(ILLUS., No. 3) ......................... **440.00**

**Vase,** 6½" h., 5½" d., bulbous
tapering ringed ovoid body
w/short wide neck, mottled
yellow & purple glaze,
No. 469-6" (ILLUS., No. 1) ....... **385.00**

**Vase,** 7" h., a wide bulbous flaring
lower body below the wide
gently sloping shoulder centered
by a short, wide cylindrical neck,
mottled overall blue glaze
w/dark yellow thick curled drips
around the neck, No. 474-7"
(ILLUS., No. 4) ......................... **440.00**

**Vase,** 7¼" h., 6¼" d., bulbous
body w/a ringed neck, covered
w/a fine raspberry matte glaze
w/green highlights (ILLUS.,
No. 5) .................................... **2,640.00**

**Vase,** 8¼" h., 7" d., ribbed
trumpet-shaped body, feathered
raspberry & green flambé glaze,
No. 476-8" (ILLUS., No. 2) .... **2,640.00**

**Vase,** 11½" h., 6½" d., wide tall
ovoid body tapering to a low,
molded mouth, yellow & dark
blue flambé glaze, No. 484-11"
(ILLUS., No. 7) ...................... **1,540.00**

**Wall pocket,** triple, tapering ringed
center container flanked by
matching smaller containers,
pointed arch backplate w/hanging
hole, mottled burnt orange &
frothy green glaze, No. 1264,
6½" h. (ILLUS. No. 6) ................ **660.00**

### JUVENILE (1916 on)

*Transfer-printed and painted on
creamware with nursery rhyme
characters, cute animals and other motifs
appealing to children.*

*"Sitting Rabbits" Feeding Dish*

**Feeding dish w/rolled edge,**
nursery rhyme, "Baby Bunting,"
8" d............................................. **98.00**

**Feeding dish w/rolled edge,**
chicks, 6½" d. ............ **95.00 to 125.00**

**Feeding dish w/rolled edge,**
chicks, 8" d. ............. **100.00 to 125.00**

**Feeding dish w/rolled edge,**
duck w/hat, 8" d. ..................... **145.00**

**Feeding dish w/rolled edge,**
nursery rhyme, "Little Jack
Horner," 8" d. ........................... **175.00**

**Feeding dish w/rolled edge,**
seated dog, 8" d. ..... **115.00 to 135.00**

**Feeding dish w/rolled edge,**
sitting rabbits, 8" d. (ILLUS. bottom
previous page)......... **100.00 to 120.00**

**Mug,** chicks, 3" h....................... **129.00**

**Pitcher,** 3½" h., chicks, matte
glaze........................ **100.00 to 125.00**

**Pitcher,** 3½" h., Sunbonnet
Girl........................... **100.00 to 125.00**

## LUFFA (1934)

*Relief-molded ivy leaves and blossoms on shaded brown or green wavy horizontal ridges.*

**Jardiniere & pedestal base,**
green ground, overall 25" h.,
2 pcs. .................................... **1,540.00**

**Vase,** 6" h., gently swelled
cylindrical body w/a wide flat
molded mouth flanked by small
pointed angular handles, brown
ground ..................... **120.00 to 150.00**

**Vase,** 7" h., tall ovoid body
tapering slightly to a wide flat
mouth flanked by small pointed
angular handles, green
ground (ILLUS. top next
column).................... **200.00 to 275.00**

**Vase,** 12¼" h., 7¼" d., footed
slender baluster-form w/a widely
flaring mouth flanked by angular
handles to the shoulder, brown
ground, gold decal mark .......... **635.00**

**Wall pocket,** conical w/tiny
angular handles beneath
rim, brown ground,
8½" h. .................... **550.00 to 575.00**

*Luffa Vase*

## MAGNOLIA (1943)

*Large white blossoms with rose centers and black stems in relief against a blue, green or tan textured ground.*

*Magnolia Cookie Jar*

**Basket,** wide round short
pedestal foot supporting a
widely flaring fanned body w/a
high curved rim, a low pointed
arch handle from side to side &
angling back to join the body
under the rim, green ground,
No. 385-10", 13" w., 10" h........ **250.00**

**Book ends,** tan ground, No. 13,
pr.............................................. **165.00**

**Candlesticks,** angular handles
rising from flat base to midsection
of stem, green ground, No. 1157-
4½", 5" h., pr. ............................ **150.00**

**Cookie jar,** cov., shoulder
handles, tan ground, No.
2-8", overall 10" h.
(ILLUS.) .................. **400.00 to 450.00**

**Cornucopia vase,** green ground,
No. 184-6", 6" h....................... **185.00**

**Ewer,** squatty bulbous base
tapering sharply to a tall slender
neck w/a forked rim & tall, long
arched spout, long angled
handle from rim to lower neck,
tan ground, No. 15-15", 15" h. ... **350.00**

**Sugar bowl,** open, blue ground,
No. 4 ......................................... **70.00**

**Teapot,** cov., blue ground, No. 4.. **200.00**

**Vase,** 6" h., a flaring foot below a
bulbous ring supporting a tall
gently flaring trumpet-form body
w/angular pointed handles from
base to midsection, blue ground,
No. 88-6".................................... **80.00**

## MATT GREEN (before 1916)

*Dark green matt finish. Some pieces
plain; others decorated with various
embossed designs such as leaves or
children's faces.*

**Basket,** hanging-type, everted
scalloped rim, embossed
design...................... **150.00 to 175.00**

**Candlesticks,** a wide flaring
round disc foot supporting a
paneled columnar standard
below the widely flaring dished
socket, embossed overall
w/stylized Persian floral designs,
unmarked, 7¼" d., 14" h., pr. .... **660.00**

**Jardiniere,** large bulbous ovoid
body w/an indented band below
the swelled incurved short neck
w/a wide flat mouth, four small
loop handles from the neck to
the shoulder, smooth green
glaze, 13½" d., 9½" h.............. **495.00**

**Umbrella stand,** flaring foot
supporting a tall slightly tapering
cylindrical body w/a flared rim,
embossed from the foot up the
sides w/stylized flowers & leaves
on tall stems, leathery green
glaze, 10½" d., 22" h. (ILLUS.).. **880.00**

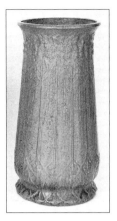

*Matt Green Umbrella Stand*

**Vase,** double-bud, 5¼" h., 6¾" w.,
modeled as the facade of an
early Spanish mission w/square
bell towers forming the vases &
flanking a Gothic arched central
door w/pierced designs at the
top, unmarked (touch-up to one
small corner chip) ................... **165.00**

**Wall pocket,** smooth conical form
w/a pointed tip & high arched &
stepped backplate w/hanging
hole, 12" h............................... **280.00**

## MING TREE (1949)

*Embossed twisted bonsai tree topped
with puffy foliage—pink-topped trees on
mint green ground, green tops on white
ground and white tops on blue ground;
handles in the form of gnarled branches.*

**Ashtray,** shaped square
w/indented rest at each
corner, blue ground,
No. 599-6" ................. **85.00 to 100.00**

**Bowl,** 11½" l., 4" h., rectangular
w/swelled sides & end rim tabs
above angled small branch
handles, white ground, No.
526-9" ..................................... **150.00**

**Candleholders,** low rounded &
lobed form w/tiny branch
handles, No. 551, pr. .............. **130.00**

**Console bowl,** oblong boat-
shaped w/angled branch end
handles, No. 528-10", 10" l. ..... **150.00**

**Ewer,** very slender, tapering &
gently curving form w/a high,
arched spout & angled branch
handle, No. 516-10", 10" h....... **225.00**

**Wall pocket,** overhead branch
handle, white ground, No.
566-8", 8½" h.......... **225.00 to 275.00**

## MOSS (1930s)

*Spanish moss draped over a brown
branch with green leaves against a
background of ivory, pink or tan shading
to blue.*

*Moss Wall Pocket*

**Bowl,** 5" d., handled spherical
body, No. 291-5" ...................... **150.00**

**Rose Bowl,** spherical body, pink
ground, No. 289-4", 4" d. ......... **185.00**

**Vase,** 6" h., footed cupped base
w/a narrow shoulder to the tall
wide cylindrical neck, long
angular handles down the
sides of the neck, pink ground,
No. 774-6" ............... **200.00 to 250.00**

**Urn-vases,** a disc base w/small
angled buttresses supporting the
wide bulbous ovoid body
tapering to a wide cylindrical
neck w/a flat mouth, large
angular handles down the sides,
ivory shaded to blue ground,
7½" d., 9" h., pr. (couple of
minor chips at base of one) ..... **605.00**

**Wall pocket,** trumpet-shaped w/a
pointed base & long angled
handles down the sides, blue
ground, No. 1278-8", 8" h.
(ILLUS.) ................................... **770.00**

## MOSTIQUE (1915)

*Incised Indian-type design of stylized
flowers, leaves or geometric shapes glazed
in bright high-gloss colors against a
heavy, pebbled ground.*

*Mostique Jardiniere & Pedestal*

**Basket,** hanging-type, a wide flat
molded mouth atop a deep
rounded body w/a pointed
bottom, stylized band of long
spade-form leaves in pale green
& yellow on a grey ground,
No. 334-6", 6½" h..................... **385.00**

**Jardiniere & pedestal base,** the
jardiniere w/a wide bulbous ovoid
body tapering to a wide short
cylindrical neck flanked by small
angled tab handles, the columnar
pedestal flaring to molded rings at
the top & base, each piece
decorated w/large four-petal white
diamond-form stylized flowers
w/yellow centers above clusters of
three dark green pointed leaves,
ringed bands accent both pieces,
tan ground, a few glaze nicks on
body, very minor, 15½" d.,
overall 34¼", 2 pcs. (ILLUS.) ...... **880.00**

**Vase,** 9¾" h., 7" d., bulbous ovoid
body below a slightly tapering
cylindrical neck w/a flat rim, a
triple-ring light brown neck band
above bluish green & pink
blossoms above light brown leaf
clusters on a tan ground ......... **330.00**

Wall pocket, elongated bullet-shape w/a rounded-arch backplate w/hanging hole, heart-shaped dark green leaves below a square pink four-petal rim blossom flanked by dark green bands, 9½" h. ........................... **350.00**

## PANEL (1920)

*Recessed panels decorated with embossed naturalistic or stylized florals or female nudes.*

*Two Panel Wall Pockets*

Candlesticks, sharply tapering round base w/a slender standard below the half-round candle socket w/a wide flat rim, panels of stylized orange leaves, dark brown ground, 6" d., 8¼" h., pr. .............................. **440.00**

Vase, 6" h., pillow-form, wide flattened ovoid form tapering to a wide rectangular molded rim, small angular handles from the rim to shoulder, panels of orange orchid blossoms on a dark green ground ... **250.00 to 300.00**

Vase, 8½" h., 6½" d., footed bulbous cylindrical form deeply rounded at the bottom & shoulder, a small closed mouth, the sides w/wide panels of orange fruit & leaves, dark brown ground .......................... **330.00**

Wall pocket, a slender trumpet-form w/a pointed base & widely flared & paneled rim, long pierced squared handles down the sides, a long narrow panel

w/an orange female nude, dark brown ground, 5" w., 7½" h. (ILLUS. left, previous colum) ..... **550.00**

Wall pocket, simple bullet-form body w/a gently flaring & undulating rim, large swirled panel of orange fruit & green leaves against a dark brown ground, 4½" w., 9" h. (ILLUS. right, previous column) ............. **385.00**

## PINE CONE (1931)

*Realistic embossed brown pine cones and green pine needles on shaded blue, brown or green ground (Pink is extremely rare.)*

*Pine Cone Ewer & Jardiniere*

Basket, footed trumpet-form body w/a widely flared rim, high pointed branch handle curved back under the rims, brown ground, No. 338-10", 10" h. ..... **368.00**

Basket, hanging-type, squatty bulbous body tapering slightly toward the base, w/a short wide cylindrical neck flanked by tiny branch hanging handles, green ground, No. 352-5", 5" ........................... **400.00 to 450.00**

Bowl, 12" l., footed, boat-shaped, No. 432-12" ............................. **350.00**

Dish, boat-shaped shell-form w/curled-up end w/pine needle sprig handle, blue ground, No. 427-8", 9" l. ....................... **175.00**

Ewer, footed bulbous ovoid body tapering to a forked neck w/a high arched spout & angled branch handle, brown ground,

original paper label, little
roughness on spout, 10¼" h.
(ILLUS. left, previous page) ..... **330.00**

**Jardiniere,** bulbous ovoid body
tapering to a flat mouth flanked
by asymmetrical small branch
handles, blue ground, original
paper label, 8½" h. (ILLUS.
right, previous page) ............... **495.00**

**Jardiniere,** bulbous spherical
form w/twig handles, brown
ground, No. 632-12", 12" h. .. **1,320.00**

**Mug,** footed cylindrical body,
brown ground, No. 960-4",
4" h. ........................ **225.00 to 250.00**

**Pitcher w/ice lip,** 8" h., ball-
shaped, branch handle, brown
ground, No. 1321 .................... **600.00**

**Planter,** single side handle rising
from base, green ground,
No. 124-5", 5" h........................ **190.00**

**Planter,** oblong egg-form bowl
w/incurved rim on a thin twig
foot w/a pine needle end handle,
green ground, No. 456-6", 6" l. .. **160.00**

**Rose bowl,** blue ground,
No. 278-4", 4" h...................... **275.00**

**Sand jar,** green ground, No.
766-14", 14" h. ..................... **1,800.00**

**Vase,** 6" h., green ground, No.
748-6" ..................................... **210.00**

**Vase,** 8" h., pillow-type, oblong disc
foot supporting a wide flattened
ovoid body w/an arched, double-
notched rim, small twig side
handles, blue or brown ground,
No. 845-8", each........................ **300.00**

**Vase,** 12" h., green, No.
712-12" ................... **375.00 to 400.00**

## PRIMROSE (1932)

*Cluster of long-stemmed blossoms and
pod-like leaves in relief on blue, pink or
tan ground.*

**Basket,** hanging-type, squatty
bulbous body w/a wide short
cylindrical neck w/hanging
holes, small angular shoulder
handles, tan ground,
No. 354-5" .............. **200.00 to 220.00**

*Primrose Jardiniere & Pedestal*

**Jardiniere & pedestal base,**
bulbous nearly spherical
jardiniere w/a wide narrow
molded mouth flanked by small
angled shoulder handles, the
baluster-form pedestal w/a disc
top & foot, pink ground, No.
634-10", jardiniere 16" d.,
10" h., overall 29" h., 2 pcs.
(ILLUS.) ................................ **1,210.00**

**Vase,** 6½" h., swelled cylindrical
body narrowing slightly at the
top to a flat mouth, angled
handles down the sides,
No. 761-6", tan ground............ **150.00**

**Vase,** 7" h., slightly flaring
cylindrical body w/a narrow
shoulder to a short, wide
cylindrical neck, low angled
handles down the sides,
No. 760-6", tan ground............ **100.00**

**Vase,** 9" h., pink ground, No.
769-9" ..................................... **160.00**

## ROSECRAFT VINTAGE

*Curving band of brown and yellow
grapevine with fruit and foliage at top,
usually on a dark brown ground.*

**Bowl vase,** squatty bulbous
tapering body w/wide molded
flat rim, 3" h. ............................. **175.00**

**Bowl vase,** bulbous tapering
body w/a wide flat molded rim,
5" h......................................... **495.00**

*Rosecraft Vintage Vase*

*Silhouette Pattern Fan Vase*

**Jardiniere,** wide bulbous tapering body w/a wide flat molded rim, No. 607-7", 9" d., 7" h. ............. **413.00**

**Vase,** double-bud, 4¾" h., 8" w., gate-form, No. 48-4½" ............... **66.00**

**Vase,** 5" h, ovoid body w/short molded rim (ILLUS. above) ...... **245.00**

**Vase,** 6" h., bulbous ovoid body tapering to short narrow cylindrical rim ........................... **295.00**

**Vase,** 8" h., slightly expanding cylindrical body w/short slightly flared rim ................................. **795.00**

**Wall pocket,** slender conical form w/an arched top & low loop handles down the sides, 9" h. ......................... **225.00 to 250.00**

## SILHOUETTE (1952)

*Recessed shaped panels decorated with floral designs or exotic female nudes against a combed background. In colors of tan, turquoise blue, deep rose and white with turquoise panels.*

**Basket,** oblong-shaped foot below upright body w/one side tall & pointed & joining long, angular handle joining the opposite side near the base, florals, blue ground, No. 709-8", 8" h. ......................................... **195.00**

**Candleholders,** sloping base tapering to a short waisted stem, florals, blue ground, No. 751-3", 3" h., pr. ................... **110.00 to 130.00**

**Candleholders,** sloping base tapering to a short waisted stem, florals, tan ground, No. 751-3", 3" h., pr. ..................................... **55.00**

**Jardiniere,** footed wide nearly spherical body w/an incurved wide irregular rim, small pointed angular shoulder handles, female nudes, blue ground, 9" d., 5¾" h. ............................. **825.00**

**Planter,** double, a thick gently arched rectangular foot supports two squared upright containers w/sloping rims & joined by a curved center buttress, florals, blue ground, No. 757-9", 9" l., 5½" h. ........................ **75.00 to 100.00**

**Urn-vase,** a disc foot w/four small pointed tabs supporting a tall pointed ovoid body w/a wide flat rim, female nudes, rose ground, No. 763-8", 8" h. ...... **350.00 to 400.00**

**Vase,** 5" h., handled, florals, blue ground, No. 779-5" .................... **75.00**

**Vase,** 7½" h., 8" w., fan-shaped, a flattened domed base w/double brackets below the widely flaring flattened body w/serrated rim, female nudes, tan ground, No. 783-7" (ILLUS. above) ....... **450.00**

## SNOWBERRY (1946)

*Clusters of white berries on brown stems with green foliage over oblique scalloping, against a blue, green or rose shaded background.*

**Ashtray,** round, shaded rose ground, No. 1AT ....................... **60.00**

**Basket,** hanging-type, shaded blue ground, No. 1 HB-5", 5" h........................................... **265.00**

**Basket,** low pedestal foot supports a flattened ovoid tall body w/a sloping rim, a half-arc handle beginning near the bottom of one side arches up to touch the upper rim & curves over & angles back to end at the lower rim, shaded blue ground, No. 1BK-10", 10" h.................. **185.00**

**Basket,** low pedestal foot supports a flattened ovoid tall body w/a sloping rim, a half-arc handle beginning near the bottom of one side arches up to touch upper rim & curves over & angles back to end at the lower, curved rim, shaded green ground, No. 1BK-12", 12½" h... **325.00 to 375.00**

**Candleholders,** squatty bulbous base centering a short cylindrical socket flanked by small angular handles at shoulder, shaded rose ground, No. 1CS1-1", 2" h., pr. .............. **60.00**

**Console set:** 14" l. long shallow pointed leaf-shaped tray & a pr. of 4½" h. tapering cylindrical candlesticks; shaded rose ground, tray No. 1BL-14", 14" l., candlesticks No. 1CS-2", the set ..................................... **245.00**

**Creamer & open sugar bowl,** No. 1C & No. 1S, shaded blue ground, pr. .............. **130.00 to 170.00**

**Jardiniere,** shaded blue ground, No. 1J-8", 8" h........................ **495.00**

**Jardiniere & pedestal base,** shaded green ground, overall 25" h., 2 pcs. ........................... **750.00**

**Sugar bowl,** pink ground, No. 1S .. **40.00**

**Vase,** 6" h., baluster-form lower body below a wide gently flaring neck, pointed handles from center of neck to center of body, shaded green ground, No. 1V-6" ................................. **85.00**

**Vase,** 7½" h., globular base w/high pointed shoulder handles, tapering to a long

slender cylindrical neck w/a flared rim, shaded green ground, No. 1V2-7" ................... **70.00**

**Vase,** 12" h., shaded rose ground, No. 1V2-12" ............ **275.00 to 300.00**

**Window box,** shaded rose ground, No. 1WX-8", 8" l.......... **125.00**

## THORN APPLE (1930s)

*White trumpet flower and foliage on one side, reverse with thorny pod and foliage against shaded blue, brown or pink ground.*

**Basket,** disc foot below tall flaring conical body w/a wide flat mouth joined at each side by a tall pointed arch handle, shaded pink ground, No. 342-10", 10" h. ...... **210.00**

**Basket,** hanging-type, wide squatty bulbous body tapering to a bottom point & tapering up to a wide, flat molded mouth, small pointed shoulder handles, shaded brown ground, No. 355-5", 7" d............. **225.00 to 275.00**

**Book end,** No. 3 ........................ **100.00**

**Flower frog,** shaded blue ground, No. 30-4"................................. **120.00**

**Flowerpot w/saucer,** shaded pink ground, No. 639-5" ........... **155.00**

**Vase,** 4" d., wide squatty bulbous base w/sharply tapering sides to a small, short rolled neck, small pointed shoulder handles, shaded blue ground, No. 308-4" ..................................... **155.00**

**Vase,** 5" h., No. 809-5".............. **165.00**

**Vase,** 9" h., low pedestal foot below a tall slender ovoid body tapering to a flat rim, small angular shoulder handles, shaded blue ground, No. 820-9" ..................................... **175.00**

**Wall pocket,** triple, three slender slightly curving conjoined cones w/an embossed leaf & apple across the front & a blossom handle at the top, shaded brown ground, No. 1280-8", 8" h. ........................ **325.00 to 425.00**

## VISTA (1920s)

*Embossed green coconut palm trees and lavender blue pool against grey ground.*

*Vista Vase & Planter*

**Jardiniere,** 6½" h. ..... **225.00 to 250.00**

**Planter,** round w/short upright sides decorated w/molded yellow, green & pink flowers on a green & lavender ground, 7" d., 3½" h. (ILLUS. right) ....... **165.00**

**Vase,** 10" h., 5½" d., bulbous ovoid base tapering to a cylindrical neck, low long double-pierced angular handles down the neck to the shoulder, molded w/tall green trees on a blue & lavender ground (ILLUS. left) .......................................... **550.00**

**Vase,** 14 12" h., 7½" d., tall slightly flaring cylindrical body w/a narrow shoulder tapering up to a thick molded rim, small pointed loop handles on the shoulder, decorated w/tall green palm trees on a creamy yellow ground, No. 121-15" ................ **990.00**

**Wall pocket,** conical w/a flattened low-domed base, a high arched, flat-topped backplate w/hanging hole, decorated w/palm trees ....................... **550.00 to 600.00**

## WATER LILY (1940s)

*Water lily blossoms and pads against a horizontally ridged ground. White lilies on green lily pads against a blended blue ground, pink lilies on a pink shading to green ground or yellow lilies against a gold shading to brown ground.*

*Water Lily Cornucopia-Vase*

**Bowl w/flower frog,** 8" l., oblong footed body w/an irregular rim & small pointed end handles, blended blue ground, bowl No. 440-8", w/4½" h. No. 48 dome-footed upright fanned five-hole frog w/angled handles from rim to base, 2 pcs. ........................ **200.00**

**Cookie jar,** cov., bulbous ovoid body tapering to a flat mouth flanked by angular shoulder handles, low domed cover w/a knob finial, pink shading to green ground, No. 1-8", 8" h. .... **500.00**

**Cornucopia-vase,** oblong tapering foot supports a blossom cluster below the slender upright curved vase w/flaring rim & curled tip, gold shading to brown ground, No. 178-8", 8" h. (ILLUS.) ................................... **175.00**

**Ewer,** footed squatty bulbous base w/a flattened shoulder centered by a tall slender tapering neck w/a forked rim & high arched spout, long angled handle from rim to shoulder, pink shading to green ground, No. 11-10", 10" h. .... **170.00 to 190.00**

**Jardiniere,** footed squatty
bulbous wide base tapering
slightly to a wide cylindrical body
w/an incurved mouth flanked by
angled handles down to the
shoulder, pink shading to green
ground, No. 663-8", 8" h. ......... **410.00**

**Rose bowl,** two-handled, gold
shading to brown ground,
No. 437-4", 4" h. ........ **75.00 to 100.00**

**Vase,** 18" h., floor-type, footed tall
wide baluster-form body
w/angular pointed handles near
the top, gold shading to brown
ground, No. 85-18".................. **750.00**

## WHITE ROSE (1940)

*White roses and green leaves against a
vertically combed ground of blended blue,
brown shading to green or pink shading
to green.*

**Basket,** hanging-type, squatty
bulbous form w/incurved rim
pierced w/hanging holes,
blended blue ground, No.
463-5", 5" h............. **250.00 to 275.00**

**Basket,** a low disc foot supports a
tall flattened & widely fanned
body w/the high arched rim
tapering down to side points, a
long pointed arch loop handle
starts on each side of the lower
body & curves up to attach to
the rim tips & terminates at a
high center point, blended blue
ground, No. 363-10",
10" h. ...................... **210.00 to 225.00**

**Book ends,** modeled as a tier of
two stacked books w/a large
blossom resting on top, blended
blue ground, No. 7,
pr. ........................... **195.00 to 225.00**

**Cornucopia vases,** a disc foot
below the slender upright vase
w/a curled up end & a widely
flaring & arched gently lobed
rim, brown shading to green
ground, No. 144-8", 8" h., pr. .... **248.00**

**Ewer,** a short flaring foot
supporting a wide ovoid body
w/a flattened shoulder tapering

to a short forked neck w/an
upright arched spout & a pointed
arch handle from the rim to the
shoulder, brown shading to
green, No. 990-10", 10" h. ....... **303.00**

**Urn,** a pedestal base supporting a
bulbous ovoid body w/a high,
wide cylindrical notched neck
flanked by arched handles,
blended blue ground, No.
147-8", 8" h. ............................. **195.00**

**Vase,** double bud, 4½" h., two
footed cylinders joined by an
arched bridge, pink shading to
green ground, No. 148 ............. **110.00**

**Vase,** 8" h., a rectangular foot
w/notched corners below flaring
fanned brackets supporting the
tall flattened ovoid body tapering
to a slightly shaped mouth,
upright pointed loop shoulder
handles, blended blue ground,
No. 984-8".............................. **229.00**

**Vase,** 12½" h., footed wide ovoid
body tapering slightly to a
short four-lobed neck flanked
by pointed angular shoulder
handles, brown shading
to green ground,
No. 991-12" .......... **350.00 to 450.00**

## WINCRAFT (1948)

*Shapes from older lines such as Pine
Cone, Cremona, Primrose and others,
vases with an animal motif, and
contemporary shapes. High gloss glaze in
bright shades of blue, tan, yellow,
turquoise, apricot and grey.*

*Wincraft Book Ends*

**Basket,** a footed curved base supports the trumpet-form body w/a forked uneven rim, a high arched handle runs from under the high rim end & terminates w/a series of three small graduated loops down the opposite side, decorated w/cactus in bloom, No. 210-12", 12" h. (minor professional restoration) ............ **325.00**

**Book ends,** blue ground, No. 259-6½", 6½" h., pr. (ILLUS. bottom previous page) ................ **150.00**

**Coffee set:** 9½" h., cov. coffeepot, creamer & sugar bowl; chartreuse ground, Nos. 250P, 271C & 271S, 3 pcs. ....................... **365.00 to 380.00**

**Cornucopia-vase,** low rectangular base supports a reclining cornucopia w/flaring upturned rim & short curled end, relief florals against a glossy green ground, No. 221-8", 9" l., 5" h. ............................................. **80.00**

**Vases,** 7" h., a round foot below an upright paneled squared body w/angled corners, the top w/a gently rounded shoulder centered by a flat round mouth, the panels decorated w/swirled Art Deco style designs in relief on a glossy yellow & tan ground, No. 274-7", pr. ........................... **220.00**

## WISTERIA (1933)

*Lavender wisteria blossoms and green vines against a roughly textured brown shading to deep blue ground, rarely found in only brown.*

**Bowl-vase,** wide squatty bulbous form tapering to a flat mouth flanked by tiny angled loop handles, vines in purple & green against an ochre & brown ground, gold foil label, No. 637-6½", 7½" d., 6¾" h. ............. **425.00 to 450.00**

**Candlestick,** domed base topped by small pointed handles below the tall cylindrical candle socket, No. 1091-4", 4" h. ...................... **150.00**

**Jardiniere & pedestal base,** bulbous spherical jardiniere w/a wide molded mouth flanked by small C-form handles, raised on a slender tapering pedestal, mottled brown & green ground, two chips & nick to base of jardiniere, jardiniere 14" d., overall 28" h., 2 pcs. ............. **1,980.00**

**Vase,** 6" h., tapering pear-shaped body w/a short cylindrical neck & flat rim, small loop shoulder handles, No. 631-6" ... **330.00 to 400.00**

**Vase,** 7" h., bulbous inverted pear-shaped body tapering sharply to a tiny mouth, small looped shoulder handles, blue ground, No. 634-7" (very small nick off one of the flowers) ....... **440.00**

**Vase,** 8" h., 6½" d., bulbous ovoid body tapering to a short cylindrical neck w/a wide flat rim, pointed angled handles from the neck to the shoulder, blue ground ............ **550.00**

## ZEPHYR LILY (1946)

*Deeply embossed day lilies against a swirl-textured ground. White and yellow lilies on a blended blue ground; rose and yellow lilies on a green ground; yellow lilies on terra cotta shading to olive green ground.*

*Zephyr Lily Basket*

**Basket,** low flaring foot below the half-spherical body w/curved-in leaf-form ends flanking a flat rim, the ends joined by an overhead curved handle, green ground, No. 393-7", 7" h. (ILLUS.) ..................... **150.00 to 175.00**

**Basket,** a low tapering round foot below tall slender swelled cylindrical body w/a widely flaring & deeply forked rim w/high spout-form sides, a low curved handle joined under the rim of each 'spout' & arching across the top, terra cotta ground, No. 395-10", 10" h. ..... **225.00**

**Book ends,** blue ground, No. 16, pr................ **200.00 to 225.00**

**Candleholder,** low tapering cylindrical form w/small loop handles, green ground, No. 1162-2", 2" h........................ **50.00**

**Console Bowl,** No. 476-10", 10" d........................................ **110.00**

**Cornucopia-vase,** blue ground, No. 204-8", 8½" h. .... **100.00 to 150.00**

**Ewer,** footed ovoid lower body w/an angled shoulder tapering to a tall slender cylindrical neck w/a deeply forked rim w/a tall upright spout, long curved handle from rim to shoulder, terra cotta ground, No. 23-10", 10" h. ....................... **135.00 to 165.00**

**Jardiniere & pedestal base,** bulbous spherical jardiniere tapering to a wide flat molded mouth flanked by low curved shoulder handles, on a tall waisted cylindrical pedestal, terra cotta ground, No. 671-8", jardiniere 12½" d., overall 24½" h., 2 pcs. ........................ **935.00**

**Vase,** 6½" h., fan-shaped, a rectangular vase supporting a flattened deep U-form body w/stepped rim ends, the foot joined to the lower body by small C-scroll handles, terra cotta ground, No. 205-6" .. **130.00 to 140.00**

**Vase,** 7" h., pillow-type, a thick rectangular foot tapering slightly to support a wide flattened three-section fanned body w/low curved handles near the foot, terra cotta ground, No. 206-7" (ILLUS. top next column) ......... **265.00**

**Vase,** 7¼" h., a round tapering pedestal foot below the trumpet-form body w/a widely flaring rim,

*Zephyr Lily Pillow Vase*

*Zephyr Lily Wall Pocket*

long curved handles from mid-body to the foot rim, terra cotta shading to green ground, No. 132-7"................................ **220.00**

**Vase,** bud, 7½" h., a round tapering foot continuing to form the slender slightly swelled cylindrical body w/a flared rim, curved handles from mid-body to the foot, terra cotta ground, No. 201-7"................................ **50.00**

**Vase,** 18½" h., floor-type, footed tall swelled cylindrical body w/a narrow shoulder to a short cylindrical neck, small C-form shoulder handles, blue ground, No. 142-18"............................. **935.00**

**Wall pocket,** long slender conical form w/rounded side lobes at the top, long curved handles near the bottom, blue ground, No. 1297-8", 8" h. (ILLUS. bottom, this column) ............... **250.00**

# ROYAL BAYREUTH

*Good china in numerous patterns and designs has been made at the Royal Bayreuth factory in Tettau, Germany, since 1794. Listings below are by the company's lines, plus miscellaneous pieces. Interest in this china remains at a peak and prices continue to rise. Pieces listed carry the company's blue mark except where noted otherwise.*

*Royal Bayreuth Mark*

## DEVIL & CARDS

*Devil & Cards Creamer*

**Creamer,** 3¾" h.
(ILLUS.) .....................**250.00 to 300.00**

**Creamer,** figural red devil,
4" h. .........................**275.00 to 350.00**

**Match holder,** hanging-type, 4"
w., 5" h. ....................................**600.00**

**Pitcher,** water, 7¼" h. ..................**575.00**

**Sugar bowl,** open, short..............**325.00**

## MOTHER-OF-PEARL FINISH

**Bowl,** 6½ x 9", oak leaf-shaped, footed, pearlized finish w/gold trim .............................................**750.00**

**Creamer,** boot-shaped, figural
Spiky Shell patt., 4¾" h. .............**125.00**

**Creamer,** figural Spiky Shell patt., pearlized finish , 4¼" h.................**95.00**

**Cup & saucer,** demitasse, footed, figural Spiky Shell patt., pearlized finish ..........................**150.00**

**Mustard pot,** cov., figural Spiky
Shell patt., pearlized finish.........**125.00**

**Sugar bowl,** cov., footed, figural
Spiky Shell patt., pearlized
finish, 3½" h. .............................**140.00**

**Pitcher,** milk, boot-shaped, figural
Spikey Shell patt., pearlized
finish, 5½" h. .............................**195.00**

**Wall pocket,** figural grape cluster, pearlized finish, 9" h...................**358.00**

## ROSE TAPESTRY

*Rose Tapestry Bowl*

**Basket,** miniature, two-color roses on yellow ground, braided decoration around rim ...............**285.00**

**Basket,** three-color roses,
4¾ x 5¼" ...................................**395.00**

**Bell,** pink American Beauty
roses .........................................**545.00**

**Bowl,** 10½" d., gently scalloped rim w/four shell-molded gilt-trimmed handles, three-color roses (ILLUS. above) ................**995.00**

**Cake plate,** open-handled, three-color roses, 10½" d. ..................**395.00**

**Clock,** table-model, three-color roses, upright rectangular case w/a flaring base & domed top, old but not original works ..........**856.00**

**Creamer,** wide cylindrical body slightly flaring at the base & w/a long buttress spout & gilt angled handle, two-color roses on a rose ground, 3" h. ......................**385.00**

**Creamer,** long pinched spout, triple pink roses, 4" h. ...............**285.00**

**Dresser box,** cov., kidney-shaped, double pink roses, 5¼" w., 2" h...............................**345.00**

**Flowerpot & underplate,** three-color roses, 3 x 4", 2 pcs............**295.00**

**Match holder,** hanging-type, three-color roses........................**460.00**

**Model of a high-top lady's shoe,** pink roses w/a band of green leaves around top, 3½" h. ..........**570.00**

**Nut set:** master footed bowl & six small footed bowls; decorated w/pink roses, 7 pcs. ...................**1,250.00 to 1,275.00**

**Plate,** 7½" d., round w/slightly scalloped rim & four sections of fanned ruffles spaced around the edge, three-color roses........**190.00**

**Powder jar,** cov., footed squatty rounded base w/a squatty domed cover, three-color roses, 3" d., 2½" h. ..............................**400.00**

**Relish dish,** oblong w/gilt-trimmed scalloped rim, decorated w/large pink roses, 4¾" w., 8" l. .....................**295.00**

**Sugar bowl,** cov., footed squatty rounded body w/D-form gold handles & inset cover w/button finial, pink American Beauty roses, 3" h................................**220.00**

**Teapot,** cov., three-color roses ....**650.00**

**Vase,** 4½" h., decorated w/American Beauty roses ..........**375.00**

### SNOW BABIES

**Creamer**....................................**125.00**

**Salt shaker** ...............................**120.00**

**Tea tile**.....................................**145.00**

### SUNBONNET BABIES

**Bell,** babies fishing, unmarked.....**275.00**

**Bell,** babies sewing, unmarked....**400.00**

*Sunbonnet Babies Plate*

**Creamer & open sugar bowl,** babies sewing, pr. ......................**475.00**

**Cup & saucer,** babies washing ...**350.00**

**Pitcher,** milk, 4¼" h., babies washing......................................**325.00**

**Plate,** 6" d., babies washing (ILLUS. above)............................**75.00**

## MISCELLANEOUS

*Poppy Pattern Chocolate Pot*

**Ashtray,** figural, oyster & pearl design .......................................**195.00**

**Basket,** "tapestry," footed, bulbous body w/a ruffled rim & ornate gold-trimmed overhead handle, portrait of lady w/horse, 5" h..............................................**595.00**

**Bell,** musicians scene, men playing a cello & mandolin .........**215.00**

**Chamberstick,** wide deeply dished, round pinched sides, central cylindrical socket w/flattened rim, S-scroll handle from side of dish to socket, dark brick red ground, decorated w/"Dancing Frogs" & flying insects ........................................**925.00**

**Chocolate pot,** cov., figural Poppy, tall pink blossom w/ruffled rim, figural poppy on cover, light green & white leafy footed base & large leaf & stem handle, 8½" h. (ILLUS. bottom previous page) ........................**1,300.00**

**Cracker jar,** cov., figural grape cluster ........................................**595.00**

**Creamer,** hunt scene decoration, 3" h................................................**85.00**

**Creamer,** figural apple, yellow & red w/green leaves ......................**95.00**

**Creamer,** figural apple, all-green ..........................**200.00 to 250.00**

**Creamer,** figural bull, grey, 3½" h..........................................**325.00**

**Creamer,** figural butterfly .............**345.00**

**Creamer,** figural cockatoo ...........**375.00**

**Creamer,** figural coachman .........**350.00**

**Creamer,** figural crow, black & white ..........................**150.00 to 200.00**

**Creamer,** figural crow, black ..........................**200.00 to 250.00**

**Creamer,** figural crow, brown bill & eyes ........................................**200.00**

**Creamer,** figural Dachshund........**350.00**

**Creamer,** figural eagle (ILLUS. top next column) ........................**450.00**

**Creamer,** figural elk .......................**95.00**

**Creamer,** figural fish head, grey ..**250.00**

**Creamer,** figural girl w/basket......**595.00**

**Creamer,** figural grape cluster, lilac................................................**95.00**

**Creamer,** figural lamp lighter .......**450.00**

**Creamer,** figural lemon ................**225.00**

**Creamer,** figural leopard...........**3,200.00**

**Creamer,** figural monkey, brown ..**425.00**

**Creamer,** figural monkey, green ..**575.00**

**Creamer,** figural mountain goat ...........................**250.00 to 275.00**

**Creamer,** figural oak leaf .............**225.00**

**Creamer,** figural orange ............. **295.00**

**Creamer,** figural owl .........**400 to 475.00**

*Eagle Creamer*

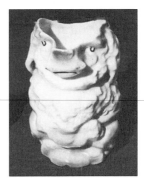

*Grey Poodle Creamer*

**Creamer,** figural oyster & pearl....**175.00**

**Creamer,** figural pelican, unmarked ...................................**295.00**

**Creamer,** figural perch ................**650.00**

**Creamer,** figural pig, grey ...........................**550.00 to 600.00**

**Creamer,** figural platypus .........**1,275.00**

**Creamer,** figural poodle, grey (ILLUS. bottom) .........**350.00 to 375.00**

**Creamer,** figural robin ..................**280.00**

**Creamer,** figural rose ...................**375.00**

**Creamer,** figural seal ...................**350.00**

**Creamer,** figural shell w/coral handle ........................................**185.00**

**Creamer,** figural shell w/lobster handle, unmarked, 2½" h.............**75.00**

**Creamer,** figural strawberry .........**300.00**

**Creamer,** figural watermelon .......**395.00**

**Creamer,** Brittany Girl decoration ..**75.00**

**Creamer,** blue cylindrical body w/flared base & figural brown & grey cat handle, 3¾" h. ..............**395.00**

**Creamer,** flow blue, Babes in Woods decoration .....................**325.00**

**Creamer,** "tapestry," wide ovoid body w/a flaring foot & a long pinched spout, ornate gilt D-form handle, sheep in the meadow decoration, 4" h..........................**355.00**

**Creamer & cov. sugar bowl,** figural purple grape cluster, pr. ...**395.00**

**Dish,** leaf-shaped, "tapestry," scenic Lady & Prince decoration ..................................**110.00**

**Dresser tray,** rectangular, "tapestry," Lady & Prince scenic decoration, 7 x 9¼" ....................**395.00**

**Hair receiver,** cov., three-footed, scene of dog beside hunter shooting ducks ..........................**335.00**

**Hatpin holder,** hexagonal shape, decorated w/pink & white roses, green leaves & gold trim on rim, satin finish .................................**295.00**

**Lamp base,** "tapestry," slender ovoid body decorated w/"The Chase" scene, hounds after stag in water, raised on a metal ring support w/four short legs w/paw feet, set on an octagonal metal base w/molded swirled leafy stems, fitted for electricity, overall 21" h. (ILLUS. top next column) .....................................**915.00**

**Match holder,** hanging-type, figural spiky shell ......................**275.00**

**Match holder,** hanging-type, scene of fishermen in boat.........**305.00**

**Match holder,** hanging-type, stork decoration on yellow ground.....................................**305.00**

**Mustard jar,** cov., figural shell .....**100.00**

**Nut set:** large pedestal-based open compote & six matching servers; each decorated w/a colorful pastoral scene w/animals, 7 pcs. .......................**450.00**

**Pipe rest,** figural basset hound, brown, 5½" l., 3" h.....................**475.00**

**Pitcher,** lemonade, 6¾" h., wide ovoid body w/flat foot & long pinched spout, ornate D-shape handle, dark brick red ground w/green "Dancing Frog" & flying insects decoration.....................**900.00**

*Royal Bayreuth Lamp Base*

**Pitcher,** milk, 4½" h., nursery rhyme scene w/Jack & the Beanstalk ..................................**325.00**

**Pitcher,** milk, figural cockatoo, 4¾" h.........................................**695.00**

**Pitcher,** milk, figural shell w/lobster handle, 3" h. ..............**150.00**

**Pitcher,** 5" h., hunting scene decoration ..................................**175.00**

**Pitcher,** water, 6¾" h., figural lobster ......................................**395.00**

**Plaque,** pierced to hang, "tapestry," round w/a scroll-molded gilt-trimmed border, center portrait of woman leaning on horse, 9½" d. (ILLUS. top next page)..............**770.00**

**Plate,** 6" d., handled, figural leaf & flower .........................................**85.00**

**Powder box,** cov., round, "tapestry," scenic Lady & Prince decoration .................................**150.00**

**Salt & pepper shakers,** figural grape cluster, purple, pr. ..............................**125.00 to 175.00**

**Sugar bowl,** cov., figural orange ..**375.00**

**Sugar bowl,** cov., figural shell w/lobster handle.........................**200.00**

*Royal Bayreuth "Tapestry" Plaque*

*Small Royal Bayreuth Vases*

**Toothpick holder,** three-handled, floral decoration, 2¼" h. .............**150.00**

**Toothpick holder,** round, one side handle, decorated w/scene of man tending turkeys ..............**155.00**

**Vase,** 3¼" d., footed, baluster-form body w/angled shoulder handles, short cylindrical silver rim, Cavalier Musicians scene on grey ground............................**60.00**

**Vase,** 3¾" h., handled, flow blue, Babes in Woods decoration, scene of girl curtseying ..............**370.00**

**Vase,** 5" h., "tapestry," bulbous ovoid body tapering to a short slender flaring neck, 'Castle by the Lake' landscape scene ........**365.00**

**Vases,** 3⅛" h., 2⅝" d., squatty bulbous lower body below the tall tapering sides ending in a ringed neck & flanked by loop handles, one w/scene of Dutch boy & girl playing w/brown dog & the other w/scene of Dutch boy & girl playing w/white & brown dog, green mark, pr. (ILLUS. bottom, this column) .....**110.00**

# ROYAL BONN & BONN

*Royal Bonn Covered Bowl & Underplate*

*Bonn and subsequently Royal Bonn china were produced in Bonn, Germany, in a manufactory established in 1755. Later wares made there are often marked Mehlem or bear the initials FM or a castle mark. Most wares were of the hand-painted type. Clock cases were also made in Bonn.*

*Royal Bonn & Bonn Mark*

**Berry or salad set:** 10" h. pedestal-based master bowl & six sauce dishes; Wild Rose patt., flow blue, Germany, 7 pcs. .....................................**$200.00**

**Bowl, cover & underplate,** decorated w/three clusters of small multicolored flowers, cobalt & gold trim on rims & finial, plate 8" d., overall 5¾" h., 3 pcs. (ILLUS. above) ..............**170.00**

**Vase,** 8½" h., portrait of lovely lady in pink, deep blue blank ....**625.00**

**Vase,** 12½" h., h.p. full-figure portrait of a cavalier, gold rococo trim, artist-signed .....................**525.00**

**Vase,** 14" h., full-figure portrait of peasant girl beside stone wall, scenic setting w/rose bush, stream & woods, lavish gold trim, artist-signed .................. **1,055.00**

# ROYAL COPENHAGEN

*This porcelain has been made in Copenhagen, Denmark, since 1715. The ware is hard paste.*

*Royal Copenhagen Mark*

**Creamer,** fluted body, blue decoration, 3" h. ........................ **$45.00**

**Figure,** Goose Girl, No. 528 ..................... **180.00 to 200.00**

**Figure,** a gentleman standing in native Scandinavian dress selling produce, base numbered "12103," 20th c., 12½" h. .......... **345.00**

**Figure,** girl w/braid, wearing country costume, No. 1223, 8" h. ........................................... **450.00**

**Figure,** Pan on grey column w/rabbit looking up at base, No. 456, 8½" h. ......................... **295.00**

**Figure,** Pan with pipes, No. 1736 ........................................ **240.00**

**Figure group,** a young girl & boy standing together & wearing traditional Scandinavian dress, the base labeled "cordless og leisbeth" & numbered "12106," 20th c., 8½" h. .......................... **489.00**

**Figure group,** two girls standing side-by-side wearing native Scandinavian dress, on a plinth base, labeled on the base "piter og trein dirchans" & numbered "12105," 20th c., 9" h. ............... **428.00**

**Model of a dog,** dachshund ......... **76.00**

**Models of lovebirds,** No. 402, pr. ................................................. **72.00**

**Vase,** 12½" h., decorated w/h.p. apple blossoms, cobalt blue ground ....................................... **275.00**

**Vase,** 16½" h., a gilt-trimmed pedestal base below the wide ovoid body tapering to a slightly flaring cylindrical neck trimmed w/molded gilt bands, high looped gilt figural dolphin handles from neck rim to shoulder, the body decorated w/a wide band of colors, h.p. flowers & green leaves flanked by narrow double gilt bands, designed by G.F. Hetesch, painted in the manner of Johan-Laurents Jensen, ca. 1840, triple-wave & dot mark in underglaze-blue .................... **6,037.00**

# ROYAL COPLEY

*Royal Copley was a trade name used by the Spaulding China Company of Sebring, Ohio during the 1940s and 1950s for a variety of ceramic figurines, planters and other decorative pieces. Similar pieces were also produced under the trade name "Royal Windsor" as well as the Spaulding China mark.*

*The Spaulding China Company stopped producing in 1957 but for the next two years other potteries finished production of their outstanding orders. Today these originally inexpensive wares are developing a dedicated collector following.*

**Head vase,** Colonial Man .......... **$55.00**

**Head vase,** Colonial Woman ........ **55.00**

**Model of bird on stump** .............. **20.00**

**Model of a dog,** 6½" h. ................. **26.00**

**Model of a dog by suitcase** ........ **35.00**

**Model of a dog in basket** ............ **30.00**

**Model of a dog w/wagon** ............. **25.00**

**Model of a duck,** baby mallard .... **15.00**

**Model of a duck,** mallard by stump ......................................... **30.00**

**Model of a hen,** Royal Windsor
mark, 6½" h............................... **25.00**
**Model of an apple**....................... **28.00**
**Planter,** angel w/star.................... **28.00**
**Planter,** barefoot girl, red trim,
7½" h......................................... **30.00**
**Planter,** model of a dog, Spaniel,
7¾" h......................................... **26.00**
**Planter,** model of a deer & a
fawn, 9" h. ................................. **26.00**
**Planter,** model of a dog at
mailbox, black & white ............... **75.00**
**Planter,** model of horse head,
yellow mane............................... **30.00**
**Planter,** model of a running horse.. **16.00**
**Planter,** model of a deer .............. **25.00**
**Smoking set,** mallard duck
decoration, 3 pcs. ...................... **35.00**
**Wall pocket,** model of a dog
head, Cocker Spaniel ................ **35.00**

# ROYAL DUX

*Ornate Royal Dux Centerpiece*

*This factory in Bohemia was noted for
the figural porcelain wares in the Art
Nouveau style which were exported
around the turn of the century. Other
notable figural pieces were produced
through the 1930s and the factory was
nationalized after World War II.*

*Royal Dux Marks*

*Royal Dux Water Carriers*

**Bust of a female nude,** emerging
form w/curling waves, long
flowing hair, white, gold & black
highlights, pink triangle mark,
large ..................................... **$1,250.00**
**Centerpiece,** an ornate oblong
dish w/deep undulating sides &
rim, the side applied w/large
flower blossoms & each rim
applied w/a full-length floating
Art Nouveau maiden w/flowing
robes, all hand-decorated,
7 x 15", 9" h. (ILLUS. bottom
previous column) ...................... **489.00**
**Figures,** woman wearing loose
beige robe, green cap & green
apron filled with flowers, holding
flowers near head of sheep,
man wearing beige robe & green
animal skin over shoulder & tied
around waist, standing next to
goat, both on base w/floral
decoration & green trim, pr. ... **1,250.00**
**Figures,** a young woman & a
young man, each dressed in
peasant outfits & leaning against
a wellhead filling either a jug or
a tall pitcher, round bases, each
w/polychrome decoration, late
19th - early 20th c., each
23½" h., pr. (ILLUS. above) ...... **605.00**
**Model of a dog,** a recumbent
German Shepherd w/an alert
pose........................ **100.00 to 150.00**

**Model of an elephant,** trunk up,
10 x 13".................................... **195.00**

**Vase,** 20½" h., 7½" d., decorated
w/raised blackberries, vines &
leaves on an ivory ground,
unmarked................................. **300.00**

# ROYAL RUDOLSTADT

*Ornate Royal Rudolstadt Urn*

    *This factory began as a faience pottery established in 1720. E. Bohne made hard paste porcelain wares from 1852 to 1920, when the factory became a branch of Heubach Brothers. The factory is still producing in what was East Germany.*

*Royal Rudolstadt Mark*

**Bowl,** 9½" d., interior decorated
w/three bouquets of pink roses
& green leaves on cream
ground, scalloped edge trimmed
in gold, artist-signed.................. **$75.00**

**Chocolate set:** 10½" h. cov.
chocolate pot & four 3" h. cups &
saucers; all w/a creamy ground
decorated w/yellow & white
roses, green leaves & gold
handles, artist-signed, the set... **400.00**

**Ice cream set:** rectangular
master tray & six small plates;
bluebird decoration, artist-
signed, 7 pcs.............................. **95.00**

**Urn,** cov., a tall square plinth
base supports a short pedestal
& the large ovoid body tapering
to a short, slender waisted
cylindrical neck fitted w/a high
domed cover w/knob finial,
curved loop gilt mask side
shoulder handles, the front of
the body painted w/a large oval
reserve of a young woman
wearing a low-cut gown
exposing her breasts, within a
'jeweled' oval frame against a
cobalt blue ground trimmed
w/ornate gilt scrolling foliage,
further gilt scrolling on the
shoulders, neck, cover, pedestal
& base, the reverse of the body
decorated w/leafage suspending
floral garlands, titled
"Printemps," artist-signed,
stamped factory mark &
impressed "7671," late 19th c.,
one handle restored, overall
24" h. (ILLUS. top previous
column) ................................. **2,300.00**

**Vase,** 14¼" h., molded body
w/pierced handles, a narrow
neck w/a flared & shaped
mouth, shell pink & cream
shaded ground decorated
w/bouquets of small yellow &
blue flowers, late 19th c. ........... **395.00**

# ROYAL VIENNA

    *The second factory in Europe to make hard paste porcelain was established in Vienna in 1719 by Claud Innocentius de Paquier. The factory underwent various changes of administration through the years and finally closed in 1865. Since then, however, the porcelain has been reproduced by various factories in Austria and Germany, many of which have also reproduced the early beehive mark. Early pieces, naturally, bring far higher prices than the later ones or the reproductions.*

*Royal Vienna Heart Bowl*

*Royal Vienna Mark*

**Bowl,** 10½" w., 3" h., heart-shaped w/a fluted flower & scroll-molded rim, center floral decoration & dark rose side panels, leafy pale green & yellow borders w/gold trim (ILLUS. top next column) ........ **$185.00**

**Candlesticks,** scenic decoration on a maroon & gold ground, after Angelica Kauffmann, 5½" h., pr. ................................ **495.00**

**Centerpiece,** cov., the tapering ovoid two-handled body raised on an oval foot, one side painted w/a scene of a young maiden surrounded by putti playing the mandolin, the other w/a reclining woman shaking a tambourine before two dancing putti, titled on the back in red "Tanz Musik," underglaze-blue shield mark, ca. 1900, 11" h. ..................... **1,725.00**

**Charger,** round, a wide paneled border band w/gilt scrolling designs on a dark ground surrounding an ornate gilt field centered by a large rectangular panel w/a colorful classical allegorical scene w/three ladies & a bound cupid in a landscape, pseudo-shield mark in blue, impressed "Carl Knoll Carlsbad 33 0," late 19th c., 19" d. ......... **4,025.00**

*Ornate Royal Vienna Plate*

**Plaque,** round, a classical landscape scene depicting Europa seated upon Jupiter disguised as a bull while her maidens adorn him w/garlands & ribbons, artist-signed & titled in German on the back, pseudo-shield mark in underglaze-blue, in a square giltwood frame w/delicate molded scrolls at each corner, late 19th c., 24" d. ....... **8,050.00**

**Plate,** 9½" d., a central classical scene showing a semi-nude Venus teasingly holding aloft the bow & arrows belonging to the young Cupid who reaches for them, the wide border w/alternating panels of ornate scrolls on a dark ground & gilt-trimmed landscape scenes, blue shield mark & titled in black, late 19th c. (ILLUS. bottom, this column) ................................... **805.00**

**Urn,** cov., the shouldered wide baluster-form body decorated

*Portrait Vase by Royal Vienna*

w/a wide band featuring a classical period scene reserved on a cobalt blue & gilt ground, scroll-trimmed female term gilt-bronze shoulder handles & domed scrolled gilt-bronze foot, the domed cover in cobalt blue w/gilt vine decoration & a gilt bud finial, scene titled on base "Golden Age," 19th c., overall 15½" h. (some restoration) .... **1,320.00**

**Vase,** 9½" h., simple baluster-form body w/gently flaring neck, the cobalt blue ground decorated w/delicate gilt scrolls & banding & a large oval medallion portrait of a late 18th c. lady wearing a large plumed hat, artist-signed, printed mark, ca. 1880 (ILLUS. above) ...................................... **575.00**

# ROYAL WORCESTER

*This porcelain has been made by the Royal Worcester Porcelain Co. at Worcester, England, from 1862 to the present. For earlier porcelain made in Worcester, see WORCESTER. Royal Worcester is distinguished from those wares made at Worcester between 1751 and 1862 that are referred to as only Worcester by collectors.*

*Royal Worcester Marks*

**Bowl,** 3" d., fluted, decorated w/h.p. flowers ........................... **$55.00**

**Butter dish, cover & drainer,** acanthus leaf molding on rim of base & around pine cone finial of the domed cover, typically gilded multicolored flowers, shape No. 1393, ca. 1890, 5¾" h. ......... **525.00**

**Candle snuffer,** figural French nun, ca. 1900 ........................... **158.00**

**Dinner service:** twelve each of dinner plates, rimmed bowls, luncheon & salad plates, finger bowls, butter pats, tea cups & saucers, a demitasse cov. pot & five cov. servers, a cov. tureen, five platters & approximately ten miscellaneous serving pieces; each piece decorated w/blue impatiens in a wide border band against a white ground, dated 1889, the set (ILLUS. of part, next page) ............................... **3,335.00**

**Ewer,** footed bulbous body w/an ornate handle & rim, decorated w/h.p. florals, dated 1890, 10" h. ......................................... **295.00**

**Figure,** "Boy with Paroquet," designed by F. Doughty, No. 3087, 1935, 6¾" h. ............. **150.00**

**Figure,** Cairo Water Carrier, a standing Arab man in traditional costume holding a large amphora in his hands, on a rounded rockwork base, enameled decoration, 1895, 8¾" h. ............. **633.00**

**Figure,** "December," signed F. Doughty, No. 3458, 1949, 6½" h. ......................................... **189.00**

**Figure,** "Lisette," by Ruth Van Ruychevelt, limited edition of 500, 1958 ................................ **750.00**

**Figure,** "Monday's Child," signed F. Doughty, No. 3519, 7½" h. ... **127.00**

*Royal Worcester Dinner Service*

**Figure,** "October," young boy
w/squirrels, he dressed in yellow
& blue, signed F. Doughty,
No. 3417, 1947, 7¾" h. ............ **189.00**

**Figure,** a Politician, a chubby
standing man wearing a long
overcoat w/his hands in his
pockets, a floppy hat on his
head, on a square base
w/chamfered corners, white-
glazed, late 19th c., 5¼" h.
(staining, chip to hat brim
restored) .................................. **288.00**

**Figure,** "Tommy," designed by
F. Doughty, No. 2913, 4½" h. ... **225.00**

**Figures,** a lady & a gentleman in
late Georgian costume ca. 1800,
she walking & wearing a turban,
shawl, long dress & carrying a
muff, he walking & wearing a top
hat, tail coat, cravat, waistcoat,
pants & high boats, each on a
rounded rockwork base,
decorated w/enamels, signed
"Hadley," 7¾" h. & 8¼" h.,
pr ........................................... **1,093.00**

**Fish plates,** each round plate
decorated w/a gilt lattice &
foliate border surrounding an
enamel-decorated h.p. fish,
artist-signed, printed marks,
ca. 1940, 9¼" d., set of 13 ..... **2,300.00**

**Model of Dairy Shorthorn bull,**
designed by Doris Lindner,
No. 3781, 1964, limited edition
of 500 ...................................... **700.00**

*Royal Worcester Floral-decorated Vase*

**Pitcher,** miniature, 1⅜" h., bird
decoration on a beige ground,
gold trim, ca. 1900 ..................... **88.00**

**Pitcher,** ice-type, 10" h., tusk-
shaped, No. 1116, ca. 1885...... **235.00**

**Vase,** 7½" d., 3" h., squatty
bulbous base w/slightly flared
rim, 4" d. collar carved &
reticulated, the body decorated
w/a detailed scene of five
swallows in flight, ca. 1903 ....... **965.00**

**Vase,** 15¾" h., bottle-form, the
tapering ovoid body raised on a
flaring gilt-trimmed foot, the sides
tapering to a slender 'stick' neck
w/flared & incurved mouth, looped
gilt dragon-form handles on the
neck, the body & neck decorated
w/colorful enameled floral sprays,
1888 (gilt rim wear) ..................... **748.00**

**Vases,** 7½" h., urn-form, a slender pedestal base supports a shouldered ovoid body below a wide, flaring neck flanked by gilt S-scroll handles, the body w/a red ground decorated w/a large colorful floral cartouche within gilt scroll borders, the ivory rim & pedestal w/gilt trim, printed marks, ca. 1901, pr. (ILLUS. of one, bottom right previous page) ..... **1,955.00**

# ROZENBURG DEN HAAG

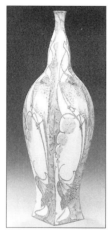

*Rare Rozenburg den Haag Vase*

This Dutch earthenware and porcelain factory was established in 1855 at The Hague. It is noted for the exceptionally thin earthenware made in the late 19th and early 20th centuries. Subtle shapes and fine enameled decoration combine to make it an exquisite production greatly influenced by the Art Nouveau movement. The ware was marked "Rozenburg den Haag" with a stork and crown.

*Rozenburg Den Haag Mark*

**Vase,** bud, 4¾" h., the bulbous bottle-form body w/a squared base, delicately painted w/morning glories, wildflowers & leafage in shades of green, yellow, red & ochre, reserved against a striated ground, decorated by Sam Schellink, printed mark "Rozenburg Den Haag," dated 1908 & numbered "282" ..................................... **$3,737.00**

**Vase,** 12½" h., the squared ovoid body tapering to a swelled neck w/a tiny flared rim, delicately painted w/parrots perched amid foliage, in shades of yellow, red, green, orange, blue, olive green, purple & aquamarine, reserved against a cross-hatched ground, printed mark & painted date of 1900 & numbered "1331," artist monogram of W.P. Hartgring (ILLUS. previous column) .... **10,925.00**

# R.S. PRUSSIA & RELATED WARES

*Ornately decorated china marked "R.S. Prussia" and "R.S. Germany" continues to grow in popularity. According to the Third Series of Mary Frank Gaston's* Encyclopedia of R.S. Prussia, *these marks were used by the Reinhold Schlegelmilch porcelain factories located in Suhl in the Germanic region known as Prussia prior to World War I, and in Tillowitz, Silesia which became part of Poland after World War II. Other marks sought by collectors include "R.S. Suhl," R.S." steeple or church marks, and "R.S. Poland."*

*The Suhl factory was founded by Reinhold Schlegelmilch in 1869 and closed in 1917. The Tillowitz factory was established in 1895 by Erhard Schlegelmilch, Reinhold's son. This china customarily bears the phrase "R.S. Germany" and "R.S. Tillowitz." The Tillowitz factory closed in 1945, but it was re-opened for a few years under Polish administration. The "R.S. Poland" mark is attributed to that later time period.*

*Prices are high and collectors should beware of the forgeries that sometimes find their way to the market. Mold names and numbers are taken from Mary Gaston's books on R.S. Prussia.*

*The "R.S. Prussia" mark and the "R.S. Suhl" mark have been reproduced, so buy with care.*

*Collectors are also interested in the porcelain products made by the Erdmann Schlegelmilch factory. This factory was founded by three brothers in Suhl in 1861. They named the factory in honor of ther father, Erdmann Schlegelmilch. A variety of marks incorporating the "E.S." initials were used. The factory closed ca. 1935. The Erdmann Schlegelmilch factory was an earlier and entirely separate business from the Reinhold Schlegelmilch factory. The two were not related to each other.*

*R.S. Germany Cup & Saucer*

## R.S. GERMANY

**Berry set:** 9" master bowl & six matching 5½" sauce dishes; Iris mold, decorated w/large red roses, 7 pcs. ...........................**$495.00**

**Bowl,** handled, Lebrun portrait, Tiffany finish, artist's palette, paintbrush ................................**900.00**

**Creamer,** Mold 640, decorated w/roses, gold trim on ruffled rim & ornate handle ...........................**35.00**

**Cup & saucer,** decorated w/blue, black & white bands on beige lustre ground, cup has center silhouette of Art Deco lady in blue dancing w/blue scarf, cup 3½" d., 2¼" h., saucer 5¾" d. (ILLUS.) .....................................**88.00**

**Mustard jar,** cov., calla lily decoration ...................................**40.00**

**Salad set:** 10½" d. lettuce bowl & six 8" d. matching plates; Mold 12, Iris decoration on pearl luster finish, 7 pcs. .....................**250.00**

**Toothpick holder,** two-handled, decorated w/roses & gold trim, artist-signed ................................**60.00**

## R.S. PRUSSIA

**Bell,** tall trumpet-form ruffled body w/twig handle, decorated w/small purple flowers & green leaves on white ground, unmarked, 3½" h........................**285.00**

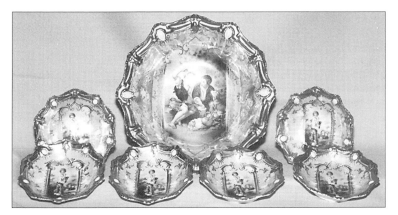

*Ribbon & Jewel Melon Eaters Berry Set*

**Berry set:** master bowl & six sauce dishes; Ribbon & Jewel mold w/Melon Eaters decoration, 7 pcs. (ILLUS. bottom previous page) ............**3,750.00**

**Bowl,** 9¾" d., Iris variant mold, rosette center & pale green floral decoration .................................**255.00**

**Bowl,** 10½" d., Point & Clover mold (Mold 82), decorated w/forget-me-nots & roses, satin finish, artist-signed....................**315.00**

**Bowl,** 10¾" d., Mold 217, "tapestry" center mill scene, gilt scroll border (ILLUS. top next column)...........**1,185.00**

**Bowl,** 11" d., 3" h., Fishscale mold, decorated w/white lilies on purple & orange lustre ground, artist-signed ..............................**325.00**

**Cake plate,** open-handled, Medallion mold, center Flora portrait, Tiffany finish w/four cupid medallions, unmarked, 10½" d.......................................**890.00**

**Cake plate,** open-handled, Carnation mold (Mold 28), dark pink roses against teal & green w/gold trim, 11" d. ......................**225.00**

**Celery tray,** Ribbon & Jewel mold (Mold 18), pink roses & white snowball blossoms within a wide cobalt blue border w/gilt trim, 12" l...........................................**275.00**

**Celery tray,** Mold 254, decorated w/green & pink roses, lavish gold tracery, artist-signed, 12" l...........................................**280.00**

**Chocolate cup & saucer,** footed, egg-shaped cup, pink & white poppies decoration ....**100.00 to 125.00**

**Chocolate set:** 10" h. cov. chocolate pot & four cups & saucers; Mold 729, pansy decoration w/gold trim, the set .....**900.00**

**Coffeepot,** cov., Mold 517, raised floral designs as part of border, unmarked..................................**250.00**

**Cracker jar,** cov., Mold 634, molded feet, surreal dogwood blossoms decoration on pearlized lustre finish, 8" d., 6½" h.......................................**245.00**

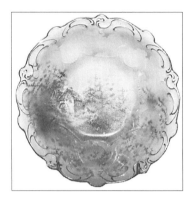

*Rare "Tapestry" Bowl*

**Cracker jar,** cov., Mold 704, grape leaf decoration, 7" h.........**440.00**

**Creamer & cov. sugar bowl,** Ribbon and Jewel mold, single Melon Eaters decoration, pr. ..**1,800.00**

**Cup & saucer,** decorated w/pink roses, peg feet & scalloped rim, cup 1¾" h., saucer, 4¼" d., pr................................................**120.00**

**Dessert set:** pedestal cup & saucer, creamer & sugar bowl, two 9¾" d. handled plates, eleven 7¼" d. plates, nine cups & saucers, oversized creamer & sugar bowl; plain mold, decorated w/pink poppies w/tints of aqua, yellow & purple, all pieces are matching, the set ..................................**1,975.00**

**Model of a lady's slipper,** embossed scrolling on instep & heel & embossed feather on one side of slipper, a dotted medallion w/roses & lily-of-the-valley on the other, shaded turquoise blue w/fancy rim trimmed w/gold, 8" l. ..................**245.00**

**Mustache cup,** Mold 502 ...........**265.00**

**Mustard pot,** cov., Mold 509a, decorated w/white flowers, glossy light green ground...........**150.00**

**Nut bowl,** footed, Point & Clover mold, decorated w/ten roses in shades of salmon, yellow & rose against a pink, green & gold lustre-finished ground, 6½" d.........................................**185.00**

*Mold 91 Rose-decorated Plate*

**Pitcher,** tankard, 10" h., Mold 584, decorated w/hanging basket of pink & white roses ......**725.00**

**Plate,** 7½" d., Carnation mold, decorated w/pink roses, lavender ground, satin finish......**225.00**

**Plate,** 8¾" d., Mold 91, yellow roses decoration on pink ground, shiny yellow border (ILLUS. above)..........................**150.00**

**Plate,** 9" d., Mold 343, spring figural scenic decoration in keyhole medallion, iridescent Tiffany purple finish at base of figure, gold finish around portrait decorated w/small pink roses .......................................**1,900.00**

**Relish dish,** Mold 82, decorated w/forget-me-knots & multicolored carnations, six jeweled domes .....................**125.00**

**Spooner/vase,** Mold 502, three-handled, decorated w/delicate roses & gold trim, unsigned, 4¼" h............................................**75.00**

**Syrup pitcher & underplate,** Mold 507, white & pink roses on a shaded brown to pale yellow ground, 2 pcs. ............................**245.00**

**Tea set,** child's: cov. teapot & four cups & saucers; decorated w/roses, the set..........................**595.00**

**Toothpick holder,** Stippled Floral mold (Mold 23), white floral decoration .................................**135.00**

**Vase,** 4" h., salesman's sample, handled, Mold 914, decorated

*Rare Melon Eaters Vases*

w/large lilies & green foliage, raised beading around shoulder, gold handles, shaded green ground, artist-signed .................**145.00**

**Vase,** 8" h., cylindrical body w/incurved angled shoulder handles, decorated w/parrots on white satin ground, unmarked...............................**2,025.00**

**Vases,** 11¾" h., Mold 901, footed slightly tapering cylindrical body w/a high flaring cupped deeply fluted neck w/jewels, beading & jewels around the shoulder & foot, ornate scrolled gilt handles, Melon Eaters decoration against a shaded dark green ground, pr. (ILLUS. above).........................**3,600.00**

## OTHER MARKS

**Bowl,** 10" d., shallow w/very ornate, large Flora portrait, front pose past waist, floral garland, veiling, four different cameo portraits of Flora, wide Tiffany border, lavish gold (E.S. Prov. Saxe)..........................**950.00**

**Chocolate pot,** cov., lemon yellow ground w/Art Deco decoration & gold trim (R.S. Tillowitz - Silesia) ......................**150.00**

**Fernery,** pedestal base, decorated w/pink & white roses, mother-of-pearl finish (R.S. Poland) ......................................**450.00**

**Plate,** 8" d., peafowl decoration
(R.S. Tillowitz - Silesia)..............**125.00**

**Plate,** 10½" d., lovely center
portrait of Madame DuBarry,
four cameos in different poses
on a deep burgundy lustre
border band (E.S. Prov. Saxe)...**400.00**

**Relish dish,** woman's portrait
w/shadow flowers & vine border
on green ground, 8" l. (E.S.
Germany Royal Saxe) ................**72.00**

**Server,** center-handled,
decorated w/orange, white &
pink poppies on a shaded bluish
grey ground w/a narrow gilt
border band, 8½" d., 3¾" h.,
E. Schlegelmilch - Thuringia .....**100.00**

**Vase,** miniature, 3½" h.,
cylindrical body w/a rounded
shoulder tapering to a tiny rolled
neck, decorated w/a colored
scene of crowned cranes (R.S.
Poland) .....................................**410.00**

**Vase,** 7½" h., wide squatty bulbous
base tapering sharply to a tall
slender cylindrical neck w/an
upturned four-lobed rim, long
slender gold handles from rim to
shoulder, decorated w/a center
reserve of a standing Art Nouveau
maiden w/her hands behind her
head & a peacock behind her
framed by delicate gold scrolls &
beading & floral bouquets all on a
pearl lustre ground (Prov. Saxe -
E.S. Germany) ............................**395.00**

**Vase,** 13½" h., twisted gold
handles, portrait of "Goddess of
Fire," iridescent burgundy &
opalescent colors w/lavish gold
(Prov. Saxe - E.S. Germany) .....**650.00**

**Vases,** 10" h., gently swelled
body tapering to narrow rounded
shoulders & a short flaring
scalloped neck, ornate C-scroll
gilt shoulder handles, gold neck
band, the body decorated w/a
colored scene of a sheepherder
leading his flock toward a mill in
the background, trees overhead,
the second identical except w/a
cottage scene, R.S. Poland, pr.
(ILLUS. of one) ..........................**640.00**

*R.S. Poland Landscape Vase*

# RUSSEL WRIGHT DESIGNS

*The innovative dinnerwares designed by Russel Wright and produced by various companies beginning in the late 1930s were an immediate success with a society that was turning to a more casual and informal lifestyle. His designs, with their flowing lines and unconventional shapes, were produced in many different colors which allowed the hostess to arrange a creative table. Although not antique, these designs, which we list below by line and manufacturer, are highly collectible. In addition to dinnerwares, Wright was also known as a trend-setter in the design of furniture, glassware, lamps, fabrics and a multitude of other household goods.*

*Russel Wright Marks*

### AMERICAN MODERN (Steubenville Pottery Company)

**Bowl,** fruit, lug handle, bean
brown ........................................ **$20.00**

Bowl, fruit, lug handle,
chartreuse .................................. **12.00**
Bowl, salad, coral ......................... **45.00**
Bowl, soup, lug handle, bean
brown ......................................... **22.00**
Casserole, cov., stick handle,
coral .......................................... **30.00**
Casserole, cov., stick handle,
seafoam blue ............................. **55.00**
Celery tray, slender oblong
shape w/asymmetrical incurved
sides, bean brown....................... **24.00**
Celery tray, slender oblong
shape w/asymmetrical incurved
sides, white ................................ **30.00**
Coffeepot, cov., demitasse,
white ........................................ **110.00**
Creamer & cov. sugar bowl,
chartreuse, pr............................. **15.00**
Cup & saucer, demitasse, cedar
green.......................................... **16.00**
Cup & saucer, bean brown .......... **22.00**
Cup & saucer, coral ...................... **8.00**
Pitcher, cov., chartreuse ............ **150.00**
Pitcher w/ice lip, white.............. **195.00**
Pitcher, water, 12" h., black
chutney ...................................... **85.00**
Pitcher, water, 12" h., chartreuse ... **60.00**
Plate, bread & butter, 6¼" d.,
coral ............................................ **4.00**
Plate, salad, 8" d., bean brown ..... **20.00**
Plate, dinner, 10" d., bean brown.. **22.00**
Plate, dinner, 10" d., coral.............. **8.00**
Plate, chop, 13" sq., chartreuse.... **30.00**
Platter, 13¾" l., bean
brown........................... **40.00 to 50.00**
Platter, 13¾" l., coral ................... **20.00**
Ramekin, cov., chartreuse...........**125.00**
Relish dish, divided w/raffia
handle, seafoam blue ............... **185.00**
Salad fork & spoon, chartreuse,
pr.................................................. **85.00**
Salt & pepper shakers,
chartreuse, pr............................. **12.00**
Salt & pepper shakers, coral, pr. .. **12.00**
Teapot, cov., granite grey ............ **45.00**
Vegetable dish, open, oval,
10" l., coral ................................. **15.00**
Vegetable dish, open, divided,
granite grey ................................ **50.00**

Woodfield salad spoon,
chartreuse .................................. **45.00**

## CASUAL CHINA (Iroquois China Company)

Bowl, cereal or soup, cov., ice
blue ........................................... **14.00**
Butter dish, cov., avocado
yellow......................................... **45.00**
Butter dish, cov.,
charcoal.................... **100.00 to 125.00**
Butter dish, cov., lemon yellow.. **125.00**
Carafe, cov., lettuce green, 10" h...**125.00**
Carafe, cov., sugar white, 10" h.. **145.00**
Casserole, cov., ice blue, 2 qt. ..... **45.00**
Casserole, cov., ripe apricot, 2 qt. .. **20.00**
Coffeepot, demitasse, ice blue... **135.00**
Coffeepot, demitasse, nutmeg
brown, 4½" h...............................**125.00**
Creamer, restyled, cantaloupe ..... **65.00**
Cup & saucer, cantaloupe ........... **25.00**
Dutch oven, cov., lettuce green,
6 qt............................................. **95.00**
Gravy w/attached undertray,
avocado yellow .......................... **75.00**
Gumbo soup bowl, handled, ice
blue, 21 oz. ................................ **25.00**
Gumbo soup bowl, handled,
lemon yellow, 21 oz. .................. **38.00**
Mug, ice blue, 13 oz...................... **70.00**
Mug, nutmeg brown, 13 oz. .......... **35.00**
Pitcher, water, avocado yellow... **125.00**
Pitcher, water, sugar white ......... **145.00**
Pitcher, water, restyled, pink
sherbet....................................... **50.00**
Plate, bread & butter, 6" d.,
cantaloupe ................................. **12.00**
Plate, bread & butter, 6" d., oyster
grey............................................ **10.00**
Plate, dinner, 10" d., cantaloupe... **27.00**
Teapot, cov., ice blue .................. **75.00**
Teapot, cov., restyled, ice blue... **100.00**
Teapot, cov., restyled, lemon
yellow........................................**125.00**
Vegetable bowl, cov., divided,
ice blue, 10" d. ........................... **45.00**
Vegetable bowl, cov., divided,
nutmeg brown, 10" d.................. **20.00**
Vegetable bowl, cov., divided,
ripe apricot, 10" d....................... **45.00**

# SAN ILDEFONSO (Maria) POTTERY

*A thin-walled and crudely polished blackware has been made at most Rio Grande Pueblos. Around 1918 a San Ildefonso Pueblo woman, Maria Montoya Martinez and her husband, Julian, began making a thicker walled blackware with a finely polished gunmetal black sheen. It was fired in the traditional manner using manure to smother the firing process and produce the black coloration. The following is a chronology of Maria's varied signatures: Marie, mid to late teens-1934; Marie & Julian, 1934-43; Maria & Santana, 1943-56; Maria & Popovi, 1956-71; and Maria Poveka, used on undecorated wares after 1956. Maria died in July of 1980. Rosalia, Tonita, Blue Corn and other signatures might also be found on pottery made at the San Ildefonso Pueblo. Considered a true artistic achievement, early items signed by Maria, or her contemporaries, command good prices. It should be noted that the strong pottery tradition is being carried on by current potters.*

**Jar,** spherical body w/flat mouth, carved & polished blackware avanyu (water serpent) on matte ground, signed "Rose," Rose Gonzales, ca. 1930s, original price tag, 4¾" d., 3" h. (some wear to polished surfaces) ...... **$220.00**

**Jar,** squatty bulbous body w/flat mouth, carved & polished blackware w/scalloped design, signed "Rose," Rose Gonzales, ca. 1935, original price tag, 5¼" d., 3" h. (misfired brown area) ........................................ **193.00**

**Jar,** squatty bulbous form w/steeply angled shoulder to flat mouth, carved & polished redware w/geometric design, signed "Rose," Rose Gonzales, ca. 1935, original price tag, 4¼" d., 3¼" h. .......................... **193.00**

**Jar,** squatty bulbous body tapering to flat mouth, black on blackware, signed "Marie &

Julian," Marie & Julian Martinez, 5⅞" d., 4¼" h. (minor wear & rim has either been varnished or repainted)............................... **1,265.00**

**Jar,** squatty bulbous body tapering to flat mouth, redware w/carved avanyu (water serpent) around shoulder, early Rose Gonzales piece w/exceptional polish, signed "Rose," w/original price tag, 7¼" d., 4½" h. (minor wear & tiny rim flake) ................ **495.00**

**Vase,** 7½" h., very wide bulbous ovoid body tapering to a flat mouth, black on blackware, lightly etched decoration of a stylized, grotesque creature w/large eyes & long horns, its open mouth exposes prominent teeth & a crooked arrow for a tongue, six pointed legs support the long-tailed body, all under two delicate bands in a design of dots, matte & glossy glazes, script signature "Maria" .......... **3,300.00**

# SASCHA BRASTOFF

*Even though Sascha Brastoff experimented with different materials and had a natural talent for sculpting, it was not until November 1953 that he felt his unique ability in ceramic design was recognized. His friend, Winthrop Rockefeller, backed him in a large, newly constructed showplace encompassing a full block on Olympic Boulevard in downtown Los Angeles, California. Brastoff designed each piece personally and the Brastoff-trained employees produced them. He created a full line of hand-painted china in about twelve designs. A pottery dinnerware line named "Surf Ballet," a marbleized treatment usually in gold and pink or silver and blue, was marketed. Artware items with patterns such as "Star Steed," a leaping fantasy horse and "Rooftops," a village scene with a batik look, are popular items. Hard-to-find resin items are an example of Brastoff's diversified talents. A line of enamels on copper was also made. Pieces signed "Sascha B." were done by his artisans; those with the full "Sascha Brastoff" signature were personally hand-painted by him. The chanticleer was a Brastoff trademark used as a backstamp in conjunction with the signature marks. Because of health problems Brastoff left his company in 1963; it would be another ten years before the business closed. Sascha Brastoff died February 4, 1993.*

Sascha Brastoff Marks

**Ashtray,** Western scene w/covered wagon, rare promotional piece, 14" w......... **$165.00**

**Ashtray,** floral decoration, No. 110AC ................................. **45.00**

**Ashtray,** round, leaf decoration, full signature, large ................... **350.00**

**Bowl,** 8" d., footed, abstract design ........................................ **38.00**

**Box,** cov., Jewel Bird decoration, No. 020 ...................................... **60.00**

**Candleholder,** resin, green or blue, 6" h., each ......................... **50.00**

**Cigarette box,** cov., Rooftops patt., No. 021, 8" l. ...................... **45.00**

**Cigarette box,** cov., "Star Steed" decoration .................................**125.00**

**Compote,** polar bear decoration, No. 085 ...................................... **65.00**

**Dish,** horse decoration on green ground, 6½" sq............................ **28.00**

**Dish,** three-footed, fish-shaped (flounder), house decoration, 8¼ x 8½"..................................... **80.00**

**Lamp base,** mosaic tile, 27" h. ... **175.00**

**Model of a polar bear,** blue resin, 10" h................................ **275.00**

**Model of a rooster,** mosaic design, 15" h. ............................ **450.00**

**Plate,** square, vegetable decoration, full signature........... **275.00**

**Tray,** 7" sq., floral decoration, marked "Sample" under glaze .... **75.00**

---

# SATSUMA

*Rare Satsuma Bowl*

*These decorated wares have been produced in Japan since the end of the 18th century. The early pieces are scarce and high-priced. Later Satsuma wares are plentiful and, with prices rising, as highly collectible as earlier pieces.*

**Bowl,** 4¾" d., rounded sides turning in toward a hexagonal rim, overall overlapping floral design, base w/seal & signature, late 19th c. .............................. **$259.00**

**Bowl,** 16" d., 8¼" h., a narrow footring supports the deep rounded sides, the interior decorated w/overlapping chrysanthemums, the exterior w/two panels, one depicting a cockerel & quail in a flowering landscape, the other w/adults & children by a riverside, divided by vertical bands each w/a central roundel containing a phoenix, patterned lappet border below the rim, Meiji Period, signed "Dai Nihon, Kyoto, Tojiki Goshigaisha, Ryozan Sho" above a Shimazu mon (ILLUS. above) ............. **17,250.00**

**Plaque,** pierced to hang, landscape scene w/floral border in polychrome & gilt, artist-signed, 9¾ x 12" ................... **1,760.00**

**Tea set:** 6½" h. cov. teapot, creamer, cov. sugar bowl, six cups & saucers & six 7¼" d. plates; each piece w/a paneled design of courtesans in courtyard settings, ca. 1900, the set ..................................... **288.00**

**Tray,** rectangular w/scalloped corners, decorated w/women playing a game in a garden setting, a border of colorful fans, signed "Ryozan," 19th c., 6½ x 9⅜" (chip, wear) .......... **1,265.00**

**Vase,** 6" h., cylindrical body w/three small cloud-form feet, decorated w/fan-shaped cartouches depicting Samurai & figures in a garden, on a floral & patterned ground, 19th c. (signature worn) ..................... **1,035.00**

**Vase,** 12" h., wide ovoid body tapering to a short flared neck, raised on a high domed base w/short scalloped legs, geometric banded borders at the top & base w/the body decorated w/a large landscape scene of an artist decorating scrolls w/trees, flowers & birds in the background, late 19th c. (feet repairs)............................... **259.00**

**Vase,** 22" h., 9" d., decorated w/three figures, elaborate gold trim & white beading & outlining, ornate handles ......................... **375.00**

**Vases,** 10" h., tall squared form, each side decorated w/figures at various pursuits within medallions reserved on a red & gold ground, signed in red, 19th c., pr. ............ **440.00**

---

# SCHAFER & VATER

*Founded in Rudolstadt, Thuringia, Germany in 1890, the Schafer and Vater Porcelain Factory specialized in decorative pieces of porcelain usually in white or colored bisque. They produced many novelty figural items such as creamers, toothpick holders, boxes and hatpin holders and also produced a line of jasper ware with white relief decoration in imitation of the famous Wedgwood jasper wares. The firm also decorated white ware blanks.*

*The company ceased production in 1962 and collectors now seek out their charming pieces which may be marked with a crown over a starburst containing the script letter "R."*

*Schafer & Vater Mark*

*Schafer & Vater Ashtrays & Match Holder*

**Ashtray,** figural, Dutch boy & girl w/match strikers on their bottoms, standing on white base in front of ashtray inscribed "Waiting for the Smacks," small holder for matches, 3" d., 3¾" h. (ILLUS. right, bottom previous page)...................................... **$150.00**

**Ashtray,** figural, little boy & little girl w/green hair ribbon white rabbits on one corner, white doves on other, inscribed on front "Everybody's Doing it," unmarked, 3⅜" d., 4" h. (ILLUS. left, bottom previous page) ....... **135.00**

**Bottle w/original stopper,** decorated w/a little child imbibing from a whiskey bottle & the quote "A Wee Scotch"........... **79.00**

**Bottle w/original stopper,** figural, a standing old woman w/her hair pulled into a bun, her smiling head forming the stopper, her long neck forming the bottle neck, wearing a cloak & long dress w/her hands held in front, mottled dark brown glossy glaze, 2¾" d., 5¾" h. .............................**125.00**

**Creamer,** figural girl holding a duck, 4½" h. .............................. **150.00**

**Jar,** cov., jasper ware, decorated w/white relief Grecian figures & female bust, medallion cover, background in shades of greens, pink, grey & white ......................**125.00**

**Match holder,** figural, round base w/Scotsman wearing a short kilt, red jacket & hat, drinking from a cup & standing by match holder barrel marked "The Thirsty First," unmarked, 2⅛" d., 4¼" h. (ILLUS. center, bottom previous page)........................................ **145.00**

**Teapot,** cov., jasper ware, globular body, light green ground, decorated w/scroll-bordered white relief cartouches front & back showing white relief courting couple on blue ground, cartouches of white relief birds on blue ground on cover, 4½" h. (ILLUS. top next column) .......... **190.00**

*Schafer & Vater Jasper Teapot*

**Vase,** 9" h., jasper ware, decorated w/white relief lady playing harp on a green ground.. **45.00**

---

# SCHOOP (Hedi) ART CREATIONS

*Hedi Schoop Chinese Woman*

*By far one of the most talented artists working in California in the 1940s and 1950s was Hedi Schoop. Almost every piece in her line she designed and modeled herself. She began her business in 1940 in Hollywood, California. Barker Brothers department store in Los Angeles discovered Schoop's work which encouraged her to open the small Hollywood studio. Shortly after a move to larger quarters, financed by her mother, Hedi began calling her business Hedi*

*Schoop Art Creations. It would remain under that name throughout Schoop's career which was ended when a fire destroyed the operation in 1958. At that time, Hedi decided to free-lance for other companies (see: CLEMINSON CLAY).*

*Probably one of the most imitated artists of the time, other people and businesses began using Schoop's designs and techniques. Hedi Schoop decided to sue in court and the results were settled in Schoop's favor.*

*Among those imitators were Kim Ward, and Ynez and Yona. Hedi Schoop saw forms differently than other artists and, therefore, was able to create with ease and in different media. While Hedi made shapely women with skirts that flared out to create bowls as well as women with arms over their heads holding planters, she also produced charming bulky-looking women with thick arms and legs. When TV lamps became popular, Hedi was able to easily add her talents to creating those designs with roosters, tragedy and comedy joined together in an Art Deco fashion, and elegant women in various poses. A variety of marks were used by Schoop including her signature (incised or stamped) which also, on occasion, shows "Hollywood, Cal." or "California," and there was also a sticker used but such pieces are hard to find.*

*Hedi Schoop*
*HOLLYWOOD CAL.*

*HEDI SCHOOP*
*HOLLYWOOD, CALIF.*
*Hedi Schoop*

*Schoop Marks*

**Figure of a ballerina dancer,** on a thin round base, long skirt flared upward revealing right foot, right arm extended & holding up skirt, left arm extended forward w/head turned to front, bluish grey w/silver overtones, impressed mark "Hedi Schoop," 9¼" h................. **$75.00**

**Figure of a Chinese woman,** standing on round black base, white floor-length skirt, black, white & green blouse w/long sleeves flaring at wrists, a white flower in black hair above each ear, right fingers bent to hold a pot w/black cloth handle & in same colors as blouse, right leg bent at knee, woman 9" h., pot 2½" h., 2 pcs. (ILLUS. bottom previous page) ...........................**125.00**

**Figure of a girl standing,** bell-shaped skirt w/scalloped edges, sunflower-shaped face & yellow hair, green blouse, yellow skirt, Model No. 703, 9" h. ................... **85.00**

**Figure of a girl,** standing on cobalt blue-glazed round base, legs slightly apart, arms stretched out to sides, hands folded to hold jump rope, rough textured black hair w/pigtails out to sides & held in place w/cobalt blue glossy ties, light blue long sleeve shirt, cobalt blue overblouse w/straps, rough textured cobalt blue short skirt & socks, inkstamp on unglazed bottom, "Hedi Schoop Hollywood, Cal.," 8½" h. ............................... **115.00**

**Lamp,** figural, TV-type, Comedy & Tragedy masks on a base w/full Comedy, part Tragedy conjoined, dark green w/gold trim, ca. 1954, 10¾" l., 12" h..... **275.00**

**Model of a cat lying down,** head up, tail wrapped around side, paws tucked under body, brown collar around neck w/two yellow bells & two small brown pots attached, white rough textured body, inkstamp under glaze, "Hedi Schoop Hollywood, Cal.," 6¾" l., 6½" h................................ **85.00**

**Planter,** model of a horse, rough textured mane & tail, white glossy glazed body w/mint green face accents, saddle, bows in assorted areas & scalloped edging at the base, inkstamp mark "Hedi Schoop," 7½" h......... **55.00**

**Tray,** divided w/irregular leaf-shaped raised edges, the rim

*Hedi Schoop Figural Tray*

production of hard paste began. Between 1850 and 1900, many biscuit and soft-paste pieces were made again. Fine early pieces are scarce and high priced. Many of those available today are late productions. The various Sevres marks have been copied and pieces listed as "Sevres-Style" are similar to actual Sevres wares, but not necessarily from that factory. Three of the many Sevres marks are illustrated below.

*Sevres Marks*

mounted w/the figure of a cherub on her knees, arms outstretched beside her, head tilted, beige & gold tray interior, beige w/pink-tinged cherub, gold wings, rose on left wrist, belt of roses around her waist w/rose-glazed bowl exterior & rose hair, bottom of tray also in a glossy rose, incised "Hedi Schoop," 11½" l., 6" h. including cherub (ILLUS.) ............ **110.00**

**Vase,** 4½" h. at lowest point, 9" h. at highest point, 9" l., seashell-form, footed oval base, fluted edge rising from the low end to the higher end, dark green base w/dark green & gold fading to light green & gold, inside in solid lime green, rim trimmed in gold, transparent textured glossy glaze, marked w/a silver label w/red block letters, "Hedi Schoop Hollywood, Calif." on two lines ..................................... **75.00**

# SEVRES & SEVRES-STYLE

*Some of the most desirable porcelain ever produced was made at the Sevres factory, originally established at Vincennes, France, and transferred, through permission of Madame de Pompadour, to Sevres as the Royal Manufactory about the middle of the 18th century. King Louis XV took sole responsibility for the works in 1759 when*

**Bowls,** cov., Sevres-Style, gilt-bronze mounted, a deep rounded porcelain bowl w/low domed cover fitted within a gilt-bronze stand w/a pierced looping metal rim band flanked by rams' head, a base ring raised on four pilaster legs joined by serpentine bars above the round, paneled plinth base on flattened ball feet, metal branch-form cover handle, the body & cover decorated w/oval reserves painted w/exotic birds & trees within scrolling gilt borders against a colored ground, 10¼" h., pr. (ILLUS. of one, top next page) .............. **$6,037.00**

**Bust of Comtesse du Barry,** white biscuit, her high swept-back hair w/long curls down the back, wearing an off-the-shoulder drapery gown, inscribed on the reverse "Portrait De Madame La Comtesse DuBarry - Pajou Sculpteur," impressed mark, 19th c., 22½" h. ................................... **2,300.00**

*Bronze-mounted Sevres Bowl*

*'Sevres' Candlesticks*

**Cache pot,** cov., gilt-bronze mounted, the front panel painted w/maidens & gentlemen in a landscape w/an opposing floral panel on a turquoise blue ground surmounted by a foliate pierced rim & flanked by lion-and-ring handles, the whole raised on a gilt-bronze base ending in paw feet, late 19th c., 12" h..................................... **1,840.00**

**Candlesticks,** Sevres-Style, a cylindrical shaft fluted on the lower portion & molded w/two oval medallions painted w/bust portraits of courtly ladies in 18th c. dress & separated by gilt rams' heads, on a stepped circular molded base, slender metal neck below a drip pan & bulbous cylindrical candle socket w/a flattened rim trimmed w/enameling, the shaft & base w/a *bleu celeste* ground w/white 'jewels' & gilt highlighting, ca. 1900, 11¼" h., pr. (ILLUS. top next column) ....... **2,300.00**

**Dresser mirror,** the oval beveled rotating mirror glass opposed by an oval porcelain plaque decorated w/a young man giving a young lady a lesson in love, reserved on a green ground, artist-signed, raised on a slender standard & square base, 15" h... **550.00**

**Figure of a classical female,** white biscuit, 19th c., 20" h. ...... **173.00**

**Figures of Cupid & Psyche,** bisque & blue glazed enamel, after the models by Falconet, each w/an inscribed & shaped enamel-decorated base, impressed & printed factory marks, ca. 1872, 12½" h., pr. (foot repair to Cupid, both bases w/chips & repairs) .................. **1,380.00**

**Figure group,** white biscuit, Sevres-Style, "Leda and the Swan," the naked Leda seated on a fabric-draped rocky outcrop w/one arm about the shoulder of her daughter who lounges at her side holding part of the drapery against her naked body, Leda petting the swan who rests his head against her thigh, raised on an oval green-glazed plinth decorated w/gilt, incised interlaced "L's" mark w/an "I" & "M" below, third quarter 18th c., 15" l., 14¼" h. (ILLUS. top next page)..................................... **4,600.00**

**Garniture set:** two baluster-form 17¾" h. urns & an oval center open compote; each decorated w/Napoleonic scenes & landscapes reserved on a green & raspberry ground w/gilt trim, bronze-mounted, 19th c., 3 pcs. (urns missing covers)............. **5,500.00**

*Leda and the Swan Figure Group*

*Ornate 'Sevres' Urn*

**Paperweight,** decorated in *pate-sur-pate* in the cameo style w/a young woman's head in profile in bright white w/the word "FLORE," her head surrounded w/flowers in brown, blue, grey & green matte glazes, incised "T DOAT - 1900 - SEVRES," 1910, 1¼ x 3½"................................ **1,980.00**

**Plaques,** round, each decorated w/a panoramic landscape w/trees, figures, hills & distant ancient ruins, marked w/interlacing "L" surmounted by a crown in blue enamel, mounted in wide square giltwood frames w/round openings, late 19th c., 7" d., pr...................... **5,175.00**

**Sauceboat & undertray,** figural, modeled as an oval swan, the exterior w/feathers & folded wings, the gracefully arched neck & head forming the handle, on a dished oval undertray w/a leaftip border all richly decorated in burnished gilt, early 19th c., marked in iron-red "Mre. Imple. de Sevres," sauceboat 4½" l., undertray 6" l., 2 pcs. ................ **690.00**

**Urn,** cov., slender baluster-form w/a tall waisted neck supporting a stepped, domed cover w/a metal ball & spearpoint finial, the shoulders mounted w/gilt-bronze looped rope handles continuing down the sides, gilt-bronze connector ring to the pedestal resting on a square gilt-bronze foot w/notched corners, the body decorated on one side w/a figure group of a young maiden & two cupids & on the opposite side w/a landscape scene, late 19th c., 27¾" h. ...................... **2,760.00**

**Urn,** cov., Sevres-Style, the wide ovoid body raised on a gilt-bronze pedestal & octagonal foot, each side of the body painted w/a large oval panel, the obverse w/a parkland setting w/an 18th c. gallant & lady buying a posy from a flower seller, artist-signed, the reverse w/a scene of a chateau in a landscape, each panel reserved on a gilt-trimmed cobalt blue ground, including the waisted neck & domed cover (restored) w/gilt-metal nut-form finial, late 19th c., 38½" h. (ILLUS. above)........................ **6,900.00**

**Urns,** a square foot & ringed pedestal supporting a gently flaring cylindrical body w/a short, wide & waisted neck, gilt-metal lion mask & fan shoulder handles, each side w/a long rectangular panel, one urn depicting Napoleon, the other Josephine, the opposite panels depicting the Chateau St. Cloud & the Chateau La Mal Maison, each against an ornately gilt-trimmed green ground, late 19th c., 24¼" h., pr. (covers missing) ................................ **6,325.00**

**Vase,** 24" h., classical urn-form w/a bulbous ovoid body w/the wide shoulder tapering to a wide, short trumpet neck w/an applied gilt-bronze gadrooned border band & inset w/a stepped & domed cover w/a gilt-bronze disc & floral finial, the body raised on gilt-bronze leaf bands joined by a narrow ring connector above the domed pedestal raised on a gilt-bronze foot w/a cast wrapped ribbon band above a square foot w/notched corners, gilt-bronze satyr head shoulder handles, the front decorated w/a large oval reserve of classical figures in a landscape framed by a scrolling gilt border, the reverse w/a large floral reserve, all against a yellow ground, artist-signed, 19th c. .................................... **1,380.00**

**Vases,** 8½" h., *pate-sur-pate*, urn-shaped, a small round domed foot tapering to a short ringed pedestal supporting a wide urn-form body w/a wide tapering neck ending in a flat rim flanked by S-scroll handles, the dark blue ground w/white slip decoration washed in the *cafe-au-lait* manner, the neck w/a stylized column & urn border w/gilt trim, the main body decorated on each w/a white slip classical female bust, each titled on the reverse & artist-signed, Louis Solon, ca. 1865, one w/a slight rim flake, pr. .................. **7,475.00**

# SHAWNEE

*The Shawnee pottery operated in Zanesville, Ohio, from 1937 until 1961. Much of the early production was sold to chain stores and mail-order houses including Sears, Roebuck, Woolworth and others. Planters, cookie jars and vases, along with the popular "Corn King" oven ware line, are among the collectible items which are plentiful and still reasonably priced. Reference numbers used here are taken from Mark E. Supnick's book,* Collecting Shawnee Pottery, The Collector's Guide to Shawnee Pottery *by Duane and Janice Vanderbilt, or* Shawnee Pottery—An Identification & Value Guide *by Jim and Bev Mangus.*

## Shawnee
### U.S.A.

Shawnee Mark

**Bank - cookie jar combination,** figural Smiley Pig, No. 61, butterscotch ........................... **$375.00**

**Bank,** figural Howdy Doody on pig, 6½" h. ................................ **395.00**

**Butter dish,** cov., "Corn King" line, No. 72 ................................. **65.00**

**Butter dish,** cov., Lobster Ware, Kenwood line, domed white cover w/lobster finial, 7¼" l. ...... **250.00**

**Casserole,** cov., individual, "Corn King" line, No. 73, 9 oz. ............. **95.00**

**Casserole,** cov., "Corn King" line, No. 74, 1½ qt. ............... **65.00 to 85.00**

**Cookie jar,** cov., "Corn King" line, No. 66 ...................................... **240.00**

**Cookie jar,** figural Drummer Boy w/gold ....................................... **795.00**

**Cookie jar,** figural Dutch girl, w/gold & decals ........ **275.00 to 300.00**

**Cookie jar,** figural Jo Jo the Clown, No. 12 (ILLUS. top next page) ......................... **300.00 to 350.00**

**Cookie jar,** figural Mammy, yellow ....................................... **600.00**

*Jo Jo the Clown Cookie Jar*

**Cookie jar,** figural Mugsey Dog,
blue scarf w/gold trim ............... **985.00**

**Cookie jar,** figural Owl w/gold
trim ............................................ **400.00**

**Cookie jar,** figural Sailor Boy,
gold trim & decals .................... **575.00**

**Cookie jar,** figural Smiley Pig,
cold paint, red scarf ................. **120.00**

**Cookie jar,** figural Winnie Pig,
gold trim ................................... **800.00**

**Creamer,** figural Puss 'n Boots,
green & yellow w/gold trim ........ **160.00**

**Creamer,** figural Smiley Pig,
yellow & blue decoration ............. **79.00**

**French casserole,** cov., Lobster
Ware, Kenwood line, 10 oz. ........ **30.00**

**French casserole,** cov., Lobster
Ware, w/brass stand & warmer,
16 oz., the set ............................ **50.00**

**Lamp base,** figural Duck Playing
Drum, cold paint.......................... **45.00**

**Mixing bowl,** "Corn King" line,
No. 5, 5" d. ................................. **20.00**

**Mug,** "Corn King" line, No. 69 ....... **28.00**

**Mug,** Lobster Ware, Kenwood
line, white w/lobster handle,
8 oz. ......................................... **150.00**

**Pie bird,** pink ............................... **40.00**

**Pitcher,** ball-type, Pennsylvania
Dutch patt., No. 12 ..................... **95.00**

**Pitcher,** ball-type, embossed
Snowflake patt., blue ................. **35.00**

**Pitcher,** figural Little Bo Peep,
decals, red ribbon under arm,
gold trim ................................... **325.00**

**Pitcher,** figural Smiley Pig, large .. **145.00**

**Pitcher,** figural Smiley Pig, large,
gold trim ................................... **375.00**

**Planter/book end,** Buddha,
marked "USA 524" ...................... **55.00**

**Planter,** figural wishing well
flanked by figural Dutch boy
& girl, No. 710 ............................ **30.00**

**Planter,** figural Tony the Peddler,
"Carioca Rum," marked "USA
621".............................................. **25.00**

**Planter,** figural Two Dogs,
marked "USA 611" ...................... **10.00**

**Plate,** 10" d., "Corn Queen" line,
No. 68 ........................................ **45.00**

**Platter,** 12" l., "Corn Queen" line,
No. 96 ........................................ **65.00**

**Relish tray,** "Corn King" line,
No. 79 ........................................ **35.00**

**Salt & pepper shakers,** figural
Chanticleer Rooster, large, pr. ..... **65.00**

**Salt & pepper shakers,** "Corn
King" line, range size, No. 77,
5¼" h., pr. .................................. **32.00**

**Salt & pepper shakers,** figural
daisy, large, pr. .......................... **30.00**

**Salt & pepper shakers,** figural
flowerpots, pr. ............................ **25.00**

**Salt & pepper shakers,** figural
fruit cluster, small, pr................... **30.00**

**Salt & pepper shakers,** figural
lobster, Lobster Ware, Kenwood
line, large, pr. ............................ **140.00**

**Salt & pepper shakers,** figural
milk can, pr. ................................ **15.00**

**Salt & pepper shakers,** figural
Mugsey Dog, range size,
five-hole, pr. .............................. **160.00**

**Salt & pepper shakers,** figural
sunflower, small, pr.................... **35.00**

**Salt & pepper shakers,** figural
watering can, pr. ........................ **15.00**

**Sugar bowl,** cov., "Corn King"
line, No. 78.................................. **42.00**

**Sugar bowl,** cov., "Corn Queen"
line, No. 78.................................. **40.00**

**Tankard,** Medallion line, bronze
glaze, marked "USA 990" .......... **50.00**

**Teapot,** cov., individual, "Corn
King" line, No. 65, 10 oz. .......... **250.00**

**Teapot,** cov., "Corn King" line,
30 oz., No. 75 ........................... **275.00**

*Tom the Piper's Son Teapot*

**Teapot,** cov., figural, Tom the
Piper's Son (ILLUS.) ................... **95.00**

**Teapot,** cov., decorated w/red
flower, gold trim .......................... **70.00**

**Vegetable dish,** open, "Corn
King" line, No. 95, 9" l. ................ **75.00**

**Wall lamp,** bracket-type, a round
mounting disc w/a fishscale
band extends a leaf-embossed
arm ending in an urn-form
flower-embossed electric socket,
colored trim................. **75.00 to 100.00**

**Wall pocket,** figural bird in nest.... **28.00**

**Wall pocket,** figural cuckoo clock.. **50.00**

**Wall pocket,** figural tulip, yellow,
matte finish ................................. **40.00**

**Water sprinkler,** figural turtle ....... **55.00**

---

# SHELLEY

*Members of the Shelley family were in the pottery business in England as early as the 18th century. In 1872 Joseph Shelley formed a partnership with James Wileman of Wileman & Co. who operated the Foley China Works. The Wileman & Co. name was used for the firm for the next fifty years, and between 1890 and 1910 the words "The Foley" appeared above conjoined "WC" initials.*

*Beginning in 1910 the Shelley family name in a shield appeared on wares, although the firm's official name was still Wileman & Co. The company's name was finally changed to Shelley in 1925 and then Shelley China Ltd. after 1965. The*
firm changed hands in the 1960s and became part of the Doulton Group in 1971.

*At first only average quality earthenwares were produced but in the late 1890s new shapes and better quality decorations were used.*

*Bone china was introduced at Shelley before World War I and these fine dinnerwares became very popular in the United States and are increasingly popular today with collectors. Thin "eggshall china" teawares, miniatures and souvenir items were widely marketed during the 1920s and 1930s and are sought-after today.*

*Shelley Mark*

**Ashtray,** Blue Rock patt. ............ **$32.00**

**Ashtray,** Daisy patt....................... **59.00**

**Bonbon,** Melody patt. ................... **50.00**

**Bonbon,** Primrose patt. ................ **50.00**

**Bowl,** 13" d., decorated w/suns,
palms & multicolored balloon
shapes, yellow lustre ................ **200.00**

**Butter dish,** cov., Sky Blue patt,
white w/gold trim ....................... **135.00**

**Cake plate,** Chintz Melody patt. .. **185.00**

**Cake plate,** Glorious Devon patt. ... **68.00**

**Coffeepot,** cov., Blue Rock patt.,
large......................................... **295.00**

**Coffeepot,** cov., Chintz Melody
patt........................................... **395.00**

**Coffeepot,** cov., Rock Garden
patt........................................... **395.00**

**Condensed milk pot,** cov.,
Chintz Melody patt. ................... **245.00**

**Creamer & cov. sugar bowl,**
miniature, Rosebud patt., pr. ...... **68.00**

**Creamer & cov. sugar bowl,**
Chintz Melody patt., pr............. **150.00**

**Creamer & cov. sugar bowl,**
Dainty Blue patt., pr. .................. **75.00**

**Creamer & cov. sugar bowl,**
Daisy patt.................................. **175.00**

**Cup & saucer,** demitasse,
Daffodil Time ............................... **55.00**

**Cup & saucer,** demitasse, Rose
& Red Daisy patt. ........................ **72.00**

**Cup & saucer,** demitasse,
Rosebud patt. ............................ **72.00**

**Cup & saucer,** Begonia patt. ........ **45.00**

**Cup & saucer,** Blue Rock patt.,
fourteen-flute ............................... **50.00**

**Cup & saucer,** Country Side patt... **95.00**

**Cup & saucer,** Daffodil patt. ......... **65.00**

**Cup & saucer,** Dubarry patt. ........ **48.00**

**Cup & saucer,** Glorious Devon
patt. ........................................... **45.00**

**Cup & saucer,** Maytime patt. ..... **100.00**

**Cup & saucer,** Old Mill patt. ......... **45.00**

**Cup & saucer,** Rose & Red Daisy
patt. ........................................... **45.00**

**Cup & saucer,** Stocks patt., fluted
shape, lavender, pink, white &
blue flowers, cups 3½" d., 2⅜" h.
(ILLUS. right, top next column) ...... **55.00**

**Cup & saucer,** Summer Glory
patt. .......................................... **145.00**

**Cup & saucer,** decorated w/large
clusters of blue flowers w/small
pink blossoms, blue-trimmed
handle & borders, saucer 5½" d.,
cup 3¼" d., 2¾" h. (ILLUS. left,
top next column) .......................... **48.00**

**Dessert set:** cup & saucer &
dessert plate; Cape Gooseberry
patt., Regency shape, 3 pcs. ...... **99.00**

**Dessert set:** cup & saucer &
dessert plate; Charm patt.,
3 pcs. ......................................... **75.00**

**Dessert set:** cup & saucer &
dessert plate, Lily-of-the-Valley
patt., six-flute shape, 3 pcs. ........ **65.00**

**Dessert set:** cup & saucer &
dessert plate, Melody patt.,
Regency shape, 3 pcs. .............. **99.00**

**Dessert set:** cup & saucer &
dessert plate; Stocks patt.,
3 pcs. ......................................... **75.00**

**Dessert set:** cup & saucer &
dessert plate; Wild Anemone
patt., Chester shape, 3 pcs. ......... **69.00**

**Dessert set:** cup & saucer &
dessert plate; Wildflowers patt.,
Chester shape, 3 pcs. ................. **69.00**

*Shelley Cups & Saucers*

**Egg cup,** Lily-of-the-
Valley patt., eight-flute shape ..... **55.00**

**Feeding dish,** scene of child
w/Boo Boos on seesaw, 6½" d. .. **145.00**

**Hot water pot,** Sky Blue patt.,
white w/gold trim ....................... **135.00**

**Jam pot,** cov., Chintz Melody
patt. .......................................... **245.00**

**Jardiniere,** floral decoration on
white ground, 9" w., 8" h. .......... **285.00**

**Muffin dish,** cov., Chintz Melody
patt. .......................................... **250.00**

**Muffineer,** Polka Dot patt.,
yellow ........................................ **275.00**

**Nut dish,** Melody patt. .................. **68.00**

**Pin dish,** Daisy patt. .................... **89.00**

**Pin dish,** Maytime patt. ................. **89.00**

**Plate,** 6" d., Blue Rock patt. .......... **20.00**

**Plate,** 6" d., scene of children
sitting in donkey cart w/Boo
Boos, artist-signed .................... **110.00**

**Plate,** 9¼" d., Blue Rock
patt. .............................. **45.00 to 50.00**

**Posy Vase,** mushroom-shaped,
Chintz Melody patt. ................... **195.00**

**Reamer,** two-piece, green &
white ........................................ **175.00**

**Teapot,** cov., Daffodil Time patt. .. **175.00**

**Teapot,** cov., Primrose patt.,
8-cup ........................................ **350.00**

**Tray,** miniature, Violets patt. ......... **33.00**

# SHENANDOAH VALLEY POTTERY

*The potters of the Shenandoah Valley in Maryland and Virginia turned out an earthenware pottery of a distinctive type. It was the first earthenware pottery made in America with a varied, brightly colored glaze. The most notable of these potters,*

*Peter Bell, Jr., operated a pottery at Hagerstown, Maryland and later at Winchester, Virginia, from about 1800 until 1845. His sons and grandsons carried on the tradition. One son, John Bell, established a pottery at Waynesboro, Pennsylvania in 1833, working until his death in 1880, along with his sons who subsequently operated the pottery a few years longer. Two other sons of Peter Bell, Jr., Solomon and Samuel, operated a pottery in Strasburg, Virginia, a town sometimes referred to as "pot town" for six potteries were in operation there in the 1880s. Their work was also continued by descendants. Shenandoah Valley redware pottery, with its colorful glazes in green, yellow, brown and other colors, and the stoneware pottery produced in the area, are eagerly sought by collectors. Some of the more unique forms can be considered true American folk art and will fetch fantastic prices.*

**Flowerpot w/attached saucer base,** coggled rim, yellowware w/mottled brown & green & clear glaze, 6¾" d., 5½" h. (chips & top edge very chipped) ........ **$1,430.00**

**Jar,** bulbous ovoid on narrow molded foot, rounded shoulder tapering to wide cylindrical neck w/molded rim, redware w/tooled lines at shoulder & lip & small loop handles, cream slip w/mottled blue & brown glaze, 5⅞" h. (wear & chips)............... **193.00**

**Jug,** semi-ovoid body, rounded shoulder w/tooled lines, applied strap handle, redware w/cream slip & greyish green mottled glaze, 6⅛" h. (chips) .............. **1,430.00**

**Mug,** tapering cylindrical body w/applied strap handle, brown running glaze, impressed "John Bell," 5½" h. (wear, hairlines & chips on base) ...................... **1,045.00**

**Pitcher,** 6" h., footed ovoid body w/flaring rim, pinched spout & applied strap handle, tooled lines, cream slip on redware

w/brown & green glaze, hairline in spout & small chips ........... **2,750.00**

**Salt dip,** redware, ovoid body w/wide flat rim on domed foot, white slip w/mottled green glaze, 2¾" h. (small flakes on rim & chips on base) ......................... **248.00**

**Salt dip,** redware, ovoid body w/wide flat rim on domed foot, white slip w/mottled green & brown glaze, 3⅛" h. ................. **413.00**

**Vase,** 7" h., redware, simple baluster shape, white slip w/brown & green running glaze (minor glaze flakes) .............. **1,155.00**

---

# SLIPWARE

*This term refers to ceramics, primarily redware, decorated by the application of slip, or semi-liquid paste made of clay. Such wares were made for decades in England and Germany and elsewhere on the Continent, and in the Pennsylvania Dutch country and elsewhere in the United States. Today, contemporary copies of early Slipware items are featured in numerous decorator magazines and offered for sale in gift catalogs.*

**Bowl,** 13½" d., 2" h., round shallow form, redware w/three parallel triple wavy bands in yellow slip, coggled rim (worn, badly chipped center) ............ **$402.00**

**Creamer,** bulbous body w/long pinched spout, ribbed strap handle, yellow slip design in green splotches, 4⅜" h. (chips) .................................... **435.00**

**Flowerpot w/attached saucer base,** canted sides w/coggled rim, redware w/cream slip, mottled green & brown glaze, 8" h. (saucer drilled & edges are very chipped, some old red paint over chipped edges) .............. **1,045.00**

**Jar,** cov., cylindrical w/low-domed lid & button finial, redware

*Slipware Loaf Pan & Pie Plates*

Photos Courtesy of Garth's Auctions

w/cream slip, brown & green
brushed arches & intersecting
lines, Pennsylvania, 7" d. (very
worn & chipped cream slip) ... **1,375.00**

**Loaf pan,** shallow oblong form,
redware w/three-line wavy band
across center, "pine tree"
designs on border, all in yellow
slip, coggled rim, rim chipped,
wear & chips in slip, 17" l.
(ILLUS. top center) .................. **523.00**

**Milk bowl,** deep, redware, yellow
slip decorated rim, 16" d., 7" h.
(wear & scratches from heavy
use) ......................................... **330.00**

**Model of a cradle,** redware,
rectangular, the arched headrail
& hood w/shaped edge
surmounted by applied molded
birds & double ringed finials
decorated w/yellow slip
continuing to rectangular sides
surmounted by applied birds
joined by a tapering rectangular
footboard w/ringed finials,
inscribed "1859 - EH," on two
rockers, 6½ x 10¾", 10" h.
(breaks, repairs) ...................... **219.00**

**Pie plate,** three line yellow slip-
quilled decoration, coggled rim,
8" d. (old edge chips & minor
wear) ......................................... **193.00**

**Pie plate,** redware w/entwined
three-line yellow slip decoration
in center flanked by three-line
"S" scroll yellow slip bands,
coggled rim, 9¾" d. (wear &
minor chips) ............................. **358.00**

*Fine Slipware Plates*

**Pie plate,** redware, three-line
yellow slip center decoration
w/yellow slip squiggly lines
above & below, coggled rim,
minor wear & small rim chips,
9¾" d. (ILLUS. top right) .......... **468.00**

**Pie plate,** redware w/stylized
floral center decoration flanked
by squiggled lines, all in yellow
slip, coggled rim, wear, old chips
including flakes in slip, 12½" d.
(ILLUS. top left) ........................ **550.00**

**Pitcher,** 10¼" h., cylindrical,
redware w/applied tooled handle &
tooled bands, cream slip w/mottled
brown & olive green glaze (wear,
chips & some glaze flaking) ... **1,155.00**

**Plate,** 8½" d., redware
w/polychrome slip "X" & star
designs in white, brown & green,
coggled rim, pinpoint edge
flakes (ILLUS. bottom left) ..... **5,060.00**

**Plate,** 11¼" d., redware w/yellow
slip decoration of wavy lines &
initials, coggled rim, minor wear
& small flakes (ILLUS. bottom
right) ......................................... **495.00**

*A large variety of Spatterware*

# SPATTERWARE

*This ceramic ware takes its name from the 'spattered' decoration, in various colors, generally used to trim pieces hand-painted with rustic center designs of flowers, birds, houses, etc. Popular in the early 19th century, most was imported from England.*

*Related wares, called "stick spatter," had free-hand designs applied with pieces of cut sponge attached to sticks, hence the name. Examples date from the 19th and early 20th century and were produced in England, Europe and America.*

*Some early spatter-decorated wares were marked by the manufacturers, but not many. 20th century reproductions are also sometimes marked, including those produced by Boleslaw Cybis in the 1940s which sometimes have "CYBIS" impressed.*

**Creamer,** footed ovoid body w/long pinched spout & leaftip handle, Peafowl patt., free-hand bird in blue, green, red & black, red spatter border, edge wear, stains & small repairs on spout, 4½" h. (ILLUS. top row, front left) .......................................... **$330.00**

**Cup & saucer,** miniature, handleless, Tulip patt., free-hand flower in blue, yellow, red & green, blue spatter border (chip on table ring of saucer) .... **990.00**

**Cup & saucer,** handleless, blue transfer-printed Eagle patt. trimmed in yellow & green, red spatter background (stains, hairlines) .................................... **385.00**

**Cup & saucer,** handleless, Peafowl patt., free-hand bird in blue, yellowish ochre, green & black, red spatter border (ILLUS. top row, front right).................... **550.00**

**Cup & saucer,** handleless, Rainbow spatter borders (pinpoint flake on table ring of cup) ............................................ **83.00**

**Cup & saucer,** handleless, Rose patt., free-hand flower in red, green & black, blue spatter border (edge roughness & saucer w/edge repair) .............. **138.00**

**Plate,** 8¾" d. Peafowl patt., free-hand bird in red, orange, green & black, blue spatter border, small flakes (ILLUS. bottom row, second from right) ....................**385.00**

**Plate,** 9¼" d., Adam's Rose patt., free-hand rose in red, green & black w/blue spatter border....... **110.00**

**Plate,** 9¼" d., Peafowl patt., free-hand bird in light blue, green, yellowish ochre & black, overall red spatter, edge wear & small chip on table ring (ILLUS. bottom row, second from left) ... **495.00**

**Plate,** 9½" d., molded edge rim, Peafowl patt., free-hand bird in blue, red, green & black, blue spatter border, minor wear, pinpoint flake in green on peafowl (ILLUS. top row, far right).......................................... **385.00**

**Plate,** 9½" d., Peafowl patt., free-hand bird in blue, yellowish ochre, red & black, overall blue spatter, chips on table ring, blue in peafowl might flake (ILLUS. bottom row, far left) ................... **275.00**

**Plate,** 9¾" d., Peafowl patt., free-hand bird in red, orange, green & black, blue spatter border, stains & small rim repair (ILLUS. bottom row, far right)................. **385.00**

**Plate,** 11" d., Peafowl patt., free-hand bird in red, yellowish ochre, green & black on blue spatter background surrounded by white band & blue spatter border, yellowish ochre flaked, edge wear & chip on table ring (ILLUS. top row, back center) ... **578.00**

**Soup plate w/flanged rim,** Rose patt., free-hand flower in red, teal green, black & blue w/red spatter border, impressed "N," 9⅜" d.......................................... **660.00**

**Soup plate w/flanged rim,** Peafowl patt., free-hand bird in purple, green, red & black, overall blue spatter, 10" d. (ILLUS. top row, back left) ....... **1,375.00**

**Sugar bowl,** cov., footed bulbous body, Peafowl patt., free-hand bird in blue, green, red & black, overall blue spatter, lid w/slight lavender to blue cast, small flakes on inner lip & lid w/professional repair, 4⅝" h. (ILLUS. bottom row, center)...... **330.00**

**Teapot,** cov., footed & paneled tall, tapering Gothic form w/angled handle & swan's-neck spout, high domed cover w/blossom finial, Fort patt., h.p. in green, black & red, blue spatter trim, 8½" h. (chips, hairlines, professional repair in cover) ........................................ **825.00**

**Toddy dish,** round, Bull's-eye patt., rainbow spatter in blue & purple, 5" d............................... **358.00**

**Waste bowl,** footed, round flaring sides, Peafowl patt., free-hand bird in blue, green, red & black w/overall blue spatter, 6½" d. (wear, stains & small flakes) .. **1,100.00**

### Stick and Cut Sponge Spatter

**Bowl,** 11" d., 2" h., stick spatter red & green flowers, spongeware design rim, marked "Imperial Royale, Belgium" ....... **115.00**

**Bowl,** 14⅜" d., "gaudy" floral decoration in blue, brown & red, black & red rim design, marked "Maastricht," Holland (stains & minor rim bruise w/short hairline) .................................... **248.00**

**Plate,** 9" d., center & outer borders of cut-sponge star design in red & green, impressed "Powell & Bishop" (wear & minor stains) ............... **110.00**

**Plates,** 9¾" d., a narrow rim band of small round cut-sponge flowerheads, the interior h.p. w/three large pointed leaf clusters alternating w/blossom clusters all around a center circle enclosing a three-petal blossom, in blue, red & green, set of 6 .................................... **121.00**

*A Group of Spongeware Pitchers*

# SPONGEWARE

*Spongeware's designs were spattered, sponged or daubed on in colors, sometimes with a piece of cloth. Blue on white was the most common type, but mottled tans, browns and greens on yellowware were also popular. Spongeware generally has an overall pattern with a coarser look than Spatterwares, to which it is loosely related. These wares were extensively produced in England and America well into the 20th century.*

**Bank,** model of a jug, semi-ovoid body centered by small cylindrical neck, wire bail w/wooden handle, blue sponging on white, 3⅞" h........ **$990.00**

**Creamer,** ovoid w/molded swirled ribs, pinched spout, C-form handle, overall blue on white, 5½" h........................................ **275.00**

**Cuspidor,** stoneware, squatty bulbous body w/widely flaring rim, blue sponged bands on rim & body on white, 8" d. ................. **61.00**

**Flowerpot w/attached saucer,** ovoid body w/crimped rim, overall coarse dark blue spatter on white, 4⅝" h. (crazing & small flakes) ...................................... **330.00**

**Pitcher,** 4½" h., brown & green sponging .................................... **75.00**

**Pitcher,** 8⅜" h., tall slender barrel shape w/low long loop handle & small pinched rim spout, overall blue sponging on white (ILLUS. second from left) ...................... **220.00**

**Pitcher,** 8⅞" h., bulbous nearly spherical base tapering to a wide cylindrical neck w/tiny pinched spout, angled branch handle, overall fine blue sponging on white, chips (ILLUS. far right) ...................... **220.00**

**Pitcher,** 8⅞" h., cylindrical body w/flat rim w/pointed spout & C-form handle, the side molded w/a rose, decorated overall w/a repeating banded design w/large blue daubing alternating w/large white spots (minor open surface blisters) ................................... **358.00**

**Pitcher,** 9" h., tankard-type, cylindrical body slightly swelled near the base, small pinched rim spout, small angled handle, bold spiraling bands of blue sponging on white around the sides, rim chip, minor flakes on base (ILLUS. far left) ........................ **275.00**

**Pitcher,** 9⅛" h., tankard-type, flat rim w/pointed rim spout, low C-form handle, decorated w/wide bands of heavy blue daubing alternating w/narrow bands of white (hairline, minor flakes) ................................... **330.00**

**Pitcher,** wash, 9¾" h., footed bulbous ovoid body tapering to a wide, high arched spout & C-scroll handle, wide dark blue bands of sponging on white around the neck, mid-body & foot, short hairline in foot, minor stains (ILLUS. second from right) ............................ **60.00 to 80.00**

**Plates,** 9¼" d., round w/wide flanged rims, overall heavy blue sponging on white, pr.............. **220.00**

**Vase,** 5" h., cylindrical w/flaring rim, overall heavy dark sponged blue on white............................ **330.00**

**Vase,** 8¾" h., cylindrical w/molded ribs in zigzag design at rim, blue sponging on white .. **413.00**

**Wash bowl & pitcher,** bulbous ovoid body w/wide flaring rim, pinched spout, coarse brown & blue sponging & brown stripe around mid-section of pitcher, 9½" d., 7¾" h., the set (wear, bowl w/professional repair) ....... **330.00**

# STAFFORDSHIRE FIGURES

*Bust of William Pitt*

*Small figures and groups made of pottery were produced by the majority of the Staffordshire, England potters in the 19th century and were used as mantel decorations or "chimney ornaments," as they were sometimes called. Pairs of dogs were favorites and were turned out by the carload, and 19th century pieces are still available. Well-painted reproductions also abound and collectors are urged to exercise caution before investing.*

**Bird,** pearlware, stylized model w/yellow, blue & ochre wings & spots on a round green base, probably Yorkshire, ca. 1800, 3½" h. (restored base) ........... **$633.00**

**Bust of William Pitt the Younger,** pearlware, finely modeled w/a shaded grey to white curled wig & long grey pigtail, fine facial detail, wearing a tan coat w/mauve vest draped w/a green sash, on a waisted square marbleized plinth base decorated in grey, orange & purple, late 18th c., 8⅞" h. (ILLUS. previous column) ......... **495.00**

**Cat,** pearlware, seated animal w/a white body sponged w/black & yellow, on a green oval base, ca. 1815, 3½" h......................... **518.00**

**Cottage,** a small double-gabled house w/a central dormer above narrow double windows flanking the double front door, center steps on the domed oblong base, applied "coleslaw" & florettes around the edges of the roof, decorated in grey, red, green & black, 19th c., 5" w., 5½" h. (some small in-the-making separations) ................. **127.00**

**Dog,** Whippet in seated position, on a blue rounded cushion, off-white w/tiny black spots & a gold collar & chain, last quarter 19th c., 6⅞" h. (overall fine crazing) .................................... **198.00**

**Dogs,** Greyhound standing holding a rabbit in its mouth, mounted on an irregular oval base w/a tree stump center support under the body, decorated in tan, black, red, green, gold & grey, applied "coleslaw" decoration on the base, 19th c., 7½" h., facing pair (one ear missing) ..................... **303.00**

**Dogs,** Spaniel in seated position, white w/red spots & painted trim, 19th c., 7¾" h., facing pr........... **385.00**

**Dogs,** Whippet, holding a rabbit in mouth, cobalt blue pillow base, 12" h., pr......................... **900.00**

**Equestrian group,** a bearded man in military uniform seated astride a prancing white horse, on an oval base w/the raised lettering "K. of Sardinia," sparsely decorated in black, fleshtone & red, two bunches of "coleslaw" grass, 19th c., 12" h. (slight restoration to front leg & tail of the horse) ........................ **127.00**

**Equestrian groups,** one showing a man & woman seated on a prancing white horse, titled in raised letters across the rectangular base "Going to Market," the matching piece titled "Returning Home," each sparsely decorated in fleshtone, black, gold, green & blue, 19th c., 8½" h., facing pr. .......... **440.00**

**Ewe & lamb,** large standing ewe in front of a leafy branched & flowered tree, raised on a high rockwork base w/a small lamb reclining below, overall enamel decoration w/a green base, impressed "Salt" on the base, 19th c., 6" h. (some slight chipping, heavy green enamel wear) ........................................ **495.00**

**Fawn,** pearlware, crudely modeled recumbent animal w/long ears, white splashed in brick red, ochre & dark brown, on an oval base, ca. 1760, 2¾" h. ............... **748.00**

**Figure of an American Naval officer of the mid-19th century,** probably Admiral David Farragut, standing & leaning on a round pink column embossed w/three white & gold American eagles, wearing a long jacket & high kneeboots, decorated in black, yellow, gold, pink, ochre, fleshtone & brown, mid-19th c., 9½" h. (meandering hairline on side of base) ......................... **1,320.00**

**Figure of a biblical woman,** standing beside a well w/a small jug, titled in script across the front of the oval base "Rebekah," sparsely decorated in fleshtone, black, brown, red &

gold, 19th c., 15" h. (three small base chips on the back, small in-the-making separation on base front) ........................................ **413.00**

**Figure of George Washington,** standing wearing civilian dress, decorated in gold, grey, black, brown, red & fleshtone enamels, early 19th c., 14½" h. (small mold separation on side of base) ...................................... **3,850.00**

**Figure of a lady in classical dress,** standing & holding a very long cornucopia w/fruits & flowers, decorated in red, pink, green & yellow, early 19th c., 10½" h. (area of discolored restoration on the base) ............ **363.00**

**Figure of Robinson Crusoe's man Friday,** a Black native standing wearing a turban & carrying a rifle, decorated in overglaze black, yellow, brown & pink, 19th c., 5" h. ..................... **330.00**

**Figure of the 'Tailor,'** a man in 18th c. costume riding on the back of a horned goat w/two baby goats in a basket on his back, brightly painted in black, fleshtone, yellow, brown, maroon, grey, green & gold, possibly Rockingham, first half 19th c., 5" h. .............................. **440.00**

**Figures of American evangelists "Sankey" & "Moody,"** title at the base of each standing man, "Moody" misspelled "Noody," each man wearing 19th c. attire & standing w/one hand resting on a pedestal, decorated in black, lavender, fleshtone, tan & blue, 19th c., 9¾" h., pr. (faint crazing on back of one, both w/some flaking black) .............................. **248.00**

**Figures,** each a standing man wearing period costume & a cape & leaning on a pedestal, one w/the name "Milton" across the front of the rectangular base, the other w/the name "Shakspere" (sic), each decorated in grey, brown, fleshtone, black & copper lustre trim, 19th c., 11¼" h., pr.... **413.00**

**Figure group,** a large castle-like structure w/two square crenelated towers flanking a tall pointed arch w/a large clock dial above a row of four rounded arch staggered windows above lower inset arches alternating with three rounded doorways, two of them opened & topped by oversized colored ivy vines, the structure resting atop a rockwork foundation molded w/a row of three inset grottos, the center one filled w/an applied young girl flanked by two recumbent lambs, ornately decorated in blue, red, green, grey, orange & black, 19th c., 15" h. (heavy crazing, network of hairlines in one tower & tip of other worn)... **413.00**

**Figure group,** farmer & his wife, he standing & holding a scythe, w/bound sheaves of wheat at his feet, she standing holding a basket of speckled eggs, finely decorated in yellow, red, green, fleshtone, bright orange, brick red & black, fine detail, oval base, 15¾" h. (small unseen chip on the back) ..................... **132.00**

**Figure group,** a standing hunter w/his dog beside him on an oval base, identified as Roualeyn George Gordon-Cumming, the Lion Slayer, well-decorated in brown, black, yellow, orange, fleshtone, purple, red & green, 19th c., 14¼" h. (seam separation on each side, glaze rub on one boot)........................................... **220.00**

**Figure group,** titled "Empress Eugenie," a young woman seated holding a baby, decorated in brown, grey, yellow, green, purple, fleshtone & ochre, 19th c., 7½" h. (some of the title worn)..... **220.00**

**Figure group,** pearlware, Night Watchman, two staggering men in 18th c. costume, one carrying a lantern & supporting his larger friend who carries a jug of beer in one hand & a mug in the other, on an oblong shaped base w/the sides decorated

*Night Watchman Group*

w/molded & painted scrolls, the figures dressed in black, one w/a brick-red coat, head of one reglued, 19th c., 9" h. (ILLUS.) .. **220.00**

**Figure group,** two peasant women standing side by side w/their skirts rolled up showing striped petticoats & their heads wrapped in scarves, one w/a pail beside her on the rockwork oval base, heavily decorated in orange, yellow, brown, pink, green, fleshtone & black, 19th c., 9" h. (in-the-making separation across the back) ....................... **193.00**

**Figure group,** a tall Whippet dog in white w/black spots seated next to a dead hare at his feet, on an oblong rockwork base, restoration to nose of the dog, 19th c., 11½" h. (ILLUS. top next page)................................ **385.00**

**Horse,** standing animal w/painted decoration, 8½" h...................... **185.00**

**Lamb,** miniature, standing animal w/a "pebbled" coat, black eyes & red mouth, on a hollow domed oval base decorated w/a single gold line, 19th c., 2" l., 2¼" h. (two minute flakes, small hairline off the base) .............................. **176.00**

**Lion,** pearlware, crudely molded recumbent animal w/a brown mane & yellow fur splashed in brown, on a green oval base, ca. 1790, 2¾" h. (very slight wear) ........................................ **288.00**

*Dog & Hare Group*

**Pastille burner,** figural, model of
a small cottage w/center
chimney & sloped roof, applied
florettes & "coleslaw" on the roof
& base, decorated in yellow,
green, blue, gold & red, 19th c.,
4" w., 4⅜" h. (in-the-making
separations in the base, roof &
rear opening) ............................ **116.00**

**Spill vase,** figural, a young boy &
young girl each holding the
products of harvesting &
standing flanking a tree trunk-
form vase, overall polychrome
decoration, 19th c., 8¼" h. ........ **154.00**

**Stag,** recumbent animal on an
oval base, hollow body & base,
applied "coleslaw" flowers in red
& yellow, grey antlers & tan
body, black eyes & muzzle,
19th c., 5" l., 4¾" h. .................... **176.00**

**Vase,** 7¼" h., creamware, figural,
a large flaring, ruffled & two-
tiered cornucopia vase held
aloft on one shoulder of a
classically garbed standing lady
wearing a striped dress &
standing on an ornate shell-
embossed base, decorated in
early blue, green & manganese,
ca. 1780-90 (two base rim
chips, flake on tip of bocage,
lower portion mellowed) .......... **440.00**

**Watch holder,** pearlware, figural,
in the form of a tall case clock
w/a round top w/opening for the
watch face, flanked by the
figures of a boy & girl, the boy
w/a blue sash covering him, the
girl w/a red blouse & bluish
green skirt, a hint of pink lustre
around dial opening, the lower
case of the clock w/a medallion
in the form of a ribbon holding a
crown done in green, blue,
yellow & red, flaking to some
paint, 19th c., 7½" h. ................ **325.00**

# STAFFORDSHIRE TRANSFER WARES

*Quadrupeds 'Rhinoceros' Platter*

*The process of transfer-printing
designs on earthenwares developed in
England in the late 18th century and by
the mid-19th century most common
ceramic wares were decorated in this
manner, most often with romantic
European or Oriental landscape scenes,
animals or flowers. The earliest such
wares were printed in dark blue but a
little later light blue, pink, purple, red,
black, green and brown were used. A
majority of these wares were produced at
various English potteries right up till the
turn of the century but French and other
European firms also made similar pieces
and all are quite collectible. The best
reference on this area is Petra Williams'*

*book* Staffordshire Romantic Transfer Patterns—Cup Plates and Early Victorian China *(Fountain House East, 1978). Also see HISTORICAL & COMMEMORATIVE WARES.*

**Basket,** oval w/lattice-pierced sides w/a wide rolled rim & loop end handles, a medium blue interior design of a piping shepherd & sheep in a bucolic landscape, floral border, early 19th c., 10¾" l., 3½" h............. **$660.00**

**Bowl,** 8¼" d., 3¾" h., deep rounded sides, the bottom interior w/an octagonal bordered scene of a Chinese tea party in a landscape setting, a series of octagonal paneled scenes around the interior & exterior sides featuring a European figure & his Chinese servant, dark blue, first half 19th c.......... **105.00**

**Creamer,** boat-shaped, Bird's Nest patt., dark blue, probably Hall, 5" h. ................................. **275.00**

**Creamer,** boat-shaped, man standing & pointing across a river at tower, foliage border, dark blue, 5½" h. (slight glaze rubbing on rim, overall mellowing)................................ **198.00**

**Cup & saucer,** handleless, scene of classical cherubs w/a goat, medium blue, pink lustre rim ..... **138.00**

**Cup & saucer,** handleless, Sleigh Ride patt., dark blue, impressed mark, Wood (slight dullness to saucer face) ............................ **193.00**

**Cup plate,** center picture of a hyena, Quadrupeds series, dark blue, Hall, 4" d.......................... **220.00**

**Mug,** cylindrical w/angled handle, Roses patt., dark blue w/large rose blossoms & leaves among smaller blossoms, beaded rim band, Rogers, 3¼" h. (tiny inner rim flake) ................................. **385.00**

**Pitcher,** jug-type, 5½" h., the exterior in lavender on a buff ground, the neck band h.p. w/small stylized leaves & blossoms, the sides w/lavender transfer-printed scenes, one side showing castle ruins, the other showing a village church & tower, molded satyr mask spout, shaped D-form handle, interior & handle in buff, early 19th c........ **220.00**

**Plate,** 5½" d., motto-type, black transfer-printed scene, "Little Strikes Fell Great Oaks, Dr. Franklin," ca. 1850 .............. **145.00**

**Plate,** 6¾" d., Shells patt., dark blue, Stubbs and Kent (trace of high point stacking wear) .......... **198.00**

**Plate,** 8½" d., Zoological series, dark blue w/a round central reserve featuring a Pointer, wide scroll & floral border, Wood, ca. 1830 ................................... **303.00**

**Plate,** 9" d., Lasso patt., medium blue w/a central scene of a wild horse round-up, the wide border w/vignettes of giraffe hunting, Pinder, Bourne & Company, first half 19th c. ............................... **193.00**

**Plate,** 9⅞" d., gently scalloped rim, wide border w/a sunrise vignette panel at the top above the script inscription "The Sun of Righteousness," alternating flower & oasis vignettes around the border, the center w/a large round scene of a praying child Samuel above the inscription "Speak Lord For Thy Servant Heareth," red, Wood, ca. 1830 ..**385.00**

**Plate,** 10¼" d., Zoological series, dark blue, central design of two running stags, floral & scroll border, Wood, ca. 1830 ............ **330.00**

**Platter,** 11" l., Caledonia patt., gently scalloped rim, mulberry, Adams, ca. 1830 (light mellowing, short hairline off the rim)............................................ **275.00**

**Platter,** 17" l., oval, dark blue transfer-printed center scene of a rhinoceros near palm trees w/a sailing ship in the background, scroll-bordered animal vignettes around the wide border, Quadrupeds series, Hall, ca. 1814-22 (ILLUS. second column previous page) ........... **1,495.00**

**Platter,** 18" l., oval w/lightly scalloped rim, Canna patt., red (minor stains & edge wear) ....... **385.00**

**Platter,** 20⅞" l., oval, well-and-tree-type, a large floral cluster in the center & smaller clusters around the flanged rim, medium blue, probably by Spode ........... **385.00**

**Puzzle jug,** a footed baluster-form pitcher w/a wide spout & angled handle, the white sides decorated w/black transfers of various figures such as Pantaloon, Harlequin & Columbine, each highlighted w/red, green, maroon, ochre & gold enamels, exterior base hole & another under the handle connected by a hollow interior piece, Elsmore & Forster, mid-19th c., 8¾" h. .................... **285.00**

**Salt dip,** wide shallow rounded bowl on a flaring pedestal foot, medium blue Willowware-type border, 2¼" h. .......................... **154.00**

**Sauce tureen, cover & ladle,** the squatty bulbous oval body raised on a short, flaring pedestal foot & w/scrolled end handles, the stepped, domed cover w/a knob finial & hole for the ladle handle, dark blue transfer-printed English landscape scene, Enoch Wood & Sons, second quarter 19th c., 8" l., 3 pcs. (tiny handle chips, some glaze wear, hairline) ......... **863.00**

**Soup plate w/flanged rim,** Asiatic Palaces patt., dark blue w/embossed white rim, Ridgway, ca. 1830-40 ................................. **99.00**

**Soup tureen,** cov., Birds & Fruit patt., stepped domed cover w/replaced blossom finial, squatty bulbous paneled body w/heavy shell-embossed loop end handles, raised on a shaped platform on paw feet, very dark blue, probably Stubbs, ca. 1830s, 14" l., 9¼" h. (excellent restoration of hairline off ladle hole) ...................................... **1,430.00**

**Sugar bowl,** cov., squatty bulbous baluster-form w/curved loop end handles, flanged &

incurved wide rim supporting the inset low domed cover w/button finial, Neptune patt., a sailing ship scene on the sides, feathery leaves on the cover & rim, black, Alcock, ca. 1830, 5¾" h. (minute unseen flakes on cover rest) ................................. **160.00**

**Toddy plate,** flanged border molded in relief w/a band of grapevines, the center w/a black transfer-printed inscription "For William" above a tiny coach & four, all within an oval painted floral panel decorated w/green, yellow & ochre, early 19th c., 5¼" d. ........................................ **413.00**

**Vegetable dish,** cov., squared body w/lightly scalloped flanged base rim w/molded scroll handles, stepped domed cover w/large fruit finial, decorated in dark blue w/"The Hunting Series - The Pause," Davenport, unmarked, ca. 1830, 10½" w., 7" h. ........................................ **1,210.00**

**Wash bowl,** footed rounded body w/widely flaring flattened rim, center scene of a large urn overflowing w/exotic flowers, flower & scroll border, dark blue, Riley, 12¾" d., 5" h. (reglued chip on interior of foot) .............. **908.00**

**Watch hutch,** figural, an arched top w/flowers & birds enclosing a round opening for the watch face above a grouping of several ladies on an oval base, polychrome & gilt trim, 19th c., 11" h. (some crazing & hairlines) ................................. **330.00**

# STANGL

*Johann Martin Stangl, who first came to work for the Fulper Pottery in 1910 as a ceramic chemist and plant superintendent, acquired a financial interest and became president of the company in 1926. The name of the firm was changed to Stangl*

*Pottery in 1929 and at that time much of the production was devoted to a high grade dinnerware to enable the company to survive the Depression years. One of the earliest solid-color dinnerware patterns was their Colonial line, introduced in 1926. In the 1930s it was joined by their Americana pattern. After 1942 these early patterns were followed by a wide range of hand-decorated patterns featuring flowers and fruits with a few decorated with animals or human figures.*

*Around 1940 a very limited edition of porcelain birds, patterned after the illustrations in John James Audubon's "Birds of America," was issued. Stangl subsequently began production of less expensive ceramic birds and these proved to be popular during the war years, 1940-46. Each bird was hand painted and each was well marked with impressed, painted or stamped numerals which indicated the species and the size.*

*All operations ceased at the Trenton, New Jersey plant in 1978.*

*Two reference books which collectors will find helpful are* The Collectors Handbook of Stangl Pottery *by Norma Rehl (The Democrat Press, 1979), and* Stangl Pottery *by Harvey Duke (Wallace-Homestead, 1994).*

*Stangl Mark*

## BIRDS

**Bluebird,** No. 3276S.................. **$50.00**

**Cardinal,** (Pyrrhuloxia), grey,
No. 3596, 4¾" h. ......................... 50.00

**Flying Duck,** No. 3443, green
(antique gold patina), 9" h. ........ **325.00**

**Hen,** No. 3446, grey & yellow,
7" h.......................................... 140.00

**Kentucky Warbler,** No. 3598,
3" h............................................ 60.00

*Key West Quail Dove*

**Key West Quail Dove,** No. 3454,
9" h. (ILLUS.) ........................... **325.00**

**Paroquet (Parrot),** No. 3449,
5½" h....................................... **150.00**

**Pair of Cockatoos,** No. 3405-D,
9½" h.......................................**125.00**

**Pair of Orioles,** No. 3402D,
5½" h....................................... **120.00**

**Pair of Parakeets,** No. 3582,
7" h.......................................... **200.00**

**Pair of Redstarts,** No. 3490-D,
9" h.......................................... **200.00**

**Pair of Wrens,** No. 3401D, dark
brown, 8" h................................. **98.00**

**Pheasant,** Della Ware, blue,
9 x 15½".................................... **500.00**

**Rooster,** No. 3445, blue & grey,
9" h.......................................... **185.00**

**Wren,** No. 3401S, 3½" h. .............. **55.00**

**Yellow (Prothonatary) Warbler,**
No. 3447, 5" h. ........................... **65.00**

## DINNERWARES & ARTWARES

**Ashtray,** fluted, Holly patt. ........... **22.00**

**Ashtray,** oval, Duck patt.,
Sportsmen's Giftware line,
No. 3926, 10" l. .......................... **40.00**

**Ashtray,** oval, Quail patt.,
Sportsmen's Giftware line,
No. 3926, 10" l. .......................... **40.00**

**Bowl,** berry, Chicory patt., small ..... **5.00**

**Bowl,** cereal, 5½" d., Festival
patt. .......................................... **12.00**

**Bowl,** fruit, 5½" d., Florette patt. ..... **8.00**

**Bowl,** soup, flat, 8¼" d., Florette patt. ........................................... **10.00**

**Bowl,** 9¾" d., Fruit patt. ............... **13.00**

**Bowl,** salad, 10" d., Provincial patt. ........................................... **35.00**

**Bowl,** salad, 12" d., Thistle patt. ... **50.00**

**Bowl,** soup, w/lug handles, Festival patt. ............................... **12.00**

**Bowl,** soup, w/lug handles, Provincial patt. ........................... **12.00**

**Bowl,** divided, ABC, Kiddieware line ........................................... **135.00**

**Cake stand,** Florette patt., 10" d... **20.00**

**Candleholders,** Early Pennsylvania Tulip patt., blue, pr........................ **450.00**

**Candle warmer,** Provincial patt. ... **22.00**

**Casserole,** w/serving lid, Festival patt. ........................................... **42.00**

**Celery tray,** Provincial patt., 10½" l. ........................................ **20.00**

**Cheese & cracker tray,** dustpan-shape, blue ................................. **55.00**

**Cigarette box,** cov., Flying Duck patt., Sportsmen's Giftware line, No. 3915, 3¾ x 4½" ................... **65.00**

**Cigarette box,** cov., Goldfinch decoration, No. 3931 ................. **55.00**

**Coaster/ashtray,** Thistle patt. ...... **15.00**

**Coffeepot,** cov., individual, Blueberry patt. ........................... **50.00**

**Coffee server,** cov., Lyic patt. ...... **95.00**

**Creamer,** Thistle patt. ................... **12.00**

**Creamer & cov. sugar bowl,** Provincial patt., pr. ..................... **20.00**

**Cup,** Little Bo Peep, Kiddieware line ........................................... **40.00**

**Cup & plate,** ABC patt., Kiddieware line ......................... **110.00**

**Cup & plate,** Ducky Dinner, Kiddieware line ......................... **195.00**

**Cup & saucer,** Thistle patt. ........... **8.00**

**Egg cup,** Thistle patt. ................... **15.00**

**Gravy boat,** Florette patt. ............. **10.00**

**Gravy boat,** Magnolia patt., 9" l.... **15.00**

**Mug,** Holly patt., low ..................... **28.00**

**Mug,** mallard decoration, Sportsmen's Giftware Line, No. 5092 ...................................... **35.00**

**Mug & saucer,** stacking-type, Florette patt., pr. ......................... **18.00**

**Pitcher,** Provincial patt., ½ pt. ...... **20.00**

**Pitcher,** Thistle patt., 1 pt. ........... **25.00**

**Plate,** 6" d., Florette patt. ............... **5.00**

**Plate,** 6" d., Provincial patt........... **10.00**

**Plate,** 6" d., Thistle.......................... **2.00**

**Plate,** 8" d., Magnolia patt............. **12.00**

**Plate,** 8" d., Provincial patt........... **12.00**

**Plate,** 8" d., Thistle patt................. **12.00**

**Plate,** 9" d., Kitten Capers, Kiddieware line ......................... **100.00**

**Plate,** 9" d., Thistle patt................. **12.00**

**Plate,** 10" d., Fruit patt. ................. **20.00**

**Plate,** 10" d., Thistle patt.............. **15.00**

**Plate,** 11" d., canvasback duck decoration, Sportsmen's Giftware line, No. 3774 .............. **58.00**

**Plate,** grill, 11⅝" d., Colonial patt., white ........................................... **25.00**

**Plate,** 12" d., Bachelor Button patt. ........................................... **30.00**

**Plate,** chop, 14¼" d., Magnolia patt. ........................................... **40.00**

**Plate,** divided, Our Barnyard Friends patt., Kiddieware line ..... **75.00**

**Relish dish,** Thistle patt. ............. **22.00**

**Salt & pepper shakers,** Florette patt., pr....................................... **12.00**

**Server,** center handle, Chicory patt. ........................................... **18.00**

**Server,** center handle, Sculptured Fruit patt................................... **18.00**

**Server,** center handle, Thistle patt. ........................................... **18.00**

**Soup,** coupe, Country Life patt., Mallard w/green head, on right, facing duck's rear sticking out of the water, 8" d................ **150.00**

**Spoon rest,** Town & Country patt., yellow................................ **38.00**

**Stoby mug,** "Archie," No. 1681, 6½" h........................................ **185.00**

**Sugar bowl,** cov., Deco Delight patt. ........................................... **50.00**

**Teapot,** cov., individual, footed, Flora patt., 5¾" h. ...................... **20.00**

**Teapot,** cov., Town & Country patt., blue ................................. **95.00**

**Vase,** 7" h., bulbous ovoid body tapering to a short trumpet-shaped neck, leaf-shaped handles from shoulder to rim, pale blue, No. 3104.................... **40.00**

**Vase,** 8" h., Tropic Ware line,
No. 2025 .................................. **275.00**

**Vegetable bowl,** open, divided,
Festival patt. .............................. **30.00**

# STONEWARE

*Stoneware Pig Bottle*

*Stoneware is essentially a vitreous
pottery, impervious to water even in its
unglazed state, that has been produced by
potteries all over the world for centuries.
Utilitarian wares such as crocks, jugs,
churns and the like, were the most
common productions in the numerous
potteries that sprang into existence in the
United States during the 19th century.
These items were often enhanced by the
application of a cobalt blue oxide
decoration. In addition to the coarse,
primarily salt-glazed stonewares, there
are other categories of stoneware known
by such special names as basalt, jasper
and others. Also see BENNINGTON.*

**Bottle,** figural, molded as a pig,
grey salt glaze, 9" l. (ILLUS.
above).................................. **$1,210.00**

**Bowl,** cylindrical w/sides flaring to
wide molded rim & applied
handles, cobalt blue "comma"
decoration & impressed "1½" in
circle of dots, 10¾" d., 6¾" h.
(wear & chips)............................ **83.00**

**Butter churn,** tall swelled
cylindrical body w/eared handles
& molded rim, large brushed
cobalt blue scrolling bush design
w/large top leaves, impressed
mark "H.M. Whitman, Havana,
N.Y. - 3," 19th c., 3 gal., 15" h.
(minor interior rim chips) ........ **1,150.00**

*Bennington Stoneware Crock*

**Butter churn,** cylindrical w/eared
handles, brushed cobalt blue
flower & "4," 4 gal., 16½" h.
(very minor chips) .................... **165.00**

**Butter crock,** cov., brushed
cobalt blue leafy design on base
& similar design on mismatched
lid, 7¼" d. (chips on lid finial) .... **303.00**

**Crock,** cylindrical body w/eared
handles, brushed cobalt blue
leaf design & impressed label
"E. & L.P. Norton, Bennington
Vt," 7" h. (rim chips & hairline).... **248.00**

**Crock,** cylindrical w/eared
handles, cobalt blue slip-quilled
stylized floral design &
impressed label "E. & L.P.
Norton, Bennington, Vt 3," 3 gal,
10¼" h. (chips)......................... **275.00**

**Crock,** cylindrical w/applied
handles, slip-quilled cobalt blue
bird on branch & impressed label
"White & Wood, Binghamton,
N.Y. 4," 4 gal., 11¼" h. (hairline &
small rim chips).......................... **380.00**

**Crock,** cylindrical w/eared handles,
brushed cobalt blue floral
decoration & impressed label "M.
Woodruff, Cortland 4," 4 gal.,
11½" h. (hairlines in base).......... **187.00**

**Crock,** cylindrical w/eared handles
& molded rim, cobalt blue slip-
quilled large basket of stylized
flowers, impressed mark of J.
Norton & Co., Bennington,
Vermont & "6," mid-19th c., 6
gal., minor chips, 13¼" h.
(ILLUS. above).......................... **489.00**

**Flask,** flattened ovoid body tapering to a short neck w/a molded mouth, front incised w/"SP July 19 - 1803" & the reverse w/an incised flower tree & "1803," 5¼" h. ..................... **3,220.00**

**Jar,** cov., ovoid w/a flat flared mouth & eared handles, cobalt blue impressed label "S. Purdy, Portage Co., Ohio," 9¼" h. (rim chips & mismatched red clay lid) ............................................ **275.00**

**Jar,** wide ovoid w/rolled molded rim, brushed cobalt blue tulips, dark brown Albany slip interior, 4¾" h. ...................................... **385.00**

**JJar,** cylindrical w/rounded shoulder & slightly flaring molded rim, brushed cobalt blue foliage design, dark brown Albany slip interior, 10¼" h. ...... **248.00**

**Jar,** ovoid w/wide molded flaring neck, tooled lines around shoulder, cobalt blue brushed decoration of large stylized flowers, impressed "2," 2 gal, 10½" h. (hairlines in base) ........ **248.00**

**Jar,** ovoid w/applied open shoulder handles, incised designs highlighted in cobalt blue w/blue at handles, 13¾" h. (hairlines & rim chips) ............... **193.00**

**Jar,** bulbous ovoid body w/wide molded mouth, eared handles, incised lines & cobalt blue impressed heart designs, 14¼" h. (chips & hairlines) ........ **220.00**

**Jar,** ovoid w/applied shoulder handles, stenciled cobalt blue label "Donaghho Co., Parkersburg, 10," 10 gal., 19½" h. (minor flakes) .............. **138.00**

**Jug,** beehive form, applied strap handle, marked "W. Lewis, Milburn" & impressed "2," 2 gal... **95.00**

**Jug,** squatty bulbous body w/molded rim & applied strap handle, impressed cobalt blue label "M. Culton & Plains Dell, No. 1 Market Sq. Portsmouth, N.H.," 7½" h. (chip on lip & small flakes) ...................................... **149.00**

**Jug,** semi-ovoid w/small molded rim & strap handle, cobalt blue slip-quilled long-tailed bird on a branch, impressed label "J. Norton & Co., Bennington, Vt.," 11" h. ......................................... **479.00**

**Jug,** ovoid w/molded neck & rim handle, impressed cobalt blue label, "I.M. Mead" (Ohio), 11¼" h. ...................................... **220.00**

**Jug,** bulbous ovoid body w/strap handle, brushed cobalt blue flower, "2" & impressed label "I.M. Mead, Mogadore, Ohio," 2 gal., 14" h. (minor chips & hairline in neck) ......................... **869.00**

**Jug,** bulbous ovoid body w/strap handle & tooled band at neck, grey salt glaze w/olive green highlights & brown daub on handle, impressed "Boston 2," 2 gal., 15" h. (hairlines in base) ... **220.00**

**Jug,** ovoid tapering to a small cylindrical neck, cobalt blue stenciled & free-hand elaborate floral design & label "From Hamilton & Jones, Greensboro, Greene Co., Pa.," 16" h. (hairlines) ................................... **770.00**

**Jug,** bulbous ovoid w/tooled neck & applied strap handle, cobalt blue brushed design & daubs of blue at handle, 16¾" h. (chips on bottom edge) ....................... **330.00**

**Milk bowl,** round flaring sides w/molded rim, cobalt blue brushed leaf designs, impressed "1" in circle, 10¾" d. (flakes on inside lip) ................................. **385.00**

**Milk bowl,** wide cylindrical w/eared handles, cobalt blue brushed leaf sprig design & "1½" black Albany slip interior, 11¼" d., 5¾" h. ......................... **275.00**

**Pitcher,** 7¾" h., tapering ovoid body w/branch handle, arched spout, decorated w/applied tooled leaves & branches, Albany slip exterior glaze (ILLUS. top next page) .............. **110.00**

**Pitcher,** 8" h., cylindrical body w/pinched spout & C-form

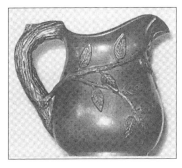

*Albany Slip-glazed Stoneware Pitcher*

handle, relief-molded tree bark w/roses & portrait, man w/tankards, highlighted in cobalt blue (very small edge flakes) .... **138.00**

**Preserving jar,** cylindrical body w/thick molded rim, cobalt blue brushed foliage scroll designs, 10⅜" h. ....................................... **171.00**

**Preserving jar,** cylindrical body w/molded rim, cobalt blue brushed tulip-like flower, impressed "H. Purdy 2" (Ohio), 2 gal., 12¾" h. (rim chip) ........... **165.00**

**Water cooler,** cov., bulbous ovoid w/applied strap handles from neck to shoulder & domed cover w/button finial, incised flowering branch highlighted w/cobalt blue w/blue at hole & handles, impressed "Cyrus Felton," 20" h. plus lid (domed lid a loose fit & is chipped, hairline in base & minor chips on lip) ................. **4,070.00**

## SUSIE COOPER

*Susie Cooper is unique in the annals of the British pottery industry in that her career covered a span of over 70 years, many of those as a designer and decorator of varied lines of earthenware and china.*

*Beginning her career at Gray's Pottery in 1922, she soon showed a great talent for design and decorating and many colorful and unique Art Deco designs were introduced by her during the 1920s*

*and 1930s. Working for a number of British potters over the years, the designs for dinnerwares by Susie Cooper evolved with the tastes of the times so more modern patterns and shapes were introduced after World War II and right up until her retirement as director of Susie Cooper Limited in 1972. Even after her retirement Ms. Cooper kept active in the pottery business and produced special limited items right into her 90s.*

**Ashtray,** Cornpoppy patt., ca. 1971 ..................................... **$37.00**

**Bowl,** fruit, 5" d., Gardenia patt., 1952 ............................................. **6.00**

**Bowl,** 6½" d., Gardenia patt., 1952 ... **8.00**

**Coffee set:** cov. coffeepot, creamer, cov. sugar bowl & four cups & saucers; Relief Polka Dot patt., green & white, Wedgwood, the set .................. **395.00**

**Creamer,** Gardenia patt., 1952 ..... **10.00**

**Creamer & cov. sugar bowl,** Tigerlily patt., 1941, pr. (crazing) .. **30.00**

**Cream soup w/underplate,** Gardenia patt., 1952, 2 pcs. ......... **8.00**

**Cup & saucer,** Gardenia patt., 1952 .. **8.00**

**Gravy boat,** Gardenia patt., 1952 .. **15.00**

**Plate,** 8" d., Gardenia patt., 1952.... **6.00**

**Platter,** 14" l., Tigerlily patt., 1941 ........................................... **55.00**

**Snack set:** cup, saucer & plate; Black Fruit patt., black on white, orange interior in cup, 3 pcs. ...... **25.00**

**Sugar bowl,** cov., Gardenia patt., 1952 ......................................... **15.00**

## TECO POTTERY

*The American Terra Cotta and Ceramic Company of Terra Cotta (Crystal Lake), Illinois introduced their line of Teco Pottery in 1902. The company had been founded by William D. Gates in 1881 and originally produced only bricks and drain tile. The company had excellent facilities for experimentation, including a chemical* laboratory, and was able to develop this art pottery line which featured mainly matte green glazes. Later pieces were produced in a wider range of colors including metallic lustre and crystalline glazes. Some hand-thrown pottery was produced by Gates preferred molded wares since they were less expensive to make. Teco Pottery was no longer produced by 1923 and the American Terra Cotta and Ceramic Company was sold in 1930. A good reference on this pottery is the book Teco: Art Pottery of the Prairie School, by Sharon S. Darling (Erie Art Museum, 1990).

*Teco Pottery Mark*

**Book ends,** upright rectangular backplate on a thick hollowed rectangular foot, molded on the upright w/the figure of a standing Indian maiden holding a jug & looking down into an openwork pool in the base, cream & orange glaze w/glossy green-glazed pool, impressed mark, 7" h., pr. ................................. **$660.00**

**Bowl,** 6¾" d., low squatty wide bulbous sides w/a wide shoulder curving up to a high, thick rolled rim, variegated brownish green matte glaze, marked twice on base .......................................... **358.00**

**Bowl-vase,** a wide sharply tapering bowl flanked by four heavy squared buttress legs w/block feet, the exterior w/a medium green matte glaze w/light charcoaling, the interior w/a rich creamy crackle glaze, impressed marks, 12" d., 6" h. (ILLUS. top next column) ....... **5,225.00**

**Ewer,** tall slender waisted form w/a pinched rim spout & arched forked handle continuing from the rim edge to halfway down

*Fine Teco Bowl-Vase*

the body, matte green glaze, designed by W.D. Gates, No. 297, impressed mark, 8½" h. (repaired rim chip).................... **358.00**

**Planter,** long, low & narrow rectangular form w/eight buttress supports topped by small raised medallions, inspired by the style of Louis Sullivan, cream matte glaze w/orange highlights, 6 x 24", 6½" h. (minor chips) ....................................... **935.00**

**Vase,** 5½" h., 8½" w., a bulbous base pulled out to the sides to form thick loop handles arching up to the rim of the short flaring neck, gunmetal grey over matte green glaze, designed by N. Forester, No. 297, impressed mark.......................................... **468.00**

**Vase,** 6¼" h., 5¼" d., bulbous ovoid body w/four small in-body handles around the pierced flat mouth & shoulder, the sides embossed w/bands of scrolled organic designs, fine darker green veined matte glaze, No. 113, die-stamped mark ... **2,090.00**

**Vase,** 8¾" h., 4" d., footed gently swelled cylindrical body w/a narrow angled shoulder to the flaring rim, molded in relief w/narcissus blossoms on tall leafy stems under a matte light pink ground, unmarked (glaze chip on base) ........................... **550.00**

**Vase,** 9" h., squared slightly tapering form w/paneled sides & broad low loop handles from the flat mouth to the shoulder, small top opening, matte green glaze,

*Large Teco Vase*

mark stamped twice, No. 184,
designed by Fritz Albert ........ **2,530.00**

**Vase,** 12" h., 6" d., four-sided lily
form w/a large cup-shaped lotus
blossom top & trailing stems &
leaves, supported by four
vertical buttresses, deep green
matte glaze, die-stamped mark
twice...................................... **2,640.00**

**Vase,** 30½" h., 18" d., a tall wide
simple ovoid form w/a small,
thick molded mouth, matte
green glaze w/black crazing,
small glaze nicks on body
(ILLUS.) ................................ **2,310.00**

# TEPLITZ - AMPHORA

*Ornate Amphora Jardiniere*

*Numerous potteries operated in the vicinity of Teplitz in the Bohemian region of what is now the Czech Republic. During the late 19th and early 20th centuries a wide range of vases and figural pieces of varying quality were*

*manufactured there by such companies as Riessner & Kessel (Amphora), Ernst Wahliss and Alfred Stellmacher. The wares were originally low-priced, but the best examples of Teplitz and Amphora wares are bringing strong prices today.*

*Teplitz-Amphora Marks*

**Bowl-vase,** jeweled porcelain,
squatty bulbous body w/a short,
wide cylindrical neck, matte
white ground decorated w/gilt
floral & geometric designs,
highlighted w/iridescent light
blue & white enameling & a
band of discs centered by
'jewels' around the shoulder,
impressed Amphora mark,
No. 461 - 3, 5½" d., 3⅞" h....... **$748.00**

**Figurine,** Austrian aristocrat
wearing kneebreeches & shirt
w/balloon sleeves & peplum,
head tilted back & one hand
holding the brim of his hat,
standing near tree stump w/a
dog at his feet, Nos. 4239 &
1345, marked w/five-pointed
crown, artist-initialed, "E.W." &
"Turn-Wien-Made in Austria,"
20¾" h. to top of hat (ding
on tip of dog's tail, barely
noticeable) .......................... **2,500.00**

**Jardiniere,** a twisted oblong
pedestal base supports a wide
oblong bowl w/the sides molded
in high-relief w/stylized large
flowers & stems continuing to
form end handles, wide incurved
mouth, decorated in shades of
pink & green w/gold highlighting,
impressed crown & "Amphora" in
a lozenge, No. 0390,52, 5½ x
13", 5⅞" h. (ILLUS. bottom,
previous column) ..................... **575.00**

**Vase,** 5" h., a thin footring supports a spherical body w/two short tapering necks w/inwardly-pointed rims, one on each side of the top shoulder, a raised decoration of delicate pine branches w/needles in gold, green & white suspended from each rim, all against a white matte ground w/gold highlights, marked "Made in Austria - Vienna," impressed "1561" & w/the Amphora mark ................... **275.00**

**Vase,** 8⅛" h., bulbous base in robin's egg blue divided into four sections by gold diamond shapes & tapering to a cylindrical, faceted slender neck of moss green ........ **375.00**

**Vase,** 9" h., Crown Oak Ware, a bulbous ovoid body w/wide vertical ribs to resemble a tree trunk w/slender curved branch handles from the angled shoulder to the tall, slender neck w/molded rim, rich caramel & greyish green matte glaze, marked "Teplitz - Austria," impressed marks & partial paper label ...................... **165.00**

**Vase,** 11" h., applied pink rose on basketweave ground w/applied child at side climbing into basket, grey lustre finish, marked "Amphora - Czechoslovakia" ..... **450.00**

# TIFFANY POTTERY

*In 1902 Louis C. Tiffany expanded Tiffany Studios to include ceramics, enamels, gold, silver and gemstones. Tiffany pottery was usually molded rather than wheel-thrown, but it was carefully finished by hand. A limited amount was produced until about 1914; it is scarce.*

*Tiffany Pottery Mark*

*Tiffany Bronze Pottery Vase*

**Bowl-vase,** deep slightly tapering cylindrical form rounded at the bottom rim & w/an incurved wide mouth, the body molded in relief w/fruiting branches, glazed in shades of cream, charcoal & pale green, inscribed on base "L C T - Tiffany-Favrile Pottery - P 228," ca. 1910, 8" d. (minor chip on base) .............................. **$6,325.00**

**Vase,** 6¼" h., bronze pottery, a bulbous base tapering to a wide cylindrical neck, the interior glazed in mottled blue & white, decorated w/prunus branches & blossoms all encased in bronze, inscribed "L.C.T." & "L.C. Tiffany-Favrile Bronze Pottery - B.P.165," ca. 1910-14 (ILLUS. above) ..... **3,450.00**

**Vase,** 12¾" h., 4" d., very tall slender slightly tapering cylindrical form, embossed w/wide bands of poinsettia blossoms & leaves separated by a wide central pebbled band, bronze overlay & silvered wash, impressed in base "LCT," & written out "LCTiffany Favrile Bronze Pottery," early 20th c.... **2,090.00**

# TILES

*Since the late 19th century many American and foreign potteries have produced lines of decorative and utilitarian tiles. Many of the firms which featured art pottery wares included tiles as part of this production and such wares were often used to decorate fireplaces, floors and walls, as well as serving as tea tiles. We list a sampling of tiles from various potteries below.*

*Rookwood Tile Panels*

**Arts & Crafts style,** square, a delicate squeezebag decoration of stylized poppies w/large teal blossoms & centers in dark blue w/aqua stamens, all atop narrow vivid green twisting stems & leaves w/prominent spines & jagged edges against a rich cream ground, 5½" w. ............. **$523.00**

**California Faience,** Berkeley, California, square, decorated in cuenca w/a large Spanish galleon in matte burgundy, dark blue & ochre on a glossy turquoise sea, stamped mark, 5½" w. ...................................... **165.00**

**Grueby Faience & Tile Company,** Boston, Massachusetts, square, decorated w/a ferocious brown lion w/open mouth, extended tongue & long twisting tail against an oatmeal ground & under two stylized trees w/green trunks & leaves backed by pale blue water & sky, 4" w. (minor chips) ............ **523.00**

**Grueby Faience & Tile Company,** Boston, Massachusetts, square, decorated w/a single tulip w/an ivory blossom atop a carved vertical stem & broad carved leaves, all in rich matte green, in original wide flat oak frame, tile 6" w. ...................................... **1,320.00**

**Marblehead Pottery,** Marblehead, Massachusetts, square, a stylized landscape of three dark green & bluish green trees atop a green rolling ground backed by a sky of tan & caramel w/a narrow border of bluish grey, in a period wide flat oak frame, paper label & large impressed mark, tile 4" w. ....... **1,760.00**

**Marblehead Pottery,** Marblehead Massachusetts, square, h.p w/a bulbous dark blue vase filled to

overflowing w/light & dark blue flowers & dark green leaves against a pale blue ground, dark blue rim band, soft matte glaze, marked, 5¾" w. (minor glaze nicks) ...................................... **523.00**

**Rhead Pottery,** Santa Barbara, California, square, carved design of a Grecian woman w/peach curling hair in a flowing tan & white toga against a mottled caramel, black & white ground, geometric border in blues, signed, 6" w. (minute chips) ...................................... **660.00**

**Rookwood Pottery,** Cincinnati, Ohio, square, decorated w/a stylized landscape w/a single tree w/a rich caramel trunk & olive green leaves atop an olive green ground backed by a medium blue lake, distant lavender mountains & pale blue sky, Matte glaze, in a wide flat oak frame, 5½" w. .................... **825.00**

**Rookwood Pottery,** Cincinnati, Ohio, twelve-sided, Blue Ship patt. on a white ground, No. M-28, ca. 1920s-30s, 6" w. (minor surface wear) ........................... **330.00**

**Rookwood Pottery,** Cincinnati, Ohio, a pair of panels each composed of eight tiles forming a full-length portrait of a classical maiden, one carrying a lamp, the other cymbals, matte glazed in ivory & cream w/brown hair, blue eyes, rosey pink

shawl, the lamp & cymbals in
ochre, the scroll in one hand in
tan, on a green background,
framed & back w/iron,
impressed "rookwood faience -
1924Y - 5" & sequenced, each
17" w., 33" h., facing pr.
(ILLUS. top previous page).... **5,750.00**

**Walrich Pottery,** Berkeley,
California, square, a glossy-
glazed landscape of tall trees
w/green leaves & blue & green
trunks among clumps of green
bushes on a rich lavender &
dark blue ground, backed by a
calm lavender body of water, a
dark green distant shoreline, a
dark blue mountain peak & a rich
lavender sky, in a period
wide flat oak frame, tile 5" w..... **5,225.00**

# TOBY MUGS & JUGS

*Two Early Tobies*

*The Toby is a figural jug or mug
usually delineating a robust, genial
drinking man. The name has been used in
England since the mid-18th century.
Copies of the English mugs and jugs were
made in America.*

*For listings of related Character
Jugs see DOULTON & ROYAL
DOULTON.*

**Pratt-type pearlware Toby,**
seated Mr. Toby wearing a
tricorn hat, dotted jacket &
kneebreeches & holding a jug of
ale, polychrome underglaze
enamels, w/an inset lid, ca.
1800, hat brim damage, foot rim
line, 9½" h. (ILLUS. right)........ **$978.00**

**Staffordshire "hearty good
fellow" pearlware Toby,**
standing man wearing a black
tricorn hat & coat, a vest
w/ornate floral sprig design,
kneebreeches & shoes
w/buckles, holding a jug in one
hand which is decorated w/a
drinking scene, on a heavy
mottled green base, face &
hands in flesh tones & brown,
1790-1820, 10½" h. (restoration
to the hat, right arm & small
chips around base, some black
enamel flaking) ........................ **440.00**

**Staffordshire pearlware Toby,**
seated Mr. Toby wearing a
tricorn hat & holding a foaming
mug of beer between his hands
on his lap, decorated in typical
"Pratt" colors of light blue,
yellow, orangish ochre, black,
light green, brick red & mottled
green, ca. 1780-1800, 8¾" h.
(invisible restoration to brim of
hat)........................................... **275.00**

**Staffordshire pearlware Toby,**
seated Mr. Toby wearing a
tricorn hat & holding a foaming
mug of ale, overglaze
polychrome enamel decoration,
chips & repairs, 19th c., 9½" h.
(ILLUS. left).............................. **345.00**

**Whitefield (George) Toby,**
earthenware, seated Mr. Toby
holding his hat in one hand, a
lantern in the other, overglazed
enamel-decorated & w/a
marbleized base, England, early
19th c., 8¾" h. (spout chips
restored, enamels retouched,
left foot repaired)...................... **259.00**

**Wilkinson "Admiral Jellicoe"
Toby,** standing figure in naval

*Three Wilkinson Character Tobies*

uniform holding a pitcher marked "Hell Fire Jack," designed by Sir Francis Carruthers Gould, printed marks, England, ca. 1918, 10" h.......................................... **575.00**

**Wilkinson "Field Marshall Haig" Toby,** seated figure in military uniform & hat holding a jug decorated w/the Union Jack, the rectangular base w/notched corners incised across the front "Push and Go," polychrome decoration, designed by Sir Francis Carruthers Gould, printed marks, ca. 1917, 10¾" h. (ILLUS. right) ........................... **460.00**

**Wilkinson "Marshall Foch" Toby,** seated figure of the French officer in uniform holding a champagne glass in one hand w/his other hand on a large bottle marked "Au Diable Le Kaiser," polychrome decoration, on a round base decorated w/various animals, modeled by Sir Francis Carruthers Gould, printed marks, ca. 1918, 11¾" h. (ILLUS. center) ...................... **345.00**

**Wilkinson "Marshall Joffre" Toby,** seated figure of an older man in military uniform w/a widely flaring hat brim forming the spout, holding a large cannon shell in his lap which reads "75mm Ce que Joffre," polychrome decoration, on a rectangular base w/notched corners, modeled by Sir Francis Carruthers Gould, printed marks, ca. 1918, hat brim restored, 10" h. (ILLUS. left) ..... **345.00**

**Wilkinson "President Wilson" Toby,** standing figure wearing a jacket & striped pants, holding a model of a bi-plane, entitled "Welcome! Uncle Sam," designed by Sir Francis Carruthers Gould, printed marks, England, ca. 1918, 10¾" h. (nicks to plane wing).... **978.00**

**Yorkshire-type Toby,** standing Mr. Toby w/a dotted pattern painted on his vest & interior of his tricorn hat as well as around the round base, typical Pratt palette, a caryatid-form handle, England, early 19th c., 7¾" h. (hat brim chip restored) .............................. **748.00**

# TORQUAY POTTERY

*Torquay Pottery is a general term referring to the products of several potteries which operated in the Torquay area of South Devon, England in the late 19th and early 20th centuries. Various decorative techniques were used to decorate these wares including sgraffito work, slip-glazed decoration and molding. Around the turn of the century hand-decorated "Motto Ware" became a popular product, often sold at area resorts as souvenirs. These pieces are among the most common and collectible of the Torquay pottery wares found on the U.S. market.*

*The three main Torquay potteries were:*

- *The Watcombe Pottery (The Watcombe Terracotta-Clay Company 1869-1962)*

- *The Torquay Terracotta Company (1875-1909)*

- *Aller Vale Art Pottery (1865-1901)*

*The Longpark Pottery of Torre was another noted maker of Motto Ware and operated from 1905 to 1940.*

*Torquay Pottery Marks*

**Basket,** ship decoration, sunset colors, 3 x 4½", 5¾" h. ............. **$105.00**

**Bowl,** pedestal base w/junket motto around outside rim, decorated w/a band of flowers, 6¾" d., 5¼" h. (ILLUS. top next column) ..................................... **190.00**

**Candlestick,** handled, saucer-shaped base, Black Cockerel patt., 4¼" h. ............................... **100.00**

*Torquay Footed Bowl*

**Candlestick,** handled, saucer-shaped base, Scandy patt., 4¼" h. ........................................ **105.00**

**Creamer,** child's, Motto Ware, Cottage patt., "Gretna Green," 1¾" d., 2¼" h. ............................. **40.00**

**Creamer,** Lucky Devon Pixie decoration on yellow ground, 3¾" h. ........................................ **120.00**

**Egg cup,** round base, Motto Ware, Cottage patt., "Fresh to-day," 3" d., 2¾" h. ................... **35.00**

**Hot water jug,** cov., Cottage patt. ............................................ **135.00**

**Jam jar,** cov., handled, Cottage patt. ............................................ **100.00**

**Mug,** three-handled, Motto Ware, Sailing Ship patt., cylindrical body w/three C-form handles, "Time and Tide for no Man Bide," 5½" d., 4⅝" h. (ILLUS. center, top next page) ................ **95.00**

**Pen tray,** oval, Scandy patt., 2½ x 9¼" .................................... **110.00**

**Pitcher,** jug-type, barrel-shaped, Scandy patt., 4½" h. ................... **125.00**

**Puzzle jug,** Sailing Ship patt., 4¼" h. ........................................ **165.00**

**Sugar bowl,** ruffled rim, colored cockerel decoration, 4" d., 3½" h. ........................................ **125.00**

**Teapot,** cov., Devon Motto Ware, "The Shamrock Green, o'er Earth is seen. Hibernia's beauty telling" ...................................... **125.00**

*Torquay Motto Ware Vases & Mug*

**Vase,** 3⅜" h., 3⅝" d., Motto Ware, Sailing Ship patt., a waisted cylindrical body w/two twisted C-form handles down the sides, "Welcome is the best cheer" (ILLUS. right) .............................. **65.00**

**Vase,** 5¾" h., 3" d., Motto Ware, Sailing Ship patt., tapering cylindrical body w/a narrow rounded shoulder to the trumpet neck, "I wish you all the joy that you may wish" (ILLUS. left)......... **60.00**

Potter *Artus Van Briggle began his career as a decorator for the famous Rookwood Pottery of Cincinnati. Due to health problems he left Rookwood and moved to Colorado Springs, Colorado where he and his wife Anna founded The Van Briggle Pottery in 1900. Artus died in 1904 but Anna carried on production for several years before others took over the operation. Pieces were dated from 1900 until 1920. Van Briggle Pottery continues in production today in Colorado Springs.*

# VAN BRIGGLE POTTERY

*Early Van Briggle Chalice*

*Van Briggle Pottery Mark*

**Bowl,** 6¾" d., 4" h., a wide flat base below the flaring rounded lower body w/a wide tapering shoulder to the wide flat mouth, robin's-egg blue matte glaze, shape No. 268, 1906 .............. **$605.00**

**Chalice,** a rounded wide foot tapering to a slender stem supporting a wide squatty bulbous bowl tapering to a flat mouth, molded in relief w/a beautiful stylized mermaid embracing the form of a fish, covered in a velvety matte light green glaze, shape No. 1, dated 1902, repaired, 11½" h. (ILLUS. bottom previous page) .................................. **14,300.00**

**Jug w/original beetle-molded stopper,** "Snake Jug" model, tall ovoid body w/a relief-molded snake wrapping around the body & forming the handle, snake in brown against a medium green ground w/a lightly molded band of stripes around the shoulder, rust-colored highlights, shape No. 23, 1902, 6⅞" h. (tight line in handle at rim) ........................ **3,190.00**

**Mug,** slightly ovoid shape w/rolled rim w/an embossed eagle in flight under a rich medium matte green glaze, incised "AA - Van Briggle - Colorado Springs - 1906 - 355 - 4," 1906, 4¾" d., 5" h. .......................................... **303.00**

**Trivet,** round w/thick raised molded rim, the center embossed w/a large stylized spider in black on a dark matte green ground, shape No. 491, 1906, 5½" d. .............................. **495.00**

**Vase,** 3½" h., 3¾" d., squatty bulbous body w/slightly rolled lip, w/heavily embossed spade-shaped leaves under a turquoise matte glaze, incised "AA - Van Briggle - Colo Spgs - 732," 1907-1912 (clay showing through leaf edges) ................... **495.00**

**Vase,** 4½" h., 4¾" d., squatty angular bulbous body tapering to short cylindrical neck w/rounded rim, decorated w/stylized poppy pods on swirling stems in relief, under variegated soft green matte glaze, incised "AA - 8 - Van Briggle - Colo. Springs - 1906 - 452," 1906 ............................... **715.00**

**Vase,** 5" h., copper-clad, wide bulbous ovoid body w/a rounded shoulder to the wide, short neck w/flat rim flanked by relief-

*Van Briggle Dragonfly Vase*

molded lizard handles down the sides, marks on the copper bottom include the Van Briggle logo, notation "Van Briggle Colo. Spgs.," a finisher number "11" & shape "No. 702 SW," ca. 1907-12 (two small breaks in copper on rim & spot on side where copper did not adhere) ........... **1,650.00**

**Vase,** 5½" h., gently swelled cylindrical body w/a narrow shoulder to the short cylindrical neck, carved decoration of large tulip blossoms atop long vertical stems backed by stylized leaves, thick mustard yellow matte glaze, incised marks, ca. 1903 .............................. **1,650.00**

**Vase,** 5¾" h., 4" d., cylindrical body w/gently swelled shoulder curving in to a closed-in mouth, long slender round-tipped leaves swirling up & around the sides, gunmetal & dark green matte glaze, 1914, marks hidden by glaze ........................................ **440.00**

**Vase,** 6½" h., 5¼" d., ovoid form w/closed-in mouth, decorated w/stylized poppy pods on swirling stems, under a leathery, curdled bluish green to robin's-

egg blue matte glaze, incised
"AA - Van Briggle - Colorado
Springs - 1906 - 4??," 1906
(clay showing through glaze)... **2,530.00**

**Vase,** 6⅞" h., simple ovoid body
w/a short cylindrical neck
flanked by relief-molded
dragonflies, matte turquoise blue
glaze over a matte brown glaze,
ca. 1906 (ILLUS. top previous
page).................................... **1,610.00**

**Vase,** 7" h., 5" d., a narrow
footring below a wide squatty
bulbous body molded w/a band
of wide spearpoint leaves
tapering up to a slender, slightly
flaring cylindrical neck, flowing
blue matte glaze, 1907-12 ........ **825.00**

**Vase,** 7½" h., 4¾" d., "Dos
Cabezos" model, bulbous ovoid
body tapering to a cylindrical
neck, molded in high-relief on
each side w/a standing Art
Nouveau woman reaching back
around the shoulder, frothy
dark purple & gunmetal glaze,
1907 .................................... **6,325.00**

**Vase,** 8¼" h., 4" d., a slender
waisted cylindrical body w/a
rounded swelled shoulder
tapering to a short tapering
narrow neck, the shoulder
embossed w/a band of large
stylized thistle heads w/slender
stems down the sides, leathery
dark bluish green matte glaze,
shape No. 380, 1905 ............ **1,045.00**

**Vase,** 9½" h., 4½" d., gently
swelled cylindrical body w/an
angled shoulder to the short
cylindrical neck, embossed
poppy pods & leaves under a
fine blue matte flowing glaze,
red clay shows through the high
spots, shape No. 173, 1905... **1,980.00**

**Vase,** 10½" h., 5" d., tall
cylindrical body w/low buttress-
type handles flanking the flat
mouth, molded w/light blue
morning glories at the top on
green & dark blue leaves on a
soft green ground, shape
No. 228, 1903 ...................... **3,575.00**

*Van Briggle "Two Bears" Vase*

**Vase,** 11" h., "Indian Chiefs"
model, tall slender swelled body
w/a flaring round foot & molded
rim, molded in bold relief under
the rim w/the busts of three
Native American chiefs, matte
brown glaze w/green
highlighting, incised marks,
ca. 1930 .................................. **460.00**

**Vase,** 14½" h., "Two Bears"
model, a tall cylindrical body
molded at the top w/two climbing
bears, brown glaze w/slight blue
overspray, shape No. 244, dated
"1918" (ILLUS. above) ........... **4,675.00**

---

# VERNON KILNS

*The story of Vernon Kilns Pottery
begins with the purchase by Mr. Faye
Bennison of the Poxon China Company
(Vernon Potteries) in July 1931. The
Poxon family had run the pottery for a
number of years in Vernon, California,
but with the founding of Vernon Kilns the
product lines were greatly expanded.*

*Many innovative dinnerware lines and
patterns were introduced during the*

1930s, including designs by such noted American artists as Rockwell Kent and Don Blanding. In the early 1940s items were designed to tie in with Walt Disney's animated features "Fantasia" and "Dumbo." Various commemorative plates, including the popular "Bits" series, were also produced over a long period of time. Vernon Kilns was taken over by Metlox Potteries in 1958 and completely ceased production in 1960.

*Vernon Kilns Mark*

## DINNERWARES

**Bowl,** cereal, tab-handled, Tam O'Shanter patt............................ **$8.00**

**Bowl,** fruit, 5½" d., May Flower patt............................................... **6.00**

**Bowl,** flower petal-shaped, green, No. 135 ...................................... **68.00**

**Bowl,** salad, Organdie patt. .......... **60.00**

**Butter dish,** cov., Tam O'Shanter patt., ¼ lb. ..................................... **28.00**

**Casserole,** cov., Tam O'Shanter patt............................................... **48.00**

**Casserole,** cov., Tickled Pink patt............................................... **55.00**

**Chicken baker,** cov., Organdie patt............................................... **25.00**

**Coaster,** Homespun patt. ............. **25.00**

**Comport,** footed, Tweed patt. (T-504), 9½" h............................ **75.00**

**Cup & saucer,** demitasse, Organdie patt. ............................. **15.00**

**Cup & saucer,** Homespun patt., oversize ................................... **155.00**

**Egg cup,** Homespun patt.............. **18.00**

**Pitcher,** large, Tam O'Shanter patt............................................... **50.00**

**Plate,** luncheon, May Flower patt. .. **12.00**

**Plate,** 10½" d., Santa Claus decoration .................................. **45.00**

**Plate,** chop, 12" d., Frontier Days (Winchester 73) patt. ................ **100.00**

**Plate,** chop, 12" d., Monterey patt. .. **25.00**

**Plate,** chop, 12½" d., Ultra California patt., (carnation) pink or ice green ................................. **12.00**

**Salt & pepper shakers,** Organdie patt., pr....................................... **10.00**

**Soup plate w/flanged rim,** Organdie patt., 8" d.................... **10.00**

**Teapot,** cov., Vernon's 1860 patt. .. **75.00**

**Trio buffet server,** Country Cousin patt................................. **35.00**

**Tumbler,** Heavenly Days patt., 14 oz. ......................................... **16.00**

**Tumbler,** Tickled Pink patt., 14 oz. ......................................... **18.00**

**Vegetable bowl,** open, oval, divided, Frontier Days (Winchester 73) patt.................. **90.00**

**Vegetable bowl,** open, oval, May Flower patt. ................................. **20.00**

**Vegetable bowl,** open, divided, Tam O'Shanter patt. .................. **28.00**

**Vegetable bowl,** open, Tam O'Shanter patt............................ **15.00**

## "BITS" SERIES

**Plate,** 8½" d., Bits of the Middle West Series, Fourth of July......... **38.00**

**Plate,** 8½" d., Bits of Old New England Series, The Whaler....... **38.00**

**Plate,** 8½" d., Bits of the Old Southwest Series, San Juan Bautista Mission......................... **35.00**

**Plate,** 8½" d., Bits of the Old Southwest Series, San Juan Capistrano Mission .................... **40.00**

**Plate,** 8½" d., Bits of the Old West, The Barfly ......................... **25.00**

## DISNEY "FANTASIA" & OTHER ITEMS

**Bowl,** 10½" d., Sprite, No. 125, blue .......................................... **240.00**

**Figure of Nubian Centaurette,** No. 24, 7½" h. ....................... **1,050.00**

**Figure of Unicorn,** sitting, white, No. 14, 5" h. ............................. **450.00**

*Winged Pegasus Vase*

**Vase,** 7½" h., 12" l., Winged Pegasus patt., a wide flat-sided tapering form w/curved ends & a long rectangular flat mouth, lightly molded w/the winged horse in a landscape, a white ground h.p. in green, brown, yellow & black, glossy glaze, ca. 1941, marked (ILLUS.) ...................... **400.00 to 800.00**

**Vase,** 10½" h., Goddess patt., footed flattened ovoid form w/a low scalloped rim, relief-molded standing figure of a nude female shorting a bow & arrow, blue ... **1,200.00**

### DON BLANDING DINNERWARES

**Charger,** Lei Lani patt., 17½" d. .. **295.00**

**Cup,** Coral Reef patt., maroon ...... **45.00**

**Cup & saucer,** Lei Lani patt. ........ **27.00**

**Plate,** 7" d., Lei Lani patt. .............. **27.00**

**Plate,** dinner, Lei Lani patt. ........... **32.00**

**Plate,** chop, 12" d., Hawaiian Flowers patt., maroon .............. **135.00**

**Plate,** chop, 14" d., Hawaiian Flowers patt., maroon ................. **95.00**

**Plate,** chop, 17" d., Lei Lani patt. ......................................... **275.00**

**Salt & pepper shakers,** Hawaiian Flowers patt., maroon, pr. ........... **35.00**

**Sugar bowl,** cov., Lei Lani patt. ..... **38.00**

### ROCKWELL KENT DESIGNS

**Bowl,** 9" d., "Our America" series, scene of New York City piers.... **140.00**

**Cup & saucer,** demitasse, Moby Dick patt., blue ........................... **50.00**

**Jam jar w/notched cover,** Moby Dick patt., maroon..................... **250.00**

**Mug,** Moby Dick patt., maroon...... **95.00**

**Plate,** 9½" d., Salamina patt. ...... **135.00**

**Plate,** 10½" d., Salamina patt. .... **145.00**

**Plate,** 12" d., Salamina patt. ....... **225.00**

**Plate,** chop, 17" d., "Our America" series ...................................... **350.00**

**Sugar bowl,** cov., Moby Dick patt................................................ **75.00**

**Teapot,** cov., Moby Dick patt., blue, 6-cup ................................. **95.00**

### MISCELLANEOUS COMMEMORATIVES

**Plate,** Mission San Gabriel, multicolored ............................... **35.00**

**Plate,** Mission Santa Barbara, multicolored ............................... **35.00**

# VOLKMAR POTTERY

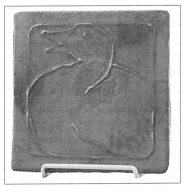

*Charles Volkmar Tile*

Charles Volkmar came from an artistic family and was able to study pottery making in Europe where he remained fourteen years before returning home in 1875. At the 1876 Philadelphia Centennial Exposition he was intrigued by the French art pottery exhibited and returned to France for further study.

Volkmar returned to the United States in 1879 and opened his first kiln in Greenpoint, Long Island, New York in

*1879. By 1882 he had established his own studio, kilns, salesroom and home at Tremont, New York.*

*The early Volkmar wares were decorated with applied and underglaze decoration done by Volkmar or an assistant using his designs. During the following years he worked in several partnerships and finally established the Volkmar Keramic Company in Brooklyn in 1895. His last venture was begun in 1902 when he was joined by his son Leon to establish the Volkmar Kilns in Metuchen, New Jersey in 1903. Charles Volkmar died in 1914 and Leon continued pottery production for some years.*

*Volkmar Marks*

**Mug,** waisted cylindrical body w/D-form handle, slip-decorated w/a bust portrait of a Boxer dog on a shaded green & brown ground, glossy glaze, Charles Volkmar, die-stamped "VOLKMAR," 5¼" d., 5¾" h. ....**$220.00**

**Pitcher,** 5" h., 4" d., hand-thrown, wide squatty bulbous base gently tapering to a wide slightly flaring cylindrical neck w/a pinched spout & C-form handle, fine dark green matte glaze, Charles Volkmar, incised "V" mark ............**83.00**

**Tile,** square, decorated in the squeezebag technique w/a stylized duck, matte green & black glaze, minor roughness to raised work, incised "V," 8" w. (ILLUS.) ....................................**495.00**

**Vase,** 6½" h., 3½" d., Charles Volkmar 'Crownpoint Ware,' slender ovoid body tapering to a short ruffled neck, decorated in Barbotine w/white, yellow & red blossoms & turquoise foliage on a mottled black & brown ground, die-stamped "VOLKMAR - 120" (invisible rim restoration)............**385.00**

**Vase,** 10" h., 9" d., wide flat-bottomed ovoid form tapering to a swelled rim w/wide flat mouth, incised w/full-length wide leaves under a satin green glaze, incised "V" ................................**935.00**

---

# WATT POTTERY

*Starflower Tea Canister*

*Founded in 1922, in Crooksville, Ohio, this pottery continued in operation until the factory was destroyed by fire in 1965. Although stoneware crocks and jugs were the first wares produced, by 1935 sturdy kitchen items in yellowware were the mainstay of production. Attractive lines like Kitch-N-Queen (banded) wares and the hand-painted Apple, Cherry and Pennsylvania Dutch (tulip) patterns were popular throughout the country. Today these hand-painted utilitarian wares are "hot" with collectors.*

*A good reference book for collectors is* Watt Pottery, An Identification and Value Guide, *by Sue and Dave Morris (Collector Books, 1993)*

*Watt Pottery Mark*

**Baker,** cov. Double Apple patt.,
No. 96, 8½" d., 5¾" h. .............**$295.00**

**Bean pot,** cov., two-handled,
Autumn Foliage patt., No. 76,
7½" d., 6½" h. ............................**145.00**

**Bean pot,** cov., two-handled,
Starflower patt., four-petal, No.
76, 7½" d., 6½" h. ......................**125.00**

**Bean server,** individual,
American Red Bud (Tear Drop)
patt., No. 75, 3½" d. ....................**35.00**

**Bowl,** cov., 7½" d., Dutch Tulip
patt., No. 66 ..............................**325.00**

**Bowl,** cov., 8¾" d., ribbed, Eagle
patt., No. 601 ............................**210.00**

**Bowl,** 5½" d., individual cereal,
Apple patt., No. 74 ......................**45.00**

**Canister,** cov., Starflower patt.,
four-petal, "Tea," No. 82
(ILLUS. previous page) ..............**175.00**

**Casserole,** cov., individual, oval
handles, Moonflower patt., pink
on black (old style) ....................**120.00**

**Chip N' Dip set,** Apple patt., No.
73 .............................................**100.00**

**Cookie jar,** cov., Rooster patt.,
No. 503 .....................................**275.00**

**Creamer,** Rooster patt., No. 62,
4¼" h. (ILLUS. top next column) ..**155.00**

**Creamer,** Starflower patt., No. 62,
4¼" h. .........................................**275.00**

**Creamer & cov. sugar bowl,**
Morning Glory patt., Nos. 97
& 98, pr. ....................................**650.00**

**Fondue pot,** cov., handled, Apple
patt., 9" l., 3" h. ..........................**500.00**

**Goodies jar,** cov., Apple patt.,
No. 59, 8½" h. ...........................**295.00**

**Grease jar,** cov., American Red
Bud (Tear Drop) patt. .................**185.00**

**Mixing bowls,** Apple patt., Nos.
5, 6, 8 & 9, the set......................**220.00**

**Mug,** Apple patt., No. 121, 3¾" h...**195.00**

**Pitcher,** 5½" h., American Red
Bud (Tear Drop) patt., No. 15 ......**50.00**

**Pitcher,** 5½" h., Cherry patt.,
No. 15, w/advertising .................**145.00**

**Pitcher,** 6½" h., Rooster patt.,
No. 16 .......................................**175.00**

**Pitcher w/ice lip,** 8" h., Starflower
patt., four-petal, No. 17 ..............**160.00**

*Watt Rooster Creamer*

*Dutch Tulip Spaghetti Bowl*

**Plate,** chop, Apple patt., No. 49 ...**375.00**

**Refrigerator pitcher,** squared
shape, Dutch Tulip patt. No. 69,
8½" w., 8" h...............................**525.00**

**Salt & pepper shakers,**
American Red Bud (Tear Drop)
patt., barrel-shaped, 4" h., pr. ....**200.00**

**Salt & pepper shakers,** Rooster
patt., barrel-shaped, pr. ............**450.00**

**Spaghetti bowl,** 13" d., Dutch
Tulip patt., No. 39 (ILLUS.
bottom, this column) .................**185.00**

**Spaghetti bowl,** 13" d.,
Starflower patt., No. 39 ...............**78.00**

**Sugar bowl,** cov., Apple patt.
w/advertising, No. 98 .................**395.00**

**Teapot,** cov., Autumn Foliage
patt., No. 112, 6" h. .................**1,500.00**

# WEDGWOOD

*Reference here is to the famous pottery established by Josiah Wedgwood in 1759 in England. Numerous types of wares have been produced through the years to the present.*

## WEDGWOOD

*Wedgwood Mark*

## BASALT

*Bust of Dryden & Milton Figure*

**Bust of Robert Burns,** mounted on a raised circular base, impressed title & mark, 19th c., 7½" h. ..................................... **$374.00**

**Bust of Dryden,** mounted on a round socle base, impressed title & mark, mid-19th c., 12" h. (ILLUS. left) .............................. **575.00**

**Bust of Shakespeare,** raised on a shaped squared base w/his name in raised letters, impressed marks, 1964, 10" h. ......................................... **374.00**

**Candlesticks,** figural, dolphin-shaped, the tail raised upright to form the candlesocket, on a shell-trimmed rectangular base, impressed marks, 1967, 8¾" h., pr. .......................................... **1,093.00**

**Figure of Milton,** standing, wearing period costume & a long cape & leaning on a round column, raised on an oblong base, titled on the reverse, impressed mark, ca. 1870, 16¼" h. (ILLUS. right) ........... **1,840.00**

**Figure group,** Cupid & Psyche, the seated nude figures modeled as youngsters on an oval base w/molded edge, impressed mark & title, 19th c., 7½" h. ..................................... **1,380.00**

**Incense burner,** a squatty bulbous wide body fitted w/a tapering domed pierced cover, the bowl supported on the upturned tails of three dolphins resting on a triangular base, impressed "Josiah Wedgwood Feb. 2, 1805," 5½" h. (restored cover chips) .......................... **1,610.00**

**Model of toucans,** potted as two conjoined birds w/glass eyes perched on a free-form circular base, modeled by Ernest Light, impressed marks, ca. 1913, 5¼" h. ..................................... **1,380.00**

**Pitcher,** club-type, 5½" h., ovoid body tapering to a short ringed neck w/a wide spout, loop handle from rim to center of the side, decorated w/scattered colored enamel florals, impressed mark, mid-19th c. .... **230.00**

**Plaques,** rectangular, decorated in relief w/scenes of bacchic revelry, set within simple walnut frames, impressed "WEDGWOOD" only, early 19th c., 9 x 22½", pr. .............. **2,875.00**

**Vase,** fixed lid-type, 9¾" h., engine-turned, a tall egg-form body w/molded stripes & an inverted acorn finial on the domed top, applied Bacchus head handles at the sides joined by a molded band of drapery swags, raised on a slender waisted pedestal foot on a square base, wafer mark of Wedgwood and Bentley, late 18th c. (handles restored) ...... **1,093.00**

*Wedgwood "First Day" Vases*

**Vases,** cov., 13¾" h., replicas of Wedgwood's First Day vase manufactured to commemorate the opening of the New York showroom, a flaring domed foot supporting a wide ovoid body w/a narrow incurved shoulder w/tall upright loop handles flanking the inset low-domed cover w/tall bullet-form finial, impressed marks, ca. 1948, pr. (ILLUS.) ............................ **2,530.00**

## CANEWARE

**Basket,** a shallow round form w/a high flat arched handle from side to side, a flattened pierced insert top, the exterior sides applied w/black basalt fruiting grapevine, impressed mark, early 19th c., 4¼" h. (rim staining) .................. **575.00**

**Game dish,** cov., deep slightly tapering oval sides w/rope borders, molded in relief w/fruiting vines & hanging game, the slightly domed inset cover w/a recumbent rabbit finial, impressed marks, w/a liner, 1865, 7" l. (liner cracked) .......... **431.00**

**Teapot,** cov., glazed, white fruiting grapevine in relief around the body, impressed mark, ca. 1830, 7" l. (base rim chip) ......................................... **173.00**

**Vase,** 7⅞" h., a sharply tapering body w/a ringed, flaring foot, the wide flat mouth w/a low rolled rim, the body decorated overall w/stylized enameled flowers & leaves, designed by Millicent Taplin, impressed marks, ca. 1930 ................................... **288.00**

## CREAMWARE

*Wedgwood Creamware Plate*

**Dish w/underplate,** oval w/reticulated borders, 9⅞" l., 2 pcs. (minor damage) ............. **275.00**

**Plate,** 9⅛" d., scene of young lady sitting on stool by kettle suspended over fire testing the cooking, basket by her side, titled on back, "Anticipation is rather dangerous," artist-signed, date marks for 1863 & marked "Wedgwood" (ILLUS.) .............. **325.00**

**Teapot,** cov., spherical body w/an inset cover & knob finial, swan's-neck spout & D-form handle, black transfer-printed decoration, one side w/a scene of male & female figures drinking in a landscape, the reverse w/the verse "Long may we live, happy may we be, blest with content, and from misfortunes free," lower case mark, ca. 1770, 5¼" h. (glaze wear, minor staining, handle restored) ........................ **633.00**

## JASPER WARE

**Barber bottle w/original stopper,** four-color, classical form w/a short pedestal & wide round foot supporting a wide ovoid body tapering to a tall cylindrical neck w/a molded rim & small domed cap w/button finial, decorated around the shoulder w/a wide white relief laurel leaf band & four Bacchus head masks above a band of floral swags separating round figural medallions w/lilac grounds, further white relief swags, leaf & beaded bands on the neck, cap, lower body & base, w/a green ground to either side of the central dark blue ground, impressed marks, late 19th c., 10½" h. ...................... **2,070.00**

**Bowl,** 7⅛" d., deep rounded sides on a small footring, white relief classical band of "Dancing Hours" on black, impressed mark, 20th c. ............................ **345.00**

**Candlesticks,** cylindrical shaft above a flaring foot & a cupped socket rim, the shaft w/a white relief classical scene & a narrow leaf band at the top & a looping scroll band around the foot on crimson, impressed marks, ca. 1920, 5" h., pr. ...................... **1,610.00**

**Cheese dish,** cov., a raised disc base w/a wide flanged rim decorated w/a band of white relief leaves on dark blue, the inset high-domed cover decorated in white relief w/a band of classical figures on dark blue, impressed marks, late 19th c., 9½" d. (ILLUS. top next column) ..................................... **460.00**

**Clock,** wall-type, a round light blue jasper ware wide frame w/a figural vignette at the top & floral swags down the sides enclosing a round clock w/enamel dial w/Arabic numerals framed by a band of rhinestones, the jasper ware mounted between an ormolu leaf cluster suspended from a ribbon, rings & bow above & a leaf cluster & pine cone below, the whole mounted on a rosewood veneer classical urn-form plaque, 19th c., overall 15½" h. (clock face damaged) .. **690.00**

*Jasper Ware Cheese Dish*

**Cracker jar,** cov., waisted cylindrical body, black relief fruiting grapevine & lion masks on a yellow ground, silver plate rim, cover & bail handle, impressed mark, late 19th c., 5¼" h. ............. **498.00**

**Cracker jar,** cov., barrel-shaped, w/wide rounded body decorated w/white relief classical figure groups w/lion mask handles at the sides & a white relief leaf top band on blue, a wide silver plate rim, swivel bail handle & ribbed & domed cover w/knob finial, impressed "Wedgwood" only, 6¼" h. ........................................ **330.00**

**Creamer,** squatty bulbous body w/pinched spout & C-form handle, white relief "Domestic Employment" scenes by Templeton on dark blue, ca. 1892-1915, marked "Wedgwood England," 3½" d., 2⅝" h. ............. **75.00**

**Jardiniere,** a narrow round foot supports a wide cylindrical body rounded at the bottom & w/a wide flat rim, a narrow white relief leafy rim band above large grapevine swags around the body joined by lion head masks w/rings, a band of classical figures around the lower body on crimson, impressed marks, ca. 1920, 7" d. (ILLUS. top left, next page) ............................. **1,093.00**

**Match holder,** footed cylindrical body w/flat rim, white relief classical figures around base & scroll & floral band flanked by white relief border around top on dark blue, ca. 1915-30, marked "Wedgwood - Made in England," 1⅝" d., 2⅛" h. ............................ **95.00**

*Crimson Jasper Jardiniere*

**Medallion,** round, white relief center scene of classical figures & a pedestal within a border of rounded loops on lilac, designed by Bert Bentley, impressed "BB 1362" & company mark, ca. 1920, enclosed in a wide, square ebonized wood frame, medallion 2½" d. ...................... **259.00**

**Perfume bottle w/silver plated screw-on top,** lay-down type, flattened teardrop form w/a white relief classical figure of a lady walking w/a cupid below a top swag drop & within a finely beaded border on green, unmarked, early 19th c., 4¾" l. (slight surface line)................... **690.00**

**Pitcher,** jug-form, miniature, 2½" h., 2¼" d., the ovoid body w/white relief groups of classical figures on dark blue, marked "Wedgwood" only (ILLUS. left, top next column) ...................... **125.00**

**Pitcher,** tankard, 3⅞" h., 2½" d., white relief classical figures & grape border around top edge, light blue ground, pre-1892, marked "Wedgwood" only .......... **95.00**

**Pitcher,** cov., 6½" h., 3¾" d., bulbous ovoid body tapering to a high arched rim & spout fitted w/a metal border & hinged cover w/serpent finial, white relief tall spearpoint leaves alternating w/cattails up the sides on dark blue, a white relief continuous horizontal band of blossoms around the neck, marked "Wedgwood" only (ILLUS. right with miniature pitcher)............... **245.00**

*Large & Miniature Pitchers*

*Round Jasper Plaque*

**Plaque,** oval, white relief classical scene of a female balancing a basket of flowers on her head on green, impressed mark, 19th c., mounted in a giltwood frame, plaque 5½ x 7½" ...................... **403.00**

**Plaque,** rectangular, white relief scene of Achilles dragging the body of Hector on solid light blue, impressed mark, late 19th c., mounted in a wide carved oak frame, plaque 5½ x 16"................................ **1,495.00**

**Plaque,** round, a central white relief scene of "Infant Academy" on lilac, a white relief acanthus leaf border band, impressed mark, mounted in octagonal giltwood frame, early 19th c., plaque 8¼" d. (ILLUS. bottom) .. **1,380.00**

**Plaques,** oval, one w/a white relief scene of "Perseus and

Andromeda" & the other w/"Ganymede and the Eagle," both on solid pale blue, one marked "BB44" & the "BB53," designed by Bert Bentley, in narrow molded frames w/name plates, impressed company marks, early 20th c., plaques 5¾ x 6½" (one restored) ........ **1,380.00**

**Teapot,** cov., squatty bulbous footed body w/an inset domed cover & button finial, short curved spout & D-form handle, white classical relief scene of figures & trees on crimson, impressed marks, ca. 1920, 10" l. (relief loss, cover restored) ........................... **690.00**

**Urn,** cov., bulbous ovoid body raised on a short flaring pedestal on a square foot, w/a short neck w/rolled rim & inset domed cover w/knob finial, white loop mask handles at the shoulders, the shoulders w/a white relief band of acanthus leaves & lancets above a wide band of white relief dancing classical figures on charcoal grey, further white relief designs on the lower body & around the foot, impressed "Wedgwood" only, 19th c., 8" h. ........................................... **770.00**

**Vase,** 5" h., bulbous body, white relief band of classical figures on charcoal grey, marked "Wedgwood" only ...................... **330.00**

**Vase,** 10½" h., Portland Vase model, wide ovoid body tapering to a short trumpet neck flanked by arched handles to shoulder, white relief continuous classical scene on black, impressed "T. Lovatt," & factory mark, ca. 1877 ............ **2,000.00 to 2,300.00**

**Vase,** cov., 11¾" h., a wide ovoid body tapering to a domed pedestal on a square plinth foot, a flattened disc cover centered by a vase-form finial, high arched applied reeded white relief shoulder handles, a band of white relief classical figures in different poses around the body

*Ornate Covered Vases*

below a narrow band of flowering swags, the upper shoulder band w/a white relief band of palmettes, the cover w/white relief bands & radiating leaves, further white relief designs on the lower body, pedestal & foot edge, all on solid blue, impressed mark, ca. 1967 ...................................... **805.00**

**Vases,** cov., 13½" h., classical form w/a square plinth below the short tapering pedestal supporting the tall egg-form body tapering to a short waisted neck w/a molded rim supporting a small domed cover w/knob finial, white jasper Bacchus mask shoulder handles, the yellow ground decorated w/various classical design bands in black, the main body w/a large frieze of "Dancing Hours," one w/chips to socle rim, early 20th c., pr. (ILLUS. above) ..... **2,300.00**

## ROSSO ANTICO

**Bust of Matthew Prior,** the turbaned figure w/draped shoulders, on a socle base, impressed mark & title, late 18th c., 7¼" h. (restorations) ..... **403.00**

**Potpourri,** cov., crater-form, a wide flaring urn-form body raised on a domed foot, a heavy rolled rim w/high loop handles continuing to the base of the urn, a pierced disc cover & insert lid, black basalt vine in relief around the upper sides, impressed mark, early 19th c., 13¼" w. (foot rim & insert flakes) .................................... **1,150.00**

## QUEENSWARE

*Victorian Queensware Platter*

**Basket & undertray,** the basketweave-molded bodies w/pierced galleries, decorated w/green & black enamel oak leaves & trim lines, impressed mark, early 19th c., basket 9" l., 2 pcs. ...................................... **288.00**

**Figure group,** "The Country Lovers," a young man & woman seated on a tree stump base, he wearing a dress suit & hat, she wearing a dress decorated overall w/flowerheads, the base decorated overall w/ivy leaves, polychrome colors, modeled by Arnold Machin, printed maker's mark, ca. 1940, 12⅜" h. ......... **1,035.00**

**Model of a duiker antelope,** the small animal in a running pose w/greenery behind, on a rectangular base, glossy glaze, designed by John Skeaping, impressed artist & factory marks, ca. 1927, 8¼" h. ........................ **201.00**

**Plate,** 9" d., octagonal w/raised oak leaf border, central enamel-decorated figural landscape signed by Emile Lessore, impressed marks, ca. 1872 ....... **316.00**

**Platter,** 15¾ x 20⅜", oval, polychrome decorated w/birds on branches in the center & butterflies & plants around the rim, in the Chelsea style, impressed mark, 1871 (ILLUS. previous column) ......... **374.00**

**Vase,** cov., 12½" h., the tall inverted pear-shaped body raised on a ringed, flaring low pedestal base, long D-form handles down the sides, the wide mouth fitted w/a stepped, domed cover w/artichoke finial, impressed & printed marks, ca. 1960 ................................... **173.00**

## MISCELLANEOUS

*Fairyland Lustre Bowl*

**Bowl,** 7" w., octagonal, Fairyland Lustre, "Castle on a Road" patt. on exterior, "Bird in a Hoop" patt. on interior, No. Z5125, ca. 1920, printed marks (ILLUS.) ........... **3,450.00**

**Bowl,** 8" w., octagonal, Hummingbird Lustre, decorated in blue lustre glaze w/hummingbirds on the exterior, the interior in bright orange w/a central hummingbird, No. 25294, ................................. **770.00**

**Candleholder,** Agate ware, classical urn-form, a short flaring pedestal supporting the tall body w/an angled shoulder to the cylindrical neck w/thick flaring rim at socket, applied creamware band & drapery swags around the shoulder, square black basalt base, wafer mark of Wedgwood and Bentley, ca. 1775, 6½" h. (restored chip to socle) ................................. **1,495.00**

*Majolica Figure of Bacchus*

*Wedgwood Model of a Flicker*

**Coffeepot,** cov., miniature, Moonlight Lustre, footed baluster-form w/a high domed cover w/knob finial, straight angled spout, D-form handle, overall mottled lustre finish, ca. 1810, impressed mark (small chips to spout & cover rim) ....... **690.00**

**Cup,** "York cup," Fish Lustre, a wide deep bowl w/a flaring rim, raised on a low ringed foot, mother-of-pearl interior, blue mottled exterior w/a band of fish, printed mark, ca. 1920s, 4½" d........................................ **403.00**

**Figure of Bacchus,** majolica, running young god nude except for an animal skin, holding a thyrus over his shoulder, game birds hanging from its end, a lute resting by his feet, impressed mark, ca. 1875, restorations, 16" h. (ILLUS. above) ............ **3,910.00**

**Figure of Long John Silver,** bone china, decorated in polychrome, modeled by Montaque Weaver-Bridgeman, impressed & printed marks, ca. 1924, 9¼" h...................... **1,150.00**

**Jardiniere,** majolica, wide cylindrical form raised on small scroll feet, a cobalt blue ground decorated w/relief-molded designs of polychrome floral swags & drops alternating w/four large oval portrait medallions in

relief alternatively depicting Queen Elizabeth I & Cardinal Woolsey, impressed marks, ca. 1871, 10½" h. (glaze loss repairs, hairlines) ..................... **460.00**

**Model of a Flicker,** bone china, the polychromed decorated bird perched on a slender tree stump w/flowers below, modeled by H.W. Palliser, painted by Arthur Dale Holland, ca. 1940, printed marks, 9½" h. (ILLUS. above)... **546.00**

**Pitcher,** 5½" h., jug-type, majolica, hexagonal body molded w/a Shell & Seaweed patt., polychrome decoration, D-form handle, impressed mark, ca. 1865 (rim line, foot rim chip, light body stains)...................... **230.00**

**Pitcher,** cov., jug-type, 6" h., the Drabware body glazed in glossy blue w/relief-molded hunting scenes & a band of short vertical bands around the base, molded hound handle & hinged pewter lid, impressed mark, ca. 1877 (base hairline) ........................... **403.00**

**Plate,** 9" d., Dragon Lustre, dished form w/a mother-of-pearl interior ground decorated w/mottled ground center w/a curled dragon, a mottled purple, blue & green exterior w/Chinese ornaments, printed mark, No. 4831, ca. 1920s (glaze wear) ... **374.00**

**Potpourri vase,** cov., slip-decorated Pearlware, a blue ground w/white floral swags in relief w/a band above engine-turned fluting, pierced cover, impressed mark, ca. 1800, 7" h. (body restoration, cover married) .................................... **230.00**

**Teapot,** cov., Moonlight Lustre, oval cylindrical body w/a flattened & slightly angled shoulder to the inset flat cover w/knob finial, straight angled spout & D-form handle, overall mottled lustre finish, impressed mark, ca. 1810, 3" h. (restored cover rim chips, nicks on spout rim)............................................ **575.00**

**Umbrella stand,** majolica, fan-form, a tall upright partially opened fan w/molded dark rim & center bands & raised on a molded rope & tassel base on a round foot, impressed marks, ca. 1883, 24½" h. (restoration) .......................... **1,150.00**

**Vase,** cov., 6¾" h., Porphory, classical urn-form raised on a flaring short pedestal, the wide flattened shoulder tapering to a short waisted neck w/a thick rolled rim & domed cover w/knop finial, the neck flanked by scroll handles w/face terminals at the top & resting on the shoulder rim, goat's head handles at the shoulder joined by heavy applied laurel garlands, mounted on a black basalt square base, gilt traces on the creamware handles, impressed wafer mark of Wedgwood and Bentley, ca. 1775 (base restored, cover manufactured)............................ **920.00**

**Vase,** 6" h., spherical body decorated w/incised engine-turned banding below the wide cylindrical neck, matte grey glaze, designed by Keith Murray, 20th c., impressed & printed marks........................ **403.00**

**Vase,** 9" h., Fairyland Lustre, wide baluster-form w/a wide, short rolled rim, "Imps on a Bridge"

*Fairyland Lustre Vase*

patt., w/a pinkish red sky, river & roc bird in blue, shape No. 2351, pattern No. Z5360, ca. 1920, restored rim chips, lines under base (ILLUS.)........................... **1,840.00**

**Wall pocket,** modeled as a large nautilus-type shell, matte green glaze, Keith Murray-type, printed & impressed marks, ca. 1937, 10½" l....................................... **173.00**

---

# WELLER

*The Weller Pottery was established by Samuel A. Weller in 1872 and operated until 1945. Originally located in Fultonham, Ohio, the factory moved to Zanesville in 1882. A wide range of lines, both of art pottery and commercial quality, were produced over the years and we list a sampling here.*

*Reference books on Weller include* The Collectors Encyclopedia of Weller Pottery, *by Sharon and Bob Huxford (Collector Books, 1979) and* All About Weller *by Ann Gilbert McDonald (Antique Publications, 1989)*

WELLER          Weller Pottery

*Weller Marks*

## AURELIAN (1898-1910)

*Similar to Louwelsa line but brighter colors and a glossy glaze.*

*Giant Aurelian Vase*

**Clock,** mantel or shelf-type, a molded flattened front & back w/an arched top above deeply waisted & scroll-molded sides ending on flaring feet, decorated on one side of the dial w/a cluster of yellow & brown jonquils & green leaves & stems against a mottled golden yellow ground against a mottled dark brown ground on the remainder of the case, round enameled clock dial w/Arabic numerals, base incised "Aurelian Weller" & stamped "6700," artist-initialed by Josephine Imlay .............. **$1,760.00**

**Mug,** decorated w/slip-painted orange & green grapes on gold & brown ground, 5½" d., 5¾" h. (minor surface scratches) ......... **193.00**

**Vase,** 60" h., very tall ovoid body tapering to a tall waisted neck w/a widely flaring rim, decorated w/large red & yellow roses w/green leaves & brown stems against a very dark brown shaded to yellow ground, exhibited at the 1904 St. Louis World's Fair, artist-signed & dated "1899" (ILLUS. above) ................................. **36,300.00**

**Whiskey jug,** wide bulbous nearly spherical body w/a wide shoulder to the short neck w/a tiny pinched spout & loop handle from rim to shoulder, decorated w/a large cluster of black & red blackberries & brown & yellow leaves against a black shaded to yellow ground, artist-initialed & incised marks, 5⅛" h................. **385.00**

## BARCELONA (late 20s)

*Colorful Spanish peasant-style designs on buff ground.*

*Barcelona Vase*

**Ewer,** bulbous body tapering to a small flared neck, strap handle from neck to shoulder, 6½" h. .... **150.00**

**Vase,** 9⅛" h., baluster-form hand-turned ridged body w/a flaring mouth flanking by two heavy strap handles to the center of the sides, decorated w/a large h.p. four-petal stylized blossom in yellow, gold, burgundy & green w/four dark blue spearpoints issuing from each side, on a yellow shaded to pale green ground, marked ............. **275.00**

**Vase,** 9¼" h., ovoid body tapering to a short flaring neck flanked by strap handles (ILLUS. above) ...................................... **375.00**

**Vase,** 10" h., w/three strap handles ................................... **475.00**

## BRIGHTON (1915)

*Various bird or butterfly figurals colorfully decorated and with glossy glazes.*

*Coppertone Bowl & Pitcher*

**Bowl,** 4¾" h., deep sharply tapering sides w/a flattened inverted rim set w/two squared loop handles, base incised "Weller Hand Made - 3X" (ILLUS. above left) ................... **138.00**

**Bowl-vase,** large spherical body w/eared handles at the sides, heavy copper-colored ground w/lightly mottled green, marked "Weller Hand Made" & "2," 6¼" h. ........................................ **220.00**

**Candleholders,** model of a turtle w/lily blossom, 3" h., pr. ......... **1,000.00**

**Flower frog,** figural, modeled as a mushroom-form w/a disc top centered by a figural frog emerging from a water lily blossom, 4½" h. ........................... **193.00**

**Pitcher,** 7⅝" h., ovoid body molded as large water pads tapering to a scalloped rim & wide spout, the figural handle in the form of an open-mouthed fish, inkstamp Weller mark, "12" & painted "T" w/original "Weller Coppertone Ware" paper label (ILLUS. above right) ................................. **770.00**

**Vase,** 6½" h., bulbous body tapering w/a widely flaring flattened neck, heavy D-form handles from rim to center of sides, mottled vivid green & brownish gold matte glaze, incised "Weller Handmade - 12" ........................................ **440.00**

*Large Brighton Parrot*

## Jardiniere & pedestal base,

decorated w/birds & chrysanthemums in crimson, blue & burnt orange on a cream ground, overall 31½" h. (professional minor repair to one circular handle) .................. **935.00**

**Model of a kingfisher,** perched on a brown branch above a disc base, 6½" h. .............................. **350.00**

**Model of a parrot,** crimson, dark blue, gold & cream on green & brown stand, 13½" h. (ILLUS. above) .................... **1,650.00**

## CHASE (late 1920s)

*White relief fox hunt scenes usually on a deep blue ground.*

**Vase,** 9" h., swelled cylindrical body tapering to a flat wide mouth, rare orange ground ....... **450.00**

**Vase,** 9" h., swelled cylindrical body tapering to a flat wide mouth, blue ground .................. **385.00**

## COPPERTONE (late 1920s)

*Various shapes with an overall mottled green glaze. Some pieces with figural frog or fish handles. Models of frogs also included.*

## DICKENSWARE 2nd Line (1900-05)

*Various incised "sgraffito" designs usually with a matte glaze.*

*Dickensware Figural Humidor*

**Bowl,** 4 × 8", four-lobed form w/flat rim, decorated w/red & green flowers on dark blue ground, impressed mark ........... **523.00**

**Humidor,** cov., figural, Turk's head, dark-skinned man w/black beard & mustache wearing a multicolored turban, two flat chips on lid, minor damage to retaining rim inside neck, 6½ × 7¼" (ILLUS.)..................... **413.00**

**Vase,** 8¾" h., ovoid w/flaring rim incised w/scene of golfer in a pink shirt & green pants, trees in background on a shaded brown ground, impressed "487/D" .... **1,210.00**

**Vase,** 10½" h., slender cylindrical body w/slightly flared shoulder tapering to a flaring rolled neck & rim, w/incised bust portrait of a Native American, "White Buffalo," polychrome w/green shaded matte glaze, signed "L.J. Burgess" & impressed "Dickensware, Weller" (firing defect w/surface chip on back edge at shoulder) ..................... **550.00**

**Vase,** floor-type, 17" h., ovoid body tapering to wide cylindrical neck & flared rim, decorated w/incised scene of three wigged men drinking at a table, polychrome on green glaze, impressed "WELLER DICKENSWARE/X279" (glaze chips to rim) ............................. **880.00**

**Vase,** bud, name card w/butterfly..................................... **300.00**

## EOCEAN and EOCEAN ROSE (1898-1925)

*Early art line with various hand-painted flowers on shaded grounds, usually with a glossy glaze.*

*Eocean Exhibition Vase*

**Basket,** late-type, spherical body raised on four small flared tab feet, high arched handle from side to side, the black handle & upper rim decorated w/bright stylized florals above the mottled shaded pink & grey lower body, artist-initialed by Mae Timberlake, 5¾" h. .......................................... **468.00**

**Jardiniere,** wide tapering bulbous ovoid body w/a wide rolled rim, decorated w/clusters of stylized pale purple grapes & vines in dark grey & black, dark grey upper ground shading to pale creamy green at the lower half, signed by Frank Ferrell, base incised "Weller - 163" (some staining under glaze from use) .. **550.00**

**Pitcher,** 6⅜" h., a thick & wide cushion-type base tapering slightly to a deeply indented band below the tapering cylindrical sides w/a flat rim, thick rim spout & thick inverted D-form handle from the rim to the edge of the base, dark grey shading to cream ground, the upper body decorated w/a wading white stork w/stylized clouds behind its head & stylized pale green lily pads on the lower base, painted by Frank Ferrell, artist's monogram, incised "Eocean Weller," embossed logo ........................................ **1,870.00**

**Vase,** 5" h., late-type, bulbous ovoid body tapering to a short cylindrical neck w/a flat rim, the black neck decorated w/pastel multicolored blossoms & leaves continuing down the sides over the yellow shaded to grey ground, unmarked..................... **193.00**

**Vase,** 8⅜" h., late-type, slender tapering ovoid body w/a small flat mouth, decorated around the rim w/several yellow roses on a black & multicolored ground shading to pale purple at the bottom, artist-initialed by Mae Timberlake ............................... **605.00**

**Vase,** 10" h., 3¼" d., tall cylindrical body w/large thumbprint indentations around the body near the top, decorated w/a small bust portrait of a pit bull terrier in white, grey & brown on a shaded grey to green to cream ground, incised marks.......................... **1,320.00**

**Vase,** 11½" h., broad ovoid slightly tapering body w/a rolled mouth, the ground shading from dark blackish green to medium & pale green to cream at the bottom, decorated w/large white water lily blossoms & buds & green lily pads & stems, base impressed "Weller Ware," incised "Eocean - 9075" .................. **12,090.00**

**Vase,** 53" h., exhibited at the 1904 St. Louis World's Fair, a tall slender ovoid body tapering to a widely flaring trumpet neck, decorated w/large chrysanthemums in shades of maroon, mauve & white w/green stems & leaves against a dark charcoal shading to pale pink ground, artist-signed, ca. 1900 (ILLUS. second column, previous page) ................................ **20,900.00**

## FOREST (mid-Teens - 1928)

*Realistically molded and painted forest scene.*

*Forest Vase & Jardiniere*

**Jardiniere,** slightly tapering cylinder decorated w/embossed trees in brown & green, blue sky, 8¾" d., 7½" h. .................... **303.00**

**Jardiniere,** "Children in the Woods" design, wide gently tapering cylindrical form, rare version w/pairs of young girls walking through the forest, only marked w/a black slip "20" on the base, 8⅝" h. (ILLUS. right, above)...... **1,760.00**

**Jardiniere,** tall slightly tapering cylindrical footed bowl, the side molded in bold relief w/a continuous forest scene in greens & browns, marked, 13" h. (several chips off the base)....... **605.00**

**Jardiniere & pedestal base,** decorated w/brown trees & green foliage on blue ground, jardiniere 11 × 12", 2 pcs. (spider line to body of jardiniere) ......... **550.00**

**Vase,** 8⅛" h., flattened flaring oval form, molded w/a continuous forest landscape, marked (ILLUS. left, above)...... **110.00**

**Vase,** 13" h., tall slender waisted cylindrical form, molded w/a continuous forest scene ........... **225.00**

## GEODE (1934)

*A line of simple forms decorated with blue stars and comets on a white background or white stars and comets on a medium blue background.*

**Vase,** 5¾" h., 6" d., footed wide squatty bulbous body tapering to a small, short flaring neck, decorated w/white comets & stars on a light blue matte ground, decorated by Hester Pillsbury, artist-initialed on the side, base w/incised pottery mark .............. **715.00**

**Vase,** 6" h., 5¾" d., footed squatty bulbous ovoid body tapering to a short flared neck, slip-painted around the sides w/six- and five-point stars & long-tailed comets in white against an azure blue ground, decorated by Mae Timberlake, incised "TM - Weller Pottery" (minute bottom rim nick) ..................................... **468.00**

## GLENDALE (early to late 1920s)

*Various relief-molded birds in their natural habitats, life-like coloring.*

*Glendale Wall Pocket*

**Console bowl w/flower frog,** relief-molded birds & a nest w/eggs, foliage in green, blue, red & brown, 2 pcs. ................... **770.00**

**Flower frog,** model of a bird's nest ......................................... **165.00**

**Vase,** double bud, 7" h., gate-form, two cylindrical slender tree trunks joined by an arched center panel w/a bird perched next to its nest........................... **265.00**

**Vase,** 8½" h., simple ovoid body tapering to a flat mouth, molded w/a pair of parakeets perched on a branch.............................. **450.00**

**Vase,** 12" h., tall slender baluster-form, bird in nest in fork of slender tree .............................. **395.00**

**Wall pocket,** cornucopia-form w/curved tail, arched & scalloped backplate pierced w/a hanging hole, the base molded w/a blue & yellow bird beside a nest of yellow baby birds against a leafy green & brown ground, unmarked (ILLUS. previous column)............ **440.00**

## HUDSON (1917-34)

*Underglaze slip-painted decoration.*

*Two Hudson Vases*

**Vase,** 7" h., slender ovoid body w/a flat molded mouth, decorated w/a stylized landscape of autumn trees & grasses in grey, blues, greens, white & some deep red, signed by Mae Timberlake, inkstamp logo mark, fairly tight three inch line from rim (ILLUS. left) .......... **990.00**

**Vase,** 9½" h., 10" d., broad bulbous footed ovoid body tapering to a short flaring neck, small loop shoulder handles, decorated w/branches of blue, pink & yellow flowers w/green leaves against a shaded light blue ground, decorated by McLaughlin & artist-signed & marked.......................... **880.00**

**Vase,** 12" h., tall wide baluster-form w/a short neck & flared rim, decorated w/pale multicolored hibiscus blossoms, buds & green leaves outlined in black, another spray of flowers on the reverse in white & pink outlined in black, all on a shaded pale green to pale pink ground, decorated by Hester Pillsbury, inkstamp logo mark (ILLUS. right, second column previous page)...................................... **1,760.00**

**Vase,** 13⅞" h., tall tapering ovoid body w/a wide rounded shoulder to the short neck w/a rolled molded rim, dark grey ground decorated w/large greyish white hibiscus blossoms w/yellow & red centers & dark blue leafage, marked w/block letters ............. **880.00**

## JAP BIRDIMAL (1904)

*Stylized Japanese-inspired figural, bird or animal designs on various solid-colored grounds.*

**Jardiniere,** wide ovoid body w/a gently flaring wide, flat mouth, decorated around the sides w/a moonlight scene of dark blue trees against a pale blue ground, marked in small block letters "Weller," 8⅜" h. .............. **275.00**

**Jardiniere & pedestal base,** decorated w/a stylized landscape design in dark blue against a light blue ground, base w/light blue & pink ground, jardiniere die-stamped "WELLER," overall 24½" h., 2 pcs. ............................ **660.00**

**Vase,** 14⅝" h., tall slender cylindrical body w/a narrow angled shoulder to the short neck w/molded rim, decorated w/a geisha girl standing in a grove of stylized Rhead-like trees w/little tufts of grass at her feet, extensive slip-trailing & slip painting, artist-initialed, base incised "570" & the name "Rhead," minor glaze abrasions on back, small drill hole in base repaired................................... **1,100.00**

## LASA (1920-25)

*Various landscapes on a banded reddish and gold iridescent ground.*

**Vase,** 4¼" h., cabinet-type, ovoid form decorated w/landscape scene of tall trees & lake, burgundy, green & gold, artist-signed ...................................... **275.00**

**Vase,** 7" h., 3¼" d., tall slender ovoid body, decorated w/iridescent bands of red, gold & green w/a lakeside landscape scene of pine trees & distant mountains, unmarked .............. **440.00**

**Vase,** 8⅞" h., simple cylindrical form, decorated w/a dark silhouetted woodland scene of bare trees against bands, golden iridescent ground, signed on the side "Weller Lasa" & "G" (minor scratch or two) .............. **413.00**

**Vase,** 12½" h., 5½" d., tall slender ovoid body tapering to a thick molded rim, decorated w/a landscape of tall trees & a lake in the foreground & mountains in the distance, in green mauve & brown against an ivory & green sky, painted mark...................... **550.00**

## LOUWELSA (1896-1924)

*Hand-painted underglaze slip decoration on dark brown shading to yellow ground; glossy glaze.*

**Chamberstick,** flared base tapering to cupped socket, angled handle, decorated w/gold & brown pansies on gold to dark brown ground, impressed "Lowelsa," 5" d., 7¼" h.............. **165.00**

**Clock,** table model, wide arched & scalloped case decorated w/a yellow wild rose on brown to dark brown ground, artist-signed & Louwelsa stamp, 5¼" w., 7" h.......................................... **440.00**

**Ewer,** squatty bulbous base tapering to a short indented neck w/a tricornered rim,

*Louwelsa Pitcher & Mug*

inverted D-form handle, decorated w/a cluster of blackberries against yellowish orange leaves on a blackish brown shaded to dark tan ground, signed "Mitchell" on the side, impressed "Louwelsa Weller - 248," 6¼" h. .................. **193.00**

**Jug,** spherical body w/loop handle at top & short angled spout, h.p. gooseberries & leaves on shaded brown ground, decorated by Minnie Mitchell, impressed "Louwelsa/painted M. Mitchell," 5½" d., 6½" h. ....... **248.00**

**Mug,** slightly ovoid body w/a molded rim & C-form handle, painted w/a bust portrait of a bald monk against a shaded brown ground, signed by Levi J. Burgess, impressed company mark & "X517," 5¾" h. (ILLUS. right with pitcher) ..................... **550.00**

**Pitcher,** tankard, 12½" h., slightly tapering cylindrical form w/an arched rim spout & D-form handle, painted w/a half-length portrait of a Native American chief against a shaded brown ground, initials by artist Levi J. Burgess, incised letter "F," tiny flake off base (ILLUS. left with mug) ..................... **1,430.00**

**Vase,** 11⅝" h., Louwelsa Blue, tall slender swelled cylindrical form w/a flat molded rim, shaded dark

blue glaze decorated w/large nasturtium blossoms & leaves, unmarked ............................... **1,430.00**

**Vase,** 12⅝" h., very tall slender & slightly waisted cylindrical body w/a sloping shoulder to the flaring trumpet neck, decorated w/reddish orange wild roses & green leaves against a dark blackish brown ground, artist-initialed, marked ....................... **275.00**

**Vase,** 17⅝" h., tall slender cylindrical body w/a narrow rounded shoulder to a low rolled rim, decorated w/a large cluster of chrysanthemum blossoms & leafy stems in yellow, golden brown, orange & green against a black shaded to dark brown ground, shape No. 548, decorated by L. McGrath, marked ................................... **1,320.00**

## MARVO (mid-1920s-33)

*Molded overall fern and leaf design on various matte-background colors.*

*Marvo Wall Pocket*

**Bowl w/flower frog,** green ground, 2 pcs. ........................... **225.00**

**Jardiniere,** grey ground, 6" d., 10" h. ......................................... **225.00**

**Jardiniere & pedestal base,** green, overall 36½" h., 2 pcs. ... **825.00**

**Vase,** double-bud, green ground .. **95.00**

**Wall pocket,** conical, green ground, 7½" h. (ILLUS.) ............ **165.00**

## MATT GREEN (ca. 1904)

*Various shapes with slightly shaded dark green matte glaze and molded with leaves and other natural forms.*

**Jardiniere,** a wide cylindrical body w/a wide flattened flanged rim w/small loop handles from under rim to upper sides, a wide gently tapering base raised on a scalloped foot, the side embossed w/rectangular panels of Glasgow roses & foliage, die-stamped mark, 7" d., 6" h.......... **440.00**

**Umbrella stand,** tall wide slightly waisted cylindrical form w/a molded band of large knobs around the base, the lightly scalloped rim above molded alternating tulip & sunflower blossoms w/leaves raised on slender stems running down to the base band, matte green glaze, unmarked, 20⅛" h. ......... **935.00**

**Vase,** 5⅛" h., a waisted cylindrical body molded in relief w/twisted ribs down the sides forming trailing stems around the flaring foot, flat incurved mouth, marked...................................... **358.00**

**Vase,** 11½" h., 6½" d., tall flaring cylindrical lower body w/a tapering ringed conical upper body w/a flat mouth flanked by rounded handles w/a triple bar forked openwork design, incised decoration of cherries & leaves under the leather matte green glaze, unmarked (tin base grinding chip) ........................ **1,320.00**

**Vase,** 12½" h., 5" d., tall slender ovoid form heavily embossed on each side w/a full-length Art Nouveau lady in a flowing diaphanous gown, richly textured green matte glaze .... **3,080.00**

## MATT WARE (ca. 1907)

*Various forms decorated with veined, streaked, or mottled glazes, often with figures molded in high- and low-relief.*

**Vase,** 5" h., 5" d., double-gourd form, a wide bulbous lower section & a small swelled upper section, the lower section embossed w/burgundy morning glories & green leaves w/green leaves around the top rim, rich feathered matte glazes, incised mark........................................... **440.00**

**Vase,** 6" h., 4 2/3" d., bulbous double-gourd body w/strap handles from side of top shoulder to lower body, decorated w/embossed nasturtium blossoms & leaves in pink, yellow & purple on a green ground, marked.......... **165.00**

**Vase,** 10½" h., 4" d., gently swelled cylindrical form tapering to closed-in rim, decorated w/sheaves of wheat in relief under a fine bluish grey & red feathered matte glaze, die-stamped "WELLER".............. **1,430.00**

## ROMA (1912-late 1920s)

*Cream-colored ground decorated with embossed floral swags, bands or fruit clusters.*

**Candelabrum,** three-light, a flaring foot below a rosette-molded knob w/a tall leaf-embossed center standard flanked by two curved ribbed arms joined to the center standard by slender straight bars, each arm w/a leaf-molded bell-form socket, 8" h. ................ **110.00**

**Jardiniere & pedestal,** overall 29½" h., 2 pcs. ...................... **1,950.00**

**Umbrella stand,** tall cylindrical form w/raised vertical narrow ribs filled w/fruits & flowers w/bands of ribbon in color alternating w/plain cream-colored panels w/short double-leaf bands at the top & base, marked, 21⅛" h. (minor scuffs) ........................... **248.00**

**Vase,** triple-bud, 8" h., a low-footed base tapering slightly to support three tall slender cylindrical bases, the two side ones angled, all three joined by an inverted horseshoe device w/embossed florals .................... **90.00**

**Wall pocket,** tapering fanned
shape w/scalloped rim, red
blossom sprig tied w/a blue bow,
7" h............................................ **195.00**

## SABRINIAN (late 20s)

*Pieces modeled as seashells with sea
plant trim and figural sea horse handles.
In pastel shades of violet, blue, green and
brown.*

*Sabrinian Pitcher*

**Bowl,** 6½" d., 3" h., round shell-
molded sides, on three small
knob feet ................................... **240.00**

**Pitcher,** 10⅝" h., a footed
baluster-form w/the sides
molded w/large upright fanned
pale purple shells against a blue
& green seaweed ground, figural
sea horse handle, pink interior,
marked (ILLUS.) ...................... **440.00**

**Vase,** 9⅝" h., upright boldly
twisted trumpet-shaped shell
form in blue & green above a
cluster of seaweed flanked by
sea horses at the base, light
pink interior, marked ................ **468.00**

**Wall pocket,** conical, 8½" h........ **475.00**

## SICARDO (1902-07)

*Various shapes with iridescent glaze of
metallic shadings in greens, blues, crimson,
purple or copper tones decorated with vines,
flowers, stars or free-form geometric lines.*

*Spectacular Sicardo Jardiniere & Pedestal*

**Jardiniere & pedestal,** a large
bulbous nearly spherical jardiniere
w/a wide, flat molded rim,
decorated w/overall iridescent
swirling leaves in green, blue &
gold, resting on a figural pedestal
w/a round disc top supported on
the raised & curved tail of a
dolphin-like sea creature
w/realistic eyes set into its head
w/a wide scrolled mouth, the head
raised on a molded, domed base
w/four grotesque mask feet, the
base also in an overall lightly
iridized green glaze, the base
painted w/the notation "S.A. Weller
J. Sicard 1-8th- 1902 Zanesville,"
possibly a presentation piece to
Weller & used in the Weller home,
small rim repair, overall
31⅜" h. (ILLUS.) .................... **4,180.00**

**Vase,** 4½" h., 4½" d., footed
bulbous nearly spherical form
tapering slightly to a tiny flared
neck, unusual lustre drippy
copper over burgundy & bluish
green glaze, painted mark ........ **523.00**

**Vase,** 6⅛" h., bulbous ovoid
tapering lobed body w/a small
crimped mouth & upturned loop
handles at the shoulders,
decorated overall w/flowers &
floating seeds in iridescent shades
of purple to mauve to gold, green,
red & blue, marked only w/an
incised "10" on the base .......... **3,080.00**

**Vase,** 8" h., 3" d., slender swelled cylindrical body w/a thick rolled mouth, decorated w/overall leaf-shaped arabesques in green, blue, gold & crimson, painted mark ...................................... **1,100.00**

**Vase,** 12⅜" h., 5"d., tall slender ovoid body w/a molded flat mouth, iridescent glaze in blue, green & red w/stylized dandelion decoration, signed in glaze, ca. 1905 ............................... **1,495.00**

**Vase,** 14" h., 6½" d., a low footring supports a rounded tapering cylindrical body w/a gently flaring rim, decorated w/peacock feathers in a bluish green lustre finish on a crimson ground, painted mark ............. **2,420.00**

## WILD ROSE (early to mid-30s)

*An open white rose on a light tan or green background, Matte glaze.*

*Wild Rose Vase*

**Basket,** a small footring supports a ball-form body w/an integral curved top handle forming an oval opening, this topped by a double-pierced branch-form handle, shaded tan ground, 6" h. ............................................ **60.00**

**Vases,** 6¾" h., disc foot below a gently flaring trumpet-form body w/small tab handles near the top, green ground, pr. (ILLUS. of one) ............................................ **75.00**

## WOODCRAFT (1917)

*Rustic designs simulating the appearance of stumps, logs and tree trunks. Some pieces are adorned with owls, squirrels, dogs and other animals.*

**Basket,** hanging-type, deep gently rounded sides, wide flat mouth, the sides molded w/leafy branches of an apple tree centered by the head of an owl peeking out of a knothole, unmarked, 9¾" d., 4¾" h. (small rim bruise) ..................... **440.00**

**Vase,** 13¼" h., 5½" d., tall tree trunk form w/pierced branch handles around the rim above an owl peeking out of a hole, marked ...................................... **605.00**

**Wall pocket,** conical form w/an arched rim, a round opening w/an owl peeking out near the top, a cluster of fruit & leaves near the base, 10" h. ................. **225.00**

## ZONA (about 1920)

*Red apples and green leaves on brown branches all on a cream-colored ground; some pieces with molded florals or birds with various glazes.*

*A line of children's dishes was also produced featuring hand-painted or molded animals. This is referred to as the "Zona Baby Line."*

*Zona Child's Feeding Dish*

**Creamer,** ovoid body w/twig handle, dinnerware line, 3½" h. .......................... **25.00 to 50.00**

**Feeding dish,** Juvenile line, rolled edge, decorated w/ducks (ILLUS. bottom previous page) .. **85.00 to 95.00**

**Pitcher,** 7" h., cylindrical body, paneled splashing duck decoration ............................... **185.00**

**Pitcher,** 8" h., cylindrical, paneled kingfisher decoration on a cream ground, brown branch handle...................... **225.00 to 250.00**

**Umbrella stand,** cylindrical, decorated w/a row of tall, standing maidens in long dresses holding a continuous garland of pink roses, green ivy vines around the top, all on a cream ground, glossy glaze, 10½" d., 20½" h. ...... **750.00 to 950.00**

---

# WHEATLEY POTTERY

*Thomas J. Wheatley was one of the original founders of the art pottery movement in Cincinnati, Ohio in the early 1880s. In 1879 the Cincinnati Art Pottery was formed and after some legal problems it operated under the name T.J. Wheatley & Company. Their production featured Limoges-style hand-painted decorations and most pieces were carefully marked and often dated.*

*In 1882 Wheatley disassociated himself from the Cincinnati Art Pottery and opened another pottery which was destroyed by fire in 1884. Around 1900 Wheatley finally resumed making art pottery in Cincinnati and in 1903 he founded the Wheatley Pottery Company with a new partner, Isaac Kahn.*

*The new pottery from this company featured colored matte glazes over relief work designs and green, yellow and blue were the most often used colors. There were imitations of the well-known Grueby Pottery wares as well as artware, garden pottery and architectural pieces. Artwork was apparently not made much after 1907. This plant was destroyed by fire in 1910 but was rebuilt and run by Wheatley until*

*his death in 1917. Wheatley artware was generally unmarked except for a paper label.*

*Wheatley Pottery Marks*

**Bowl,** 9" d., 2½" h., wide flat-bottomed shallow form w/incurved sides molded as broad vertical overlapping leaves, thick matte green glaze, incised "W - 681"......................**$468.00**

**Tile,** square, molded in relief w/a grotesque face of a smiling man w/long hair & beard, in olive green, caramel & tobacco brown matte glaze, in a wide flat oak frame, early 20th c., tile 7½" w...**770.00**

**Vase,** 8¾" h., 6½" d., wide ovoid body tapering slightly to a low rolled neck, impressed around the center w/a narrow band of geometric chain-like design, rich green matte glaze, mark hidden by glaze .....................................**825.00**

**Vase,** 10½" h., 10½" d., very wide squatty bulbous base tapering to a wide cylindrical neck w/a molded flat mouth, the lower body heavily embossed w/a band of wide pointed & veined leaves alternating w/slender floral stems & buds up the sides, rich textured flowing green matte glaze, impressed "WP" mark & original paper label ................**3,850.00**

**Vase,** 12" h., wide ovoid form w/an angled shoulder & four in-body flat handles flanking the waisted neck & curving up to the thick rolled rim, covered in a thick mottled dark green matte glaze, based on a Teco design, incised "WP 611," small buttress handle repair (ILLUS. top next page)......................................**2,750.00**

*Matte-glazed Wheatley Vase*

*Ridgways Willow Platter*

& pepper shakers w/wooden
center-handled holder; Japan,
overall 7½" h., 6 pcs. .................**100.00**

**Creamer,** medium size, Japan.......**20.00**

**Creamer,** Allerton, England ..........**95.00**

**Creamer & sugar bowl,** oval,
Japan, pr. ....................................**30.00**

**Cup & saucer,** child's ....................**12.00**

**Cup & saucer,** Allerton, England...**32.00**

**Cup & saucer,** ca. 1907, Arthur J.
Wilkinson, England ......................**18.00**

**Cup & saucer,** interior design .........**6.00**

**Cup & saucer,** handled,
porcelain, lightly scalloped rims,
light blue w/gold rim, 19th c. ........**66.00**

**Egg cup,** double, marked
"Booth's Old Willow" ....................**40.00**

**Lamp,** miniature, Japan .................**60.00**

**Mug,** 4" h., Royal Doulton .............**95.00**

**Mug,** Japan ...................................**12.00**

**Mug,** interior design & on handle,
Japan .........................................**20.00**

**Pie plate,** unmarked ......................**40.00**

**Pitcher,** 8¼" h., Allerton,
England.....................................**250.00**

**Pitcher,** jug-form, 8¾" h., wide
ovoid body w/C-scroll handle &
low arched rim spout, pale light
blue, England, ca. 1830-60 ........**220.00**

**Plate,** 6" d., Allerton, England ..........**9.00**

**Plate,** 6" d., Japan...........................**2.00**

**Plate,** 6¼" d., England ....................**5.00**

**Plate,** 7" d., Ridgway, England ......**13.00**

**Plate,** 10½" d., Ridgway, England ..**22.00**

**Plate,** 10½" d., marked "Booth's
Old Willow".................................**35.00**

**Plate,** 12" d., Royal China
Company ....................................**10.00**

**Plate,** dinner, Homer Laughlin .......**12.00**

# WILLOW WARES

*This pseudo-Chinese pattern has been used by numerous firms throughout the years. The original design is attributed to Thomas Minton about 1780 and Thomas Turner is believed to have first produced the ware during his tenure at the Caughley works. The blue underglaze transfer-print pattern has never been out of production since that time. An Oriental landscape incorporating a bridge, pagoda, trees, figures and birds, supposedly tells the story of lovers fleeing a cruel father who wished to prevent their marriage. The gods, having pity on them, changed them into birds enabling them to fly away and seek their happiness together.*

*Also see BUFFALO POTTERY.*

## BLUE

**Bowl,** 5" d., unmarked ...................**$3.00**

**Bowl,** fruit, 5½" d., Japan.................**3.00**

**Bowl,** cereal, 6½" d., Japan.............**4.00**

**Bowl,** 6¾" d., Allerton, England .....**13.00**

**Bowl,** 8" d., marked "Crown
Pottery Warranted," American-
made ........................................**200.00**

**Bowl,** 9" d., Royal China
Company. ...................................**10.00**

**Coffeepot,** cov., 7½" h., Allerton,
England....................................**250.00**

**Condiment set:** oil cruet
w/stopper, vinegar cruet
w/stopper, cov. mustard pot, salt

Plate, grill, Japan ...........................**10.00**

Plate, grill, Shenango China
Company .....................................**12.00**

Plate, salad, England....................**13.00**

Plate, salad, unmarked ...................**5.00**

Platter, 9 x 12", Ridgways,
England (ILLUS. second column
previous page) ............................**80.00**

Platter, 18" l., oval, England,
ca. 1830 ...................................**165.00**

Pudding mold, 5¾" d. ..................**60.00**

Soup plate w/flanged rim,
Japan, 7½" d................................**5.00**

Soup plate w/flanged rim, Royal
China Co., 8½" d...........................**7.00**

Soup plate w/flanged rim,
Ridgways, England .....................**22.00**

Vegetable bowl, cov., footed
octagonal form w/flaring sides &
a domed, stepped cover
w/blossom finial, medium light
blue, impressed "Stone China"
mark, England, ca. 1850-75,
6¾" h........................................**198.00**

Vegetable bowl, cov., 9" d.,
Brown & Steventon ...................**160.00**

Vegetable bowl, cov., 9¼" l.,
Allerton, England ......................**250.00**

Vegetable bowl, cov., 9½" d.,
marked "Booth's Old Willow" .....**200.00**

Vegetable bowl, cov., oval,
ca. 1902, Doulton......................**295.00**

Vegetable bowl, open, 9" d.,
Alfred Meakin, England...............**35.00**

Vegetable bowl, open, oval,
marked "Booth's Old Willow" .....**100.00**

## OTHER COLORS

Pudding mold, red ........................**35.00**

Soup plates w/flanged rims,
large, red, Shenango Pottery, pr..**48.00**

---

# WORCESTER

*The famed English factory was established in 1751 and produced porcelains. Earthenwares were made in the 19th century. Its first period is known as the "Dr. Wall" period; that from 1783 to 1792 as the "Flight" period; that from 1792 to 1807 as the "Barr, Flight & Barr" period. The firm became Barr, Flight & Barr from 1807 to 1813; Flight, Barr & Barr from 1813 to 1840; Chamberlain & Co. from 1840 to 1852; and Kerr and Binns from 1852 to 1862. After 1862, the company became the Worcester Royal Porcelain Company, Ltd., known familiarly as Royal Worcester. Also included in the following listing are examples of wares from the early Chambelains and early Grainger factories in Worcester. Also See ROYAL WORCESTER.*

*Worcester Marks*

Basket, deep round gently flaring
reticulated latticework sides
punctuated by rosettes &
decorated w/a floral spray in the
center bottom, First Period,
ca. 1765, 7⅛" d., 2¼" h...........**$863.00**

Bowl, 10" d., flaring rounded
shell-molded sides below a
scalloped rim, transfer-printed in
dark blue w/fruit & floral sprays,
First Period, mid-18th c..............**345.00**

Creamer, footed tapering ovoid
body w/a rim spout & C-form
handle, dark blue ground
decorated w/shaped white
reserves filled w/polychrome
birds & insects w/gilt trim, Dr.
Wall period square mark, 4¼" h.
(small flakes & short hairline in
spout) .......................................**715.00**

Mustard pot, cov., cylindrical
body, the cover w/a floral finial,
decorated w/blue transfer-
printed floral clusters, First
Period, mid-18th c., 4" h. ..........**374.00**

**Plate,** 7¼" d., Blind Earl patt., decorated w/a raised rose spray surrounded by polychrome floral sprays within a scalloped border, mid-18th c...................**1,265.00**

**Plate,** dinner, 10¼" d., shaped gadrooned rim surrounding floral spray cartouches & a coat-of-arms, Chamberlain Worcester, early 19th c. ...........................**316.00**

**Sauceboats,** footed boat-shaped body w/a C-scroll handle w/thumbrest, decorated w/a narrow geometric rim band above a foliate-molded body decorated w/color floral sprays, First Period, ca. 1765, 4¼" h., pr................................................**316.00**

**Sugar bowl,** cov., deep rounded body & domed cover w/floral finial, decorated w/blue transfer-printed butterfly & florals, First Period, mid-18th c., 5½" h. ........**196.00**

**Tea cup & saucer,** handleless, the lobed cup painted w/a rocaille border surrounding a reserve painted w/a bird & floral spray, First Period, ca. 1765, cup 2" h. ....................................**288.00**

**Teapot,** cov., globular body decorated w/a chinoiserie vignette within foliate & cartouche borders w/gilt highlights, First Period, ca. 1765, 5½" h. .............**345.00**

**Tea set:** cov. teapot & six handleless teacups & saucers; a small globular teapot & cover w/an applied floral sprig finial, all pieces transfer-printed in blue w/a bouquet of garden flowers & two hovering butterflies, underglaze-blue crescent mark, late 18th c., teapot 5" h., the set .......................................**805.00**

**Vase,** 5" h., baluster-form, decorated w/colorfully painted exotic birds within a landscape, First Period, ca. 1765.................**259.00**

**Vegetable dishes,** cov., Royal Lily patt., the cover w/a floral finial above gilt highlighted leaves, ca. 1800, pr. ..................**633.00**

# YELLOW-GLAZED EARTHENWARE

*In the past this early English ware was often referred to as "Canary Lustre," but recently a more accurate title has come into use.*

*Produced in the late 18th and early 19th centuries, pieces featured an overall yellow glaze, often decorated with silver or copper lustre designs or black, brown or red transfer-printed scenes.*

*Most pieces are not marked and today the scarcity of examples in good condition keeps market prices high.*

**Mug,** child's, cylindrical, a black transfer-printed design w/oval reserves w/bust portraits of Lafayette & Washington below a spread-winged eagle, Wood, England, ca. 1820s, 2½" h. (slight hairline at rim) ...........**$1,760.00**

**Pitcher,** jug-type, 5¼" h., the ovoid body decorated w/a red transfer-printed landscape scene of a shepherd & sheep in front of ruins on one side & a couple in front of ruins on the other side, red enamel border bands & a band of leaves around the neck, ca. 1830 (tiny chip on tip of spout, deteriorating repair to crack on lower handle) .............................**165.00**

**Tea set,** child's: cov. teapot, cov. sugar bowl, creamer, waste bowl & five handleless cups & saucers; rounded forms, the teapot w/an angled spout, C-form handle & domed cover w/button finial, each piece decorated w/black & red floral sprigs w/dark brown rims & finials, ca. 1800-15, the set (various minor damages) ...........**1,980.00**

# YELLOWWARE

*Yellowware is a form of utilitarian pottery produced in the United States and England from the early 19th century onward. Its body texture is less dense and vitreous (impervious to water) than stoneware. Most, but not all, yellowware is unmarked and its color varies from deep yellow to pale buff. In the late 19th and early 20th centuries bowls in graduated sizes were widely advertised. Still in production, yellowware is plentiful and still reasonably priced.*

**Cups & saucers,** black transfer-printed European scenes, impressed "N.J.," two sets (small chips on table rings of cups .......**$99.00**

**Jar,** cov., cylindrical w/eared handles at mid-section, slightly domed lid w/button finial, deep gold w/blue & white stripes, 9½" d., 7" h. (chips, hairline & stains) .........................................**165.00**

**Mixing bowl,** footed sides flaring to wide rim, decorated w/blue & white stripes, marked "Warrented Fireproof," 12¼" d., 5¾" h. (interior wear) ...................**83.00**

**Mug,** cov., white & brown stripes, overall 5 5/8" h. (small chips on rim & lid, lid is a close mismatch) ..................................**385.00**

**Pitcher,** jug-type, 8½" h. ................**65.00**

**Preserving jar,** cov., cylindrical body w/rounded shoulder tapering to slightly flaring rim, inset flat cover w/tab finial, impressed "John Bell," lid fits but color varies, wear & crazing, 5¾" h....................**550.00**

**Rolling pin** (small chip on end of cylinder) .....................................**395.00**

**Tobacco jar,** cov., footed cylindrical body embossed w/drapery swags & women's heads, figural finial of a young woman wearing turban, 6½" h. (rim chips & hairlines in base)......**94.00**

# ZSOLNAY

*This pottery was made in Pecs, Hungary, in a factory founded in 1862 by*

*Vilmos Zsolnay. Utilitarian earthenware was originally produced but by the turn of the century ornamental Art Nouveau-style wares with bright colors and lustre decoration were produced and these wares are especially sought today. Currently Zsolnay pieces are being made in a new factory.*

*Reticulated Zsolnay Bowl*

**Bowl,** 7½" d., 5" h., deep bulbous rounded body w/seven rounded & flaring pierced rim lobes above the fully reticulated body, raised on four lobed & reticulated feet, flower & leaf decoration in steel blue, rust, yellow & pink w/dark rust rim banding (ILLUS.)......................**$260.00**

**Figurine,** stylized geometrically angular figure of a woman carrying a deep ovoid dish-form vessel on her head, one arm up supporting its rim, glossy white ground w/black geometric trim & facial details, stamped blue towers mark, impressed "T-...67 - R," 8 3/8" h..............................**316.00**

**Vase,** 16¾" h., figural, cast w/a maiden w/wind-blown gown & tresses standing & clasping the side of the cylindrical vase w/a wave-molded cushion base, glazed in iridescent shades of mustard yellow, orange & reddish blues reserved against a golden chartreuse ground, impressed "ZSOLNAY PECS - 5955 - 6," designed by Mack Lajos, ca. 1900 ......................**2,875.00**

# GLOSSARY OF SELECTED CERAMICS TERMS

**Abino Ware**—A line produced by the Buffalo Pottery of Buffalo, New York. Introduced in 1911, this limited line featured mainly sailing ship scenes with a windmill on shore.

**Agate Ware**—An earthenware pottery featuring a mixture of natural colored clays giving a marbled effect. Popular in England in the 18th century.

**Albany slip**—A dark brown slip glaze used to line the interiors of most salt-glazed stoneware pottery. Named for a fine clay found near Albany, New York.

**Albino line**—A version of Griffen, Smith and Hill's Shell & Seaweed majolica pattern with an off-white overall color sometimes trimmed with gold or with pink or blue feathering.

**Albion Ware**—A line of majolica developed by Edwin Bennett in the 1890s. It featured colored liquid clays over a green clay body decorated with various scenes. Popular for jardinieres and pedestals.

**Bas relief**—Literally "low relief," referring to lightly molded decorations on ceramic pieces.

**Bisquit**—Unglazed porcelain left undecorated or sometimes trimmed with pastel colors. Also known as bisque.

**Bocage**—A background of flowering trees or vines often used as a backdrop for figural groups which were meant to be viewed from the front only.

**Bone china**—A porcelain body developed in England using the white ashes of bone. It has been the standard English porcelain ware since the early 19th century.

**Coleslaw**—A type of decoration used on ceramic figurines to imitate hair or fur. It is finely crumbled clay applied to the unfired piece and resembling coleslaw cabbage.

**Crackled glaze**—A glaze with an intentional network of fine lines produced by uneven contracting of the glaze after firing. First popular on Chinese wares.

**Crazing**—The fine network of cracks in a glaze produced by uneven contracting of the glaze after firing or later reheating of a piece during usage. An unintentional defect usually found on eathernwares.

**Creamware**—A light-colored fine earthenware developed in England in the late 18th century and used by numerous potters into the 19th century. Josiah Wedgwood marketed his version as Queensware.

**Crystalline glaze**—A glaze containing fine crystals resulting from the presence of mineral salts in the mixture. It was a popular glaze on American art pottery of the late 19th century and early 20th century.

**Eared handles**—Handles applied to ceramic pieces such as crocks. They are crescent or 'ear' shaped, hence the name.

**Earthenware**—A class of fine-grained porous pottery fired at relatively low temperature and then glazed. It produces a light and easily molded ware that was widely used by the potteries of Staffordshire, England in the late 18th and early 19th century.

**Faience**—A form of fine earthenware featuring a tin glaze and originally inspired by Chinese porcelain. It includes early Dutch Delft ware and similar wares made in France, Germany and other areas of Europe.

**Fairyland Lustre**—A special line of decorated wares developed by Susannah 'Daisy' Makeig-Jones for the Josiah Wedgwood firm early in the 20th century. It featured fantastic or dreamlike scenes with fairies and elves in various colors and with a mother-of-pearl lustre glaze. Closely related to **Dragon Lustre** featuring designs with dragons.

**Flambé glaze**—A special type of glaze featuring splashed or streaked deep reds and purple, often dripping over another base color. Popular with some American art pottery makers but also used on porcelain wares.

**Flint Enamel glaze**—A version of the well known brown mottled Rockingham pottery glaze. It was developed by Lyman Fenton & Co. of Bennington, Vermont and patented in 1849. It featured streaks and flecks of green, orange, yellow and blue mixed with the mottled brown glaze.

**Glaze**—The general term for vitreous (glass-like) coating fired onto pottery and porcelain to produce an impervious surface and protect underglaze decoration.

**Hard-paste**—Refers to 'true' porcelain, a fine, white clay body developed by the Chinese and containing **kaolin** and **petuntse** or china stone. It is fired at a high temperature and glazed with powdered feldspar to produce a smooth, shiny glaze.

**Lead glaze**—A shiny glaze most often used on cheap redware pottery and produced using a dry powdered or liquid lead formula. Since it would be toxic, it was generally used on the exterior of utilitarian wares only

**Lithophane**—A panel of thin porcelain delicately molded with low-relief pattern or scenes which show up clearly when held to light. It was developed in Europe in the 19th century and was used for decorative panels or lamp shades and was later used in the bottom of some German and Japanese steins, mugs or cups.

**Majolica**—A type of tin-glazed earthenware pottery developed in Italy and named for the island of Majorca. It was revived in Europe and America in the late 19th century and usually featured brightly colored shiny glazes

**Married**—A close match or a duplicate of the original missing section or piece, such as a lid.

**Mission Ware**—A decorative line of pottery developed by the Niloak Pottery of Benton, Arkansas. It featured variously colored clays swirled together and was used to produce such decorative pieces as vases and candlesticks.

**Moriage**—Japanese term for the slip-trailed relief decorations used on various forms of porcelain and pottery. Flowers, beading and dragon decoration are typical examples.

**Pâte-sur-pâte**—French for 'paste on paste,' this refers to a decorative technique where layers of porcelain slip in white are layered on a darker background. Used on artware produced by firms like Minton, Ltd. of England.

**Pearlware**—A version of white colored creamware developed in England and widely used for inexpensive eathenwares in the late 18th and early 19th century. It has a pearly glaze, hence the name.

**Pillow vase**—a form of vase designed to resemble a flattened round or oblong pillow. Generally an upright form with flattened sides. A similar form is the **Moon vase** or **flask**, meant to resemble a full moon.

**Porcelain**—The general category of translucent, vitrified ceramics first developed by the Chinese and later widely produced in Europe and America. Hard-paste is 'true' porcelain, while soft-paste is an 'artificial' version developed to imitate hard-paste using other ingredients.

**Pottery**—The very general category of ceramics produced from various types of clay. It includes redware, yellowware, stoneware and various earthenwares. It is generally fired at a much lower temperature than porcelain.

**PUG**—An abbreviation for "printed under glaze," referring to colored decorations on pottery. Most often it is used in reference to decorations found on Mettlach pottery steins.

**Relief-molding**—A decorative technique, sometimes erroneously referred to as "blown-out," whereby designs are raised in bold relief against a background. The reverse side of such decoration is hollowed-out, giving the impression the design was produced by 'blowing' from the inside. Often used in reference to certain Nippon porcelain wares.

**Rocaille**—A French term meaning 'rockwork.' It generally refers to a decoration used for the bases of ceramic figurines.

**Salt-glazed stoneware**—A version of stoneware pottery where common rock salt is thrown in the kiln during firing and produces hard, shiny glaze like a thin coating of glass. A lightly pitted "orange peel" surface is sometimes the result of this technique.

**Sanded**—A type of finish usually on pottery wares. Unfired pieces are sprinkled or rolled in fine sand, which, when fired, gives the piece a sandy, rough surface texture.

**Sang-de-boeuf**—Literally French for "ox blood," it refers to a deep red glaze produced with copper oxide. It was first produced by the Chinese and imitated by European and American potters in the late 19th and early 20th century.

**Sgrafitto**—An Italian-inspired term for decorative designs scratched or cut through a layer of slip before firing. Generally used on earthenware forms and especially with the Pennsylvania-German potters of America.

**Slip**—The liquid form of clay, often used to decorate earthenware pieces in a process known as **slip-trailing** or **slip-quilling**.

**Soft-paste**—A term used to describe a certain type of porcelain body developed in Europe and England from the 16th to late 18th centuries. It was used to imitate true hard-paste porcelain developed by the Chinese but was produced using a white clay mixed with a grit or flux of bone ash or talc and fired at fairly low temperatures. The pieces are translucent, like hard-paste porcelain, but are not as durable. It should **not** be used when referring to earthenwares such as creamware or pearlware.

**Sprigging**—A term used to describe the ornamenting of ceramic pieces with applied relief decoration, such as blossoms, leaves or even figures.

**Standard glaze**—The most common form of glazing used on Rookwood Pottery pieces.

It is a clear, shiny glaze usually on pieces decorated with florals or portraits against a dark shaded backhground.

**Stoneware**—A class of hard, high-fired pottery usually made from dense grey clay and most often decorated with a salt glaze. American 19th century stoneware was often decorated with slip-quilled or hand-brushed cobalt blue decorations.

**Tapestry ware**—A form of late 19th century porcelain where the piece is impressed with an overall linen cloth texture before firing. The Royal Bayreuth firm is especially known for their fine "Rose Tapestry" line wherein the finely textured ground is decorated with colored roses.

**Tin glaze**—A form of pottery glaze made opaque by the addition of tin oxide. It was used most notably on early Dutch Delft as well as other early faience and majolica wares.

**Underglaze-blue**—A cobalt blue produced with metallic oxides applied to an unfired clay body. Blue was one of the few colors which does not run or smear when fired at a high temperature. It was used by the Chinese on porcelain and later copied by firms such as Meissen.

# APPENDIX I

## CERAMICS CLUBS
## & ASSOCIATIONS
### For Ceramic Collectors

Abingdon Pottery Club
210 Knox Hwy. 5
Abingdon, IL 61410

American Art Pottery Association
P. O. Box 525.
Cedar Hill, MO 63016

American Ceramic Circle
419 Gate Lane
Philadelphia, PA 19119

Pottery Lovers Reunion
4969 Hudson Dr.
Stow, OH 44224

Bauer News
P.O. Box 91279
Pasadena, CA 91109-1279

Belleek Collectors Society, The
c/o Reed & Barton Co.
144 West Britannia St.
Taunton, MA 02780

Blue & White Pottery Club
224 12th St., NW
Cedar Rapids, IA 52405

Blue Ridge Collectors Club
Rte. 3, Box 161
Erwin, TN 37650

Carlton Ware International
P. O. Box 161
Sevenoaks
Kent Tn15 6GA England

Ceramic Arts Studio Collectors
P.O. Box 46
Madison, WI 53701-0046

Chintz China Collector (The)
P.O. Box 6126
Folsom, CA 95630

Clarice Cliff Collector's Club
Fantasque House
Tennis Drive, the Park
Nottingham NG1 1AE England

The Dedham Pottery Collectors Society
Newsletter
248 Highland St.
Dedham, MA 02026-5833

Heartland Doulton Collectors
P.O. Box 2434
Jolliet, IL 60434

Mid-America Doulton Collectors
P.O. Box 483
McHenry, IL 60050

Fiesta Club of America
P.O. Box 15383
Loves Park, IL 61115

Fiesta Collectors Club
P.O. Box 361280
Strongsville, OH 44136

Flow Blue International Collectors' Club
2774 E. Main St., Suite 136
St. Charles, IL 60174

Frankoma Pottery Collectors Club
5632 N.W. 58th Terrace
Oklahoma City, OK 73122

Gonder Collectors Club
P.O. Box 21
Crooksville, OH 43731

Goss Collectors Club
4 Khasiaberry
Walnut Tree
Milton Keynes MK7 7DP England

Hall Collector's Club
P.O. Box 360488
Cleveland, OH 44136

National Autumn Leaf Collectors Club
   Rt. 16, Box 275.
   Tulsa, OK 74131-9600

Haviland Collectors Internationale
   Foundation
   P.O. Box 11632
   Milwaukee, WI 53211-0632

Head Vase Society
   P.O. Box 83H
   Scarsdale, NY 10583-8583

*Hull Pottery News* (Newsletter)
   466 Foreston Place
   St. Louis, MO 63119-3927

*Hull Pottery Newsletter*
   11023 Tunnell Hill NE
   New Lexington, OH 43764

Foundation for Historical Research of
   Illinois Potteries
   2108 Church St.
   Streator, IL 61364-3831

Collectors of Illinois Pottery &
   Stoneware
   1527 East Converse St.
   Springfield, IL 62702

Homer Laughlin
   Newsletter: *The Laughlin Eagle*
   1270 - 63rd Terrace So.
   St. Petersburg, FL 33705

Majolica International Society
   1275 First Ave., Suite 103
   New York, NY 10021

*Our McCoy Matters* (Newsletter)
   P. O. Box 14255
   Parkville, MO 64152-7255

Arkansas Pottery Collectors Society
   (Niloak and Camark Pottery)
   P. O. Box 7617
   Little Rock, AR 72217

New England Nippon Collectors Club
   64 Burt Rd.
   Springfield, MA 01118

Long Island Nippon Collectors Club
   145 Andover Pl.
   West Hampstead, NY 11552

Lakes & Plains Nippon Collectors Club
   4305 W. Beecher Rd.
   P.O. Box 230
   Peotone, IL 60468

International Nippon Collectors Club
   112 Oak Ave. N.
   Owatonna, MN 55060

Noritake Collectors' Society
   1237 Federal Ave., East
   Seattle, WA 98102-4329

North Dakota Pottery Collectors Society
   P.O. Box 14
   Beach, ND 58621-0014

*Old Ivory Newsletter*
   P.O. Box 1004
   Wilsonville, OR 97070-1004

Phoenix Bird Collectors of America
   685 S. Washington
   Constantine, MI 49042-1325

Pickard Collectors Club
   300 E. Grove St.
   Bloomington, IL 61701-5232

Purinton Pottery
   Newsletter: *Purinton Pastimes*
   P.O. Box 9394
   Arlington, VA 22219

Red Wing Collectors Society, Inc.
   P.O. Box 184
   Galesburg, IL 61402-0184

Roseville's of the Past Pottery Club
   P.O. Box 656
   Clarona, FL 32710-0656

Royal Bayreuth International Collectors'
   Society
   P. O. Box 325
   Orrville, OH 44667-0325

Royal Copley
   Newsletter: *The Copley Courier*
   1639 N. Catalina St.
   Burbank, CA 91505-1605

International Association of R.S. Prussia
  Collectors Inc.
  14215 Turtle Rock
  San Antonio, TX 78232

Shawnee Pottery Collectors Club
  P.O. Box 713
  New Smyrna Beach, FL 32170-0713

Shelley China
  Newsletter: *Shelley Group Newsletter*
  12 Lilleshall Rd.
  Clayton Newcastle - Under-Lyme
  Staffordshire ST5 3BX England

Southern Folk Pottery Collectors Society
  1224 Main St.
  Glastonbury, CT 06033

Stangl/Fulper Collectors Association
  P.O. Box 64-M
  Changewater, NJ 07831

American Stoneware Association
  208 Cresent Ct.
  Mars, PA 16066-3308

Susie Cooper Collectors Group
  P.O. Box 7436
  London, England N12 7QF

Tea Leaf Club International Membership
  324 Powderhorn Dr.
  Houghton Lake, MI 48629

Tile Heritage Foundation
  P.O. Box 1850
  Healdsburg, CA 95448

North American Torquay Society
  604 Orchard View Dr.
  Maumee, OH 43537

Torquay Pottery Collectors Society
  P.O. Box 373
  Schoolcraft, MI 49087-0373

Uhl Collectors Society
  233 E. Timberlin Lane
  Huntingburg, IN 47542

*Vernon Views Newsletter*
  P. O. Box 945
  Scottsdale, AZ 85252

Watt Collectors Association
  Box 184
  Galesburg, IL 61401

Watt Pottery Collectors
  P.O. Box 26067
  Fairview Park, OH 44126

Wedgwood Society
  The Roman Villa
  Rockbourne, Fordingbridge
  Hants SP6 3PG England

Wedgwood Society of New York
  5 Dogwood Ct.
  Glen Head, NY 11545

International Willow Collectors
  P.O. Box 13382
  Arlington, TX 76094-0382

# APPENDIX II

## Museums & Libraries
## with Ceramic Collections

**BENNINGTON**

Bennington Museum, The
    W. Main St.
    Bennington, VT 05201

**CERAMICS (AMERICAN)**

Everson Museum of Art of Syracuse &
Onondaga County
    401 Harrison St.
    Syracuse, NY 13202

Museum of Ceramics at East Liverpool
    400 E. 5th St.
    East Liverpool, OH 43920

**CERAMICS (AMERICAN ART
    POTTERY)**

Cincinnati Art Museum
    Eden Park
    Cincinnati, OH 45202

Newcomb College Art Gallery
    1229 Broadway
    New Orleans, LA 70118

Zanesville Art Center
    620 Military Rd.
    Zanesville, OH 43701

**CHINESE EXPORT PORCELAIN**

Peabody Museum of Salem
    East India Square
    Salem, MA 01970

**COWAN POTTERY CO.**

Cowan Pottery Museum at the Rocky
River Public Library
    1600 Hampton Rd.
    Rocky River, OH 44116-2699

**DEDHAM**

Dedham Historical Society
    612 High St.
    Dedham, MA

**PENNSYLVANIA GERMAN**

Hershey Museum
    170 W. Hersheypark Dr.
    Hershey, PA 17033

**GENERAL COLLECTIONS:**

The Bayou Bend Collection
    #1 Wescott
    Houston, TX

Greenfield Village and Henry Ford
Museum
    Oakwood Blvd.
    Dearborn, MI 48121

Jones Museum of Glass & Ceramics
    Douglas Hill Rd.
    East Baldwin, ME 04024

Museum of Early Southern
Decorative Arts
    924 Main St.
    Winston-Salem, NC 27101

Abby Aldrich Rockefeller Folk
Art Collection
    England St.
    Williamsburg, VA 23185

The Margaret Woodbury Strong Museum
    700 Allen Creek Rd.
    Rochester, NY 14618

Henry Francis DuPont Winterthur Museum
    Winterthur, DE 19735

# APPENDIX III

## References to Pottery and Porcelain Marks

*DeBolt's Dictionary of American Pottery Marks—Whiteware & Porcelain*
Gerald DeBolt
Collector Books,
Paducah, Kentucky, 1994

*Encyclopaedia of British Pottery and Porcelain Marks*
Geoffrey A. Godden
Bonanza Books,
New York, New York, 1964

*Kovel's New Dictionary of Marks, Pottery & Porcelain, 1850 to the Present*
Ralph & Terry Kovel
Crown Publishers,
New York, New York, 1986

*Lehner's Encyclopedia of U.S. Marks on Pottery, Porcelain & Clay*
Lois Lehner
Collector Books,
Paducah, Kentucky, 1988

*Marks on German, Bohemian and Austrian Porcelain, 1710 to the Present*
Robert E. Röntgen
Schiffer Publishing, Ltd.,
Atglen, Pennsylvania

# APPENDIX IV
## English Registry Marks

Since the early nineteenth century, the English have used a number of markings on most ceramics wares which can be very helpful in determining the approximate date a piece was produced.

The 'registry' mark can be considered an equivalant of the American patent number. This English numbering system continues in use today.

Beginning in 1842 and continuing until 1883, most pottery and porcelain pieces were printed or stamped with a diamond-shaped registry mark which was coded with numbers and letters indicating the type of material, parcel number of the piece and, most helpful, the day, month and year that the design or pattern was registered at the Public Record Office. Please note that a piece may have been produced a few years after the registration date itself.

Our Chart A here shows the format of the diamond registry mark used between 1842 and 1867. Accompanying it are listings of the corresponding month and year letters used during that period. In a second chart, Chart B, we show the version of the diamond mark used between 1868 and 1883 which depicts a slightly different arrangement. Keep in mind that this diamond registry mark was also used on metal, wood and glasswares. It is important to note that the top bubble with the Roman numeral indicates the material involved; pottery and porcelain will always be Numeral IV.

After 1884, the diamond mark was discontinued and instead just a registration number was printed on pieces. The abbreviation "Rd" for "Registration" appears before the number. We list here these design registry numbers by year with the number indicating the first number that was used in that year. For instance, design number 494010 would have been registered sometime in 1909.

## CHART A

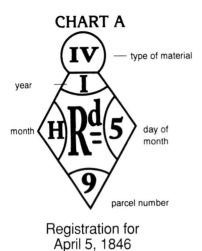

Registration for
April 5, 1846

## CHART B

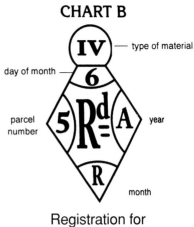

Registration for
August 6, 1871

# LIST
### Month of the Year of Registration

| | |
|---|---|
| C—January | I—July |
| G—February | R—August |
| W—March | D—December |
| H—April | B—October |
| E—May | K—November |
| M—June | A—December |

# LIST
### Year of Registration—1842-1867

| | | |
|---|---|---|
| 1842—X | 1851—P | 1860—Z |
| 1843—H | 1852—D | 1861—R |
| 1844—C | 1853—Y | 1862—O |
| 1845—A | 1854—J | 1863—G |
| 1846—I | 1855—E | 1864—N |
| 1847—F | 1856—L | 1865—W |
| 1848—U | 1857—K | 1866—Q |
| 1849—S | 1858—B | 1867—T |
| 1850—V | 1859—M | |

# LIST 3

## Year of Registration — 1868-1883

| | | |
|---|---|---|
| 1868—X | 1874—U | 1879—Y |
| 1869—H | 1875—S | 1880—J |
| 1870—C | 1876—V | 1881—E |
| 1871—A | 1877—P | 1882—L |
| 1872—I | 1878—D | 1883—K |
| 1873—F | | |

# LIST 4

## DESIGN REGISTRY NUMBERS — 1884-1951

| | | |
|---|---|---|
| Jan. 1884—1 | 1907—493900 | 1929—742725 |
| 1885—20000 | 1908—518640 | 1930—751160 |
| 1886—40800 | 1909—535170 | 1931—760583 |
| 1887—64700 | Sep. 1909—548919 | 1932—769670 |
| 1888—91800 | Oct. 1909—548920 | 1933—779292 |
| 1889—117800 | Jan. 1911—575817 | 1934—789019 |
| 1890—142300 | 1912—594195 | 1935—799097 |
| 1891—164000 | 1913—612431 | 1936—808794 |
| 1892—186400 | 1914—630190 | 1937—817293 |
| 1893—206100 | 1915—644935 | 1938—825231 |
| 1894—225000 | 1916—635521 | 1939—832610 |
| 1895—248200 | 1917—658988 | 1940—837520 |
| 1896—268800 | 1918—662872 | 1941—838590 |
| 1897—291400 | 1919—666128 | 1942—839230 |
| Jan. 1898—311677 | 1920—673750 | 1943—839980 |
| 1899—332200 | 1921—680147 | 1944—841040 |
| 1900—351600 | 1922—687144 | 1945—842670 |
| 1901—368186 | 1923—694999 | Jan. 1946—845550 |
| 1902—385180 | 1924—702671 | 1947—849730 |
| 1903—403200 | 1925—710165 | 1948—853260 |
| 1904—424400 | 1926—718057 | 1949—856999 |
| 1905—447800 | 1927—726330 | 1950—860854 |
| 1906—471860 | 1928—734370 | 1951—863970 |

# INDEX